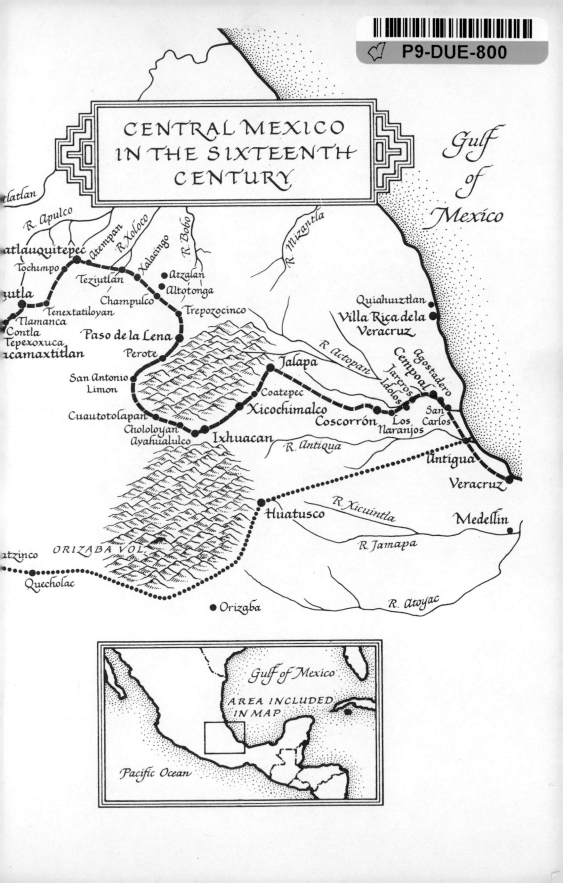

CENTRAL MEXICO IN THE SIXTEENTH CENTURY

Gulf of Mexico

...latlan
R. Apulco
...atlauquitepec
Tochimpo
...utla
Teziutlan
R. Atempan
R. Xoloco
Xalacingo
R. Bobo
Atzalan
Altotonga
Champulco
Tenextatiloyan
Tlamanca
Contla
Tepexoxuca
...camaxtitlan
Paso de la Lena
Perote
San Antonio Limon
Cuautotolapan
Chololoyan
Ayahualulco
Ixhuacan
Trepozocinco
R. Mizantla
Quiahuiztlan
Villa Rica de la Veracruz
R. Actopan
Cempoal
Agostadero
Tarros Idolos
Jalapa
Coatepec
Xicochimalco
Coscorrón
Los Naranjos
San Carlos
R. Antigua
Antigua
Veracruz
Huatusco
R. Xicuintla
Medellin
R. Jamapa
...atzinco
Quecholac
ORIZABA VOL.
Orizaba
R. Atoyac

Gulf of Mexico

AREA INCLUDED IN MAP

Pacific Ocean

HERNÁN CORTÉS: *Letters from Mexico*

HERNAN CORTES

Letters from Mexico

Translated and edited by Anthony Pagden

With an Introduction by J. H. Elliott

YALE UNIVERSITY PRESS

NEW HAVEN AND LONDON · 1986

To Peter Russell

First published in 1971 by Grossman Publishers,
New York. Reprinted in this edition with
revisions in 1986 by Yale University Press.

Printed in Great Britain at the Bath Press, Avon.

ISBN 0-300-03724-4 (cloth)
ISBN 0-300-03799-6 (paper)
LC 86-50363

Acknowledgments

My greatest single debt is to Professor J. H. Elliott who read through the work at every stage of its development and was generous with both his advice and encouragement. Mr. Max Wheeler read through the text of the translation itself and suggested numerous emendations; to him it owes much of its accuracy, though the responsibility for whatever errors may be found remains entirely my own. I would also like to thank Professor Charles Gibson who read through the entire work in proof and made numerous suggestions from which I have greatly benefitted. I would further like to record my gratitude to Professor P. E. Russell and to Dr. R. Highfield who answered my questions on sixteenth century Spain; and to Professor Lewis Hanke who also supplied me with information. I would like to thank for their assistance with the preparation of the manuscript, my father J. B. D. Pagden, Miss C. M. Chaytor, Mr. John Clibborn, and Miss E. M. Purves. Mr. Peter Storrei of the University of Sheffield made the original drawings on which the maps of Bruce Kennedy and Anita Karl are based; Mrs. Fiorella Ljunggren prepared the Index. Finally I would like to thank the Provost and Fellows of Oriel College Oxford for granting me a subvention towards the cost of typing this work.

Contents

List of Illustrations

Cortés, Velázquez and Charles V[1]

When Cortés landed on the coast of Mexico on April 22, 1519, he was on the point of committing himself to an enterprise of unknown proportions against an enemy of unknown character and strength. After the meeting with the Totonac chief Tentlil on Easter Sunday he knew at least that, somewhere in the interior, there lived a powerful ruler called Motecuçoma, whose dominion included the peoples of the coastal plain. But this fact of

1. This brief survey has drawn heavily on the illuminating studies of Cortés and his ideas by Victor Frankl: "Hernán Cortés y la tradición de las Siete Partidas"; "Die Begriffe des Mexicanischen Kaisertums und der Weltmonarchie in den 'Cartas de Relación' des Hernán Cortés"; "Imperio particular e imperio universal en las cartas de relación de Hernán Cortés." Frankl's critical reassessment of Cortés as a reliable source for his own exploits is to some extent inspired by Eulalia Guzmán, *Relaciones de Hernán Cortés a Carlos V sobre la invasión de Anáhuac,* an annotated edition of the first two letters which is often shrewd and penetrating in its judgments but is vitiated by the author's antipathy toward Cortés. The most interesting and suggestive attempt so far made to reconstruct the political scene in Spain and the Indies in the first decades of the sixteenth century is to be found in the massively ambitious biography of Las Casas by Manuel Giménez Fernández, to which his *Hernán Cortés y su Revolución Comunera en la Nueva España* may be regarded as a useful pendant.

In addition to these works, I have also made use of the following: Robert S. Chamberlain, "La controversia entre Cortés y Velázquez sobre la gobernación de la Nueva España, 1519–1522," and his "Two unpublished documents of Hernán Cortés and New Spain, 1519 and 1524"; Richard Konetzke, "Hernán Cortés como poblador de la Nueva España"; José Valero Silva, *El Legalismo de Hernán Cortés como Instrumento de su Conquista;* H. R. Wagner, *The Rise of Fernando Cortés.*

Motecuçoma's existence was the fact he most needed to know. From Easter Sunday, 1519, a single, supreme objective established itself clearly in his mind. He must reach Motecuçoma and somehow induce him to acknowledge the supreme overlordship of Juana and her son Charles, the sovereign rulers of Castile.

Although everything else was surrounded by innumerable uncertainties, the central objective of Cortés's Mexican strategy was therefore clearly defined, and he pursued it undeviatingly until it was triumphantly attained. The march into the interior, the entry down the causeway into Tenochtitlan on November 8, the taking of Motecuçoma into custody on the fourteenth, and the "voluntary" donation of Motecuçoma's empire to Charles—these represented the critical moments in an exceptionally hazardous but carefully calculated military and political exercise, which worked with greater precision than even Cortés himself could have dared to hope. Within nine months of landing, he had made himself master of Motecuçoma's empire in the name of the sovereigns of Castile.

The magnitude and the brilliance of this achievement can all too easily obscure the fact that Motecuçoma was in some respects the least dangerous of the enemies whom Cortés had to face, and that he had more to fear from some of his own countrymen than from the emperor of the Mexica. From the moment of his hasty departure from Santiago, in Cuba, he found himself in a highly equivocal position, both in relation to his immediate superiors and to the Spanish Crown.

Technically, Cortés was commanding an expedition on behalf of the governor of Cuba, Diego Velázquez, who himself was merely the deputy of the hereditary admiral of the Indies, Diego Colón (Columbus). Velázquez, however, was an ambitious man, eager to conquer new lands in his own right. To do this, he must somehow break free from Colón's jurisdiction, and obtain from the Crown his own license to explore, conquer and colonize. In the two or three years before the dispatch of Cortés, he had made a number of moves directed toward this end. In 1517 and 1518 he had sent out the exploring and trading expeditions of Hernández de Córdoba and Juan de Grijalva; and for the second of these expeditions he had taken care to obtain authorization from the Hieronymite governors of Hispaniola, who were the Crown's direct representatives in the Indies, and were independent of Diego Colón. He had also dispatched, in succession, two personal agents to the Spanish Court—Gonzalo de Guzmán, and his chaplain, Benito Martín —to urge the Crown to grant him the title of *adelantado* of Yucatán, with the right to conquer and settle the newly discovered lands.

Apart from some further lucrative trading, Velázquez's principal purpose in dispatching Cortés in the wake of the two previous expeditions of Hernández de Córdoba and Grijalva seems to have been to keep his claims alive during the period when he was impatiently awaiting the outcome of his initiative at Court. This would explain the nature of his instructions for Cortés, dated October 23, 1518.[2] The purpose of Cortés's expedition, according to these instructions, was to go in search of Grijalva's fleet (of whose return to Cuba Velázquez was still unaware) and of any Christians held captive in Yucatán. Cortés was also authorized to explore and to trade, but had no permission to colonize. The reason for this was that Velázquez himself was still awaiting such authorization from Spain, and had no legal authority to confer a right that was not yet his.

Recent changes in Spain, however, made it reasonably certain that Velázquez would soon secure his title of adelantado, and the rights of conquest and jurisdiction for which he was petitioning. Ferdinand the Catholic had died in 1516, and in September, 1517, Charles of Ghent arrived in Castile from Flanders to take up his Spanish inheritance. Charles's arrival in the peninsula was followed by a purge of the officials who had governed Spain and the Indies during the regency of Cardinal Jiménez de Cisneros. Among the councilors and officials who acquired, or returned to, favor

2. *Cedulario*, doc. 1.

with the coming of the new regime was the formidable figure of the
bishop of Burgos, Juan Rodríguez de Fonseca, the councilor principally responsible for the affairs of the Indies during the reigns of
Ferdinand and Isabella. Fonseca had always had fierce enemies and
devoted partisans; and among the latter was Diego Velázquez, who
was married to Fonseca's niece.[3] There was every reason, then, to
assume that he would use all his newly recovered influence to support the pretensions of Velázquez.

      Cortés, who kept himself well informed of what went on at
Court, must have been well aware that, with the return to power of
Fonseca, the tide of events in Spain was moving in Velázquez's
favor. If he were ever to be a great conqueror in his own right, it
was therefore essential for him to act with speed, and to obtain as
much freedom for maneuver as possible. Cortés, who had been
quick to learn the tragic lessons of the Spanish Caribbean, had
grasped the crucial fact that the key to empire was settlement. It
was exactly this which Velázquez's instructions denied him. But
Cortés was skillful enough to secure the insertion of a clause which
gave him a certain amount of latitude. Velázquez admitted that it
was impossible to foresee all eventualities; and he authorized
Cortés, in the event of unexpected emergencies, to take such measures as would conform most closely to "the service of God and
their highnesses." [4] Clearly, Velázquez did not know his man.
Cortés had his own ideas about God's service, and Their Highnesses', and they were not quite the same as those of the governor of
Cuba. Thanks to Article 27, he was now empowered to take such
measures as he might consider necessary, and which were not specifically covered by his instructions. But this useful legal weapon,
which he had devised to justify an unauthorized act of settlement,
would be rendered useless if Velázquez should receive permission
to conquer and settle while Cortés was still in Cuba. Hence the

3. The relationship is reported by Francisco López de Gómara, *Cortés,
The Life of the Conqueror by His Secretary*, p. 327. Giménez Fernández,
Hernán Cortés, p. 53, suggests that the "niece" was a daughter.
4. Clause 27, *Cedulario*, p. 30.

indecent haste of his departure from Santiago. On no account must he still be accessible when Velázquez's warrant arrived from Spain.

In sailing so precipitately from Santiago, Cortés had therefore defied his own immediate superior, Velázquez, and had potentially antagonized Velázquez's powerful friends at Court. He knew well enough the grave risks he was running. But to Cortés and his friends—Puertocarrero, the Alvarado brothers, Gonzalo de Sandoval—the risks paled before the attractions of the anticipated prize. Nothing could more quickly obliterate the stigma of treachery and rebellion than a brilliant military success and the acquisition of fabulous riches. If new peoples were won for the Faith, and rich new lands won for the Crown, there was reason to hope that the original defiance of Velázquez would be regarded as no more than a peccadillo, and that Velázquez's friends and protectors would be silenced by a *fait accompli*.

The king was the fountainhead of justice. It rested with him to punish the wicked, reward the good, and forgive the occasional act of insubordination—especially when the act was committed, as it would be this time, in the king's own interest and for the greater glory of God. It was well known that God had specifically entrusted the sovereigns of Castile with the task of winning for the Church the peoples of the newly discovered Indies, and that this divine mission had been confirmed by decision of the papacy. Cortés, therefore, would from the first act in the name of the king, in order to further this providential mission; and then, insofar as he had offended against the letter of the law, would throw himself on his mercy. This meant that, from the moment of his departure from Cuba, Cortés totally ignored any claims to jurisdiction of Velázquez or Colón and behaved as if he were directly subordinate to the Crown alone. Any Indians he met as he cruised along the Mexican coast were regarded as being *already* the vassals of the Crown of Castile,[5] by virtue of the papal donation. Similarly, he took formal possession of the land at the Tabasco River in the name of the

5. Below, p. 452, n. 15.

Crown, in spite of—or, more accurately, precisely because of—the inconvenient fact that Grijalva had already taken formal possession at the same spot, on behalf of the governor of Cuba.

That Cortés and his close associates were banking on eventual vindication by the Crown is further suggested by the jocular exchange on board ship just before the landing at San Juan de Ulúa, as reported by Bernal Díaz.[6] Alonso Hernández de Puertocarrero came up to Cortés, quoting a snatch from one of the romances in the Castilian *romancero general*:

> "Look on France, Montesinos,
> Look on Paris, the city,
> Look on the waters of the Duero,
> Flowing down into the sea."

The lines came from the ballad of Montesinos, who was exiled from court because of a false accusation by his mortal enemy, Tomillas. Montesinos, the innocent exile, was seeking permission from his father to return to court in disguise and take service with the king, in order to avenge his wrong. If Montesinos was Cortés, then Tomillas, his enemy, was Velázquez; and Cortés could hope to resolve his difficulties, as Montesinos resolved his, by taking service under the king. "He who takes the king's pay," continued the ballad, "can avenge himself of everything." Cortés promptly responded in kind, with a quotation from another ballad about another exile: "God give us the same good fortune in fighting as he gave to the Paladin Roland."

Success in arms, and resort to the highest authority of all, that of the king himself—these were the aims of Cortés and his fellow conspirators as they prepared in April, 1519, to compound their defiance of Velázquez by a landing which would mark the real beginning of their attempt to conquer an empire. They were concerned, like all conquistadors, with fame, riches and honor. But

---

6. Chap. 36. Frankl, in "Hernán Cortés y la tradición de las Siete Partidas," was the first to appreciate the cryptic references in the exchange.

behind the willful defiance of the governor of Cuba there existed, at least in Cortés's mind, a philosophy of conquest and colonization which made his action something more than an attempt at self-aggrandizement at the expense of Velázquez. He entertained, like so many Castilians of his generation, an exalted view of the royal service, and of Castile's divinely appointed mission. Both the divine and the royal favor would shine on those who cast down idols, extirpated pagan superstitions, and won new lands and peoples for God and Castile. But there was a wrong way, as well as a right way, of going about this great work. In the Antilles, the Castilians had gone about it the wrong way, with disastrous consequences. Cortés had seen with his own eyes how captains and soldiers whose sole concern was the quest for gold and the capture of slaves and booty had destroyed the islands and peoples discovered by Columbus only a generation ago. The extension to the New World of a style of warfare reminiscent of the war against the Moors in medieval Spain had made a desert of a paradise and had left even the Spaniards themselves shiftless and discontented. The failure of Grijalva's expedition had only served to drive home the lesson already learned by Cortés—that conquest, to achieve any long-term success, required intelligent colonization. Whether Velázquez had learned the same lesson seems doubtful; and Cortés could always point to the absence from his instructions of any order to colonize, to prove that he had not. But in any event Velázquez would be given no opportunity to put the question to the test. Cortés would conquer Mexico, and not only conquer it but settle it as well.

It was, then, with the intention of establishing a permanent settlement that Cortés dropped anchor in the harbor of San Juan de Ulúa on April 21, 1519. But some careful preliminary maneuvers were needed before he could openly flout Velázquez's orders by formally founding a town. There was a strong faction of Velázquez's partisans in the expedition, headed by Francisco de Montejo and Juan Velázquez de León. This faction had first to be neutralized, and the rank and file of the army be induced to support

Cortés. The first months on Mexican soil were therefore taken up, not only with reconnaissance surveys designed to discover the nature of Motecuçoma's empire and the extent of his power, but also with attempts to detach the soldiers from their adherence to Velázquez's men. This was done with considerable skill, by playing on their desire for gold and land. Bernal Díaz's account[7] suggests how cleverly Cortés forced the Velázquez faction into the open with a demand that the expedition should return to Cuba—a demand with which Cortés seemed ready to comply. At this point the troops, whose expectations had been aroused and now looked like being dashed, came out with what seemed to be a spontaneous demand that the expedition should continue.

Cortés had been given his cue, and the Velázquez faction had been outmaneuvered. But although the practical difficulties in the way of settlement had been overcome, there still remained the problem of finding some legal justification for disregard of Velázquez's orders. It was at this point that Cortés's knowledge of Castilian law came into its own. That great medieval compilation, the *Siete Partidas* of Alfonso X, dating from 1256–1263, presented a cogent picture of the organic unity that should naturally prevail between the king and his subjects, bound together in mutual concern for the upholding of the commonweal against selfish private interest. In the context of events in the New World in 1519, Velázquez and his friends could be depicted as self-interested officials, moved by greed and ambition, while Cortés and his army represented the true community, motivated by concern for the commonweal and the desire to serve God and the king. Whereas the private interest of Velázquez busied itself solely with trade and barter, which would fill his own capacious pockets, the commonweal demanded an expedition of conquest and colonization, which would promote the true interests of the realm.

It was in pursuance of this simple but time-honored political philosophy that the remarkable events of June and July, 1519, were

7. Chap. 41.

enacted. According to the *Siete Partidas*, the laws could only be set aside by the demand of all the good men of the land. On the soil of Mexico, these were clearly the rank and file of Cortés's army, and it was in deference to their demand that he now set aside his instructions. They were united in agreeing that the expedition should not return to Cuba but should remain to attempt the conquest of Motecuçoma's empire; and they formally constituted themselves a community—the Villa Rica de Vera Cruz—in order to ensure that the king's interests were upheld. As a municipality, they then proceeded to appoint the usual municipal officials, the *alcaldes* and *regidores*. From this point, Velázquez's instructions were regarded as inoperative, and the authority conferred by them on Cortés was deemed to have lapsed. Supreme jurisdiction in Mexico now resided in the municipality of Vera Cruz, and the charade was duly completed when the municipality, acting on behalf of Charles and Juana, appointed Cortés *alcalde mayor* and *justicia* of Vera Cruz, and captain of the royal army.

The effect of this brilliant legalistic maneuver was to free Cortés from his obligations to his immediate superior, Velázquez, and to make him directly dependent on the king. But what seemed plausible enough in Mexico was bound to seem highly implausible in Cuba and at the Spanish Court. Clearly it was essential to win support in Spain for an action which Fonseca and his friends would certainly represent to the king as an act of open rebellion; and this became all the more urgent with the arrival at San Juan de Ulúa on July 1 of a ship commanded by Francisco de Saucedo bearing the not unexpected news that Velázquez, by royal decree of November 13, 1518, had been appointed adelantado of Yucatán, and had been granted the right to conquer and settle. Now that Velázquez had obtained his authorization, Cortés's action seemed to lack even the shadow of legality.

Everything now depended on the successful presentation of his case at Court, where the Fonseca group would certainly do all in its power to destroy him. If possible, Charles and his advisers must be reached and won over before they had time to learn from Velázquez himself of Cortés's act of rebellion. For this purpose, Puertocarrero and Montejo, who had been detached from the Velázquez faction, were appointed *procuradores*, or representatives, of Vera Cruz, with full powers to present the municipality's case to the king in person. To assist them in their mission, they were to take with them, as a gift for the king, all the gold and jewels brought to Cortés by Motecuçoma's envoys, together with the traditional royal fifth of all the booty so far acquired. They took with them, too, such documentation as was needed to justify their cause. This documentation included the "lost" First Letter of Relation of Cortés—unless, as is perfectly conceivable, he never wrote such a letter, for it would necessarily have involved a number of personal explanations which could well have offered embarrassing hostages to fortune.

The most important document carried to Spain by Puertocarrero and Montejo was the letter from the new municipality of Vera Cruz, addressed to Charles and Juana. This letter, which customarily replaces Cortés's "missing" First Letter, bears all the stamp of his personality, and was no doubt written largely to his dictation. It should therefore be read, as it was written, not as an accurate historical narrative but as a brilliant piece of special pleading, designed to justify an act of rebellion and to press the claims of Cortés against those of the governor of Cuba.

For all Cortés's eager insistence that he was providing a "true" relation,[8] he displayed a masterly capacity for suppression of evidence and ingenious distortion. Great care was taken to play down the expeditions of Hernández de Córdoba and Grijalva, and the awkward fact that the latter had taken formal possession of the land was quietly ignored. The letter also missed no opportunity to blacken the reputation of Velázquez—"moved more by cupidity than any other passion" [9]—and to suggest that his financial contri-

8. Below, p. 18.
9. Below, p. 5.

bution to the expedition was insignificant. The persistent denigra-
tion of Velázquez only served to emphasize, by contrast, the loyalty and the high ideals of Cortés himself, as a man passionately
determined to serve God and the king by extirpating idolatry, converting the heathen and conquering rich new lands for the Crown
of Castile. At the same time, Cortés was careful to imply that he
broke with Velázquez's instructions only under pressure from the
popular will, as represented by the army. It was the soldiers, eager
to convert a trading expedition into a military and colonizing enterprise, who had demanded a change of plan; and Cortés, after due
deliberation, had accepted their demand as conducive to the royal
interest.

  Having offered this tendentious explanation of the founding
of Vera Cruz, the letter then dwelt at some length on the alleged
riches of the country and on the abominable customs of its inhabitants. The object of this was to appeal both to Charles's cupidity—
an appeal skillfully reinforced by the gift of Motecuçoma's treasures—and to his sense of religious obligation, as a ruler specially
entrusted by God and the Pope with the duty of winning new
peoples to the Faith. But the letter's real climax came only after the
description of Mexico and the Mexicans, and consisted of a direct
appeal to Charles and Juana "on no account to give or grant
concessions to Diego Velázquez . . . or judicial powers; and
if any shall have been given him, that they be revoked." [10] Since
the arrival of Saucedo, Cortés was perfectly well aware that Velázquez's commission had in fact already arrived. Ignorance, however,
was the better policy; and Cortés drove home his request with a
final denunciation of the governor of Cuba as a man of such patent
wickedness as to make him totally unfitted to receive the least token
of royal favor.

  The first letter from Mexico, then, was essentially a political
document, speaking for Cortés in the name of his army, and designed to appeal directly to the Crown over the heads of Velázquez

10. Below, p. 37.

and his friends in the Council of the Indies. Cortés was now involved in a desperate race against time. Montejo and Puertocarrero
left for Spain on July 26, 1519, with their bundle of letters and the
gold; and unless, or until, they could persuade Charles to sanction
retrospectively the behavior of Cortés and his men, Cortés was
technically a traitor, liable to arrest and persecution at the hands of
an irate governor of Cuba, fully empowered to act in the royal
name. The danger was acute, and the blow could fall at any time,
perhaps even from within Mexico itself. For there was still a strong
group of Velázquez partisans in the expedition, and these men
would do all they could to sabotage Cortés's plans. But Cortés,
who had his spies posted, was well aware of the dangers. The
friends of the governor of Cuba appear to have been plotting to
send him warning of the mission of Montejo and Puertocarrero, so
that he could intercept their ship. The plot was discovered, the conspirators arrested, and two of them, Juan Escudero and Diego
Cermeño, put to death.[11]

This abortive conspiracy seems to have convinced Cortés
that it was not enough simply to cut the bonds of legality that tied
him to Cuba. He must also cut the physical links. This was probably the major consideration in his famous decision to scuttle or
beach his ships, although their destruction would have the added
advantage of enabling him to add their crews to his tiny army.
Once the ships were destroyed, all contact with Cuba was broken.
A garrison was left at Vera Cruz under the command of Juan de
Escalante, and the army began its march from Cempoal into the
interior on August 16, knowing that it had openly defied the governor of Cuba and that there could be no turning back.

As long as Cortés could command the loyalties of his army
—and this would ultimately depend on his ability to capture and
distribute the fabulous riches of Motecuçoma's empire—he was
now reasonably safe from subversion within the ranks. But he was a
good deal less safe in the rear than he had anticipated. Montejo and

11. Below, p. 51.

Puertocarrero had received strict instructions to avoid Cuba and make straight for Spain, but Montejo had other ideas. Needing provisions—or perhaps prudently hedging his bets—he chose to put in on the west of the island to make a brief visit to his estate. He arrived on August 23, left letters for a friend, and, on his last night, displayed the Mexican treasures to his major-domo before sailing again on the twenty-sixth. The major-domo duly informed Veláz-quez, who immediately dispatched two ships in pursuit of the pro-curadores. But their pilot, Alaminos, took the ship by a new route through the Bahamas Straits, and Montejo and Puertocarrero made their escape into the Atlantic and thence to Seville.

Thwarted of his prey, Velázquez made two moves which were to be crucial for the future course of events. Gonzalo de Guzmán, who had already acted on his behalf at the Spanish Court, was sent back to Spain again in mid-October to counter the activi-ties of the Vera Cruz procuradores, and to convince the Crown and the Council of the Indies that Cortés was a traitor and should be treated as such. Simultaneously, Velázquez began to organize an army to be sent to Mexico against Cortés. News of these prepara-tions greatly alarmed the judges of the highest tribunal in the In-dies, the *Audiencia* of Santo Domingo. Conflicts among rival bands of conquistadors were all too common an occurrence, and the Audi-encia was anxious to prevent still more shedding of blood. It there-fore sent the *licenciado* Lucas Vázquez de Ayllón to halt the prepa-rations, but Velázquez was in no mood to listen to the Audiencia, and the expedition was already preparing to sail by the time of the licenciado's arrival.

At a time when a smallpox epidemic was raging in Cuba, Velázquez felt unable to lead his army in person, and handed over the command to one of his more reliable but less intelligent friends, Pánfilo de Narváez. The army, twice the size of that of Cortés, set sail from Cuba on March 5, 1520, accompanied by Vázquez de Ayllón, who clearly felt that, having failed to prevent it from sail-ing, the least he could do was to act as a witness and perhaps as an umpire. He was rewarded for his pains by being placed under arrest when Narváez landed at San Juan de Ulúa on April 20.

During the autumn and winter of 1519, therefore, at the time when Cortés was securing the submission of Motecuçoma and had established himself precariously in Tenochtitlan, he was faced with the prospect of a military confrontation with his immediate superior, the governor of Cuba, who himself was acting in defiance of the Audiencia of Santo Domingo. The outcome was likely to be determined on the battlefield, in an internecine struggle of Spaniard against Spaniard, which could well jeopardize and even destroy Cortés's uncertain hold over the Aztec empire. But in the Spanish monarchy of the sixteenth century a military solution could never be final. Legality was paramount, and the key to legality lay with the king.

Everything therefore turned on the success of Montejo and Puertocarrero in Spain. They duly reached Seville at the beginning of November, 1519, only to find their country on the verge of revolt. Charles had been elected Holy Roman Emperor on June 28. Once elected, his immediate aim was to extract the largest possible subsidies from the Cortes of the various Spanish kingdoms, and then to leave for Germany. When the procuradores arrived in Seville, the emperor was still in Barcelona, heavily preoccupied with plans for his departure; and the Castilian cities were beginning to voice their dissatisfaction at the prospect of heavy new fiscal demands and an absentee king.

At this particular moment the chances of winning the emperor's support for a still-unknown adventurer on the other side of the world hardly looked very promising. It was also unfortunate for the procuradores that Velázquez's chaplain, Benito Martín, happened to be in Seville at the time of their arrival. Martín persuaded the officials of the Casa de la Contratación to embargo their ships, together with the Mexican treasure, and so deprived them of their most powerful argument, gold. In spite of this, Montejo and

Puertocarrero set out for Barcelona, accompanied by the most faithful of Cortés's agents in Spain, his own father, Martín Cortés de Monroy. They reached Barcelona near the end of January, 1520, only to find that the emperor had already left for Burgos. But their visit to Barcelona at least enabled them to make a number of influential contacts, and they were lucky to find there Francisco Núñez, a royal official and a cousin of Cortés, who agreed to act as his legal representative. From Barcelona they moved across Spain in the tracks of the emperor, finally catching up with him at Tordesillas, near Valladolid, early in March. Here, seven months after leaving Vera Cruz, they could at last petition the emperor in person to confirm Cortés in his position as captain general and *justicia mayor*.

Their petition was fiercely contested, not only by Velázquez's agent, Gonzalo de Guzmán, but also by his patron, the bishop of Burgos. Fonseca's position, however, was not quite as strong as it had been. Charles's Flemish advisers were falling out with Fonseca and his friends, whose collective reputation in the affairs of the Indies had been tarnished by the denunciations made before the emperor in December by that zealous apostle of Indian liberty, Fray Bartolomé de las Casas. Above all, there was Motecuçoma's treasure to speak on behalf of Cortés. The precious gold objects and the delicate featherwork had created a sensation in Seville, and such treasures could hardly be left indefinitely impounded in the hands of the officials of the House of Trade. On the emperor's orders, the treasure was dispatched from Seville and reached him early in April, although Cortés's friends were able to allege that not everything was there, and that Fonseca had deliberately held some of it back. As was to be expected, the treasure powerfully reinforced the arguments of Montejo and Puertocarrero, who put their case again at Corunna, just before Charles was due to sail. The emperor deferred his decision, but declined to follow Fonseca's advice and declare Cortés a rebel. This at least was an encouraging start, and the procuradores gained another victory when a royal decree, dated May 10, 1520, ordered the officials in Seville to return their confiscated funds.

When Charles sailed for Germany on May 20, therefore, Cortés's friends could claim at least a partial success. Their gold, too, would now come into its own. But there was still a very long way to go, and the political climate was menacing. Castile was now in open revolt. Fonseca remained a highly influential figure, and his brother was the royalist army commander. In these circumstances, it was easy enough to tar Cortés with the same brush of rebellion as the *Comuneros* of Castile. Both in the Indies and in Castile, the emperor was faced with treason and revolt. Could the rebellions be crushed, and the emperor's authority be preserved? As far as Mexico was concerned, Fonseca pinned his hopes on the expedition of Pánfilo de Narváez. But in fact, a few days after Charles left for Germany, the fate of Narváez had been decided. Cortés, marching back to the coast from Tenochtitlan, outmaneuvered, defeated and captured him on May 27.

Narváez's defeat left the governor of Cuba a ruined and broken man. Cortés had defeated Velázquez—geographically his nearest enemy—but he was still without news from the Spanish Court. Moreover, his march to the coast to defeat Narváez had fatally weakened the Spanish position in Tenochtitlan. When Cortés got back to the capital on June 25 it was already too late. The behavior of Alvarado and his men in Tenochtitlan during Cortés's absence had precipitated an Indian uprising, and neither Cortés's troops, nor the diminished authority of Motecuçoma, proved sufficient to quell the revolt. Motecuçoma, rejected by his own subjects, died his strange death on June 30. During the course of the same night, the *noche triste*, the Spaniards made their famous retreat from Tenochtitlan. Cortés might have defeated the governor of Cuba, but he had also lost the empire he had promised to Charles.

It was during the autumn months of 1520, while Cortés was preparing for the siege and reconquest of Tenochtitlan, that he wrote the Second Letter. This letter, like its predecessor from Vera Cruz, is both more and less than a straightforward narrative of events, for it, too, has an essentially political purpose. Cortés, when writing it, was influenced by three major considerations. In the first place, he still did not know what decision, if any, had been reached in Spain on his plea for retrospective authorization of his unconventional proceedings. In the second place, he had by now heard the news of Charles's election to the imperial throne. Finally, he had won a new empire for Charles and had proceeded to lose it. His letter, therefore, had to be so angled as to suggest that, at the most, he had suffered no more than a temporary setback (attributable to other men's crimes), and that he would soon be in a position to render the most signal new services to a king who had now become the mightiest monarch in the world.

With these considerations in mind, Cortés carefully contrived his letter to convey a predominantly "imperial" theme. Its opening paragraph contained a graceful allusion to Charles's new empire in Germany, which was skillfully coupled with a reference to a second empire across the Atlantic, to which he could claim an equal title.[12] This reference set the tone for the document as a whole. The fact that Cortés was no longer at this moment the effective master of the Mexican empire was no doubt inconvenient, but could be played down as far as possible. For the thesis of the letter was that Charles was already the *legal* emperor of this great new empire, and that Cortés would soon recover for him what was rightfully his.

The entire story of the march to Tenochtitlan and the imprisonment of Motecuçoma was related in such a way as to support this general thesis. Motecuçoma, by his speeches and his actions, was portrayed as a man who voluntarily recognized the sovereignty of Charles V, and voluntarily surrendered his empire into his hands. Whether Motecuçoma did indeed speak anything like the words which Cortés attributes to him will probably never be known for

12. Below, p. 48.

certain. Some passages in his two speeches contain so many Christian overtones as to be unbelievable coming from a pagan Aztec. Others, and in particular the identification of the Spaniards with the former rulers of Mexico wrongly banished from their land, may be an ingenious fabrication by Cortés, or may conceivably reflect certain beliefs and legends, which Motecuçoma himself may or may not have accepted. Whatever its origins, the story of the expected return of lords from the east was essential to Cortés's grand design, for it enabled him to allege and explain a "voluntary" submission of Motecuçoma, and the "legal" transfer of his empire—an empire far removed from the jurisdiction of the Audiencia of Santo Domingo and from the Caribbean world of Diego Colón and Velázquez—to its rightful ruler, Charles V.

Motecuçoma's death at the hands of his own subjects left Charles the undisputed master of the field. It was unfortunate that the Mexicans were now in open rebellion—a situation which could only be ascribed to the nefarious activities of the governor of Cuba, acting through his agent Pánfilo de Narváez. But although Narváez's invasion had nearly brought disaster, the tide had now been turned, because God was on the emperor's side. With divine help, and through the agency of that most loyal of lieutenants, Hernán Cortés, the land would soon be recovered; and what better name could be bestowed upon it than that of New Spain?[13]

It is clear that this entire letter was superbly designed to appeal directly to Charles over the heads of Fonseca and his friends in the Council of the Indies and the imperial entourage. But Fonseca was still far from ready to admit defeat. It was always possible that Cortés would suffer the fate of other conquistadors, and be unseated by conspirators among his own men. The abortive plot of Antonio de Villafaña during the siege of Tenochtitlan[14] showed that Velázquez still had his friends, and that this was by no means an unreasonable hope. There was a chance, too, that Fonseca could

13. Below, p. 158.
14. Below, pp. 277-278.

rid himself of Cortés by more subtle means. With Narváez's defeat, military overthrow had become unlikely; but as long as Charles V declined to pronounce on Cortés's status, he remained intensely vulnerable to legal action.

When news of Narváez's defeat reached Spain, Fonseca persuaded Adrian of Utrecht, who headed the regency government during Charles's absence in Germany, to appoint a royal official to intervene in Mexico. The chosen official was Cristóbal de Tapia, a royal inspector in Hispaniola. He received his commission in April, 1521—the month when the Castilian Comuneros were defeated and crushed at Villalar—and he was apparently ordered to take over the government of New Spain, and, if possible, to arrest Cortés and ship him home. Tapia landed at Vera Cruz on December 4, 1521, four months after Cortés's army had captured Tenochtitlan. The Aztec empire had been destroyed; but, for all his success, Cortés was in a delicate position. To defy Tapia, who had come to New Spain as the legally appointed representative of the royal authority, would be the height of imprudence, and yet to surrender the empire into his hands would be intolerable.

Once again, however, as the Third Letter makes clear, Cortés showed himself equal to the occasion. Carefully avoiding a personal meeting with Tapia, who would at once have presented him with a royal warrant, he sent a Franciscan, Fray Pedro de Melgarejo, to greet Tapia, and no doubt to pass him an appropriate bribe. At the same time, he had recourse to the device which he had already employed at the beginning of the conquest, and arranged another "spontaneous" assertion of the popular will. The representatives of the various municipalities of New Spain, usefully reinforced for the occasion by the rapid founding of the new town of Medellín, met Tapia at Cempoal on December 24, 1521, and went through the time-honored Castilian procedure followed by those who were prepared to obey but not to comply. With honor thus satisfied on both sides, Tapia took the next ship back to Hispaniola, a wiser, and no doubt a richer, man.

Tapia's intervention provided Cortés, in his Third Letter of May 15, 1522, with a *diabolus ex machina*, equivalent to Narváez in the Second Letter. While the letter related in great detail the siege and capture of Tenochtitlan, it also enabled him to smear by implication all those royal officials who placed their own interest before the emperor's. It was scarcely necessary to contrast their conduct with that of Cortés, who had not only conquered an empire for Charles, but was now offering him yet another vision of fabulous riches—a vision, this time, of the Spice Islands of the Pacific and the world of Cathay.[15]

It must have been bitterly frustrating for Cortés that, in spite of all these services, no word of royal approval had yet been received. This could only be explained, he concluded, by the machinations of his enemies, who were concealing the truth from the emperor. Nor could there any longer be real doubt that the chief among these enemies was Fonseca, the bishop of Burgos. It was Fonseca who had been responsible for the unwelcome intervention of Tapia. It was Fonseca, too, who was responsible in 1523 for a further challenge to Cortés's position—the intervention of Juan de Garay.

In 1521 Garay, the governor of Jamaica, obtained from Fonseca a warrant authorizing him to conquer and colonize the Pánuco region, to the north of Vera Cruz. He landed at Pánuco in July, 1523, with an army of four hundred infantry and 120 cavalry. This could easily have been another Narváez affair, and Cortés at once recalled his captains, now dispersed over Mexico, to meet the new challenge to his authority. It was this challenge which he described in the opening pages of his Fourth Letter of October 15, 1524, where for the first time Fonseca is mentioned by name.[16] Tapia and Garay, like Narváez in the Second Letter, are portrayed as self-interested men whose ill-chosen and ill-timed intervention in the affairs of New Spain placed the imperial authority and the

15. Below, pp. 267, 327, 444.
16. Below, p. 289.

achievements of Cortés at risk. Cortés himself emerges, not for the first time, as the loyalist, confronted by a quartet of enemies—Fonseca, Diego Colón, Velázquez and Garay—united in their sinister machinations to accomplish his ruin.

By the time this letter was written, however, Cortés's battle for recognition had long since been won. During the course of 1521 the balance of power in the emperor's councils had perceptibly shifted. This year, which saw the defeat of the Comuneros, saw also the siege and capture of Tenochtitlan. If Fonseca's brother had emerged victorious in Castile, Fonseca's enemy had emerged victorious in New Spain; and as more and more wealth flowed in from Mexico, something of the significance of Cortés's achievement began to be realized. His agents were lobbying hard in the regency council of Adrian of Utrecht, and duly convinced the regent that the bishop of Burgos had done the emperor an ill service in persistently supporting the governor of Cuba. He therefore deprived Fonseca of jurisdiction in the suit between Cortés and Velázquez, instituted to determine which of the two could rightfully lay claim to the spoils of New Spain.

Charles V returned to Spain in July, 1522, and received Cortés's representatives in audience the following month. After hearing their arguments, he confirmed Adrian's decision, but appointed a new tribunal to receive representations from both parties and to reach a final verdict. This tribunal, which included among its members the grand chancellor Gattinara, eventually decided in Cortés's favor. It was left open to Velázquez to sue Cortés for debts, but it was ruled that Velázquez's financial contribution to the original expedition, even if it were larger than that of Cortés, did not entitle him to claim credit for the conquest of Mexico.

The tribunal's recommendations were accepted by the emperor and embodied in a decree dated October 15, 1522, which named Cortés governor and captain general of New Spain.[17] At last, some three and a half years after his original act of insubordination,

17. *Cedulario*, doc. 2.

Cortés had received the vindication for which he and his agents had worked so hard. The original strategy, so tenaciously pursued, of appealing directly to the sovereign over the heads of his officials, had yielded its expected dividend. Cortés was no longer a rebel—another Comunero—but the emperor's official governor of the newly conquered realm of New Spain.

The news, however, still had to reach Cortés. It was conveyed to Mexico by his brother-in-law Francisco de las Casas, and his cousin, Rodrigo de Paz, who in due course secured appointment as Cortés's personal secretary and major-domo. When Garay landed in July, 1523, it had not yet come, but it arrived in September, just in time to give a decisive turn to events. Cortés at once had the contents of the emperor's decree publicly announced in Mexico City—now rising on the ruins of Tenochtitlan—along with those of another imperial decree forbidding Garay to interfere in the affairs of New Spain. Copies of the decrees were also dispatched to Garay, who saw that he was beaten and gave up without a fight. He duly traveled to Mexico City to visit Cortés, and died there suddenly on December 27.

One after another, then, Cortés's opponents and rivals, from Velázquez to Garay, had been worsted in the intricate political game which Cortés had played with such skill since the moment he first took ship for Mexico. It was a game whose ground rules he had studied closely, and which he had fought with every weapon at his command. Events in Mexico itself were crucial, because success in Mexico was the prerequisite for success at Court. However skillful the maneuvers of Cortés's relatives and agents at home in Spain, their chances of success ultimately turned on Cortés's ability to conquer Motecuçoma's empire and to replenish the imperial coffers with Mexican gold. But Cortés knew well enough that victory in Mexico would be nothing without victory at Court, and the entire presentation of his case through his letters to the emperor was most cunningly designed to bring this about.

He achieved what he intended to achieve; and yet, in the

end, his very success proved his own undoing. By consistently emphasizing his own absolute loyalty to the emperor, he had delivered himself into the emperor's hands. His acutely sensitive political antennae, which had told him that he must win at Court if he were to win at all, failed him at the very moment of success. For if the Court could make a man, it could also unmake him; and there were reasons enough for unmaking Cortés.

When Fonseca fought his protracted battle with Cortés, he may to some extent have been motivated by personal animosity, but at the same time he was profoundly conscious of his position as the Crown's principal minister in the government of the Indies. It was the policy of the Castilian Crown, firmly laid down in the reign of Ferdinand and Isabella, that no subject should be permitted to grow overmighty, and that acts of insubordination should be promptly punished without fear or favor. In persecuting Cortés, Fonseca was doing his duty, even if he did it with some personal relish. But Cortés, in the end, proved too strong for him. The intuitive political genius outmaneuvered and outclassed the bureaucratic mind.

The bureaucratic mind, however, is distinguished by its tenacity; and even if Fonseca himself had failed, his successors in the government of the Indies could hardly afford to let Cortés get away with his success. If the Crown's authority were to be effectively established on the far shores of the Atlantic, acts of private initiative must at all costs be curbed. It was symptomatic of the Court's concern at the very magnitude of Cortés's success that the decree of October 15, 1522, appointing him governor of New Spain, should be accompanied by another, appointing four royal officials to assist him in government.[18] Already the bureaucrats were preparing to wrest power from the military in New Spain.

The four officials—Alonso de Estrada, Gonzalo de Salazar, Rodrigo de Albornoz and Pedro Almindez Chirinos—duly arrived in Mexico in 1524. In the course of this same year, Cortés's two

18. *Cedulario*, doc. 3.

great enemies, Velázquez and Fonseca, both died: Velázquez in June and Fonseca in October. But each in his way secured a posthumous revenge.

Once central Mexico had been conquered, Cortés turned his attention to the west and the south. As part of the project for southward expansion, Pedro de Alvarado was dispatched in 1523 to conquer Guatemala, while another of Cortés's captains, Cristóbal de Olid, was given the task of occupying Honduras. Olid, a former partisan of Velázquez, left Mexico for Havana in January, 1524, to collect reinforcements. In Cuba he met Velázquez, now approaching the end of his life, and was persuaded to defy Cortés, as Cortés himself had once defied the governor of Cuba. Once Olid reached Honduras and had taken possession, he disavowed Cortés's authority. Velázquez had obtained his revenge at last.

The terrible news of Olid's treachery helps to account for the bitterness of Cortés's Fourth Letter. Having at last, after years of waiting, secured the authority that he regarded as rightfully his, he found himself betrayed by one of his own captains, at the prompting of his old enemy, Diego Velázquez. The irony of the situation rubbed salt in the wound. But his fresh denunciations of the archvillain, Velázquez, were this time accompanied by a highly imprudent threat to send a force to Cuba and arrest Velázquez for trial in Spain.[19] Nothing could have been better calculated to alarm the already nervous members of the Council of the Indies. Cortés's proposal to take the law into his own hands, and pursue a personal vendetta in the royal name, could only be regarded as conclusive evidence of the dangers in leaving Cortés in untrammeled exercise of his powers. The emperor's reaction was predictable enough. A special *juez de residencia*, Ponce de León, was appointed in November, 1525, to visit New Spain and conduct a full inquiry into Cortés's activities.

The threat to arrest the governor of Cuba was not the only

19. Below, p. 332.

misjudgment made by Cortés after receiving the news of Olid's treachery. Francisco de las Casas was sent to bargain with Olid, who promptly took him into custody. Cortés, in exasperation, then decided to lead a force to Honduras under his own command to deal with his insubordinate captain. The Honduras expedition, which provides the theme of the Fifth Letter, was an extraordinary saga of heroism and suffering. Cortés emerged from it alive, but a different, and in some ways a broken, man. A heightened religious intensity pervades the letter, as if Cortés had suddenly been made aware of man's weakness in face of the inscrutable ways of a Providence that had seemed for so long to be on his side. The Cortés who staggered ashore at Vera Cruz on May 24, 1526, so thin and weak that people had difficulty in recognizing him, contrasted strangely with the arrogant royal governor who had set out as if on a triumphal procession a year and a half before.

Yet, from the moment of its conception, the Honduras expedition seemed such a wild undertaking that it is questionable whether Cortés had not already lost his touch. The long years of waiting for the emperor's approval had imposed an intolerable strain upon him, perhaps sufficient in itself to affect his judgment. But it is just as likely that the unwelcome presence of royal officials also played a significant part. As soon as the bureaucrats began to arrive in any number, Cortés would cease to be the real ruler of New Spain. Already by the autumn of 1524 he was beginning to feel hemmed in, and the decision to leave for Honduras may well have been prompted by an impulsive desire to escape into a world where he could again enjoy the delights of supreme command.

Whatever the balance of motives, Cortés's decision proved to be the most disastrous of his life. No one else in New Spain enjoyed even a shadow of his personal authority, and his departure was the signal for anarchy. As soon as his back was turned, his enemies came out into the open, and the old faction feuds reasserted themselves in a vicious quarrel over the spoils of conquest. The old

Velázquez faction, which had felt cheated in the distribution of booty and land, turned for leadership to Gonzalo de Salazar. The followers of Cortés, for their part, grouped themselves around the person of his major-domo, Rodrigo de Paz. There was virtual civil war in Mexico in 1525, and Paz was captured, tortured and killed. But the unexpected news of Cortés's survival, and of his imminent return to New Spain, encouraged his followers to launch a counter-offensive; and when Cortés made his triumphal entry into Mexico City in June, 1526, he returned to a capital once again controlled by his own partisans.

But the triumph of 1526 was ephemeral. The violent faction feuds in New Spain merely confirmed the determination of the Council of the Indies to bring it under the effective control of the Crown. A few days after Cortés's return to the capital, Ponce de León arrived to conduct his *residencia*, and suspended him from his office of governor. The net was slowly closing on Cortés, and each new official pulled it a little tighter around him. Fonseca's hand stretched beyond the grave.

Embittered by the apparent neglect of his services, Cortés decided to seek redress, as he had always attempted to seek it, with the emperor in person. He left Mexico for Spain in March, 1528, and was duly accorded a magnificent reception at Court. He was raised to the nobility with the title of Marqués del Valle de Oaxaca, and the emperor confirmed him in the possession of numerous vassals and vast estates. But he did not reappoint him to the governorship of New Spain. When he returned to Mexico in 1530 he returned with no office or special authority, and he found that the royal officials assiduously kept him at arm's length. In the Spanish-style bureaucratic state that was being constructed on the ruins of Mote-cuçoma's empire, there was no place for the conqueror of Mexico. In 1540 he retired to Spain, where he lived out the remaining seven years of his life, a disappointed and disillusioned man. He had played the game according to the rules, but these had been laid down by the Spanish Crown. And Cortés, who had devoted such time and thought to their study, had overlooked the most important fact of all: that those who devise the rules are likely, in the last round, to win the match.

J. H. Elliott
King's College, University of London

⸎ *Translator's Introduction*

I

The years described in these letters were the most brilliant of Cortés's career. Between 1519 and 1526 he rose from being a small landowner in Cuba to become the master of vast territories which reached even beyond the old Mexica domain, and the owner of one of the largest estates anywhere in the world.[1] But the journey to Honduras, described in the fifth and final letter, was the beginning of the end. When he returned to Mexico in 1526 his personal power, which the Castilian crown had been trying to weaken for so long, had been irrevocably undermined, and barely four years later he was denied access to the very city he had overthrown.[2] But despite his final defeat Cortés remained, in fact and popular opinion, the most obviously successful of the *conquistadores*, for the invasion of the Mexica "empire" not only established effective Spanish hegemony throughout Central America, it also provided a model on which nearly all subsequent conquests—most obviously Pizarro's—were consciously based.

Cortés was also the only *conquistador* to have written a detailed narrative account of his deeds. All the "captains"—as they called themselves—of the Spanish crown were required by law to

1. On Cortés's lands see, G. Michael, Riley, *Fernando Cortés and the Marquesado in Morelos.*
2. Gayangos, pp. 497–498.

xxxix

send regular reports (*relaciones*) on their activities, and most did; but none of these are anything more than perfunctory, usually disingenuous, accounts of services rendered. Cortés's letters are also disingenuous, but they are never perfunctory. They are far longer than the conventional *relación* and provided with a conscious, if often clumsy, narrative structure. They were also written in the form not, as was usual, of itemized accounts but of letters.[3] Cortés spoke to his monarch respectfully but also directly and sometimes even threateningly as any great feudal lord would. It is unlikely that Charles V ever himself read any of these letters. During the 1520s he was engaged in more urgent matters than the internal affairs of what was then the least significant of his domains. But it was crucial to Cortés's ambitious enterprise for him to insist on the personal nature of his relationship with his king, since his success depended— as J. H. Elliott has indicated[4]—on his ability to represent himself as a loyal, and frequently maligned and misrepresented, vassal. And in order to do this he had to describe his actions, and in particular the less obviously legitimate of them, in the context of his longer-term achievements and objectives. His letters, then, are, at one level, an exercise in legitimation. They describe a series of events which begins with an act of usurpation, and continues with repeated, more or less legal, rejections of any attempt by the crown—or, as Cortés always insisted, by the crown's officers—to weaken or deprive him of his authority. Cortés had had power conferred on him first by a contract between himself and a largely fictitious town-council, and, after 1522 when he was made Captain-General of New Spain, by the crown itself. Both as the chosen instrument of the town of Vera Cruz and as a royal office-holder he claimed high executive prerogative. He was bound as the servant of the king to ensure that the king's commands were executed; but he also possessed the right to interpret those commands if circumstances required, and, if cir-

---

3. The term "letters of relation" (*Cartas de relación*) was not, however, used by Cortés himself. It appears for the first time in the title of the first printed edition of the Second Letter.
4. Above, pp. xv–xvi.

cumstances required, to set them aside altogether. "A new fact", as he himself put it, "elicits a new opinion".[5] He had the right, and the duty, in the Castilian phrase, "to obey but not comply". The early-modern state was compelled to rely heavily on the loyalty of its servants, since royal ordinances might well be long out of date by the time they reached their destination. The office holder had always to be prepared to act in accordance with the king's wishes even if this required him to act in defiance of his express commands. Thus Cortés sent the royal overseer (*veedor*), Cristóbal de Tapia, who, rather naively, "had come to this land for the purpose of assuming control of the government thereof on behalf of Your Majesty" back to Hispaniola, because Tapia's presence, and Cortés's absence, would, in Cortés's view, have resulted in an Indian uprising. And he arranged to have an Indian plot uncovered shortly after Tapia's arrival just to drive the point home. Under such circumstances, it was clearly not in the interest of the king, or of the Spanish "towns" in Mexico, for him to carry out the king's commands.[6]

Attempts such as this to deprive the conquerors of what they regarded as their rights, the result of the crown's long-term strategy to bring the unruly world of the Americas more firmly under centralised official control, led to a series of local revolts. Cortés's own captains, Cristóbal de Olid and Francisco de las Casas, rebelled against his authority and attempted to create for themselves independent kingdoms in the jungles of Honduras; while in 1544 Francisco Pizarro's younger brother, Gonzalo, seized control of Peru and was only defeated after four years of fighting. Cortés, although frequently suspected of planning a similar uprising, always remained loyal to the crown. He was perhaps the only one among the the *conquistadores* to recognise that the potential wealth of America depended upon the planned exploitation of all her resources. Cortés had seen for himself the ruin of the Antilles in the

5. Below, p. 337.
6. See pp. 272–3 below.

rush for quick returns, and he was not prepared to watch this dismal example repeated in Mexico.[7] He had come not only to conquer but to settle and to "people" (*poblar*), to create a thriving new Spanish community over which he could rule. He therefore refused to allow his men to return to Spain once the conquest was over, and compelled them either to send for the wives they already had "within one year and a half"[8] or to marry locally. His writings are also filled with requests for assistance in developing European agriculture and for the tools required to build European-style towns. The prosperous Spanish community he planned for "New Spain" could, he knew, only be created as a province (none of the American dependencies were ever referred to, nor were they, under law, colonies) of the Castilian crown; and in order to win the crown's recognition and support, he had first to convince its wearer that his acts of insubordination had all been carried out in the royal interest and by the rights which his position, and the services he had done the crown, had conferred upon him. In order to make good this claim in the face of suspicion and distrust, he had to argue his case at far greater length than any of the other *conquistadores* with more immediate ambitions had had to do.

A similar motive lies behind Cortés's attempt to legitimate the conquest itself as first a voluntary donation and thereafter as the suppression of a rebellion. In the light of the subsequent conquests, and in particular of Pizarro's invasion of Peru, this legal posturing might seem curiously unnecessary. But in 1519 no clear pattern of legitimate occupation had been established. Cortés faced an unknown enemy, and was uncertain about the possible response to his actions in Spain. He had, after all, been witness in Hispaniola to several attempts to regularize the crown's political relationship with its new subjects, and he must have been aware that the official

7. See J. H. Elliott, *The Spanish Conquest and Settlement of America*, pp. 192–194.
8. Sánchez Barba, p. 352. He even offered to meet the cost of their passage.

attitude at least insisted that Indians were, in the terms of Isabel's instructions to Nicolas de Ovando, the governor of Hispaniola, "to be well treated as our subjects and our vassals."[9] He also wished to present the "empire" he was conquering in his king's name, *as* an empire. If Motecuçoma's domains could be overrun with the same ease and disregard for the divinely-ordained rights of sovereign peoples, as Cuba had been, then his, Cortés's, achievements would be incapable of sustaining his claims to be worthy of the king's favour. Cortés understood, far better than any of the other *conquistadores*, the truth of Aristotle's claim that a man may be judged by the quality of the things he can command. Motecuçoma had—since the only political model for his conquest Cortés knew was the *reconquista*— to be treated as an Arab ruler would have been. Charles V's claims to sovereignty, *dominium jurisdictionis*, in America had to be grounded in an act of donation, and in a war fought in just defence of that donation.[10] For this reason, too, Cortés had to describe, and describe in considerable detail, the Mexica "empire" as if it truly was, as he said in the beginning of his second letter, "of such a kind that that one might call oneself the emperor of this kingdom with no less glory than of Germany, which, by the Grace of God, Your Sacred Majesty already possesses".[11] Cortés's accounts of Mexico, and in particular of the city of Tenochtitlan, are, therefore, suitably fantastic. Although many of the details are evidently correct, the overall effect is that of barbarian, and predominantly Oriental splendor.[12]

Cortés's elaborate rhetoric also served another purpose, for it is clear that his letters were not written for his king alone. Cortés took detailed notes of his exploits, recorded the names of all those

9. Quoted by A. Pagden, *The Fall of Natural Man*, pp. 34–5.
10. See Eberhard Strauss, *Das bellum iustum des Hernán Cortés in Mexico*, pp. 47–87.
11. Below, p. 48.
12. They are certainly not the "premières donnés proprement ethnographiques sur la civilisation prehispanique" Georges Baudot takes them to be. *Utopie et histoire au Mexique*, p. 7.

he had dealings with, of the places he visited and of the things he saw.[13] The two surviving manuscripts of the letters, one in Vienna, the other in Madrid,[14] are both compiled as if they constituted a history of the conquest, which in a sense they do. No other royal official, either in America or Europe, had two complete scribal copies made of his correspondence, each provided with lengthy prefaces providing details of his early life. Cortés seems to have arranged for each letter to be carried back to Spain as soon as it was ready, and it is likely that his father was responsible for arranging for their immediate publication.[15] Like Columbus and Vespucci before him, Cortés realised the full political importance of the printing press. The open public legitimation of his behavior would be far harder for the crown to ignore than a private request, which is probably one of the reasons why the letters were banned in 1527.[16] But Cortés was also aware of the importance of arguing his case before posterity. If his *fama et gloria* which, as he knew, were the nobleman's most precious, and most precarious, possession were to survive they had to be preserved for later generations on his own terms, and in print.

II

Despite his carefully nurtured public image Cortés the man remains a curiously hazy figure. We know a great deal about his later life because he shared it with so many who wrote about him or engaged in lawsuits against him. He was a royal office-holder, which meant that a great number of documents were drawn up about his activities; and like all office-holders in Spain he had finally

13. See p. 404 below.
14. See p. liii below.
15. An *información* of October 1532 says that one Diego de Garrido "came to this land with the Marquis [Cortes] and then returned immediately to Spain with the account of the land by order of the Captain General, and he returned after the city had been won". Quoted by Baudot, *Utopie et histoire au Mexique*, p. 7.
16. See p. lviii below.

to submit to a *residencia*, a legal investigation into his administration which gave all those—and in Cortés's case they were many—who had any complaint against him full opportunity to make their grievances known. His own writings, however, give remarkably little away, which has made it possible to create a number of personae for him: the soldier-scholar of the Renaissance, a bandy-legged syphilitic liar and, most improbable of all, a humane idealist aiding an oppressed people against tyranny.[17]

We also know remarkably little about his early life. Even López de Gómara, who knew him personally and is even said to have been his chaplain, is frequently uncertain of the facts. He was born, probably in 1484,[18] in Medellín, a small town on the banks of the Guadiana in the province of Extremadura from which so many of the *conquistadores*, Pizarro among them, came. His father, Martín Cortés de Monroy, although poor, was, according to Bartolomé de las Casas who claims to have known him, "an old Christian and, they say, an hidalgo".[19] He fought with Alonso de Monroy, warden of the military order of Alcántara (who may have been his cousin),[20] in the latter's rebellion against the crown, which suggests that he must have been of at least hidalgo status, a member that is of the lesser aristocracy, titleless but with the duty to bear arms for his feudal lord, and exempt from taxation. Monroy was still powerful enough when finally defeated to demand a pardon for himself and his followers, and Martín Cortés does not seem to have suffered for his part in the rebellion. Cortés's mother is an even more shadowy figure. According to Juan Suárez de Peralta she was the daughter of Diego Altamirano de Pizarro, but little or nothing is known about him, although Gómara claimed that both the Pizarro

17. Eulalia Guzmán, *Relaciones de Hernán Cortés* and Ramon Menéndez Pidal, ¿Codicia insacíable? ¿Ilustres hazañas?
18. The usual date, provided by Gómara (p. 296), is 1485. Cortés, however, stated in a petition of February 3 1544 that he was sixty (Wagner, p. 9). In the preface to the Madrid manuscript the birth date has been erased. But the copyist says that he was "eighteen and nearly nineteen" in 1504, which would have meant that he was born in 1486. (f. 1r.)
19. Bk. III, cap. 27.
20. See Federico Gómez de Orozco, "Cual ere el linaje paterno de Cortes".

and the Altamirano families were of noble lineage, and the anonymous compiler of the Madrid manuscript of the *Cartas de relación*
says that they came from Trujillo (a town close to Medellín and
the future birthplace of Francisco Pizarro).[21]

At the age of fourteen Hernán Cortés is said to have enrolled
in the law faculty of the University of Salamanca. Much has been
made of his supposed university training, but it is by no means certain that this was not also merely a pious fabrication by later
chroniclers eager to credit a man who was now a marquis with a
respectable ancestry. If Cortés could make no undisputed claim to
membership of the military aristocracy, then his supposed training
in law made him a fitting candidate for the rising service nobility.
Las Casas, who had no love for "that oppressor of men",[22] said that
he was a Latin scholar "only because he had studied at Salamanca and
was a Bachelor of Law", implying, with some justification, that the
amount of Latin known to bachelors of law was not very great. The
only evidence he provides for Cortés's latinity consist merely of
the commonplace Biblical quotation, "qui non intrat per ostium fur
est et latro".[23] Bernal Díaz also claimed that Cortés was a Bachelor
of Law and that "when he spoke with jurists [*letrados*] and Latin
scholars [*hombres latinos*] he replied to what they said in Latin."[24]
I doubt that there were many *letrados* or *hombres latinos* among
Cortés's followers and Díaz is surely only copying Gómara, from
whom he took far more than he was ever prepared to admit. Since
the records of student admissions for this period are missing, we
shall never know whether Cortés ever went to Salamanca or, if he
did, how much he learnt there. The one person, however, who never
made any claim to being a Bachelor of Law—and he made claims,
many of them exaggerated, to every other one of his accomplish-
ments—was Cortés himself.

21. *Tratado del descubrimiento de las Indias*, p. 30; Gomára, p. 296; and
Biblioteca nacional (Madrid), ms. 3020, f. 1r. Suárez de Peralta says that
Cortés was "the son of hidalgo parents, although extremely poor".
22. *Los tesoros de Perú*, pp. 309–311.
23. Las Casas, Bk. III, cap. 16.
24. Bk. III, cap. 20.

Another version of this phase in Cortés's life is provided by Juan Suárez de Peralta, who heard it from his father (Cortés's brother-in-law).[25] In Suárez's account, Cortés is said to have spent over a year, not in Salamanca, but at a notary's office in Valladolid, where "he learnt to write and to take notes like a notary which he did very well". He then set out to make his fortune in the Italian wars, but turned back when he heard of Columbus's discovery. He then traveled to Seville, where he was again employed by a notary for a short while before leaving for Hispaniola. If Cortés spent, as this account suggests, slightly over one year in Spain, and later five or six years in Hispaniola, working for a notary, then this could have provided him with the slight knowledge of Latin which is apparent in his writings.

Cortés's supposed university training has allowed a number of scholars to impute to him an extensive familiarity with classical and legal literature. Some of the remarks in his letters have been traced to such unlikely sources—unlikely even for a Bachelor of Law in early sixteenth-century Spain—as Livy and Aristotle.[26] Manuel Alcalá has even attempted to show the influence of Latin on Cortés's epistolary style.[27] But on closer examination, all this classical learning disappears. It is only apparent, and then only faintly, in the opening paragraphs of the letters, when he is simply using a conventional mode of address. Moreover, as so much of the substance of his letters is dedicated to the legal or quasi-legal legitimation of his actions, it would be surprising not to find Latinate constructions and even distant echoes of classical historians (although not of Greek philosophers). What are lacking from Cortés's works are precisely the self-conscious literary devices to be found in the work of the university-trained historians. Because of the conditions under which he was writing, his need to mix different genres within a single narrative, his style is often disjunctive, clumsy and verbose.

25. *Tratado del descubrimiento de las Indias*, p. 30 ff.
26. See e.g., Frankl, "Imperio particular e imperio universal en las cartas de relación de Hernán Cortés".
27. *César y Cortés*, pp. 135–138.

But it is also unadorned. There are no direct references to any theological, philosophical or even legal source, and only one quotation from the Gospels which, as J. H. Elliott has pointed out, is produced with such a flourish as to leave the reader in some doubt as to his ability to provide any more.[28]

It is hard to say what other sources, besides the standard legal texts, Cortés had read. Bernal Díaz, who had a great weakness for Roman stories, puts a number of speeches into Cortés's mouth which are full of high-sounding references to classical heroes. These have often been assumed to be, as Díaz claimed, transcripts of Cortés's own words and have been used as evidence of his classical education. But all of them can be traced to more obvious sources, the ballads and romances of chivalry, so beloved of Don Quixote, which were immensely popular in Spain at the time.[29] To judge from a remark made in his instructions to Francisco Cortés, Cortés was also a reader of the romances and may well, as many clearly did, have taken them to be the "true histories" they usually claimed to be.[30]

III

Suárez de Peralta claims that Cortés had originally intended to go, not to the Indies, but to Italy to serve under Hernández de Córdoba, the Great Captain.[31] Why he changed his mind is not apparent. Gómara says that he was to have sailed to Hispaniola with Nicolás de Ovando, the governor of the Indies, and intimates that

28. "The mental world of Hernán Cortés", p. 54.
29. See Irving A. Leonard, *Romances of chivalry in the Spanish Indies*, p. 3.
30. Sánchez Barba, p. 369. Francisco Cortés was told to look for a tribe of women who "reproduce in the manner of the Amazons as described in the ancient histories", by which he probably meant the romances. See Irving A. Leonard, *Books of the Brave*, p. 50.
31. Gómara (p. 296), however, says that "He considered which of the two routes would suit him best and decided to cross over to the Indies because he knew Ovando who would give him a position and because it seemed to him a more profitable journey than the one to Naples on account of the great quantity of gold which had come from there."

Ovando was an acquaintance of the Cortés family.[32] At this point Gómara interpolates the now famous story of Cortés's fall from a wall one night while out to meet a woman.[33] This is supposed to have laid him up for a while and, when he recovered, Ovando had already left. Cortés then returned to his former plan and set out for Italy. Cortés belonged to an overpopulated social class for whom Spain herself had little to offer. As an hidalgo could only honorably achieve success by arms, there were but two roads open to him: the wars in Italy, or the Indies with their as yet unfulfilled promises of wealth. Cortés, perhaps by force of circumstance, decided on the latter alternative.

He finally sailed from the little port of Sanlúcar de Barrameda in 1504. Soon after his arrival in Hispaniola he was made a notary of the recently founded town of Azúa,[34] a post which he held for some five or six years, until in 1511 he accompanied Diego Velázquez in the conquest of Cuba. Afterwards, Cortés settled on the island as Velázquez's secretary, but after a while came to blows with the governor. The reasons for this are not clear. Gómara claims that the dispute arose out of Cortés's refusal to marry Catalina Suárez Marcaida, to whom he had been betrothed early in 1513.[35] Velázquez married María de Cuéllar, who may have been related to the Xuárez sisters,[36] that same year and may have been protecting the family interests. According to Las Casas, however, Cortés had joined a group of conspirators with grievances against Velázquez and had agreed to take their complaints to the Hieron-

32. This seems a little unlikely, although Ovando also came from Extremadura. Ursula Lamb says that Cortés was a distant relation of Ovando but does not give her source. Ursula Lamb, *Frey Nicolás de Ovando*, p. 190.
33. *Loc. cit.*
34. Richard Konetzke, "Hernán Cortés como poblador de la Neuva España", p. 342.
35. p. 297.
36. Velázquez's wife was not Catalina's sister. Gómara (p. 297) says that the governor was enamored of one of the Xuárez sisters but does not say that he married her, and it is likely that María de Cuéllar was in no way related to the Xuárez'. Velázquez himself was also a native of Cuéllar and probably married a local girl.

ymite commission in Hispaniola.[37] Velázquez heard of the plot, had Cortés arrested and threatened to hang him. But, after a number of people had interceded on his behalf, he was pardoned and transferred to a ship to await deportation to Hispaniola. Cortés managed to escape and took refuge in a church, but he was captured while walking about outside and imprisoned for a second time. Gómara also mentions this incident but claims that Cortés was the victim of a plot to discredit him. Juan Suárez speaks of the dispute with Velázquez but says that Cortés had been married to Catalina for some years before it happened.[38] He says that his father helped Cortés make his peace with Velázquez, and tells how Cortés went to the governor to ask his pardon and so startled poor Velázquez that he agreed to drop all charges. Gómara repeats this story in a modified form, adding that Cortés and Velázquez dined together and then spent the night in the same bed.[39]

Sometime before his betrothal to Catalina Suárez, Cortés had settled in Baracoa, later renamed Santiago de Cuba. Here, after making his peace with Velázquez, he twice acted as *alcalde*, and lived with Catalina in the house he had built in 1514. Las Casas, who knew him in "those days of his poverty, humility and low estate", claims that he was as happy with his wife "as if she were the daughter of some duchess".[40]

By the time Hernández de Córdoba sailed on the first expedition from Cuba to Yucatán in 1517, Cortés had acquired a good *encomienda* and some gold mines. But despite this apparent prosperity he was, according to Bernal Díaz, relatively poor. "He spent everything on his own person and on finery for his wife, for he was recently married, and on the guests who gathered in his house because he was of good conversation and amiable."[41] If his accounts

37. Bk. III, chap. 27.
38. *Tratado*, pp. 32–33. Cortés probably married Catalina in 1515 (Wagner, p. 15).
39. *Tratado, loc. cit.* Gómara, p. 298.
40. *Loc. cit.*
41. Chap. 20.

of Cortés's later displays of ceremony are to be believed,[42] Díaz is not exaggerating.

By 1517 Cortés must have achieved some standing on the island, but what his ambitions were at this point it is impossible to say. He appears to have shown no interest in either the Córdoba expedition or in that of Juan de Grijalva, which sailed the following year. If he was dissatisfied with his life in Cuba and the meager prospects it afforded, he must have been fully aware of every development that offered him some possibility for advancement. On the other hand, the expeditions of 1517 and 1518 were trading ones with no license to settle. [43] They would have given Cortés very little scope, and even if he had invested and sailed in them he would only have been one among many. Furthermore, it was only when Pedro de Alvarado was detached from Grijalva's main fleet and sent back to Cuba with some twenty thousand *pesos* that there was any proof that the mainland held any riches at all.

Why Cortés was chosen to command the largest of the fleets to leave Cuba under Velázquez's auspices is still something of a mystery. Cortés had no experience, and it seems unlikely that he contributed enough toward the cost of the expedition to secure his appointment as captain that way.[44] There is probably some truth in the story that Amador de Lares, Velázquez's *contador*, and the merchant Andrés de Duero had entered into a partnership with Cortés and used their money and influence to bring about his appointment.[45]

The original purpose of the Cortés expedition was supposedly to find Grijalva, who had been away too long. But Grijalva returned before Cortés left, having reached the west coast of Cuba on October 1 or 2. Whether or not Velázquez knew of Grijalva's subsequent arrival in Santiago before he drew up his instructions

42. Cf. Bernal Díaz, chap. 204.
43. See, however, the First Letter, n. 17.
44. See the First Letter, n. 20. Suárez de Peralta says that he was not made a captain but only a *caudillo* (*Tratado*, p. 35).
45. Bernal Díaz, chap. 19. See also the First Letter, n. 20.

for Cortés on October 23 is uncertain. Shortly afterwards he seems to have turned against Cortés and, according to Gómara, tried to prevent him from being supplied with provisions,[46] but it is hard to believe that Velázquez intended to abandon a profitable trading venture simply because Grijalva need no longer be looked for. Bernal Díaz provides what is probably the most likely answer, that Velázquez's kinsmen, led by someone called Juan Millán, had poisoned the governor's mind against Cortés.[47] No doubt Velázquez was also a little apprehensive about Cortés's increasing power.

Cortés now decided to depart as soon as possible and before Velázquez had time to prevent him. After raiding the town slaughterhouse, he left Santiago on November 18. Velázquez must have heard of his departure almost immediately because he is said to have come down to the harbor and to have called out after Cortés, "Why, *compadre*, is this the way you leave? Is this a fine way to say farewell to me?" On hearing this, Cortés came across to him in a heavily armed boat and called back, "Forgive me, Your Worship, for this and similar things have to be done rather than thought about."[48]

The fleet left Santiago short of food. Once clear of the port, Cortés sent a caravel to Jamaica for provisions and led the rest of the ships to Macaca where he bought three hundred loads (*cargas*) of bread and some pigs. He then moved on to Trinidad, from where a caravel was sent, under Diego de Ordaz, to intercept a shipload of provisions in the care of Juan Núñez Sedeño. Ordaz was successful, and four thousand *arrobas* of bread, fifteen hundred flitches of pork and a number of chickens passed into Cortés's holds. Sedeño decided to cut his losses and joined Cortés.

46. P. 300.
47. Bernal Díaz. chap. 22.
48. Las Casas, bk. III, chap. 115, Gómara, *loc. cit.* Suárez de Peralta tells a slightly different version of these events. He claims that Velázquez revoked the orders that he had issued to Cortés and transferred his authority to one Luís de Medina. Xuárez got wind of this maneuver, overtook Velázquez's messenger to Medina, killed him and took the papers to Cortés, who embarked at once. (*Tratado*, pp. 34–35.) See also Bernal Díaz, chap. 20, who denies the whole affair.

The fleet now moved swiftly around the south coast of the island, collecting provisions and reinforcements. It then rounded Cabo Corrientes and headed toward Havana, while Cortés traveled overland. Here, however, the people remained loyal to Velázquez and refused to supply him, with the exception of the bishop's tithe collector and the vendor of papal bulls: these last sold him "2,000 flitches of pork and a like number of loads of maize, yucca and chili."

Cortés was now sufficiently well equipped and had swelled his army with two hundred of Grijalva's men, collected on the course of his journey. He returned along the coast to a port near the Cabo San Antonio, called Guaniguanico. Here he held a muster and delivered a speech to his men. On February 18, 1519, after having heard Mass, the fleet put out into the Yucatán Channel, sailing toward Cape Catoche, "the nearest point of Yucatán."[49]

IV

There are two surviving manuscript compilations of the *Cartas de relación*, one in the Biblioteca nacional in Madrid (ms. 3020), the other in the Österreichische national bibliothek in Vienna (ms. 1600).[50] The Madrid copy contains a long preface by the scribe but omits the so-called "first letter". The Vienna codex is, in a number of ways, obviously the more complete manuscript and contains the only known transcript of the first letter. It was first discovered in 1777 by the Scottish historian William Robertson, who, in his

49. This account is taken from Gómara (pp. 300–301). Andrés de Tapia gives a slightly different version; see *The Conquistadors*, Patricia de Fuentes, trans. and ed., pp. 19–20.
50. There is a facsimile edition published in Graz in 1960 with an introduction and bibliography by Charles Gibson. The compiler of the codex and the date of compilation are unknown. Gibson (p. XIV) offers very cogent reasons for dating it 1527 or 1528, and Pascual de Gayangos thinks that it was probably compiled by Juan de Sámano, secretary to the Consejo Real y Supremo de las Indias, who had the Fifth Letter in his possession at that time (Gayangos, p. IX. See p. lxiv below).

researches for *The History of America*, had failed to locate in Spain the letter that Cortés mentions at the beginning of the Second Letter as a "very long and detailed account." Robertson, however, reasoned that as Charles V was preparing to leave for Germany at the time when Cortés's representatives arrived in Spain, the missing letter might be in Vienna. He then obtained permission to have the Imperial Library searched.[51] This brought to light the codex which, although it did not contain the missing letter, did contain a notarial copy of a letter from the municipal council of Vera Cruz, the *Carta de la Justicia y Regimiento de la Rica Villa de la Vera Cruz a la Reina Doña Juana y al Emperador Carlos V, su Hijo, en 10 de julio de 1519* (hereinafter referred to as *Carta*).[52] This was first published by Navarrete in 1842 in *CDHE*, vol. I, pp. 410–472.

Although called *Primera Relación* for the sake of convenience, it was not written by Cortés and is not the account referred to in the Second Letter. The *Carta* is prefaced by a short account of the conquest by the compiler of the codex. This preface, which has been omitted from the present translation, was included in a copy of the codex made in 1778 by a Spanish diplomat, Domingo de Iriarte, and sent to the Academia de la Historia in Madrid. It was printed, together with the *Carta*, by Navarrete and has been reprinted in some subsequent editions of Cortés's writings, including the most recent one by Manuel Alcalá (see p. lxv below).

The actual First Letter has never been found. A number of hypotheses have been put forward as to its fate on arrival in Spain, but these have not helped to locate it. Recently, the Mexican historian Josá Valero Silva[53] has suggested that although Cortés may in fact have written such a letter he never sent nor ever intended to send it. The lost First Letter, he argues, would have provided evi-

51. William Robertson, *The History of America*, I: X–XI.
52. Fols. 2v–19r.
53. *El Legalismo de Hernán Cortés como instrumento de su conquista*, pp. 31–35.

dence against Cortés. He could have added little to what had already been said, but by attempting to explain his position himself he ran the risk of undoing his whole strategy, which depended for its success on convincing the emperor that his break with Velázquez had been in response to a demonstration of the popular will. There are, in fact, only two things of importance which the *Carta* actually omits: an account and justification of Cortés's hasty departure from Cuba and an explanation of why he was taking a fifth of the booty instead of the tenth to which he was entitled.

It is difficult indeed to imagine how a "very long and detailed account [*relación*]" could have been made out of the events leading up to the founding of Vera Cruz, unless this account were nothing more than a retelling of the story as it is related in the *Carta*, for to differ in any particular from the *Carta* would have been disastrous. But the "sort of bibliographical tradition" which argues for the existence of a lost First Letter is too strong to be ignored. It is mentioned by a number of writers, and it may be helpful at this point to examine the statements of two of them.

Bernal Díaz makes a direct reference to the letter but provides little information about it: "Cortés also wrote, on his own account, a true report [*relación*] of the events, or so he told us but we never saw his letter." [54] If the army did not actually see the letter, although Cortés declared publicly that he had written one, the representatives of the municipal council of Vera Cruz, Montejo and Puertocarrero, may have been instructed to pretend that they were carrying such a letter or to suppress it. Montejo was one of the Velázquez faction, and by all accounts far from easy to handle. By choosing to send him to Spain, Cortés succeeded in keeping him out of the way and, at the same time, of implicating Velázquez's supporters in his scheme. [55] About Puertocarrero we know very

54. Chap. 54.
55. Bernal Díaz (chap. 53) says that Cortés bribed Montejo with two thousand *pesos*, "to have him on his side."

little, but Cortés seems to have treated him well, giving him first a horse in Trinidad and later Marina; certainly he could have been trusted either not to take the letter or at least not to deliver it.

The only author who gives evidence of having both seen and used the missing letter is Gómara. H. R. Wagner[56] has shown fairly conclusively that at the time of writing his history Gómara had in his possession a letter from Cortés which is now lost, and that a copy of that same letter was also in the possession of José de Sigüenza, a Hieronymite friar and the author of a history of his order.[57] Wagner's theory is based on one short but telling sentence that occurs with identical wording both in Gómara and Sigüenza. The sentence, which refers to the financing of the expedition to Mexico, reads, "He [Cortés] bought two ships, six horses and much clothing."[58] Although much was said about his contribution toward the cost of the expedition both during and after the conquest, nowhere in any of his writings that have so far come to light, does Cortés make any specific claims about what he purchased.

Sigüenza's book was published in 1605, but he does not seem to have known Gómara's work and so presumably could not have been copying from him. Gómara's reference to the missing letter is also the only one that provides substantial details of its contents.

"By the hands of the delegates [procuradores] he sent the Emperor the report [relación] and notarized statement of events [autos] which he had and he also wrote a very long letter to the Emperor (he was called that although they did not know it then), in which he gave a summarized account of all that had happened since he had left Santiago de Cuba; the quarrels and differences between him and Diego Velázquez, the bickerings in his camp, the hardships they had suffered, the good they had accomplished in the royal service, the greatness and the wealth of the country and his hope to subject it to the royal crown of Castile. He undertook to

56. "The lost first letter of Cortés."
57. The *Tercera Parte* was published in Madrid in 1605.
58. "*. . . compro dos naos, seys cavallos y muchos vestidos.*"

win Mexico for the Emperor, and to take the great king Moctezuma dead or alive. Finally he begged the Emperor's assistance in
the performance of his duties, and the money for the purchase of
supplies that would have to be sent to the new land, which he had
discovered at his own cost, to compensate him for his hardship and
expenses."[59]

The *relación* mentioned at the beginning of this paragraph
must be the lost letter. Yet Gómara does no more than note its existence. What he describes at such length would appear to be a letter
similar to the private ones that accompany the Third and Fourth
Letters; not a *relación* but a personal plea for assistance and recognition.

It is possible, therefore, that Cortés pretended both to his
men and the emperor that he had sent his own account of the events
described in the *Carta*. As captain of the expedition he was bound
to do this and had even been instructed by Velázquez to do so.[60]
Instead he sent a personal letter, a copy of which was before
Gómara when he wrote his history and later came into the possession of Sigüenza. This letter was probably not a true *relación* and
contained no information not to be found in the *Carta* except that
already quoted, which would be quite likely to occur in a letter
endeavoring to show that Cortés had discovered Mexico "at his
own cost."

The problem remains of how this letter, which may have
been given to Gómara by Cortés himself, came into the possession
of Sigüenza. Sigüenza was the librarian at the Escorial, probably
until his death in 1606, and Wagner suggests that he might have
examined Gómara's papers, which were taken there after Gómara's
death by Honorate Juan, the bishop of Osma, and later came into

59. Gómara, p. 323. The translation is by L. B. Simpson, *Cortés, the Life
of the Conqueror*, pp. 87–88. The letter is also mentioned by Herrera
(dec. II, bk. IX, chap. 7), but it is unlikely that he ever saw it. It is also
said to have been used by Peter Martyr in the Fourth Decade of *De
Orbe Novo*, but there is little evidence to support this. See H. R. Wagner, "Peter Martyr and his works," pp. 255–256.
60. *Cedulario*, p. 19.

the hands of Philip II's son, Don Carlos, who may have deposited them in the Escorial. Wagner also suggests two other possibilities: first that Charles V took the letter to the Hieronymite monastery of Juste; second, that the letter was in the convent of Sisla in Toledo where Sigüenza was living in 1592 and where a number of other documents about the Hieronymite commission of 1516 were kept.[61] If Cortés's letter was also in the Sisla, he may have sent a copy of it to Santo Domingo. But no ship was sent to the islands until Alonso de Ávila went there for supplies in 1520, by which time the Hieronymite Fathers had returned to Spain. It is possible, therefore, that Ávila took the letter with him when he sailed with Quiñones in 1522. This last hypothesis makes an otherwise inexplicable statement by Andrés González Barcía particularly interesting. He suggests that the lost letter was either suppressed on the instance of Narváez or "what is more certain is that it is the one Juan Florín took from Alonso de Ávila or was lost in the fight he had with him."[62] Unless he is referring to a copy of the letter from the Hieronymites, why should he suppose that Ávila was carrying to Spain an account of events already two years old?

The Second Letter was printed in November 1522 by Jacobo Cromberger, the third in March 1523, also by Cromberger, and the fourth in 1525. All three letters went through several editions in Latin, French and Italian. But in March 1527 any further printings in Spanish were forbidden by royal decree. In 1553 the crown issued another decree forbiding the export to the Indies of all the histories of the conquest and later the same year placed a ban on the works of López de Gómara.[63] The crown, concerned as it was with increasing its own precarious hold over the government of

---

61. Elsewhere, Sigüenza mentions other papers "in my care," and on p. 109, discussing the *residencia* of Rodrigo de Figueroa, he says, "And our religious greatly favored him (as may be seen in the papers preserved in the Sisla in Toledo)," which suggests that he was in fact in the Sisla at the time of writing.

62. *Epitome de la bibliotheca de don Antonio de León Pinelo*, II: 598, and see p. 330 below.

63. Marcel Bataillon, "Hernán Cortés, autor prohibido"; *Cedulario*, p. 95; Cuevas, p. 259 and Wagner, pp. XIII–XIV.

its American dependencies, found Cortés's mythologizing of the conquest, which had become a powerful ideological weapon in the hands of the rebellious *conquistador* elite, an obvious political embarrassment.

Like the *Carta*, the Fifth Letter was also first discovered in the Vienna Codex. In the opening paragraph Cortés mentions another letter which has never been found. This is sometimes referred to as the Fifth, and the actual Fifth as the Sixth. But it is impossible to say whether this was a true *relación* or simply one of the private letters, of the kind which were sent with both the second and the third *Carta de relación*. All Cortés himself says is, "I wrote to your Majesty concerning certain events which took place in that gulf they call Las Hibueras between the two captains I had sent there and another called Gil González, and also about my own arrival there later", which, given the content of the Fifth Letter, does not sound like material for an independent account of any length. The John Carter Brown Library possesses a sixteenth-century copy of the Fifth Letter,[64] which contains the following note by an unknown hand: "I do not think that the fifth letter or relation has been printed, for I have not been able to see it, but I hope to have it from the secretary Sámano. The sixth letter or relation has also not been printed. However, I had it written down and transcribed, and it is as follows." If Sámano did, in fact, have the so-called Fifth Letter in his possession and was responsible for the compilation of the Vienna Codex as Pascual de Gayangos, Cortés's first modern editor, believed, then it is difficult to understand why he did not include it with the others.

The transcript in the Vienna Codex lacks the final paragraph. Both the Madrid manuscript and the John Carter Brown copy, however, conclude: "From the city of Temistitan of this New Spain on the Third day of the month of September in the year of the birth of Our Lord and Saviour Jesus Christ, 1526".

The Fifth Letter was first published by Navarrete in 1844

64. Call number, Codex Sp. 15.

in CDHE, vol. IV, pp. 8–167. All five letters were printed together for the first time by Pascual de Gayangos in Paris in 1866 in an edition based on the Madrid manuscript and filled with incorrect readings. There is still no satisfactory modern Spanish text, although in 1958 the Mexican archaeologist and *indigenista*, Eulalia Guzmán, published a heavily annotated version of the First and Second Letters based on a new reading of the Vienna Codex. In 1960 Manuel Alcalá edited a new text of all five letters which was again based, albeit somewhat loosely, on the Vienna Codex and this was reprinted in 1963 together with a number of Cortés's other writings in a useful volume edited by Sánchez Barba.

In preparing this translation I, too, have relied largely on the text of the Vienna Codex. I have also consulted the Madrid manuscript, the Gayangos, Guzmán and Alcalá editions as well as the first printed versions of the Second, Third and Fourth Letters. But as any translation must necessarily deviate too far from the original to make textual precision possible, I have taken the liberty of dividing the text into a greater number of paragraphs and shorter sentences than the original. The spelling of proper and place names have been retained as they appear in the original, and the correct orthography or modern equivalent, where possible, given in the endnotes. Where confusion might arise as to the position of towns and villages, the modern state to which they now belong has also been given. There are, however, a large number of Mexican names about which I was unable to discover anything.

Anthony Pagden
King's College, Cambridge

HERNÁN CORTÉS: *Letters from Mexico*

The First Letter

Sent to the Queen Doña Juana and to the Emperor, Charles V, Her Son, by the Justiciary and Municipal Council of the Muy Rica Villa de la Vera Cruz on the Tenth Day of July, 1519.

Most high, mighty and excellent princes, most catholic and powerful kings and sovereigns:

We have reason to believe that Your Royal Highnesses have been informed, by letters of Diego Velázquez, the admiral's[1] lieutenant in the island of Fernandina (Cuba), of a new land that was discovered in these parts some two years ago more or less, and which was first called Cozumel and later Yucatan,[2] without it being either the one or the other as Your Royal Highnesses shall see from our report. For the accounts previously made of this land to Your Majesties, as to its wealth, and the way in which it was discovered and other details which have been described, were not, nor could have been true, as in this report we are sending Your Majesties, because until now no one has known any of these things. Here we will treat of the beginning, when it was first discovered, up until its present state, so that Your Highnesses may know what land it is, what people live in it, the way in which they live, their rites and ceremonies, religions and customs and what profit Your Highnesses may gain

3

from it, or have already gained; and by whom Your Majesties have been served, so that Your Highnesses may in all things do as You see fit. This very true and trustworthy account is as follows.

It was some two years ago, more or less, that in the city of Santiago,[3] which is on the island of Fernandina where we then lived, three citizens of that same island met together. Their names were Francisco Fernández de Córdoba, Lope Ochoa de Caycedo and Cristóbal Morante; and, as it is customary in these islands which have been settled by Spaniards in Your Highnesses' name to bring Indian slaves from the other islands where Spaniards have settled, these men sent two ships and a brigantine for this purpose.[4] We believe, although we do not know for certain as yet, that Diego Velázquez owned a fourth share of this fleet. One of the owners, Francisco Fernández de Córdoba, went as captain and took with him Antón de Alaminos,[5] of the town of Palos, as pilot; and we ourselves have taken on this Antón de Alaminos as our pilot and now send him to Your Highnesses so that he may further inform Your Majesties.

They continued their journey and landed on the aforementioned land, named Yucatán, which is situated some sixty or seventy leagues from the island of Fernandina and from this land of the Rica Villa de la Vera Cruz, where we, in Your Highnesses' Royal name now are. There they landed at a village named Campoche,[6] to whose lord they gave the name Lázaro, and gave him two spindles with a cloth of gold for a bed, and other gold articles. As the natives, however, would not permit them to remain on their land, they then sailed some ten leagues down the coast, where they landed near another town, called Mochocobon, whose chief was called Champoton.[7] There the Spaniards were well received by the natives, although they did not allow them to enter their town. That night the Spaniards left the ships and slept on shore. When the natives saw this, they attacked them on the following morning, killing twenty-six Spaniards and wounding all the others. When Francisco

Fernández de Córdoba saw this he fled with those who remained to take refuge in the ships.

When this same captain discovered that more than a quarter of his men had been killed, that all the rest were wounded and that he himself had received more than thirty wounds and was lucky to be alive, he returned with his ships to the island of Fernandina, where he informed the above-mentioned Diego Velázquez that they had discovered a land rich in gold; for he had seen that all the natives wore gold rings, some in their nostrils and some in their ears and in other parts; and likewise that there were buildings of stone and mortar. He spoke also of a host of other things for which that land was renowned, and told Velázquez, if he could, to send ships in order to barter for gold, because there was much to be had.

On hearing this, Diego Velázquez, moved more by cupidity than any other passion, dispatched his representative to Hispaniola with a request made to the Reverend Fathers of St. Jerome,[8] who acted as governors of the Indies, asking that they, with the powers invested in them by Your Highnesses, should grant him license to explore that coast. He added that he would be doing a great service to Your Majesties, if they permitted him to trade with the natives for gold, pearls, precious stones and other things which, save for the Royal fifth,[9] would all become his. The Fathers granted him his license because he knew the whereabouts of this land and claimed to have discovered it at his own expense; also because such an under-taking would further Your Highnesses' interests. At the same time, without informing the Fathers, he sent Gonzalo de Guzmán[10] as his representative with the same account to Your Royal Highnesses, adding that he wished to conquer the land at his own expense and begging Your Majesties to make him *adelantado* and governor of it, in addition to requesting certain other privileges which Your Majesties will have already seen from his account.

In the meantime, as he had received permission in Your Majesties' name from the Reverend Fathers of St. Jerome, he made haste to equip three ships and a brigantine so that if it should not have pleased Your Majesties to grant the requests conveyed by Gonzalo de Guzmán, the fleet would already have set sail with the other permission. Once they were ready, he appointed Juan de Grijalba,[11] a relation of his, as their captain, and with him went 170 men from that same island; and some of us were among them as captains, in Your Highnesses' service. Not only did we and those others go and risk our lives, but we supplied almost all the provisions of the fleet from our own stocks, spending a large part of our fortunes. Antón de Alaminos went as pilot, for he had first discovered the land with Francisco Fernández de Córdoba.

On this journey they followed the same route as previously, but, before reaching that land, they discovered a small island to the south of it, some thirty leagues round the coast: this island is called Cozumel.[12] On it they came to a village which they called San Juan de Portalatina; and they renamed the island Santa Cruz. The day they arrived, some 150 Indians came out to watch them, but on the following day, as it later appeared, they all left their villages and fled into the forest. As the captain was in need of water, he had sailed off that same day, but while pursuing his journey decided to return to the island. When he landed, the villages were totally deserted, and once he had taken his water he returned to the ships without exploring the island or learning anything about it as he ought to have done, so as to render a true account of it to Your Royal Highnesses. He then set sail and continued on his way until he reached the land which Francisco Fernández de Córdoba had discovered; afterwards they followed the coast in a southwesterly direction until they reached a bay to which Grijalba and Alaminos gave the name of the Bahía de la Ascensión.[13] The pilots thought that bay was very close to the Punta de las Veras, which is the land that Vicente Yáñez[14] discovered and marked down, and which runs into the middle of that bay. And so large is the bay itself that it is thought to reach to the Northern Sea.

Thence they returned back along the same coast until they

1. Cortés at the age of sixty-three with the arms granted to him as Marqués de la Valle de Oaxaca. From *El Cortés Valeroso y Mexicana* by Lasso de la Vega, 1588. *Courtesy of the British Museum.*

rounded the point of that land, and sailed along the north coast, reaching the port of Campoche, whose lord is called Lázaro, to trade on behalf of Diego Velázquez, who had ordered them to do so, and also because they had much need of water. When the natives saw them approach they lined themselves in battle order to bar their way into the village. The captain then called to them through an interpreter he had with him,[15] and made the Indians who came forward understand that he came only to trade with them and to take water; and so he went with them to a spring which was close to the village. While taking the water he began to tell them through the interpreter how he would give them the ornaments he was carrying in exchange for gold. When the Indians understood they told him to go away, as they had no gold; but he asked them to let him take the water, after which he would go. Despite his requests, however, the following morning at the hour of Mass he was attacked by the Indians armed with bows and arrows, spears and shields. One Spaniard was killed in the fighting and the captain Grijalba and many others were wounded; that evening they embarked in the caravels without having entered the Indian village or learnt anything to report to Your Royal Majesties.

From there they traveled along the coast until they reached a river which they called the Grijalba[16] and which they entered about the hour of vespers. On the following morning a great number of Indian warriors lined up on both sides of the river to defend their land; and some of us believed that there were as many as five thousand. When the captain saw this, he ordered that no one should go ashore but spoke from the ships to the Indians through his interpreters, asking them to come closer so that he might explain the reason for his coming; twenty natives then boarded a canoe and very cautiously approached the ships. The captain told them that he had come only to trade and that he wished to be their friend. He asked them to bring gold, which he would exchange for the ornaments he was carrying.

So, on the following morning they brought some ornaments

of fine gold, and the captain gave them, in exchange, what he thought appropriate. He remained there that day and sailed away on the next without learning anything more about the land. He continued along the coast until he reached a bay which they called San Juan, and the captain landed with certain of his men on some deserted beaches. As the natives had seen the ships coming along the coast, they gathered there, and the captain spoke to them through his interpreters, and had a table brought on which he laid his goods, giving them to understand that he came to trade and to be their friend. When they saw and understood this, the Indians began to bring strips of cloth and some gold ornaments which they traded with the captain. The captain then sent one of the caravels back to Diego Velázquez with all they had obtained.[17] The captain himself sailed on down the coast with the remaining ships; and he went some forty-five leagues without landing or seeing anything, save what was visible from the sea. He then turned back for the island of Fernandina without seeing any other thing on that land worthy of note, from which Your Royal Highnesses may see that none of the other accounts of this land can have been true, for they learnt nothing of its secrets, but have written according to their fancies.

When the ship which Grijalba had dispatched from the bay of San Juan reached the island of Fernandina, and Diego Velázquez saw the gold it carried, and learnt from Grijalba's letters of the cloth and ornaments which he had been given in exchange, it seemed to him that the profit was small, in view of the stories he had heard from the people who returned in the caravel, and in relation to his own lust for gold. He forthwith put it about that he had not covered the cost of equipping the fleet, which distressed him, and that he was ill-pleased to see how little Grijalba had achieved. But Diego Velázquez had in fact little cause for complaint, because he covered the cost of the fleet with some skins and barrels of wine and some boxes of linen shirts and barter beads and other goods which he sent with it, which he sold to us here at four *pesos de oro* for the wine, which is two thousand *maravedís* the *arroba*, and the linen shirts he sold for two *pesos de oro* and the bags of green beads at two *pesos*.[18] With this he covered the cost of his fleet and even made some money. We make such a detailed account of this to Your Majesties so that You may know that the fleets which have been sent by Diego Velázquez up to now have been equipped by him as much by ordinary trade as by proper outfitting; and that we have, although we suffered many hardships, served Your Royal Highnesses with our persons and the wealth of our estates, and shall continue to serve as long as our lives permit.

While Diego Velázquez was thus vexed on account of the little gold he had been brought, and eager to acquire more, he decided, without even informing the Hieronymite Fathers, to gather a fleet and to send it to look for his relative Juan de Grijalba. So as to do it at somewhat less cost to himself, he spoke with Fernando Cortés,[19] citizen and *alcalde* of the city of Santiago on Your Majesties' behalf, and suggested that between them they should fit out some eight or ten ships, for at that time Fernando Cortés was better equipped than anyone else on the island, having three ships of his own, and ready cash and being well thought of on the island. It was thought that many more people would follow him than anyone else, as in fact occurred. When Fernando Cortés heard what Diego Velázquez proposed, he, being most eager to serve Your Royal Highnesses, decided to spend his entire fortune in equipping the fleet and paid for nearly two-thirds of it, providing not only ships and supplies but also giving money to those who were to sail in the fleet but were unable to equip themselves with all they required for the journey.[20]

Once the fleet had been made ready, Diego Velázquez appointed Fernando Cortés captain of it in Your Majesties' name, in order to explore the land and trade for gold and do all that Grijalba had not done. The fleet, however, was disposed according to Velázquez's orders, although he contributed but a third of the cost, as Your Royal Highnesses may see from the instructions and authority which Fernando Cortés received in Your Majesties' name, and which we now send by our deputies.[21] And Your Majesties should also know that the third part contributed by Velázquez consisted in the main of wine and cloth and other things of no great value, to be sold to us later at a much higher price than he paid for them, so that we might say that it is with us Spaniards, Your Royal Highnesses' subjects, that he has traded, and has invested his funds very profitably.

And when the above-mentioned fleet was ready Your Royal Highnesses' captain Fernando Cortés left the island of Fernandina with ten caravels and four hundred soldiers, among whom were many gentlemen and knights, sixteen of them with horses. The first land they reached was the island of Cozume[1], which is now called Santa Cruz—as we said above; and when they landed in the port of San Juan de Portalatina they found the village deserted as though it had never been occupied by a living soul. And Fernando Cortés, wishing to know why that place was so deserted, ordered his men to leave their ships and quarter themselves in the village. While he was there he learnt from three Indians, whom they had captured in a canoe fleeing to the land of Yucatán, that the chieftains of Cozume[1], when they saw the Spaniards land, had left their villages and fled into the forest with all their people, for fear of the Spaniards, not knowing with what intentions they were coming. Cortés then spoke to them through his interpreter and told them that he had not come to do them harm but to instruct and bring them to the knowledge of our Holy Catholic Faith, so they might become Your Majesties' vassals and serve and obey You, as do all the other Indians in these parts which are inhabited by Spaniards. On being reassured in this fashion by the captain, they lost much of their fear and said they would go and call their chieftains who were in the forests in the interior. The captain then gave them a letter of safe-conduct for their chieftains. They departed, saying they would return within five days. When, however, the captain had waited three or four days more than the agreed time, and had seen that they were not coming, he decided, in order to prevent all

the Indians from leaving the island, to send an expedition along the
coast. He sent two captains, each with a hundred men, and ordered
them to go, one to each end of the island, and speak with any chieftains they might meet, telling them how he was waiting to speak
with them on Your Majesties' behalf in the port of San Juan de
Portalatina; and that they were to beg and persuade them as best
they could to come to the aforementioned port; but they were in
no way to harm their persons, houses or properties, so as to avoid
alarming them and driving them still farther away. The two captains departed, as Fernando Cortés had commanded, and within
four days returned saying that all the villages they had come across
were deserted. They brought with them, however, some ten or
twelve people amongst whom was one of rank; and Fernando
Cortés spoke with him on Your Highnesses' behalf, telling him to
call the other chieftains, for he, Cortés, would on no account leave
that island until he had seen and spoken with them. The Indian
replied that he would do so and departed with a safe-conduct to
look for those chieftains. After two days he returned with one who
said he was lord of the island and had come to see what the Spaniards wanted. The captain replied that he had not come to do them
harm, but to persuade them to the knowledge of our Holy Faith;
and they should know that we were subjects of the most powerful
monarchs in the world, whom most of the world obeyed. What he,
Francisco [sic.] Cortés, required of them was only that the chieftains and people of the island should also owe obedience to Your
Highnesses; and told them that by doing so they would be much
favored, and no one thereafter would molest them. The chieftain
replied that he was happy to do so and sent for all the other chieftains of the island who, when they arrived, expressed satisfaction
with all that Hernando Cortés had told their lord. He then commanded them to return, and so reassured had they been that within
a few days the villages were as full of people as before, and the
Indians went among us with so little fear that it seemed as if they
had known us for a long time.

In the meantime the captain learnt that some Spaniards had been held captive in Yucatán for seven years by the command of certain chieftains; their caravel [22] had been wrecked in the shallows off Jamaica while sailing from *Tierra Firme* and they had escaped in an open boat which had brought them to this land where they were captured by the Indians. The captain had left the island of Fernandina with instructions to look for these Spaniards, and as he had now received news of them and where they were to be found, it seemed to him that he would be rendering great service to God and Your Majesties in attempting to rescue them from captivity. He wished, therefore, to go in person with the entire fleet, and would have done so had not the pilots prevented him, saying that they would all be lost, for the coast was very rocky, as indeed it is, and with no harbor or bay where the ships might put ashore. He therefore abandoned the idea and sent instead some Indians in a canoe, who had said they knew the chieftain who was holding the Spaniards; and he wrote to these Spaniards saying that, if he did not come himself with the fleet to rescue them, it was only because the coast difficult and dangerous to land on; but he asked them to attempt to escape by canoe and said that he would wait for them there on the island of Santa Cruz.

Three days later the captain, dissatisfied with his plans and believing that the Indians would be unable to do everything as he wished, sent two brigantines and one smaller vessel with forty men on board to that land, to recapture the captive Spaniards if they could find them. He also sent another three Indians with a letter, and orders to land and search for the Spaniards.[23] When the ships reached the land the three Indians were sent ashore to search for the Spaniards as the captain had ordered; and they waited six days for them on that coast with such difficulty that they almost foundered and were lost, for the sea was very rough as the pilots had said. Seeing that neither the Spaniards nor the Indians who had been sent to look for them had come, they decided to return to where Fernando Cortés was waiting for them, on the island of Santa Cruz.

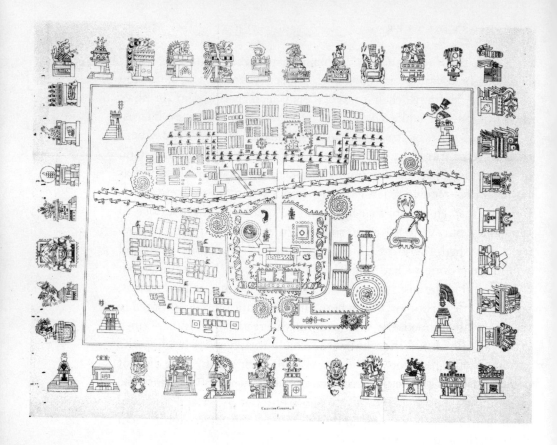

2. Map of Tlaxcala. The top right-hand sector is Tizatlan, the bottom right-hand sector Quiahuixtlan, the top left-hand sector Octelolco and the bottom left-hand sector Tepeticpac. The river Atzompa crosses the city from North to South (left to right, the map being oriented along an East-West axis). From Alfredo Chavero, *Pintures Jeroglíficas*, Mexico 1901. *Courtesy of the British Museum.*

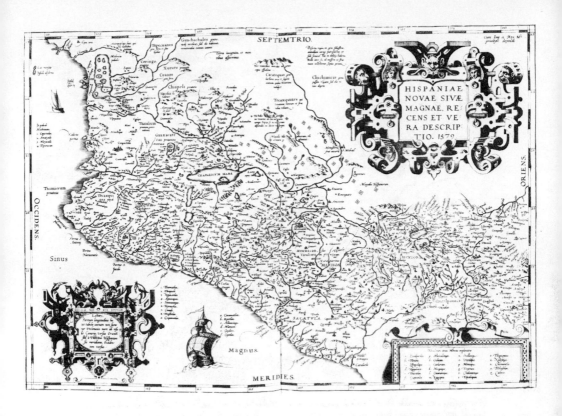

3. Map of New Spain by Abraham Ortelius. From *Additamentum Theatri Orbis Terrarum*. 1579. *Courtesy of the British Museum.*

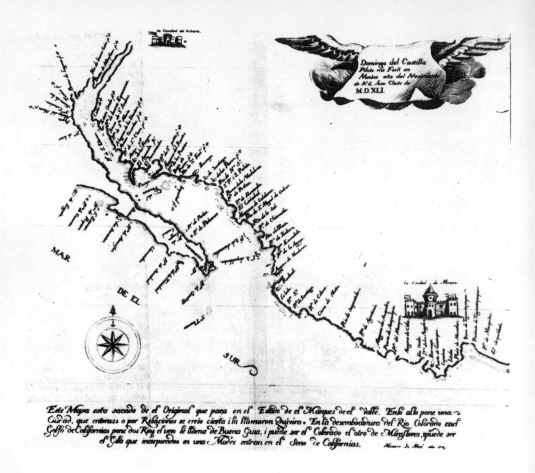

4. Map of the Southern Sea made by the pilot Domingo de Castillo. From Archbishop Lorenzana's edition of Cortés letters, Mexico 1770. The legend reads: "This map is taken from the original in the possession of the Marqués de la Valle. In the upper part it shows a city which, according to all the accounts, was actually thought to exist and given the name Quivira. Two rivers are drawn in the estuary of the Colorado river in the Gulf of California. One of these is called the Buena Guia and may be the Colorado itself; the other, called Miraflores, may be the Gila. Together they merge into one current and flow down into the Gulf of California." *Courtesy of the British Museum.*

When they reached the island, and the captain heard of their failure, he was much distressed, and proposed to embark the following
day, with every intent of reaching that land even if the whole fleet
were lost; also to discover if there was any truth in the report
which the captain Juan de Grijalba had sent to the island of Fernandina, since he suspected that it was all a fiction, and that no Spaniards had ever landed on that coast or been held captive there.

    With this resolve, the captain had embarked all his men
save for himself and twenty others; and while the weather was most
favorable for their departure, there suddenly sprang up a contrary
wind followed by heavy showers, and the pilots urged the captain
not to leave port, for the weather was now most unfavorable.
When the captain saw this he duly disembarked the rest of his men.
On the following day at noon a canoe was sighted sailing toward
the island, and, when it reached us, we saw that Gerónimo de Aguilar,[24] one of the Spanish captives, was aboard. He told us how he
had come to be lost and how long he had remained in captivity,
which was all as we have described to Your Royal Highnesses
above. And we held that sudden bad weather which came upon us a
great miracle and divine mystery, whereby we have come to believe
that nothing can be undertaken in Your Majesties' service which
does not end in good. From this Gerónimo de Aguilar was also
learnt that the others who were shipwrecked with him were scattered throughout the land, which, he told us, was very large, and it
would be impossible to rescue them without spending much time
there.[25]

    Then, as Fernando Cortés saw that the provisions for the
fleet were already running low, and that his men would suffer
greatly from hunger if he delayed and remained there any longer,
and, furthermore, that he still had not accomplished the purpose of
his voyage, he resolved with the consent of those in his company to
depart. And so setting sail, they left the island of Cozume[l], now
called Santa Cruz, very peaceful and in such a manner that were it
to be settled the natives would serve the Spaniards willingly. The

chieftains were very pleased and contented with what the captain had told them on Your Royal Highnesses' behalf and with his having given them so much finery for their persons: and we are certain that all the Spaniards who come to this island in the future will be as well received as in any of those which have been settled for a long time. This island is small, and nowhere is any river or stream to be found, so that all the water which the Indians drink comes from wells. The land consists entirely of crags and rocks and forests; the only produce the Indians have is from beehives, and our deputies are conveying to Your Highnesses samples of the honey and beeswax from the hives, for Your inspection.

Be it known to Your Majesties that the captain urged the chieftains of that island to renounce their heathen religion; and when they asked him to give them instead a precept by which they might henceforth live, he instructed them as best he could in the Catholic Faith. He left them a wooden cross fixed on top of a high building and an image of Our Lady the Virgin Mary, and told them most fully all they were to do to be good Christians; and they showed him that they had received everything with great goodwill, and thus we left them very happy and contented.

After we departed from this island we sailed for Yucatan and ran along the northern coast until we reached that great river called Grijalba, which is, as Your Royal Highnesses have already been informed, where Captain Juan de Grijalba, a relation of Diego Velázquez, landed; and so shallow is the mouth of the river that none of the large ships could enter. However, as Captain Hernando Cortés is so devoted to Your Majesties' service, and greatly desired to render a true account of all that is to be found in this land, he determined to proceed no farther until he had discovered the secret of that river and the towns along its banks, for they were said to be famous for their wealth. So he transferred all the men in the fleet to the small brigantines and open boats, and we sailed up the river until we could see the towns in that country. When we arrived at the first town[26] we found the people standing by the riverbank, and the captain spoke with them through his interpreter and also through Gerónimo de Aguilar, who spoke and understood that language very well. He made them understand that he had not come to do them any harm but only to speak to them on Your Majesties' behalf, and to this end begged them to permit us to land, for we had nowhere to sleep that night save in those brigantines and open boats, in which we had barely room to stand; it was too late to return to our ships, which we had left beyond in the open sea. When the Indians heard this they replied that he might say all he wished from there, but neither he nor any of his men were to attempt a landing, for if they did so they would be repelled. Then after saying this their archers were drawn up and they threatened us and shouted for us to leave. Because the day was much advanced and the sun almost set, the captain decided that we should go to some beaches which lay in front of that town; and there we landed and slept that night.

On the following morning certain Indians came to us in a canoe bringing some chickens and a little maize, which was barely enough for a single meal, and told us to take it and leave their land. The captain then answered them, giving them to understand that on no account would he leave until he had learnt the secrets of the land and might send Your Majesties a true account of it; and again he entreated them not to take it ill, nor to prevent him from entering the town, for they were Your Royal Highnesses' vassals. Yet still they replied forbidding us to enter their town and ordering us to be gone.

After they had left, the captain decided to proceed to the town, and therefore sent a captain of his company with two hundred men along a road to the town, which we had discovered the previous night, while he, Fernando Cortés, embarked with about eighty men in the boats and brigantines and anchored in front of the town, waiting to land if they permitted him to do so. When he arrived, he found the Indians prepared for war, armed with bows, arrows, lances and bucklers, and shouting to us to leave the land, but if we wanted war, to begin at once, for they were men who knew how to defend their homes. After having read the *requerimiento* to them three times and having asked Your Royal Highnesses' notary[27] to witness that he did not want war, but seeing that the Indians were most resolutely determined to prevent him from landing, and indeed had already begun to shoot arrows at us, he had ordered us to fire the guns and attack. A few of us were wounded when the shots were fired and as our men were landing, but at last the speed of our attack, and the attack on their rear of our men who had come by the road, drove them out of the village. Thus we took it and occupied what seemed to us to be the strongest part.

On the following day, at the hour of vespers, there came two Indians on behalf of their chieftains bringing certain gold ornaments which were very thin and of little value; and they told the captain that they were bringing these trinkets so that he should depart without doing them further harm, and leave their land as it had been before. To which the captain replied saying that he would be well pleased to do them no further harm, but, as to leaving the land, they must know that from henceforth they must hold as their lords the greatest monarchs on earth and must serve them as their vassals: once they had done this, Your Majesties would grant them many favors and aid and protect them from their enemies. They replied that they were content to do so but still required us to leave their land: and so we became friends.

Having arranged this friendship, the captain informed them that the Spaniards who were with him had nothing to eat nor had brought any food from the ships and begged them therefore to bring us provisions for as long as we might remain in their land. They replied that they would bring it the next day and then they left; but neither on the following day nor on the day after did they come with any food, and because of this we were very short of provisions. On the third day some Spaniards asked leave of the captain to go to the farms nearby in search of food. And when the captain saw that the Indians had not come as promised, he sent four captains with more than two hundred men to search the outskirts

of the town for food. While they were searching, however, they
came across a large number of Indians who shot at them with arrows and wounded twenty Spaniards; and had not the captain at
once been informed and rescued them, more than half the Christians would have perished. Following this, we all withdrew to our
camp and those who had been wounded were attended to, and
those who had fought rested.

When the captain saw the harm the Indians had done by
attacking us with arrows instead of bringing supplies as they had
promised, he ordered all the men to arm themselves and ten of the
horses we had brought in the ships to be landed, for he believed that
those Indians, encouraged by what had happened on the previous
day, would attack our camp intending to do us harm. On the next
day, when everyone had thus been prepared, he sent some captains
with three hundred men to the place where the battle had been
fought on the previous day to see if the Indians were still there or, if
not, to discover what had become of them. Soon afterwards he sent
out another two captains with a rear guard of a hundred men, and
he himself went secretly along one side with the ten horsemen.
While advancing in this order, the vanguard encountered a large
number of Indian warriors coming to attack us in our camp, and
had we not that day gone out to meet them on the road we might
have found ourselves in dire peril. When the captain of artillery
read the requerimiento before a notary to these Indians, telling
them, through the interpreters, that we did not desire war but only
peace and love between us, they replied not in words but with a
shower of arrows. While the vanguard was thus fighting with the
Indians, the two captains of the rear guard arrived, and, after two
hours of fighting, Fernando Cortés and the ten horsemen came up,
in a part of the forest where the Indians were beginning to surround the Spaniards, and there he fought with the Indians for an
hour. And so great was their number that neither could the Indians
who were fighting the Spanish infantry see the horsemen or know
where they were, nor could the horsemen, as they charged in

and out of the Indians, see one another. As soon as our foot soldiers saw the horsemen, however, they attacked fiercely and put
the Indians to flight, pursuing them for half a league. When the
captain saw that the Indians had been routed and that there was
nothing further to be done, and, moreover, that his men were very
fatigued, he ordered them to gather in some farmhouses that were
close by; and, after they had gathered, twenty were found to have
been wounded, none of whom died, not even those wounded the
previous day.[28] Once we had regathered, and attended to the sick,
we returned to our camp; and we took with us two Indians whom
we had captured, but the captain ordered them to be freed and gave
them letters for the chieftains saying that if they came to the camp
he would forgive them their crime and they would be his friends.
That same afternoon there came two Indians who seemed to be
persons of importance, and said that they were very grieved by all
that had happened, and that those chieftains on whose behalf they
came begged him to forgive them and do them no further harm
than he had already, nor kill any more of their people, for almost
220 had been killed; the past should be forgotten and henceforth
they wished to be vassals of those monarchs of whom we had
spoken, and as such did offer themselves, and bound themselves to
serve them whenever they were required to do anything in Your
Majesties' name; thus an agreement was reached and a peace made.
The captain then asked these Indians through his interpreters who
the people were he had been fighting with in the battle; they replied
that they had assembled from eight provinces, and that according
to the written records they had, there were in all some forty thousand men, for they were well able to count on such a number.
Your Royal Highnesses may truly believe that this battle was won
more by the will of God than by our own might, for what could
our four hundred have done against forty thousand?[29]

      After having all become good friends, they gave us, during
the four or five days we remained there, some 140 *pesos de oro* in
all, but comprised of pieces so thin yet valued so highly by them

that it seems their land is very poor in gold, for it was thought that the little they possessed had come from other parts by means of trading.

The land is very fertile and abounds in maize, fruit and fish and other things which they eat. The town is situated on the banks of the aforementioned river, up which we sailed, in a plain which has many farms and arable lands which they own and cultivate. The captain reproved them for their evil practice of worshipping their idols and gods, and made them understand how they must come to the knowledge of our Holy Faith; and he left them a wooden cross planted on a height, with which they were well pleased and said they would hold it in great veneration and adore it; thus these Indians became our friends and Your Royal Highnesses' vassals.

Fernando Cortés then left that place and continued on his voyage; and we reached the port and bay which is called San Juan,[30] where the aforementioned captain Juan de Grijalba had traded, of which a detailed account has been given to Your Majesty above. As soon as we arrived, the natives of that land came to discover what caravels those were that had reached their shores, but as the day was already much advanced, and it was almost night, the captain remained in the ships and ordered that no one should land. On the following day the captain, with a great part of his men, went ashore, and found there two chieftains to whom he made certain gifts of his own garments; and he spoke with them through his interpreters, giving them to understand that he had come to these parts by Your Royal Highnesses' command to tell them what they must do in Your service, and to this end he asked them to return to their village and call forth the chieftain or chieftains who were there to come and speak with him. And so they might more surely come, he gave them for the chieftains two shirts, gold belts and two doublets, one of satin, the other of velvet, and for each a scarlet bonnet and a pair of breeches, and thus they departed with these gifts.

A little before noon on the following day a chieftain arrived with those from the town and spoke to the captain, who made him understand through the interpreters that he had come to do them no harm but to make known to them how they were to be Your Majesties' vassals and must henceforth serve and give of what they had in their land, as do all who are such. He replied that he was very content to be so and to obey, and it pleased him to serve them and to have such high princes for sovereigns, as the captain had made them understand Your Royal Highnesses were. Then the captain told him that as he had shown such goodwill toward his king and lord he would soon see the favors which henceforth Your Majesties would bestow on him. So saying, he had him dressed in a shirt of fine Dutch linen, a coat of velvet and a gold belt, with which the chieftain was very happy and contented. He told the captain to wait there while he returned to his land, for on the following day he would bring things of his own that we might more fully appreciate his will to serve Your Royal Highnesses; and so he took his leave and went. On the following day he returned as promised, and had a white cloth spread before the captain, and offered him certain precious gold ornaments which he placed on it; of these and of others which were later obtained we make a special report to Your Majesties in a list which our representatives bear with them.

After this chieftain had taken leave of us and returned much contented to his own house, we in this fleet[31] who were of noble lineage, gentlemen and knights, zealous in the service of God and of Your Royal Highnesses, and most eager to honor the Royal Crown, extend its dominions and increase its revenues, came together and urged the aforementioned captain Fernando Cortés, saying that this land was very good and, to judge by the samples of gold which the chieftain had brought, most wealthy also, and, moreover, that the chieftain and his Indians had shown us great goodwill: for these reasons, therefore, it seemed to us not fitting to Your Majesties' service to carry out the orders which Diego Velázquez had given to Hernando Cortés, which were to trade for as

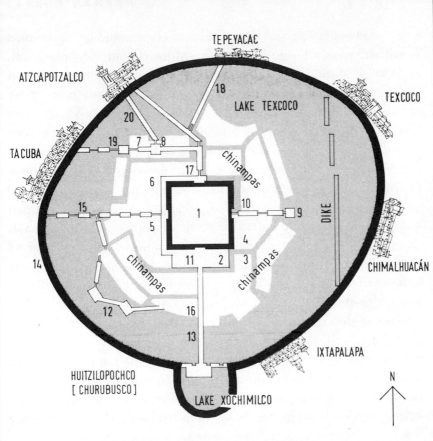

ATZCAPOTZALCO

TEPEYACAC

TACUBA

TEXCOCO

LAKE TEXCOCO

chinampas

DIKE

CHIMALHUACÁN

chinampas

chinampas

IXTAPALAPA

HUITZILOPOCHCO
[CHURUBUSCO]

LAKE XOCHIMILCO

N

INTERPRETATION OF THE NUREMBURG PLAN

KEY

1. Main Temple Enclosure
2 and 3. Palace of Motecucoma
4. Menagerie
5. Palace of Axayacatl
6. Palace of Cuauhtemoc
7. Temple of Tlaltelolco
8. Market at Tlaltelolco
9. Temple
10. Palace
11. Square

12. Motecuçoma's "House of Pleasure"
13. Fortress at Xoloc.
14. Chapultepec. Beginning of
      the acqueduct to Tenochtitlan.
15. Tacuba Causeway
16. Ixtapalapa Causeway
17 and 18. Tepeyac Causeway
19. Nonoalco Causeway
20. Vallejo Causeway.

Based on a drawing by Manuel Toussaint

much gold as possible and return with it to the island of Fernandina in order that only Diego Velázquez and the captain might enjoy it, and that it seemed to all of us better that a town with a court of justice be founded and inhabited in Your Royal Highnesses' name so that in this land also You might have sovereignty as You have in Your other kingdoms and dominions. For once the land has been settled by Spaniards, in addition to increasing Your Royal Highnesses' dominions and revenues, You may be so gracious as to grant favors to us and to the settlers who come in future.

Having decided on this, we joined together with one mind and purpose and made a petition to the captain in which we said: that he well knew how advantageous it would be to the service of Our Lord God and Your Majesties if this land were settled, giving him the reasons which we have set forth to Your Highnesses above, and we therefore requested him to cease trading in the manner he was doing, for it would to a large extent destroy the land, which would do Your Majesties much disservice. Likewise we requested that he should forthwith appoint alcaldes and *regidores* for the town which we were to found in Your Royal Highnesses' name; all this was accompanied by certain intimations that we would protest against him if he did not do as we required. When this request was made, the captain said he would give us his reply on the following day. And as the captain saw that what we asked was beneficial to Your Royal Highnesses' service, he answered us on the following day saying that he was more devoted to Your Majesties' service than to any other cause. Therefore, he disregarded his personal interest in continuing trading, by which he had expected to recover his investment and the great expense of fitting out the fleet together with Diego Velázquez, but rather set all this aside, and was pleased and willing to do all that we requested, for it would greatly benefit the service of Your Royal Highnesses. At once, with great diligence he set about founding and settling a town which he named the Rica Villa de la Vera Cruz and appointed those whose names are signed at the foot of this paper as alcaldes and regidores of the town, and received from us in Your Royal Highnesses' name the solemn vow customary in such cases.[32]

This done, on the following day we assembled in council and called captain Fernando Cortés and asked him in Your Royal Highnesses' name to show us the authority and instructions which the aforementioned Diego Velázquez had given him when coming to these parts.[33] Whereupon he sent for them, and once we had seen and read them and examined them most carefully, it seemed, to the best of our understanding, that by this authority and instructions Captain Fernando Cortés no longer had any authority, and as it had expired he could no longer exercise the office of captain or judicial officer.

It seemed to us, Most Excellent Princes, that in order to preserve peace and concord amongst ourselves and to govern us well it was necessary to elect someone for Your Royal service who might act in Your Majesties' name, in the aforementioned town and in these parts, as chief justice, captain and our leader, whom we might all respect, until an account of these events had been sent to Your Royal Highnesses so that You might provide for what is best suited to Your service. And seeing that no person was better fitted for such a responsibility than Fernando Cortés, for in addition to being the person most suited, he is most zealous in the service of Your Majesties, and also has much experience in these lands through the Royal offices and commands he has held from Your Majesties in the islands, in which he has always given good account of himself: moreover he spent all he had to come with this fleet in Your Majesties' service and held of small account, as we have already related, all he might have gained if he had continued to trade as had been agreed, we appointed him therefore, in the name of Your Royal Highnesses, chief justice and *alcalde mayor* and received from him the oath required in such cases. When this was done, as is appropriate to Your Majesties' service, we received him in Your Royal name, into our council and chamber, as chief justice and captain of Your Royal armies, and so he is and shall remain until Your Majesties provide whatever is more suitable to Your service. We desire to relate all this to Your Royal Highnesses so that You may be acquainted with all that has passed here and our present position and circumstances.

Having thus completed our business and being all together in our council, we decided to write to Your Majesties and send You all the gold, silver and jewels which we have obtained in the land, over and above the fifth which belongs to Your Royal revenues by law, for we decided that by sending You all the first spoils from these lands, and in keeping nothing for ourselves, we should serve Your Royal Highnesses and demonstrate the very great satisfaction we have in Your service, as we have shown before by venturing our persons and our possessions. When this had been agreed upon we elected as our representatives Alonso Fernández Puerto Carrero and Francisco de Montejo, whom we send to Your Majesties with all that we mention above that they may kiss Your Royal hands on our behalf and in our name, and in the name of this town and council beg Your Royal Highnesses to favor us with certain things necessary for the service of God and Your Majesties and for the common and public good of this town, as is set down at greater length in the instructions which we have given them. Which representatives we do most humbly beseech Your Majesties, with all the reverence which we owe You, to receive, and give Your Royal hands for them to kiss on our behalf, and to grant us all the favors which they, in the name of this council and ourselves, shall request of You, for besides doing a great service to Our Lord thereby, this town and council would reckon it a most singular grace such as we daily hope Your Royal Highnesses may see fit to bestow upon us.

In a previous section of this letter we said that we were sending Your Royal Highnesses an account of this land so that Your Highnesses might be better acquainted with its customs and riches, of the people who inhabit it, and of the laws and beliefs, rites and ceremonies by which they live. Most Powerful Lords, this land which we have now settled in Your Majesties' name extends for fifty leagues along the coast on either side of this town: the coast is completely flat with sandy beaches which in some places stretch for two leagues or more. The country inland is likewise very flat with most beautiful meadows and streams; and among these are some so beautiful that in all Spain there can be none better, for they are both pleasing to the eye and rich in crops, and well cared for and well situated; and there are places to walk and to graze all kinds of herds.

In this land there is every kind of game, and animals and birds similar to those of our acquaintance, such as deer, and fallow deer, wolves, foxes, partridges, pigeons, several kinds of turtledove, quails, hares and rabbits: so that in the kinds of birds and animals there is no difference between this land and Spain, and there are lions and tigers as well.

Some five leagues inland from the sea, and in certain places less, runs a great range of the most beautiful mountains, and some of these are exceedingly high, but there is one which is much higher than all the others from which one may see a great part of the sea and land; indeed it is so high that if the day is not fine one cannot even see the summit, for the top half of it is all covered by cloud. At other times, however, when the day is very fine one can see the peak rising above the cloud, and it is so white we think it to be covered in snow, and even the natives say it is snow, but as we have not seen it very clearly, although we have come very close to it, and because this region is so hot, we cannot be certain that it is.[34]

We shall endeavor to see and learn the secret of this and other things of which we have heard so that we may render Your Royal Highnesses a true account, as of the wealth in gold and silver and precious stones which Your Majesties may judge according to the samples we are sending. In our view it cannot be doubted that there must be in this land as much as in that from which Solomon is said to have taken the gold for the temple. But so little time has passed since we first landed that we have been unable to explore more than five leagues inland and some ten or twelve leagues along the coast on either side of the place where we landed, although from the sea there appears to be much more, and indeed we saw more while sailing hither.

The people who inhabit this land, from the island of Cozume[1] and the cape of Yucatan to the place where we are now, are of medium height and of well-proportioned bodies and features, save that in each province their customs are different; some pierce their ears and put very large and ugly objects into them; others pierce their nostrils down to the lip and put in them large round stones which look like mirrors;[35] and others still split their lower lips as far as the gums and hang there some large stones or gold ornaments so heavy that they drag the lips down, giving a most deformed appearance. The clothes they wear are like large, highly colored yashmaks; the men cover their shameful parts, and on the top half of their bodies wear thin mantles which are decorated in a Moorish fashion. The common women wear highly colored mantles from the waist to the feet, and others which cover their breasts, leaving the rest uncovered. The women of rank wear skirts of very thin cotton, which are very loose-fitting and decorated and cut in the manner of a rochet.

The food they eat is maize and some chili peppers, as on the other islands, and *patata yuca*,[36] just the same as is eaten in Cuba, and they eat it roast, for they do not make bread of it; and they both hunt and fish and breed many chickens such as those found on *Tierra Firme*, which are as big as peacocks.

There are some large towns and well laid out. The houses in those parts where there is stone are of masonry and mortar and the rooms are small and low in the Moorish fashion. In those parts where there is no stone they make their houses of adobes, which are whitewashed and the roofs covered with straw. There are houses belonging to certain men of rank which are very cool and have many rooms, for we have seen as many as five courtyards in a single house, and the rooms around them very well laid out, each man having a private room. Inside there are also wells and water tanks

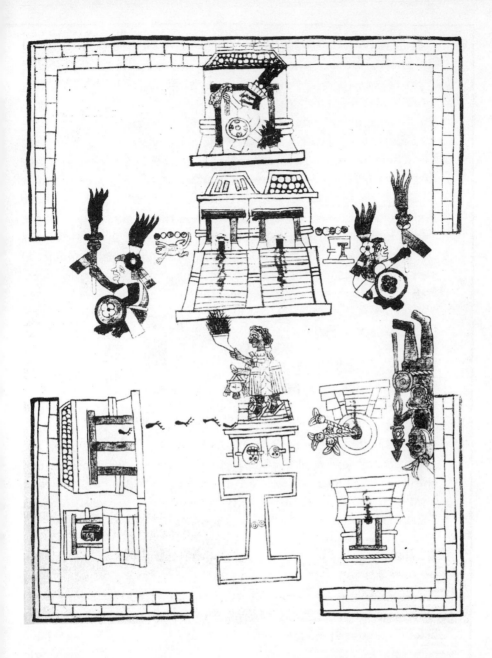

5. The Great Temple Enclosure at Tenochtitlan. From Sahagún, *Historia de las Cosas de Nueva España*. Madrid MS, f. 269.

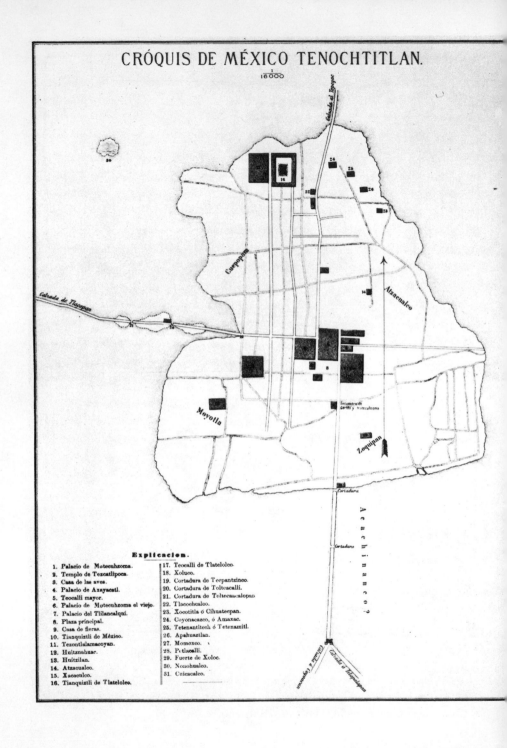

CRÓQUIS DE MÉXICO TENOCHTITLAN.

$$\frac{1}{16000}$$

Explicacion.

1. Palacio de Motecuhzoma.
2. Templo de Tezcatlipoca.
3. Casa de las aves.
4. Palacio de Axayacatl.
5. Teocalli mayor.
6. Palacio de Motecuhzoma el viejo.
7. Palacio del Tlilancalqui.
8. Plaza principal.
9. Casa de fieras.
10. Tianquiztli de México.
11. Tezontlalamacoyan.
12. Huitznahuac.
13. Huitzilan.
14. Atzacualco.
15. Xacacualco.
16. Tianquiztli de Tlatelolco.

17. Teocalli de Tlatelolco.
18. Xoluco.
19. Cortadura de Teepantzinco.
20. Cortadura de Tolteacalli.
21. Cortadura de Toltecacalopan
22. Tlacochcalco.
23. Xocotitla ó Cihuateepan.
24. Coyonacazeo, ó Amaxac.
25. Tetenantitech ó Tetenamitl.
26. Apahuaztlan.
27. Momoxco.
28. Petlacalli.
29. Fuerte de Xoloc.
30. Nonohualco.
31. Cuicacalco.

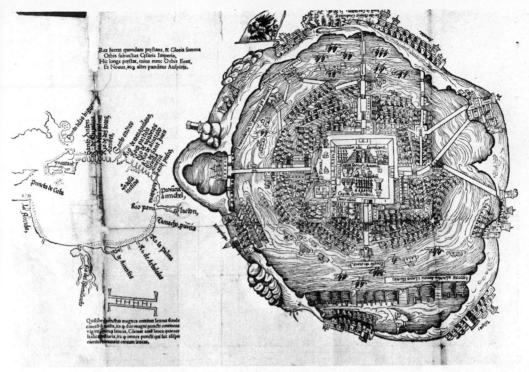

7. Map of Tenochtitlan and the Gulf of Mexico, supposedly made on Cortés's orders. From Latin edition of Cortés's Second Letter, printed in Nuremburg in 1524. *Courtesy of the British Museum.*

6. Ground plan of Tenochtitlan from Manuel Orozco y Berra's *Historia Antigua y de la Conquista de Mexico*, Mexico 1880.

The key reads:

1. Palace of Motecuçoma II	16. *Tianquiztli* of Tlatelolco
2. Temple of Tezcatlipoca	17. Temple of Tlatelolco
3. The Aviary	18. Xoluco
4. Palace of Axayacatl	19. Tecpantzinco bridge
5. Temple of Huitzilopochitl	20. Tolteacalli bridge
6. Palace of Motecuçoma I	21. Toltecaacalopan bridge
7. Palace of Tlilancalqui	22. Tlacochcalco
8. Main square	23. Xocotitla or Cihuatecpan
9. Menagerie	24. Coyonacazco or Amaxac
10. *Tianquiztli* of Mexico	25. Tetenantitech or Tetenamitl
11. Tezontlalamacoyan	26. Apahuaztlan
12. Huitznahuac	27. Momoxco
13. Huitzilan	28. Petlacalli
14. Atzacualco	29. Fortress of Xoloc
15. Xacaculco	30. Nonohualco
	31. Cuicacalco

Courtesy of the British Museum.

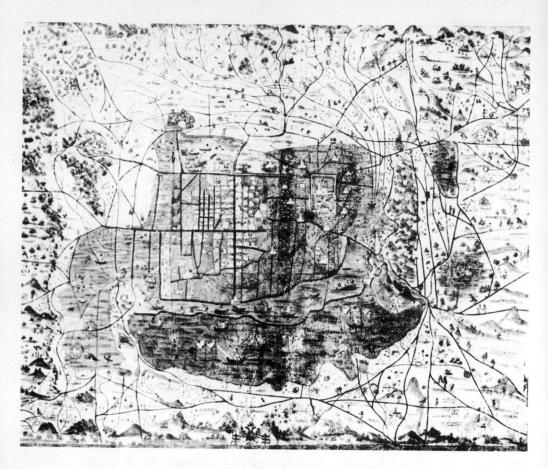

8. Map of Tenochtitlan formerly attributed to Alonso de Santa Cruz, cosmographer to Charles V. Although of post-Cortesian origin, it was drawn before 1555 and is therefore the earliest extant native map of the city. It consists of two strips of parchment, joined vertically, and the whole measures 114 x 75 centimeters. The inscription in the bottom right-hand corner is apparently a dedication to Charles V, though only a partial reading of the text has so far been possible. The map is orientated along the cardinal points but has been turned through 90° so that North now lies to the right. Beyond the city itself the orientation is less exact. The easternmost region (at the bottom of the map) and the North-South axis from Amecameca to Otumba are fairly accurate, but the corresponding axis on the West side is more difficult to place since it bends visibly toward the Northeast. For a detailed discussion of this map and its importance see, S. Linné, *El Valle y la Ciudad de Mexico.*

and rooms for slaves and servants of which they have many. Each of these chieftains has in front of the entrance to his house a very large courtyard and some two or three or four of them raised very high with steps up to them and all very well built. Likewise they have their shrines and temples with raised walks which run all around the outside and are very wide: there they keep the idols which they worship, some of stone, some of clay and some of wood, which they honor and serve with such customs and so many ceremonies that many sheets of paper would not suffice to give Your Royal Highnesses a true and detailed account of them all. And the temples where they are kept are the largest and the best and the finest built of all the buildings found in the towns; and they are much adorned with rich hanging cloths and featherwork and other fineries.

Each day before beginning any sort of work they burn incense in these temples and sometimes sacrifice their own persons, some cutting their tongues, others their ears, while there are some who stab their bodies with knives. All the blood which flows from them they offer to those idols, sprinkling it in all parts of the temple, or sometimes throwing it into the air or performing many other ceremonies, so that nothing is begun without sacrifice having first been made. They have a most horrid and abominable custom which truly ought to be punished and which until now we have seen in no other part, and this is that, whenever they wish to ask something of the idols, in order that their plea may find more acceptance, they take many girls and boys and even adults, and in the presence of the idols they open their chests while they are still alive and take out their hearts and entrails and burn them before the idols, offering the smoke as sacrifice. Some of us have seen this, and they say it is the most terrible and frightful thing they have ever witnessed.[37]

This these Indians do so frequently that, as we have been informed, and, in part, have seen from our own experience during the short while we have been here, not one year passes in which they do not kill and sacrifice some fifty persons in each temple; and this is done and held as customary from the island of Cozumel to this land where we now have settled. Your Majesties may be most certain that, as this land seems to us to be very large, and to have many temples in it, not one year has passed, as far as we have been able to discover, in which three or four thousand souls have not been sacrificed in this manner. Let Your Royal Highnesses consider, therefore, whether they should not put an end to such evil practices, for certainly Our Lord God would be well pleased if by the hand of Your Royal Highnesses these people were initiated and instructed in our Holy Catholic Faith, and the devotion, trust and hope which they have in these their idols were transferred to the divine power of God; for it is certain that if they were to worship the true God with such fervor, faith and diligence, they would perform many miracles. And we believe that it is not without cause that Our Lord God has been pleased that these parts be discovered in the name of Your Royal Highnesses so that Your Majesties may gain much merit and reward in the sight of God by commanding that these barbarous people be instructed and by Your hands be brought to the True Faith. For, as far as we have been able to learn, we believe that had we interpreters and other people to explain to them the error of their ways and the nature of the True Faith, many of them, and perhaps even all, would soon renounce their false beliefs and come to the true knowledge of God; for they live in a more civilized and reasonable manner than any other people we have seen in these parts up to the present.

To attempt to give Your Majesties all the details about this land and its people might lead us to make some mistakes in our account, for there is much we have not seen but only heard from the natives, and therefore we venture only to render account of those things which Your Majesties may hold to be most true and certain. Your Majesties may, if You see fit, send a report to the Holy Father, so that diligence and good order may be applied to the work of converting these people, for it is hoped that much may be gained thereby; also that His Holiness may permit and approve that the wicked and the rebellious, after having first been admonished, may be punished as enemies of our Holy Catholic Faith. This will be the occasion of a fearsome warning and example to those who are obstinate in coming to the knowledge of the truth; and the great evils which they practice in the service of the Devil may be prevented. For in addition to those which we list above, of the children and men and women which they kill and offer in their sacrifices, we have been informed, and are most certain it is true, that they are all sodomites and practice that abominable sin.[38] In all of which we entreat Your Majesties to provide as You judge most fitting to the service of God and Your Royal Highnesses and that we who are here in Your service be favored and rewarded.

Among other things which we are sending to Your Highnesses by way of these, our representatives, are instructions that they beseech Your Majesties on no account to give or grant concessions to Diego Velázquez, the admiral's lieutenant in the island of Fernandina, of *adelantamiento* or governorship in perpetuity (or of any other kind) or judicial powers; and if any shall have been given him, that they be revoked, for it is not to the benefit of the service of Your Royal Crown that the aforementioned Diego Velázquez, or any other person, should have authority or be granted any concessions, whether in perpetuity, or of any other kind, in this new land of Your Highnesses, unless it be by the express will of Your Majesties, for it is, as far as we are able to judge or have reason to hope, very rich. And, moreover, were the aforementioned Diego Velázquez granted some office, far from benefiting Your Majesties' service, we foresee that we, the vassals of Your Royal Highnesses, who have begun to settle and live in this land, would be most ill used by him, for we believe that what we have now done in Your Majesties' service, namely to send You such gold and silver and jewels as we have been able to acquire in this land, would not have been his intention, as has been most clearly demonstrated by four

servants of his who passed this way; for, when they saw our intention to send it all to Your Royal Highnesses, they proclaimed publicly that it would be better to send it to Diego Velázquez; and they
said other things to prevent it being sent to Your Majesties. For this
we had them seized, and they are still in custody awaiting sentence;
and when that has been carried out we shall inform Your Majesties
of what we have done with them.[39] And for what we have seen of
the doings of Diego Velázquez and our experience of them, we are
afraid that if he should come to this land with some commission he
would treat us badly, as he did on the island of Fernandina when he
had charge of the government, dealing justice to no one except as it
pleased him, and punishing those whom he chose out of anger or
animosity rather than justice or reason; in this manner he has ruined
many good men and reduced them to great poverty by refusing to
give them Indians as servants, taking all for himself, and likewise by
taking all the gold which they have collected, without giving them
any part of it: for this purpose he has bands of outlaws at his command; also as he is governor and *repartidor*,[40] no one dare oppose
him for fear that they may be ruined. Of this Your Majesties know
nothing, nor has any account of it been sent to You, for the representatives who have gone to Your Court from that island are all of
the same die, or his servants, and he keeps them contented giving
them Indians whenever they ask; and the representatives who come
to him from the towns on matters concerning the communities do
always as he wishes, for he rewards them with gifts of Indians.
When these representatives return to their towns and are ordered
to give an account of what they have done, they complain that
poor people should not be sent, for by giving them a single Indian
chieftain, Diego Velázquez can have them do as he wishes. Furthermore, as all the alcaldes and regidores who own Indians fear that
Diego Velázquez will take them, they dare not reprove the representatives who have done what they ought not to have done in
order to please Diego Velázquez; and in this respect and in many
others he is most cunning. By which Your Majesties may see that all

the accounts which the island of Fernandina has submitted on behalf of Diego Velázquez, and the favors which they ask for him,
are in exchange for the Indians which he gives to the representatives
and not because the communities are satisfied and so desire it; indeed they would rather such representatives were punished. As the
above-said is well known to all the citizens and inhabitants of this
town of Vera Cruz, they had a meeting with the representatives of
this council and begged and required us by a signed petition that, in
their name, we should beseech Your Majesties not to grant the
aforementioned concessions, nor any others to Diego Velázquez,
rather to order him to submit to a *residencia* and deprive him of the
governorship of the island of Fernandina; for by such a residencia
the truth of our account would be plainly seen. For which purposes
we therefore entreat Your Majesties to send a judge to investigate
all we have reported to Your Royal Highnesses, not only as con-
cerns the island of Cuba but also in other parts, for we believe we
can prove accusations whereby Your Majesties may see whether it
is just or right that he hold Royal commissions in these parts or in
those others where he at present resides.

The representatives, inhabitants and citizens of this town
have likewise asked us, in the aforementioned petition, to entreat
Your Majesties on their behalf to order and provide a decree and
letters patent in favor of Fernando Cortés, captain and chief justice
of Your Royal Highnesses, so that he may govern us with justice
until this land is conquered and pacified, and for as long as Your
Majesties may see fit, knowing him to be a person well suited for
such a position. Which petition and request we send to Your Majesties with these our representatives and humbly supplicate Your
Royal Highnesses to grant us this and all the other favors which in
the name of this council and town may be asked of You by the
aforementioned representatives, and that You hold us as Your most
loyal vassals, as we have been and always shall be.

The gold, silver, jewels, bucklers and garments which we
are sending to Your Royal Highnesses with these representatives,

over and above the one-fifth which belongs to Your Majesty, Fernando Cortés and the council of this town offer in Your service, and are sending together with a list signed by the same representatives as Your Royal Highnesses may observe. From the Rica Villa de la Vera Cruz, the tenth day of July, 1519.

The gold, jewels, precious stones and articles of featherwork which have been acquired in these newly discovered lands since our arrival here, which you, Alonso Fernández Puerto Carrero and Francisco de Montejo, who go as representatives of this Villa Rica de la Vera Cruz to the Very Excellent Princes and Most Catholic and Very Great Kings and Sovereigns, the Queen Doña Juana and the King, Don Carlos her son, are the following:[41]

First a large gold wheel with a design of monsters on it and worked all over with foliage. This weighed 3,800 *pesos de oro*. From this wheel, because it was the best that has been found here and of the finest gold, a fifth was taken for Their Highnesses; this amounted to two thousand *castellanos* which belonged to Them of Their fifth and Royal privilege according to the stipulation that the captain Fernando Cortés brought from the Hieronymite Fathers who reside on the island of Hispaniola and on the other islands. The eighteen hundred *pesos* that remained and all the rest that goes to make up twelve hundred *pesos*, the council of this town bequeath to Their Highnesses, together with everything else mentioned in this list, which belonged to the people of the aforementioned town.

Item: Two necklaces of gold and stone mosaic, one of which has eight strings of 232 red jewels and 163 green jewels. Hanging from the border of this necklace are twenty-seven small gold bells; and in the center of them are four figures in large stones inlaid with gold. From each of the two in the center hang single pendants, while from each of the ends hang four double pendants. The other necklace has four strings of 102 red jewels and 172 which appear to be green in color; around these stones there are twenty-six small gold bells. In this necklace there are ten large stones inlaid with gold from which hang 142 pendants.

Item: Four pairs of screens,[42] two pairs being of fine gold leaf with trimmings of yellow deerskin, and the other two (pairs) of fine silver leaf with trimmings in white deerskin. The remainder are of plumes of various colors, and very well made. From each of these hang sixteen small gold bells, all with red deerskin.

Another item: One hundred *pesos de oro* for melting, so that Their Highnesses may see how the gold is taken from the mines here.

Another item: In a box, a large piece of featherwork, lined with animal skin which, in color, seems like that of a marten. Fastened to this piece, and in the center of it, is a large disk of gold which weighed sixty *pesos de oro*, and a piece of blue and red stone mosaic in the shape of a wheel, and another piece of stone mosaic, of a reddish color; and at the end of the piece there is another piece of colored featherwork that hangs from it.

Item: A fan of colored featherwork with thirty-seven small rods cased in gold.

Another item: A large piece of colored featherwork to be worn on the head and encircled by sixty-eight small pieces of gold, each of which is as large as a half *cuarto*.[43] Beneath them are twenty little gold towers.

Item: A miter of blue stone mosaic with a design of monsters in the center of it. It is lined with an animal skin which by its color appears to be that of a marten, and has a small piece of featherwork which, together with the one mentioned above, is of the same miter.

Item: Four harpoons of featherwork with their stone heads

fastened by a gold thread, and a jeweled scepter with rings of gold and the rest of featherwork.

Item: A bracelet of blue jewels and, in addition, a small piece of black featherwork and with other colors.

Item: A large pair of sandals of leather whose color resembles that of a marten. The soles are white and sown with gold thread.

Furthermore, a mirror set in a piece of blue and red jewelry, with a piece of featherwork and two strips of red leather attached to it, together with a skin which seems to be from those same martens.

Item: Three pieces of colored featherwork that belong to a large gold head which seems to be that of an alligator.

Item: Some screens of blue stone mosaic, lined with a skin which by its color seems to come from a marten; and from each one of them hang fifteen small gold bells.

Another item: A maniple of wolfskin with four strips of leather that look like martenskin.

Another item: Some fibers placed in some colored feathers; the which fibers are white and look like locks of hair.

Another item: Two pieces of colored featherwork that are for two helmets of stone mosaic which are mentioned below.

Furthermore, two pieces of colored featherwork which are for two pieces of gold, made like large shells and worn on the head.

Furthermore, two birds with green plumage and their feet, beaks and eyes made of gold. These are put on one of those pieces of gold that resemble shells.

Furthermore, two large ear ornaments of [44] blue stone mosaic which are for the large alligator head.

In another square box, a large alligator head in gold, which is the one mentioned above where the aforementioned pieces are to be put.

Also, a helmet of blue stone mosaic with twenty small gold bells hanging round the outside of it with two strings of beads above each bell: and two ear ornaments of wood with gold plates.

Also, a bird with green plumage and with feet, beak and eyes of gold.

Another item: Another helmet of blue stone mosaic with twenty-five little gold bells and two beads of gold above each bell, which hang round it, with some wooden ear ornaments with gold plates; and a bird with green plumage and feet, beak and eyes of gold.

Another item: A reed container with two large pieces of gold to be worn on the head; they are made like gold shells with ear ornaments of wood with gold plates. Also two birds with green plumage and feet, beaks and eyes of gold.

Also, sixteen bucklers of stone mosaic with pieces of colored featherwork hanging round the outside of them, and with a wide-angled board of stone mosaic with its pieces of colored featherwork. In the center of this board is a cross inside a wheel made of the same stone mosaic, and lined with leather the color of martenskin.

Furthermore, a scepter of a red stone mosaic, made to resemble a snake with head, teeth and eyes in what seems to be mother-of-pearl. The hilt is adorned with the skin of a spotted animal, and beneath this hilt there hang six small pieces of featherwork.

Another item: A fan of featherwork in a reed adorned with the skin of a spotted animal, in the manner of a weathercock. Above it has a crown of featherwork and finally many long green feathers.

Item: Two birds made of thread and featherwork. The quills of their wings and tails, the claws of their feet, their eyes and the tips of their beaks are of gold, each placed in its respective gold-covered reed. And below some feather down, one white and the other yellow, with some gold embroidery between the feathers; and from each of these hang seven strands of feathers.

Item: Four pieces made after the manner of skates, placed in their respective gold-covered canes. Their tails, gills, eyes and mouths are of gold; below, on their tails, are some pieces of green featherwork, while toward their mouths each has a crown of colored featherwork, and in some of the white feathers there is some gold embroidery, and beneath the handle of each one hang six strands of colored featherwork.

Item: A small copper rod lined with a skin in which is placed a piece of gold in the manner of a piece of featherwork, which has some pieces of colored featherwork above and below it.

Another item: Five fans of colored featherwork, four of which have ten small quills covered with gold while the fifth has thirteen.

Item: Four harpoons of white flint, fastened to four rods of featherwork.

Item: A large buckler of featherwork trimmed on the back with the skin of a spotted animal. In the center of the field of this buckler is a gold plate with a design such as the Indians make, with four other half plates of gold round the edge, which together form a cross.

Another item: A piece of featherwork of various colors made in the manner of a half chasuble, lined with the skin of a spotted animal. This, the lords of these parts, which we have seen up to now, hang from about their necks. On the front it has thirteen pieces of gold very well fitted together.

Item: A piece of colored featherwork, made in the manner of a jousting helmet, which the lords of this land wear on their heads. From it hang two ear ornaments of stone mosaic with two small bells and two beads of gold; and above there is a piece of featherwork of broad green feathers, while below hang some white hairs.

Furthermore, four animal heads, two of which seem to be wolves, the other two tigers, with some spotted skins: from these heads hang some small bronze bells.

Item: Two animal skins of spotted animals, lined with some cotton mantles: these skins appear to be those of a mountain cat.

Item: The red and gray skin of another animal, which seems to be a lion, and two deerskins.

Item: Four skins of small deer from which here they make small tanned gloves.

And, moreover, two books which the Indians have: also half a dozen fans of colored featherwork and a perfume container of colored featherwork.

Furthermore, a large silver wheel which weighed forty-eight silver marks, and also some bracelets, some beaten [silver] leaves; and one mark five ounces and forty *adarmes*[45] of silver; and a large buckler and another small one of silver, which weighed four marks and two ounces; and another two bucklers which appear to be silver and which weighed six marks and two ounces; and another buckler, which likewise appears to be of silver, which weighed one mark and seven ounces, which is in all sixty-two marks of silver.

[COTTON CLOTHING][46]

Another item: Two large pieces of cotton richly woven in white, black and tawny.

Item: Two pieces woven with feathers and another piece woven in various colors; another piece woven in patterns of red, black and white, and on the back these patterns do not show.

Item: Another piece woven with patterns and in the center a black wheel of feathers.

Item: Two white cotton cloths woven with some pieces of featherwork.

Another cotton cloth with some white cords(?) attached. A peasant smock.

A white piece with a large wheel of white feathers in the middle.

Two pieces of gray cord with some wheels of feathers, and another two of tawny cord.

Six painted pieces; another red piece with some wheels and another two pieces painted blue; and two women's shirts.

[Twelve veils.][47]

Item: Six bucklers, each one with a gold plate covering the whole buckler.

Another item: A half miter of gold.

The which things, and each one of them, as is laid down and established by these declarations, we, Alonso Fernández Puerto Carrero and Francisco de Montejo, the abovementioned representatives, do acknowledge that it is true that we have received them and that they were entrusted to us to take to Their Highnesses, from you, Fernando Cortés, chief justice for Their Highnesses in these parts, and from you, Alonso de Ávila and Alonso de Grado, treasurer and *veedor* for Their Highnesses. And because it is true we sign it with our names. Dated the sixth day of July in the year 1519. —PUERTO CARRERO, FRANCISCO DE MONTEJO.

The things above-mentioned in the said memorial, with the aforementioned letter and account sent by the municipal council of Vera Cruz, were received by the King Don Carlos, Our Sovereign, as already stated, in Valladolid, in Holy Week, in the beginning of the month of April of the year of Our Lord, 1520.[48]

The Second Letter   🎴

Sent to His Sacred Majesty the Emperor, Our Sovereign, by Don Fernando Cortés, Captain General of New Spain.

In which he gives an account of the lands and provinces without number that he has newly discovered in Yucatán in the year 1519 and subjected to His Majesty's Royal Crown. And in particular he gives an account of a very large and very rich province called Culua,[1] in which there are large cities and marvelous buildings, much commerce and great wealth. Among these cities there is one more marvelous and more wealthy than all the others, called Temixtitan,[2] which has, with extraordinary skill, been built upon a great lake, of which city and province a powerful lord called Mutezuma[3] is king: here things terrible to relate befell the captain and the Spaniards. He tells at length of the great dominion of the said Mutezuma and of its rites and ceremonies and how they are performed.

Most high and powerful and catholic prince, most
invincible emperor and our sovereign:

In a ship which I dispatched to Your Sacred Majesty from
New Spain on the sixteenth day of June, 1519, I sent a very long and
detailed account of all that had occurred in these lands from the
day I arrived until that date. This relation was carried by Alonso
Hernández Puerto Carrero and Francisco de Montejo, representatives of the town of Vera Cruz, which I founded in Your Highness's name. Since then, because I have had neither the opportunity
nor the ships, and because I was occupied in the conquest and pacification of these lands, and, moreover, because I knew nothing of
the aforementioned representatives and their ship, I have not acquainted Your Majesty with all that has happened since. God alone
knows how much this has troubled me; for I wished Your Highness
to know all the things of this land, which, as I have already written
in another report, are so many and of such a kind that one might
call oneself the emperor of this kingdom with no less glory than of
Germany, which, by the Grace of God, Your Sacred Majesty already possesses. And because to attempt to inform Your Highness
of every detail of these lands and new realms would be to continue
almost forever, I beg Your Highness's pardon if I do not render as
long an account as I should. Neither my natural aptitudes nor the
conditions in which I find myself favor me in the task. Despite this,
however, I shall make every effort to acquaint Your Highness, as
best I can, with the truth and with all that at the present time Your
Majesty should know. Likewise I beg Your Highness to forgive me
if I do not record all that is necessary and am uncertain of time and
details, or if I do not give the correct names either of some of the

9. Title page of the first printed edition of Letter II, Seville, 1522.
Courtesy of the British Museum.

¶Carta de relació ẽbiada a su. S. majestad del ẽpa-
dor nr̄o señor por el capitã general dela nueua spaña: llamado fernãdo cortes. Enla q̄l haze relació dlas tierras y prouicias sin cuẽto q̄ hã descubierto
nueuamẽte enel yucatã del año de. xix. a esta pte: y ha sometido ala corona
real de su .S.A. En especial haze relació de vna grãdissima prouicia muy
rica llamada Culua: ẽla q̄l ay muy grãdes ciudades y de marauillosos edi-
ficios: y de grãdes tratos y riq̄zas. Entre las q̄les ay vna mas marauillosa
y rica q̄ todas llamada Timixtitã: q̄ esta por marauillosa arte edificada sobre vna grãde laguna. dela q̄l ciudad y prouicia es rey vn grãdissimo señor
llamado Muteeçuma: dõde le acaecierõ al capitã y alos españoles espãto-
sas cosas de oyr. Cuenta largamẽte del grãdissimo señorio del dicho Muteeçuma y de sus ritos y cerimonias. y de como se sirue.

towns and cities, or of their rulers, who have offered themselves in the service of Your Highness as your subjects and vassals. For in a certain misfortune which has recently befallen me, of which I shall render complete account later in this report, I lost all the proceedings and agreements I had made with the natives of these lands, and many other things besides.

Most Excellent Prince, in the other report I told Your Majesty of the cities and towns which at that time had offered themselves to the service of Your Highness and which I held subject. I also spoke of a great lord called Mutezuma, whom the natives of these lands had spoken to me about, and who, according to the number of days they said we would have to march, lived about ninety or a hundred leagues from the harbor where I disembarked. And, trusting in God's greatness and in the might of Your Highness's Royal name, I decided to go and see him wherever he might be. Indeed I remember that, with respect to the quest of this lord, I undertook more than I was able, for I assured Your Highness that I would take him alive in chains or make him subject to Your Majesty's Royal Crown.

With that purpose I set out from the town of Cempoal, which I renamed Sevilla, on the sixteenth of August with fifteen horsemen and three hundred foot soldiers, as well equipped for war as the conditions permitted me to make them. I left in the town of Vera Cruz two horsemen and 150 men, to construct a fortress which is now almost completed; and I left all that province of Cempoal and all the mountains surrounding the town, which contain as many as fifty thousand warriors and fifty towns and fortresses, very secure and peaceful; and all of these natives have been and still are faithful vassals of Your Majesty, for they were subjects of Mutezuma and, according to what I was told, had been subdued by force not long previously. When they heard through me of Your Highness and of Your very great Royal power, they said they wished to become vassals of Your Majesty and my allies, and asked me to protect them from that great lord who held them by tyranny and by force, and took their children to sacrifice to his idols; and they made many other complaints about him. Because of this, they have been very loyal and true in the service of Your Highness, and I believe that they will always be so, as they are now free of his tyranny, and because they have always been honored and well treated by me. But to ensure further the safety of all who remained in Vera Cruz, I brought with me some of their chieftains with their servants, who were of no small use to me on my journey.

Because, as I believe I wrote to Your Majesty in the first report, some of those who joined my company were servants and friends of Diego Velázquez, it troubled them to see what I was doing in the service of Your Highness, and some of them even wanted to overthrow me and to leave this land, especially four Spaniards, Juan Escudero and Diego Cermeño, a pilot, and Gonzalo de Ungría, also a pilot, and Alonso Peñate, all of whom voluntarily confessed that they had determined to seize a brigantine which was in the port with bread and salt pork aboard. They intended to kill the master of it, return to the island of Fernandina and inform Diego Velázquez of how I had sent a ship to Your Highness, and also of what she was carrying and what course she was to take, so that the said Diego Velázquez might send ships to lie in wait and take her. As soon as he knew this, he did so, for, as I have been informed, he sent a caravel after that same ship which, if she had not already passed, would have been taken. Likewise they confessed that there were others who also intended to warn Diego Velázquez. On hearing the confessions of these miscreants, I punished them according to the law and as, in the circumstances, I judged would do Your Majesty greatest service.

As well as the friends and servants of Diego Velázquez who wished to leave the land, there were others who, when they saw how big it was, and how few Spaniards we were against so many, were of the same mind. Believing, therefore, that if the ships remained there would be a rebellion, and once all those who had resolved to go had gone I would be left almost alone, whereby all that in the name of God and of Your Highness has been accomplished in this land would have been prevented, I devised a plan, according to which I declared the ships unfit to sail and grounded them;[4] thus they lost all hope of escape and I proceeded in greater safety and with no fear that once my back was turned the people I had left in the town would betray me.

Eight or ten days after I ran the ships aground, and having already left the town of Vera Cruz for that of Cempoal, which is four leagues distant and whence I was to continue my journey, I heard from Vera Cruz that four ships were sailing off the coast and that the captain[5] whom I had left in charge had gone out to them in a boat, and they had told him that they were from Francisco de Garay, lieutenant and governor of the island of Jamaica, and that they had come to explore. The captain had told them how I, in the name of Your Highness, had settled in this land and had founded a town there, one league from where the ships were; that they might go there and I would be informed of their arrival. If they were short of anything they could obtain it there; he would lead them into the port which he pointed out to them. They replied that they had already seen the port as they had sailed past it, and that they would do as he said. He returned to the port, but the ships did not follow him and were still sailing along the coast, with what purpose he did not know.

On hearing this, I left at once for Vera Cruz, where I learnt that the ships were anchored three leagues down the coast and that no one had landed from them. From there I set off with a few followers to gather information, but when I had come within almost one league of them I met three men from the ships, one of whom said he was a notary. The other two were to be witnesses, or so I was told, of the serving of a notice. They said that their captain had told them to give me a document they had brought with them which informed me that he had discovered that land and wished to colonize it. He therefore desired to discuss frontiers with me, for he wished to set up a base five leagues down the coast beyond Nautecal, which is a city twelve leagues from Vera Cruz and which is now called Almería.[6] I told them to rejoin their captain and to sail to Vera Cruz, where we would talk and discover what they had come for. And if his ships were in need of anything I would help him as best I could. Since he said that he came in the service of Your Sacred Majesty, I too said I desired nothing except insofar as I might serve Your Highness thereby, which in helping him I believed I was doing.

They replied that on no account would Captain Garay or anyone else land, not even to meet me; and seeing how reluctant they were to appear before me, I thought that they must have done some damage in the land.

When night fell I crept very silently up to the shore just opposite where the ships were anchored, and there I lay hidden until almost noon the following day, thinking that the captain or pilot would come ashore and that I might discover from them what they had done or where they had been; and if they had done any damage in the land, I would send them to Your Holy Majesty. But neither they nor anyone else came ashore, so I made those who had brought the summons remove their clothes, which I put on three men of my own company whom I ordered to go down to the beach and signal to the ships. As soon as they saw them, they sent out a boat with as many as ten or twelve men aboard armed with cross-bows and harquebuses. The men who had been signaling from the shore then left the beach as though seeking the shade of some bushes which were nearby. Four men landed, two crossbowmen and two harquebusiers, who, as they were surrounded by the Spaniards I had placed on the beach, were taken. One of these was master of one of the ships, and he tried to fire his harquebus, which would have killed the captain I had put in charge of Vera Cruz had not Our Lord prevented the fuse from igniting. Those who remained in the boat put out to sea, but, before they had reached them, the ships had hoisted their sails without waiting or wishing to discover anything from them. Those who remained behind told me that they had reached a river[7] thirty leagues down the coast from Almería, and that they had been well received by the natives and had bartered with them for food. They had seen some gold which the Indians brought but not much. And they had bartered for as much as three thousand gold *castellanos*. They had only gone ashore when they saw some villages by the riverbanks which were so close they could see them clearly from the ships. There were no stone buildings, all of the houses being built of straw, although some of the floors were raised and made by hand. All of which I later heard more fully from Mutezuma and from certain interpreters of that land which he had with him.

I sent these men I had captured, together with an Indian whom they had brought from that river, and some other messengers of Mutezuma, to the lord of that river, who is called Pánuco, to persuade him to the service of Your Holy Majesty. He sent back with them an important person and, they told me, the chief of a village, who gave me some clothes, stones and featherwork from him, saying that he and all his subjects were very well pleased to be Your Highness's vassals and my friends. I then gave them things from Spain with which he was very pleased, so much so that when other ships arrived from Francisco de Garay (of which I will tell Your Majesty later) this Pánuco sent me word that these ships were in another river, five or six days' journey from there. He wished to know if those who traveled in them were of my party, for if so, he would give them whatever they needed; and that he had sent them some women, and chickens and other things to eat.

Most Powerful Lord, I traveled for three days through the country and the kingdom of Cempoal, where I was very well received and accommodated by all the natives. On the fourth day I entered a province which is called Sienchimalem,[8] in which there is a town which is very strong and built in a defensible position on the side of a very steep mountain. There is only one entrance, up steep steps which can only be climbed on foot and that with considerable difficulty. In the plain there are many villages and hamlets of five or three or two hundred inhabitants, so that there are in all as many as five or six thousand warriors; and this land is in the kingdom of Mutezuma. Here they received me very well and generously provided the provisions I needed for the journey. They told me that they knew I was going to visit their lord Mutezuma, and that I should be confident he was my friend and had sent word that they were to give me every facility, for they served him by so doing. I responded to their great kindness by saying that Your Majesty had received news of him and had sent me to see him, and that I was going for no other purpose. Then I went over a pass which is at the frontier of this province, and we called it Nombre de Dios, because it was the first we had crossed in these lands: it is so rough and steep that there is none in Spain so difficult. But I did cross it, safely and without adverse incident. On the slopes below the pass there are other villages and a fortress called Ceyxnacan,⁹ which also belongs to Mutezuma; here we were no less well received than at Sienchimalen; also, they told us, because Mutezuma wished it. And I replied as before.

From there I continued for three days through desert country which is uninhabitable because of its infertility and lack of water and because of the extreme cold. God knows how much my people suffered from thirst and hunger, and especially from a hail- and rainstorm that hit us there, which I thought would cause the deaths of many people from cold; and indeed several Indians from the island of Fernandina who had not enough to wear did die from it. After three days we crossed another pass not so steep as the first. At the top of it there was a small tower, almost like a wayside shrine, in which they kept a number of idols, and around the tower were more than a thousand cartloads of firewood, all very well stacked; for this reason we called it the Firewood Pass.¹⁰ On the descent from this pass, between some very steep mountains, there is a valley thickly inhabited with people who seemed to be very poor. After going two leagues through this region without learning anything about it, I reached a flatter place where the chief of that valley appeared to live; for he had the largest and the best-constructed buildings we had seen in that land so far. They were all of dressed stone and very well built and very new, and they had very large and beautiful halls in them and many rooms, also well built: this valley and town are called Caltanmí.[11.] By the chief and the people I was very well received and lodged.

After I had spoken to him on behalf of Your Majesty and of the reason for my coming to these parts, I asked him if he was a vassal of Mutezuma or owed some other allegiance. And he showed surprise at my question, and asked who was not a vassal of Mutezuma, meaning that here he is king of the whole world. I replied by telling him of the great power of Your Majesty and of the many other princes, greater than Mutezuma, who were Your Highness's vassals and considered it no small favor to be so; Mutezuma also would become one; as would all the natives of these lands. I therefore asked him to become one, for if he did it would be greatly to his honor and advantage, but if, on the other hand, he refused to obey he would be punished. And to acknowledge that he had been received into Your Royal service, I begged him to give me some gold to send to Your Majesty. He replied that he had gold but would give me none unless Mutezuma commanded it, but that once this had been done he would surrender to me the gold and his own person and all that he had. So as not to offend him and for fear that some calamity might befall my endeavor and my journey, I dissembled as best I could and told him that very soon I would have Mutezuma order him to give the gold and all that he owned.

Here two other chieftains who held lands in that valley came to see me: one lived four leagues down the valley and the other two leagues up the valley, and they gave me several gold necklaces of little weight and value and seven or eight female slaves. After staying there four or five days, I left them all very pleased and went up the valley to the town of the other chief I spoke of, which is called Ystacmastitán.[12] His territory consists of some three or four leagues' extent of built-up land, lying in the valley floor beside a small river which runs through it. On a very high hill is this chief's house, with a better fortress than any to be found in the middle of Spain, and fortified with better walls and barbicans and earthworks. On top of this hill live some five or six thousand inhabitants with very good houses and somewhat richer than those living in the valley. Here likewise I was very well received, and this chief said that he was also a vassal of Mutezuma. I remained in this town three days, to allow my people to recover from the hardships they had suffered in the desert as well as to await the return of four native messengers from Cempoal who had come with me and whom I had sent from Catalmy to a very large province called Tascalteca,[13] which they told me was very close by, and so it seemed to be. They had also told me that the natives of this province were their friends and very hated enemies of Mutezuma, and they wished to be my allies for they were many and very strong. They shared a large frontier with Mutezuma and fought continual wars with him and would help me if Mutezuma wished to oppose me. But the whole time I was in that valley, which was eight days in all, the messengers did not return; so I asked those chieftains of Cempoal who traveled in my company why the messengers had not returned. They replied that the land must be far away and they could not return so quickly. When I saw how long they were in coming, and that the chieftains of Cempoal so assured me of the friendship and good faith of those of that province, I set out thither.

On leaving this valley I found a great barrier built of dry stone and as much as nine feet high, which ran right across the valley from one mountain range to the other.[14] It was some twenty paces wide and all along the top was a battlement a foot and a half thick to provide an advantageous position for battle; it had only one entrance, some ten paces wide. At this entrance one wall doubled over the other, in the manner of a ravelin, within a space of forty paces, so that the entrance was not direct but had turns in it. When I asked the reason for this wall they replied that that was the frontier of the province of Tascalteca, whose inhabitants were Mutezuma's enemies and were always at war with him. The natives of the valley, because I was going to see Mutezuma their lord, begged me not to go through the territory of his enemies, for they might be hostile to me and do me some harm; they themselves would lead me to Mutezuma without leaving his territory, in which I would always be well received.

But those of Cempoal told me not to do this, but to go through Tascalteca, for what the others had said was only to prevent me from forming an alliance with that province. They said that all Mutezuma's people were wicked traitors and would lead me to a place whence I could not escape. As I held those of Cempoal in greater esteem than the others, I took their advice, leading my men with as much caution as possible. And I, with some six horsemen, rode half a league ahead, not in anticipation of what later befell me, but to explore the land, so that if anything should happen I might have time to gather and instruct my men.

After proceeding four leagues, we reached the brow of a hill, and the two horsemen who went in front of me saw some Indians dressed in the feathers they wear in battle, and bearing swords and bucklers, who when they saw the horses began to run away. I arrived soon after and I called out to them to return and not to be afraid; as we approached them (there must have been about fifteen Indians) they banded together and began to throw spears and to call to others of their people who were in a valley. They fought so fiercely with us that they killed two horses and wounded three others and two horsemen. At this point the others appeared who must have been four or five thousand. Some eight horsemen were now with me, not counting the dead, and we fought them making several charges while we waited for the other soldiers whom I had sent a horseman to fetch; and in the fighting we did them some damage, in that we killed fifty or sixty of them and ourselves suffered no harm, although they fought with great courage and ferocity. But as we were all mounted we attacked in safety and retreated likewise.

When they saw our men approaching, they withdrew, for they were few, and left us the field. After they had gone, several messengers arrived, who said they came from the chieftains of that province and with them two of the messengers I had sent, who said that the lords of the province knew nothing of what those others had done; for they were of an independent community and had done it without his permission. They regretted what had happened and would pay me for the horses which had been killed; they wanted to be my friends, wished me good fortune and said I would be welcomed by them. I replied that I was grateful to them and that I held them as friends and would go where they said. That night I was forced to sleep in a river bed one league beyond where this happened, for it was late and the men were tired.

There I took all the precautions I could, with watchmen and scouts both on foot and on horseback. When it was light I departed, keeping my vanguard and baggage in close formation and my scouts in front. When, at sunrise, I arrived at a very small village I found the other two messengers weeping, saying that they had been tied up to be killed, but had escaped that night. Only a stone's throw from them there appeared a large number of Indians, heavily armed, who with a great shout began to attack us with many javelins and arrows. I began to deliver the formal requerimiento through the interpreters who were with me and before a notary, but the longer I spent in admonishing them and requesting peace, the more they pressed us and did us as much harm as they could. Seeing therefore that nothing was to be gained by the requerimiento or protestations we began to defend ourselves as best we could, and so drew us fighting into the midst of more than 100,000 warriors who surrounded us on all sides. We fought all day long until an hour before sunset, when they withdrew; with half a dozen guns and five or six harquebuses and forty crossbowmen and with the thirteen horsemen who remained, I had done them much harm without receiving any except from exhaustion and hunger. And it truly seemed that God was fighting for us, because from such a multitude, such fierce and able warriors and with so many kinds of weapons to harm us,[15] we escaped so lightly.

That night I fortified a small tower on top of a hill, where they kept their idols. When it was day I left two hundred men and all the artillery behind and rode out to attack them with the horsemen, one hundred foot soldiers and four hundred Indians of those I brought from Cempoal, and three hundred from Yztaemestitan [*sic*]. Before they had time to rally, I burnt five or six small places of about a hundred inhabitants, and took prisoner about four hundred persons, both men and women; and returned to the camp having suffered no loss whatever. The following day at dawn, more than 149,000 men, who covered the entire ground, attacked the camp with such force that some of them broke in and fought the Spaniards hand to hand. We then went out and charged them, and so much did Our Lord help us that in four hours' fighting we had advanced so far that they could no longer harm us in the camp, although they still made some attacks. And so we fought until late, when they retired.

The following day I left before dawn by a different route, without being observed, with the horsemen, a hundred foot soldiers and my Indian allies. I burnt more than ten villages, in one of which there were more than three thousand houses, where the inhabitants fought with us, although there was no one there to help them. As we were carrying the banner of the Cross and were fighting for our Faith and in the service of Your Sacred Majesty in this Your Royal enterprise, God gave us such a victory that we killed many of them without ourselves receiving any hurt. Having gained our victory, we returned to camp a little after midday, for the enemy was gathering from all directions.

The following day messengers arrived from the chieftains saying that they wished to be vassals of Your Highness and my friends; and they begged me to forgive them for what they had done. I replied that they had done wrong, but that I was content to be their friend and to forgive what they had done. The next day some fifty Indians who, it seemed, were people of importance among them, came to the camp saying they were bringing food, and began to inspect the entrances and exits and some huts where we were living. The men from Cempoal came to me and said I should take notice of the fact that the newcomers were bad men and had come to spy and see how we could be harmed, and I could be certain that that was their only purpose in coming. I ordered one of them to be captured discreetly so that the others did not see, and I took him aside and through the interpreters threatened him so that he should tell me the truth. He confessed that Sintengal,[16] who is captain general of this province, was waiting with many men behind some hills opposite the camp to fall on us that night, because, they said, they had fought with us by day and gained nothing and now wished to try by night, so that their people should fear neither the horses nor the guns nor the swords. They had been sent to spy out our camp and to see where it could be entered, and how they might burn the straw huts. Then I had another Indian seized and questioned him likewise, and he repeated what the other had said and in the same words. Then I took five or six and they all confirmed what I had heard, so I took all fifty and cut off their hands and sent them to tell their chief that by day or by night, or whenever they chose to come, they would see who we were. I had the camp fortified as best I could, and deployed my men where I thought most advantageous, and so remained on the alert until the sun set.

When night fell the enemy began to come down through two valleys, thinking that they were unobserved and could draw close to us the better to accomplish their purpose. But as I was well prepared I saw them, and it seemed to me that it would be disadvantageous to allow them to reach the camp; for at night they would be unable to see the damage my people inflicted on them, and would be all the more intrepid. I was also afraid that as the Spaniards would not be able to see them, some of them might show less boldness in their fighting. Moreover, I was afraid they might set fire to the camp, which would have been so disastrous that none of us would have escaped. I therefore determined to ride out to meet them with all the horsemen to frighten and scatter them so they would be unable to reach the camp. And so it was that when they saw that we intended to attack them on horseback they, without stopping or shouting, made off into the maize fields of which this land is full. They unloaded some of the provisions they were carrying for the celebrations they intended to hold once they had utterly defeated us; and so they left us in peace for the rest of the night. After this occurrence I did not leave the camp for several days except to defend the entrance from some Indians who came to shout and skirmish.

When we had rested somewhat, I went out one night, after inspecting the first watch, with a hundred foot soldiers, our Indian allies and the horsemen; and one league from the camp five of the horses fell and would go no further, so I sent them back. And although all those who were with me in my company urged me to return, for it was an evil omen, I continued on my way secure in the belief that God is more powerful than Nature. Before it was dawn I attacked two towns, where I killed many people, but I did not burn the houses lest the fires should alert the other towns nearby. At dawn I came upon another large town containing, according to an inspection I had made, more than twenty thousand houses. As I took them by surprise, they rushed out unarmed, and the women and children ran naked through the streets, and I began to do them some harm. When they saw that they could not resist, several men of rank of the town came to me and begged me to do them no more harm, for they wished to be Your Highness's vassals and my allies. They now saw that they were wrong in not having been willing to assist me; from thenceforth I would see how they would do all that I, in Your Majesty's name, commanded them to do, and they would be Your faithful vassals. Then, later, more than four thousand came to me in peace and led me outside to a spring and fed me very well.

And so I left them pacified and returned to our camp where I found that those who had remained behind were very afraid that some danger had befallen me because of the omen they had seen in the return of the horses the night before. But after they heard of the victory which God had been pleased to give us, and how we had pacified those villages, there was great rejoicing, for I assure Your Majesty that there was amongst us not one who was not very much afraid, seeing how deep into this country we were and among so many hostile people and so entirely without hope of help from anywhere. Indeed, I heard it whispered, and almost spoken out loud, that I was a Pedro Carbonero[17] to have led them into this place from which they could never escape. And, moreover, standing where I could not be seen, I heard certain companions in a hut say that if I was crazy enough to go where I could not return, they were not, and that they were going to return to the sea, and if I wished to come with them, all well and good, but if not, they would abandon me. Many times I was asked to turn back, and I encouraged them by reminding them that they were Your Highness's vassals and that never at any time had Spaniards been found wanting, and that we were in a position to win for Your Majesty the greatest dominions and kingdoms in the world. Moreover, as Christians we were obliged to wage war against the enemies of our Faith; and thereby we would win glory in the next world, and, in this, greater honor and renown than any generation before our time. They should observe that God was on our side, and to Him nothing is impossible, for, as they saw, we had won so many victories in which so many of the enemy had died, and none of us. I told them other things which occurred to me of this nature, with which, and Your Highness's Royal favor, they were much encouraged and determined to follow my intentions and to do what I wished, which was to complete the enterprise I had begun.

On the following day at ten o'clock, Sintengal, the captain general of this province, came to see me, together with some fifty men of rank, and he begged me on his own behalf, and on behalf of

10. The Emperor Charles V, by Cranach the Elder. Galleria Thyssen. *Photo Brunel, Lugano.*

11. Queen Juana of Castille, by John of Flanders. Galleria Thyssen.
Photo Brunel, Lugano.

Magiscasin,[18] who is the most important person in the entire province, and on behalf of many other lords, to admit them to Your Highness's Royal service and to my friendship, and to forgive them their past errors, for they did not know who we were. They had tried with all their forces both by day and by night to avoid being subject to anyone, for this province never had been, nor had they ever had an over-all ruler. For they had lived in freedom and independence from time immemorial and had always defended themselves against the great power of Mutezuma and against his ancestors, who had subjugated all those lands but had never been able to reduce them to servitude, although they were surrounded on all sides and had no place by which to leave their land. They ate no salt because there was none in their land;[19] neither could they go and buy it elsewhere, nor did they wear cotton because it did not grow there on account of the cold; and they were lacking in many other things through being so enclosed.

All of which they suffered willingly in return for being free and subject to no one, and with me they had wished to do the same; to which end, as they said, they had used all their strength but saw clearly that neither it nor their cunning had been of any use. They would rather be Your Highness's vassals than see their houses destroyed and their women and children killed. I replied that they should recognize they were to blame for the harm they had received, for I had come to their land thinking that I came to a land of friends because the men of Cempoal had assured me that it was so. I had sent my messengers on ahead to tell them that I was coming and that I wished to be their friend. But without reply they had attacked me on the road while I was unprepared and had killed two horses and wounded others. And after they had fought me, they sent messengers to tell me that it had been done without their consent by certain communities who were responsible; but they were not involved and had now rebuked those others for it and desired my friendship. I had believed them and had told them that I was pleased and would come on the following day and go among them as I would among friends. And again they had attacked me on the road and had fought all day until nightfall. And I reminded them of everything else that they had done against me and many other things which in order not to tire Your Highness I will omit. Finally, they offered themselves as vassals in the Royal service of Your Majesty and offered their persons and fortunes and so they have remained until today and will, I think, always remain so for what reason Your Majesty will see hereafter.

I did not then leave the camp for six or seven days, for I dared not trust them, although they begged me to come to a great city of theirs where all the chiefs of the province are accustomed to live. These chiefs even came themselves and pleaded with me to go to the city, for there I should be better entertained and supplied with all the things I needed which were not available in the country-side. They were ashamed to see me so poorly accommodated, for they held me as their friend, and both they and I were Your High-ness's vassals; and because of their pleas I went to the city, which is six leagues from our camp.

The city is so big and so remarkable that, although there is much I could say of it which I shall omit, the little I will say is, I think, almost unbelievable, for the city is much larger than Granada and very much stronger, with as good buildings and many more people than Granada had when it was taken, and very much better supplied with the produce of the land, namely, bread, fowl and game and fresh-water fish and vegetables and other things they eat which are very good.[20] There is in this city a market where each and every day upward of thirty thousand people come to buy and sell, without counting the other trade which goes on elsewhere in the city. In this market there is everything they might need or wish to trade; provisions as well as clothing and footwear. There is jew-elry of gold and silver and precious stones and other ornaments of featherwork and all as well laid out as in any square or marketplace in the world. There is much pottery of many sorts and as good as the best in Spain. They sell [21] a great deal of firewood and charcoal and medicinal and cooking herbs. There are establishments like barbers' where they have their hair washed and are shaved, and there are baths. Lastly there is amongst them every consequence of good order and courtesy, and they are such an orderly and intelligent people that the best in Africa cannot equal them.

In this province, which is in size ninety leagues or more about, there are many beautiful valleys and plains, all cultivated and harvested, leaving no place untilled; and the orderly manner in which, until now, these people have been governed is almost like that of the states of Venice or Genoa or Pisa, for they have no overlord. There are many chiefs, all of whom reside in this city, and the country towns contain peasants who are vassals of these lords and each of whom holds his land independently; some have more than others, and for their wars they join together and together they plan and direct them.

It is thought that there must be some form of law for punishing wrongdoers, because one of the natives of this province stole some gold from a Spaniard and I told Magiscasin, who is the greatest of all the chiefs, and they searched for him and pursued him to a city that is close by, called Churultecal,[22] and from there they brought him prisoner and delivered him to me together with the gold and told me to punish him. I thanked them for the diligence they had shown in this matter, and told them that since I was in their land they should punish him as they were accustomed, and that I did not wish to interfere by punishing their own people, for which they thanked me and took him and with a crier who announced his crime publicly had him marched through that great marketplace. They made him stand below a kind of stage which is in the middle of this marketplace, and the crier climbed to the top of the stage and in a loud voice again announced his crime; when they saw him they all beat him over the head with cudgels until he died. Many others we have seen in captivity, where they say they are held for thefts and other crimes.[23] There are in this province, according to the investigation I had made, 150,000 inhabitants to-

gether with another small province which is adjacent, called Guasyn-
cango,[24] and there they live as these do with no natural lord; and
these are no less Your Highness's vassals than those of Tascalteca.

Most Catholic Lord, while I was in the camp which I had in
the country during the war with this province, six chieftains of
rank, vassals of Mutezuma, came to see me with as many as two
hundred men in attendance. They told me that they had come on
behalf of Mutezuma to inform me how he wished to be Your
Highness's vassal and my ally, and that I should say what I wished
him to pay as an annual tribute to Your Highness in gold and silver
and jewels as well as slaves, cotton, clothing and other things which
he possessed; all of which he would give, provided that I did not go
to his land, the reason being that it was very barren and lacking in
all provisions and it would grieve him if I and those who came with
me should be in want. With them he sent me almost a thousand
pesos de oro and as many cotton garments, such as they wear.

They stayed with me during much of the war and remained
until the end, when they saw clearly what Spaniards are capable of
and the peace we made with those of this province and how the
lords and all the inhabitants offered themselves to the service of
Your Sacred Majesty. It appeared that they were rather displeased
at this, since they made many and varied attempts to cause trouble
between me and those people, saying that they were not speaking
the truth nor was the friendship they offered me sincere, but that
all this was done so that they might dispel my suspicions and thus
betray me with impunity. The people of Tascalteca, on the other
hand, warned me many times not to trust Mutezuma's vassals, for
they were traitors and everything they did was done with treachery and cunning; and that in this manner they had subjugated the
whole land. They warned me of all this as true friends, and inas-
much as they were people who were well acquainted with their
behavior. When I saw the discord and animosity between these two
peoples I was not a little pleased, for it seemed to further my purpose considerably; consequently I might have the opportunity of

subduing them more quickly, for, as the saying goes, "divided they fall." . . . And I remember that one of the Gospels says, "*Omne regnum in seipsum divisum desolabitur*." [25] So I maneuvered one against the other and thanked each side for their warnings and told each that I held his friendship to be of more worth than the other's.

After having spent twenty days in this city, those lords, Mutezuma's messengers, who were always with me, asked me to go to a city called Churultecal, which is six leagues from Tascalteca, for the people there were Mutezuma's allies, and there we should know Mutezuma's wishes, whether I was to go to his land or not, and some of their number would go and tell him what I had said, and would return with his reply, although they knew that certain of his messengers were waiting there to speak with me. I told them that I would go and advised them on what day I would leave. And when those of Tascalteca heard what the others had planned with me, and that I had agreed to go to that city with them, the chiefs came to me much distressed and warned me on no account to go, for a trap had been prepared to kill me in that city and all my companions, and that for this purpose Mutezuma had sent from his land (for some part of it bordered with this state) fifty thousand men who were garrisoned two leagues from the city. They had closed the highroad by which they usually traveled, and had made a new one full of holes and with sharpened stakes driven into the ground and covered up so that the horses would fall and cripple themselves; they had walled up many of the streets and piled stones on the roofs of the houses so that after we had entered the city they might capture us without difficulty and do with us as they wished. And if I wished to confirm all they said, I should take notice of the fact that the chiefs of that city had never come to see me, although it was so near, while the people of Guasincango, which is farther away, had come; and I should send for them and I would see that they would refuse to come. I thanked them for their warning and asked them to give me messengers that I might send for them. This they did, and I sent them to ask those chiefs to come to me, for I wished to speak to them about certain matters on behalf of Your Highness and to explain to them the reason of my coming to this land.

These messengers went and delivered my message to the chiefs of that city, and they sent back two or three persons of no great importance who told me that they had come on behalf of those chiefs who could not come themselves because they were sick; and that I should tell them what I wanted. The people of Tascalteca said that this was a trick; for those messengers were men of little consequence and that I should on no account depart from there until the chiefs of that city had come. I spoke to those messengers and told them that an embassy from so high a prince as Your Sacred Majesty should not be received by persons such as they, and that even their masters were hardly worthy to receive it; therefore the chiefs should appear before me within three days to owe obedience to Your Highness and offer themselves as your vassals. I warned them that if they did not appear within the period I specified, I would march against them and destroy them as rebels who refused to subject themselves to the dominion of Your Highness. For this purpose I sent them a command signed in my name and witnessed by a notary, together with a long account concerning the Royal person of Your Sacred Majesty and of my coming, telling them how these parts and other much greater lands and dominions all belonged to Your Highness, and that those who wished to be Your vassals would be honored and aided, but that on the other hand, those who rebelled would be punished in accordance with the law.

On the following day, some or nearly all the chiefs of the above-mentioned city came and said that if they had not come before it was because the people of that province were their enemies and they dared not enter their land because they did not feel safe there. They believed I had been told things unfavorable to them, but I should not believe what I heard because it was the word of enemies and not the truth, and I should go to their city, for there I would recognize that all I had been told was false and that what they said was indeed true. From thenceforth they offered themselves as vassals of Your Sacred Majesty and swore to remain so always and to serve and assist in all things that Your Highness commanded them. A notary set all this down through the interpreters which I had. Still I determined to go with them; on the one hand, so as not to show weakness and, on the other, because I hoped to conduct my business with Mutezuma from that city because it bordered on his territory, as I have said, and on the road between the two there is free travel and no frontier restrictions.

When the people of Tascalteca saw my determination it distressed them considerably, and they told me many times that I was mistaken, but since they were vassals of Your Sacred Majesty and my friends they would go with me to assist me in whatever might happen. Although I opposed this and asked them not to come, as it was unnecessary, they followed me with some 100,000 men, all well armed for war, and came within two leagues of the city. After much persuasion on my part they returned, though there remained in my company some five or six thousand of them. That night I slept in a ditch, hoping to divest myself of these people in case they caused trouble in the city, and because it was already late enough and I did not want to enter too late. The following morning, they came out of the city to greet me with many trumpets and drums, including many persons whom they regard as priests in their temples, dressed in traditional vestments and singing after their fashion, as they do in the temples. With such ceremony they led us into the city and gave us very good quarters, where all those in my company were most comfortable. There they brought us food, though not sufficient. On the road we had come across many of the signs which the natives of that province had warned us about, for we found the highroad closed and another made and some holes, though not many; and some of the streets of the city were barricaded, and there were piles of stones on all the roofs. All this made us more alert and more cautious.

There I found several of Mutezuma's messengers who came

and spoke with those who were with me, but to me they said merely that they had come to discover from those others what they had agreed with me, so as to go and inform their master. So after they had spoken with them, they left; and with them went one of the most important of those who had been with me before. During the three days I remained in that city they fed us worse each day, and the lords and principal persons of the city came only rarely to see and speak with me. And being somewhat disturbed by this, my interpreter, who is an Indian woman[26] from Putunchan, which is the great river of which I spoke to Your Majesty in the first letter, was told by another Indian woman and a native of this city that very close by many of Mutezuma's men were gathered, and that the people of the city had sent away their women and children and all their belongings, and were about to fall on us and kill us all; and that if she wished to escape she should go with her and she would shelter here. All this she told to Gerónimo de Aguilar, an interpreter whom I acquired in Yucatán, of whom I have also written to Your Highness; and he informed me. I then seized one of the natives of this city who was passing by and took him aside secretly and questioned him; and he confirmed what the woman and the natives of Tascalteca had told me. Because of this and because of the signs I had observed, I decided to forestall an attack, and I sent for some of the chiefs of the city, saying that I wished to speak with them. I put them in a room and meanwhile warned our men to be prepared, when a harquebus was fired, to fall on the many Indians who were outside our quarters and on those who were inside. And so it was done, that after I had put the chiefs in the room, I left them bound up and rode away and had the harquebus fired, and we fought so hard that in two hours more than three thousand men were killed. So that Your Majesty should realize how well prepared they were, even before I left my quarters they had occupied all the streets and had placed all their people at the ready, although, as we took them by surprise, they were easy to disperse, especially because I had imprisoned their leaders. I ordered some towers and fortified houses from which they were attacking us to be set on fire. And so I proceeded through the city fighting for five hours or more, leaving our quarters, which were in a strong position, secure. Finally all the people were driven out of the city in many directions, for some five thousand Indians from Tascalteca and another four hundred from Cempoal were assisting me.[27]

When I returned I spoke to those chiefs I had imprisoned, and asked them for what reason they had wished to kill me treacherously. They replied that they were not to blame, for those of Culua, who were Mutezuma's vassals, had forced them to it, and that Mutezuma had garrisoned in a place, which later was found to be a league and a half from there, fifty thousand men for that purpose. But now they knew that they had been tricked, and they asked that one or two of them should be freed so as to fetch into the city the women and children and the belongings which they had outside. They begged me to forgive them their mistake and assured me that they would not be deceived in future, and they would be Your Highness's very true and faithful vassals and my allies. After having spoken to them at length concerning their error, I freed two of them, and on the following day the whole city was reoccupied and full of women and children, all unafraid, as though nothing had happened. Then I set free all the other chiefs on the condition that they promised to serve Your Majesty most loyally.

After fifteen or twenty days which I remained there the city and the land were so pacified and full of people that it seemed as if no one were missing from it, and their markets and trade were carried on as before. I then restored the friendly relations between this city of Curultecal [sic] and Tascalteca, which had existed in the recent past, before Mutezuma had attracted them to his friendship with gifts and made them enemies of the others.[28]

This city of Churultecal is situated in a plain and has as many as twenty thousand houses within the main part of the city and as many again in the outskirts. It is an independent state having fixed frontiers; the people owe obedience to no overlord but are governed like those of Tascalteca. The people of this city wear somewhat more clothes than those of Tascalteca, for the respected citizens among them wear burnooses over their other garments, but they are different from those worn in Africa because they have armholes, although in the shape and the cloth and in the hems they are very similar. Since those troubles, they have all been and continue to be very faithful vassals of Your Majesty and very obedient in whatever I, in Your Royal name, have requested of them, and I believe that they will remain so.

This state is very rich in crops, for it possesses much land, most of it irrigated. The city itself is more beautiful to look at than any in Spain, for it is very well proportioned and has many towers. And I assure Your Highness that from a temple I counted more than 430 towers, and they were all of temples. From here to the coast I have seen no city so fit for Spaniards to live in, for it has water and some common lands suitable for raising cattle, which none of those we saw previously had, for there are so many people living in these parts that not one foot of land is uncultivated, and yet in many places they suffer hardships for lack of bread. And there are many poor people who beg from the rich in the streets as the poor do in Spain and in other civilized places.

I spoke to those of Mutezuma's messengers who were with me of the treachery attempted upon me in that city, and how the chiefs had said that it had been done on Mutezuma's orders, and that I could scarcely believe that such a great lord should send his messengers and such esteemed persons as he had sent me to say that he was my friend, and meanwhile should be seeking a way to attack me by another's hand so that he might avoid responsibility if all did not turn out as he hoped. But since it was true that he did not keep his word or speak the truth, I had changed my plans: whereas, before, I had been going to his land with the intention of seeing him and speaking with him in order to have him as a friend and to converse with him in harmony, now I intended to enter his land at war doing all the harm I could as an enemy, though I regretted it very much, for I had always wished rather to be his friend and ask his advice on all the things that must be done in this land.

They then replied that they had been with me many days and had known nothing of such an agreement save what they had heard in the city after the fighting was over, and they could not believe that it had been done by order of Mutezuma. They therefore begged me that before I resolved to cast aside his friendship and make war on him as I had said, I should be certain of the truth; I should allow one of them to go and speak with him, and he would return very soon. There are but twenty leagues between the city and the place where Mutezuma lives. I told them I agreed and allowed one of them to go, who, after six days, returned with another who had gone before. And they brought me ten gold plates and fifteen hundred articles of clothing and many provisions of chickens and *panicap*,[29] which is a certain beverage they drink; and they told me that Mutezuma was much distressed at the hostilities that had been attempted in Churultecal because he knew I could not but believe that it had been done by his orders. But he assured me that it was not so, and although it was true that the men who were garrisoned there were his, they had taken part without his orders, induced by those of Churultecal, for they came from two of his provinces, one of which was called Acancingo and the other Yzcucan,[30] which bordered on the territory of that city. Between these there were certain neighborly agreements of mutual assistance, and for this reason they had gone there, and not because he ordered it. But in future I would see by his deeds whether what he said was true or not; even so, he urged me not to trouble to come to his land, for it was very barren and we would go hungry, and that, wherever I might be, I should send to him for what I required and he would provide it for me. I replied that the journey to his land could not be avoided, for I had to send an account of it and of him to Your Majesty; I believed what he said, but as I had perforce to go and see him he should accept the fact and not make any other plans, because it would cause him great harm, and I would be distressed if any harm befell him. Once he understood my determination to go and see him and his land, he sent to tell me that I was welcome, and that he would accommodate me in that great city where he lived; and he sent to me many of his men to accompany me, for I was now entering his land. These men wished to lead me by a certain road where they must have planned to prepare an ambush, or so it seemed afterwards, for many Spaniards whom I later sent through the land saw the road. There were on it so many bridges and difficult stretches that had I gone that way they could have accomplished their purpose with no trouble. But as God has always shown diligence in guiding the Royal affairs of Your Sacred Majesty ever since Your childhood, and as I and those of my company traveled in Your Royal service, so He showed us another road which, although somewhat rough, was not so dangerous as the one by which they wished to lead us and it happened in the following manner:

Eight leagues from this city of Churultecal are two very high and very remarkable mountains;[31] for at the end of August there is so much snow on top of them that nothing else can be seen, and from one of them, which is the higher, there appears often both by day and by night a great cloud of smoke as big as a house which goes straight as an arrow up into the clouds, and seems to come out with such force that even though there are very strong winds on top of the mountain they cannot turn it. Because I have always wished to render Your Highness very particular account of all the things of this land, I wished to know the explanation of this which seemed to me something of a miracle; so I sent ten of my companions, such as were qualified for such an undertaking, with some natives to guide them; and I urged them to attempt to climb the mountain and discover the secret of the smoke, whence it came, and how. These men went and made every effort to climb the mountain but were not able to on account of the great quantity of snow that is there and the whirlwinds of ash which come out of the mountain, and also because they could not endure the great cold which they encountered there. But they came very close to the summit; so much so that while they were there the smoke started to come out, with such force and noise, they said, it seemed the whole mountain was falling down, so they descended and brought much snow and icicles for us to see, for this seemed to be something very rare in these parts, so the pilots have believed until now, because of the warm climate; especially as this land is at twenty degrees, which is on the same parallel as the island of Hispaniola, where it is always very hot.

When they were going toward this mountain, they came across a road and asked the natives who were with them where it led, and they replied, to Culua, and that it was a good one and that the other, by which the people of Culua had wished to lead us, was not good. And the Spaniards traveled along it until they had crossed the mountains, between which the road ran, and there they looked down on the plains of Culua and the great city of Temixtitan and the lakes which are in that province, with all of which I will acquaint Your Highness later. So they returned very pleased at having discovered such a good road; and God knows how glad I was about it. After these Spaniards who had gone to see the mountain had returned, and I had questioned both them and the natives about the road they had found, I spoke to those messengers of Mutezuma who came with me to lead me through their land, and told them that I wished to go by that road because it was shorter, and not by the one they had mentioned. They replied that it was true it was shorter and easier, but that they had not taken us by it because we would have had to spend a day in Guasucingo, which was the land of their enemies, and there we would have had none of the things we required as we would in the land of Mutezuma, but that if I wished to go that way they would have provisions brought from the other road. So we left, in some fear lest they should persist in trying to set a trap for us; but as we had announced that that was the road we were to travel by, it did not seem wise to me to leave it or to turn back, for I did not wish them to believe we lacked courage.

On the day I left the city of Churultecal, I traveled four leagues to some villages of the state of Guasucingo, where I was very well received by the natives, who gave me some female slaves and clothing and some small pieces of gold, which in all was very little, because they own very little on account of their being allies of the Tascaltecans and surrounded on all sides by Mutezuma's land, so they have no trade save with the people of their own province; because of this they live very poorly. On the following day I climbed the pass which goes between the two mountains I have mentioned, and on the descent we entered Mutezuma's land through a province of it called Chalco. Two leagues before we reached the villages,[32] I found a dwelling, newly built and so large that I and all those of my company were quartered there very comfortably, although I brought with me more than four thousand Indians, natives of the provinces of Tascalteca, Guasucingo, Churultecal and Cempoal. There was plenty to eat for all, and in all the rooms very great fires and plenty of firewood, for it was very cold on account of our being very close to those two mountains which have so much snow on them.

Certain persons, who seemed to be chieftains, came here to speak with me, one of whom was said to be Mutezuma's brother. He brought me some three thousand *pesos de oro* from Mutezuma, and begged me on his behalf to turn back and not persist in going to his city, for the land was scarce of food and the roads were bad; furthermore, the city was built entirely on the water and I might only enter it by canoe. He also told me of many other inconveniences I would find on the journey. He then said that I had only to say what I wanted and Mutezuma, their lord, would command it to be given me and would likewise agree to give me each year a *certum quid*, which he would send to the coast or wherever else I wished. I received them very well and gave them some of the things from Spain which they hold in great esteem, especially to him who was said to be Mutezuma's brother. To his embassy I replied that were it in my power to return I would do so to please Mutezuma, but that I had come to this land by Your Majesty's commands, and the principal thing of which I had been ordered to give an account was of Mutezuma and his great city, of which and of whom Your Highness had known for many years. And I told him to beg Mutezuma on my behalf to acquiesce in my journey, because no harm would come of it to his person or his land, rather, it would be to his advantage; and that once I had seen him, should he still not wish me to remain in his company, I would then return; and that we could better decide between ourselves in person how Your Majesty was to be served than through ambassadors, even if they were men in whom we placed the utmost confidence. With this reply they departed. To judge by all we had seen and the preparations which had been made in this dwelling of which I have spoken, it seemed to the Indians that they planned to attack us that night. When I heard this I set up such a guard that once they saw it they changed their minds, and very secretly sent away that night many of their people who had gathered in the woods which were close to the camp, as was seen by our sentries and scouts.

At daybreak I departed for a town which is two leagues from there and is called Amaqueruca.[33] It is in the province of Chalco, which contains, in the principal town and in the villages which are two leagues away, more than twenty thousand inhabitants. In the aforementioned town we were quartered in some very good houses belonging to the lord of the place. And many persons who seemed to be of high rank came to speak with me, saying that Mutezuma, their lord, had sent them to wait for me there and to provide me with all that I might need. The chief of this province and town gave me as many as forty slave girls and three thousand castellanos, and, in the two days that we were there, he provided us very adequately with all the food we needed. On the following day, traveling with those messengers of Mutezuma who said that they had come to wait for me, I left and put up for the night four leagues from there in a small town which is by a great lake. Almost half of it is built on the water, and on the land side there is a very rugged mountain strewn with many stones and boulders; and there we were very well quartered.[34] Here likewise they wished to pit their strength against us, only it seemed that they wished to do it without risk by falling on us at night unawares. But as I was on the alert I anticipated their plans, and that night kept such watch that when dawn broke my men had taken or killed some fifteen or twenty of their spies, some of whom had come in canoes and others of whom had descended from the mountain to see if there was an opportunity of achieving their intention. Consequently, few of them returned to report what they had discovered; and, seeing that we were always so well prepared, they decided to abandon their original intent and treat us well.

On the following morning, as I was preparing to leave the town, ten or twelve lords, of great importance, as I later discovered, came to see me, and among them there was one great chief, a young man of about twenty-five[35] to whom they all showed great reverence, so much so that after he stepped down from the litter in which he came all the others began to clear the stones and straw from the ground in front of him. When they came to where I was they told me they had come on behalf of Mutezuma, their lord, and that he had sent them to accompany me, and he begged me to forgive him for not coming himself to receive me, for he was indisposed; but his city was close by, and since I was determined to go there we should meet and I would learn from him his willingness to serve Your Highness. But still he begged me, if it were possible, not to go there, for I would suffer many hardships and he was very ashamed not to be able to provide for me as he wished. To this end those chiefs urged and earnestly persisted, so much so that finally there was nothing left for them to say, save that they would bar the road if I still insisted on going.

I answered, and appeased them as eloquently as I could, making them understand that no harm could ensue from my coming, but rather much profit. I then gave them some of the things that I had with me and they departed. I followed immediately after them accompanied by many people who seemed of some account, as afterwards they were shown to be. I continued on the road by the side of that great lake, and one league from the quarters we had just left I saw in the middle of it, well beyond bowshot, a small city, with perhaps some thousand or two thousand inhabitants, constructed entirely on the water and with many towers and no place to enter, or so it seemed from a distance.[36] Another league beyond we entered upon a causeway as wide as a horseman's lance and two-thirds of a league into the middle of the lake, and there we came upon a city, which, although small, was the most beautiful we had seen, both in regard to the well-built houses and towers and in the skill of the foundations, for it is raised on the water.[37] In this city, which has some two thousand inhabitants, they received and fed us very well. The chief and important persons of the place came to me and begged me to rest there for the night. But Mutezuma's messengers told me not to stay, but to go to another city three leagues from there, called Yztapalapa, belonging to a brother of Mutezuma, and I did so.[38] And to leave this city, where we ate, whose name I cannot now recall, we passed along another causeway for a league or more before reaching dry land. When I arrived at the city of Yztapalapa, the lord and that of another city called Caluaacan,[39] which is three leagues distant, came out to meet me together with other chiefs who were waiting there, and they gave me some three or four thousand *castellanos* and some clothing and slave girls, and made me very welcome.

In this city of Yztapalapa live twelve or fifteen thousand inhabitants. It is built by the side of a great salt lake, half of it on the water and the other half on dry land. The chief of this city has some new houses which, although as yet unfinished, are as good as the best in Spain; that is, in respect of size and workmanship both in their masonry and woodwork and their floors, and furnishings for every sort of household task; but they have no reliefs or other rich things which are used in Spain but not found here. They have many upper and lower rooms and cool gardens with many trees and sweet-smelling flowers; likewise there are pools of fresh water, very well made and with steps leading down to the bottom. There is a very large kitchen garden next to the house and overlooking it a gallery with very beautiful corridors and rooms, and in the garden a large reservoir of fresh water, well built with fine stonework, around which runs a well-tiled pavement so wide that four people can walk there abreast. It is four hundred paces square, which is sixteen hundred paces around the edge. Beyond the pavement, toward the wall of the garden, there is a latticework of canes, behind which are all manner of shrubs and scented herbs. Within the pool there are many fish and birds, wild ducks and widgeons, as well as other types of waterfowl; so many that the water is often almost covered with them.

On the following day I left this city and after traveling for half a league came to a causeway which runs through the middle of the lake for two leagues until it reaches the great city of Temixti- tan, which is built in the middle of the lake. This causeway is as wide as two lances, and well built, so that eight horsemen can ride abreast. In the two leagues from one end to the other there are three towns, and one of them, which is called Misicalcango, is in the main built on the water, and the other two, which are called Nici- aca and Huchilohuchico,[40] are built on the shore, but many of their houses are on the water. The first of these cities has three thousand inhabitants, the second more than six thousand, and the third an- other four or five thousand, and in all of them there are very good houses and towers, especially the houses of the chiefs and persons of high rank, and the temples or oratories where they keep their idols.

In these cities there is much trading in salt, which they ex- tract from the water of the lake and from the shallow area which is covered by the waters of the lake. They bake it in some way to make cakes, which are sold to the inhabitants and also beyond.

Thus I continued along this causeway, and half a league be- fore the main body of the city of Temixtitan, at the entrance to another causeway which meets this one from the shore, there is a

very strong fortification with two towers ringed by a wall four
yards wide with merloned battlements all around commanding
both causeways. There are only two gates, one for entering and
one for leaving. Here as many as a thousand men came out to see
and speak with me, important persons from that city, all dressed
very richly after their own fashion. When they reached me, each
one performed a ceremony which they practice among themselves;
each placed his hand on the ground and kissed it. And so I stood
there waiting for nearly an hour until everyone had performed his
ceremony. Close to the city there is a wooden bridge ten paces wide
across a breach in the causeway to allow the water to flow, as it
rises and falls. The bridge is also for the defense of the city, because
whenever they so wish they can remove some very long broad
beams of which this bridge is made. There are many such bridges
throughout the city as later Your Majesty will see in the account I
give of it.

After we had crossed this bridge, Mutezuma came to greet
us and with him some two hundred lords, all barefoot and dressed
in a different costume, but also very rich in their way and more so
than the others. They came in two columns, pressed very close to
the walls of the street, which is very wide and beautiful and so
straight that you can see from one end to the other. It is two-thirds
of a league long and has on both sides very good and big houses,
both dwellings and temples.

Mutezuma came down the middle of this street with two
chiefs, one on his right hand and the other on his left. One of these
was that great chief who had come on a litter to speak with me, and
the other was Mutezuma's brother, chief of the city of Yztapalapa,
which I had left that day. And they were all dressed alike except
that Mutezuma wore sandals whereas the others went barefoot; and
they held his arm on either side. When we met I dismounted and
stepped forward to embrace him, but the two lords who were with
him stopped me with their hands so that I should not touch him;
and they likewise all performed the ceremony of kissing the earth.

When this was over Mutezuma requested his brother to remain with me and to take me by the arm while he went a little way ahead with the other; and after he had spoken to me all the others in the two columns came and spoke with me, one after another, and then each returned to his column.

When at last I came to speak to Mutezuma himself I took off a necklace of pearls and cut glass that I was wearing and placed it round his neck; after we had walked a little way up the street a servant of his came with two necklaces, wrapped in a cloth, made from red snails' shells, which they hold in great esteem; and from each necklace hung eight shrimps of refined gold almost a span in length. When they had been brought he turned to me and placed them about my neck, and then continued up the street in the manner already described until we reached a very large and beautiful house which had been very well prepared to accommodate us. There he took me by the hand and led me to a great room facing the courtyard through which we entered. And he bade me sit on a very rich throne, which he had had built for him and then left saying that I should wait for him. After a short while, when all those of my company had been quartered, he returned with many and various treasures of gold and silver and featherwork, and as many as five or six thousand cotton garments, all very rich and woven and embroidered in various ways. And after he had given me these things he sat on another throne which they placed there next to the one on which I was sitting, and addressed me in the following way:

"For a long time we have known from the writings of our ancestors that neither I, nor any of those who dwell in this land, are natives of it, but foreigners who came from very distant parts; and likewise we know that a chieftain, of whom they were all vassals, brought our people to this region. And he returned to his native land and after many years came again, by which time all those who had remained were married to native women and had built villages and raised children. And when he wished to lead them away again they would not go nor even admit him as their chief; and so he departed. And we have always held that those who descended from him would come and conquer this land and take us as their vassals. So because of the place from which you claim to come, namely, from where the sun rises, and the things you tell us of the great lord or king who sent you here, we believe and are certain that he is our natural lord, especially as you say that he has known of us for some time. So be assured that we shall obey you and hold you as our lord in place of that great sovereign of whom you speak; and in this there shall be no offense or betrayal whatsoever. And in all the land that lies in my domain, you may command as you will, for you shall be obeyed; and all that we own is for you to dispose of as you choose. Thus, as you are in your own country and your own house, rest now from the hardships of your journey and the battles which you have fought, for I know full well of all that has happened to you from Puntunchan[41] to here, and I also know how those of Cempoal and Tascalteca have told you much evil of me; believe only what you see with your eyes, for those are my enemies, and some were my vassals, and have rebelled against me at your coming and said those things to gain favor with you. I also know that they have told you the walls of my houses are made of gold, and that the floor mats in my rooms and other things in my household are likewise of gold, and that I was, and claimed to be, a god; and many other things besides. The houses as you see are of stone and lime and clay."

Then he raised his clothes and showed me his body, saying, as he grasped his arms and trunk with his hands, "See that I am of flesh and blood like you and all other men, and I am mortal and substantial. See how they have lied to you? It is true that I have some pieces of gold left to me by my ancestors; anything I might have shall be given to you whenever you ask. Now I shall go to other houses where I live, but here you shall be provided with all that you and your people require, and you shall receive no hurt, for you are in your own land and your own house." [42]

I replied to all he said as I thought most fitting, especially in making him believe that Your Majesty was he whom they were expecting; and with this he took his leave. When he had gone we were very well provided with chickens, bread, fruit and other requisites, especially for the servicing of our quarters. In this manner I spent six days, very well provisioned with all that was needed and visited by many of those chiefs.

Most Catholic Lord, as I said at the beginning of this account, when I departed from Vera Cruz in search of this Mutezuma I left behind 150 men to complete a fortress which I had begun; I also related how I had left many towns and fortresses in the countryside around that town under Your Highness's Royal command and the natives pacified.

When I was in the city of Churultecal I received letters from the captain whom I had left in the aforementioned town in which he informed of how Qualpopoca, chief of the city which is called Almería, had sent messengers to him to say that he wished to be Your Highness's vassal, and if he had not come before or now to swear allegiance and offer himself and all his lands as he was obliged, it was because he would have to pass through the lands of his enemies and feared that he would be attacked. He therefore asked the captain to send four Spaniards to accompany him, for those through whose land he must pass, knowing his purpose, would not trouble him. The captain, believing what Qualpopoca said to be true, for many others had done the same sort of thing, sent the four Spaniards, but once Qualpopoca had them in his house, he ordered them to be killed in such way as to appear he had not done it. Two of them were killed, but the others escaped, wounded, through the woods.

And so the captain had marched on the city of Almería with fifty Spaniards and the two horsemen, as well as two guns and with some eight or ten thousand of our Indian allies. They had attacked the inhabitants of that city, and with the loss of six or seven Spaniards had captured it and killed many of the inhabitants, driving out the rest. They had set fire to the city and destroyed it, for the

Indians who came with them were the enemies of that city and had taken great care over it. But Qualpopoca, chief of that city, together with other chiefs, allies of his, who had come to assist him, had escaped. From some prisoners he took in that city the captain had discovered who had been defending it and for what reason they had killed the Spaniards whom he had sent. They said that it was done because Mutezuma had commanded Qualpopoca and the others who had come there, as his vassals, that once I had left the town of Vera Cruz to fall upon those who had rebelled and offered themselves to the service of Your Highness, and to seek every possible means of killing the Spaniards whom I had left behind, so that they should not help or favor them.

Most Invincible Lord, six days having passed since we first entered this great city of Temixtitan, during which time I had seen something of it, though little compared with how much there is to see and record, I decided from what I had seen that it would benefit Your Royal service and our safety if Mutezuma were in my power and not in complete liberty, in order that he should not retreat from the willingness he showed to serve Your Majesty; but chiefly because we Spaniards are rather obstinate and persistent, and should we annoy him he might, as he is so powerful, obliterate all memory of us. Furthermore, by having him with me, all those other lands which were subject to him would come more swiftly to the recognition and service of Your Majesty, as later happened. I resolved, therefore, to take him and keep him in the quarters where I was, which were very strong.

Thinking of all the ways and means to capture him without causing a disturbance, I remembered what the captain I had left in Vera Cruz had written to me about the events in the city of Almería, and how all that had happened there had been by order of Mutezuma.[43] I left a careful watch on the crossroads and went to Mutezuma's houses, as I had done at other times, and after having joked and exchanged pleasantries with him and after he had given me some gold jewelry and one of his daughters and other chiefs' daughters to some of my company, I told him that I knew of what had happened in the city of Nautecal (or Almería, as we called it), and the Spaniards who had been killed there; and that Qualpopoca excused himself by saying that all had been done by Mutezuma's command, and that as his vassal he could not have done otherwise. I told him, however, that I did not believe it was as Qualpopoca had said, but that as he was trying to exculpate himself, I thought that he ought to send for Qualpopoca and for all the other lords concerned in the death of those Spaniards, so that the truth might be known, and they might be punished so that Your Majesty should see clearly his good intentions. For, if he provoked Your Highness's anger, instead of receiving favors as he should, he would suffer much harm on account of what those men had said, but I was well satisfied that the truth was the reverse of what they claimed, and I had confidence in him. He immediately sent for certain of his men to whom he gave a small stone figure in the manner of a seal, which he carried fastened to his arm, and he commanded them to go to the city of Almería, which is sixty or seventy leagues from Temixtitan, and to bring Qualpopoca, and to discover who were the others who had been concerned with the death of the Spaniards and to bring them likewise. If they did not come voluntarily, they were to be brought as prisoners, and if they resisted capture, Mutezuma's messengers were to request of certain communities close to the city, which he indicated to them, to send forces to seize them, but on no account to return without them.

These left at once, and after they had gone I thanked Mutezuma for the great care which he had taken in this matter, for it was my responsibility to account to Your Highness for those Spaniards, but asked that he should stay in my quarters until the truth were known and he was shown to be blameless. I begged him not to take this ill, for he was not to be imprisoned but given all his freedom, and I would not impede the service and command of his domains, and he should choose a room in those quarters where I was, whichever he wished. There he would be very much at his ease and would certainly be given no cause for annoyance or discomfort, because as well as those of his service my own men would serve him in all he commanded. In this we spent much time reasoning and discussing, all of which is too lengthy to write down and too tedious and too little pertinent to the issue to give Your Highness an account; so I will say only that at last he said he would agree to go with me. Then he ordered the room where he wished to stay to be prepared, and it was very well prepared. When this was done many chiefs came, and removing their garments they placed them under their arms, and walking barefoot they brought a simple litter, and weeping carried him in it in great silence. Thus we proceeded to my quarters with no disturbance in the city, although there was some agitation which, as soon as Mutezuma knew of it, he ordered to cease; and all was quiet and remained so all the time I held Mutezuma prisoner, for he was very much at his ease and kept all his household—which is very great and wonderful, as I will later relate —with him as before. And I and those of my company satisfied his needs as far as was possible.

Fifteen or twenty days after his imprisonment, those he had sent to find Qualpopoca and the others who had killed the Spaniards returned, bringing with them the aforementioned Qualpopoca and one of his sons and fifteen other persons whom they said were of high rank and had been concerned in the killing. And Qualpopoca was borne in a litter like a lord, which indeed he was. When they arrived they were handed over to me and I had them well guarded in chains. After they had confessed to the killing of the Spaniards I had them questioned to see if they were Mutezuma's vassals. Qualpopoca replied asking if there were any other lord of whom he could be a vassal, as much as to say that there was no other, and that he was. Likewise I asked them if what they had done was by Mutezuma's command, and they replied that it was not, although when the sentence that they should be burnt was carried out, they said unanimously that it was true that Mutezuma had ordered it to be done, and by his command they had done it. Thus they were burnt publicly in a square, with no disturbance whatsoever. But on the day of their execution, because they had confessed that Mutezuma had ordered them to kill those Spaniards, I ordered him to be put in irons, from which he received no small fright, although later that same day, after having spoken with him, I had them removed, and he was very pleased.

From then on I did all I could to please him, especially by announcing publicly to all the natives, the chiefs as well as those who came to see me, that it was Your Majesty's wish that Mutezuma should remain in power, acknowledging the sovereignty which Your Highness held over him, and that they could best serve Your Highness by obeying him and holding him for their lord, as they had before I came to this land. So well did I treat him and so much satisfaction did he receive from me that many times I offered him his liberty, begging him to return to his house, and each time he told me that he was pleased to be where he was and he did not wish to go, for he lacked nothing, just as if he were in his own home. Also, his going might permit certain chiefs, his vassals, to induce or oblige him to do something against his will and prejudicial to the service of Your Highness; for he had resolved to serve Your Majesty in all that he could. As long as these chiefs were informed of all he wanted he was content to remain there, as he might excuse himself, should they wish to demand anything of him, by replying that he was not at liberty. Many times he asked my permission to go and spend some time at certain residences which he owned both inside and outside the city, and not once did I refuse him. Many times he went with five or six Spaniards to entertain himself one or two leagues beyond the city, and he always returned very happy and content to the quarters where I held him. Whenever he went out he gave many gifts of jewels and clothing, both to the Spaniards who escorted him and to the natives by whom he was always so well attended that when the least number went with him there were more than three thousand men, most of whom were chiefs and persons of high rank; he also gave many banquets and entertainments, of which those who went with him had much to relate.

After he had demonstrated very fully to me how great was his desire to serve Your Highness, I begged him to show me the mines from which they obtained the gold, so that I could give Your Majesty a more complete account of the things of this land, and he replied that he would be very pleased to do so. Then he called certain of his servants and sent them in pairs to four provinces where he said it was obtained; and he asked me to send Spaniards with them to see it being mined, so I gave him two Spaniards to accompany each two of his men.

Some went to a province which is called Cuçula,⁴⁴ and is eighty leagues from the great city of Temixtitan. The natives of that province are Mutezuma's vassals, and there the Spaniards were shown three rivers, and from these and others they brought me samples of gold, of good quality, although extracted with little skill, for they had no tools save that which the Indians traditionally use. On their journey these Spaniards passed through three provinces with very beautiful lands and many towns and cities and other communities in great numbers, and with so many and such good buildings that they said in Spain there could be none better. In particular they said that they had seen fortified lodgings larger and stronger and better built than the Burgos Castle. The people of one of these provinces, which is called Tamazulapa,⁴⁵ wore more clothes than any others we have seen, and as it seemed to them, well designed.

Some of the others went to a province called Malinaltebeque,⁴⁶ which is likewise seventy leagues or so from the capital, and more toward the coast. And likewise they brought me samples of gold from a great river which passes through there. Others went to another land which is upstream of this river and is of a people who speak a different language from that of Culua; the land is called Tenis,⁴⁷ and the lord of the land is called Coatelicamat. Because he has his lands among some very high and steep mountains and also because the people of that province are very warlike and fight with lances some twenty-five or thirty spans long, he is not subject to Mutezuma.

Thus, because these people were not Mutezuma's vassals, the messengers who went with the Spaniards dared not enter the land without first making their presence known to the lord thereof and asking his permission, saying that they came with Spaniards to see the gold mines he had in his land, and they begged him on my behalf and on behalf of Mutezuma their lord to let them pass. Coatelicamat replied that he was very pleased for the Spaniards to enter his land and see the mines and all else they wished to see, but that the people of Culua, who are Mutezuma's subjects, might not enter because they were his enemies. The Spaniards were somewhat undecided whether to enter alone or not, because their companions had warned them not to go, saying that they would be killed, with which intention the Culuans had been denied entry. At last they resolved to go alone and were very well received by the lord and all those of his land; and they were shown seven or eight rivers from which they were told that the gold was taken, and in their presence the Indians extracted some; and they brought me back samples from all the rivers. With these Spaniards the aforementioned Coatelicamat sent several of his messengers to offer me his person and his land in the service of Your Sacred Majesty; and he also sent me certain gifts of gold and of native clothing. The others went to another province called Tuchitebeque,[48] which lies in the same direction toward the coast, twelve leagues from the province of Malinaltebeque, where, as I have said, there is gold, and there they were shown other rivers from which they also brought samples of gold.

According to the Spaniards who went there, that province of Malinaltebeque was very well provided for setting up farms. I therefore asked Mutezuma to have a farm built there for Your Majesty; and he was so diligent in all this that in two months about ninety-five bushels of maize were sown, and fifteen of beans and two thousand cacao plants. Cacao is a fruit like the almond, which they grind and hold to be of such value that they use it as money throughout the land and with it buy all they need in the markets and other places. They built four very good houses, in one of which, apart from the rooms, they made a water tank, and in it put five hundred ducks, which here they value highly, and pluck them every year, because they use their feathers to make clothes. And they put there as many as fifteen hundred chickens and other things for dairy farming, which the Spaniards who saw them many times valued at twenty thousand *pesos de oro*.

Likewise I asked Mutezuma to tell me if there was on the coast any river or cove where the ships that came might enter and be safe. He replied that he did not know, but would have them make a map of all the coast for me with all its rivers and coves; and that I should send some Spaniards to see it, and he would give me guides to accompany them; and so it was done. On the following day they brought me a cloth with all the coast painted on it, and there appeared a river which ran to the sea, and according to the representation was wider than all the others. This river seemed to pass through the mountains which we called Sanmin,[49] and are so high they form a bay which the pilots believed divided a province called Mazamalco. He told me to decide whom to send, and he would provide the means and the guide to show it to them. Then I chose ten men, and among them some pilots and other persons who knew about the sea. With the provisions which he had given them, they departed and traveled up all the coast from the port of Calchilmeca,[50] which is called San Juan, where I landed; and they went more than seventy leagues along the coast and nowhere did they find a river or bay where any ships might enter, although on that coast there were many and very large ones and they sounded them all from canoes. Finally they reached the province of Quacalcalco,[51] where the aforementioned river is to be found.

The ruler of that province, who is called Tuchintecla, received them very well and gave them canoes to explore the river, and in the shallowest part of its mouth they found two and a half fathoms and more. They then went upriver for twelve leagues, and the shallowest they found there was five or six fathoms; and from what they saw of it they concluded that it continued for more than thirty leagues at that depth. On the banks of this river are many great towns, and all the province is very flat and fertile, and abounds in all manner of crops, and the population is almost without number.

The people of this province are not vassals or subjects of Mutezuma; rather his enemies. Thus when the Spaniards arrived the lord of the land sent to say that the Culuans might not enter his domain because they were his enemies. When the Spaniards returned to me with this report, he sent with them several messengers who brought gold jewelry, and tigerskins and featherwork and precious stones and clothing; they told me, on his behalf, that Tuchintecla,[52] their lord, had known of me for some time, because the people of Puchunchan [sic]—which is the river of Grijalba—who are his allies, had told him how I had passed by there and had fought with them because they would not allow me to enter their town; and how afterwards they became our friends and Your Majesty's vassals. He likewise offered himself to Your Royal service, together with all his lands, and begged me to take him as a friend, on condition that the Culuans should not enter his land, although I might see all that he had which might be of service to Your Highness, and that each year he would give all that I indicated.

When the Spaniards who had been to that province told me that it was suitable for settling and that they had found a port there, I was greatly pleased, for ever since I arrived in this land I have been searching for a port, so that I might settle here, but I had never found one, nor is there one on all the coast from the river of San[t] Antón, which is next to the Grijalba, to the Pánuco, which is down coast, where certain Spaniards went to settle by order of Francisco de Garay, of which I will inform Your Highness later.

In order to acquaint myself better with the state of that province and port and with the intentions of the inhabitants and other things pertinent to settling, I sent back certain members of my company, who had some experience in these matters, to discover all this. They went with the messengers which that lord Tuchintecla had sent me and with several things which I gave them for him. When they arrived they were very well received by him and they again sounded the port and the river and looked to see what sites there were on which to build a town. They brought me a very long and accurate report of all this and said that there was everything we required for settling, and the lord of the province was very pleased and very willing to serve Your Highness. When they arrived with this report I sent a captain with 150 men to lay out the town and to build a fort, for the lord of that province had offered to do it and anything else I might need or demand of him; and he even built six dwellings there himself, saying that he was very pleased that we had gone there to settle in his land.

Most Powerful Lord, in the preceding chapters, I told how at the time I was going to the great city of Temixtitan, a great chief had come out to meet me on behalf of Mutezuma, and, as I learnt afterwards, he was a very close kinsman of Mutezuma and ruled a province called Aculuacan, next to the territory of Mutezuma. The capital of it is a very great city which stands beside the salt lake; and by canoe it is six leagues from there to the city of Temixtitan, and by land ten. This city is called Tesuico, and there are as many as thirty thousand inhabitants in it.[53] It has very remarkable houses and temples and shrines, all very large and well built; and there are very large markets.

In addition to this city he has two others, one of which is three leagues from Tesuico and is called Acuruman, and another six leagues away which is called Otumpa.[54] Each of these has three or four thousand inhabitants. The aforementioned province and dominion of Aculuacan has many other villages and hamlets and very good lands and farms. This province borders on one side with

the province of Tascalteca, of which I have already spoken to Your
Majesty. After Mutezuma had been imprisoned, the lord of this
province, who is called Cacamazin,[55] rebelled both against the service of Your Highness, to which he had pledged himself, and against
Mutezuma. Although he was many times required to obey Your
Majesty's Royal commands, he would not, even though, as well as
the demands I sent, Mutezuma sent orders also. On the contrary, he
replied that if we required anything from him we should go and get
it, and that there we should see what sort of man he was and what
service he was obliged to render! According to the information I
received, he had collected together a large force of warriors who
were all very well prepared for war.

As neither warnings nor commands could persuade him, I
spoke to Mutezuma and asked him what he thought we should do
so that his rebellion should not go unpunished. To which Mutezuma replied that to try and take him by force would be very dangerous, for he was a very great lord and had many troops and that
he could not be defeated without the risk of a large number being
killed. But he, Mutezuma, had in Cacamazin's land many important
persons who received salaries from him, and he would speak to
them so as to win some of Cacamazin's people over to our side; and
once this had been done we might take him in safety. So it was that
Mutezuma made his arrangements in such a way that those persons
induced Cacamazin to meet them in the city of Tesuico to settle
matters concerning their status as persons of rank, and because it
grieved them to see that he was acting in a way which might lead to
his downfall.

They met in a beautiful house belonging to Cacamazin himself, which was by the lakeside and so built that canoes might pass
underneath it. There they had canoes secretly prepared and many
men ready lest Cacamazin attempt to resist capture. Once he was in
their presence, all those lords took him before his own people realized it, and put him into those canoes, and went out onto the lake,
from whence they went to the great city which is six leagues from

there, as I have said. When they arrived they placed him in a litter, as his position demanded, and as they were accustomed to do, and brought him to me; and I had irons put on him and ordered him to be closely guarded. And on Mutezuma's advice I, in Your Highness's name, appointed a son of his, called Cocuzcacin,[56] as ruler of that province. And I made all the communities and chiefs of that province and dominion obey him as their lord until such time as Your Highness might make other arrangements. Thus it was done, and from then on they all took him as their lord and obeyed him as they had Cacamazin; and he was obedient in all that I, on Your Majesty's behalf, commanded him.

A few days after the imprisonment of this Cacamazin, Mutezuma summoned to an assembly all the chiefs of the cities and lands thereabouts. When they were gathered he sent for me to join him, and as soon as I arrived addressed them in the following manner:

"My brothers and friends, you know that for a long time you and your forefathers have been subjects and vassals of my ancestors and of me, and that you have been always well treated and honored by us, and likewise you have done all that loyal and true vassals are obliged to do for their rightful lords. I also believe that you have heard from your ancestors how we are not natives of this land, but came from another far away, and how they were brought by a lord who left them there, whose vassals they all were. After many years this lord returned but found that our ancestors had already settled in this land and married the native women and had had many children; consequently, they did not wish to return with him and refused to welcome him as their sovereign. He departed, saying that he would return or would send such forces as would compel them to serve him. You well know that we have always expected him, and according to the things this captain has said of the Lord and King who sent him here, and according to the direction whence he says he comes, I am certain, and so must you be also, that this is the same lord for whom we have been waiting, especially as he says that there they know of us. And because our predecessors did not receive their lord as they were bound, let us now receive him and give thanks also to our gods that what we have so long awaited has come to pass in our time. And I beg you—since all this is well known to you—that just as until now you have obeyed me and held me as your rightful lord, from now on you should obey this great King, for he is your rightful lord, and as his representative acknowledge this his captain. And all the tributes and services which, until now, you have rendered to me, render now to him, for I also must contribute and serve in all that he may command; and in addition to doing your duty and all that you are obliged to do, you will give me great satisfaction thereby."

All this he said weeping with all the tears and sighs that a man is able; and likewise all the other lords who were listening wept so much that for a long time they were unable to reply. And I can assure Your Holy Majesty that among the Spaniards who heard this discourse there was not one who did not have great pity for him.

After they had restrained their tears somewhat, those chiefs replied that they held him as their lord and had sworn to do all he commanded, and that for this reason and on account of what he had said they were very pleased to obey, and from then on they submitted themselves as Your Highness's vassals. Then all together and each one by himself they promised to obey and comply with all that was demanded of them in the name of Your Majesty, as true and loyal vassals must do, and to provide all the tributes and services which formerly they paid to Mutezuma and whatever else might be required of them in Your Highness's name. All of this was said before a notary public, who set it down in a formal document, which I asked for, attested by the presence of many Spaniards who served as witnesses.

When the submission of these chiefs to Your Majesty's service was complete, I spoke one day with Mutezuma and told him that Your Highness had need of gold for certain works You had ordered to be done. I asked him therefore to send some of his people together with some Spaniards to the countries and dwellings of those chiefs who had submitted themselves, to ask them to render to Your Majesty some part of what they owned, for, as well as the need which Your Highness had, they were now beginning to serve Your Highness, who would have thereby higher regard for their good intentions. I also asked him to give me something of what he possessed, for I wished to send it to Your Majesty, as I had sent the gold and other things with the messengers. Later he asked for the Spaniards he wished to send, and by twos and fives dispatched them to many provinces and cities, whose names I do not remember, because I have lost my writings, and they were so many and so varied, and, moreover, because some of them were eighty and a hundred leagues from the great city of Temixtitan. With them he sent some of his own people, and ordered them to go to the chiefs of those provinces and cities and tell them I demanded that each of them should give me a certain quantity of gold. And so it was done, and all the chiefs to whom he sent gave very fully of all that was asked of them, both in jewelry and in ingots and gold and silver sheets, and other things which they had.

When all was melted down that could be, Your Majesty's fifth came to more than 32,400 *pesos de oro*, exclusive of the gold and silver jewelry, and the featherwork and precious stones and many other valuable things which I designated for Your Holy Majesty and set aside; all of which might be worth a hundred thousand ducats or more.[57] All these, in addition to their intrinsic worth, are so marvelous that considering their novelty and strangeness they are priceless; nor can it be believed that any of the princes of this world, of whom we know, possess any things of such high quality.

And lest Your Highness should think all this is an invention, let me say that all the things of which Mutezuma has ever heard, both on land and in the sea, they have modeled, very realistically, either in gold and silver or in jewels or feathers, and with such perfection that they seem almost real. He gave many of these for Your Highness, without counting other things which I drew for him and which he had made in gold, such as holy images, crucifixes, medallions, ornaments, necklaces and many other of our things. Of the silver Your Highness received a hundred or so marks, which I had the natives make into plates, both large and small, and bowls and cups and spoons which they fashioned as skillfully as we could make them understand. In addition to this, Mutezuma gave me many garments of his own, which even considering that they were all of cotton and not silk were such that in all the world there could be none like them, nor any of such varied and natural colors or such workmanship. Amongst them were very marvelous clothes for men and women, and there were bedspreads which could not have been compared even with silk ones. There were also other materials, like tapestries which would serve for hallways and churches, and counterpanes for beds, of feathers and cotton, in various colors and also very wonderful, and many other things which as there are so many and so varied I do not know how to describe them to Your Majesty.

He also gave me a dozen blowpipes,[58] such as he uses, whose perfection I am likewise unable to describe to Your Highness, for they were all painted in the finest paints and perfect colors, in which were depicted all manner of small birds and animals and trees and flowers and several other things. Round their mouthpieces and muzzles was a band of gold a span in depth, and round the middle another, finely decorated. He also gave me pouches of gold mesh for the pellets and told me that he would give me pellets of gold as well. He also gave me some gold bullet-molds[59] and many other things which are too numerous to describe.

Most Powerful Lord, in order to give an account to Your Royal Excellency of the magnificence, the strange and marvelous things of this great city of Temixtitan and of the dominion and wealth of this Mutezuma, its ruler, and of the rites and customs of the people, and of the order there is in the government of the capital as well as in the other cities of Mutezuma's dominions, I would need much time and many expert narrators. I cannot describe one hundredth part of all the things which could be mentioned, but, as best I can, I will describe some of those I have seen which, although badly described, will, I well know, be so remarkable as not to be believed, for we who saw them with our own eyes could not grasp them with our understanding. But Your Majesty may be certain that if my account has any fault it will be, in this as in all else of which I give account to Your Highness, too short rather than too long, because it seems to me right that to my Prince and Lord I should state the truth very clearly without adding anything which might be held to embroider it or diminish it.

Before I begin to describe this great city and the others which I mentioned earlier, it seems to me, so that they may be better understood, that I should say something of Mesyco, which is Mutezuma's principal domain and the place where this city and the others which I have mentioned are to be found.[60] This province is circular and encompassed by very high and very steep mountains, and the plain is some seventy leagues in circumference: in this plain there are two lakes which cover almost all of it, for a canoe may travel fifty leagues around the edges. One of these lakes is of fresh water and the other, which is the larger, is of salt water.[61] A small chain of very high hills which cuts across the middle of the plain separates these two lakes. At the end of this chain a narrow channel which is no wider than a bowshot between these hills and the mountains joins the lakes. They travel between one lake and the other and between the different settlements which are on the lakes in their canoes without needing to go by land. As the salt lake rises and falls with its tides as does the sea, whenever it rises, the salt water flows into the fresh as swiftly as a powerful river, and on the ebb the fresh water passes to the salt.

This great city of Temixtitan is built on the salt lake, and no matter by what road you travel there are two leagues from the main body of the city to the mainland. There are four artificial causeways leading to it, and each is as wide as two cavalry lances. The city itself is as big as Seville or Córdoba. The main streets are very wide and very straight; some of these are on the land, but the rest and all the smaller ones are half on land, half canals where they paddle their canoes. All the streets have openings in places so that the water may pass from one canal to another. Over all these openings, and some of them are very wide, there are bridges made of long and wide beams joined together very firmly and so well made that on some of them ten horsemen may ride abreast.

Seeing that if the inhabitants of this city wished to betray us they were very well equipped for it by the design of the city, for once the bridges had been removed they could starve us to death without our being able to reach the mainland, as soon as I entered the city I made great haste to build four brigantines, and completed them in a very short time. They were such as could carry three hundred men to the land and transport the horses whenever we might need them.

This city has many squares where trading is done and markets are held continuously. There is also one square twice as big as that of Salamanca,[62] with arcades all around, where more than sixty thousand people come each day to buy and sell, and where every kind of merchandise produced in these lands is found; provisions as well as ornaments of gold and silver, lead, brass, copper, tin, stones, shells, bones, and feathers. They also sell lime, hewn and unhewn stone, adobe bricks, tiles, and cut and uncut woods of various kinds. There is a street where they sell game and birds of every species found in this land: chickens, partridges and quails, wild ducks, flycatchers, widgeons, turtledoves, pigeons, cane birds, parrots, eagles and eagle owls, falcons, sparrow hawks and kestrels, and they sell the skins of some of these birds of prey with their feathers, heads and claws. They sell rabbits and hares, and stags and small gelded dogs which they breed for eating.[63]

There are streets of herbalists where all the medicinal herbs and roots found in the land are sold. There are shops like apothecaries', where they sell ready-made medicines as well as liquid ointments and plasters. There are shops like barbers' where they have their hair washed and shaved, and shops where they sell food and drink. There are also men like porters to carry loads.[64] There is much firewood and charcoal, earthenware braziers and mats of various kinds like mattresses for beds, and other, finer ones, for seats and for covering rooms and hallways. There is every sort of vegetable, especially onions, leeks, garlic, common cress and watercress, borage, sorrel, teasels and artichokes; and there are many sorts of fruit, among which are cherries and plums like those in Spain.

They sell honey, wax, and a syrup made from maize canes, which is as sweet and syrupy as that made from the sugar cane. They also make syrup from a plant which in the islands is called *maguey*,[65] which is much better than most syrups, and from this plant they also make sugar and wine, which they likewise sell. There are many sorts of spun cotton, in hanks of every color, and it seems like the silk market at Granada, except here there is a much greater quantity. They sell as many colors for painters as may be found in Spain and all of excellent hues. They sell deerskins, with and without the hair, and some are dyed white or in various colors. They sell much earthenware, which for the most part is very good; there are both large and small pitchers, jugs, pots, tiles, and many other sorts of vessel, all of good clay and most of them glazed and painted. They sell maize both as grain and as bread and it is better both in appearance and in taste than any found in the islands or on the mainland. They sell chicken and fish pies, and much fresh and salted fish, as well as raw and cooked fish. They sell hen and goose eggs, and eggs of all the other birds I have mentioned, in great number, and they sell *tortillas* made from eggs.

Finally, besides those things which I have already mentioned, they sell in the market everything else to be found in this land, but they are so many and so varied that because of their great number and because I cannot remember many of them nor do I know what they are called I shall not mention them. Each kind of merchandise is sold in its own street without any mixture whatever; they are very particular in this. Everything is sold by number and size, and until now I have seen nothing sold by weight. There is in this great square a very large building like a courthouse, where ten or twelve persons sit as judges. They preside over all that happens in the markets, and sentence criminals. There are in this square other persons who walk among the people to see what they are selling and the measures they are using; and they have been seen to break some that were false.

There are, in all districts of this great city, many temples or houses for their idols. They are all very beautiful buildings, and in the important ones there are priests of their sect who live there permanently; and, in addition to the houses for the idols, they also have very good lodgings. All these priests dress in black and never comb their hair from the time they enter the priesthood until they leave; and all the sons of the persons of high rank, both the lords and honored citizens also, enter the priesthood and wear the habit from the age of seven or eight years until they are taken away to be married; this occurs more among the first-born sons, who are to inherit, than among the others. They abstain from eating things, and more at some times of the year than at others; and no woman is granted entry nor permitted inside these places of worship.

Amongst these temples there is one, the principal one, whose great size and magnificence no human tongue could describe, for it is so large that within the precincts, which are surrounded by a very high wall, a town of some five hundred inhabitants could easily be built. All round inside this wall there are very elegant quarters with very large rooms and corridors where their priests live. There are as many as forty towers, all of which are so high that in the case of the largest there are fifty steps leading up to the main part of it; and the most important of these towers is higher than that of the cathedral of Seville. They are so well constructed in both their stone and woodwork that there can be none better in any place, for all the stonework inside the chapels where they keep their idols is in high relief, with figures and little houses, and the woodwork is likewise of relief and painted with monsters and other figures and designs. All these towers are burial places of chiefs, and the chapels therein are each dedicated to the idol which he venerated.

There are three rooms within this great temple for the principal idols, which are of remarkable size and stature and decorated with many designs and sculptures, both in stone and in wood. Within these rooms are other chapels, and the doors to them are very small. Inside there is no light whatsoever; there only some of the priests may enter, for inside are the sculptured figures of the idols, although, as I have said, there are also many outside.

The most important of these idols, and the ones in whom they have most faith, I had taken from their places and thrown down the steps; and I had those chapels where they were cleaned, for they were full of the blood of sacrifices; and I had images of Our Lady and of other saints put there, which caused Mutezuma and the other natives some sorrow. First they asked me not to do it, for when the communities learnt of it they would rise against me, for they believed that those idols gave them all their worldly goods, and that if they were allowed to be ill treated, they would become angry and give them nothing and take the fruit from the earth leaving the people to die of hunger. I made them understand through the interpreters how deceived they were in placing their trust in those idols which they had made with their hands from unclean things. They must know that there was only one God, Lord of all things, who had created heaven and earth and all else and who made all of us; and He was without beginning or end, and they must adore and worship only Him, not any other creature or thing. And I told them all I knew about this to dissuade them from their idolatry and bring them to the knowledge of God our Saviour. All of them, especially Mutezuma, replied that they had already told me how they were not natives of this land, and that as it was many years since their forefathers had come here, they well knew that they might have erred somewhat in what they believed, for they had left their native land so long ago; and as I had only recently arrived from there, I would better know the things they should believe, and should explain to them and make them understand, for they would do as I said was best. Mutezuma and many of the chieftains of the city were with me until the idols were removed, the chapel cleaned and the images set up, and I urged them not to sacrifice living creatures to the idols, as they were accustomed, for, as well as being most abhorrent to God, Your Sacred Majesty's laws forbade it and ordered that he who kills shall be killed. And from then on they ceased to do it, and in all the time I stayed in that city I did not see a living creature killed or sacrificed.

The figures of the idols in which these people believe are very much larger than the body of a big man. They are made of dough from all the seeds and vegetables which they eat, ground and mixed together, and bound with the blood of human hearts which those priests tear out while still beating. And also after they are made they offer them more hearts and anoint their faces with the blood. Everything has an idol dedicated to it, in the same manner as the pagans who in antiquity honored their gods. So they have an idol whose favor they ask in war and another for agriculture; and likewise for each thing they wish to be done well they have an idol which they honor and serve.[66]

There are in the city many large and beautiful houses, and the reason for this is that all the chiefs of the land, who are Mutezuma's vassals, have houses in the city and live there for part of the year;[67] and in addition there are many rich citizens who likewise have very good houses. All these houses have very large and very good rooms and also very pleasant gardens of various sorts of flowers both on the upper and lower floors.

Along one of the causeways to this great city run two aqueducts made of mortar. Each one is two paces wide and some six feet deep, and along one of them a stream of very good fresh water, as wide as a man's body, flows into the heart of the city and from this they all drink. The other, which is empty, is used when they wish to clean the first channel. Where the aqueducts cross the bridges, the water passes along some channels which are as wide as an ox; and so they serve the whole city.

Canoes paddle through all the streets selling the water; they take it from the aqueduct by placing the canoes beneath the bridges where those channels are, and on top there are men who fill the canoes and are paid for their work. At all the gateways to the city and at the places where these canoes are unloaded, which is where the greater part of the provisions enter the city, there are guards in huts who receive a *certum quid* of all that enters. I have not yet discovered whether this goes to the chief or to the city, but I think to the chief, because in other markets in other parts I have seen this tax paid to the ruler of the place. Every day, in all the markets and public places there are many workmen and craftsmen of every sort, waiting to be employed by the day. The people of this city are dressed with more elegance and are more courtly in their bearing than those of the other cities and provinces, and be-cause Mutezuma and all those chieftains, his vassals, are always com-ing to the city, the people have more manners and politeness in all matters. Yet so as not to tire Your Highness with the description of the things of this city (although I would not complete it so briefly), I will say only that these people live almost like those in Spain, and in as much harmony and order as there, and considering that they are barbarous and so far from the knowledge of God and cut off from all civilized nations, it is truly remarkable to see what they have achieved in all things.

Touching Mutezuma's service and all that was remarkable in his magnificence and power, there is so much to describe that I do not know how to begin even to recount some part of it; for, as I have already said, can there be anything more magnificent than that this barbarian lord should have all the things to be found under the heavens in his domain, fashioned in gold and silver and jewels and feathers; and so realistic in gold and silver that no smith in the world could have done better, and in jewels so fine that it is impos-sible to imagine with what instruments they were cut so perfectly;

and those in feathers more wonderful than anything in wax or embroidery.

I have not yet been able to discover the extent of the domain of Mutezuma, but in the two hundred leagues which his messengers traveled to the north and to the south of this city his orders were obeyed, although there were some provinces in the middle of these lands which were at war with him. But from what I have discovered, and what he has told me, I imagine that his kingdom is almost as big as Spain, for he sent messengers from the region of Putunchan, which is the Grijalba River, seventy leagues to a city which is called Cumantan commanding the inhabitants thereof to offer themselves as vassals to Your Majesty, and that city is 230 leagues from the capital; the remaining 150 leagues have been explored by Spaniards on my orders. The greater part of the chiefs of these lands and provinces, especially those from close by, resided, as I have said, for most of the year in this capital city, and all or most of their eldest sons were in the service of Mutezuma. In all these domains he had fortresses garrisoned with his own people, and governors and officials to collect the tributes which each province must pay; and they kept an account of whatever each one was obliged to give in characters and drawings on the paper which they make, which is their writing.[68] Each of these provinces paid appropriate tributes in accordance with the nature of the land; thus Mutezuma received every sort of produce from those provinces, and he was so feared by all, both present and absent, that there could be no ruler in the world more so.

He had, both inside the city and outside, many private residences, each one for a particular pastime, and as well made as I can describe—as is befitting so great a ruler. The palace inside the city in which he lived was so marvelous that it seems to me impossible to describe its excellence and grandeur. Therefore, I shall not attempt to describe it at all, save to say that in Spain there is nothing to compare with it.

He also had another house, only a little less magnificent than this, where there was a very beautiful garden with balconies over it; and the facings and flagstones were all of jasper and very well made. In this house there were rooms enough for two great princes with all their household. There were also ten pools in which were kept all the many and varied kinds of water bird found in these parts, all of them domesticated. For the sea birds there were pools of salt water, and for river fowl of fresh water, which was emptied from time to time for cleaning and filled again from the aqueducts. Each species of bird was fed with the food which it eats when wild, so that those which eat fish were given fish, and those which eat worms, worms, and those which eat maize or smaller grain were likewise given those things. And I assure Your Highness that the birds which eat only fish were given 250 pounds each day, which were taken from the salt lake. There were three hundred men in charge of these birds who knew no other trade, as there were others who were skilled only in healing sick birds. Above these pools were corridors and balconies, all very finely made, where Mutezuma came to amuse himself by watching them. There was also in this house a room in which were kept men, women and children who had, from birth, white faces and bodies and white hair, eyebrows and eyelashes.

He had another very beautiful house, with a large patio, laid with pretty tiles in the manner of a chessboard. There were rooms nine feet high and as large as six paces square. The roofs of each of these houses are half covered with tiles while the other half is covered by well-made latticework. In each of these rooms there was kept a bird of prey of every sort that is found in Spain, from the kestrel to the eagle, and many others which have never been seen there. There were large numbers of each of these birds, and in the covered part of each of the rooms was a stick like a perch, and another outside beneath the latticework, and they were on one during the night or when it rained and on the other during the day when the sun was out. All these birds were given chickens to eat each day and no other food. In this house there were several large

low rooms filled with big cages, made from heavy timbers and very
well joined. In all, or in most of them, were large numbers of lions,
tigers, wolves, foxes and cats of various kinds which were given as
many chickens to eat as they needed. Another three hundred men
looked after these birds and animals. There was yet another house
where lived many deformed men and women, among which were
dwarfs and hunchbacks and others with other deformities; and each
manner of monstrosity had a room to itself; and likewise there were
people to look after them. I shall not mention the other entertainments which he has in this city, for they are very many and of many
different kinds.

He was served in this manner: Each day at dawn there arrived at his house six hundred chiefs and principal persons, some of
whom sat down while others wandered about the rooms and corridors of the house; there they passed the time talking but without
ever entering his presence. The servants of these persons and those
who accompanied them filled two or three large courtyards and the
street, which was very big. And they remained all day until nightfall. When they brought food to Mutezuma they also provided for
all those chiefs to each according to his rank; and their servants and
followers were also given to eat. The pantry and the wine stores
were left open each day for those who wished to eat and drink.
Three or four hundred boys came bringing the dishes, which were
without number, for each time he lunched or dined, he was brought
every kind of food: meat, fish, fruit and vegetables. And because
the climate is cold, beneath each plate and bowl they brought a
brazier with hot coals so that the food should not go cold. They
placed all these dishes together in a great room where he ate, which
was almost always full. The floors were well covered and clean and
he sat on a finely made, small leather cushion. While he ate, there
were five or six old men, who sat apart from him; and to them he
gave a portion of all he was eating. One of the servants set down and
removed the plates of food and called to others who were farther
away for all that was required. Before and after the meal they gave

him water for his hands and a towel which once used was never used again, and likewise with the plates and bowls, for when they brought more food they always used new ones, and the same with the braziers.

He dressed each day in four different garments and never dressed again in the same ones. All the chiefs who entered his house went barefoot, and those he called before him came with their heads bowed and their bodies in a humble posture, and when they spoke to him they did not look him in the face; this was because they held him in great respect and reverence. I know that they did it for this reason because certain of those chiefs reproved the Spaniards, saying that when they spoke to me they did so openly without hiding their faces, which seemed to them disrespectful and lacking in modesty. When Mutezuma left the palace, which was not often, all those who went with him and those whom he met in the streets turned away their faces so that in no manner should they look on him; and all the others prostrated themselves until he had passed. One of those chiefs always walked before him carrying three long thin rods, which I think was done so that all should know he was coming. When he descended from the litter he took one of these in his hand and carried it to wherever he was going. The forms and ceremonies with which this lord was attended are so many and so varied that I would need more space than that which I have at present to recount them, and a better memory with which to recall them, for I do not think that the sultans nor any of the infidel lords of whom we have heard until now are attended with such ceremony.

While in this great city I was seeing to the things which I thought were required in the service of Your Sacred Majesty and subduing and persuading to Your service many provinces and lands containing very many and very great cities, towns and fortresses. I was discovering mines and finding out many of the secrets of Mutezuma's lands and of those which bordered on them and those of which he had knowledge; and they are so many and so wonderful that they seem almost unbelievable. All of which was done with such good will and delight on the part of Mutezuma and all the natives of the aforementioned lands that it seemed as if *ab initio* they had known Your Sacred Majesty to be their king and rightful lord; and with no less good will they have done all that I, in Your Royal name, have commanded them.

In these matters and in others no less useful to the Royal service of Your Highness I spent from the eighth of November, 1519, until the beginning of May of this year. While all was quiet in this city, having sent many of the Spaniards to many and diverse places and having pacified and settled this land, I was anxiously waiting for ships to arrive with a reply to the report I had sent to Your Majesty concerning this land and by them to send this one, and all the gold and jewels which I had collected for Your Highness, when there came to me certain natives of this land, vassals of Mutezuma, who live by the sea. They told me how close by the mountains of Sanmyn, which are on the coast, before reaching the harbor or bay of Sant Juan, eighteen ships had arrived, but they did not know to whom these ships belonged, because as soon as they had seen them they had come to inform me.[69] Following these came an Indian from the island of Fernandina, who brought me a letter from a Spaniard whom I had posted on the coast, so that if he saw ships he should tell them about me and the town which was close by that harbor, so they should not get lost. This letter contained the following: That on such and such a day a single ship had anchored in front of the harbor of Sant Juan, and he had looked all along the coast as far as he was able but had seen no other; and therefore he believed that it was the ship which I had sent to Your Sacred Majesty, because it was time for it to return. To make certain, however, he was waiting for this ship to enter the port so that he might learn what it was. Then he would immediately inform me.

When I saw this letter I sent two Spaniards, one by one road and one by another so that they should not miss any messenger coming from the ship. I told them to go to the port and discover how many ships had arrived, whence they came, and what they were carrying, and to return to me as swiftly as possible to inform me. Likewise I sent another to the town of Vera Cruz to tell them all that I had discovered about those ships so that they might make enquiries there and send me their information. I sent yet another to the captain whom, together with 150 men, I had ordered to build a town in the province and port of Quacucalco,[70] and I wrote to him that, no matter where the messenger might reach him, he should not move from there until I wrote again, for I had received news that certain ships had arrived at the port, which, so it appeared later, he already knew by the time my letter arrived.

After I had sent these messengers, fifteen days passed without my knowing anything or receiving a reply from any of them, and this perturbed me not a little. After fifteen days, however, there came other Indians, also Mutezuma's vassals, and from these I learnt that the ships were anchored in the port of Sant Juan, and that the people had landed. They had counted eighty horses, and eight hundred men and ten or twelve guns, all of which they had represented on a piece of their paper,[71] to show it to Mutezuma. The Indians told me how the Spaniard I had posted on the coast and all the other messengers whom I had sent were with those people, and had explained to the Indians that the captain would not let them leave and asked them to inform me of the fact. When I heard all this I resolved to send a friar[72] whom I had brought in my company with a letter from me and another from the alcaldes and regidores of the town of Vera Cruz who were with me in the city. These I addressed to the captain and his people who had landed at that port, informing them very fully of all that had happened in this land and how I had taken many cities, towns and fortresses and had subjected them to Your Majesty's Royal service, and how I had captured the lord of these parts. I spoke of the nature of the capital city and of the gold and jewels which I had for Your Highness; and also of how I had sent a report concerning this land to Your Majesty. I

begged them to inform me as to who they were, and if they were
true vassals of the realms and dominions of Your Highness, and to
write to me whether they came by Your Royal command to settle
and remain in the land, or were going on, or had to return. If they
lacked for anything, I would equip them with all that was in my
power. If they came from outside Your Highness's domains they
should also let me know whether they had need of anything, for I
would likewise help them as best I could; but if they refused to
inform me, I required them on behalf of Your Majesty to depart
from Your lands at once and not to disembark. Furthermore, I
warned them that if they did not do so I would march against them
with all I had, Spaniards as well as natives of the land, and I would
capture or kill them as foreigners invading the realms and dominions
of my lord and king.

Five days after the aforementioned friar had left with this
dispatch, there arrived in the city of Temixtitan twenty Spaniards
from Vera Cruz, and they brought with them a friar and two lay-
men whom they had taken in the aforementioned town.[73] From
them I learnt that the fleet in the port was from Diego Velázquez
and had come by his command, under the captaincy of one Pánfilo
de Narváez, an inhabitant of the island of Fernandina. He brought
eighty horsemen and many guns and eight hundred foot soldiers,
among whom they said there were eighty harquebusiers and 120
crossbowmen; and he called himself captain general and lieutenant
governor in all these parts for Diego Velázquez, and for this had
brought decrees from Your Majesty. The messengers I had sent and
the man I had posted on the coast were all with this Pánfilo de
Narváez and he would not allow them to return. From them he had
learnt how I had founded a town, twelve leagues from the port, and
of the people who were in it and likewise he heard of those people
I had sent to Quacucalco and those who were in a province called
Tuchitebeque, which is thirty leagues from the aforementioned
port; and of all the things which I, in the service of Your Highness,
had done in the land: of the towns and cities which I had conquered

and pacified; of that great city of Temixtitan; of the gold and jewels which had been acquired in the land; and of all the other things which had happened to me.

Narváez had sent these men to Vera Cruz to speak to the people there on his behalf and see if they could win them over to his purpose and make them rise against me. With them they brought more than a hundred letters which this Narváez and his companions had sent to Vera Cruz telling the people of the town to believe what the cleric and the others who were with him said on his behalf, and promising them that if they did as he asked, he, in the name of Diego Velázquez, would reward them well; but if they refused, they would be very harshly treated. This and many other things contained in these letters were told to me by those envoys.

Almost at the same time one of the Spaniards from Quacucalco arrived with letters from the captain, one Juan Velázquez de León.[74] He informed me that the people who had come to that port were those of Pánfilo de Narváez. This captain also forwarded me a letter which Narváez had sent to him with an Indian, for he was a relation of Diego Velázquez and Narváez's brother-in-law, in which Narváez said that he had learnt from my messengers how Juan Velázquez was there with those men, and asked that he should bring them to him for it was his duty to a kinsman, and that he, Narváez, believed that I held him by force; and other things which Narváez had written. This captain, Juan Velázquez, as he was more bound to serve Your Majesty, not only refused to do as Narváez bade him, but, after he had sent me this letter, came to join forces with me.

I learnt from that cleric and from the other two who accompanied him many things about the intentions of Diego Velázquez and Pánfilo de Narváez and how they had sent that fleet and their men against me because I had sent the report concerning this land to Your Majesty and not to the aforementioned Diego Velázquez; and how they came with pernicious intent to kill me and many of my company whom they had already singled out in Cuba. I like-

wise learned that the *licenciado* Figueroa, a judge residing on the
island of Hispaniola, and all Your Highness's judges and officials,
when they heard that Diego Velázquez was preparing a fleet, and
his purpose in doing so, had seen the harm and disservice to Your
Majesty that this might cause and had therefore sent the licenciado
Lucas Vázquez de Ayllón,[75] one of the aforementioned judges, with
their authority to command Diego Velázquez not to send the fleet.
When he arrived he found Diego Velázquez on the headland of the
island of Fernandina with all his men armed and prepared to leave.
He commanded Diego Velázquez and all those in the fleet not to
go, for Your Highness would be ill served by their doing so, and he
threatened them with severe penalties, but they, in defiance of all
this licenciado had commanded them, departed with the fleet nonetheless.

     I also learnt that this same Ayllón was in the port, for he had
sailed with the fleet hoping thereby to prevent the harm which
would ensue from its arrival, because the evil intents with which it
came were well known to him and to everyone else. I sent the
aforementioned cleric with a letter of mine for Narváez,[76] in which
I told him how I had learnt from the same cleric and his companions
that Narváez was the captain of the fleet, and I was pleased that it
was so, for, as my messengers had not returned, I had thought
otherwise; but that as he knew I was in this land in Your Highness's
service, I was surprised that he had neither written nor sent any
messenger advising me of his arrival, for he knew how pleased I
would be, both because he had been my friend for a long time and
because I knew that he came to serve Your Highness, which was
what I most desired. Furthermore, it surprised me to hear that he
had sent suborners and letters of inducement to the people, whom I,
in the service of Your Majesty, had in my company, to rise against
me and join him as though one of us were a Christian and the other
an infidel or as if one were Your Highness's vassal and the other his
enemy. I, therefore, begged him to cease behaving in this fashion,
and to let me know the reason for his coming. I also informed him

that I had been told he had taken the title of captain general and lieutenant governor for Diego Velázquez, and had had himself proclaimed throughout the land as such; and that he had appointed alcaldes and regidores and executed justice, all of which was a great disservice to Your Highness and contrary to all Your laws; because as this land pertained to Your Majesty and had been colonized by Your vassals, and as there was both justice and a municipal council, he could not assume the aforementioned titles or exercise them without first being instated, for in order to do so he needed Your Majesty's decree. If he brought such a decree, I asked and required him to present it before me and before the municipal council of Vera Cruz, and they would be observed as letters and decrees from our king and rightful lord insofar as was appropriate to Your Majesty's Royal service.

I was myself in that city where I held the lord captive, and I had a great quantity of gold and jewels, belonging to Your Highness, to the people in my company, and to myself, and for this reason I dared not leave the city for fear that once I had done so the inhabitants would rebel and I would lose all the gold, the jewels, and even the city itself; for once that was lost the whole country would be lost also. Likewise I gave this cleric a letter for Ayllón, who, as I later discovered, by the time the cleric arrived, had been seized by Narváez and sent back with two ships.[77]

On the day this cleric left, a messenger arrived from the people in Vera Cruz, who informed me that all the natives had rebelled and joined Narváez, especially those of the city of Cempoal and their followers, and that none of them would come and serve in the town or the fortress or provide any of the other assistance as they used to; for they said Narváez had told them that I was wicked and he had come to seize me and all my company and take us away. The men that he brought were many, while those who were on my side were few, and he brought many horses and guns and they wished to be on the winning side. This messenger also informed me that they had learnt from the Indians how Narváez had moved his quarters to the city of Cempoal, and, knowing how near it was to Vera Cruz, they believed from all they had heard of Narváez's evil intentions that he would move against them with the help of those Indians. They, therefore, informed me that they were leaving the town so as not to fight them; and to avoid a disturbance they were going into the mountains to the house of a chieftain who was Your Highness's vassal and our friend, and there they would remain until I sent to tell them what they should do.

When I saw the great harm which was being stirred up, and how the country was in revolt because of Narváez, it seemed to me that if I went to where he was the country would, in great part, become calm, for the Indians would not dare to rebel once they had seen me. I also intended to make an agreement with Narváez so that the great harm which was begun should cease. So I departed that same day, leaving the fortress well provided with maize and water, and garrisoned by five hundred men with some guns.[78] And together with the remaining seventy or so men, I set out accompanied by some of Mutezuma's chieftains. Before I left I spoke to Mutezuma at length, telling him to bear in mind that he was Your Highness's vassal and would now receive favors from Your Majesty for the services he had rendered, and that I left in his care those Spaniards, with all the gold and jewels which he had given me and had ordered to be given to Your Highness, for now I was going to meet those people who had newly arrived in the land, to discover who they were, for as yet I did not know, but I believed that they must be hostile, and not Your Highness's vassals. He promised me to provide those I left behind with everything they might need and to guard closely all that I left there belonging to Your Majesty; and those of his people who went with me would lead me by a road which never left his lands, and on it he would have them provide me with everything I required. He begged me to inform him if those people were hostile, for he would straightaway send many warriors to fight them and drive them from the land. For all of which I thanked him and assured him that he would be well re-

CAP.º 69.º

CAP.º 71.

The Engagem.^(nt) between y.^e Spanish Brigantines and the Canoes of the Mexicans.

13. From the English translation by Thomas Townsend of Antonio de Solis's *Historia de la Conquista de México* (1724). Although a hypothetical reconstruction, this drawing gives a very good idea of what Cortés's brigantines must have looked like. *Courtesy of the British Museum.*

12. The arrival of the Spaniards at San Juan de Ulúa. From Vol. II of Fray Diego de Durán's *Historia de las Indias de Nueva España e Islas de Tierra Firme*, Mexico, 1880. *Courtesy of the British Museum.*

warded by Your Highness, and I gave many jewels and articles of clothing to him and to a son of his and to many of the lords who were with him at that time.

In a city called Churultecal I met Juan Velázquez, the captain whom, as I have said, I had sent to Quacucalco, together with all his men; and after having sent some who were sick on to the capital, I continued my journey with him and the rest. Fifteen leagues beyond Churultecal I met the friar whom I had sent to the port to discover whose fleet it was that had arrived there. He brought me a letter from Narváez which informed me that he, Narváez, brought certain decrees to hold this land for Diego Velázquez, and that I should go to where he was to comply with them; and that he had founded a town and appointed alcaldes and regidores. From this same friar I also learnt how Narváez had seized the licenciado Ayllón, his notary and *alguacil*, and had sent them away in two ships; how certain of Narváez's men had attempted to bribe him into persuading some of my company to go over to Narváez; and how the same Narváez had paraded all his men, both horsemen and foot soldiers, before him and certain Indians who were with him, had fired all the ordinance both in the ships and on land in order to frighten them, and then had said, "See how you cannot defend yourselves if you do not do as we ask." He also told me how he had seen Narváez with a native chief, a vassal of Mutezuma and his governor in all the lands from the mountains to the coast. He knew that this chief had spoken to Narváez on Mutezuma's behalf and had given him certain gold ornaments; in return Narváez had given him some few things, and had sent messengers to Mutezuma to tell him he would be freed and that he, Narváez, had come to seize me and all my company and would afterwards leave the land. He said he did not want gold but that once he had captured me and all those with me he would leave the people of this land in complete freedom. Finally this friar said I should know that Narváez's intention was to take possession of this land on his own authority, without being subject to anyone, and if I and my company would not acknowledge him as captain general and chief justice, in the name of Diego Velázquez, he intended to proceed against us and take us by force. To this end he was in league with the natives, especially with Mutezuma by way of his messengers.

As I foresaw so clearly the harm and disservice to Your Majesty which would ensue from the above-mentioned, especially as they told me he had powerful forces with him, and brought a decree from Diego Velázquez that as soon as I and certain of my companions, whom he had singled out, were taken we should be hanged, I still determined to go to him, thinking it wise to make him recognize the great disservice which he was doing to Your Highness and to dissuade him from his evil intent. So I continued on my way, and fifteen leagues before the city of Cempoal, where Narváez was quartered, the cleric whom the people of Vera Cruz had sent, and with whom I had dispatched a letter to Narváez and Ayllón, came to me together with another cleric[79] and one Andrés de Duero, an inhabitant of the island of Fernandina and also one of Narváez's company. They, in reply to my letter, told me, on Narváez's behalf, that I should still go and obey him and acknowledge him as captain general and hand over the country to him, and that if I did not do so I would suffer greatly, for he, Narváez, had many forces and I, few, because in addition to the Spaniards whom he brought, most of the natives were on his side. If I delivered the country to him, he said he would give me all that I needed of the ships and provisions which he had and would allow me, and all those who wished to go with me, to leave with all we wished to take without impeding us in any way. One of those clerics also told me that Diego Velázquez had empowered Narváez and the two clerics jointly to make this offer and any concessions I might wish. I replied that I saw no decree from Your Highness instructing me to deliver the land to them, and that, if indeed they brought one, they should present it before me and the municipal council of Vera Cruz in accordance with the practice in Spain; and that I was very diligent in my obedience and, therefore, until this was done, I would not be persuaded by bribes to do as they asked, for I, and those who were with me, would rather die in defense of the land which we had won and now held in subjection for Your Majesty than be disloyal or traitors to our king.

They made many other suggestions to win me to their purpose, but none of them would I accept before I had seen a decree from Your Highness ordering me to do so, which they were never willing to show me. Finally these clerics, Andrés de Duero and I agreed that Narváez, with ten of his men, and I, with as many of mine, should meet with a surety on both sides, and there he would make known to me the decree, if indeed he brought one, and I would reply to him. I, for my part, signed and dispatched a safe-conduct, and he likewise sent me another signed in his name which, it seemed to me, he had no intention of keeping, for he had planned to find a way to kill me at our meeting without more ado. To that end he instructed two of the ten who were to come with him to fall on me while the others fought with my men. For they said that once I was dead their task was accomplished, which, indeed, it would have been if God, who so often intervenes at such times, had not intervened then with a warning, which one of those who was party to the treachery sent me together with the safe-conduct.

Once I had learnt all this I wrote a letter to Narváez and another to the mediators telling them that I had discovered his evil designs and that I had no wish to meet them in the manner they planned. I then sent them several requests and commands in which I demanded that if Narváez brought any decree from Your Highness, he should make it known to me, and until he did so he should not call himself captain general or chief justice or exercise any of the functions of those offices under pain of certain punishments which I imposed. Likewise I commanded all those who were with Narváez not to obey him as captain general or chief justice, and summoned them to appear before me within a certain time, which I also set down, when I would tell them what they should do in the service of Your Highness. But I warned that if they did not do so, I would proceed against them as against traitors and perfidious vassals who had rebelled against their sovereign and sought to usurp his realms and dominions and deliver them to a man who had no claim to them nor competent authority over them. In the execution whereof, if they did not appear before me or perform what was required of them in my commandment, I would march against them and seize them and hold them prisoner as justice demanded.

Narváez's reply was to seize the notary and his companion, who was carrying the order, and also some Indians in their company, all of whom were detained until I sent another messenger to inquire about them.[80] All Narváez's men were paraded before them, and they and I were threatened if we refused to surrender the land. Once I had seen that there was no way by which I could avoid the great harm that would ensue, and, furthermore, that the natives of the land were becoming more rebellious each day, I entrusted myself to God, and, setting aside all fear of what might ensue, and considering that to die in the service of my king and in defense of his lands against usurpation would win for us all great glory, I ordered Gonzalo de Sandoval, *alguacil mayor*, to seize Narváez and all those who called themselves alcaldes[81] and regidores; and to do this I gave him eighty men. I, with another 170 men (for we were 250 all together) but with no horses or guns, followed the aforementioned alguacil mayor on foot to assist him should Narváez and the others resist arrest.

On the same day the alguacil mayor, and I and all the men arrived at the city of Cempoal, where Narváez and his people were camped. He learnt of our arrival and rode out of his camp with eighty horsemen and five hundred foot soldiers, still leaving a strong force behind in the great temple of the city where he had his quarters. Thus he came to within a league of where I was, but, as all he knew of my arrival he had heard from the Indians, when he failed to find me he thought they were deceiving him and he returned to the city, alerting all his men and placing two spies almost one league outside the city. As I wished to avoid any disturbance, I thought it best to go by night without being observed if possible, and proceed directly to Narváez's quarters, which I and all my company knew very well, and seize him, for I believed that once he was taken there would be no disturbance, because the others would be willing to follow justice, particularly since most of them had been forced to come by Diego Velázquez and for fear that if they refused he might confiscate the Indians they had in the island of Fernandina.[82]

So a little after midnight on the Feast of Pentecost,[83] I entered Narváez's camp. First, however, I met the aforementioned spies Narváez had stationed and my vanguard captured one of them, from whom I learnt how they were disposed. The other escaped and so that he should not arrive before me and warn them of my coming I advanced as rapidly as possible, although not fast enough to prevent the spy from arriving almost half an hour before me.

When I reached Narváez's camp all his men were armed and mounted and well prepared, two hundred men in each section, but we came with such stealth that when they observed us and sounded the alarm I was already inside the courtyard of the camp where all the men were gathered together; and they had occupied the three or four towers there and all the other strong positions. On the steps of the tower where Narváez himself was quartered were some nineteen guns. But we climbed those steps so quickly that they had time to fire only one gun, which, thank God, did not go off or cause any harm whatsoever. We reached the place where Narváez slept, and he and some fifty men fought with the alguacil mayor and the men who were with him, and although they commanded Narváez many times in Your Highness's name to give himself up, he would not until they had set fire to the place, at which he surrendered. While the alguacil mayor was seizing Narváez, I, with the rest of the men, defended the tower against those who came to his assistance, and I seized the artillery and with it strengthened my defense.

With the loss of only two men who were killed by one shot, in one hour all those whom we wished to capture were taken, together with the arms of all of them. They all promised to abide by Your Majesty's justice, for they claimed to have been deceived into believing that Narváez had decrees from Your Majesty and that I had usurped the land and was a traitor to Your Highness, and many other things besides. When they all knew the truth and how Diego Velázquez and Narváez had acted with evil intent and their campaign had been misconceived, they were very glad that God had so provided. For I assure Your Majesty that if God had not mysteriously assisted us and the victory had gone to Narváez, it would have been the greatest harm that Spaniards had done to each other for a long time past. For he would have carried out his intentions and what Diego Velázquez had ordered him to do, namely, to hang me and many of my company so that no one might recount what had happened. Furthermore, I was informed by some Indians that they had agreed that if Narváez had captured me as he intended he could not have done it without many of his own people being killed as well as mine. Meanwhile the Indians would have killed all those I had left in the city, as indeed they attempted to. Afterwards they would have united and fallen on all those who remained here so that they and their land might be free, and all memory of the Spaniards obliterated. Your Highness may be certain that had they accomplished all they intended, this land which has now been conquered and subdued could not be regained in twenty years.

Two days after Narváez's capture, as I could not now maintain so many people together in that city, especially as it was almost in ruins, for those who were with Narváez had looted it and all the inhabitants had fled, leaving their houses empty, I sent two captains with two hundred men each, one to build a town at the port of Quicicalco, which, as I told Your Highness, I had previously ordered to be built, and the other to that river which the ships of Francisco de Garay said they had seen, for I was now sure of its existence there.[84] Likewise I sent another two hundred men to the town of Vera Cruz, where I ordered Narváez's ships to be brought. I myself remained in the city with the rest of the men to provide for all that might be necessary in Your Majesty's service. I also sent a messenger to the city of Temixtitan to inform the Spaniards who remained there of all that had happened to me. This messenger returned within twelve days bringing me letters from the alcalde who had remained there in which he informed me of how the Indians had attacked the fortress and set fire to it in many places and tried to mine it, and that the Spaniards had been greatly pressed and in great danger, and might yet be killed if Mutezuma did not order a cease fire, for although they were not at present being attacked, they were still surrounded and not permitted to venture outside the fortress at all. In the battle they had lost much of the provisions which I had left them and the four brigantines I had built there were burnt. They were in dire need and I must, for the love of God, come to their aid as swiftly as possible.[85]

I saw how hard pressed these Spaniards were, and knew that if I did not go to their aid not only would they be killed by the Indians and all the gold and silver we had acquired that belonged to Your Highness as well as to the Spaniards and myself be taken, but the greatest and most noble city of all the newly discovered part of the world would be lost, and with it all we had gained, for it was the capital city of the land which all others obeyed. I immediately sent messengers to the captains whom I had dispatched informing them of all I had heard from the capital and ordering them to return, no matter where they might be, and travel by the shortest main road to the province of Tascalteca, where I would join them with all the artillery I could command and seventy horsemen. There we met, and when we had paraded our men we found that we had seventy horsemen and five hundred foot soldiers.

I left in all possible haste for the capital, and not once on my journey did any of Mutezuma's people come to welcome me as they had before. And all the land was in revolt and almost uninhabited, which aroused in me a terrible suspicion that the Spaniards in the city were dead and that all the natives had gathered waiting to surprise me in some pass or other place where they might have the advantage of me. Fearing this, I proceeded with the greatest possible caution until I arrived at the city of Tesuico,[86] which, as I have already informed Your Majesty, is on the shores of that great lake. There I asked the inhabitants about the Spaniards who had remained in the capital and was told that they were still alive. I then instructed them to bring me a canoe, for I wished to send a Spaniard to find out; and I said also that when he left, one of them, who seemed to be of importance, was to remain with me, for nowhere could I see any of the chiefs and nobles who were known to me. He then ordered a canoe to be brought and sent several Indians with the Spaniard, while he himself remained with me.

As this Spaniard was embarking for the city of Temixtitan, he saw another canoe approaching across the lake and waited for it to reach the port. In it came one of the Spaniards from the city from whom I learnt that they were all alive, except five or six whom the Indians had killed; but the rest were still surrounded and not allowed to leave the fortress nor were they provided with any of the things they needed except at a great price. Since hearing of my arrival, however, the Indians had treated them better, and Mutezuma had said that he was only waiting for me to arrive before allowing them to move freely about the city as they were accustomed. With this Spaniard, Mutezuma sent me one of his own messengers, who told me that as I must by now be informed of all that had happened in the city he believed I would be angry and intent on doing him harm. But he begged me not to be angry, for what had happened grieved him as deeply as it did me and that nothing had been done by his will and consent. He sent me word of many other things to placate the anger he thought I bore against him, and begged me to go and live in the city as I had done before, for nothing would be done there save what I commanded, as had been the case before. I answered saying that I was not angry with him, for I well knew his good intention and wanted to do as he requested.

On the following day, which was the eve of St. John the Baptist's day, I departed and slept on the road three leagues from the city; and on the day of St. John, after having heard Mass, I entered the city, almost at midday. I saw very few people about the city and some of the gates at the crossroads and entrances to streets had been removed, which did not seem well to me, although I thought that they did it for fear of what they had done, and that my arrival would reassure them. With this I went to the fortress where, together with the great temple which was beside it, all my people were quartered. The garrison in the fortress received us with such joy it seemed we had given back to them their lives which they had deemed lost; and that day and night we passed in rejoicing, believing that all was quiet again.

The next day, after Mass, I sent a messenger to Vera Cruz to give them the good news of how all the Christians were alive and how I had entered the city which was now secure. But after half an hour this messenger returned, beaten and wounded and crying out that all the Indians in the city were preparing for war and had raised all the bridges. And almost behind him there came upon us from all sides such a multitude that neither the streets nor the roofs of the houses could be seen for them.[87] They came with the most fearful cries imaginable, and so many were the stones that were hurled at us from their slings into the fortress that it seemed they were raining from the sky, and the arrows and spears were so many that all the walls and courtyards were so full we could hardly move for them. I went out to attack the Indians in two or three places, and they fought very fiercely with us. In one place a captain went out with two hundred men, and before he could withdraw they had killed four and wounded him and many others; and in the place where I was engaged they wounded me and many of the other Spaniards. We killed few of them, for they were sheltered from us on the other side of the bridges and threw stones on us from the roofs and terraces, some of which were captured and burnt.

But they were so many and so strong and so well provided

with stones and other arms that we were unable to take them all, for we were few, nor even to prevent them from being able to attack us at their ease. The fighting in the fortress was so fierce that they set fire to it in many places, and in one burnt down a great part of it, about which we could do nothing until we knocked down a part of the wall, which extinguished the fire. And if I had not placed there a strong force of harquebusiers and crossbowmen with some guns, they could easily have broken in without our being able to resist. In this fashion we fought all that day until well after dark; and even after nightfall they continued to scream at us and make a commotion until dawn. That night I had the breaches in the wall caused by fire repaired, and wherever else I thought the fortress was weak. I organized the watches and the men who were to keep them and chose those of us who would go outside to fight the next day. I also had the wounded, of which there were more than eighty, attended to.

Later, when it was light, the enemy attacked us very much more fiercely than on the previous day, and there was so great a number of them that the artillery had no need to aim but only to point their guns at the Indian forces. And although the artillery did much damage, for there were thirteen harquebuses besides the guns and some crossbows, it seemed to make no impression, for where ten or twelve were killed by the firing others came immediately to take their place, so that it was as if none had fallen. Leaving behind in the fortress all the men I could spare, I took the others and went out and captured some of the bridges and burnt some of the houses and killed many of those who were defending them, but they were so many that although we did all the harm we could we made very little impression on them. We had to fight all day, whereas they fought in shifts and still they seemed to have plenty of men to spare. That day they wounded sixty or seventy more Spaniards but killed none, although we fought until nightfall, by which time we were so tired we withdrew to the fortress.

Seeing the great harm that the enemy had done us and how

they wounded and killed us as they chose, and how, although we did great harm to them there were so many that it did not seem so, we spent all that night and all the following day in constructing three wooden engines. Each one of these carried twenty men inside, and the stones the Indians threw from the roof tops could not harm them for they were covered by boards. The people who went inside were some of them harquebusiers and crossbowmen; the rest carried pikes and pickaxes, and iron bars to break into the houses and throw down the barricades the Indians had built in the streets. While we were constructing these machines the enemy continued to attack; whenever we left the fortress they tried to break in, and we repulsed them only with great difficulty. Mutezuma, who together with one of his sons and many other chiefs who had been captured previously was still a prisoner,[88] asked to be taken out onto the roof of the fortress where he might speak to the captains of his people and tell them to end the fighting. I had him taken out, and when he reached a breastwork which ran out beyond the fortress, and was about to speak to them, he received a blow on his head from a stone; and the injury was so serious that he died three days later.[89] I told two of the Indians who were captive to carry him out on their shoulders to the people. What they did with him I do not know; only the war did not stop because of it, but grew more fierce and pitiless each day.

That same day they called to me from the place where they had wounded Mutezuma, asking me to go there, for certain captains wished to speak with me. This I did, and we had many discussions and I begged them not to fight me, for they had no cause to, and to consider the good deeds I had done for them and how they had always been well treated by me. They replied saying that once I had left their land they would stop the war; otherwise they had all determined to die or put an end to us. This they said, or so it seemed, to persuade me to leave the fortress, for then they could have taken us easily at the bridges. I replied that they should not think I asked for peace because I feared them, but because it distressed me to see the harm we had done them, and would still have to do them, for I did not want to destroy so fine a city as theirs; yet still they answered that they would not end the war until I left the city.

On the following day, when we had finished the engines, I went out to capture some of the roof tops and bridges. The engines went in front, and behind them came four guns, many crossbow-men and shield-bearers and more than three thousand Indians from Tascalteca who had come with me and served the Spaniards. When we reached one of the bridges we placed the engines against the wall of a house and set up ladders with which to climb onto the roof, but there were so many people defending that bridge and the roof top, and so many and so large were the stones which they threw down at us, that they put our engines out of action and killed one Spaniard and wounded many more. We were unable to ad-vance one step, although we fought hard from morning until mid-day, at which hour we returned to the fortress sorely disappointed. This gave the enemy such heart that they almost reached our gates. They captured the great temple, and some five hundred Indians, who seemed to me to be persons of rank, climbed up the main tower carrying provisions of bread and water and other things to eat, and many stones. All the rest had very long lances with flint heads wider than ours and no less sharp. From there they did much damage to the people in the fortress which stood close by. Once or twice the Spaniards attacked this tower and attempted to climb it, but because it was very high and the ascent very difficult, for there were a hundred or more steps, and because those at the top were well provided with stones and other weapons, and at an advantage because we had failed to take the other roof tops, every time the Spaniards began to climb they were driven back down again; and many were wounded thereby. When those of the enemy who were engaged elsewhere saw this, they became so elated that they came fearlessly right up to the fortress. When I saw that by continu-ing to hold that tower they not only inflicted great damage from it, but also gained fresh courage to attack us, I left the fortress, although I had lost the use of my left hand from a wound I received on the first day, and strapping my buckler to my arm went to the tower with a few Spaniards.[90] I made them surround it from below, which was easily done, although not without danger, for they fought on all sides with the enemy who brought in many reinforcements. I then began to climb the tower with several Spaniards behind me, and, although they defended it so very fiercely that three or four Spaniards were thrown down, with the help of God and his Blessed Mother, for whose house that tower had been set aside and where we had placed her image, we reached the top and fought so hard with the people there that they were forced to jump down onto some terraces round the tower which were about a pace wide. The tower had three or four of these, and all were about five yards high, one above the other. Some of the Indians fell all the way down and they were killed by the Spaniards below. Those who remained on the top, however, fought so fiercely that it was more than three hours before we had killed them all (for none escaped); and I assure Your Sacred Majesty that the capture of this tower was so difficult that if God had not clipped their wings, twenty of them would have sufficed to hold off a thousand; even so, they fought very bravely until death. I ordered my men to set fire to this tower and the others in the temple from which they had already removed the holy images that we had placed there.

The loss of this tower so much damaged their confidence that they began to weaken greatly on all sides. Afterwards, I returned to that roof top and addressed the captains who had spoken to me before and who were now somewhat dismayed by what they had seen. These then came and I told them to observe how they could not triumph, and how each day we did them great harm and killed many of them and we were burning and destroying their city; and that we would not cease until there was nothing left either of it or of them. They replied that they had indeed seen how much they had suffered and how many of them had died, but that they were all determined to perish or have done with us, and that I should look and see how full of people were all those streets and squares and roof tops. Furthermore, they had calculated that if 25,000 of them died for every one of us, they would finish with us first, for they were many and we were but few. They told me that all the causeways into the city were dismantled—which in fact was true, for all had been dismantled save one—and that we had no way of escape except over the water. They well knew that we had few provisions and little fresh water and, therefore, could not last long because we would die of hunger if they did not kill us first. And truly they were right, for even if we had had nothing to fight but hunger and thirst, we would have died in a very short while. We discussed many other things, each one expressing his own opinions.

After nightfall I went out with several Spaniards, and as we fell on them unawares we took a street where we burnt more than three hundred houses. Then I returned by another street, for the enemy was massing in the first, and there likewise I burnt many houses, especially some which were close to the fortress and from whose roof tops they did us much harm. They were very frightened by what had happened, and that same night I ordered the engines which had been damaged the previous day to be repaired and made ready.

To follow up this victory which God had given us, I went out at dawn to that street where they had defeated us the day before but found it as well defended as before. As we were fighting for our lives and our honor, for that street lead to the only unbroken causeway crossing to the mainland—although on the way were eight deep and wide bridges, and the street itself was lined by many high houses and towers—we were so brave and determined that with the help of Our Lord we won four of them that day and burnt every single house and tower. The previous night, however, they had erected at all the bridges many very strong walls of adobe and clay, in such a manner that the guns and the crossbows could not harm them. We filled in the channels beneath the four bridges with the adobe and earth of the walls and with stones and wood from the burnt houses, although this was not accomplished without danger and they wounded many Spaniards. That night I placed a careful watch on those bridges so that they should not retake them.

The following morning I went out again and God gave us such a lucky victory that, although there were innumerable people defending the bridges and the very great walls and openings which they had made that night, we won them all and closed them up. At the same time some horsemen pursued the defeated enemy to the mainland. While I was repairing and closing up those bridges, they called to me to come in great haste, for the Indians were asking for peace and certain of their captains were waiting for me at the fortress. I left behind the men and guns and went alone with two horsemen to see what they wanted. They told me that if I assured them that they would not be punished for what they had done, they would raise the siege, replace the bridges, repair the roads and serve Your Majesty as they had done before. They asked me to bring one of their priests whom I held prisoner, and who was a kind of superior in their religion.[91] He came and spoke to them and made agreements between us; and then it seemed that they sent messengers, as they had promised, to the captains in the field to end the attack on the fortress and all further hostilities; and with this we parted.

I returned to the fortress to eat, and as I was about to begin they came in a great hurry to tell me that the Indians had retaken the bridges which we had won that day and had killed several Spaniards. God knows how much this perturbed me, for I believed our task had been completed when we had opened a way out. I rode as fast as I was able down the whole length of the street with some horsemen following me, and without stopping I broke through those Indians, recovered the bridges and pursued the fugitives to the mainland. But because the foot soldiers were tired and wounded and frightened and saw the great danger they were in, none of them followed me, so that when, having crossed the bridges, I now wished to return, I found they had been taken and many which we had closed up had now been dug much deeper than before. Both sides of the causeway were full of people, on the land and also in canoes, who speared and stoned us in such a fashion that if God had not mysteriously deigned to save us, we should never have escaped, and even so it had been put about among those in the city that I was dead. When I reached the last bridge outside the city I found that all those horsemen who were with me had fallen into the water and that one horse was loose. I could not cross and was forced to stand alone against the enemy, and in fighting I made enough room for the horses to pass. When the bridge was freed I passed over, although with great difficulty, for the horse had to jump almost five feet from one side to the other; but neither he nor I, as we were both well armored, were wounded but only bruised and beaten.

That night they held those four bridges; but I had the other four well guarded and went to the fortress and had a wooden bridge made to be carried by forty men. Because I had seen the great danger we were in and the great harm which the Indians did us every day, and because I feared they would demolish that causeway as they had demolished the others, after which we could have done nothing save resign ourselves to death, and because all of my company, the greater part of whom were so badly wounded they could no longer fight, had often entreated me to depart, I determined to leave that same night. I took all Your Majesty's gold and jewels which we could carry and placed them in a room where, in several bundles, I entrusted them to Your Highness's officials that I in Your Royal name had chosen, and I begged and commanded the alcaldes and regidores and all those who were present to help me to carry it out and save it; and for this purpose I gave them one of my mares onto which they loaded as much as possible. I chose certain Spaniards, servants of mine as well as of others, to go with the mare and the gold, and the rest of the alcaldes and regidores and myself distributed the remainder among the Spaniards. Having abandoned the fortress with great riches belonging to Your Highness, the Spaniards and myself, I went out as secretly as possible taking with me a son and two daughters of Mutezuma, and Cacamazin, lord of Aculmacan, and also his brother whom I had appointed in his stead, and other chiefs of cities and provinces, whom I held prisoner.

When we reached the first of the bridges which the Indians had removed we threw across the space, with little difficulty, the bridge which we had made, for there was no one to impede us except a few guards. These, however, raised such a shout that before we had reached the second bridge an infinite number of the enemy were upon us, attacking us from all sides both from the land and from the water. I crossed quickly with five horsemen and a hundred foot soldiers, and we swam across each of the channels until we reached the mainland. Leaving these people on the far side, I returned to the rest and found that, although they were fighting fiercely, the harm which both the Spaniards and the Indians of Tascalteca who were with us had received was beyond compare, for nearly all had been killed. The Spaniards had also killed many of the enemy, but many had perished together with their horses, and all the gold had been lost together with jewels, clothing, all the artillery and many other things besides. I collected all those who were still alive and sent them on ahead while I, with three or four horsemen and some twenty foot soldiers who were bold enough to remain with me, took the rear guard and fought with those Indians until we reached a city called Tacuba at the end of the causeway. God alone knows how dangerous and how difficult it was, for each time I turned on the enemy I came back full of arrows and bruised by stones. For as there was water on both sides they attacked in safety with no fear of those who were fleeing to the land. When we attacked them they jumped into the water, so that they received very little hurt except that there were so many that some of them fell on each other and were killed. With great danger and difficulty I led all my men to the city of Tacuba, without a single Indian or

Spaniard being killed or wounded save for one horseman who came with me in the rear guard. The people in the front and on the sides fought no less fiercely, although the worst attack came from behind where the enemy pursued us out of the great city.[92]

When I arrived in Tacuba I found all my people crowded together in a square not knowing where to go. I therefore made haste to move them out into the countryside before more of the enemy arrived in the city and occupied the roof tops, from which they could do us great harm. The vanguard said they did not know which road to take, so I sent them to the rear and took the lead myself until we had left the city, and then waited in the fields. When the rear guard arrived I saw that they had received some damage and that some of the Spaniards and Indians had been killed; and also that much of the gold had been lost by the road and captured by the enemy. I remained behind until all the men had passed, holding the Indians in check so that the foot soldiers might take a hill on which stood a tower and a fortified house.[93] They succeeded without being injured, but God alone knows how exhausted I was in keeping back the Indians until the tower was taken, for of the twenty-four horses that remained not one could gallop, nor was there a horseman who could raise his arm nor barely a foot soldier well enough for action. When we arrived at the aforementioned house we barricaded ourselves in, and there the enemy surrounded us until nightfall without letting us rest for a single hour. We discovered that 150 Spaniards had died in the rout and forty-five horses and more than two thousand Indians, who had helped the Spaniards, among whom were the son and daughters of Mutezuma and all the other lords we had held prisoner.[94]

That night, at midnight, thinking that we were unobserved, we quit that house very silently, leaving behind many fires; and we knew no road nor where we were going, save that an Indian from Tascalteca led us, saying that he would take us to his land if the road was free. But there were some guards close by who saw us and raised all the people from the villages thereabouts, who pursued us until daybreak. At dawn, five horsemen who were riding ahead as scouts came across a squadron of the enemy on the road and killed several of them, whereupon the rest fled, believing that more horsemen and foot soldiers were coming up behind.

When I saw that the enemy was massing on all sides, I concentrated my people there, and from those who were still capable of action made squadrons, placing them in front and behind and on the sides with the wounded in the middle; and I distributed the horsemen likewise. In this manner we marched all that day, fighting on all sides and so fiercely that we covered no more than three leagues during a whole day and night. Just at nightfall our Lord showed us a tower and fortified house on a hill where we barricaded ourselves as before.[95] That night they left us in peace, although shortly before dawn the alarm was raised, though for no reason save the fear which we all had of the great multitude of people who continued to follow us.

On the following day I left an hour after daybreak in the formation already mentioned, keeping my rear guard and vanguard well protected; and still they pursued us on both sides, shouting and calling to arms all that land which is thickly populated. Those of us who were on horseback, although we were few, attacked them but did them little harm, for as the land there was somewhat uneven they retreated into the hills. In this manner we traveled that day close by some lakes until we reached a good town[96] where we expected to have some encounter with the inhabitants. But as we arrived they abandoned it and fled to other villages which were thereabouts. I remained there that day and the following because all the men, both the wounded and the fit, were exhausted and weary with hunger and thirsty, as indeed were the horses. We also found some maize there which we ate boiled and roasted for the journey.

We left the next day, still pursued by the enemy, who, with terrible cries, attacked us from time to time in front and behind. We followed the directions of the Indian from Tascalteca, suffering many hardships, for we were often obliged to leave the road. When it was already late we reached a plain with some small houses[97] where we camped that night, in great need of food. On the morning of the following day we began to depart, but even before we had reached the road the enemy was pursuing us, and skirmishing with them we reached a large village,[98] which was two leagues from there, and to the right of it were some Indians on a small hill.[99] Intending to take them, for they were very close to the road, and also to discover if there were more people behind the hill, I went with five horsemen and ten or twelve foot soldiers and circled the hill. Behind it lay a great city of many inhabitants,[100] with whom we fought fiercely, but as the ground was strewn with boulders, and the Indians were many and we were few, I considered it wise to withdraw to the village where our people were.

In the fighting I had been very badly wounded in the head from two stones. After having bound up my wounds, I made the Spaniards leave that village, for it did not seem a safe place for us to camp. Thus we left, the Indians still following in great numbers, and fighting so fiercely with us that they wounded four or five Spaniards and as many horses. One horse was killed and, although God knows how much we needed it, and how sorry we were to have lost it, for after God we had no help save from the horses, its flesh was some consolation, for we ate it, leaving neither the skin nor any other part of it. For we were very hungry as we had eaten nothing since we left the great city save boiled and roasted maize—and there was not always even enough of that—and herbs which we picked in the fields.

When I saw how each day the enemy grew in number and became more daring while we were weakening, I ordered crutches and other aids to be made for the wounded and the sick, whom we had hitherto carried on the haunches and backs of the horses, so that they could stand and walk, and leave the horses and the Spaniards who were well free to fight. And it seemed, from what happened the following day, that the Holy Spirit had inspired me in this, for, after we had struck camp in the morning and traveled on a league and a half, there came to meet us such a multitude of Indians that the fields all around were so full of them that nothing else could be seen. We could hardly distinguish between ourselves and them, so fiercely and so closely did they fight with us.[101] Certainly we believed that it was our last day, for the Indians were very strong and we could resist but feebly, as we were exhausted and nearly all of us wounded and weak from hunger. But Our Lord was pleased to show His power and mercy, for with all our weakness we broke their great arrogance and pride, and many of them died, including many important persons, for they were so many that they got in each other's way, and could neither fight nor run. We spent most of that day in the fight until God ordained that one of their chieftains should die, and he, it seemed, was of such importance that the battle ended. So we proceeded more easily but still somewhat harassed, until we reached a small house[102] in the plain, and there, and in the fields round about, we camped that night. From there we caught sight of some mountains of the province of Tascalteca, which brought no small joy to our hearts, for we knew the land and where we had now to go, although we were not very certain that we would find the natives of that province still our friends. For we believed that on seeing us so dispirited they would seek to put an end to our lives and regain their former liberty. This thought distressed us as much as the fighting with the Culuans.

On the following day, when it was light, we began to travel along a very flat road which led directly to the aforementioned province of Tascalteca. Here very few of the enemy followed us, although there were several large towns nearby; and those who did remained far in the rear and shouted after us from some hills. And so that day, which was Sunday, the eighth of July, we left Culua and reached a town of the province of Tascalteca, called Gualipán,[103] which had some three or four thousand inhabitants by whom we were well received; and there we were, in some measure able to satisfy our great hunger and need for rest, although they gave us many of our provisions only in exchange for money and would accept nothing but gold, which, on account of our great need, we were obliged to give them. In this town I remained three days, and here Magiscacin and Sicutengal came to see me together with all the chiefs of the province and some of those from Guazucingo. They all seemed much distressed by what had happened to us, and tried hard to console me, saying that many times they had told me that the people of Culua were traitors, and I should beware of them, but I had not wished to believe it. But I had escaped alive, for which I should be thankful, and they would die to help me avenge the harm which I had been done, for apart from the duty they owed Your Highness as his vassals, they grieved for their sons and brothers who had been killed in my company.

In times past they had received many other injuries from the Culuans, and I might be certain that they would remain faithful to me until death. As I was wounded and all those in my company exhausted, they said we should go to the city which is four leagues from this town, and there we could rest, and they would attend to our wounds and restore us after our exhaustion. I thanked them and accepted their offer and gave them some few jewels that had escaped, which greatly pleased them. Thus I accompanied them to the aforementioned city, where we were likewise very well received. And Magiscacin brought me a finely made wooden bed with some of the bedclothes they use, in which I slept, for we had brought none with us; and he gave to every one of us all that he had and could.

When I set out for Temixtitan I had left behind in this city some who were wounded and some of my servants with silver and clothing of mine and other personal effects which I was carrying, so that I might be less burdened should anything befall us. All the written agreements I had made with the natives of these parts were lost. Likewise all the Spaniards' clothing had been left behind, and they brought nothing save what they were wearing and their cloaks.

I now learnt how another of my servants had come from the

town of Vera Cruz,[104] accompanied by five horsemen and forty-five foot soldiers, with provisions and other things for me; and how he had taken back with him all the people whom I had left behind with the silver and clothes and other things belonging to me and my companions, together with seven thousand *pesos de oro* which I had left in two chests, not to mention other valuables, and also fourteen thousand *pesos de oro* which, in the province of Tuchitebeque, had been given to that captain whom I had sent to build the town of Quacucalco. And there were many other things besides, worth in all more than thirty thousand *pesos de oro*. But the Indians of Culua had killed them on the road and taken all they were carrying. Likewise I learnt that many other Spaniards had been killed on the road to Temixtitan, believing that the city was at peace and the roads safe as they had been before. I assure Your Majesty that this caused us the greatest sadness, for in addition to the loss of these Spaniards and the others, this reminded us of how many had died and how much had been lost in the city and on the bridges and on the road; it also made me suspect that they might have attacked the people in Vera Cruz, and that those whom we held as allies, when they learnt of our defeat, might have rebelled against us. Then I sent certain messengers to learn the truth, with some Indians to guide them, and I ordered them to return as swiftly as possible but not to travel by the usual roads. It pleased Our Lord, however, that they should find all the Spaniards quite safe and the natives loyal. And this made up greatly for our losses, although the Spaniards were very distressed to hear of our rout.

In this province of Tascalteca I remained twenty days to heal my wounds, which on account of the journey and the ill treatment I had received had greatly worsened, especially those in the head;[105] and likewise to recover from the toil of the days past and to heal the wounds of my companions. Some of them died and others were crippled, for they were very badly wounded and we had few means by which to cure them. I myself lost two fingers of my left hand.

When those of my company saw that many had died and that those who remained were weak and wounded and discouraged by the dangers they had endured, and being afraid of those who might very soon come, they many times begged me to return to Vera Cruz, where we could make ourselves secure before the natives of the land, whom we held as our allies, on seeing our defeat and feeble strength, could join with our enemies, seize the mountain passes by which we were to travel, and fall on us and on those in Vera Cruz. Once we were all together and had ships, we would be stronger and better able to defend ourselves, should they attack us, until such time as we sent for help from the islands. But I saw that to show the natives, especially those who were our allies, that we lacked courage would suffice to turn them against us the sooner, and I remembered that Fortune always favors the bold, and furthermore that we were Christians who trusted in the great goodness of God, who would not let us perish utterly nor allow us to lose so great and noble a land which had been, or was to be, subject to Your Majesty; nor could I abandon so great a service as continuing the war whereby we would once more subdue the land as it had been before. I determined, therefore, that on no account would I go across the mountains to the coast. On the contrary, disregarding all the dangers and toil that might befall us, I told them that I would not abandon this land, for, apart from being shameful to myself and dangerous for all, it would be great treason to Your Majesty; rather I resolved to fall on our enemies wherever I could and oppose them in every possible way.

After I had been in this province twenty days, although my wounds were not fully healed and those in my company were still rather weak, I departed for another province which is called Tepeaca, which belongs to the league and confederation of Culua, our enemies, and where, I was informed, ten or twelve Spaniards had been killed on the road, which passes through there, from Vera Cruz to the great city. This province of Tepeaca is very large and in part borders on Tascalteca and Churultecal. When we crossed the border many of the natives came out to fight with us and defend the road against us as best they could, attacking us from strong and dangerous positions. But so as not to give an account of all the details of what befell us in this battle, which would be too lengthy, I will say only that after we had made our demands for peace on Your Majesty's behalf and they had not complied, we made war on them and they fought many times with us. With God's help and the Royal fortune of Your Majesty we always routed them and killed many, without their killing or wounding a single Spaniard. And, although, as I have said, this province is very large, within twenty days we had subdued and pacified many towns and villages, and the lords and chieftains have come and offered themselves as Your Majesty's vassals. Furthermore, I have driven from these provinces many of the people of Culua who had come to help the natives of Tepeaca make war on us and to assure that they did not become our allies, willingly or unwillingly. Thus I have been engaged in this war, which is still not finished, for there are still some towns and villages to be pacified, which with the aid of Our Lord will soon, like these others, be subject to Your Majesty's Royal command.

In a certain part of this province,[106] where they killed the ten or twelve Spaniards, the natives have always been very warlike and rebellious. I made certain of them slaves of which I gave a fifth part to Your Majesty's officers, for, in addition to their having killed the aforementioned Spaniards and rebelled against Your Highness's service, they are all cannibals, of which I send Your Majesty no evidence because it is so infamous.[107] I was also moved to take those slaves so as to strike some fear into the people of Culua and also because there are so many people that if I did not impose a great and cruel punishment they would never be reformed. In this war the natives of Tascalteca, Churultecal and Guasucingo have fought with us, and by so doing have so assured us of their friendship that we are certain they will always serve Your Highness as loyal vassals.

While I was in this province of Tepeaca I received letters from Vera Cruz, informing me of how there had arrived in the port in disarray two ships belonging to Francisco de Garay, who, it seems, had sent them back with more men to that great river, of which I have already rendered Your Highness account, and that the natives had fought with them and killed seventeen or eighteen Christians and wounded many others. Likewise seven horses had been killed, but the Spaniards who remained swam out to the ships and only escaped because they had strong legs. The captain and the others were in a sorry state and wounded, but the lieutenant whom I had left in the town had welcomed them and ordered their wounds to be attended to. So that they might recover in greater comfort, he had sent some of them to the land of a friendly chieftain that lay close by, and there they were very well cared for. All of which distressed us as much as our past hardships; but perhaps such misfortune would never have befallen them if they had joined me on that first occasion, about which I have already written to Your Highness, for, as I was very well acquainted with these parts, I could have advised them and this disaster would have been avoided, especially as the chieftain of that river, which is called Pánuco, had offered himself as Your Majesty's vassal, in recognition of which he had sent certain gifts with his messengers to me in the city of Temixtitan, as I have already said. I have written to Vera Cruz saying that if Garay's captain and his people wish to leave they should give them every assistance in dispatching both themselves and their ships.[108]

After having pacified all that which in this province of Tepeaca has now been pacified and subjected to the service of Your Royal Highness, Your Majesty's officers and I many times discussed the manner by which the security of this province was to be maintained. Seeing that the natives, having offered themselves as Your Highness's vassals, had rebelled and killed many Spaniards, and seeing that the road inland from the seacoast passes through here, we considered that if this province were left unattended as before, the natives of Culua, their neighbors, might once again incite these others to rebel, from which great harm would follow and hindrance to the subjection of these parts and to the service of Your Highness, for the road would be closed, especially as there are only two mountain passes leading to the sea, both of which are very steep and rocky and could be easily defended by the natives. So for these and for many other reasons touching this matter, we decided that to avoid these evils we would have a town built in the best part of this province of Tepeaca, where conditions were best suited to the needs of the settlers. When this had been decided, I, in Your Majesty's name, called this town Segura de la Frontera, and appointed alcaldes, regidores and other officials as is customary. For the greater security of the inhabitants of this town, I have ordered a fortress to be built in a place which I indicated, and building materials to be brought, as these are very good hereabouts; and all possible haste will be made to complete it.

While engaged in writing this report there came to me several messengers from the chief of a city five leagues from this province, called Buacachula,[109] and situated at the entrance to one of the passes into the province of Mesico. These messengers told me, on behalf of their lord, that some while previously they had come and offered themselves as Your Majesty's vassals. And so that I should not accuse them of complicity, they were informing me that several captains from Culua were quartered in their city, and that in it and one league away thirty thousand men were garrisoned to prevent us from crossing by that pass, and also to prevent the inhabitants of the city or of any of the surrounding provinces from becoming Your Highness's vassals or our allies. They said that some of those would have come to offer themselves in Your Royal service had they not been prevented. They told me this so that I should remedy it, for in addition to preventing all those of goodwill from coming, the Culuans had done great harm to the inhabitants of that city and to the people thereabouts. For, as there were many warriors, their people had been greatly injured and ill treated and their women and belongings and other things had been taken from them. If I would grant them protection, they promised to do as I commanded. Then, after thanking them for their information and their offer, I sent thirteen horsemen and two hundred foot soldiers[110] to accompany them together with some thirty thousand of our Indian allies. We agreed that they should travel by roads where they would not be discovered, and once they were outside the city the chief and inhabitants and all his other vassals and supporters would be alerted and would surround the place where the captains were quartered, so they might seize and kill them before their people had time to come to their assistance. When they did come the Spaniards would already be in the city and would fight with them and set them to rout.

So they left and went by way of the city of Churultecal and through some of the province of Guasucingo, which borders on the land of Buacachula four leagues from the city. In a village of the aforementioned province of Guasucingo it is said that they told the Spaniards that the natives of that province had plotted with the people of Buacachula and Culua to trick the Spaniards into going to that city, where, once they were all together, they would fall on the Spaniards and kill them. As they had not yet dispelled the terror with which they had been filled by the Culuans, this intelligence terrified the Spaniards; their captain made investigations as well as he could, and seized all the chiefs of Guasucingo he had with him, together with the messengers from the city of Buacachula, and returned to the city of Churultecal, which is four leagues from there, and sent me the prisoners accompanied by several horsemen and foot soldiers to inform me of what had happened. The captain also wrote to me saying that our men were alarmed and dispirited, and that the expedition now seemed very hazardous.

When the prisoners arrived I questioned them most diligently through my interpreters to learn the truth, and it appeared that the captain had misunderstood them. I at once set them free and placated them, saying that I believed them to be loyal vassals of

Your Sacred Majesty and that I would go in person to rout the Culuans, for, in order to show no weakness before the natives of this land, whether friends or enemies, it seemed to me that we should not abandon an enterprise we had begun. To dispel some of the fear of the Spaniards I decided to lay aside all other business and the dispatch which I was writing for Your Majesty, and departed that same hour with the greatest possible speed. I arrived that day at the city of Churultecal, which is eight leagues from this city [Segura de la Frontera], and there I found the Spaniards who still believed firmly in the treachery.

On the following day I slept at the town in Guasucingo where the chiefs had been seized. The next day after having agreed with the messengers from Buacachula as to where and how we were to enter the city, I set out an hour before dawn and arrived there just before ten o'clock. When I was still about half a league distant certain messengers from the city came out to meet me on the road; they told me how everything was prepared and how the Culuans knew nothing of our arrival, for certain inhabitants of that city had seized the spies which the captains from Culua had placed on the roads, and likewise those who had been sent to the walls and towers of the city to survey the countryside. The enemy was therefore unprepared, confident that they were well protected by their spies and scouts; and so my advance would pass unnoticed. Thus I hastened to enter the city without being discovered, because we were marching across a plain where they could easily have seen us. When the inhabitants of the city saw how close we were they surrounded the houses where the captains were quartered and began to attack the others scattered throughout the city. When I came within a crossbowshot of the city they brought me some forty prisoners, and I made all the more haste to enter. There was a great uproar throughout all the streets of the city. While fighting with the enemy I was guided by a native to the place where those captains were quartered, which I found surrounded by more than three thousand men who had captured the roofs and high places and were fighting to get in. But the captains and their men fought so well and so fiercely that although they were few they repulsed their attackers. For not only were they most valiant men but also the building they were in was very strong. As soon as I arrived we entered, but so many natives came with us that I was unable to save those captains from being killed almost immediately. I had wished to take some alive in order to learn of the affairs of the great city and who was lord now that Mutezuma was dead, and other things besides; but I was only able to capture one, more dead than alive, who informed me as I shall hereafter relate.

Many of those Culuans who were quartered in the city were killed and the rest, as soon as they heard of my arrival, began to flee to where the others were garrisoned; but many of them died in their attempt to escape. The disturbance was soon heard by the garrison, which commanded a height overlooking the city and the surrounding plain. They came to see what it was and to help, almost at the same time as the others arrived who had fled from the city. They were more than thirty thousand men and the most magnificent we have ever seen, for they wore many jewels and much gold and feathers. As the city is large, they began to set fire to it in the place where they had entered; this was soon discovered by the inhabitants, however, and I went out with only the horsemen, for the foot soldiers were very exhausted. We broke through them and they retreated to a pass which we took and then pursued them, overtaking many on an upward slope so steep that when we reached the top of the hill neither the enemy nor ourselves could either retreat or advance. Thus many of them fell suffocated by the heat without receiving a single wound. Two horses also fell, one of which died. In this manner we did great harm, for we had with us many of our Indian friends who, as they were refreshed and the enemy half dead, killed many of them: so in a short while the battlefield was empty of the living, though somewhat cluttered with the dead. We reached the quarters and shelters they had recently built in the countryside: these were in three groups, each, it seemed, as large as a small village, for in addition to the warriors, there were many servants and supplies for their camp, because, as I learnt afterwards, they had had some persons of high rank with them. All this was plundered and burnt by our Indian allies of whom, I assure Your Majesty, there were more than a hundred thousand altogether. Having with this victory now driven the enemy from the land to beyond some difficult mountain passes which they still held, we returned to Buacachula, where we were very well received and accommodated by the inhabitants; and in that city we rested for three days, for we were in great need of rest.

At this time there came to offer themselves in Your Majesty's Royal service the inhabitants of a large town called Ocupatuyo,[111] which stands two leagues above the hills where the enemy camp was, and at the foot of that smoking mountain. They said that their chief had fled with the Culuans when we had pursued them, believing we would not stop at his town; and that for some while they had desired my friendship and would have come to offer themselves as Your Highness's vassals, but their chief would not permit it, although they asked him many times. They now wished to serve Your Majesty; and there remained behind a brother of that chief, who had always been of their opinion and still was. They begged me, therefore, to approve his succession, and that if the other lord returned not to receive him as such, for they themselves would not do so. I told them that as they had until now been allied with the Culuans and in revolt against Your Majesty's service, they deserved great punishments, which I had intended to execute on their persons and possessions; but as they had come and told me that the cause of their rebellion had been their lord, I, in Your Majesty's name, forgave them their past errors and admitted them to Your Royal service. But I cautioned them that if another such crime were committed they would be punished; promising them on the other hand that if they were loyal vassals they would be much honored and assisted by me in Your Royal name.

This city of Guacachulla [sic] is situated in a plain bounded on the one side by some high and rugged mountains and on the others by two rivers about two crossbowshots apart which run through large and deep ravines. Thus the approaches to the city are few, and all of them are so steep that the horses can barely pass either up or down them. The whole city is surrounded by a very strong wall built of stone and mortar which is as high as twenty-four feet on the outside and almost level with the ground on the inside. All along the top of this wall runs a battlement three feet high to protect them while fighting. And there are four gateways wide enough for a man to enter on horseback. At each entrance there are three or four bends in the wall, doubling back on one another; and there are also battlements on each of these bends. On this wall they keep a great number of stones, both small and large and of various shapes, which they use for fighting. This city has some five or six thousand inhabitants, and there are as many more in the hamlets which are subject to it. It occupies a very large area, for within the city are many gardens with fruit and sweet-smelling flowers as is their custom.

When I had rested in this city three days I went to another which is called Yzçucan[112] and is four leagues from Buacachula, because I was told that there also many Culuans were garrisoned, and that the inhabitants of the city and of the towns and other places subject to it appeared to be closely allied with the Culuans, for their lord was a native of that country and a relative of Mutezuma too. I was accompanied by such a great number of the natives, Your Majesty's vassals, that they covered the fields and hills for almost as far as we could see; indeed, we must have been more than 120,000 men.

We arrived at that city of Yzçucan at ten o'clock, and found it empty of women and children, but there remained as many as five or six thousand warriors, all very well armed. When the Spaniards who had taken the vanguard arrived, the enemy began to defend their city somewhat, but soon abandoned it because it was easy for us to enter by the place we had been led to. We pursued them through the city until they were forced to jump over the parapet into a river which ran alongside all that part of the wall. As they had destroyed the bridges, we spent a little time in crossing, but then pursued them for a league and a half or more; and I think that few of those who remained escaped.

When we returned to the city I sent two of the native prisoners to speak to the men of rank, for their lord had gone with the Culuans, to persuade them to return to the city; and I promised them in Your Majesty's name that if they became Your Highness's loyal vassals, they would thenceforth be well favored by me and their past errors would be forgiven.

These messengers departed, and after three days some chieftains came and begged forgiveness for their crimes, pleading that they could not have done otherwise because their lord had so commanded them; but they promised that as their lord had fled and abandoned them they would thenceforth serve Your Majesty most loyally. I reassured them and told them to return to their homes and bring back their women and children who had been taken to towns and other places of their allies; likewise I told them to speak to the inhabitants of those places so that they should come to me, for I forgave them for what had happened. Otherwise I would be obliged to move against them and would surely do them much harm, which would distress me greatly. Thus it was done, and within two days the city of Yzçucan was repopulated, and all the dependencies thereof had offered themselves as Your Highness's vassals; and that province remained very secure, in friendship and alliance with both ourselves and the people of Buacachula.

Some dispute arose about whom the sovereignties over the city and province of Yzçucan belonged to in the absence of the lord who had gone to Mesico. There had arisen some controversy between a bastard son of the rightful lord of the land (whom Mutezuma had put to death, and in his stead placed the present lord, marrying him to one of his nieces) and a grandson of the same rightful lord, son of his legitimate daughter and the ruler of Buacachula. At last it was decided that as the son of the ruler of Buacachula came from the legitimate line, he should inherit, because, although the other was the lord's son, he was a bastard and therefore should not rule. In my presence they paid homage to that boy, who is some ten years old; and they decided that as he was not of age to rule that his illegitimate uncle and three other chieftains, one from the city of Buacachula, and the other two from Yzçucan, should govern the land and care for the boy until he came of age.

This city of Yzçucan has some three or four thousand citizens, and its streets and marketplaces are very well ordered; it had a hundred temples and shrines, well fortified with towers, all of which were burnt. It is in a plain at the foot of a medium-sized hill where there is a very good fortress. On the other side, which faces toward the plain, it is bordered by a deep river that runs very close to the walls and is surrounded by the deep gorge of the river, on the edge of which they have built battlements two yards high which run all the way around the city; and all along this wall they have piled many stones. The valley is circular and very fertile in fruit and cotton, which does not grow anywhere above the passes on account of the great cold; but here the land is warm, for it is well sheltered by mountains. The whole valley is irrigated by well-built channels which are well dug and laid out.

I remained in this city until it was secure and all the inhabitants had returned; and while I was there the lord of the city of Guasucingo and the lord of another which is ten leagues from Yzçucan, both of which share borders with Mesico, came to me offering themselves as Your Majesty's vassals. Chieftains also came from eight of the towns in the province of Coastoaca,[113] which I have mentioned in previous chapters, as the province which those Spaniards visited who went to look for gold in Cucula, and Tamazula nearby, where there were very large towns, better built than any seen in these parts. This province is forty leagues from Yzçucan; and the natives of the aforementioned eight towns likewise offered themselves as Your Highness's vassals and said that four others from the same province who had remained behind would come very soon. They asked me to forgive them for not having come before, but they had not dared to for fear of the Culuans. They had never taken arms against me, however, nor killed any Spaniard, and after they had offered to serve Your Highness they had always been loyal and true vassals, but had not dared show it. So Your Highness may be assured that if it please Our Lord to favor Your Royal good fortune, all that was lost, or a great part of it, will shortly be regained, for each day many of the provinces and cities which had been subject to Mutezuma come and offer themselves as Your Majesty's vassals, for they see how those who do so are well received and favored by me, whereas those who do not are destroyed daily.

From those who were captured in the city of Bacachula [sic], and especially from that wounded captain, I learnt in great detail of all that had happened in the great city of Temixtitan, and how, after the death of Mutezuma, a brother of his, called Cuetravacin,[114] lord of the city of Yztapalapa, had inherited the land because Mutezuma's son and heir had been killed on the bridges;[115] of his other two sons they said that one was mad and the other palsied. For these reasons the brother succeeded him, and also because he had made war on us and they held him to be a wise and valiant man. I learnt also how they were fortifying that city and all the others in the land and had built many walls and earthworks and trenches and every type of weapon. I learnt above all how they had made long lances like pikes for the horses, and indeed we have already seen some of these, because in the province of Tepeaca we found some with which they had been fighting; and in the houses where the Culuans had been quartered in Buacachula we likewise found many of them. Many other things I learnt besides but will not mention them lest I bore Your Majesty.

I sent to the island of Hispaniola four ships to bring at once horses and men to aid us; and likewise from Hispaniola and the city of Santo Domingo horses, arms, crossbows and powder, for those are what we most require in this country, for the foot soldiers with bucklers can do very little alone, as the enemy are so numerous and have such great and strong cities and fortresses. I have also written to the licenciado Rodrigo de Figueroa and to Your Highness's officials who reside on that island asking them to give all the help they can. For it will be a great service to Your Majesty and to the security of our persons, since I intend, as soon as such help arrives, to return to that country and its great city, and I believe, as I have already told Your Majesty, that it will shortly be restored to the state in which I held it before, and thus all our past losses shall be made good.

Meanwhile I am building twelve brigantines with which to cross the lake, and already the decks and other parts are being constructed, so that they may be carried overland in pieces and swiftly assembled on arrival. Likewise nails, pitch, tow, oars and sails and other essential things are being made. I assure Your Majesty that until I have achieved this I shall not rest, nor leave untried any way or means open to me, ignoring all the hardships, danger and expense that this may cost me.

Three days or so ago I learnt in a letter from the lieutenant[116] whom I had left at Vera Cruz how there had arrived at the port a small caravel with some thirty sailors and soldiers aboard, who said that they had come in search of the people whom Francisco de Garay had sent to this land and about whom I have already given Your Highness an account. They had arrived in great want of provisions, so much so indeed that had they not found help there they would have died of hunger and thirst. From them I learnt how they reached the Pánuco River and anchored there for thirty days during which time they saw no one on land or on the river; and from this we believe that the people have abandoned the land because of what happened. The men from this caravel also said that two other ships belonging to Francisco de Garay were to have followed them with men and horses, but were thought to have sailed on down the coast. It seemed to me therefore to be in Your Highness's service, in order that the ships and their passengers might not be lost, to send that caravel in search of them, to warn them of all that had happened, for, being ignorant of this land, they might receive greater harm from the natives than the first party, and once they had found them to bring them to Vera Cruz, where the first captain sent by Francisco de Garay awaited them. I pray to God that they may be found before they land, because, as the natives are already prepared and the Spaniards are not, I fear they may be much harmed, and this would be a great disservice to the Lord our God and Your Highness; because it would enrage those curs still further and give them the courage and daring to attack those who may follow after.

In a previous chapter I told how I had learnt that, on the death of Mutezuma, Cuetravacin, his brother, had become lord and had stored up all manner of arms and fortified the great city and others by the lake. And a little while ago, I learnt how he has sent word throughout all the provinces and cities in his domain that he will grant his vassals exemption for one year from all tributes and services they are obliged to render him, provided that they, by every possible means, wage very savage war on the Christians until they are all killed or driven from the land; and to do likewise with all the natives who are our friends and allies. Although I trust in the Lord God that in nothing will they achieve their purpose, I find myself in great need of help, for each day the Indians who are our friends come from many cities and towns and villages to seek our aid against the Culuans, their enemies and ours, who make war on them because they are our allies, and I am unable to help them as I desire. But, as I have said, I pray to God to assist our small forces and speedily to send us His help as well as that I have asked for from Hispaniola.

From all I have seen and understood touching the similarity between this land and that of Spain, in its fertility and great size and the cold and many other things, it seemed to me that the most suitable name for it was New Spain of the Ocean Sea,[117] and so in Your Majesty's name I called it that. I humbly entreat Your Highness to look favorably on this and order it to be so called.

I have written to Your Majesty, although in poor style, the truth about all that has happened in these parts and all that is most necessary for Your Highness to know. And in another letter which I send with this one, I beg Your Royal Excellency to send a trustworthy person to make an examination and inquiry of everything and to inform Your Sacred Majesty thereof. In this report I likewise humbly entreat the same, for I would hold such a singular favor as giving entire credit to all I say.

Very High and Most Excellent Prince, may Our Lord God preserve for very many years the life and Very Royal Person and Most Powerful Estate of Your Sacred Majesty and grant You the increase of much greater Kingdoms and Dominions, as Your Royal heart so desires. From the town of Segura de la Frontera in New Spain on the thirtieth day of October, 1520. From Your Sacred Majesty's very humble servant and vassal, who kisses the Very Royal feet and hands of Your Highness—FERNÁN CORTÉS.[118]

After this, there came on the first of the month of the March past news from New Spain, of how the Spaniards had taken by storm the great city of Temixtitan, in which there had died more Indians than Jews in Jerusalem during the destruction of that city by Vespasian and, even so, there were more people in it than in the Holy City. They found little treasure because the natives had thrown it deep in the water; in all only 200,000 pesos de oro were taken. But the Spaniards, of whom there are at present fifteen hundred foot soldiers and five hundred horsemen, are very well fortified in that city, and they have more than a hundred thousand Indian allies in the countryside.

These are great and wonderful things and it is without doubt like another world, which we who live beyond are most envious merely to see. This news is all that we here have for certain up to the beginning of April, 1522.[119]

The Third Letter

Sent by Fernando Cortés, Captain and Chief Justice of Yucatán, called New Spain of the Ocean Sea, to the Most High and Powerful Caesar and Invincible Lord, Don Carlos, Ever August Emperor and King of Spain, Our Sovereign Lord.

Concerning the very remarkable things which took place during the reconquest of the very great and marvelous city of Temixtitan and of the other provinces subject thereto which had rebelled. In which city and provinces the aforementioned captain and the Spaniards achieved great and notable victories worthy of perpetual memory. Likewise he relates how he discovered the South Sea and many more great provinces, very rich in gold and pearls and precious stones; and how he has even heard tell that there are spices.

Most high and powerful prince, most catholic and invincible emperor, king and sovereign:

With Alonso de Mendoza, a native of Medellín whom I dis-

patched from New Spain on the fifth of March of last year, 1521, I
sent a second report to Your Majesty of all that had happened here;
which report I completed on the thirtieth of October, 1520. But on
account of bad weather and the loss of three ships, one of which
was to have carried the aforementioned report to Your Majesty,
and the other two I wished to send to Hispaniola for help, the
aforementioned Mendoza's departure was much delayed, as I explained at length to Your Majesty in a letter which was also sent
with him. Toward the end of this same report I informed Your
Majesty how, after the Indians of Temixtitan had driven us from the
city by force, I had come upon the province of Tepeaca, which was
subject to Temixtitan which had rebelled, and with the remaining
Spaniards and our Indian allies I had made war upon it and had
brought it to the service of Your Majesty; and how I said that as
the past treachery and the great harm we had been done, and the
death of the Spaniards were so recent in our hearts, I had determined to return against the people of that great city which had
been the cause of all our misfortune. For this purpose I had begun
to build thirteen brigantines to do them every possible damage from
the lake if they persisted in their evil intent. I wrote to Your Majesty
that while the aforementioned brigantines were being built, and I
and our Indian allies were fitting ourselves out to return against the
enemy, I wrote to Your Majesty's officials who reside in the island
of Hispaniola for supplies of men, horses, artillery and arms and
sent sufficient money to cover the cost. I assured Your Majesty that
until I had triumphed over my enemies I would not rest nor cease to
direct my every effort toward that end, putting aside whatever
dangers, hardships and expense I might have to face; and that, so
determined, I was preparing to depart from the aforementioned
province of Tepeaca.

    I likewise informed Your Majesty how a caravel from Fran-
cisco de Garay, lieutenant governor of the island of Jamaica, had
arrived in the port of Vera Cruz, in great need of help, with some
thirty men on board, who said that two other ships had left for the

Pánuco River, where one of Garay's captains had been routed, and it was feared that if they put into the river they too would be attacked by the natives. I also wrote to Your Majesty that I had sent a caravel in search of those two ships to warn them of all that had happened. After I had written this it pleased God that one of these ships, in which there was a captain with some 120 men, should arrive at Vera Cruz, where they were informed of how Garay's men who had come previously had been defeated. They spoke with the captain who had been defeated, and he assured them that if they went to the river it was almost certain they would be much harmed by the Indians. And while they were in the port, still resolved to go to that river, a storm blew up which drove the ship out to sea, breaking the rigging and then driving them into a port which is called Sant Juan, twelve leagues further up the coast. There, after having disembarked all the men, and the seven or eight horses and as many mares which they had brought with them, they beached the ship because it was leaking badly. When I was informed of this, I wrote to the captain telling him how sorry I was at what had befallen him, and that I had given orders to my lieutenant in Vera Cruz to make him and his men welcome, to give them whatever they might require, and to ascertain what they now intended to do; and, furthermore, if all or some of them wished to return in the ships which were anchored there, to grant them leave and send them on their way as they wished. But the captain and those who came with him resolved to join me; of the other ship we have heard nothing, and as so much time has passed we hold little hope of its safety. I pray God that it may have reached a good harbor.

As I was about to depart from that province of Tepeaca, I learnt how two provinces, which are called Cacatamy and Xalaçingo[1] and are subject to the lord of Temixtitan, had rebelled and

14. Title page to Letter III from the Latin translation of Cortés letters published in Nuremburg in 1524. *Courtesy of the Britis Museum.*

Tertia Ferdinãdi Cor

tesii Sac. Caesar. et Cath. Maiesta.
IN NOVA MARIS OCEANI HYSPANIA GENE-
ralis præfecti p̃clara Natratio, In qua Celebris Ciuitatis Temix
titan expugnatio, aliarũcp Prouintiarũ, quę defecerant recupe-
ratio continetur, In quarũ expugnatione, recuperationecp Præfe
ctus, una cum Hyspanis Victorias œterna memoria dignas con
sequutus est, p̃terea In ea Mare del Sur Cortesium detexisse re-
cẽfeʃ, quod nos Australe Indicũ Pelagus putam9, & alias innume
ras Prouintias Aurifodinis, Vnionibus, Variiscp Gemmarum
generibus refertas. Et poʃtremo illis innotuisse in eis quocp Aro
matac ontineri, Per Doctorẽ Petrum Sauorgnanũ Foroiuliensem
Reueñ. in Christopatris dñi Io. de Reuelles Episcopi Viẽensis
Secretarium Ex Hyspano ydiomate In Latinum Versa.

had killed some Spaniards on the road between here and Vera Cruz, which passes through there. Thus, to ensure the safety of that road and to punish those Indians in some manner if they refused to submit peaceably, I sent a captain with twenty horsemen and two hundred foot soldiers and some of our allies; and I charged this captain and commanded him in Your Majesty's name to require the natives of those provinces to come in peace and offer themselves as Your Majesty's vassals, as they had done before; and to be as mild with them as possible; but if they would not receive him in peace to make war on them. And once this had been done and those two provinces were subdued, I told him to return with all his company to the city of Tascalteca where I would await him. He departed at the beginning of the month of December, 1520, and proceeded to the aforementioned provinces which are twenty leagues hence.

Having completed this, Most Powerful Lord, I departed from the town of Segura [de] la Frontera, which is in the province of Tepeaca, in mid-December of the same year, leaving behind a captain[2] with sixty men because the inhabitants begged it of me. I sent all the foot soldiers to the city of Tascalteca, where the brigantines are being built, which is some nine or ten leagues from Tepeaca, while I, with twenty horsemen, went that day to spend the night in the city of Cholula, for the inhabitants desired my presence, as many of their lords had died of the smallpox, which also affects those of the mainland as it does the islanders; and they wished me to appoint new ones on their advice. When we arrived we were very well received by them. And after we had concluded this business to their satisfaction, I informed them that I intended to go in arms against the province of Mexico and Temixtitan and asked them, as they were Your Majesty's vassals, to stand fast in their friendship with us until death, as we would with them. I therefore requested them to provide me with men for the war when the time came, and to welcome and treat the Spaniards who came and went through their lands as friends are bound to do; and they promised to do so.

I remained with them two or three days and then left for the city of Tascalteca, which is six leagues from there; when I arrived all the Spaniards and the inhabitants of the city were very pleased to see me. On the following day all the chiefs of that city and province came to speak with me and told me how Magiscacin, who was their overlord, had died of the smallpox; they knew well how much this would grieve me, as he was a great friend of mine. There remained, however, a son of his who was twelve or thirteen years of age, and it was to him that his father's dominion now belonged; they entreated me, therefore, to recognize him as heir; and I did so in Your Majesty's name, and they were all very gratified.

When I arrived in this city I found that the craftsmen and carpenters working on the brigantines were making great haste to complete the crossbeams and the planking and had achieved much of the work. I then sent to Vera Cruz for all the iron and nails they had, and also for sails and rigging and other necessary things, and as we had no pitch I had certain Spaniards make it on a hill close by. All the equipment for the brigantines was thus made ready so that when, God willing, I arrived in the province of Mexico and Temixtitan I might send for them from there, a distance of some ten or twelve leagues from the city of Tascalteca. And during the fifteen days I remained in that city I concerned myself only with urging on the carpenters and with preparing arms for our journey.

Two days before Christmas the captain who had gone to the provinces of Cacatamy and Xalaçingo returned with the horsemen and foot soldiers. I learnt how certain of the Indians had fought with him but that in the end they had all sued for peace, some willingly, some by force. He also brought me several of the lords of those provinces whom, although they clearly deserved punishment for rebellion and causing the death of Christians, I pardoned in Your Royal name and sent back to their lands, for they promised that from then on they would serve Your Majesty as loyal and true vassals. Thus this task was ended and Your Majesty was well served, for not only were the natives of this province pacified, but also the safety of the Spaniards who had to pass that way to the town of Vera Cruz was assured.

Two days after Christmas I reviewed my company in the aforementioned city of Tascalteca; there were forty horsemen and 550 foot soldiers, eighty of whom were crossbowmen and harquebusiers; and there were eight or nine field guns but very little powder. I formed the horsemen into four troops of ten, and of the foot soldiers made nine companies of sixty men each. When they had all assembled on parade I addressed them and told them that they already knew how they and I had, in Your Sacred Majesty's service, settled in this land and how the inhabitants thereof had offered themselves as Your Majesty's vassals, and had remained as such for some time, receiving many benefits from us and we from them. Likewise I reminded them how, for no good reason, all the natives of Culua, that is, those from the great city of Temixtitan, and those from all the other provinces which are subject thereto, had not only rebelled against Your Majesty, but moreover had killed many men who were our friends and kinsmen and had driven us from their land. I urged them to remember the dangers and hardships we had undergone, and to consider how much it would benefit the service of God and Your Majesty if we were to return and recover all that had been lost, for we had just cause and good reason for it. First, because we were fighting against a barbarian people to spread our Faith; second, in order to serve Your Majesty; third, we had to protect our lives; and, last, many of the natives were our allies and would assist. All of which were very powerful reasons why we should be strong in heart: I therefore urged them to be joyful and courageous. In Your Majesty's name I had drawn up certain ordinances for good government and other matters[3] concerning war which I then had publicly announced. I likewise urged them to abide by these ordinances, for they would render a great service to God and Your Majesty by so doing. They all promised to do so, declaring that they would very gladly die for our Faith, and in Your Majesty's service, or recover all we had lost and avenge the great treachery which the people of Temixtitan and their allies had perpetrated against us. I thanked them in Your Majesty's name, and we all returned to our quarters in high spirits.

On the following day, which was the feast of St. John the Evangelist, I called together all the lords of the province of Tascalteca, and when they were assembled told them that, as they knew, I was to leave the next day for the land of our enemies, and that they had seen how the city of Temixtitan could not be won without those brigantines which were being built there; so I asked them to give the carpenters and all the other Spaniards whom I left there all they might require, and to treat them as well as they had always treated us. I asked them also to be ready for when I sent from the city of Tesuico, if God should grant us victory, for the crossbeams and planking, and for the other equipment of those brigantines. This they promised to do, and furthermore said they wished to send some warriors with me, declaring that once the brigantines were finished they would all go, for they wanted to die where I died, or be revenged on the people of Culua, their mortal enemies. And so, on the following day, which was the twenty-eighth of December, the Feast of the Innocents, I departed with my company in good array, and we put up for the night six leagues from Tascalteca in a village called Tezmoluca,[4] which lies in the province of Guasucingo, and whose inhabitants have always maintained their friendship and alliance with us like the people of Tascalteca; we slept there that night.

Most Catholic Lord, in the earlier account I said that I had learnt that the people of the province of Mexico and Temixtitan were storing up arms and building walls and earthworks and forts to prevent us from entering their lands, for they knew now that I intended to return against them. And I, knowing this and knowing also how cunning and astute they are in war, had often considered how we might invade and attack them relatively unprepared; for they knew that we had been informed of the three roads by which we might enter their land. I therefore determined to go by way of Tezmoluca, as the pass there was steeper and rougher than the others, and we would, no doubt, encounter little resistance and find them unprepared.

Thus on the day after the Feast of the Innocents, having heard Mass and commended ourselves to God, we left that village of Tezmoluca; I led the vanguard with ten horsemen and sixty lightly armed foot soldiers, all skilled in battle. We followed the road up the pass in the best order we could and spent the night four leagues from the above-mentioned village, on top of the pass and already on the border with Culua. Although it was very cold, we managed to warm ourselves with the great quantity of firewood we found there; and on the following morning, which was a Sunday, we began to descend to the plain. I sent four horsemen and three or four foot soldiers on ahead to spy out the land, and then, as we were leaving the pass, I ordered the rest of the horsemen to advance, then the harquebusiers and crossbowmen, and finally the others, for no matter how unprepared we might find the enemy, they were certain to set an ambush or some other trap to attack us on the road. As the four horsemen and the foot soldiers proceeded on their journey, they found the road blocked with trees and branches; very large and thick pine and cypress trees, which seemed to have been cut very recently, had been felled across it. Thinking that the road ahead would not be so obstructed, they continued, but the farther they went the more they found it obstructed with pine trees and branches. As, in addition to this, the path was lined on both sides with very dense trees and large bushes, they proceeded with great difficulty. When they saw how the road was, they were greatly alarmed and imagined that the enemy was hidden behind every tree. Because of these dense woods they were unable to make use of the horses, and the farther they went the more afraid they became.

When they had gone for some while in this fashion, one of the four horsemen said to his companions: "Brothers, if you agree, let us go no further, but return to our captain and inform him of the obstruction we have encountered and the great danger in which we all find ourselves because we are unable to use the horses; if, however, you do not agree to this proposal, let us proceed, for I am as willing as you to surrender my life to accomplish our task." The others replied that although they thought his advice sound they did not think it a good idea to return until they had sighted the enemy, or discovered how far the road continued in that manner. So they began to proceed, but, when they saw that it continued for a long way, they halted and sent one of the foot soldiers to inform me of what they had seen. When I came up with the vanguard, we continued on that bad road, commending ourselves to God, and I sent word to the rear guard urging them to make haste and not to be afraid, for soon we would reach open ground. I caught up with the four horsemen, and we went on together, although with great difficulty, and after half a league it pleased God that we should begin to descend across open ground. There I halted to wait for the others, and when they arrived I told them to give thanks to Our Lord for having carried us that far in safety. From there we could see before us the province of Mexico and Temixtitan, which lies in the lakes and by their shore. Although we were greatly pleased to see it, recollecting how much harm we had suffered there, we were somewhat sad and all swore never to leave that province alive if we did not do so victorious. And with this resolution we moved on as joyfully as if we were on an outing. The enemy, who had already observed us, now suddenly began to send up great smoke signals all over the land; and I begged and entreated the Spaniards again to do as they had always done, and as was expected of them; no one should leave the path, but all should keep together and in formation on the road.

Already the Indians were shouting at us from some nearby farms and villages, calling on all the people of the land to unite and attack us at some bridges and narrow stretches which lay ahead. We made such haste, however, that we had reached the plain before they had time to gather their forces. Then certain troops of Indians came out to meet us on the road, and I ordered fifteen horsemen to break through them; this they did, spearing some of them without receiving any hurt. Then we continued on our way toward Tesuico, which is one of the largest and most beautiful cities in these parts; but as the foot soldiers were somewhat tired and it was getting late we slept in a village called Coatepeque,[5] which is subject to Tesuico and three leagues away from it; we found it deserted. That night it occurred to us that as the city and its province, which is called Aculuacán, is very large and thickly populated, there might well be at that time more than 150,000 men waiting to fall on us, so I, with ten horsemen, took the first watch and ordered all the men to be well prepared.

On the following day, Monday, the last day of December, we continued on our journey in the usual order, and a quarter of a league from that village of Coatepeque, while we were all wondering and discussing amongst ourselves whether the people of Tesuico would come in war or peace, believing that war was more likely, there came toward us four Indian chieftains with a flag of gold, which weighed some four gold marks, on a pole, and by this they gave us to understand that they came in peace; God knows how much we desired and needed peace, being, as we were, so few, so far from help and so deep into the land of the enemy. When I saw those four Indians, one of whom I knew, I halted my men, and went toward them. After we had greeted each other they told me that they had come on behalf of the lord of that city and province, who is called Guanacacin,[6] and begged me, on his behalf, to do no damage in their land nor to countenance any, for the people of Temixtitan, not they, were responsible for the hurt I had suffered previously. They wished to be Your Majesty's vassals and our friends, as they would always preserve our friendship; they asked us to enter their city, where we might judge their sincerity by their deeds.

I welcomed them through the interpreters and replied that I welcomed their offer of peace and friendship, but, though they sought to exculpate themselves from the war which had been made on me in Temixtitan, they well knew that in certain of their subject villages five or six leagues from the city of Tesuico they had killed five horsemen and forty-five foot soldiers, and more than three hundred Indians from Tascalteca who were carrying much gold and silver and clothing and other things, all of which they had taken. As they could not therefore excuse themselves from all blame, their punishment would be to return what belonged to us, and if they did so, although they all deserved to die for having killed so many Christians, I would make peace with them because they begged me to do so. But if they did not, I would proceed against them with all severity. They answered that the lord and chieftains of Temixtitan had taken everything they had stolen, but that they would search for all they could find and return it to me. They then asked me if I was going that day to the city or would camp in one of the two villages called Coatinchan and Guaxuta.[7] which are like suburbs to the city, and lie a league and a half from it, though the space between is all built up; this it later appeared was what they wished me to do. I told them in reply that I would not stop until I had reached Tesuico; they agreed to this and said that they would go on ahead to prepare quarters for the Spaniards and myself; and so they departed. When we reached the aforementioned villages some of their chieftains came out to meet us and brought us food; and at midday we reached the center of the city, where we were to be quartered in a large house which had belonged to the father of Guanacacin, chieftain of the city. But before we settled in I called together all my people and commanded them, under pain of death, not to leave the house without my permission. The house was so large that had we Spaniards been twice as many we could still have put up there very comfortably. I did this so that the natives might be reassured and return to their homes, for it seemed to me that we had not seen a tenth of the people who are normally to be found in the city, nor any women or children, which was a rather alarming sign.

The day we entered this city, which was New Year's Eve, we arranged our quarters, and although we were still somewhat perturbed at seeing so few people, and those whom we did see very well wrapped up, we suspected that it was out of fear that they did not appear on the streets, and this relieved us somewhat. Toward sunset, certain Spaniards climbed onto some high roofs from where they could survey the whole city, and they saw how all the natives were leaving; some, with their possessions, were going out into the lake in canoes, which they call *acales*, and some up into the mountains. Although I immediately ordered their flight to be halted, it was already so late that night soon fell, and they made such haste that we could not prevent them. Thus the chief of the city, whom I dearly wished to have in my power, escaped with many of the chieftains and all their belongings to the city of Temixtitan, which is six leagues away across the lake. For this reason, to carry out their plans in safety, those messengers whom I mentioned above came to meet me, hoping to detain me awhile so I should do them no harm; later that night they abandoned us, and their city also.

We remained in the city for three days, without any encounter with the Indians, for they dared not come to meet us nor were we disposed to go far in search of them, for my considered intention was always, when they wished it, to receive them in peace, and always to require it of them. At this time the lords of Coatynchan and Guaxuta and Autengo,[8] which are three large villages near to the city and, as I have said, incorporated and joined with it, came to speak to me; and, weeping, they begged me to forgive them for abandoning their land, but said that for the rest they had not fought against me or at least not willingly, and from now on would do all I commanded them in Your Majesty's name. I replied through the interpreters that they knew how well we had always treated them and that in leaving their land and everything else they were to blame; and so if they wished to be our friends they must return to their homes and bring also their women and children, for we would treat them according to their actions. And so they departed not much pleased, as it seemed to us.

When the lord of Mexico and Temixtitan and all the other lords of Culua (for the name Culua comprises all the lands and provinces in this region subject to Temixtitan) heard that the lords of those villages had come to offer themselves as Your Majesty's vassals, they sent some messengers to tell them that they had behaved very badly; and if they had done this through fear, they should have been well aware that they were many and had such strength that they must very soon kill me and the Spaniards and all the Indians of Tascalteca; and that if they had done it so as not to have to leave their lands, they should indeed leave them and go to Temixtitan, where they would be given bigger and better villages to live in.

These lords of Coatinchan and Guaxuta seized these messengers and bound them and brought them to me. They confessed that they had come on behalf of the lords of Temixtitan, but it was only to persuade those chieftains, as they were my friends, to go to the capital as mediators, to negotiate peace terms between us. This the chiefs of Guaxuta and Coatinchan denied, saying that the lords of México and Temixtitan wanted nothing but war, and although I believed them—and what they said was indeed the truth—because I wished to persuade the people of Tesuico to become our friends, because on that depended whether we had peace or war with the other provinces which were in revolt, I freed these messengers and told them not to be afraid, for I would send them back to Temixtitan. I begged them to tell their lord that, although I had every reason to do so, I did not wish to fight them, but to be their friend as I had been once before. And so as to assure them further and bring them to the service of Your Majesty, I sent to say that I was well aware that the chieftains who had made war on me before were now dead, and that the past should be forgotten, and they should not give me cause to destroy their lands and cities, for I would be very sorry to have to do so. With this I freed the messengers and they departed promising to bring me an answer. The lords of Coatinchan and Guaxuta and I were by this good deed more closely united, and I, in Your Majesty's name, forgave them their past misdeeds, and thus they were satisfied.

After having remained in this city of Tesuico seven or eight days without any disturbance or conflict with the inhabitants, during which time we fortified our quarters and prepared other things necessary for our defense and for attacking the enemy, I saw that they were not going to take the offensive and left the aforementioned city with two hundred Spaniards, among whom were eighteen horsemen, thirty crossbowmen and ten harquebusiers, together with three or four thousand of our Indian allies.[9] I marched along the lake shore to a city called Yztapalapa, which by water is two leagues from Temixtitan and six from Tesuico; it has some ten thousand inhabitants and half, or perhaps even two-thirds of it, is built over the water.

The lord of the city, who was Mutezuma's brother, had, after his brother's death, been made king by the Indians, and was the chieftain most to blame for making war on us and driving us from the great city. For this reason, and because I had heard that the inhabitants of Yztapalapa were ill-disposed toward us, I determined to march against them. When they saw me more than two leagues from the city some came out into the fields and others appeared on the lake in canoes. Thus for two leagues we struggled both with those on land and those who landed from the canoes until we reached the city. They then opened a causeway some two-thirds of a league outside the city, which served as a dike between the salt and fresh-water lakes, as Your Majesty may have seen from the map of Temixtitan which I sent. When this dike was opened the salt water began to flow into the fresh with tremendous force, although the lakes are more than half a league apart. We were so eager for victory we did not notice this subterfuge and passed on until, still fighting with the enemy, we entered the city. As the inhabitants had already been alerted, all the houses on the land had been abandoned and the people with their belongings had taken refuge in the houses over the lake; and there all those who had fled rallied and fought with us very fiercely. But Our Lord gave so much strength to His own that we drove them back into the water, some up to their chests and others swimming, and we took many of the houses on the water. More than six thousand of them, men, women and children, perished that day, for our Indian allies, when they saw the victory which God had given us, had no other thought but to kill, right and left.

Because it was now growing dark, I collected my men together and set fire to some of those houses; and while they were burning it seemed that Our Lord inspired me and brought to my memory that causeway or dike we had seen broken, and revealed to me the great danger we were in. So I left the city as swiftly as possible with all my men, although it was now quite dark. When I reached the water, which must have been at about nine o'clock, it was so deep and it flowed with such force that we had to leap across it; some of our Indian allies were drowned, and we lost all the spoil we had taken in the city. I assure Your Majesty that if that night we had not crossed the water, or had waited but three hours more, none of us would have escaped, for we would have been surrounded by water with no means of escape.

When day broke we saw that the water from the one lake was level with that of the other and flowed no more; the salt lake was full of warriors in canoes expecting to seize us there. I returned that day to Tesuico, fighting at times with some who landed from the lake, although we could do them little harm, for they retreated immediately to their canoes. When I reached Tesuico I found the people I had left there quite safe, having had no encounters at all with the enemy; and they were greatly pleased by our return and the news of our victory. The day after we returned, a Spaniard who had been wounded died, and he was the first of my company to be killed by the Indians on this campaign.

On the following day there came to this city several messengers from the city of Otumba and four other cities which are near it: these cities are five or six leagues from Tesuico. These messengers entreated me to pardon them for the part they had played in the past war, because Otumba was the place where all the forces of Mexico and Temixtitan had gathered when we were fleeing the city, intending to put an end to us. These people of Otumba well knew that they could not avoid blame, although they excused themselves by saying that they had been under orders; but in order to incline me to leniency they told me how the chiefs of Temixtitan had sent messengers to persuade them to join their cause and to make no alliance with us because, if they did so, they would be destroyed. They said, however, that they would rather be Your Majesty's vassals and obey my commands. I told them in reply that they were well aware how much they were to blame for what had happened, and before I would pardon them or believe what they said, they must bring those messengers to me as captives and all the other natives of Mexico and Temixtitan who were in their land; otherwise I would not pardon them. I told them to return to their homes and show me by their deeds that they were Your Majesty's true vassals. Although we argued at length, they could extract nothing from me, and so they returned to their land, assuring me that they would in future do all that I commanded them, and from then on they have been loyal and obedient to Your Majesty's service.

Most Fortunate and Excellent Prince, as I told Your Majesty in the second report, when we were defeated and driven from the city of Temixtitan, I took with me one son and two daughters of Mutezuma, together with the lord of Tesuico, who was called Cacamacin, two of his brothers and many other chiefs whom I held captive, and all of them had been killed by the enemy (although

they were all of the same race, and some of them were their chiefs)
except the two brothers of Cacamacin, who by great good fortune
were able to escape. One of these brothers, called Ypacsuchyl, or by
another name Cucascacin,[10] whom I, in Your Majesty's name and
with Mutezuma's accord, had made lord of that city of Tesuico and
of the province of Aculuacán, had escaped from captivity at the
time of my arrival in Tascalteca, and returned to the aforementioned city of Tesuico. But as another of his brothers, called Guanacacin, of whom I have spoken earlier, had been chosen as chief,
this brother had Cucascacin killed in the following manner: When
he arrived in the province of Tesuico he was seized by the guards
who informed their lord, Guanacacin, who likewise informed the
lord of Temixtitan, who, unable to believe that Cucascacin could
have escaped from us, thought that he must be acting on our behalf
to give us information about what was happening in that province.
He therefore ordered the aforementioned Guanacacin to kill his
brother, and he obeyed at once. Guanacacin, the youngest of the
brothers, stayed with me, and, as he was only a boy, our conversation made a greater impression on him and he became a Christian,
and we gave him the name of Don Fernando. When I departed
from the province of Tascalteca for Mexico and Temixtitan I left
him behind with certain Spaniards; and I shall relate hereafter to
Your Majesty what happened to him afterwards.[11]

On the day following my arrival in Tesuico from the city of
Yztapalapa, I resolved to send Gonzalo de Sandoval, Your Majesty's
alguacil mayor, as captain of twenty horsemen and two hundred
foot soldiers, among whom were crossbowmen, harquebusiers and
bucklers, for two very necessary purposes: first, to escort from this
province certain messengers whom I was sending to Tascalteca to
discover in what state the thirteen brigantines were which were being built there, and to provide for other things which both the
people of the town of Vera Cruz and those of my company required; second, to make safe that region so the Spaniards might
come and go in safety, for until then neither could we leave this

province of Aculuacán without passing through enemy land, nor could the Spaniards in Vera Cruz and other places come to us without being in great danger of attack. I commanded the aforementioned alguacil mayor that, once he had conducted the messengers to safety, he was to go to a province which is called Calco and borders on this of Aculuacán, for I had been assured that the natives thereof, although of the league of Culua, wished to offer themselves as Your Majesty's vassals but had not dared do so by reason of a garrison which had been stationed near them by the Culuans.

This captain then departed, taking with him all the Indians of Tascalteca who had carried our baggage, and others who had come to help us and had gained some spoils from the fighting. These Indians went some way ahead, for the captain believed that, as the Spaniards were marching in the rear, the enemy would not dare attack; but when the inhabitants of the towns and villages on the lake and by the lake shore saw them, they fell on the rear of the Tascaltecans and robbed them of their spoils, even killing some. But when the captain arrived with the horsemen and the foot soldiers he attacked them fiercely and many were speared and killed; and those who remained were routed and fled into the water and to villages nearby. The Indians of Tascalteca, accompanied by my messengers, returned to their country with all that they had left. Once they had all reached safety, Gonzalo de Sandoval continued his journey to the province of Calco, which is close by there. Early on the following morning a large number of the enemy gathered to do battle with the Spaniards; and once they were both in the field our men opened the attack and the horsemen routed two of their squadrons so that they soon fled the field, and the Spaniards pursued them killing and burning. When this was done and the road cleared, the people of Calco came out to welcome the Spaniards and both sides welcomed each other.

The lords said that they wished to come and see me; so they left and came to spend the night at Tesuico. When they arrived they came before me accompanied by two sons of the chief of Calco, who gave me some three hundred pesos de oro and told me that their father had died, and how at the time of his death he had told them that the greatest grief he had to bear was that of not having seen me before he died, for he had been expecting me for many days. He had commanded them to visit me as soon as I arrived in this province and to look upon me as their father. So when they heard that I was in the city of Tesuico, they had wished to come and see me but had not dared do so for fear of the Culuans. Nor would they now have dared had the captain I sent not arrived in their land, and, they added, I would have to send many Spaniards with them when they returned to ensure that they arrived in safety. They said that I well knew how they had never been against me either in battle or otherwise, and that I also knew how, when the Culuans were attacking our quarters in Temixtitan and the Spaniards I had left there when I went to Cempoal to see Narváez, there were two Spaniards in their land guarding some maize which I had sent them to collect. They had taken these Spaniards to the province of Guaxoc[a]ngo, since they knew that the people of that province were our friends, to save them from being killed, as the Culuans had killed all the Spaniards they found outside Temixtitan. They told me this and many other things, weeping all the while, and I thanked them for their loyalty and their good deeds, promising that I would do always as they wished and that they would be very well treated. They have always until now shown great goodwill, and have been most obedient to all that I, in Your Majesty's name, have commanded them.

These sons of the lord of Calco and those who had come with them remained with me for one day, and then told me that they wished to return to their land and asked me to give them some of my people to conduct them in safety. Gonzalo de Sandoval, with several horsemen and foot soldiers, escorted them, with orders that, once he had taken them to their land, he should thence proceed to the province of Tascalteca, and bring back with him certain Spaniards who were there, and Don Fernando, brother of Cacamacin, whom I have already mentioned. After four or five days this alguacil mayor returned, bringing the Spaniards and Don Fernando with him. A few days later I discovered that as he was a brother of the lords of this city the sovereignty belonged to him, although there were other brothers. For this reason, and also because the province was without a ruler, for Guanacacin, his brother, had left it and gone to Temixtitan, and, moreover, because Don Fernando was a very good friend of the Christians, I, in Your Majesty's name, ordered that he should be acknowledged as the lord. The inhabitants of the city, although at that time there were few present, did so, and from thenceforth obeyed him. Many of the people who had fled now began to return to the city and province of Aculuacán, and they also obeyed and served Don Fernando; from then on the city began to be rebuilt and reinhabited.

Two days after this the lords of Coatinchán and Guaxuta came to me and said that they knew for certain that all the forces of Culua were proceeding against the Spaniards and the land was full of the enemy. They asked if they should bring their women and children to where I was or should take them into the mountains, because they were very much afraid. But I encouraged them, and told them not to be afraid and to remain where they were in their houses, for I desired nothing so much as to meet the Culuans on the field. I told them to be watchful and send spies and scouts out all over the land; and once they knew the enemy was coming to advise me. Thus they departed much concerned with my orders. That night I alerted my men and positioned watchmen and sentries in every place where it was necessary; we did not sleep at all that night, nor think of anything save the matter in hand. Thus, believing what we had been told by those lords of Guaxuta and Coatinchán, we waited all that night and the following day. The day after, I learnt how some of the enemy were moving along the lake shore, making surprise attacks and hoping to seize some Indians from Tascalteca who fetched and carried things for the camp. I learnt also how they had been joined by two towns, subjects of Tesuico, which were close by the water's edge, whence they would do us all the harm they were able. They had barricaded themselves in with ditches and earthworks and other things for their defense. After I heard this I set out on the following day with twelve horsemen, two hundred foot soldiers and two small field guns, and rode to the place where they were camped, which lay about a league and a half from the city. As I was leaving, I came across certain scouts and others of the enemy who were waiting to attack, and we scattered them, killing some in the pursuit, while the rest fled into the water. We then burnt a part of those towns and returned to the camp very pleased with our victory.

On the following day three chieftains from those towns came begging my forgiveness for what had happened and asking me to destroy nothing more, for they promised that they would never again receive anyone from Temixtitan. And because these were men of little consequence, and vassals of Don Fernando, I pardoned them in Your Majesty's name. Then, on the following day, several Indians from those towns came to me, injured and ill-treated, saying that when the people of Mexico had returned to their town and had not received the welcome to which they were accustomed, they had turned on them and had taken some of them prisoners; and if they had not defended themselves they would all have been seized. They begged me to be well prepared, so that when the Culuans returned I might know in time to go to their relief; and so they departed home.

The people whom I had left in the province of Tascalteca to construct the brigantines received news that a ship had arrived at the port of Vera Cruz, in which there came, besides the sailors, thirty or forty Spaniards, eight horses, and some crossbows, harquebuses and powder; but as they did not know how the war was going for us, nor were certain of being able to reach me in safety, they were very anxious; and some of the Spaniards stayed there not daring to come, although they desired to bring me such good news. When a servant of mine, whom I had left there, heard that some of them wished to make an attempt to join me, he had it announced that no one, under pain of the most severe punishments, should leave until I had sent orders to do so. But one of my lads, who knew that nothing in the world would give me such pleasure as to learn of the arrival of this ship and the aid it brought, set out by night, although the road was dangerous, and came to Tesuico. We were very surprised to see him arrive safely and greatly pleased by his news, for we were in extreme need of help.[12]

That same day, Most Catholic Lord, there arrived in Tesuico several reliable messengers from the people of Calco, and they told me that on account of their having offered themselves as Your Majesty's vassals the people of Mexico and Temixtitan were intent on destroying them, and for this purpose had called together and alerted all their neighbors; they asked me to help them in such great danger, for if I did not, they expected to find themselves in the direst straits. I assure Your Majesty that, as I said in my previous letter, apart from our own hardships and privations, the greatest distress was caused us by not being able to help our Indian allies, who, for being Your Majesty's vassals, were harassed and illtreated by the Culuans, although I and my companions wished always to do our utmost in this, for we believed that in no way could we better serve Your Caesarean Majesty than in helping and supporting Your vassals. But the people of Calco found me in such circumstances that I was unable to do for them all I wished; and so I told them that as I now wanted to send for the brigantines, and for that purpose had alerted the whole province of Tascalteca, whence the parts were to come, I must send horsemen and foot soldiers for that purpose and so could spare them none of my men. I also told them, however, that as they knew the natives of Guaxocingo, Churultecal and Guacachula[13] were also Your Majesty's vassals and our allies they should go to them, for they live close by, and request them on my behalf to give them help and succor, and to garrison troops there until such time as I was able to help them, for at present I could give them no other assistance. Although they were not so content as if I had given them some Spaniards, they thanked me and begged me to give them a letter so that they might be believed, and might venture to ask in greater safety, because between Calco and the two other provinces, as they belonged to different alliances, there had been some strife.

While I was occupied in this, certain messengers happened to arrive from the aforementioned provinces of Guaxocingo and Guacachula, and in the presence of the people at Calco, they told me how they had neither seen nor heard of me since I left Tascalteca, even though they had placed lookouts on all the hills which circle their land and overlook Mexico and Temixtitan, so that, should they see many smoke signals, which are the signs of war, they might come to help me with their own people and with their vassals. And because a short while previously they had seen more smoke signals than ever before, they had come to discover how I was and if I required anything, so that they might send me their warriors. I thanked them greatly, and told them that, God be praised, the Spaniards and I were all well, and had always triumphed over the enemy; and that besides being much pleased by their presence and their goodwill, I would be still more pleased to form an alliance and bond of friendship between them and the people of Calco, who were there present; so I requested them, as both parties were Your Majesty's vassals, to become good friends, and help each other against the Culuans, who were wicked and perverse; especially now, as the people from Calco were in need of help, because the Culuans were preparing to attack them; and thus they became firm friends and allies. And after staying with me for two days, they departed well pleased, and thenceforth gave each other assistance.

Three days later, having heard that the work on the thirteen brigantines had been finished and the people who were to bring them were ready to depart, I sent Gonzalo de Sandoval, alguacil mayor, with fifteen horsemen and two hundred foot soldiers to bring them to me. I also commanded him to raze to the ground a large town,[14] subject to Tesuico, which stands on the borders of Tascalteca, because the inhabitants had killed five horsemen and forty-five foot soldiers who had been coming from Vera Cruz to Temixtitan when I had been besieged in that city, not suspecting that such a treacherous act could be perpetrated against us. When we entered Tesuico this time we had found in their temples or shrines the skins of the five horses with their hoofs and shoes, sewn up and as well tanned as anywhere in the world; and as a sign of victory they had offered these and much clothing and other things belonging to the Spaniards to their idols. Likewise we found the blood of our companions and brothers sacrificed and spilled in all those towers and temples, and it was such a pitiful sight that all our past tribulations were revived. The traitors of that town and of others in the neighborhood had received the Christians well when they passed by there, in order to make them feel secure and then inflict on them the greatest cruelty that has ever been done, for when the Spaniards were going down through a steep pass, every one on foot and leading their horses so that they were unable to use them to advantage, the Indians ambushed them from both sides of the path; some they killed and others were taken alive to Tesuico, where they were sacrificed and their hearts were torn out before the idols. This seemed to be what had happened, for when the alguacil mayor passed by there, some of the Spaniards who were with him found in a house, in a village which lies between Tesuico and the place where the Christians were killed, a white wall with these words written in charcoal: "Here the unhappy Juan Yuste was held prisoner." [15] He was one of the five horsemen. Surely a sight fit to break the hearts of all who saw it. When the alguacil mayor arrived at the town, the inhabitants, conscious of their great crime and guilt, began to flee, but the Spaniards and our Indian friends overtook them and killed many, and took many women and children as slaves. But Sandoval was moved by compassion and chose not to kill and destroy all he might have, and before he departed from there he even ordered those who survived to be led back to the town; and so now it is inhabited once again and very repentant of the past.

The alguacil mayor then proceeded five or six leagues to the town in Tascalteca which is closest to the borders of Culua, and there he met the Spaniards and the people who were bringing the brigantines. And the day after he arrived they left there with the timbers and planks, which were carried by more than eight thousand men, all in perfect array; and it was a remarkable sight to see and I think even to hear of: thirteen ships carried overland for eighteen leagues. I assure Your Majesty that there were more than two leagues from the vanguard to the rear. And when they set out there went in front eight horsemen and a hundred Spaniards, and with them and on the flanks went more than ten thousand warriors who had as their captains Yutecad and Teutipil, who are two of the principal lords of Tascalteca. In the rear guard came another hundred or so Spaniards, and with them another ten thousand men, all very well armed, who had as their captain Chichimecatecle,[16] who is one of the principal lords of that province; and he also brought with him other captains.

When they set out, this Chichimecatecle had gone in the vanguard with the deck planks, while the other two captains remained in the rear with the cross timbers. But when they passed over into Culua the masters of the brigantines ordered the cross timbers to be brought to the fore, and the deck planks to be sent behind because they were the more clumsy of the two, and if anything should happen it would happen in front. But Chichimecatecle, who went with the deck planks, and until then had always gone with his warriors in the vanguard, took this as an affront, and it was a matter of some difficulty to quieten him and persuade him to remain in the rear, for he wished to meet any danger that might present itself. When he finally agreed to this, he asked that no Spaniards should remain accompanying him, for he is a most valiant man and wished to keep all the glory for himself. These captains had brought with them two thousand Indians to carry their provisions. After proceeding in this order for three days, on the fourth they entered this city with much rejoicing and noise of drums as I went out to greet them.[17] And as I said above, there were so many people in this train that from the moment the first one had entered until the arrival of the last more than six hours passed, and not once was that long line broken. When those lords had arrived I thanked them for the good service they had done us and ordered that they be quartered and provided for as well as we were able. They told me that they wished to meet the Culuans and that I should see, when I commanded them, that they and their people were determined to avenge themselves or die with us. I thanked them but told them to rest, for soon I would be giving them plenty to do.

When all these warriors from Tascalteca, who for Indians are certainly very fine men, had rested for three or four days in Tesuico, I prepared twenty-five horsemen and three hundred foot soldiers and fifty crossbowmen and harquebusiers and six small field guns, and without telling anyone where I was going left this city at nine in the morning; and with me went the captains already mentioned, with more than thirty thousand men, all very well organized into battalions, after their fashion. When it was already late, we came upon a group of enemy warriors some four leagues from the city, but the horsemen broke through and routed them, and as the warriors of Tascalteca are very agile they followed us and together we killed many of our foes; that night we slept in the open, under careful guard.

On the following morning we continued our journey, and still I had not said where I intended to go, which I did because I distrusted some of those from Tesuico who were with us, for as yet I had no confidence in them and feared they might betray my intention to the people of Mexico and Temixtitan. We now reached a town called Xaltoca,[18] which is situated in the middle of the lake, and all around were a great many channels full of water, which made the town very strong because the horsemen could not cross them. The enemy yelled at us loudly and attacked us with darts and arrows, but the foot soldiers succeeded in entering the town, although with some difficulty, and drove them out and burnt much of the place. That night we put up a league from there. When it was light we continued on our way and soon came upon the enemy, who began to shout at us from afar as they do in war, which is truly a terrifying thing to hear. We followed them and came upon a very large and beautiful city called Goatitan;[19] this we found deserted and so slept there that night.

On the following day we moved on and came to a city called Tenayuca,[20] where we encountered no resistance whatever and then proceeded to another called Acapuzalco,[21] also by the lake shore; but we did not stop there either because I greatly wished to reach another city which is close by; this city is called Tacuba[22] and is very near to Temixtitan. When we came close to it we found that there also the enemy had dug a great number of ditches and were well prepared for our arrival. When we saw them, we and our allies attacked them, entered the city, killed some, and drove the inhabitants out. But as it was now late we did nothing more that night and lodged in a house which was so large that we were all very comfortable. At dawn our Indian allies began to sack and burn the whole city except for the house where we were quartered, and they were so diligent in this that they destroyed a quarter of it. They did this because after we had been driven from Temixtitan before, we had passed through this city, and the inhabitants, together with those of Temixtitan, had attacked us fiercely and killed many Spaniards.

Of the six days which we spent in Tacuba, not one passed without many engagements and skirmishes with the enemy. The captains of the Tascaltecans and their men many times challenged those of Temixtitan and fought most beautifully with them; they argued at length, shouting insults and threats at each other, all of which was a truly remarkable sight. During all this time many of the enemy were killed without any of our people being endangered, for many times we entered by the causeways and bridges of the city, although as their defenses were very good they resisted us fiercely. Often they pretended to open a way for us, saying, "Come in, come in and enjoy yourselves!" or, at other times, "Do you think there is now another Mutezuma to do whatever you wish? " Once, while they were engaged in these exchanges, I approached a bridge which they had raised, they being on the other side of the water. I signaled my men to be silent; and they also, when they saw I wished to speak to them, silenced their men. I called to them, asking if they were mad and wished to be destroyed. I asked if amongst them there was a lord of the city to whom I might speak. They replied that all the multitude of warriors I saw there were lords, so I might say what I wished. But as I made no answer they began to insult me. And one of my men, I do not know which, told them that they would die of hunger, for we would not let them escape in search of food. They replied that they were not short of food, and that when they were they would eat us and the Tascaltecans. One of them took some maize loaves and threw them toward us saying, "Take these and eat them if you are hungry, for we are not." And then they began to yell and fight with us.

As the reason for my coming to Tacuba had been principally to have talks with the Indians from Temixtitan and discover their intentions, I saw that by remaining I was achieving nothing; and so after six days had passed I decided to return to Tesuico in order to hasten the assembly of the brigantines, so as to be able to surround the enemy both by land and water. The day of our departure we put up for the night in the city of Goatitan, which I have already mentioned, and the ænemy followed us continuously, though from time to time the horsemen turned to attack them, with the result that some of them fell into our hands.

On the following day we set out again, and when the enemy saw us leaving they believed it was out of fear, so they gathered together a great number of their people and began to pursue us. When I saw this I ordered the foot soldiers to march on ahead without stopping, and sent five horsemen to bring up their rear, while twenty remained with me. Six of these I placed in ambush in one place, and six in another and five in another, while I went with three to another. I ordered that as the enemy passed, believing that we were all going on ahead, and on hearing me shout "Señor Santiago" they should come out and fall on them from behind. When it was time we emerged and rode down on them with our lances; the chase continued for nearly two leagues over land as flat as the palm of a man's hand; and it was a most beautiful sight. Thus a great many died by our hands and by those of our Indian allies. Those who remained pursued us no farther, and we hastened to join the rest of our people. That night we slept in a pleasant village called Aculman[29] that lies two leagues from Tesuico, for which we departed the following day and arrived about noon. We were very well received by the alguacil mayor, whom I had left there as captain, and by all the other people, who rejoiced greatly at our coming, for since the day we had left they had heard nothing of us or of what had happened, and they were very eager to know. The day after we arrived the lords and captains of the Tascaltecans asked my permissions to depart; and they went away to their land very pleased and with some spoils from the enemy.

Two days after my return to Tesuico there came to me certain messengers from the lords of Calco who told me that they had been ordered to inform me that the people of Mexico and Temixtitan were coming to destroy them. They again begged me to send help, as they had done before. Immediately I arranged to send Gonzalo de Sandoval with twenty horsemen and three hundred foot soldiers. I urged him to make haste, and once he arrived to do all he was able to assist Your Majesty's vassals and our friends.

When he arrived in Calco he found awaiting him many people from that province and from those of Guajocingo and Guacachula. And once he had left orders as to what was to be done, he departed for a town called Guastepeque,[24] where the Culuans had a garrison and from where they were attacking the people of

Calco. At a town on the way there appeared a great number of the enemy; but as our allies were many and furthermore had the advantage of the assistance of Spaniards and the horsemen, together they broke through them and, driving them from the field, killed many of them. They spent that night in a village outside Guastepeque and set out again on the following day. As they drew close to the aforementioned town of Guastepeque, the Culuans began to fight with the Spaniards, who soon, however, scattered them and, killing some, drove them from the town. The horsemen then dismounted so as to feed their horses and accommodate themselves, and while they were thus unprepared the enemy returned to the square where their quarters were, and shouting and screaming ferociously attacked them with stones and arrows and spears. The Spaniards armed themselves and together with our allies dashed out against them. Once again they drove them out, and pursuing them for more than a league killed a large number. They were very tired when they returned that night to Guastepeque, where they rested for two days.

At this time the alguacil mayor discovered that there were many enemy warriors in a town called Acapichtla,[25] and he resolved to go there and require them to surrender peacefully. This town was very strong and built on a high place such that the horses could not reach it. As soon as the Spaniards arrived the people of the town immediately began to attack them and throw stones down on them. And although many of our allies were with the alguacil mayor, when they saw the strength of the town they dared not attack the enemy. When the alguacil mayor and the Spaniards saw this they determined to take the heights of the city or die in the attempt, and with a shout of "Señor Santiago" they began to climb; and it pleased God to grant them so much strength that despite fierce resistance they took the town, although many were wounded in the attempt. When the enemy saw they were defeated and began to flee, our Indian allies followed them, and there was such a massacre at the hands of our allies and through their being thrown down from the heights that all who were there agree that the small river which runs past that village was dyed with blood for more than an hour, and they were unable to drink from it, although it was hot and they badly needed to. Having brought this assault to a conclusion, and leaving those two towns in peace, although severely punished for their having earlier refused it, the alguacil mayor returned to Tesuico with all his men; and Your Catholic Majesty may be assured that this was a most notable victory, in which the Spaniards showed singular courage.[26]

When the people of Mexico and Temixtitan heard how the Spaniards and the people of Calco had done them such harm they resolved to send several captains with a large force against them. When the people of Calco heard of this they sent me a request to send aid as quickly as possible. Again I sent the same alguacil mayor with several horsemen and foot soldiers, but when he arrived the Culuans and the people of Calco were already engaged in a fierce struggle. It pleased God, however, that the people of Calco should be victorious, and they killed many of the enemy and captured some forty persons, among whom was a Mexican captain and two other chieftains, all of whom the people of Calco handed over to the alguacil mayor so that he might bring them to me. Some of these he sent to me and others he kept, because, for the greater safety of the people of Calco, he remained with all his men in a Calco village on the border with Mexico. Afterwards, when he thought his presence was no longer needed, he returned to Tesuico and brought with him the remaining prisoners. Meanwhile we had had many encounters with the Culuans, which, to avoid prolixity, I shall not recount.

As the road between this city of Tesuico and Vera Cruz was now safe, those in Vera Cruz received news of us every day, and we of them, which was not possible before. They now sent me a messenger with some crossbows, harquebuses and powder, which pleased us greatly. Then, two days later, they sent me another messenger to say that three ships had arrived at the port bringing many men and horses, and that they would be sent to me at once; and so, miraculously, God granted us assistance in proportion to our need.[27]

I have always sought, Most Powerful Lord, by all the means at my disposal, to bring the people of Temixtitan into friendship with us; partly so that they might not be destroyed, and partly so that we might rest from the hardships of all the past battles, but principally because I knew that it would promote the service of Your Majesty. Whenever I captured anyone from the city I always sent him back to require and demand that they make peace. So on Wednesday of Holy Week, which was the twenty-seventh of March, 1521, I had the lords of Temixtitan whom the people of Calco had captured brought before me. I asked if there were any among them who would go to the city and speak on my behalf to their lords and entreat them to cease the war and submit themselves as Your Majesty's vassals as they had been before, because I did not wish to destroy them but to be their friend. And although they took it badly, for they were afraid they would be killed if they took such a message, two of those prisoners resolved to go and asked me for a letter because, though they would not understand what was in it, they knew it was the custom among us, and by carrying it they would be given more credence by the people in the city. Through my interpreters, however, I explained to them what was in the letter, which was what I had said to them personally. Thus they departed, and I commanded five horsemen to escort them to safety.

On Easter Saturday the people of Calco and some of their friends and allies sent to tell me that the Mexicans were marching against them, and on a large white cloth they showed the symbols for all the towns which were to attack them and the routes they were to follow. They asked me at all costs to send them assistance, and I answered that within four or five days I would send it, and that if in the meanwhile they found themselves in great need they were to tell me and I would help them. On the third day after Easter they returned and entreated me to send help at once, because the enemy was advancing rapidly. I replied that I would help them and ordered that twenty-five horsemen and three hundred foot soldiers should be ready for the following Friday.

On the Thursday before, certain messengers from the provinces of Tuzapan, Masicalcingo and Nautan[28] and from other cities in that neighborhood came to Tesuico and told me they wished to offer themselves as Your Majesty's vassals and our allies, for they had never killed any Spaniard nor risen against Your Majesty's service. They brought with them some cotton clothes, for all of which I thanked them and promised that if they behaved well they would be well treated; with this they left well pleased.

On Friday, which was the fifth of April of the same year, 1521, I left Tesuico with the thirty [sic] horsemen and three hundred foot soldiers who had been prepared, and I left behind there another twenty horsemen and three hundred foot soldiers. As their captain I appointed Gonzalo de Sandoval, the alguacil mayor. More than twenty thousand men from Tesuico came with me, and we marched in good order until we reached a town of Calco called Tlamanalco,[29] where we were well received and quartered; and there we spent the night. As there are good defenses there, ever since the people of Calco became our friends they have maintained a garrison there, for it lies on the borders of Culua. We arrived at Calco on the following day at about nine in the morning, but stopped no more than to speak with their chiefs and explain my intention, which was to follow a route around the lakes, for I believed that once I had finished this task, which was most important, I would find the brigantines completed and ready for launching. After I had spoken to the people of Calco I left that day at vespers and reached a village where more than forty thousand of our allies joined us in arms and we slept there that night. And because the inhabitants of this village told me that the Culuans were waiting in the fields, I ordered that the men should rise and be prepared by a quarter before dawn.

On the following day, after hearing Mass, we set out. I took the vanguard with twenty horsemen, while ten others rode in the rear, and in this fashion we crossed some very steep mountains. At about two o'clock we reached a very high and steep rock on top of which were many women and children. The slopes were covered with warriors, who soon began to howl and make smoke signals, attacking us with stones, which they hurled down by hand or from slings and with spears and arrows, so that in approaching them we received much harm. Even though we had seen that they dared not face us in the field, it seemed to me that, although our road led elsewhere, it would be cowardly to pass by without giving them a lesson, and our allies might think we were afraid; so I began by examining the circumference of the foot of the hill, which was almost a league round. Certainly it was so strong that it seemed madness to attempt to take it, for I could not spare the time to lay siege to it and force them to surrender from hunger. Being thus perplexed, I resolved to scale the slopes in three places that I had seen, and so I ordered Cristóbal Corral, ensign [*alférez*] of sixty foot soldiers, whom I kept always in my company, to scale the steepest part with his flag, with certain harquebusiers and crossbowmen behind him. The captains Juan Rodríguez de Villafuerte and Francisco Verdugo I sent to attack in the second place with some harquebusiers and crossbowmen, and the captains Pedro Dircio and Andrés de Monjaraz with another few harquebusiers and crossbowmen were assigned the third place. I told them that when they heard a harquebus fired they should ascend, and triumph or die.

When the harquebus was fired they immediately began to ascend, and captured from the enemy two sides of the slope but could advance no farther, for the steepness and roughness of that crag was without compare and they could not find hand- or footholds. A large number of stones were hurled and rolled down on them, which shattered into fragments doing infinite harm. So fierce was the defense that two Spaniards were killed and more than twenty wounded, and in no manner could they advance farther. When I saw that they could do no more than what they had already done, and that large numbers of the enemy were arriving to reinforce those on the crag, so that the countryside was full of them, I ordered the captains to withdraw. When the horsemen had descended we fell upon those in the plain and drove them from the field, spearing and killing many of them during a chase which lasted for more than an hour and a half. As there were a large number of them, the horsemen had spread out on either side, and when they re-formed again I learnt from some how they had come upon another rock with many people on it about a league and a half from there, but this one was not so strong as the other; and there were many people in the plain thereabouts. Furthermore, we would find there two things which we lacked at the first crag: one was water, and the other that the hill was not so well defended, and we might capture it without danger. Although we were greatly saddened by not having won a victory, we left and slept that night close to the other rock, where we endured considerable hardship and privation for we found no water there, and neither we nor the horses had drunk all day. Thus we passed that night to the sound of drums and trumpets and the shouts of our enemies.

When it was light I took with me certain captains and began to examine the slopes of the rock, which seemed to us almost as strong as the other, save that before it there were two hills which were higher but looked easier to climb; these were defended by many warriors. Those captains and myself together with some other gentlemen took our bucklers and went on foot (for the horses had been taken to drink at a place a league from there) toward the hill merely to see how strong the crag was and where we might best attack; yet when the rest of our people saw us go, they followed, although we had said nothing to them. When we reached the foot of the crag those who defended the two hills, believing we planned to attack in the center, rushed to the assistance of their companions. When I saw the mistake they had made, and that once those two hills had been captured we might do much harm from them, I quietly ordered a captain to quickly climb and capture the steepest of the two hills which they had abandoned; and so it was done. I took the rest of the men and began to climb the hill where the enemy was strongest; and it pleased God that we should take one side of it and reach a height almost level with where they were fighting, which had seemed an impossible thing to do, at least without extreme danger. One of the captains had already placed his banner on the highest point of the hill, and from there he began to assail the enemy with crossbows and harquebuses. When they saw the harm they were suffering and that all hope was lost, they signaled that they wished to surrender, and laid down their arms. And as it has always been my intent to persuade these people that we wish them no harm, no matter how guilty they may be, especially if they wish to be Your Majesty's vassals, and they are so intelligent a people that they understand this very well, I ordered that they should be done no further harm, and welcomed them well. When they saw how well they were treated, they informed those of the other crag, who, although they were victorious, likewise resolved to become Your Majesty's vassals and came to me asking forgiveness for what had occurred.

For two days I remained in this town by the rock, and from there I sent the wounded back to Tesuico and later departed myself, reaching Guastepeque, which I have mentioned above, at ten in the morning. There we were all quartered in a chief's country house amid the most beautiful and refreshing gardens ever seen. They are two leagues round about and through the middle of them runs a pleasant stream. There are summer houses spaced out at distances of two crossbowshots, and very bright flower beds, a great many trees with various fruits, and many herbs and sweet-smelling flowers. Certainly the elegance and magnificence of this garden make a remarkable sight. We rested there that day and the natives provided us with all the services and pleasures that they could.

On the following day we departed and at eight o'clock in the morning reached a fine town called Yautepeque,[30] where large numbers of the enemy were awaiting us. As we arrived, however, it

seemed as if they wished to make some sign of peace, either through
fear, or in the hope of deceiving us, but immediately after, without
more ado, they began to flee, abandoning their town. I had no desire to remain there and so pursued them with thirty horses for
some two leagues, until we trapped them in another town which is
called Gilutepeque,[31] where we speared and killed many. We found
the people in this town unprepared, for we had arrived ahead of
their spies; some were killed and many women and children were
taken, and all the rest fled. I stayed there two days, thinking that
the lord would come and offer himself as Your Majesty's vassal, but
as he did not come I ordered the town to be set on fire before I left.
Before I did so, however, certain persons from the previous town of
Yautepeque came, begging me to forgive them and offering themselves as Your Majesty's vassals. I received them willingly, for they
had already been well punished.

On the day I departed, at nine o'clock, I came within sight
of a very strong town called Coadnabacad,[32] in which a large force
of enemy warriors had gathered. So strong was the town and surrounded by so many hills and ravines, some of which were sixty
feet in depth, that the horsemen could not enter except by two
places, which were unknown to us at that time, and even they required that we make a detour of a league and a half to reach them.
There were also entrances across wooden bridges, but they had
raised them, and were thus very strong and so safe that had we been
ten times our number they could have held us with scorn. As we
approached, they propelled many arrows and javelins and stones at
as at their ease. While they were thus engaged with us an Indian
from Tascalteca crossed over a ravine in a manner so dangerous that
at first he was unobserved,[33] but when at last they did catch sight of
him they believed that the Spaniards were coming the same way
and fled in terror, with the Indian following behind. Three or four
youths, who were servants of mine, and two from another company saw the Indian cross, followed him and reached the other side.
I then went with the horsemen up into the mountains to find an

entrance into the town, and all the while the enemy attacked us with arrows and javelins, for between us and them there was only a narrow ravine. As they were so busy fighting with us they had not seen the five Spaniards who took them suddenly from behind and began to attack them with their swords. They were so surprised and unprepared that they were quite unable to turn and defend themselves, for they did not know that their people had abandoned the path by which the Indian and the Spaniards had come. They were so terrified they dared not fight, and the Spaniards killed many of them until, realizing the trick, they began to flee. Our foot soldiers were already in the town and had begun to set it on fire; the Indians all fled before them and retreated to the mountains, although the horsemen pursued and killed many.

When, at about midday, we discovered a way into the town, we lodged in some houses in a garden, although the place was almost entirely burnt. When it was already very late, the chief and other chieftains, seeing that they had been unable to defend themselves despite the strength of their town, and fearing that we would go and kill them in the mountains, decided to come and offer themselves as Your Majesty's vassals, and as such I received them, and they promised me that thereafter they would always be our friends. These Indians and the others who came to offer themselves as Your Majesty's vassals, after we had destroyed and burnt their houses and land, explained that they had delayed their coming in the belief that they might atone for their wrongs by allowing us to do them harm; thus they hoped that once we had finished we would not be so angry with them.

We slept that night in the town and in the morning continued our journey through pine forests without habitation or drinking water, and a pass which we crossed with much difficulty, without being able to drink, so that some of the Indians in our company died of thirst. Seven leagues from the town we camped for the night in some farms. When it was light we set out again and came within sight of a pleasant city called Suchimilco, which is built on the fresh-water lake.[34] As the inhabitants had been warned of our coming, they had constructed many earthworks and ditches and had raised all the bridges leading into the city, which is three or four leagues from Temixtitan. Within the city there were very many brave-looking people all resolved to defend themselves or die.

As soon as we arrived, and all our men had been collected and drawn up in good array, I dismounted and, followed by certain of the infantry, advanced toward a dike which they had made, on the far side of which were an infinite number of warriors. When we began to attack the dike the crossbowmen and harquebusiers did them so much harm they abandoned it, whereupon the Spaniards threw themselves into the water and crossed to the other side. After fighting with them for half an hour we captured the greater part of the city and forced them back along the waterways in their canoes. They fought until dusk, however, when some of them sued for peace, but the rest did not cease fighting for all that, and they made so many overtures without fulfilling them that at last we realized that they were doing it for two reasons: first, so that they might salvage their property while we talked, and, second, to gain time for help to arrive from Mexico and Temixtitan. This day they killed two Spaniards who had separated themselves from the others in order to pillage and found themselves cut off from all hope of assistance.

In the evening the enemy debated as to how they might cut off our retreat and prevent us leaving their city alive. They collected together a large number of their men and came against us in the place where we had entered. As we saw them advancing so rapidly, we were alarmed at their cunning and speed; six horsemen and myself, who were more prepared than the others, broke through the middle of them. They were frightened by the horses and began to flee, so we rode out of the city, killing many of them, although we found ourselves hard pressed, for they were courageous men, many of whom dared to face the horses with their shields and bucklers. While we were engaged with them and in great confusion, the horse I rode collapsed from exhaustion; and when some of the enemy saw me on foot they rushed upon me. I had begun to defend myself with my lance, when an Indian from Tascalteca saw the danger I was in and came to my aid; together with a servant of mine[35] who arrived soon after, we raised the horse. Meanwhile the Spaniards arrived, whereupon the enemy fled the field altogether, and as I and all the other horsemen were very weary we returned to the city. Although it was now almost night and time to rest, I ordered that all the bridges which had been removed should be filled up with stones and adobes which were at hand, so that the horses might enter and leave the city without hindrance; and I did not leave there until all those dangerous crossings had been well repaired. That night we were most vigilant and kept special watch.

On the following day all the natives of Mexico and Temixtitan, who already knew that we were in Suchimilco, resolved to come with great forces by land and water and surround us, for they believed that this time we could not escape their clutches. I then climbed one of the towers where they keep their idols, to see how they were coming and where they would attack us, so that I might make preparations accordingly. When I had completed all the preparations there arrived from across the water a fleet of canoes so large that I think there were more than two thousand of them; in these canoes were more than twelve thousand warriors, and over the land came such a multitude of people that all the fields were covered with them. Their captains went in front, carrying our captured swords and crying the names of their provinces, "Mexico! Mexico! Temixtitan! Temixtitan!" They hurled insults at us, saying that they would kill us with those swords which they had taken from us before in the city of Temixtitan.

When I had allotted to each captain his position, I took twenty horsemen and five hundred Indians from Tascalteca and went out against a horde of the enemy gathered on the mainland. We divided into three companies, and I ordered them, as soon as they had broken through the enemy, to rally at the foot of a hill which was half a league away, where there was also a large number of the enemy. When we separated, each company pursued the enemy on its own side; and once we had routed them and killed many we regrouped at the foot of the hill. I then ordered certain foot soldiers, servants of mine, who had served me and were very able, to attempt to scale the hill in the steepest part. I, with the horsemen, would circle around behind, where the ground was more even and we would take them in the middle. Thus, when the Indians saw the Spaniards climbing the hill, they turned their backs, thinking that by so doing they were safe and encountered us, who were some fifteen horsemen. We fell on them and those of Tascalteca did likewise, so that, in a brief while, more than five hundred of the enemy were killed and the rest fled to the mountains. The other six horsemen determined to follow a very wide flat path and attack the enemy with their lances. Half a league from Suchimilco they met a company of Indians in very bright array who were coming to the help of their companions; these the horsemen routed, killing some with their lances. Now that all the horsemen were together—it was about ten o'clock in the morning—we returned to Suchimilco, and at the entrance to the town I found many Spaniards who desired our return and wished to know how it had gone with us. They told me they had been hard pressed, but had done all they could to drive out the enemy, many of whom had been killed. They gave me two of our own swords that they had recaptured, and told me how the crossbowmen had no bolts nor any supplies whatsoever. While we were thus occupied, before we had even dismounted, a large number of the enemy appeared on a broad causeway, screaming fiercely; we attacked them at once and drove them into the water on either side of the causeway. Thus we routed them, and once the men had collected we returned, much exhausted, to the city, where I ordered everything except the house in which we were quartered to be burnt. We remained three days in that city and not once did the fighting cease. In the end we left it burnt and ruined, and it was a notable sight, for there had been many houses and towers for their idols all built of stone and mortar; but in order not to be prolix I shall forbear to list the many remarkable things in this city.[36]

On the day I departed I went out into a square on dry land, where the inhabitants hold their markets, and I gave orders that ten horsemen should ride in front; another ten went in the middle with the foot soldiers, while I, with a further ten, brought up the rear. When the inhabitants of Suchimilco saw that we were leaving, they thought that it was through fear of them, and, shouting fiercely, they fell on us from behind. The ten horsemen and myself turned and drove them into the water; thus they troubled us no further and we were able to continue our journey. At ten o'clock in the morning we reached the city of Cuyoacan, which is two leagues distant from Suchimilco, and near to Temixtitan, Culuacan, Uchilubuzco, Yztapalapa, Cuitaguaca and Mizqueque,[37] all of which are built on the water, the most distant lying about a league and a half away. We found it deserted and lodged in the chief's house, where we remained that day and the next.

As I intended to surround the city of Temixtitan as soon as the brigantines were complete, I wished first to know the plan of the city, its entrances and exits and where the Spaniards could make an attack or might receive one. On the following day, therefore, I took six horsemen and two hundred foot soldiers and went down to the lake, which is close by, along a causeway that leads into the city of Temixtitan; and there we saw a great many canoes on the water and an infinite number of warriors in them. Then we came to a barricade which they had built across the causeway, and the foot soldiers began to fight; and although it was very strong and well defended, and ten Spaniards were wounded, at last they captured it and killed many of the enemy, although the crossbowmen had no bolts, nor had the harquebusiers any powder. From there we could see how the causeway led over the water straight into Temixtitan, a full league and a half away, and both on that one and the other, which goes to Yztapalapa, there were countless numbers of people.

As soon as I had seen all I needed to see, and had decided that a garrison of horsemen and foot soldiers would have to be established in this city, I called together my men and we returned, burning the houses and towers where they keep their idols.

On the following day we left Cuyoacan for Tacuba, which is some two leagues distant, and we arrived at nine in the morning, attacking with our lances in one place or another as the enemy came from the lake to assail the Indians who carried our baggage; finding themselves worsted, however, they soon left us in peace. Because, as I have already said, my prime intent was to make a reconnaissance tour of all the lakes in order to inspect and acquaint myself better with the land, and also to give assistance to some of our allies, I did not wish to stop in Tacuba. When the inhabitants of Temixtitan, which is so close to there that it almost reaches dry land at Tacuba, saw us leaving they recovered much of their courage and with intrepidity fell upon our baggage train; but as the horsemen were well placed, and the ground was level, we were able to take advantage of the enemy without placing ourselves in danger. As we galloped hither and thither, some youths, servants of mine, had been accustomed to follow us, but on that occasion two failed to do so, and found themselves trapped and were captured, and we feared that the enemy would put them to death in the most cruel fashion, as was their custom.[38] God alone knows how grieved I was, for not only were they Christians but also most courageous men who had served Your Majesty well in this campaign.

After leaving this city we proceeded on our journey through other towns close by and drew near to the enemy. Here I learnt how the Indians had taken those youths, and to avenge their death, and also because the enemy was following us with the greatest arrogance possible, I concealed myself with twenty horsemen behind some houses. As the Indians saw the remaining ten horsemen with all the men and baggage moving on ahead, they followed them fearlessly along a very broad and level road. When we saw that some of them had passed, I cried out the name of the apostle St.

James (Santiago) and we fell upon them most fiercely. Before they could escape into the canals nearby we had killed more than a hundred chieftains, all brilliantly arrayed, and they followed us no farther. This day we spent the night two leagues farther on in a city called Coatinchán, which we found deserted; we were tired and wet, for it had rained heavily that afternoon. On the following day we set out again, charging from time to time at some Indians who came and yelled at us; and we slept in a town called Gilutepeque, which we likewise found deserted. On the following morning at twelve o'clock we reached the city of Aculman, which lies within the domain of Tesuico, where we slept that night. We were very well received by the Spaniards, who rejoiced exceedingly at our arrival as if we had brought them their salvation, because after my departure they had had no word of me until the day I returned. There had been several disturbances in the city, whose inhabitants had told them daily that the people of Mexico and Temixtitan would fall on them while I was away. Thus, by the Grace of God, this undertaking was completed, and it was a very great achievement by which Your Majesty was well served for many reasons, which I shall explain later.

Most Powerful and Invincible Lord, when I was in the city of Temixtitan on the previous occasion I ordered, as I informed Your Majesty in a previous account, that certain farms should be built for Your Majesty, in two or three of the most suitable provinces, and that each farm should produce grain and other things according to the disposition of the province. To accomplish this I sent two Spaniards to one of these provinces, which is called Chinantla,[39] and is not subject to Culua. In the others, which were subject, they killed the Spaniards on the farms at the same time as they were making war against me in Temixtitan, and seized all that was there which, after the manner of this land, was a substantial amount. Of the Spaniards who were in Chinantla, however, I knew nothing for almost a year, because as all those provinces were in

revolt, we could not hear from them, nor they from us. The natives
of Chinantla, as they were Your Majesty's vassals and enemies of
the Culuans, had told those Christians that on no account should
they leave that land, because the Culuans had been fighting us
fiercely, and they believed that few or none of us remained alive. So
these two Spaniards stayed in that land, and one of them, who was a
youth and of warlike disposition, was made their captain; and at
that time he went out with them to fight their enemies and often
returned victorious. Later, when it pleased God that we should re-
organize, and obtain some victories over those who had routed and
driven us from Temixtitan, the people of Chinantla told those
Christians that they had heard there were Spaniards in the province
of Tepeaca, and that if they wished to learn what was really happening, they would risk two Indians, who, although they must
travel a long way through the lands of their enemies, would journey by night and off the main roads until they reached Tepeaca.
With those two Indians, the more reliable of the two Spaniards[40]
sent a letter, the substance of which was the following:

> Noble Sirs, I have written two or three letters to Your Lordships
> but do not know if they ever reached you; and as I have received
> no reply from the others I doubt that I will receive one now. I
> wish to make it known to you that all the natives of the land of
> Culua have rebelled and are in arms and many times have at-
> tacked us; but always, praise be to God, we have been victorious.
> Likewise we fight daily with those of Tuxtepeque who are allies
> of the Culuans. Seven towns in Tenez still serve His Highness
> and remain his vassals, and Nicolás and I have remained in Chi-
> nantla, which is the capital. I would greatly like to know where
> the captain is, so that I may write and inform him of all that has
> happened here. If by chance you should reply and tell me where
> he is, send me twenty or thirty Spaniards and I will come with
> two chieftains from here who desire to see and speak with the
> captain. It would be well for them to come now for it is time

to harvest the cacao and the Culuans hinder us with the fighting. May Our Lord watch over and preserve Your Lordships. From Chinantla, I do not know what day of the month of April, 1521. At Your Lordships' service: Hernando de Barrientos.

When the two Indians arrived in the aforementioned province of Tepeaca with this letter, the captain whom I had left there with several Spaniards sent it on to me at Tesuico. When it arrived we were all greatly pleased, for although we had always trusted in the friendship of the people of Chinantla, we thought that if they had allied themselves with the Culuans, they might have killed those two Spaniards. I then wrote to them telling all that had happened and urging them to have hope for, although they were surrounded by the enemy on all sides, if it pleased God, they would soon be freed and might come and go in safety.

Once I had made a tour of the lakes and learnt thereby many things which would be useful in laying siege to Temixtitan by land and water, I returned to Tesuico, equipped myself as best I could with men and arms, and hastened to finish the brigantines and a canal by which they were to be transported to the lake. This had been begun as soon as the planks and crossbeams had arrived. It reached from our quarters right down to the lake, and was fully half a league in length from the place where the brigantines were constructed to the lake shore. More than eight thousand natives from Aculuacán and Tesuico provinces worked for fifty days on this task because the canal was more than twelve feet deep and as many wide. It was well lined with stakes, so that it would fill with water from the lake, and thus the brigantines might be transported without danger or effort; it was certainly a magnificent achievement and a notable sight.

When, on the twenty-eighth of April of the same year, the brigantines were ready and launched into the canal,[41] I called all my men out on parade and reckoned eighty-six horsemen, 118 crossbowmen and harquebusiers, some seven hundred foot soldiers with swords and bucklers, three large iron guns, fifteen small bronze field guns and ten hundredweight of powder. When I had finished the inspection I charged and exhorted all the Spaniards to abide, as far as they were able, by the ordinances which I had drawn up concerning war, and to take fresh courage and fight hard, for they had seen how Our Lord was guiding us to victory over our enemies. They knew well how we had entered Tesuico with no more than forty horsemen, and that God had helped us more than we had hoped, and ships had come with horses, men and arms, as they had seen. Above all, they were fighting to increase and spread our Faith and to submit to Your Majesty's service all those lands and provinces which had rebelled; this should fill them with courage and the desire to conquer or die. They all responded readily, showing that they were most willing in all this; and so that day we spent rejoicing, hoping soon to see ourselves engaged in the siege whereby this war, which would decide whether or not these parts would be subdued, would be brought to an end.

On the following day I sent messengers to the provinces of Tascalteca, Guaxocingo and Churultecal to inform them that the brigantines were ready and that I and all my people were prepared to surround the great city of Temixtitan. I requested them, therefore, that, as they had already been advised by me and had alerted their own people, they should come, as many and as well armed as possible, to Tesuico, where I would wait ten days for them; and that on no account should they exceed this, for it would most seriously disconcert my plans. When the messengers arrived the natives of these provinces were already prepared and eager to face the Culuans; those from Guaxocingo and Churultecal came to Calco, for so I had ordered them to do, as the siege was to begin close by there. The captains from Tascalteca with all their men, well armed and in splendid array, arrived in Tesuico four or five days before Whitsunday, which was the time I had assigned to them. As I knew that they were arriving on that day, I went joyfully out to meet them; and they arrived so confident and well disciplined that none could be better. According to the count which the captains gave us, there were more than fifty thousand warriors, who were all very well received and well quartered by us.

On the day after Whitsun, I ordered all the foot soldiers and the horsemen to gather in the square of Tesuico, and there I allotted them to three captains who were to lead them to three cities close to Temixtitan. I made Pedro de Alvarado captain of one company, and gave him thirty horsemen and eighteen crossbowmen and harquebusiers, and 150 foot soldiers with swords and bucklers, and more than 25,000 warriors from Tascalteca; these were to encamp in the city of Tacuba.

I made Cristóbal de Olid captain of another company and gave him thirty-three horsemen, eighteen crossbowmen and harquebusiers, 160 foot soldiers with swords and bucklers and more than twenty thousand warriors of our allies; these were to quarter themselves in the city of Cuyoacán.

I made Gonzalo de Sandoval, the alguacil mayor, captain of the third company, and I gave him twenty-four horsemen, four harquebusiers and thirteen crossbowmen, and 150 foot soldiers with swords and bucklers, fifty of whom were chosen from those of my own company, together with all the people from Guaxocingo, Churultecal and Calco, who numbered more than thirty thousand men. They were to go by way of the city of Yztapalapa and destroy it, and thence continue along a causeway over the lake, supported by the brigantines, until they met with my garrison at Cuyoacan, so that after I had entered the lake with the brigantines the alguacil mayor might set up camp where he saw fit.

For the thirteen brigantines with which I was to cross the lake, I left three hundred men, most of whom were sailors and very able, so that there were twenty-five Spaniards in each brigantine, and each one had a captain, a lookout and six crossbowmen and harquebusiers.

When I had given these orders the two captains who were to go to Tacuba and Cuyoacan, after they had received their instructions, left Tesuico on the tenth of May and spent the night two leagues and a half from there in a good town called Aculmán.[42] That day I learnt that there had been a dispute between the captains over their quarters, so, that night, in order to settle this dispute and make peace, I sent someone to reprove and pacify them.[43] On the following morning they left there and spent the night in a city called Gilutepeque, which they found deserted, for they were now on enemy soil. On the following day they continued their journey as instructed and slept in a city called Guatitlan, of which I have already written to Your Majesty, which they likewise found deserted. That day they also passed through two other cities and towns, and found no people in them. At the hour of vespers they entered Tacuba, which was also deserted, and quartered themselves in the houses of the chieftain of the city, which are very large and beautiful. And although it was already late, the Indians of Tascalteca went to examine the entrance of two causeways leading into the city of Temixtitan; they fought valiantly for two or three hours with its inhabitants, and when the night separated them they returned to Tacuba in safety.

On the following morning the two captains arranged, as I had ordered them, to cut off the fresh water which flowed along the aqueducts to the city of Temixtitan. One of them, with twenty horsemen and some crossbowmen and harquebusiers, went to the source, which was a quarter of a league away, and destroyed the pipes, which were made of wood and stone and mortar. He fought and defeated the enemy, who tried to prevent him by land and from the water, thus succeeding in his purpose, which was to deprive the city of fresh water, which was a cunning stratagem.

That same day the captains had some bad places on the causeways, bridges and channels in the vicinity leveled, so that the horses might pass freely from one part to another.

This occupied them for three or four days, and during that time they had many encounters with the people of the city, in which some Spaniards were wounded and many of the enemy killed and many bridges and barricades taken. Many arguments and insults were exchanged between the Tascaltecans and the Culuans which were most remarkable and worthy of note. Then the captain Cristóbal de Olid left together with those who were to proceed to Cuyoacan, which is two leagues from Tacuba. Meanwhile, Pedro de Alvarado remained with the garrison at Tacuba, where he had daily battles and skirmishes with the Indians. Cristóbal de Olid arrived at ten in the morning in Cuyoacan and lodged in the house of the lord of that city, which they found abandoned.

On the following morning they went to examine the causeway leading to Temixtitan with about twenty horsemen and some crossbowmen, and with six or seven thousand Indians from Tascalteca. They found that the enemy was prepared and had broken the causeway and put up many barricades. They fought with them, the crossbowmen killing and wounding some; and this continued for six or seven days, on every one of which there were many skirmishes and encounters. One night, at about midnight, certain enemy scouts from the city came and shouted close to the camp; the Spanish sentries sounded the alarm, whereupon our men rode out but found none of them, for the shouting which had caused the scare had been far from the camp. As our force was divided into so many parts, the people in those two garrisons dearly desired my arrival with the brigantines as if it were to be their salvation; with this hope they held out those few days until I arrived, as later I will relate. The people from those garrisons met on every one of those six days, for they were very close to each other; the horsemen overran the countryside, spearing many of the enemy, and in the mountains collected much maize which is the staple food of these parts, and much superior to that of the Islands.

In previous chapters I have told how I remained in Tesuico with three hundred men and the thirteen brigantines, for, as soon as I knew that the garrisons had set up their camps, I would embark and inspect the city and do some harm to the canoes. Although I greatly wished to go overland to take command of the camps, as the captains were men who could well be trusted with what they had in hand, I resolved to embark in the brigantines, which were of the greatest importance and required much care and discipline; furthermore, I expected to encounter the greatest dangers and risks on the water. Nevertheless, I was requested by certain officers of my company to go with the soldiers, for they believed that they would bear the greatest risks. On the day following the feast of Corpus Christi,[44] on Friday at dawn, I sent Gonzalo de Sandoval, alguacil mayor, with all his men, out of Tesuico and ordered him to go straight to the city of Yztapalapa, which is rather less than six leagues from there. They arrived a little after midday and began to burn the city and to fight with the inhabitants. But when they saw the superior forces of the alguacil mayor, for more than thirty-five or forty thousand of our allies had gone with him, they took to the water in their canoes. The alguacil mayor, with all his forces, lodged in that city, remaining there that day to await my orders and discover what had happened to me.

When I had dispatched the alguacil mayor I immediately boarded one of the brigantines and we set out using both sail and oar. At the time the alguacil mayor was burning the city of Yztapalapa we came within sight of a large and well-fortified hill [45] near the city, surrounded by water; on it were many people who had come from Temixtitan and all the villages around the lake; they knew that our first encounter would be with the people of Yztapalapa, and so they had gathered there to defend themselves and attack us if possible. When they saw the fleet approaching they began to shout and make smoke signals, so that the other cities by the lakes should know and be prepared. Although my intention had been to attack that part of the city which is in the water, we turned back to that hill or knoll, and I landed with 150 men, although it was very steep and high. With great difficulty we began to climb, and at last captured the fortifications which they had built for their defense on the top. We broke through them in such a manner that none of them escaped, save the women and children; in the struggle twenty-five Spaniards were wounded, but it was a most beautiful victory.

As the inhabitants of Yztapalapa had made smoke signals from some temple towers that stood on a very high hill close to the city, the people of Temixtitan and the other cities on the water knew that I was already crossing the lake in the brigantines and quickly gathered a large fleet of canoes to attack us and discover what sort of thing these brigantines were; as far as we could judge there were more than five hundred canoes. When I saw that they were sailing straight for us, I and all the men who were on the hill embarked with great haste, but I ordered the captains of the brigantines not to move, so that the canoes, thinking that we did not go out to them through fear, might themselves attack us; and indeed they began to direct their fleet toward us with considerable force. But when they had come within some two crossbowshots of us they stopped and remained motionless. I was anxious that this first encounter with them should result in a great victory, so that they would be inspired with a terror of the brigantines, for the key to the war lay with them, as both the Indians and ourselves were most exposed on water. And it pleased God that as we were watching one another a land breeze, very favorable to attacking them, sprang up, and I ordered the captain to break through the fleet of canoes and to drive them back into the city of Temixtitan. As the wind was good, we bore down through the middle of them, and although they fled as fast as they were able, we sank a huge number of canoes and killed or drowned many of the enemy, which was the most remarkable sight in the world. We then pursued them for three leagues or more until we had confined them among the houses of the city; and so it pleased Our Lord to grant us a greater and better victory than we could have asked or desired.

The garrison of Cuyoacan, which was better able than the one at Tacuba to witness the arrival of the brigantines, assured me afterwards that there was to them nothing in the world so desirable nor anything which gave them so much joy as to see all thirteen sails over the water with a fair wind, and us scattering the enemy canoes. For, as I have said, they and those at Tacuba eagerly

awaited my arrival, and with good reason, for both garrisons were
in the midst of a multitude of the enemy. But Our Lord miraculously gave them courage and quelled the spirits of the enemy so
that they did not attack the camp; for, had they done so, the Spaniards would most certainly have suffered greatly, although they
were always well prepared and determined to conquer or die, realizing that they were cut off from all help save that which they hoped
to receive from God.

When the garrison at Cuyoacan saw us pursue the canoes
they set out with most of the horsemen and foot soldiers, proceeding toward Temixtitan, and fought very bravely with the Indians
on the causeway. They reached and took the barriers that the
enemy had built, and on foot and on horseback, with the support of
the brigantines, which sailed close to the causeway, crossed many
channels where the bridges had been removed by the defenders.
The Spaniards and our Tascaltecan allies pursued the enemy, killing some, while others threw themselves into the water on the far
side from where the brigantines were sailing. In this fashion they
advanced for more than a league along the causeway until they arrived where I had stopped with the brigantines, as I shall hereafter
relate.

We chased the canoes with the brigantines for fully three
leagues, and those that escaped us sought refuge among the houses
in the city. As it was late and already after vespers, I collected the
brigantines together and sailed with them up to the causeway, and
there I resolved to land with thirty men and seize two small temple
towers which were surrounded by a low stone enclosure.[46] When
we landed, they fought most fiercely to defend those towers, but at
last with great danger and much effort we captured them. I then
ordered three heavy iron guns to be landed; and as the rest of the
causeway from there to the city, which was half a league, was full
of the enemy, and the water on either side of the causeway covered
with canoes full of warriors, I had one of the guns loaded and discharged along the causeway, which did much damage to the

enemy. Owing to the carelessness of our gunner, however, all the powder we had in that place was ignited. It was no great quantity, however, and that night I sent a brigantine some two leagues to Yztapalapa, where the alguacil mayor was, to bring all the powder that was there.

At first my intention, once I had embarked with the brigantines, had been to go to Cuyoacan and ensure that the garrison there was well protected and might do the enemy every possible harm, but, after I had landed that day on the causeway and captured those two towers, I decided to set up camp there and keep the brigantines close by the towers. I ordered half of the people at Cuyoacan together with fifty of the alguacil mayor's foot soldiers to come there the following day. Having made these provisions, we kept careful watch that night, for we were in great danger and all the people from the city had gathered there on the causeway and on the water. At midnight a great multitude of people arrived in canoes and poured along the causeway to attack our camp; this caused us great fear and consternation, especially as it was night, and never have they been known or seen to fight at such an hour unless they were certain of an easy victory. But as we were all well prepared, we began to fight with them, and the brigantines, each of which carried a small fieldpiece, began to fire at them and the crossbowmen and harquebusiers likewise. After this they dared advance no further, nor did they even come close enough to do us any harm;[47] and so they left us in peace for what remained of the night and attacked us no more.

On the morning of the following day there arrived at my camp fifteen crossbowmen and harquebusiers and fifty soldiers with swords and bucklers and seven or eight horsemen from the garrison at Cuyoacan; and, even as they were arriving, the people from the city fought with us on the causeway and from their canoes. So great was the multitude that neither by land nor water could we see anything but people, shouting and screaming so it seemed the world was coming to an end. We began to fight with them up the causeway and gained a channel whose bridge they had removed and an earthwork which had been built behind it. We did them so much harm with the guns and from horseback that we drove them back almost as far as the first houses of the town. As on the far side of the causeway, where the brigantines could not go, there were many canoes from which they did us much harm with the arrows and javelins they hurled at us, I ordered a breach to be opened in the causeway near to our camp and sent four brigantines through. These drove the canoes in among the houses of the city so that in no place dared they come out into the open. On the other side of the causeway the remaining eight brigantines fought with the canoes and drove them in amongst the houses, even pursuing them there, which they had not dared do before, for there were so many stakes and shallows to hinder them. But as now they found canals by which they might enter in safety, they fought with those in the canoes, taking some of them and burning many houses in the suburbs of the city. We spent the whole day fighting the enemy in this manner.

On the following day the alguacil mayor, together with all the people he had in Yztapalapa, Spaniards as well as allies, departed for Cuyoacán, which is joined to the mainland by a causeway, a league and half long. After the alguacil mayor had covered about a quarter of a league he reached a small town, which is also built on the water, but it is possible to ride through it in many places; the inhabitants began to attack him, but he routed them, killing many, and destroyed and burnt their town. When I learnt that the Indians had destroyed much of the causeway so that the men could not cross without difficulty, I sent two brigantines to help them cross, which they used as bridges for the foot soldiers. When they had crossed they set up camp at Cuyoacan, and the alguacil mayor with ten horsemen took the road to the causeway where we had pitched our camp, and when he arrived he found us fighting. He and his men then began to fight alongside us with the Indians on the causeway. While the aforementioned alguacil mayor was fighting he was pierced through the foot with a javelin; but although he and some others were wounded that day, we did so much harm to the enemy with the heavy ordnance, the crossbows and harquebuses, that neither those in the canoes nor those on the causeway dared approach us very close, and showed more fear and less arrogance than before. In this manner six days were spent, and on each day we fought them; the brigantines burnt all the houses they could around the city, having discovered a canal whereby they might penetrate the outskirts and suburbs. This was most advantageous and kept back the canoes, which now dared not come within a quarter of a league of our camp.

The following day Pedro de Alvarado, who was captain of the garrison at Tacuba, informed me how on the other side of the city the people of Temixtitan came and went as they chose along a causeway, and another smaller one which joined it, to some towns on the mainland. He believed that once they were hard pressed they would all abandon the city by these causeways. Although I desired them to leave more than they did themselves, for we could take greater advantage of them on the mainland than in that huge fortress on the water, I thought it wise to surround them on all sides so that they might avail themselves of nothing on the mainland. I ordered the alguacil mayor, wounded though he was, to move his camp to a small town at the end of one of these causeways. He left with twenty-three horsemen, a hundred foot soldiers and eighteen crossbowmen and harquebusiers, leaving me the other fifty foot soldiers which I kept in my company. On the following day, he arrived and set up camp as I had ordered, and thenceforth the city of Temixtitan was surrounded at all the points where it might be possible to escape along the causeways.

Most Powerful Lord, I had in the camp on the causeway two hundred Spanish foot soldiers among whom were twenty-five crossbowmen and harquebusiers, without counting the men on the brigantines who numbered more than 250. As we had the enemy somewhat confined, and many warrior allies, I resolved to penetrate

along the causeway as far as possible into the city, with the brigantines covering us on either side. I sent word for some horsemen and
foot soldiers from Cuyoacan to come to the camp and join us in the
assault, and that ten horsemen should remain at the entrance to the
causeway guarding our rear. Some others were to remain behind in
Cuyoacan, for the natives of the cities of Suchimilco, Culuacan,
Yztapalapa, Chilobusco, Mexicalcingo, Cuitaguaca and Mizqueque, all of which are on the lake, had rebelled in support of Temixtitan; should they attempt to take us from behind, we were protected by those ten or twelve horsemen I ordered to guard the
causeway, and the same number who remained in Cuyoacan with
more than ten thousand of our Indian allies. Likewise I ordered
Pedro de Alvarado and the alguacil mayor to attack from their positions at the same time, because I wished to gain as much as possible
on my side.

I left the camp in the morning, and moved up the causeway
on foot. There we found the enemy in defense of a breach in the
causeway as wide and as deep as a lance, and they had built a barricade. We fought with them and they with us, both very coura-
geously, but at last they were defeated and we proceeded up the
causeway until we reached the entrance to the city, where there
was a temple tower, at the foot of which had been a very large
bridge which they had removed, over a broad channel of water,
with another strong earthwork. When we arrived they began to
fight with us, but as the brigantines attacked from both sides we
were able to capture it without danger, which would have been
impossible without them. As the enemy began to abandon the barricade, the men from the brigantines came ashore and we crossed the
water together with the Indians of Tascalteca, Guaxocingo, Calco
and Tesuico, who numbered more than eighty thousand men.
While we filled in that broken bridge with stone and adobes, the
Spaniards took another barricade on the principal and widest street
in the city, and as there was no water nearby it was easier to capture. They then pursued the enemy up the street until they reached

a bridge which had been destroyed save for a broad beam over which the Indians crossed, and, once they were on the other side and protected by the water, they drew it after them. On the far side of the bridge they had built another great earthwork with clay and adobes. When we arrived we found that we could not cross without throwing ourselves into the water, which was very dangerous as the enemy fought most bravely. On both sides of the street there was an infinite number of them, who attacked us very fiercely from the roof tops, but when the force of crossbowmen and harque-busiers arrived and we fired two guns up the street we were able to do them great harm. When we saw this certain of the Spaniards threw themselves into the water and struggled toward the other side, which took more than two hours to capture. But when the enemy saw them cross they abandoned the earthwork and the roof tops and fled up the street, whereupon all our people crossed over. I then ordered the earthworks to be destroyed and the channel filled up. Meanwhile the Spaniards and our Indian allies continued for about two crossbowshots, until they reached another bridge which was next to the square containing the principal dwellings of the city. But this bridge they had not removed nor had they built any earthwork in front of it, for they had not believed that we could have gained any part of what we had won that day, nor had we imagined that it would be even half as much.

At the entrance to the square I had a gun placed, and with it we did much harm to the enemy, who were so many that there was no room for them all in the square. When the Spaniards saw that there was no water there, the thing by which they were most endangered, they resolved to enter the square. When the inhabitants of the city saw them put this into effect and beheld the great multitude of our allies—although without us, they would have had no fear of them—they fled, and our allies pursued them until they were confined in the enclosure where they keep their idols, which is surrounded by a stone wall, and, as I explained in my earlier account, is large enough to hold a town of four hundred inhabitants.

They soon abandoned it, and the Spaniards and our allies captured
the place and remained inside it and inside the towers for a considerable while.[48] But when the enemy saw that there were no horsemen they returned and drove the Spaniards out of the towers and
the courtyard and the enclosure, where they found themselves hard
pressed and in great danger; and as they were retreating rather too
hastily, they turned and faced them beneath the arches of the forecourt. But the enemy attacked them so fiercely that they were
forced to withdraw to the square, whence they were driven down
the main street, abandoning the gun which was there.[49] The Spaniards, as they were unable to resist the enemy, continued to retreat
in great peril of their lives, and indeed they would have been much
harmed had it not pleased God that at that moment three horsemen
arrived. When the enemy saw them enter the square they thought
that there were more and began to flee. The horsemen then killed
some of them and regained the courtyard and enclosure that I have
mentioned. Ten or twelve of the principal lords of the city barricaded themselves into the largest and highest of the towers, which
has a hundred or more steps to the top; but four or five Spaniards
fought their way up and killed them all, although they fought most
bravely in their defense.[50] Afterwards, another five or six horsemen
arrived, and they and the others prepared an ambush in which they
killed more than thirty of the enemy.

As it was already late I ordered my people to collect and
withdraw, and in withdrawing we were assailed by such a multitude of the enemy that were it not for the horsemen the Spaniards
would have been much injured. But as I had had all those dangerous
crossings in the street and on the causeway, where we expected
most danger, filled in and leveled by the time we withdrew, the
horsemen could come and go with ease. When the enemy attacked
us in our rear they charged them, killing some with the lances; as
the street was very long they were able to do this four or five times.
Although the enemy had witnessed the hurt they received, they
came at us like mad dogs, and in no way could we halt them or

prevent them from following us. The whole day would have been so spent had they not already recaptured many of the roof tops overlooking the street, and so placed the horsemen in great danger. For this reason we retreated up the causeway to our camp, and no Spaniard was endangered, although some were wounded. We set fire to most of the better houses in that street, so that when we next entered they might not attack us from the roof tops. This same day the alguacil mayor and Pedro de Alvarado fought very fiercely from their own positions; and at the time of the fighting we were about a league from the one, and a league and a half from the other, but the built-up area of this city extends so far that it made these distances seem less. Our allies who were with them in infinite numbers fought very well and withdrew that day without loss.[51]

In the meantime, Don Fernando,[52] lord of the city of Tesuico and the province of Aculuacan, whom I have already mentioned to Your Majesty, had attempted to win over to our friendship all the inhabitants of his city and province, especially the chieftains, who were not then so firm in their friendship as they afterwards became; and every day there came to Don Fernando many chiefs and brothers of his, all resolved to join us and fight against Mexico and Temixtitan. As Don Fernando was only a boy and bore a great love for the Spaniards, for he recognized that he had been granted his great dominion by favor of Your Majesty, because there were others who took precedence over him, he did all he could to persuade his vassals to come and fight against Temixtitan and expose themselves to the same danger and hardships as ourselves. He spoke with his brothers, who were six or seven in number and all well-disposed youths, and entreated them to go to my assistance with all the people in their domains. He sent as captain one of them called Istlisuchil, a very valiant youth of twenty-three or twenty-four years, loved and respected by all. He arrived at the camp on the causeway with thirty thousand warriors, all well armed after their fashion, while another twenty thousand went to the other camps. I received them joyfully, thanking them for their good intention and for having come so readily. Your Caesarean Majesty may well imagine how valuable this help and friendship of Don Fernando was to me, and what the people of Temixtitan must have felt on seeing advance against them those whom they held as vassals and friends, relatives and brothers, even fathers and sons.

Two days after this was the battle in the city, as I have related, and when these people had come to our assistance, the natives of Suchimilco, which is on the water, and certain of the Utumies[53] who are a mountain people more numerous than those of Suchimilco, and were once slaves of the lord of Temixtitan, came to offer themselves as Your Majesty's vassals, begging me to forgive them for having delayed so long. I received them very well and was much pleased by their coming, for had the garrison at Cuyoacan received any harm it would have been from them.

As we had burnt many houses in the outskirts of the city from the brigantines operating from the camp on the causeway, and now no canoe dared venture near us there, it seemed to me that seven brigantines were sufficient to guard our camp, and so I decided to send three brigantines each to the alguacil mayor and Pedro de Alvarado. I instructed their captains to cruise by night and day from one camp to the other, for thereabouts the natives obtained much support from the land, and carried water, fruit and other supplies in their canoes; I told them, moreover, to cover the rear of the people from the camps every time they attacked the city. So these six brigantines departed for the other two camps; this was a necessary and advantageous move, for each day and night they made remarkable raids, taking many of the enemy and their canoes.

When this had been seen to, and all the peoples I have mentioned had come willingly to our assistance, I spoke to them all, telling them that two days later I intended to enter the city, and therefore they should all be prepared for war by that time, for by this I would know whether they were truly our friends; and they promised to do as I said. On the following day I prepared and

equipped my men, and wrote informing the camps and the brigantines of all I had arranged and of what they had to do.

On the following morning, after I had heard Mass and instructed the captains in what they were to do, I left the camp with
fifteen or twenty horsemen and three hundred Spaniards and all
our Indian allies of whom there was an infinite number. When we
had gone three crossbowshots along the causeway from the camp
we found the enemy awaiting us with loud cries. As we had not
attacked them for three days they had undone all we had achieved
by filling up the breaches in the causeway, and had made them very
much stronger and more dangerous to capture than before. But the
brigantines arrived on both sides of the causeway, and as they could
come in close to the enemy with their guns, crossbows and harquebuses they did them much harm. When our men saw this they
landed and captured the first earthwork and the bridge; and we
crossed over to the other side and began to pursue the enemy, who
barricaded themselves in behind other breaches and earthworks
which they had made. These we also captured, although with
greater difficulty and danger than before, and we drove them from
the street and the square containing the principal houses of the city.
I then ordered the Spaniards to advance no farther, while I went
with our allies filling in with stones and adobes the breaches in the
causeway, which were so many that, although more than ten thousand Indians were engaged in this task, by the time we had finished
it was already the hour of vespers. During all this time the Spaniards and our allies were fighting and skirmishing with the people of
the city and setting ambushes for them in which many of them
were killed.

I rode with the horsemen for a while through the city, and
in the streets where there was no water we attacked with our lances
all those whom we met, and drove them back so that they dared not
venture onto dry land. When I saw how determined they were to
die in their defense I deduced two things: that we would regain
little, or none, of the riches which they had taken from us, and

that they gave us cause, and indeed obliged us, to destroy them utterly. On this last I dwelt with more sorrow, for it weighed heavily on my soul, and thus I sought to find a way whereby I might frighten them and cause them to recognize their error and the harm they would receive from us; so for this reason I burnt and tore down the towers of their idols and their houses. In order that they should feel it the more, I commanded my men to set on fire those big houses in the square where the Spaniards and I had previously been quartered before we were expelled from the city. These were so large that a prince with more than six hundred people in his household and his retinue might be housed in them. There were also some others next to them which, though somewhat smaller, were very much prettier and more delicate; Mutezuma had kept in them every species of bird found in these parts. Although it distressed me, I determined to burn them, for it distressed the enemy very much more; and they showed great grief, as did their allies from the cities on the lakes, for they never believed that our force was sufficient to penetrate so far into the city, and this greatly dismayed them.

Once we had burnt these houses, I called together the men, as it was late, and returned to the camp; and when the people of the city saw that we were withdrawing, an infinite number fell upon us and attacked our rear guard with enormous force. But as the horsemen could gallop the whole length of the street we turned to attack them, killing many at every charge; but for all that they did not cease to come, shouting loudly at our backs. That day they showed great dismay, especially when they saw us enter their city, burning and destroying it, and with us the people of Tesuico, Calco and Suchimilco,[54] and the Utumies, each calling out the name of his province, and in another part the Tascaltecans, who all showed them their countrymen cut to pieces, saying that they would dine off them that night and breakfast off them the following morning, which in fact they did. Thus we returned to our camp to sleep, for we had labored hard that day; moreover the seven brigantines I had with me had sailed up the canals in the city and burnt a large part of it. The captains of the other camps and the six brigantines all fought very well, and I could speak at length of their exploits, but to avoid prolixity I will state only that they returned to their camps victorious and without having received any harm.

Early on the following morning,[55] after having heard Mass, I returned to the city with my people in the same order so that the enemy should have no time to open the breaches and put up the barricades. Early as we were, however, of the three canals that cross the street which runs from our camp to the great houses in the square, two were as they had been on the previous days, and were so hard to capture that we fought from eight in the morning until one o'clock in the afternoon, during which time nearly all the bolts, ammunition and shot which the crossbowmen and harquebusiers had were expended. Your Majesty may well believe that the dangers we encountered each time we captured these bridges were beyond compare, for to take them the Spaniards were required to swim across to the other side, and many were unable or unwilling to do this, for the enemy thrust us back with the blades and butts of their spears to prevent us from reaching the other side. But as they now had no roof tops from which to do us harm and we, being but a stone's throw away, showered them with bolts, the Spaniards became each day less afraid and more determined to cross; they also saw how determined I was and that, sink or swim, it could not be avoided. Your Majesty may think that once we had gained those bridges at such risk we were negligent in not holding them, so that we were obliged to return each day to the same danger and toil, which were indeed great; and thus it would appear to all who were not present. But I assure Your Majesty that in no manner could it have been done, for to achieve it two things would have been necessary—either for us to move our camp to the square and enclosure of the temple towers, or to mount a guard on the bridges by night, both of which were most dangerous, and indeed impossible, for once we had set up our camp in the city we would have had to fight

15a. PLATE 9. The Massacre at Cholula. In the middle of the drawing a priest tells two Tlaxcalteca of a plot and they in turn warn Marina. The mounted horseman to the left of Marina looks like Sandoval but may have been intended to be Cortés though he is usually depicted with a beard. The figures in the top right-hand corner are the Tlatoque of Cholula.

15. Plates 9, 14, 18, 28, and 48 of the *Lienzo de Tlaxcala* from the edition published by Alfredo Chavero in *Antigüedades Mexicanas*, Mexico, 1892, 2 vols. (For a description of the *Lienzo* and its history see Charles Gibson, *Tlaxcala in the Sixteenth Century*, New Haven, 1952, pp. 247–253). *Courtesy of the Bodleian Library, Oxford.*

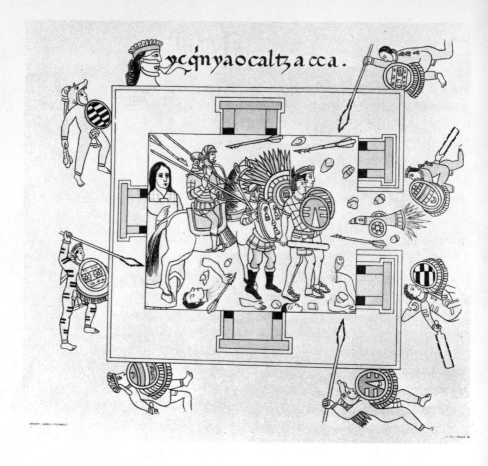

15b. PLATE 14. The attack upon Alvarado's forces in the palace of Axayacatl. The legend reads: *Icquinyaocaltzacca,* "They have shut them into the
palace with war."

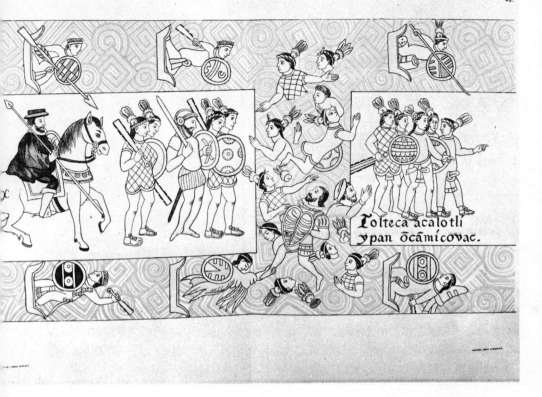

Tolteca acalotli ypan ōcāmícovac.

15c. PLATE 18. The flight from Tenochtitlan on the *noche triste*. The horseman is presumably Cortés. The legend reads: *Tlotecaacalotli ypanoncan micovac*, "In the breach called *Tlotecaacalotli* there they died."

veyotlipan.

Tonca qnamicq3 mtlatoque qmaca qyxqch qualom.

15d. PLATE 28. The arrival of the Spaniards in Hueyotlipan. Cortés is received by Maxixcatzin (?) who is carrying a bunch of flowers and is accompanied by a number of Tlaxcalteca nobles. The legend reads: *Quenamicque intlatoque quemacaque yxquechqualoni*, "Here they went out to meet the Tlatoque (the Spaniards) and gave them all manner of foods."

15e. PLATE 48. The fall of Tenochtitlan and the surrender of Cuauhtemoc.
Cortés is shown with some outlandish feathers in his cap seated on the roof
of the house of Aztacoatzin whose glyph, a white urn and water, appears
beneath it. According to Chavero the figures in the bottom right-hand corner are the defeated Mexica warriors; to me they look more like the victorious Tlaxcalteca. Marina is standing behind Cortés and above the heads of
Cuauhtemoc and his companion are those of a group of women. Only the
queen Tecuhichpoch is distinguished by a glyph. (The head of an old
woman, *tecul*, a cotton flower, *ichcatl* and the symbol for smoke *poch*[*tli*].)
The legend reads, *Yc palinque Mexica*, "Here ended the Mexica."

with them all night long; they would have caused us intolerable difficulty and attacked us on all sides, for we were few and they were many. As for placing guards by night, the Spaniards were so tired with fighting during the day that we could spare no one for the night; thus we were obliged to capture them again each day we entered the city.

That day, as we spent so long in recapturing and repairing those bridges, there was little time left for anything else, save that on another main street which leads to the city of Tacuba two other bridges were captured and filled in and many good houses were burnt. By then it was late and time to withdraw, which was hardly less dangerous than capturing the bridges, for once they saw us retreat they recovered as much strength as if they had won the greatest victory in the world and we were fleeing before them. For this withdrawal it was necessary that the channels should be well filled in and level with the road, so that the horses might gallop freely across them. Sometimes, when we were thus withdrawing and they pursued us so eagerly, the horsemen would pretend to be fleeing, and then suddenly turn on them; we always took a dozen or so of the boldest. By these means and by the ambushes which we set for them, they were always much hurt; and certainly it was a remarkable sight for, even though they well knew the harm they would receive from us as we withdrew, they still pursued us until we had left the city. With this we returned to our camp, and the captains of the other camps informed me that they had done very well that day and that many people had been killed on land and in the water. Pedro de Alvarado, who was captain in Tacuba, wrote informing me that he had won two or three bridges, for, as he was on the causeway which runs from the market in Temixtitan to Tacuba, and the three brigantines which I had given him could tie up on one side of the causeway, he had not been in such danger as previously. Where he was, there were more bridges and gaps in the causeway than in other places but fewer roof tops.

During all this time the natives of Yztapalapa, Uchilubuzco,

Mexicalcingo, Culuacan, Mizqueque and Cuitaguaca, which, as I
have recounted, are on the fresh-water lake, would never come
peaceably to us, although we had never been attacked by them. But
as the people of Calco were Your Majesty's very loyal vassals and
saw that we were fully occupied with the people in the great city,
they joined forces with some other towns which are around the lake
and did as much harm as they were able to the aforementioned
towns who, seeing that we were each day victorious over the people
of Temixtitan, and realizing the injuries they were suffering and
might further suffer from our allies, decided to submit.[56] When they
reached our camp they begged me to forgive them the past and to
command the people of Calco and their other neighbors to do them
no more harm. I told them that I was well pleased and harbored
anger against no one save the people of the city, but so that I might
have proof of the sincerity of their friendship, I asked them, as I
would not raise the siege until the city surrendered, or was captured,
and as they had many canoes with which they might help me, to
make ready as many as they could, with all the warriors in their
towns, in order to help us thenceforth on the water. I also asked
them, as the Spaniards had for their quarters but a few ruinous huts,
and it was now the rainy season, to build as many houses as possible
in the camp and to carry adobes and timber in their canoes from the
houses in the city which were nearest to the camp. They replied
that the canoes and the warriors would be ready each day; and they
were so diligent in building the houses that on both sides of the two
towers on the causeway where I was encamped they built so many
that from the first to the last was a distance of more than three or
four crossbowshots. From this Your Majesty may see how wide
this causeway is which traverses the deepest part of the lake, for
these houses were built on both sides of it, and yet there still was
space for us to pass most comfortably between them on horseback.
There were continuously more than two thousand people in the
camp, counting the Spaniards and the Indians who served them. All
the other warriors, our allies, were stationed at Cuyoacan, a league

and a half from the camp. The people from those towns, which I have already mentioned, also supplied us with provisions, of which we were in great need, especially with fish and cherries, of which latter there are such quantities hereabouts that in the six months which their season lasts they are sufficient for twice the population of this land.

As we had entered the city from our camp two or three days in succession, besides the three or four previous attacks, and had always been victorious, killing with crossbow, harquebus and field gun an infinite number of the enemy, we each day expected them to sue for peace, which we desired as much as our own salvation; but nothing we could do would induce them to do it. In order to put them in greater difficulties and to see if we might oblige them to surrender, I proposed to enter the city each day and to attack the inhabitants in three or four different places. I therefore commanded all the people from those cities on the water to come in their canoes; and on the morning of that day there gathered in the camp more than a hundred thousand of our allies. I then ordered that four brigantines with half the canoes, of which there were as many as fifteen hundred, should approach on one side, while the other three brigantines, with the same number of canoes, were to go to the other; and they were all to circle the city and burn and do all the damage they could. I entered along the main street and found it free from obstruction right up to the great houses in the square; nor had any of the breaches been reopened. I then advanced to the street which led to Tacuba, where there are six or seven bridges. From there I ordered a captain to enter another street with sixty or seventy men. Six horsemen went to guard his rear, and with them went more than ten or twelve thousand of our Indian allies. I then ordered another captain to do the same along another street, and I myself, with all the men who were left, proceeded up the road to Tacuba, where we won three bridges. These we filled in, but because it was already late we left the others for another day when they could be better taken, for I greatly desired to capture that street so that the people from Pedro de Alvarado's camp might communicate with ours and pass from one camp to the other, and the brigantines likewise. That day was one of great victory both on land and in the water, and we took some spoil from the city. The alguacil mayor and Pedro de Alvarado were also victorious.

On the following day I re-entered the city in the same order as before, and God granted us such a victory that in the places where I entered with my people there seemed to be no resistance, and the enemy retreated so swiftly that we appeared to have won three-quarters of the city. Pedro de Alvarado also drove them quickly back, and I was certain, on this day as on the previous one, that they would sue for peace, which, I assured them in every possible way, I greatly desired, with or without a victory; but, for all that, they never gave any sign of peace. That day we returned joyfully to our camp, although we could not but be saddened by their determination to die.

In these days past Pedro de Alvarado had won many bridges, and in order to hold them had placed a guard of foot soldiers and horsemen on them during the night, while the rest of his men returned to the camp, which was three-quarters of a league from there. But because this task became intolerable, he decided to move his camp to the end of the causeway leading to the market-place of Temixtitan, which is a square much larger than that of Salamanca, and all surrounded by arcades. To reach this he had only to capture two or three bridges, but the channels there were very broad and dangerous, so he had to fight for several days, although he was always successful. On that day, of which I have already spoken, when he saw the enemy weaken, and saw how I constantly attacked them with great ferocity, he became so enamored of the taste of victory, with all those bridges and fortifications he had captured, that he resolved to cross and take a breach where more than seventy paces of causeway had been torn up and replaced by water to a depth of eight or nine feet. As they attacked that same day and were greatly assisted by the brigantines, they crossed the water, gained the bridges and pursued the enemy who fled. Pedro de Alvarado then made haste to fill in that breach so that the horses might also cross over, and because I had cautioned him each day, both in writing and in person, not to take an inch of ground without first making it safe for the horsemen, who were the mainstay of the fighting. When the people of the city saw that there were only forty or fifty Spaniards and some of our allies on the other side, and that the horsemen were unable to cross, they turned on them so swiftly that they drove them back into the water. Three or four Spaniards were taken alive to be sacrificed and some of our allies were killed.[57]

Finally Pedro de Alvarado succeeded in retreating to his camp, and when that day I returned to mine and heard of all that had happened it distressed me more than anything else in the world, because it might have encouraged the enemy and led them to believe that we dared not enter the city again. The reason why Pedro de Alvarado wished to capture that dangerous breach was partly because, as I have said, he had defeated a great part of the enemy forces and they had shown some weakness; but above all he did it because his men were urging him to capture the marketplace, for, once that was taken, the city was almost won, as all the Indian forces had gathered there and placed all their hopes in it. As Alvarado's men saw how I continually defeated the Indians, they feared that I might capture the marketplace before they did, and, as they were closer to it than we, they held it a point of honor to take it first. For this reason Pedro de Alvarado was much importuned, and the same happened to me in my camp, for all the Spaniards greatly urged me to enter by one of the three streets leading to the marketplace, for we should meet with no resistance and, once it was captured, we would have less trouble thereafter. I made every possible excuse for not doing this, although I concealed the real reason, which was the disadvantages and dangers which I had observed; for in order to reach the marketplace we would have had to pass an infinite number of roof tops and broken roads and bridges, so that every house on our way would be like an island.

When I returned to my camp that afternoon and learned of Alvarado's defeat, I decided to go to his camp on the following morning to rebuke him, and to see what he had gained and where he had moved his camp, advising him as to what he must do for his own defense and for an attack on the enemy. When I reached his camp, however, I was truly astonished to see how far into the city he had gone and the dangerous bridges and passes which he had won, and I no longer blamed him as much as he had seemed to deserve. And when I had discussed with him what was to be done, I returned to my camp that same day.[58]

Once this was over I made several sorties into the city in the usual places. The brigantines and canoes attacked in two places while I fought in the city in four others. We were always victorious and killed great numbers of the enemy, for every day a multitude of people came to join our forces. I hesitated, however, to advance farther into the city, because the enemy might still abandon their stubborn resistance; furthermore, our entry could not be effected without much danger, for they were all united, full of courage and determined to die. But when the Spaniards saw this delay, for they had been fighting without cease for more than twenty days, they urged me strongly, as I said above, to enter and take the marketplace; for once that was captured the Indians would have very little left to defend and would be forced, if they did not surrender, to die of hunger and thirst, there being nothing left to drink except salt water from the lake. When I excused myself, Your Majesty's treasurer told me that the whole camp demanded it and that I must therefore comply. To him and to the other good people who were there I replied that their intention and desire were commendable, and that no one wished to see this business finished so much as I; but I would not attempt it for the reason which his demands had forced me to reveal, namely, that although he was willing there would be others who, on account of the dangers, would not be. But finally they pressed me so much that I agreed to do all I could once I had spoken to the people in the other camps.

The following day I conferred with some of the officers among us, and we agreed to inform the alguacil mayor and Pedro de Alvarado that next day we would enter the city and attempt to take the marketplace. I wrote telling them what they were to do on the Tacuba side, and as well as writing, I sent two of my servants to inform them of the entire operation. The order they were to follow was that the alguacil mayor should go with ten horsemen, a hundred foot soldiers and fifteen crossbowmen and harquebusiers to Alvarado's camp, leaving ten horsemen behind in his own. With these he should arrange that on the following day they should lie in ambush behind some houses; he would then remove his baggage as if he were breaking camp; when the enemy began to pursue him, the horsemen would fall on them from behind. The alguacil mayor, with three of his brigantines and three of Pedro de Alvarado's, was to take that dangerous breach where Alvarado had been driven back, and fill it in with all haste, and then continue his advance; but on no account was he to leave a bridge which he had won without having it repaired and leveled. I also told them that if they could reach the marketplace without exposing themselves to extreme danger, they should make every effort to do so, for I would do the same; but they should note that, although I told them to do this, it did not oblige them to take any step that might lead to their defeat or misfortune; this I told them, for I knew that they would follow where I led, even if they knew it might cost them their lives. My two servants then went with my message to the camp, where they found the alguacil mayor and Pedro de Alvarado, whom they informed of the plan, as we had agreed in our camp. As they were to fight only in one place, but I in many, I sent asking for seventy or eighty foot soldiers to enter with me the following day; these arrived that same night with my servants and slept in our camp, as they had been ordered.

Everything having been arranged as mentioned, on the following day, after Mass, the seven brigantines left our camp with more than three thousand allied canoes; I, with twenty-five horsemen and the other men I had, together with those seventy from the camp at Tacuba, marched forward into the city. When we arrived I disposed my men in this manner: From where we were, three roads led into the marketplace, which the Mexicans call Tianguizco[59] (and the whole place where it is located is called Tlatelulco). I told Your Majesty's treasurer and *contador*[60] to take the principal one with seventy men and more than fifteen or twenty thousand of our allies and to place in the rear guard seven or eight horsemen. As soon as he captured the canals and earthworks he was to level them, for which purpose he took a dozen men with picks, as well as some of our allies whose task it was to fill up breaches. The other two streets, which ran from the Tacuba causeway to the marketplace, were narrower and consisted more of causeways, bridges and canals. I sent two captains with eighty men and more than ten thousand of our Indian allies along the broader of the two, at the entrance to which I placed two large guns with eight horsemen to guard them. With eight horsemen and some hundred foot soldiers, among whom were more than twenty-five crossbowmen and harquebusiers, and a huge number of our allies, I continued my march and moved as far up the other, narrower road as I was able. But at the entrance to it I halted the horsemen and ordered them on no account to move from there, nor to follow me unless I first ordered them to do so. I then dismounted and we arrived at a barricade they had built at the end of a bridge which we took with a small field gun, supported by the crossbowmen and harquebusiers. We then moved on along a street which they had breached in two or three places.

Apart from these three attacks which we made on the inhabitants of the city, our allies who attacked them on the roof tops and other places were so numerous it seemed that nothing could resist us. When we had taken these two bridges, the barricades and the causeway, our allies followed up the street without any protection from us while I remained on a small island with some twenty Spaniards, for I had seen that certain of our allies were engaged with the enemy and were sometimes driven back into the water; with our help they might return to the attack. In addition to this, we took care that the enemy was prevented from attacking the Spaniards in the rear from certain side streets in the city. These same Spaniards sent to inform me at this time that they had gained much ground and were not far from the marketplace; they greatly wished to press on, for they could already hear the attack being made by Sandoval and Alvarado on their side. I sent to tell them that on no account should they advance a step until they had first made certain that all the bridges were well filled in; thus, should they be obliged to retreat, the water would not hinder them at all, for it was there, as they knew, that the greatest danger lay. They answered that all they had won was well repaired, and I might go there and see for myself if it was so. And I, fearing that they might have been thoughtless and not taken enough care in filling up the bridges, went there and discovered that they had crossed a breach in the road ten or twelve paces wide, in which the water was more than eight feet deep. When they crossed they had thrown wood and reed grass into the breach, and because they had passed over one at a time and with great care this had not sunk; now they were so drunk with the joy of victory they imagined that they had made it quite safe. But at the very moment I arrived at that feeble bridge I saw the Spaniards and many of our allies in full retreat, with the enemy like hounds at their heels; and as I could see the impending disaster I began to cry, "Stop! Stop!" But when I reached the bank I found the water full of Spaniards and Indians as though not a straw had been thrown into it. The enemy attacked so fiercely that in attempting to kill the Spaniards they leapt into the water after them. Then some enemy canoes came up the canals and took some of the Spaniards away alive. As this affair happened so suddenly and I saw that my men were being killed, I determined to make a stand and die fighting. The best that I and my companions could do was to help out some wretched Spaniards who were drowning; some of these were wounded, some half-drowned and others had lost their weapons. I sent them on ahead, at which point we were attacked by such a multitude of the enemy that I and another twelve or fifteen were surrounded on all sides. As I was so intent on rescuing the drowning, I neither saw nor gave a thought to the harm I might receive. Certain Indians then came to seize me and would have carried me off were it not for a captain of fifty men, who always accompanied me, and a youth in his company, who, after God, was the one to save my life, and in doing so, like a valiant man, gave his own.[61]

Meanwhile, the Spaniards who had escaped the rout were retreating along the street, which was narrow and level with the water, the dogs having made it so on purpose; as many of our allies were also fleeing that way, the road was soon so blocked with people who moved so slowly that the enemy was able to attack them from the water on both sides and kill and capture as they chose. The captain who was with me, who was called Antonio de Quiñones, said to me: "Let us go and save at least your own person, for you know that if you are killed we are all lost," but he could not persuade me to go away. When he saw this, he seized me by the arms to turn me back, and, although I would have rather died than escape, as a result of the insistence of that man and other companions of mine who were close by, we began to retreat, fighting with swords and bucklers against the enemy, who pursued us and wounded some of us. At this moment a servant of mine arrived on horseback and cleared a little room; but they speared him through the throat from a low roof top and forced him to retreat. While we were engaged in this desperate struggle to detain the enemy until our men had passed up that narrow street to safety, there came a servant of mine with a horse for me to ride; the people who had escaped from the water had brought so much mud onto the street that no one could stand upright, especially as we were being pushed about by those who were trying to escape. I mounted, but not to fight, because that was impossible then on horseback; had it not been so, those eight horsemen whom I had left on a small island farther up the causeway would have been there, whereas they were unable to do anything except retreat. Retreat, however, was so perilous that two mares, ridden by two of my servants, fell from that causeway into the water, one of which was killed by the Indians and the other saved by the foot soldiers. Another of my servants, a youth named Cristóbal de Guzmán, took a horse which they had given him on that island to bring to me so that I might escape, but both he and the horse were killed by the enemy before they could reach me. His death caused such sorrow to the entire camp that those who knew him still bear the grief to this day.

Now, after all our hardships, it pleased God that those of us who remained should reach the Tacuba causeway, which was very wide. There I mustered my men and took the rear guard myself with nine horsemen. The enemy came after us so swollen with the pride of victory that it seemed not one of us would escape alive; and withdrawing as best I could I sent word to the treasurer and contador to retire to the square in as orderly a fashion as possible. I sent the same orders to the other two captains who had gone along the street which led to the market; both parties had fought most bravely and captured many bridges and barricades, which they had also leveled very well, which was the cause of their being able to retreat unharmed. Before the treasurer and contador began to retreat, the people of the city had thrown, over the barricade where they were fighting, two or three of the heads of the captured Christians, although they did not at that time know whether they came from Pedro de Alvarado's camp or our own. When we had all gathered in the square, the enemy pressed upon us from every quarter, and in such numbers that it was all we could do to resist them, and in places where before our defeat they would never have dared attack. Then suddenly in a high temple tower close to the square they offered up to their gods as a sign of victory many perfumes and incense of a gummy substance which is found in these parts and resembles resin.[62] And although we greatly desired to put a stop to this we were unable to do so, for our people were already retreating to the camp as fast as possible.

In this rout the enemy slew thirty-five or forty Spaniards, and more than a thousand of our Indian allies; more than twenty Christians were wounded, I myself being injured in the leg; we lost a small field gun and many harquebuses, crossbows and other arms.[63]

Once they had gained their victory, the people of the city, in order to terrify the alguacil mayor and Pedro de Alvarado, took all the Spaniards they had captured dead or alive to Tlatelulco, which is the market, and on some high towers which are there sacrificed them naked, opening their chests and tearing out their hearts as an offering to the idols. The Spaniards of Alvarado's camp could see this clearly from where they were fighting, and recognized those who were being sacrificed as Christians by their white naked bodies. And, although they were grieved and greatly dispirited by the sight, they retreated to their camp, having fought very well that day and won through almost to the marketplace, which would have been taken if God, on account of our sins, had not permitted such a great disaster. We returned to our camp somewhat earlier than usual, and much saddened, for we had heard that the brigantines were lost, as the enemy canoes had fallen on us from behind, but, thank God, this was not true, although the brigantines and the canoes of our allies had been in great difficulties. So much so, indeed, that one brigantine was almost lost, and the captain and master were both wounded; the captain died within a week. All during that day and the following night the enemy celebrated with drums and trumpets so loudly it seemed as if the world was coming to an end. They opened all the streets and canals as before, and lit fires and posted sentries only two crossbowshots from our camp. And as we were so sorely defeated and wounded and without weapons, we needed to rest and recuperate.

In the meantime the people of the city sent messengers to many subject provinces, informing them of how they had won a great victory and had slain many Christians and that shortly they would have done with us, and advising them on no account to discuss terms with us. The proof they sent of their victory was the heads of those two horses which they had killed and of some Christians. These they carried about and displayed wherever they saw fit, which served further to confirm the rebels in their obstinacy. In order, however, that our enemies should not become too arrogant or perceive our own weakness, each day some Spaniards on horse and foot, together with many of our allies, went to fight in the city, although they could never gain more than a few bridges in the first street before reaching the square.

Two days after our defeat, news of which had now spread throughout the countryside, the natives of a town called Cuarnaguacar,[64] who were once subjects to Temixtitan but had declared themselves our allies, arrived in the camp. They told me how the inhabitants of Malinalco, who were their neighbors, were doing them much harm and ravaging their land, and had now allied themselves with the province of Cuisco,[65] which is a large one, and intended to fall upon them and kill them for having offered themselves as Your Majesty's vassals and our allies; furthermore, they said that once they had destroyed the people of Cuarnaguacar they would attack us. And although our defeat was so recent and we needed help more than we could give it, I determined to go to their aid because they entreated me with such insistence; so, in the face of opposition from some who claimed that I would destroy us all by reducing our numbers in the camp, I sent back with those messengers eighty foot soldiers and ten horsemen under the command of the captain Andrés de Tapia. I greatly urged him to do whatever was most convenient to Your Majesty's service and our safety, since he saw the difficulties in which we found ourselves, and therefore to return within ten days. He departed, and arriving at a small town between Malinalco and Coadnoacad he found the enemy

awaiting him. Then he and his men together with the people of
Coadnoacad began the battle in the fields, and our men fought so
well that they routed the enemy and drove them back to Malinalco,
which is situated on top of a very high hill where the horsemen
could not follow. When the Spaniards saw this, they destroyed all
they found on the plain and returned victorious to our camp within
ten days. In the upper part of this town of Malinalco are many
springs of good clear water, which is most refreshing.

While this captain was away some Spaniards on horse and
on foot, together with our allies, entered the city, as I have already
said, and reached close to the great houses in the square; but they
could advance no farther, for the enemy had opened a deep broad
canal at the entrance to the square, and on the far side had built a
large and strong barricade where fighting took place until night
overtook them.

A chieftain of the province of Tascalteca, called Chichimecatecle, of whom I have already spoken, the man who brought
the planks for the brigantines from that province, had, since the
beginning of the war, been staying with all his people in Alvarado's
camp; when he saw that after our defeat the Spaniards did not fight
as well as before, he determined to enter the city alone with his own
people. He posted four hundred archers at a dangerous bridge
which he had won from the enemy (though he could never have
done so without our help), and then advanced at the head of his
men, who made a terrible noise, screaming and calling out the name
of their province and lord. They fought very fiercely that day and
there were many wounded and many killed on both sides. The
people of the city, however, believed they had trapped their enemies, for as they are a people who, whether they are victorious or
not, pursue their adversaries in retreat with great determination,
they thought that once the Tascaltecans came to cross the water,
where the danger was greatest, they would make good their revenge. For this reason Chichimecatecle had stationed his four hundred archers at this point. As soon as the people of the city saw that

their enemies were retreating, they at once charged down on them, whereupon the Tascaltecans threw themselves into the water, and with the help of the archers reached the other side. The enemy, faced with such resistance, halted, much surprised by Chichimeca-tecle's daring.

Two days after the Spaniards had returned from fighting the people of Malinalco—as Your Majesty will have seen in the chapter before—there arrived at our camp ten Indians of the Utumies who were slaves of the Culuans and, as I have said, had offered themselves as Your Majesty's vassals and each day fought by our side. They now told me that the chieftains of the province of Matalcingo, who are their neighbors, were making war on them and laying waste their land; they had burnt a village and carried off some of its inhabitants and were now advancing, destroying all they could, and intending to come to our camps and attack us, so that those within the city could come out and have done with us for-ever. We were all the more ready to believe their story because, for the past few days, each time we entered the city the enemy had threatened us with the arrival of reinforcements from this province of Matalcingo, of which we had heard little, save that it was large and lay some twenty-two leagues from our camps. From the com-plaints these Utumi people made against their neighbors, we were given to understand that they required assistance, and although the request came at a most difficult time, we trusted in God's help to clip the wings of those defending the city, who each day threatened us with these reinforcements, and seemed to place a great deal of confidence in their aid; for, indeed, they could expect help from no other quarter; I therefore determined to send Gonzalo de Sandoval, alguacil mayor, with eighteen horsemen and one hundred foot sol-diers, among whom was but a single crossbowman; he departed with some of our Utumi allies in his company.

God alone knows the danger in which they went, and, in-deed, that in which we remained; but as we had now to show greater courage than ever before and to die fighting if need be, we concealed our weakness from friend and foe alike. And not once but many times the Spaniards declared that they asked of God only that they should live to triumph over the defenders of the city, even if this should mean that they gained nothing else in the entire land. From this may be seen the risks and extreme hardships our lives and persons were forced to bear.

That day the alguacil mayor spent the night in a village of the Utumies on the border with Matalcingo; very early on the morning of the following day he departed, and came to some farms belonging to the Utomi, which he found deserted and mostly burnt, and, descending to the plain, beside a small river he found a large number of the enemy, who had just burnt another village. When they saw the Spaniards they turned and fled; and while pursuing them, our men came across many sacks of maize and roasted babies which the enemy carried as provisions and had abandoned when they saw the Spaniards. Once they had crossed a river which was farther up the valley, the enemy began to muster their troops, whereupon Sandoval and the horsemen broke their ranks and pursued them as they fled back toward Matalcingo, which lies three leagues from there. The horsemen then drove them all the way to the town and confined them there, and awaited the other Spaniards and our Indian allies, who were killing those whom the horsemen had intercepted but left behind. More than two thousand of the enemy were slain during this chase. As soon as the foot soldiers arrived, they, together with our allies, who numbered more than seventy thousand men, began to run toward the town, where the enemy turned and faced them while their women and children and their belongings were carried to safety in a fortress, built on a high hill close by. But so fierce was the attack that the defenders were likewise forced to retreat to this fortress on the hill, which was very steep and almost impregnable. The town was burnt and sacked in a very short time, but as it was late and as the men were very tired, for they had fought all day, the alguacil mayor decided not to attack the fortress. The enemy spent most of that night howling and beating drums and blowing trumpets.

On the following morning the alguacil mayor began to lead his men up toward the fortress, although he was afraid that he would find himself hard pressed by their resistance. When he arrived, however, the place seemed to be deserted, and several of our Indian allies came down and said that they had found no one, for the enemy had left shortly before dawn. While they were thus occupied they saw that all the valleys thereabouts were full of people. These were Utumies, but the horsemen, thinking that they were the enemy, charged them and killed three or four with their lances. As the Utomi language is different from that of the Culuans, they could understand nothing, except that they saw the Indians throw down their arms and approach them; yet even after that they killed three or four more. But our allies understood that it was because they had not been recognized. As the enemy had departed, the Spaniards decided to move against another of their towns which was also involved in the fighting; but when the inhabitants saw so many advancing toward them they sued for peace. The alguacil mayor then spoke with the chieftain of that town, telling him how I always welcomed those who offered themselves as Your Majesty's vassals, however guilty they might be, and begged him to persuade the people of Matalcingo to come over to me. This lord promised to do as he was asked and also to bring the people of Malinalco to surrender. With this victory the alguacil mayor returned to his camp.

That same day some Spaniards had been fighting in Temixtitan, and the enemy had sent asking for our interpreter to come because they wished to talk peace, which, however, it seemed, they wanted only on condition that we leave the entire land. They made this move only to gain a few days in which to rest and refurnish their supplies, for we never succeeded in breaking their will to fight. While we stood arguing through the interpreter, with nothing more than a fallen bridge between us and the enemy, an old man, in full view of everyone, very slowly extracted from his knapsack certain provisions and ate them, so as to make us believe that they were in no need of supplies, for we had told them they would all die of hunger. Our allies warned us that these talks were insincere and urged us to attack them, but we fought no more that day, for the lords had told the interpreter to convey their proposals to me.

Four days after Sandoval [66] returned from Matalcingo the lords of that province and of Malinalco and of the province of Cuiscon,[67] which is very large and important and had also rebelled, came to our camp and begged forgiveness for the past and offered to serve us well, which they did and have done until now.

While the alguacil mayor was at Matalcingo, the people of Temixtitan decided to attack Alvarado's camp by night, and struck shortly before dawn. When the sentries on foot and on horseback heard them they shouted, "To arms!" Those who were in that place flung themselves upon the enemy, who leapt into the water as soon as they saw the horsemen. Meanwhile the rest of our men came up and fought with them for more than three hours. We heard in our camp a field gun being fired, and, fearing that our men might be defeated, I ordered my own company to arm themselves and march into the city to weaken the offensive against Alvarado. And the Spanish attack was so fierce that the Indians decided to retreat. And that day we entered and fought in the city once more.

By this time those of us who had been wounded during our defeat were now healed. News arrived from Vera Cruz that a ship had arrived belonging to Juan Ponce de León,[68] who had been defeated on the mainland or island of Florida; and with this news the citizens of Vera Cruz sent me some powder and crossbows, of which we were in dire need. Now, thanks be to God, all the lands round about had come over to our side. But when I saw how rebellious the people of this city were, and how they seemed more determined to perish than any race of man known before, I did not know by what means we might relieve ourselves of all these dangers and hardships, and yet avoid destroying them and their city which was indeed the most beautiful thing in the world. They paid no heed to us when we told them that we would not strike camp, nor would the brigantines cease to attack them from the water, that we had destroyed the peoples of Matalcingo and Malinalco and that there was no one in all the land who could help them, nor could they acquire maize or meat or fruit or water or any other provision. The more such things were told them, the less signs they showed of weakening; rather they seemed to attack each time with greater spirit. Then, seeing that the affair was continuing in this way, and that we had been besieging the city for more than forty-five days, I decided to take steps to ensure our greater safety and to place the enemy in further difficulties; my plan was to raze to the ground all the houses on both sides of the streets along which we advanced, so that we should move not a step without leaving everything behind us in ruins; and all the canals were to be filled in, no matter how long it took us.[69] To this end I called together all the chiefs and principal persons among our allies and told them what I had decided, and asked them, in consequence, to call up many of their farm laborers, asking them to bring their *coas*, which are sticks which they use much as workmen in Spain dig with spades. They replied that they would willingly do as I asked, and that they welcomed my decision, for it seemed to them a way to destroy the city and this they desired more than anything else in the world.

Two or three days passed while arrangements were being made. The enemy were well aware that we were planning an offensive and they, as it afterwards appeared, were making every preparation for their defense, as we guessed they would. Having agreed with our allies, therefore, that we would fight the enemy on land and water, we left the next morning after Mass and took the road to the city. When we reached the bridge and barricade close to the great houses in the square the enemy called to us to advance no farther, for they desired peace. I ordered the men not to attack and told the enemy to call the lord of the city to come there and speak to me about terms. They then told me that they had sent for him and so detained me more than an hour, for in reality they had no wish for peace, and soon demonstrated the fact by beginning, as we stood quietly by, to hurl arrows, javelins and stones. When I saw this we attacked the barricade and captured it; but on entering the square we found it strewn with boulders to stop the horses crossing it, because on land it is they who carry the attack. Likewise we found a street walled up with stones and another covered with stones so that the horses could not pass up them. From that day forward we filled in that canal so thoroughly that the Indians never opened it again; and thenceforth we began, little by little, to destroy the houses and block all the canals we had won. As we were accompanied that day by more than 150,000 warriors, we made much progress. So we returned to our camp, and the brigantines and the canoes of our allies, which had likewise done much damage, also returned to rest.

On the following day we again entered the city in the same array, and when we reached that enclosure and the forecourt of the temple towers I ordered the captains and their men to do no more than block up the canals and level out the dangerous areas which we had won. Some of our allies I sent to burn and raze the houses and others to fight in the usual places while the horsemen were placed on guard in the rear. I myself climbed the highest of those towers, for the Indians recognized me and I knew it would distress them greatly to see me there. From there I encouraged our allies and sent them help when necessary; for, as they fought without pause, they sometimes forced the enemy to retreat and at other times were forced to retreat themselves. When this happened they were reinforced by three or four horsemen, which gave them immense courage to turn again upon our enemies. In this manner we entered the city five or six days in succession; and every time we withdrew we sent our allies out in front and positioned certain Spaniards in ambush in some houses while the horsemen remained behind and pretended to retreat suddenly, so as to bring the enemy out into the square. With these devices and the ambushes set by the foot soldiers we killed a number of them with our lances every afternoon. On one particular day seven or eight horsemen were waiting in the square for the enemy to emerge, and when we saw that they would not, we feigned a retreat, but the enemy, fearing that the horsemen would turn and charge them, as they had done before, placed themselves in vast numbers behind walls and on roof tops. The horsemen then turned and charged them, but they defended, from above, the entrance to a narrow street, where the horsemen could not follow and were at last forced to retire. The enemy, encouraged that they had caused our men to retreat, ran eagerly forward to kill, but so cautious were they even so, that they took up positions where they could not be harmed, and from along the walls some of them forced the horsemen to retreat, wounding two of their horses. This gave me an opportunity to set a most successful trap for them, as I shall later recount to Your Majesty. That evening we returned to our camp leaving all that we had gained most secure and leveled, and the enemy very boastful, believing we had retreated through fear. That same evening I sent a messenger to the alguacil mayor asking him to appear at my camp before dawn with fifteen horsemen from his own and from Pedro de Alvarado's camp.

On the following morning the alguacil mayor arrived with fifteen horsemen. I had there another twenty-five from Cuyoacan, which made forty in all. Ten of them I sent out together with the rest of our people and the brigantines, ordering them to enter the city as before and to capture and destroy all they could. I would be there with the thirty horsemen when the time came to retreat, for as they knew that we had leveled much of the city I ordered them to pursue the enemy in force until they were confined in their canals and strongholds, and to hold them there until the hour came to retreat. Then I and the thirty horsemen, unobserved, would set an ambush in some large houses near to the other large ones on the square. The Spaniards did as I commanded, and half an hour after midday I set out for the city with the thirty horsemen. When we arrived I left my companions in the aforementioned houses and I myself climbed the high tower as I was accustomed to do. While I was present, some Spaniards opened a grave which contained more than fifteen hundred castellanos worth of gold ornaments.

When the time came I gave orders for my men to retreat in good order and for the horsemen to begin a charge when they reached the square, but to pretend to be afraid and stop short. This they were to do as soon as they saw a large force of people in and around the square; my men in ambush were eagerly awaiting the signal to begin their attack. They were keen to do a good job, and somewhat tired of waiting. I then joined them, and already the Spaniards, both on horse and on foot, and our Indian allies who knew of the ambush, were retreating across the square. The enemy pursued them with such wild cries that one might have thought they had conquered the world. The nine [*sic*] horsemen made as if to attack them across the square and then withdrew suddenly. When they had done this twice the enemy were so enraged that they attacked at the horses' flanks until they drove us into the entrance of the street where we were waiting in ambush. When we saw the Spaniards pass in front of us and heard a harquebus shot, which was the signal to attack, we knew it was time to emerge; and so with the cry of "Señor Santiago" we fell suddenly upon them, and charged up the square spearing them, cutting them down and overtaking many of them, who were then slain by our allies, so that in this ambush more than five hundred of their bravest and most notable men were lost. That night our allies dined sumptuously, for all those they had killed were sliced up and eaten. So great was the surprise and shock they received in seeing themselves so suddenly beaten, that not once did they shout or scream that evening nor dared they appear on the roof tops or in the streets unless they were quite certain of being safe. As it was almost dark when we finally withdrew, it seems that the enemy sent certain slaves to see whether we were retreating or what we were doing. When they appeared in the street ten or twelve horsemen attacked and pursued them so that not one escaped alive.

The enemy was so terrified by this victory of ours that never again during the whole course of the war dared they enter the square when we withdrew, even if there was only a single horseman there, nor dared they attack so much as one of our foot soldiers or Indian allies, thinking that an ambush would be sprung on them from beneath their very feet. And the victory which Our Lord God gave us that day was the principal cause of the city being won the sooner, for the inhabitants were much dismayed by it and our allies greatly encouraged. So we returned to our camp resolved to bring a speedy end to the war, and not to let one day pass without entering the city. That day there were no casualties in our camp, except that when we emerged from our ambush some of the horsemen collided with each other, and one fell from his mare, which rushed straight at the enemy, who shot at and wounded her with arrows; whereupon, seeing how badly she was being treated, she returned to us but so badly wounded that she died that night. And although we were much grieved by this loss, for our lives were dependent on the horses, we were pleased that she had not perished at the hands of the enemy, as we thought would happen, for their joy at having captured her would have exceeded the grief caused by the death of their companions. The brigantines and the canoes of our allies wrought great havoc that day in the city and returned unharmed.

We already knew that the Indians in the city were very scared, and we now learnt from two wretched creatures who had escaped from the city and come to our camp by night that they were dying of hunger and used to come out at night to fish in the canals between the houses, and wandered through the places we had won in search of firewood, and herbs and roots to eat. And because we had already filled in many of the canals, and leveled out many of the dangerous stretches, I resolved to enter the next morning shortly before dawn and do all the harm we could. The brigantines departed before daylight, and I with twelve or fifteen horsemen and some foot soldiers and Indians entered suddenly and stationed several spies who, as soon as it was light, called us from where we lay in ambush, and we fell on a huge number of people. As these were some of the most wretched people and had come in search of food, they were nearly all unarmed, and women and children in the main. We did them so much harm through all the streets in the city that we could reach, that the dead and the prisoners numbered more than eight hundred; the brigantines also took many people and canoes which were out fishing, and the destruction was very great. When the captains and lords of the city saw us attack at such an unaccustomed hour, they were as frightened as they had been by the recent ambush, and none of them dared come out and fight; so we returned with much booty and food for our allies.

The following day we returned to the city, and, as our allies now saw how far we had advanced toward destroying it, they came to our camp in such multitudes we could no longer count them. That day we finally captured the Tacuba road and leveled the difficult stretches, so that the people in Alvarado's camp could communicate with us by way of the city; and on the main street which leads to the market two more bridges were captured and filled in. We also burnt the houses of the lord of the city, the second since Mutezuma's death, a boy of eighteen years of age called Guatimucín;[70] these houses had been very strong, for they were large, well fortified and surrounded by water. Two other bridges on other streets which run close to the main road to the market were also captured, so that three-quarters of the city was now in our hands, and the Indians were forced to retreat to the strongest part of the city, which consisted of the houses farthest out over the water.

On the following day, which was that of St. James (Santiago),[71] we entered the city in the same manner as before, following the main street which leads to the market, and we captured a very wide canal which they had thought a great safeguard, although, indeed, it took us a long time and was hard to win, and because it was so wide we were unable that day to fill it in so that the horses could cross over. As we were all on foot and the Indians saw that the horses had not crossed, they turned on us afresh and many of them were fine warriors. But we resisted their attack and, as we had many crossbowmen, forced them to retreat behind their barricades, although not before we had done them much injury with the bolts. In addition to this all the Spaniards carried pikes which I had ordered to be made after our defeat, and these proved most advantageous. That day we did nothing save burn and raze to the ground the houses on either side of that main street, which indeed was a sad sight; but we were obliged to do it, there being no other way of accomplishing our aims. When the enemy saw how much we had laid waste they cheered themselves by telling our allies to get on with burning and destroying the city, for if they were victorious they would, as they well knew, make them rebuild it, and if we were victorious, it would make little difference, since they would have to rebuild it for us; which latter was, thank God, the case, save that it is the inhabitants of the city who are rebuilding it, not our allies.

The following morning we entered the city in the usual manner and found the breach in the main street closed, as we had left it the previous day. We then advanced two crossbowshots and captured two large channels which they had broken in the middle of the street, and reached a small temple tower where we found the heads of several Christians whom they had killed, and this caused us much sorrow. From that tower, the right-hand road, which was where we were, ran straight until it reached the causeway where Sandoval had pitched his camp; on the left another street led to the marketplace, which was now free of water except for one canal that the Indians still defended against us; although we fought hard with them we were unable to advance any farther that day, and as it was already late we returned to our camp. But each day Our Lord God gave us victory, and they always suffered the worst of it.

On the following day, at nine o'clock, as we were preparing to re-enter the city, we saw from our camp smoke rising upward from the two very high towers in the Tlatelulco or market of the city; we could not guess what it meant, for it seemed to be more than that from the incense the Indians are accustomed to burn to their idols. We surmised, however, that Alvarado had reached there, which, though it later proved to be true, we hardly dared believe at the time. And in fact that day Alvarado and his men carried off a valiant achievement, for we still had many bridges and barricades to capture, and the greater part of the inhabitants continually came to defend them. When, however, he saw that we were harassing the enemy on our side, he made every effort to break through into the marketplace, which was their strongest point. But he only succeeded in coming within sight of it and in capturing those two towers and many others close to the market, which is in size almost equal to the whole area enclosed by the many towers of the city. The horsemen found themselves hard pressed and were forced to retreat, and in doing so three of their horses were wounded. Pedro de Alvarado and his men then withdrew to their camp; and we failed that day to take a canal and bridge, which was all that now stood between us and the market square, except for leveling off or filling in all the dangerous places. When we withdrew they pressed us hard, although it was to their cost.

The following morning we entered the city[72] and launched an attack upon the last channel and barricade before the marketplace, next to the small tower, as I have said. An ensign [alférez] and two or three other Spaniards threw themselves into the water, whereupon the enemy fled the bridge and we began to fill in and level the ground so that the horses might cross. While this was being done, Pedro de Alvarado rode up along this same road with four horsemen, and both his men and mine rejoiced greatly at his arrival, for now we were together we might put a swift end to the war. Alvarado left sentries in the rear and on the flanks both for his own defense and to preserve all that we had won. As soon as the crossing had been repaired I took some of the horsemen and went to look at the market square, ordering the rest of my company, however, not to advance beyond the bridge. We then rode around the market square for a while and saw that the roofs above the archways were full of the enemy, but as the square was very large and we were mounted they dared not approach. I climbed that high tower which is close to the market, and there I found, as in other such towers, the heads of Christians as offerings to their idols, and also the heads of our Tascaltecan allies, for between them and the people of Culua there is a most ancient and bitter feud. And looking down from that tower, I saw all that we had won of the city, for, indeed, of eight parts we had taken seven. Seeing also that it was not possible for so many people to survive in such a confined area, especially as all the houses that remained to them were small and built almost on top of one another in the water; and, moreover, that they suffered greatly from hunger, for in the streets we had found roots and strips of bark which had been gnawed, I decided therefore not to fight that day but to offer them terms so that so large a multitude of people might not perish. For it caused me the greatest sorrow and pain to see the harm that was being done them, so I continually called on them to surrender but they replied that they would never on any account give in, and when only a single warrior remained he would die fighting. They also swore to burn or throw deep into the water all that they possessed so that we should not have it. And I, so as not to repay evil with evil, dissimulated by not attacking them.

As we now had very little powder, we had been discussing for a fortnight or so whether to build a catapult.[73] And although we had no engineers for the task, some carpenters had offered to make a small one, and, although I did not expect they would succeed in their hopes, I permitted them to try. While we were keeping the Indians confined to a corner of the city, the machine was finished and carried to the market square and placed on a kind of stage which is in the middle of it, built of masonry, rectangular, about fourteen feet high and some thirty paces from corner to corner. Here they used to hold celebrations and games on their feast days, so the participants could be seen by all the people in the square, and also by those under and on top of the arcades. The catapult then took three or four days to set up while our Indian allies threatened the inhabitants of the city with it, saying that it was going to kill them all. Even if it were to have had no other effect, which indeed it had not, the terror it caused was so great that we thought the enemy might surrender. But neither of our hopes was fulfilled, for the carpenters failed to operate their machine, and the enemy, though much afraid, made no move to surrender, and we were obliged to conceal the failure of the catapult by saying that we had been moved by compassion to spare them.

The day after we had set up the catapult we again entered the city, and as we had not fought for three or four days we found the streets along which we passed full of women and children and other wretched people all starving to death, thin and exhausted; it was the most sorrowful of sights, and I ordered our allies to do them no harm. But not one of their effective warriors came near us, although we could see them on the roof tops, unarmed and wrapped in the cloaks they use. That day I again sued for peace, but their replies were evasive. For most of the day they kept us occupied in this fashion until at last I told them that I intended to attack and that they should withdraw their people, for, if they did not, I would give our allies permission to kill them. They then answered that they wanted peace; and I replied that I saw no chief with whom I might treat; once he came, and I would give him all the security he wished, we would talk of peace. We soon realized, however, that it was all a trick and that they were all prepared to fight us. Having then warned them many times, so as to press them into still greater straits, I ordered Pedro de Alvarado to take all his men and enter a large quarter still held by the enemy where there were more than a thousand houses; I entered by another place with the foot soldiers because there we could not make use of the horses. And although they fought fiercely with us we at last captured the whole quarter. So great was the slaughter that more than twelve thousand perished or were taken prisoner, and these were so cruelly used by our allies that not one was left alive, even though we severely censured and reprimanded them.

On the following day we returned again to the city, but this time I ordered that the enemy should not be attacked or harmed. When they saw such a multitude of people coming against them, that their own vassals, over whom they had formerly held sway, were coming to kill them; when they realized their great privations and that they had no place to stand save on the bodies of their own dead, they were so eager to be delivered from their misery that they begged us to have done with them, and hurriedly asked that I should be called, for they wished to speak with me. As all the Spaniards were most eager for the war to be ended and much grieved by the harm that was being done, this pleased them greatly, for they believed that the Indians desired peace, and most willingly came and called and begged me to go to a barricade where certain lords were waiting to speak to me. Although I knew that nothing would be gained thereby, I nevertheless resolved to go, for I well knew that it was only the lord of the city and three or four others of the principal persons who had determined not to surrender; the rest wished only to see themselves out of this pass dead or alive. When I reached the barricade they said that as they held me to be a child of the Sun which, in the short space of one day and one night could make a circuit of the whole earth, why did I not slay them all in so short a time and put an end to their suffering, for they already wished to die and go to heaven to rest with their Uchilobus, who was awaiting them; for this is the idol whom they most venerate. I said many things to persuade them to surrender but all to no avail, although we showed them more signs of peace than have ever been shown to a vanquished people, for we, by the grace of Our Lord, were now the victors.

Having now reduced the enemy to the last extremity, as

may be gathered from what I have said, and in order to persuade them from their evil intention, which was for every one of them to perish, I spoke to a person of great standing among them, a prisoner whom an uncle of Don Fernando, lord of Tesuico, had captured in the city two or three days before; although he was badly wounded, I asked him if he would be willing to return, and he replied that he would. So when, on the following day,[74] we again entered the city, I sent him with some Spaniards who handed him over to his people. I had spoken to this man at length, asking him to persuade the lord of the city and the other rulers to come to terms; and he promised to do all he could. The Indians received him with much reverence as a person of rank, but when he was taken before Guatimucín his lord, and began to speak of peace, they tell me he was immediately sent to be sacrificed; and the reply which we awaited they gave us by coming with loud screams and shouting that they wished only to die. Whereupon they rained javelins, arrows and stones down upon us and fought so fiercely with us that they killed a horse with a saber made from one of our swords. But in the end it cost them dear, for very many of them were killed; and thus we returned that day to our camp.

On the following day we returned to the city,[75] and so en-feebled were the enemy that huge numbers of our allies dared to spend the whole night there. When we came within sight of the enemy we did not attack but marched through the city thinking that at any moment they would come out to us. And to induce them to it I galloped up to a very strong barricade which they had set up and called out to certain chieftains who were behind and whom I knew, that as they saw how lost they were and knew that if I so desired within an hour not one of them would remain alive, why did not Guatimucín, their lord, come and speak with me, for I swore to do him no harm; and if he and they desired peace, they would be well received by me. I then used other arguments which moved them to tears, and weeping they replied that they well knew their error and their fate, and would go and speak to their lord, begging me not to leave, for they would return very soon. They went, and returned after a while and told me that their lord had not come because it was late, but that he would come on the following day at noon to the marketplace; and so we returned to our camp. I then gave orders that on the following day a platform, such as they are accustomed to, should be erected on that high stage in the middle of the square; I also ordered food to be prepared, and so it was done.

On the following day we went to the city and I warned my men to be on the alert lest the enemy betray us and we be taken unawares; and likewise I warned Pedro de Alvarado, who was there with me. When we reached the market I sent to inform Guatimucín that we awaited him, but he, it seemed, had decided not to come, and sent me in his stead five principal persons whose names, as they are not pertinent, I shall not give here. When they arrived they said that they had come on behalf of their lord, who begged my forgiveness for not coming himself, but he was afraid of appearing before me and, furthermore, had fallen ill; they, however, would do all that was asked of them. And although the lord had not come himself, we rejoiced that those other lords were present, for it seemed to us that we might now put a speedy end to this affair. I received them cheerfully and ordered food and drink to be given them, in consuming which they plainly showed their extreme privations. Once they had eaten I told them to speak to their lord, telling him that he need fear nothing, and that I promised him that in appearing before me he would suffer no indignity nor be detained, for without his presence no agreement or understanding could be reached. I ordered them to be given some refreshment to take away to eat, with which they departed, promising to do all they could in this matter. After two hours they returned, bringing me some fine cotton wraps of the sort they use, and told me that on no account would Guatimucín, their lord, come, so it was pointless to discuss the matter further. I repeated that I knew no reason why he should be afraid to appear before me, for he saw that they, whom I well knew to be the principal instigators of the war and responsible for prolonging it, were well treated and were allowed to come and go in safety without any harassment. I therefore begged them to speak to him again and to try very hard to persuade him to come, for it was greatly to his own benefit. They replied that they would indeed do so and would return the following day with his reply; and so they departed and we returned to our camps.

Early the following morning those chieftains came to our camp, asking me to go to the marketplace, for their lord wished to speak to me there; and I, believing this was so, rode out to the marketplace and waited there three or four hours, but he did not come. When I saw that I had been tricked and that although it was already late neither the lord nor his messengers had appeared, I called our Indian allies who had remained behind at the entrance to the city, almost a league away. I had given them orders not to advance beyond that point, for the enemy had asked that none of them should be within the city while we were discussing terms. Neither they nor Alvarado's men were slow in coming, and when they arrived we attacked some barricades and canals which were the enemy's last defenses, and both we and our allies broke through with ease.

On leaving my camp, I had commanded Gonzalo de Sandoval to sail the brigantines in between the houses in the other quarter in which the Indians were resisting, so that we should have them surrounded, but not to attack until he saw that we were engaged. In this way they would be surrounded and so hard pressed that they would have no place to move save over the bodies of their dead or along the roof tops. They no longer had nor could find any arrows, javelins or stones with which to attack us; and our allies fighting with us were armed with swords and bucklers, and slaughtered so many of them on land and in the water that more than forty thousand were killed or taken that day. So loud was the wailing of the women and children that there was not one man amongst us whose heart did not bleed at the sound; and indeed we had more trouble in preventing our allies from killing with such cruelty than we had in fighting the enemy. For no race, however savage, has ever practiced such fierce and unnatural cruelty as the natives of these parts. Our allies also took many spoils that day, which we were unable to prevent, as they numbered more than 150,000 and we Spaniards were only some nine hundred. Neither our precautions nor our warnings could stop their looting, though we did all we could. One of the reasons why I had avoided entering the city in force during the past days was the fear that if we attempted to storm them they would throw all they possessed into the water, and, even if they did not, our allies would take all they could find. For this reason I was much afraid that Your Majesty would receive only a small part of the great wealth this city once had, in comparison with all that I once held for Your Highness. Because it was now late, and we could no longer endure the stench of the dead bodies that had lain in those streets for many days, which was the most loathsome thing in all the world, we returned to our camps.

That evening I arranged that when we entered the city on the following day three heavy guns should be prepared and taken into the city with us, for I feared that the enemy, who were so massed together that they had no room to turn around, might crush us as we attacked, without actually fighting. I wished, therefore, to do them some harm with the guns, and so induce them to come out to meet us. I also ordered the alguacil mayor to make ready the brigantines, so that they might sail into a large lake between the houses, where all the canoes had gathered; for they now had so few houses left that the lord of the city lived in a canoe with certain of his chieftains, not knowing where else to go. Thus we made our plans for the morrow.

When it was light I had all the men made ready and the guns brought out. On the previous day I had ordered Pedro de Alvarado to wait for me in the market square and not to attack before I arrived. When all the men were mustered and all the brigantines were lying in wait behind those houses where the enemy was gathered, I gave orders that when a harquebus was fired they should enter the little of the city that was still left to win and drive the defenders into the water where the brigantines were waiting. I warned them, however, to look with care for Guatimucín, and to make every effort to take him alive, for once that had been done the war would cease. I myself climbed onto a roof top, and before the fight began I spoke with certain chieftains of the city whom I knew, and asked them for what reason their lord would not appear before me; for, although they were in the direst straits, they need not all perish; I asked them to call him, for he had no cause to be afraid. Two of those chieftains then appeared to go to speak with him. After a while they returned, bringing with them one of the most important persons in the city, whose name was Ciguacoacin,[76] and he was captain and governor of them all and directed all matters concerning the war. I welcomed him openly, so that he should not be afraid; but at last he told me that his sovereign would prefer to die where he was rather than on any account appear before me, and that he personally was much grieved by this, but now I might do as I pleased. I now saw by this how determined he was, and so I told him to return to his people and to prepare them, for I intended to attack and slay them all; and so he departed after having spent five hours in such discussions.

The people of the city had to walk upon their dead while others swam or drowned in the waters of that wide lake where they had their canoes; indeed, so great was their suffering that it was beyond our understanding how they could endure it. Countless numbers of men, women and children came out toward us, and in their eagerness to escape many were pushed into the water where they drowned amid that multitude of corpses; and it seemed that more than fifty thousand had perished from the salt water they had drunk, their hunger and the vile stench. So that we should not discover the plight in which they were in, they dared neither throw these bodies into the water where the brigantines might find them nor throw them beyond their boundaries where the soldiers might

see them; and so in those streets where they were we came across
such piles of the dead that we were forced to walk upon them.[77] I
had posted Spaniards in every street, so that when the people began
to come out they might prevent our allies from killing those
wretched people, whose number was uncountable. I also told the
captains of our allies that on no account should any of those people
be slain; but they were so many that we could not prevent more
than fifteen thousand being killed and sacrificed that day. But still
their warriors and chieftains were hiding in corners, on roof tops, in
their houses or in canoes on the lake, but neither their dissimulations
or anything else availed them anything, for we could clearly see
their weakness and their suffering. When I saw that it was growing
late and that they were not going to surrender or attack I ordered
the two guns to be fired at them, for although these did some harm
it was less than our allies would have done had I granted them license to attack. But when I saw that this was of no avail I ordered
the harquebus to be discharged, whereupon that corner which they
still held was taken and its defenders driven into the water, those
who remained surrendering without a fight.

    Then the brigantines swept into that inner lake and broke
through the fleet of canoes; but the warriors in them no longer
dared fight. God willed that Garci Holguín, a captain of one of the
brigantines, should pursue a canoe which appeared to be carrying
persons of rank; and as there were two or three crossbowmen in the
bows who were preparing to fire, the occupants of the canoe signaled to the brigantine not to shoot, because the lord of the city
was with them. When they heard this our men leapt aboard and
captured Guatimucín and the lord of Tacuba and the other chieftains with them.[78] These they then brought to the roof close to the
lake where I was standing, and, as I had no desire to treat Guatimucín harshly, I asked him to be seated, whereupon he came up to me
and, speaking in his language, said that he had done all he was
bound to do to defend his own person and his people, so that now
they were reduced to this sad state, and I might do with him as I

pleased. Then he placed his hand upon a dagger of mine and asked me to kill him with it; but I reassured him saying that he need fear nothing. Thus, with this lord a prisoner, it pleased God that the war should cease, and the day it ended was Tuesday, the feast of Saint Hippolytus, the thirteenth of August, in the year 1521. Thus from the day we laid siege to the city, which was on the thirtieth of May of that same year, until it fell, there passed seventy-five days, during which time Your Majesty will have seen the dangers, hardships and misfortunes which these, Your vassals, endured, and in which they ventured their lives. To this, their achievements will bear testimony.

Of all those seventy-five days not one passed without our being engaged in some manner with the enemy. On the day that Guatimucín was captured and the city taken, we gathered up all the spoils we could find and returned to our camp, giving thanks to Our Lord for such a favor and the much desired victory which He had granted us.[79]

I spent three or four days in the camp attending to many items of business and then departed for the city of Cuyoacan,[80] where I have remained until now, concerning myself with the good order, government and pacification of these parts.

When the gold and other things had been collected they were melted down with the agreement of Your Majesty's officials and valued at more than 130,000 *castellanos*, a fifth of which was accorded to Your Majesty's treasurer, together with a fifth of other things such as slaves, which also belonged to Your Majesty, as will later be shown in a list of everything that belongs to Your Majesty, which will be signed with our names. The remainder of the gold was divided up between myself and the other Spaniards, according to the rank, service and merit of each. In addition to the aforementioned gold, there were certain gold objects and jewelry, a fifth part of which, consisting of the best items, was given to Your Majesty's treasurer.

Among the spoils taken from the city were many gold bucklers, plumes, feather headdresses and things so remarkable that they cannot be described in writing nor would they be understood unless they were seen; and because they were of such a kind it seemed to me that they should not be divided, but all of them be given to the service of Your Majesty. For this purpose I called together all the Spaniards and entreated them to approve of all these things being sent to Your Majesty, and that the part due to them and to me should be used in Your Majesty's service; this they rejoiced in doing with much goodwill. This was then forwarded to Your Majesty with the delegates sent by the councils of New Spain.[81]

As the city of Temixtitan was so renowned throughout these parts, it seems that it came to the notice of the lord of a very great province called Mechuacan,[82] which lies some seventy leagues from Temixtitan, how we had destroyed and razed it to the ground. It seemed to the lord of that province that, considering the great size and strength of the city, if it could not resist us then nothing could; thus, out of fear or because it pleased him, he sent some messengers to me. These spoke to me through the interpreters of their language and told me how their lord had heard that we were vassals of a great lord, and, if I would accept, he and his people wished to be his vassals also, and to hold us as their friends. I replied that we were, in truth, all Your Majesty's vassals, and that their lord had been wise in wishing to become one also, for we were obliged to make war on those who did not.

As I had some time ago received news of the Southern Sea I enquired of them whether it could be reached by crossing their land. They replied that it could, so I requested them, in order to inform Your Majesty better of that sea and of their province, to allow two Spaniards to return with them.[83] They replied that they would willingly do so, but that in order to reach the sea it was necessary to pass through the land of a powerful lord with whom they were at war, and for that reason they were, for the moment, unable to reach the coast. These messengers remained with me for three or four days, and during that time I ordered the horsemen to skirmish before them so that they might take word of it back, and after I had given them certain jewels I dispatched them and the Spaniards to the aforementioned province of Mechuacan.

Most Powerful Lord, as I informed You in the previous chapter, I had received news a while before of the Southern Sea and knew that in some two or three places it was but twelve to fourteen days' march from here. This pleased me greatly, for it seemed to me that by discovering this sea we would render a great and memorable service to Your Majesty, especially as all those who have some learning and experience in the navigation of the Indies are quite certain that once the route to the Southern Sea has been discovered we shall find many islands rich in gold, pearls, precious stones and spices, and many wonderful and unknown things will be disclosed to us. This is also confirmed by men of learning and those tutored in the science of cosmography. Thus, as I wished to render Your Majesty such a singular and notable service, I dispatched four Spaniards, two of whom traveled through one province and the others through another; and once they had been shown the roads they were to take, and been assigned some of our allies to guide them, they left. I ordered them not to stop until they reached the sea, when they should take Royal and entire possession of it in Your Majesty's name.

The first pair of these traveled some 130 leagues through many beautiful provinces without encountering opposition; and when they reached the sea took possession of it, planting crosses by the shore as a sign. After some days they returned with an account of their discovery, informing me of everything at length. They also brought back with them some natives from the shores of that sea, together with good samples of gold from the mines in some of the provinces through which they had passed, which together with other samples of gold I am now sending to Your Majesty. The other two Spaniards returned somewhat later, for they had traveled close on 150 leagues before reaching the sea, of which they likewise took possession, and brought me a lengthy account of the coast.

They also brought back some natives, all of whom I received kindly, and after informing them of Your Majesty's great power and giving them some gifts, I sent them back to their land.

Most Catholic Lord, in my previous report I informed Your Majesty how, when the Indians defeated us and drove us from the city of Temixtitan, all the provinces subject to the city had rebelled against Your Majesty's service and had made war on us. In this report Your Majesty may judge how we have once again subjected most of these rebellious territories to Your Royal service. But certain provinces, which lie on the coast of the Northern Sea, some ten, fifteen and thirty leagues from here, had rebelled at the same time as the city of Temixtitan, and the natives of these provinces had killed by treachery more than a hundred Spaniards who had safe-conducts. Until the city had fallen I had been unable to move against them, but now, as soon as I had dispatched those Spaniards to the Southern Sea, I determined to send Gonzalo de Sandoval, alguacil mayor, with thirty-five horsemen and two hundred foot soldiers, together with some of our Indian allies and some chieftains and natives of Temixtitan, to those provinces, which are called Tatactetelco, Tuxtepeque, Guatuxco[84] and Aulicaba;[85] and once he had received his orders he began to prepare for the journey.

At this time the lieutenant whom I had left in the town of Segura de la Frontera, which is in the province of Tepeaca, came to this city of Cuyoacán, and informed me how the natives of that province and others in the neighborhood, Your Majesty's vassals, were being attacked by the natives of a province called Guaxacaque because they were our allies; besides it being essential to remedy this, it would be most advantageous to pacify the province of Guaxacaque, as it lay on the route to the Southern Sea, as well as for other reasons with which I will in due course acquaint Your Majesty. The aforementioned lieutenant also told me that he had received most detailed information concerning that province, and it could be subdued by a small force; for while I was encamped before Temixtitan he had gone there, on the instigation of the people of Tepeaca, to make war on the natives; but as he had taken only twenty or thirty Spaniards with him he had been forced to return—and somewhat more hurriedly than he might have wished. When I had read his account I gave him twelve horsemen and eighty foot soldiers. He and the alguacil mayor[86] then departed from Cuyoacán on the thirtieth of October of 1521.

When they reached the province of Tepeaca they mustered their men and each departed to his conquest. After twenty-five days the alguacil mayor wrote to me saying that he had reached the province of Guatuxco, and although he had been much afraid lest he find himself hard pressed, for the enemy were very skillful in war and had many forces in their land, it had pleased Our Lord that they should come in peace; and although he had not yet reached the other provinces he was certain they would offer themselves as Your Majesty's vassals. Fifteen days later he wrote again, telling me how he had advanced farther and how all that land was now at peace. It therefore seemed to him that it would be well to settle in the most suitable places, thus ensuring the continued subjection of the province, as we had discussed many times before, and he asked me to inform him what he was to do in this matter. I then wrote thanking him for all he had done on that expedition in Your Majesty's service, and informing him that I was in agreement with what he had said about settling. I instructed him to build a town for Spaniards in the province of Tuxtepeque and to call it Medellín. I also appointed alcaldes, regidores and other officials, whom I commanded to look after Your Majesty's service and to ensure that the natives were well treated.[87]

The lieutenant of the town of Segura de la Frontera left with his men and many Indian allies from that region for the province of Guaxaca, and, although the natives resisted him and he fought fiercely with them two or three times, at last they surrendered without receiving any hurt. He wrote me a detailed account of all that had happened and informed me that the land was very fertile and rich in mines, from one of which he sent me a sample of gold which I now forward to Your Majesty. He himself remained in that province awaiting my further orders.

After I had dispatched these two expeditions and heard the good news of their success, I realized that although I had now established three colonies of Spaniards there were many still with me in Cuyoacan. I therefore discussed where we might found another colony by the lakes; for the peace and security of all these parts required such a town; and, considering that Temixtitan itself had once been so renowned and of such importance, we decided to settle in it and also to rebuild it, for it was completely destroyed. I distributed plots of land among those who wished to settle there and appointed alcaldes and regidores in Your Majesty's name as is customary throughout Your realms.[88] While the houses are being built, however, we have agreed to live in the city of Cuyoacan, where we are at present. In the four or five months that we have been rebuilding the city it is already most beautiful, and I assure Your Majesty that each day it grows more noble, so that just as before it was capital and center of all these provinces so it shall be henceforth. And it is being so built that the Spaniards will be strong and secure and well in charge of the natives, who will be unable to harm them in any way.[89]

In the meantime, the lord of the province of Tecoantapeque, which lies by the Southern Sea and through which the two Spaniards passed on their journey there, sent me certain of his chieftains, through whom he offered himself as Your Majesty's subject; he also made me a gift of gold ornaments, jewelry and articles of featherwork, all of which I handed over to Your Majesty's treasurer. I then thanked those messengers for what they had said to me on their lord's behalf, and gave them certain things with which they returned very happy.

Likewise at this time, the two Spaniards returned who had gone to the province of Mechuacán (whence those messengers had arrived saying that the Southern Sea could also be reached through their land except that they would have to cross the domain of a lord who was their enemy), and with them came a brother of the lord of Mechuacán, and also other chieftains and their attendants, who numbered more than a thousand persons. I received them with much friendship, and they on behalf of their lord, who is called Calcucin,[90] gave me for Your Majesty a gift of silver shields of considerable weight in marks,[91] and many other things besides, all of which were handed over to Your Majesty's treasurer. So that they should see our strength and report it to their lord, I ordered the horsemen to parade and skirmish before them in a square. The foot soldiers were then sent out in formation, the harquebusiers fired their weapons and I attacked a tower with the artillery. They were all much alarmed by this and by the speed of the horses; I also sent them to see how Temixtitan had been destroyed and razed to the ground; and when they saw the strength and size of it and how it was built on the water they were even more impressed. After four or five days I made them gifts of some of the things they most prize for their lord and for themselves, and they departed very happy and contented.

I have already written to Your Majesty concerning the Pánuco River, which is fifty or sixty leagues down the coast from the town of Vera Cruz; and how the ships of Francisco de Garay had gone there two or three times but had been much harmed by the natives, because the captains had been imprudent in their dealings with the Indians. Afterwards, when I saw that there were few harbors along the north coast and none so good as that river, and also because the natives of those parts had previously come to me offering themselves as Your Majesty's vassals, but have made and are still making war upon our allies, I decided to send a captain with some people to pacify the whole province. I instructed him, if it was land suitable for settling, to set up a town by that river to ensure the peace of the surrounding countryside. And although we were few and separated into three or four groups, for which reason there was some opposition to my further depleting our forces here, nevertheless, both in order to assist our allies and because, since the fall of Temixtitan, ships had arrived carrying men and horses, I equipped twenty-five horsemen and 150 foot soldiers, whom I placed under the charge of a captain and sent to the aforementioned river.

As I was dispatching this company, I received word from the town of Vera Cruz of how there had arrived in the port a ship, bearing Cristóbal de Tapia, veedor of the foundries of Hispaniola, from whom I received on the following day a letter, informing me that he had come to this land for the purpose of assuming control of the government thereof on behalf of Your Majesty, and that to this end he brought decrees from Your Majesty which he did not wish to present anywhere until we met.[92] This he had hoped would be immediately; but as his horses had been made ill by the crossing he had been unable to set out. He asked me to arrange a meeting either by his coming to me or by my going to him on the coast. When I received his letter I answered it immediately, saying that I was glad he had come and, as we had lived as neighbors on Hispaniola and knew each other well, I could wish for no better person to take over the government of these parts by Your Majesty's command. But because the pacification of these lands was not yet so complete as we desired, and any change might arouse the natives, I requested Father Pedro Melgarejo de Urrea, Commissioner of the Crusade, who had shared all our hardships and was well acquainted with the state of things here—indeed, Your Majesty has been well served by him and we have benefited from his learning and advice—to go and see Tapia and examine Your Majesty's decrees. Since he better than anyone knew what would be most expedient for Your Majesty's service and the well-being of these parts, I entreated him to reach an agreement with Tapia in whatever was most advantageous, as I had confidence in him that he would not accept anything unjust. I made this request of him in the presence of Your Majesty's treasurer, who also impressed it upon him.

Then he left for Vera Cruz, where Tapia was quartered;

and so that the aforementioned veedor should be well received and attended there and in any town through which he might pass, I dispatched with the aforementioned priest two or three worthy people from my company. When these had left I remained awaiting Tapia's reply, preparing meanwhile for my own departure and arranging certain matters concerning Your Majesty's service and the pacification and subjugation of these parts. After ten or twelve days had passed, the justiciary and municipal council of Vera Cruz wrote to me saying that Tapia had presented to them the decrees which he brought from Your Majesty and Your governors in Your Royal name, and that they had respected them with all the reverence they required; but as to putting them into effect, they had replied that the greater part of the municipal council was at present with me and must be informed, whereupon they would all do whatever was most expedient for Your Majesty's service and the good of the land.[93] This reply had somewhat displeased Tapia, who had attempted certain scandalous things. Although this distressed me, I replied entreating and requesting them, that, having regard primarily to Your Majesty's service, they should attempt to satisfy Tapia and to give no occasion for any disturbance; furthermore, I was traveling to meet him to carry out all that Your Majesty commanded and was most appropriate to Your service. Having first recalled the captain and those men who were going to the Pánuco River, so that this region might be well defended in my absence, I had already departed when the representatives of the councils of New Spain demanded with many protestations that I should not leave the area, for this province of Mexico and Temixtitan had been so recently conquered that, were I to leave, it would surely rebel, which might result in unrest throughout the land and grave disservice to Your Majesty; and in their demands they gave many other reasons for my not leaving this city at present. They said that they, with the authority of the councils, would go to Vera Cruz and examine Tapia's decrees and do all that they were able in Your Royal service. As there now seemed to me to be no alternative, I dispatched the aforementioned representatives, and with them sent a message to Tapia, informing him of what was being done and how I was sending Gonzalo de Sandoval, alguacil mayor, as my deputy, and that he and Diego de Soto and Diego de Valdenebro, who were there present in Vera Cruz, would act on my behalf together with the municipal council of Vera Cruz and the representatives of other municipal councils, in seeing that everything was done in the interests of Your Majesty's service and the good of the land; for they were and are people who can be trusted in that respect.

They encountered Tapia, accompanied by Brother Pedro, on the road leading from the town and requested him to return. Together they went to the town of Cempoal, where Cristóbal de Tapia presented Your Majesty's decrees, which were received by all with the respect due to them. As for putting them into effect, however, they replied that they would first send a petition to Your Majesty, as this was in Your Majesty's best interests, for the several causes and reasons set down in this same petition which they enumerated at the time. The representatives from New Spain are carrying it signed by a notary public. After further statements and requests had passed between Tapia and the representatives, he embarked on his own ship as he had been requested to do, for his presence and his having announced publicly that he had come as governor and captain general of these parts had caused some disturbance. The people of Mexico and Temixtitan had agreed with the natives of these parts to rebel and perpetrate so great a piece of treachery that, had it succeeded, it would have been worse than the past one.[94] It happened that certain Indians from Mexico had agreed with some of the natives of those provinces which the alguacil mayor had gone to pacify to come in great haste to me, and they told me that twenty ships with many men on board were sailing off the coast but would not land. They must therefore be hostile, and, if I wished to go there to see who it was, they would arm themselves and go with me; and so that I should believe them they drew these ships on a piece of paper.

But as they brought this information to me in secret I realized immediately that their intentions were pernicious and that it was a ruse to rid the province of me; for certain chieftains had known for some days that I intended to leave, but seeing that I did not move they had devised this plan. I dissimulated with them and then seized some of the ringleaders. Thus, as Tapia had no experience of the land or its people, his arrival caused much upheaval and his presence would have caused great harm if God had not remedied it. He would have served Your Majesty better had he remained in Hispaniola, and consulted Your Majesty, and acquainted You with the affairs of these parts, which he must have known from the ships I sent to that island for help. He must also have known how we had remedied the disturbances which we had anticipated would be caused by the arrival of the fleet of Pánfilo de Narváez—which were largely prevented by the governors and Your Majesty's Royal Council—and so should not have come, especially as the admiral, judges and officers who reside in Hispaniola had many times required Tapia under threat of certain penalties to desist from his intention to come to these parts without first informing Your Majesty of all that had happened in them. But he, looking more to his own profit than to what might best serve Your Majesty, persuaded them to lift their ban against his coming. I have only now made account of all this to Your Majesty because, when Tapia departed, the representatives and I agreed that he would not prove a reliable bearer of our letters, and so that Your Majesty may now see that in not receiving him Your Majesty was well served, as will be more fully proved whenever such proof be required.

In a previous chapter I told Your Majesty how the captain I had sent to the province of Guaxaca had pacified it and was there awaiting my orders. But because I required his presence, as he was alcalde and lieutenant of Segura de la Frontera, I wrote commanding him to give the ten horsemen and eighty foot soldiers under his command to Pedro de Alvarado, whom I then sent to conquer the province of Tatutepeque,[95] which lies forty leagues beyond Guaxaca beside the Southern Sea. The inhabitants of this province had done much harm to those who had offered themselves as Your Majesty's vassals, and to the people of Tecoantepeque because they had permitted us to pass through their lands on our way to the Southern Sea. Pedro de Alvarado left this city on the last day of January this year, and with the men he took from here and those he received in the province of Guaxaca he assembled forty horse and some two hundred foot, among whom were forty crossbowmen and harquebusiers and two small field guns. After twenty days I received letters from Pedro de Alvarado informing me that he was on the road to Tatutepeque, and had captured several enemy spies, who had told him that the lord of Tatutepeque and his men were awaiting him in the fields; he intended to go and do whatever he could to pacify that province, for which purpose, in addition to the Spaniards, he had brought many good Indian warriors. I waited anxiously to receive further news from him about his attempt, and on the fourth of March of this year he sent me letters saying he had entered the province, and that three or four towns had tried to resist him but had not held out for long. He had entered the city of Tatutepeque, where they had to all appearances been welcomed. The lord of the city had asked them to lodge in some large houses of his whose roofs were thatched with straw, but because these were situated in a place where the horses could hardly be used to advantage, they had insisted on moving down to a flatter part of the city; they also did this because just then they had heard that the natives planned to kill them all by setting fire to the houses during the night when all the Spaniards were inside. But God had disclosed this plot to him, and he had dissimulated and taken with him to that flatter part the lord of the city and one of his sons as prisoners. Alvarado had been given 25,000 *castellanos* and he believed from what the lord's vassals had told him that their lord was very wealthy. The whole province was now completely pacified, and the natives carried on their markets and commerce as before. He said that the land was very rich in gold mines, from which they had, in his presence, taken a sample which he sent to me. Three days previously he had been by the sea and taken possession of it in Your Majesty's name; and in his presence they had brought up a sample of pearls, which he also sent and which, together with the gold, I am forwarding to Your Majesty.

As Our Lord God has so favored this business, and was so fulfilling my desire to serve Your Majesty in this matter of the Southern Sea, which is of such importance, I have, with much diligence, provided, in one of the three places where we have reached the sea, for the building of two medium-sized caravels and two brigantines; the two caravels for voyages of discovery and the brigantines for charting the coast. For this I have sent, under the care of a trustworthy person, some forty Spaniards, among whom are master carpenters, shipwrights, woodcutters, blacksmiths and seamen; and I have sent to Vera Cruz for sails, nails and other necessary equipment. All possible haste will be made to complete and launch these vessels, and when this is done Your Majesty may be assured that it will be the greatest achievement and the one from which Your Majesty will derive the most benefit since the Indies were first discovered.

While we were in the city of Tesuico before leaving to lay siege to Temixtitan, preparing and supplying ourselves with all we required for that siege and quite unaware of a plot which certain persons were hatching, one of those involved in the conspiracy came to me and informed me how certain friends of Diego Velázquez, who were in my company, had plotted to kill me, and that they had elected from amongst themselves a captain, an alcalde mayor, an alguacil and other officers. He begged me to prevent it at all cost, for, besides the disturbance which would follow my death, if we turned against each other, it was certain that no Spaniard would escape alive, for not only would we find the enemy alerted but even those whom we held as allies would make every effort to put an end to us. When I saw how great was this treachery that had been disclosed to me I gave thanks to God, for in my knowledge of it lay the remedy. I then had the chief man among the conspirators seized, and he voluntarily confessed that he had plotted and conspired with many others to seize and kill me, and to usurp the government of the land in the name of Diego Velázquez; and that it was true they had appointed a new captain and alcalde mayor and that he himself was to have been alguacil mayor and to have taken or killed me himself. Many people were involved in this, but when the list of them was found in his quarters it had been torn to pieces. He admitted, however, to having plotted with some of the aforementioned persons and not only in Tesuico, for they had also discussed it during the fighting in the province of Tepeaca. When I had heard the confession of this man, a native of Zamora, whose name was Antonio de Villafaña, and was assured that he spoke the truth, an alcalde and I condemned him to death, and the sentence was duly executed. And even though there were others involved in this crime who had a large share of the guilt, I dissimulated with them and treated them as friends, for, as this was a personal matter, though perhaps I might more accurately say Your Majesty's, I did not wish to deal harshly with them.[96] This has done me little good, however, for Velázquez's men have since set me many traps and secretly caused many disturbances and quarrels against which I have found I have to be more on my guard than against the enemy. Our Lord God, however, has always guided us in such a manner that without punishing those men there is complete peace and tranquillity; but if I hear of anything further I will punish them as justice demands.

After the fall of Temixtitan, while we were in Cuyoacan, Don Fernando,[97] lord of Tesuico, died, which caused grief to us all, for he was a very loyal vassal of Your Majesty and a friend of the Christians. With the consent of the lords and chieftains of that city and province, in Your Majesty's name I entrusted the position to his younger brother, who was baptized and christened Don Carlos; and until now he has followed in his brother's footsteps and our customs and conversations please him greatly.

In the earlier report I told Your Majesty that close to the provinces of Tascalteca and Guaxocingo there was a high circular mountain from which an almost continuous column of smoke rose upwards as straight as an arrow. The Indians gave us to believe that it was a most evil thing and all those who climbed it died. I therefore ordered certain Spaniards to climb it and see what it was like up there. When they ascended, however, that smoke came out with such a noise that they neither could nor dared approach the opening. Then, later, I sent some more Spaniards, and they climbed it twice until they reached the opening from which the smoke comes. From one side to the other it measures two crossbowshots; it is nearly three-quarters of a league round, and so deep they were unable to see the bottom. They found some sulphur round about which is deposited by the smoke. When they were there they heard the great noise the smoke makes and hurried down, but before they had reached halfway a huge number of stones began to roll down toward them, from which they found themselves in great danger. The Indians thought it a great thing to have dared go where those Spaniards had gone.

In a letter of mine I informed Your Majesty how the natives of these parts are of much greater intelligence than those of the other islands; indeed, they appeared to us to possess such understanding as is sufficient for an ordinary citizen to conduct himself in a civilized country. It seemed to me, therefore, a serious matter at this time to compel them to serve the Spaniards as the natives of the other islands do; yet if this were not done, the conquerors and settlers of these parts would not be able to maintain themselves. In order therefore to avoid enslaving these Indians, and at the same time to provide the Spaniards with their needs, it seemed to me that Your Majesty should command that from the income which belongs to Your Majesty here we should obtain assistance for the expenses and maintenance of the settlers; and in this matter Your Majesty should decree as You saw most fitting to Your service. Since then, however, I have been almost forced to deliver the chieftains and other natives of these parts to the Spaniards in recognition of the services they have rendered to Your Majesty, because Your Majesty's expenses have been continuous and considerable, and we ought rather to try by every means to increase Royal revenues than to give cause for spending them; also we have been at war for a long time and have all contracted debts thereby and find ourselves in difficulties. Furthermore, on account of the inevitable delay in ascertaining Your Majesty's commands on this matter, and because I was so pressed by Your Majesty's officials and the other Spaniards, I could not in any way avoid it. So until some new order is made, or this one confirmed, the aforementioned chieftains and natives will serve the Spaniards with whom they have been deposited in all they may require in their affairs.[98] This conclusion was reached on the advice of persons who have considerable knowledge and experience in this land; moreover, nothing better or more convenient could be devised either for the maintenance of the Spaniards or for the safety and good treatment of the Indians; of all this the representatives who are now leaving New Spain will give a more detailed account to Your Majesty. Your Majesty's farms and estates have been established in the cities and provinces which seem the best and most suitable. I entreat Your Majesty to approve this and command how You may best be served in these matters.

Most Catholic Lord: May Our Lord God preserve the Life and Very Royal Person and the Most Powerful Estate of Your Caesarean Majesty, and increase it with yet greater realms and dominions, as Your Royal Heart desires. From the city of Cuyoacan in this New Spain of the Ocean Sea on the fifteenth day of May in the year 1522. Most Powerful Lord—From Your Caesarean Majesty's very humble servant and vassal who now kisses Your Majesty's Very Royal hands and feet—HERNANDO CORTÉS.

Most Powerful Lord: As Your Majesty may observe, Fernando Cortés, Your Captain and Chief Justice in this New Spain of the Ocean Sea, hereby sends a report to Your Caesarean Majesty.

We the officials of Your Catholic Majesty are obliged to give an account of events and state of these parts, and as all this is described in great detail here in this letter, and is the truth as we ourselves would have written it, there is no need for us to add anything, but only to refer You to the aforementioned Captain's account.

Most Invincible and Very Catholic Lord, may Our Lord God preserve the Life and Very Royal Person and most Powerful Estate of Your Majesty and increase it with many more realms and dominions as Your Royal Heart desires—From the city of Cuyoacán, on the fifteenth day of May in the year 1522. Most Powerful Lord—From Your Caesarean Majesty's most humble servants and vassals who kiss the Very Royal Feet and Hands of Your Majesty. JULIÁN ALDERETE. ALONSO DE GRADO. BERNARDINO VÁZQUEZ DE TAPIA.[99]

The Fourth Letter

MOST HIGH, MOST POWERFUL AND VERY EXCELLENT PRINCE,
VERY CATHOLIC AND MOST INVINCIBLE EMPEROR, KING AND LORD:
In the report which I sent to Your Majesty with Juan de
Ribera,[1] concerning the things which befell me in these parts since
the dispatch of my second letter to Your Highness, I told how, in
order to pacify and subject to Your Majesty's Royal service the
provinces of Guatusco, Tus[te]peque, and Guasaca and others
nearby on the north coast, all of which had been in revolt since the
uprising in Temixtitan, I had sent the alguacil mayor[2] with a company of men; and I described what happened to them on the road
and told how I had given them orders to found a town in the
aforementioned provinces and to call that town Medellín. It now
remains for me to inform Your Highness how the aforementioned
colony was built and all those lands and provinces subdued.

When all those parts had been pacified I sent more men and
commanded the alguacil mayor to proceed up the coast to the province of Guazacalco, which is fifty leagues from where the above-
mentioned town was built and 120 from this city. For when I was
first in this city, before the death of Mutezuma, and was trying
always to learn as much about these parts as I could, so that I might
send a detailed account of them to Your Majesty, I dispatched
thither Diego de Ordaz—who now resides at the court of Your
Majesty—and the natives of the aforementioned province received

him with much goodwill and offered themselves as vassals and subjects of Your Highness. I also learnt that at the mouth of a very
large river which runs through that province there was a good harbor for ships, for Ordaz and those in his company had explored it;
likewise the land was very suitable for settling; and because of the
scarcity of harbors along this coast I wished to find a good one and
build a town there.[3]

I gave orders to the alguacil mayor that before entering the
province he should wait on the border, and send some messengers,
natives of this city, that I gave him, to inform the inhabitants that he
went there by my command to discover if they were constant in
their intention to serve Your Majesty and in the friendship which
they had previously shown; to tell them that on account of the
battles that I had had with the lord of this city and his lands, I had
sent no one to visit them for a long time, but that I had always
considered them as friends and vassals of Your Highness, and that
as such they should find me most willing to assist them in anything
they required; and, in order to be able to favor and help them in
any need they might have, I was sending some people to settle in
their province. The aforementioned alguacil mayor and his company went and did as I commanded, but they did not find the natives as well disposed as they had previously claimed to be; on the
contrary, they were ready to make war on him should he attempt
to enter their province. But he was so skillful that by falling upon a
town one night and seizing a lady whom everyone in those parts
obeyed, he pacified the land, because she called all the lords and
ordered them to obey whatever was commanded them in Your Majesty's name, for she herself had so to do.

Thus they reached that river, and four leagues from the
mouth, because they could find no suitable site nearer the sea, they
founded and settled a town, to which they gave the name Espíritu
Santo. There the alguacil mayor remained for some time, until
many of the neighboring provinces were pacified and brought to
the service of Your Catholic Majesty: these were Tabasco, which is

by the Victoria River, or Grijalva, as it is called, and Chimaclan and Quechula and Quizaltepeque and others which because they are small I shall not name. The natives of these were distributed and put under the protection of the citizens of the town, and they have served and indeed still do serve them, although some of them, namely, those from Chimaclan, Tabasco and Quizaltepeque, have again rebelled. About a month ago I sent a captain with some people from this city to reduce them to Your Majesty's service and punish them for their rebellion, but I have, as yet, received no news from this captain. I believe that, if Our Lord so wishes, he will succeed, because he was well equipped with artillery and munitions, crossbowmen and horsemen.

Most Catholic Lord, in the report which the aforementioned Juan de Ribera took with him, I also informed Your Caesarean and Catholic Majesty how the lord, whose name was Casulcy,[4] of a great province called Mechuacán, had sent messengers offering himself and his people as Your Caesarean Majesty's subjects and vassals, and how these messengers had also brought certain gifts which I sent with the representatives of New Spain who went to Your Highness. Because the province and dominion of that lord Casulci, according to the reports of certain Spaniards whom I sent there, was large and had shown signs of being very rich, and because it was so close to this great city, after I had received some reinforcements of men and horses, I sent a captain with seventy horsemen and two hundred foot soldiers, well equipped with side arms and artillery, to investigate and explore the whole of that province; and if the report was true, they were to settle in Huicicila,[5] the capital city. When they arrived they were well received by the lord and natives of that province and quartered in that city; and, in addition to all the provisions they required, they were also given some three thousand marks of silver mixed with copper, in

16. Title page of the first printed edition of Letter IV, Toledo, 1525. *Courtesy of the British Museum.*

La quarta relacion q̃ ꝼernãdo cortes gouer
nadoꝛ y capitan general poꝛ su majestad en la
nueua España dl mar oceano embio al muy
alto ⁊ muy potentissimo inuictissimo señoꝛ
don Carlos emperadoꝛ semper. augusto y
rey de España nuestro señoꝛ: en la qual estan
otras cartas ⁊ relacioñes que los capitanes
ꝑedro de aluarado ⁊ Diego godoy embia
ron al dicho capitan ꝼernãdo coꝛtes.

proportion of about one-half silver, and some five thousand *pesos de oro*, which, in a like fashion, was mixed with an unknown proportion of silver; also some cotton clothing and other small things which they use. After Your Majesty's fifth had been taken, these were distributed among the Spaniards who participated in this expedition. As the land did not attract them much as a place to settle, they showed no great willingness to do so, and a few arguments arose for which certain of them were punished. For this reason, however, I ordered those who wished, to return, and the rest I sent with a captain to the Southern Sea, where I have founded a town called Zacatula,[6] which lies a hundred leagues from the city of Huicicila, and there I have four ships under construction to explore as much of that sea as I am able and Our Lord God permits. While this captain and his people were going to Zacatula, they heard of a province called Coliman,[7] which lies fifty leagues to the right, which is the west, of this road; and without my permission this captain went there, taking all his men, together with many of our allies from the province of Mechuacán. He crossed the border and marched on for several days and had several encounters with the natives, but although he had forty horsemen and more than a hundred foot soldiers, crossbowmen and shield-bearers, they routed him and drove him from their land, killing three Spaniards and many of our allies; he then went to the aforementioned city of Zacatula. When I learnt of this I had the captain brought to me and punished him for his disobedience.

In the account which I sent to Your Caesarean Majesty of how I had dispatched Pedro de Alvarado to the province of Tututepeque, which is by the Southern Sea, I had nothing to say save that he had arrived there and had imprisoned the lord and one of his sons, and that they had given him some gold and also some samples from the gold mines and some pearls, because at that time there was nothing further to report. Your Excellency will recall that in reply to the news which this same Pedro de Alvarado sent me I ordered him to find a convenient site in that province and to found a town there. I also ordered the citizens of Segura de la Frontera to move to the new town as soon as it had been built, for there was no further need for one so close to this city. And so it was done, and the new town was likewise called Segura de la Frontera. The natives of that same province and also of Guaxaca, Coaclán, Coasclahuaca, Tachquyaco and others in the neighborhood were distributed amongst the settlers, and they were most willing to serve and make themselves useful. Pedro de Alvarado remained there as chief justice and captain in my stead. And it happened that, while I was conquering the province of Pánuco, as I shall hereafter relate to Your Majesty, the alcaldes and regidores of that town requested Pedro de Alvarado to go with their authority to negotiate with me certain matters which they had suggested to him. This he agreed to do, and, when he had left, these alcaldes and regidores gathered together and formed a conspiracy; they convened the settlers, appointed alcaldes and, against the will of the captain whom Pedro de Alvarado had left there, abandoned the town and went to the province of Guaxaca, which was the cause of much unrest and disturbance in these parts. When that captain informed me of this, I sent Diego de Ocampo, alcalde mayor, to investigate what had happened and to punish those responsible. On hearing this, they took fright and remained hidden for a few days until I finally captured them; thus the aforementioned alcalde mayor was able to find only one of the rebels, whom he duly sentenced to death; this man appealed to me. After I had captured all the others I handed them over to the alcalde mayor, who likewise proceeded against them, sentencing them as he had the other one; and they also appealed. The cases are now concluded and ready to be executed before me in the second instance; but on examination I have decided, although their crime was a serious one, considering the long time they have been imprisoned, to commute the death penalty to that of civil excommunication; that is, to banish them from these lands and to forbid them to return without license from Your Majesty under pain of incurring the penalty of their first sentence.[8]

During this time the chief of the aforementioned province of Tututepeque died, and it and the neighboring provinces rebelled; so I sent some people under Pedro de Alvarado together with the son of the previous lord, whom I had in my power. Although there were a few encounters with the natives and some Spaniards died, they made them return to Your Majesty's service, and they are now pacified, serving the Spaniards to whom they have been assigned without complaint, although the town was not repopulated for lack of people, and because at present there is no need. They have been so subdued by their punishment that they will even come to this city when they are ordered to.

As soon as this city of Temixtitan and the lands subject to it were recovered, two other provinces, lying forty leagues to the north on the borders of the province of Pánuco, called Tututepeque and Mezclitan,[9] were subjected to the Imperial Crown of Your Caesarean Majesty; their lands are well defended and the people themselves are skilled in the use of arms, because they are surrounded by enemies on all sides. Seeing what had been done with these people and that nothing could hinder Your Majesty's cause, they sent me their messengers offering themselves as Your Majesty's subjects and vassals. I received them in Your Majesty's Royal name, and they remained loyal until the arrival of Cristóbal de Tapia, but with the disturbances and unrest which this caused amongst these people, they not only renounced their obedience but even did great harm to their neighbors who were vassals of Your Catholic Majesty, burning many villages and killing many people. I had no men to spare at that time, as they were scattered in so many places, but seeing that if I failed to act in this matter great damage might be caused, and fearing that the peoples of adjacent provinces to those might join the rebels lest they be likewise attacked; and since, furthermore, I was not convinced of their loyalty, I sent a captain with thirty horsemen and a hundred foot soldiers, crossbowmen, harquebusiers and bucklers, together with many of our allies. There were a few encounters with the enemy, in which some of our allies and two Spaniards were killed, but it pleased Our Lord that the natives should come in peace of their own accord. They brought me their lords whom I pardoned because they had come without being captured.

Later, while I was in the province of Pánuco, the natives of these parts put it about that I was returning to Castile, which caused much disturbance. One of these two provinces, the one called Tututepeque, again rebelled, and its lord came down with many people and killed and captured many of our allies, burning more than twenty of their villages. Thus, while on the road from Pánuco I turned aside to suppress them, and although at first they killed some of our allies who were in the rear and ten or twelve horses were ruined on account of the roughness of the mountain passes, the entire province was subdued, and the lord and a young brother of his were captured together with a captain general who guarded one of the frontiers. The lord and his captain general were immediately hanged and all those taken in the war—some two hundred people—were made slaves. They were branded and sold by auction; and once Your Majesty's fifth had been reserved, the rest of the money was distributed among those who had participated in the war, although there was not enough to pay for even a third part of the horses which died, because, as the land was poor, we took no other spoils. The rest of the inhabitants of that province surrendered and have remained at peace with the brother of the dead ruler as their lord. At present, however, it is of no benefit to us because the land, as I have said, is poor; so that we may be certain they will not stir up those who do serve us, and for greater security, I have sent there some of the natives of this land.

Invincible Caesar, at this time there arrived at the harbor and colony of Espíritu Santo, which I have already mentioned in previous chapters, a very small brigantine coming from Cuba. In her was one Juan Bono de Quejo, who had come to this land with Pánfilo de Narváez as master of one of the ships in his fleet; it appeared from the dispatches which he brought that he came by order of Don Juan de Fonseca, bishop of Burgos, in the belief that Cristóbal de Tapia, whom the bishop had contrived to send as governor of this land, was here. In case Tapia should meet with an unfavorable reception, as the bishop feared, and had every reason to fear, and so that Tapia should receive every possible assistance, the bishop sent Bono by way of Cuba to inform Diego Velázquez, which he did, and was given by him the brigantine in which he came. The aforementioned Juan Bono carried some hundred letters, all with the same purport, signed by the bishop and even, I believe, with the names left blank so that Juan Bono could give them to the people here he thought fit, saying that they would be rendering Your Caesarean Majesty a great favor by receiving Tapia. To this end he promised many singular rewards, adding that they must know they were serving in my company against the wishes of Your Excellency, and many other things clearly calculated to stir up sedition and unrest. To me he sent another letter saying the same thing, and that if I obeyed the aforementioned Tapia he would obtain great favors for me from Your Majesty, but if not, I might be certain that he would always be my mortal enemy. The arrival of this Juan Bono and the letters he brought caused such a disturbance amongst my people that I assure Your Majesty there would have been few means to quieten them had they not been reassured by my telling them why the bishop had written such letters and bidding them not to fear his threats, and that the greatest service they could do Your Catholic Majesty, and through which they would receive the highest favors, was to prevent the bishop or any of his hirelings from meddling in these parts, because it was his intention to hide the truth of them from Your Highness and to ask for concessions in them without Your Majesty knowing what You were giving him.

Furthermore, I was informed, although I feigned ignorance of it at the time, that some of them had suggested that, as they received nothing but threats in payment for their services, it would be as well to form a *comunidad* [10] as had been done in Castile, until Your Majesty should be informed of the truth; for the arm of the bishop extended so far in this matter that he prevented their ac-

counts from reaching Your Highness, and he also had control over
the Casa de la Contratación[11] in Seville, where their messengers
were ill-treated and their reports, letters and money seized, and reinforcements of men, arms and supplies prevented from ever reaching
them. But when I had told them all I have mentioned above, and
assured them that Your Majesty had no knowledge of all these doings, and said they might be certain that once Your Highness had
been informed their services would be rewarded, and that those
favors would be bestowed upon them which all loyal and good vassals of their king and lord, who serve as they have, deserve, they
were reassured, and, by the use which Your Excellency so graciously commanded me to make of the Royal provisions, they are
most content and serve most willingly, to which fact the fruits of
their service bear witness. Because of this they deserve that Your
Majesty should grant them great favors, which I on my part do beg
most humbly of Your Majesty, for I consider anything granted to
any one of them no less a favor than if I myself had received it, for
without them I could not have served Your Highness as I have.
Above all, I most humbly entreat Your Highness to write to them,
acknowledging the hardships which they have suffered in Your
Majesty's service and offering them some reward, for, besides dis-
charging Your Majesty's debt in this matter, it would inspire them
to serve henceforth with yet greater determination.

By a decree which Your Caesarean Majesty had granted on
the request of Juan de Ribera, concerning the adelantado Francisco
de Garay, it appears that Your Highness was informed as to how I
was about to set out, or send an expedition, to the Pánuco[12] River to
pacify it, because I had heard that it might provide a good harbor,
and because many Spaniards had perished there; not only those
under a captain which the aforementioned Francisco de Garay had
sent, but also the entire complement of another ship which sometime afterwards reached that coast, not one of whom escaped alive.
Some of the natives of those parts had come to me to excuse themselves for those deaths, saying that they had only killed the Span-

iards because they knew that they were not of my company and because they had been ill-treated by them. If, however, I wished to send some of my own people there, they would consider it a great favor and would serve them as best they could; indeed, they would be most grateful, for they feared that certain people with whom they had fought might return against them seeking revenge. Also, they had certain neighbors who were their enemies and by whom they were being much harmed, and if I sent them Spaniards they would be protected.

When these people arrived I was short of men and unable to comply with their requests, but I promised that I would do so as soon as I was able. This satisfied them and they departed, some ten or twelve villages in the regions closest to the frontier having offered themselves as Your Majesty's vassals. After a few days they returned and anxiously entreated me to send some Spaniards to settle there, as I had done in many other places, for they were being much harmed by their enemies and even by those of their own people who lived on the coast, because they had become our friends. In response to this and in order to settle in the land, I ordered a captain, for I now had more people, to go with several companions to that river. When they were about to depart I learnt from a ship which had come from Cuba how the admiral Don Diego Colón and the adelantados Diego Velázquez and Francisco de Garay were together on that island and had agreed to set out from there as my enemies and to do me all the harm they could.[13] In order to prevent their evil intent from having effect, and to avoid what their coming would cause; that is, such disturbances and unrest as followed on Narváez's arrival, I decided to leave this city as well defended as possible and to go in person, so that if all or any of them did go there, they should meet me before anyone else, because I would be best able to avoid the damage.

I set out with 120 horsemen, three hundred foot soldiers and some artillery, together with some forty thousand warriors from this city and the surrounding country. When I reached the frontier of that land, a good twenty-five leagues from the harbor in a large settlement called Ayntuscotaclan,[14] a large number of warriors came out against us, and we fought with them; but because there were so many of our allies with us and because the ground was flat and well suited to the horses, the battle did not last long; although they wounded a few horses and Spaniards and killed a few of our allies, they had the worst of it, for many of them were killed or put to flight.

I remained in that town two or three days to care for the wounded, and also because those who had already offered themselves as Your Highness's vassals came to me there, whence they followed me to the harbor, and from then on served in all they could. I traveled until I reached the port, and nowhere did I have any further encounters with them; on the contrary, those through whose lands we passed came to ask forgiveness for their crime and to offer themselves in the Royal service of Your Highness. When we reached the aforementioned harbor and river, I set up camp in a village called Chila,[15] which lies five leagues from the sea; we found it burnt and abandoned, because it was there that Francisco de Garay's captain and his people had been routed.[16] From there I sent messengers to the other side of the river and through those lakes, among which there is a number of large towns with many inhabitants, to tell them not to be afraid, that I would do them no harm on account of what had happened, for I knew well that they had rebelled because of the ill-treatment they had received from those other Spaniards and were therefore not to blame. Despite this, however, they would not come; on the contrary, they maltreated the messengers and even killed some of them. Moreover, because we took our fresh water from the other side of the river, they took up positions there and fell upon those who went to fetch it.

I waited more than fifteen days in this position, thinking that they might be persuaded by peaceful means, that seeing how well treated those who had come were, they might do likewise; but they had such confidence in the strength of their position among those lakes that they would not submit. And seeing that I had gained nothing by peaceful means, I began to seek another remedy, and in some canoes which we had had with us from the beginning, together with some others which were captured, I sent some men and horses across to the other side of the river, and by the time day broke a force of them had been collected on the far side of the river without being seen. Then I went across myself, leaving the camp well guarded. When the enemy saw us they came in large numbers and fell to fighting with us so furiously that never, since my arrival in these parts, have I seen so bold an attack in the field. They killed two horses and wounded more than ten others so badly they could no longer walk. But that day, with the help of Our Lord, they were routed and we pursued them for nearly a league, killing many of them.

With the thirty horsemen who remained and a hundred foot soldiers, I continued on my way and slept that night three leagues from the camp in a village which we found deserted. In the temples we found many things belonging to the Spaniards from Francisco de Garay's company who had been killed. On the following day I set out along the shore of a lake in search of a passage to the other side because we had seen people and villages there. I marched all day without reaching the end of the lake or finding anyplace to cross, but at the hour of vespers we came in sight of a most beautiful town and took the road toward it, which still followed the shore of that lake. When we drew close it was already late and the town seemed abandoned, but to make certain I sent ten horsemen straight into the town by the main road while I, with another ten, skirted round by the lake; for the remaining ten were bringing up the rear guard and had not yet arrived.

As soon as we entered the town, there suddenly appeared a large number of people who had been hiding in ambush inside the houses to take us unawares. They fought so fiercely that they killed a horse and wounded nearly all the others and many of the Spaniards. They were such tenacious fighters and the battle lasted so long that although we broke through them three or four times they always managed to re-form. They made a circle, kneeling on the ground, and awaited us in silence, not screaming or shouting as the others do, and every time we entered among them they fired so many arrows at us that had we not been well armored they would have got the better of us, and I suspect not one of us would have escaped. But it pleased Our Lord that some of those who were closest to a river which flowed nearby, emptying into the lake whose coast we had followed all day, began to throw themselves into the water, whereupon the others began to run to the same river; and so they were routed, although they only fled to the other side of the river. So we remained, they on the one bank and we on the other, until nightfall, for the river was too deep for us to cross, and we were not sorry to see them go. We then returned to the town, which lay a stone's throw from the river, and there, having mounted the best guard we could, we passed that night, eating the horse they had killed, because there was no other food.

On the following day we set out again, there now being no sight of the people we had fought the day before, and came upon three or four villages where we found neither people nor anything else save for some stores of the wine they make, where we found a fair number of earthenware jars filled with it. That day we came across no one at all and slept in the open, because we found some maize fields where both the men and horses satisfied their hunger. We continued in this fashion for two or three days without seeing anyone, although we passed through many villages; and because we were hampered by lack of provisions, for in all this time there were not fifty pounds of bread between us, we returned to the camp. I found the people I had left there were in good shape and had had no clashes with the enemy. And so, because it seemed to me that all the Indians were keeping to the far side of the lake I had been unable to cross, one night I sent out men and horses in the canoes, including some crossbowmen and harquebusiers; these were to proceed up the lake while the rest of the men went overland. In this manner they fell upon a large town and, as they took it by surprise, killed many people. This attack so frightened them, for they saw that, even surrounded by water as they were, they could be taken unawares, that they began to come peacefully, and in less than twenty days the whole region had offered themselves as Your Majesty's vassals.

Now that this land had been pacified, I sent people to visit all parts of it and to bring back accounts of the people and towns. When these were brought to me, I chose the site which seemed best and founded there a town, to which I gave the name Santisteban del Puerto;[17] and to the people who wished to remain there as settlers I assigned those villages, in Your Majesty's name, for their sustenance. Alcaldes and regidores were appointed, and I left a captain there as my lieutenant, together with thirty horsemen and a hundred foot soldiers. I also left them a ship and a small rowing boat which had been sent to me from Vera Cruz with provisions. Likewise a servant of mine had come from Vera Cruz in a ship loaded with supplies of meat, bread, oil, wine, vinegar and other things, but everything was lost, save for three men who were cast away on a small island, five leagues out to sea. When later I sent a ship for them they were found alive, having fed on seals, of which there were many round that island, and fruit which they said were like figs.[18] I assure Your Majesty that this expedition cost me alone more than thirty thousand *pesos de oro*,[19] as Your Majesty may see if You be pleased to examine the accounts; and those who went with me had to spend as much again on horses, provisions, arms and horseshoes, for at that time they cost their weight in gold or twice that in silver. But to serve Your Majesty well in that venture we would willingly have spent more, for, besides bringing those Indians under Your Majesty's Imperial Yoke, our journey was of great benefit, as shortly afterwards a ship with many people and supplies aboard was forced onto that coast. If the land had not been at peace, the crew would all have perished like those from the previous ship, the skins of whose faces we found in the native oratories, preserved in such a fashion that many of them could still be recognized. When the adelantado Francisco de Garay arrived in this land, as I will later relate to Your Caesarean Majesty, neither he nor any of those who came with him would have escaped alive when they were driven by bad weather onto the coast some thirty leagues below the Pánuco River. They lost some of their ships and were in such a state when they reached land that if the Indians had not been at peace and had not carried them on their shoulders and helped them until they were brought to the town of the Spaniards they would all have perished, even if they had not been attacked. And so it was of no little advantage to have pacified that land.

Most Excellent Prince, in the previous chapters I told how, after having pacified the province of Pánuco, we reconquered that of Tututepeque, which had rebelled; and I related all that was done there. I received news of a province by the South Sea called Impilcingo, which is much the same as Tututepeque in the impassability of its mountains and roughness of the terrain; and the people, who are quite as warlike, had done much harm to Your Majesty's vassals who live on their borders, and these had come to me to complain and ask for help. Although my people were not much rested, because there is a journey of two hundred leagues from one sea to the other, I immediately collected twenty-five horsemen and seventy or eighty foot soldiers, whom I placed under a captain and sent to that province. In my instructions I commanded him to attempt to win the inhabitants to Your Highness's Royal service by peaceful means, and, if they refused, to make war on them. He went there and had several encounters with them, but because the land was so rugged he could not claim to have conquered all of it. I had also commanded him in the same instructions to proceed, once he had accomplished his first task, to the city of Zacatula, and with all the people he already had and with as many more as he could find there to continue to the province of Colimán (where, as I said in previous chapters, the Indians had defeated that captain and his people who went from the province of Mechuacán to the city of Colimán), and to try and win them over by peaceful means, but if that failed to subjugate them.

He departed thither, and with his own people and those whom he collected there he assembled fifty horsemen and 150 foot soldiers and went to that province, which is some sixty leagues from the city of Zacatula, down the coast of the Southern Sea. He pacified some towns on his way and reached that province, and at the place where the other captain had been routed he found many warriors waiting for him and hoping to do to him what they had done to the others. So they began to break through each other's lines, and it pleased Our Lord that the victory fell to us, not one Spaniard being killed, although many of them and their horses were wounded. The enemy paid dearly for the harm which they had done, and so successful was this punishment that without need of further war the whole country at once surrendered. And not only this province but also many of the neighboring ones now came to offer themselves as vassals of Your Caesarean Majesty; these were: Alimán,[20] Colimonte and Ciguatán.

From there the captain wrote to me reporting all that had befallen him, and I sent him orders to find a good site and to found a colony there which he was to call Colimán, after the province. I also sent him appointments of alcaldes and regidores and ordered him to visit the towns and the peoples of those provinces, and to bring me a complete account of all he could discover about the land. This he did, and brought also some samples of pearls which he had found. And in Your Majesty's name I distributed the villages of those provinces among the settlers who remained there; these numbered twenty-five horsemen and 120 foot soldiers. In his account of these provinces he brought news of a very good harbor which he had found on that coast, and of this I was very glad because there are few. Likewise he brought me word from the lords of the province of Ciguatán, who affirm that there is an island inhabited only by women, without a single man, and that at certain times men go over from the mainland and have intercourse with

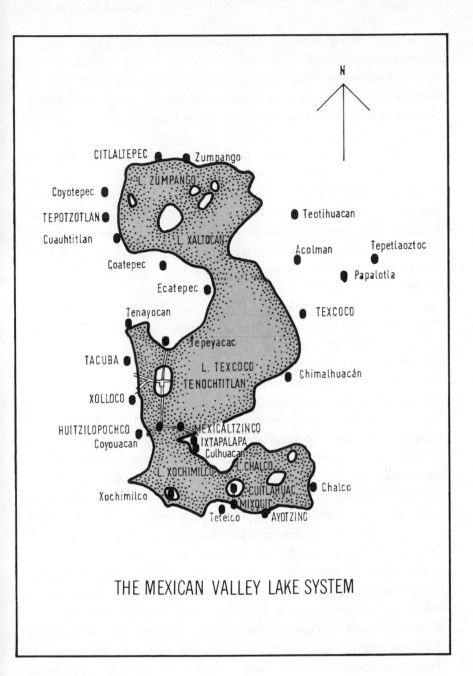

THE MEXICAN VALLEY LAKE SYSTEM

them; the females born to those who conceive are kept, but the males are sent away. This island is ten days' journey from this province and many of those chiefs have been there and have seen it. They also told me that it was very rich in pearls and gold. I will strive, as soon as I am equipped for it, to learn the truth and send Your Majesty a full account thereof.[21]

While returning from the province of Pánuco, in a city called Tuzapan,[22] two Spaniards arrived whom I had sent with some of the natives of the city of Temixtitan and others from the province of Soconusco[23] (which lies up the coast on the shores of the Southern Sea, toward where Pedro Arias de Ávila resides as Your Highness's governor, two hundred leagues from this great city of Temixtitan) to two cities, called Uclaclán[24] and Guatemala, of which I had known for some while and which lie another seventy leagues from this province of Soconusco. With these Spaniards there came some hundred natives of those cities sent by their lords to offer themselves as the subjects and vassals of Your Caesarean Majesty. I received them in Your Royal name and assured them that if they remained true to their promise they would be very well treated and honored by me and all my company in Your Highness's Royal name. I then gave them, for themselves and for them to take back to their lords, some of the things I had with me and which they value. I also sent two other Spaniards with them to arrange for things necessary on the journey. I have since been informed by certain Spaniards whom I have in the province of Soconusco that those cities and their provinces, together with another nearby called Chiapan,[25] have not maintained that goodwill which they showed at first; on the contrary, they are said to have harassed those villages of Soconusco because they are our allies. On the other hand, the Christians tell me that they are constantly sending messengers excusing themselves, saying that it is not they who are to blame, but others. To learn the truth of this matter, I decided to send Pedro de Alvarado with some eighty horsemen and two hundred foot soldiers, among whom were many crossbowmen and harquebusiers, and four pieces of artillery with an abundance of powder and shot.[26] Likewise I had a fleet of ships built in which I sent as captain Cristóbal de Olid, who came in my company, to go up the north coast and found a settlement on the point or cape of Las Hibueras, which lies sixty leagues from the bay of La Ascensión,[27] which is on the windward side of the land called Yucatán, up the coast of the mainland toward Darién.[28] I have had much information that the land there is very rich, and many pilots believe that there is a strait between that bay and the other sea, and this is the one thing in the world which I most desire to discover, because of the great service which I am certain Your Caesarean Majesty will receive thereby.

When each of these two captains had prepared everything for his journey and was about to depart, a messenger arrived from Santisteban del Puerto, which I founded on the Pánuco River, by whom the alcaldes of that town informed me how the adelantado Francisco de Garay had arrived at that river with 120 horsemen, four hundred foot soldiers and many pieces of artillery;[29] he proclaimed himself governor of that land and had told the natives so through an interpreter he had with him. Furthermore, he told them that he would avenge the wrongs which they had suffered at my hands during the past war, and that they should join him in driving out those Spaniards I had there and any more that I might send, for he would help them do it, and many other scandalous things besides, which caused considerable unrest among the natives. To confirm further the suspicions I had of his alliance with the admiral and Diego Velázquez, a few days later a caravel arrived at that river from Cuba, and in her came several friends and servants of Diego Velázquez together with a servant of the bishop of Burgos who claimed to come as agent in Yucatán; the rest of the company were servants and relatives of Diego Velázquez or servants of the admiral. On hearing this news, although I was in bed, having lost the use of one arm though a fall from my horse, I determined to go there and see him to prevent an uprising, and I immediately sent Pedro de Alvarado[30] on ahead with all the people he had ready for his journey, preparing myself to follow within two days. When my bed and everything else was already on the road and we had gone ten leagues to where I was to spend the following night, a messenger arrived from Vera Cruz, when it was almost midnight, bringing me certain letters which had arrived in a ship from Spain. With them was a decree signed with Your Majesty's Royal name, commanding the aforementioned adelantado Francisco de Garay not to interfere in that river or in any other place which I had settled, because Your Majesty was pleased that I should hold it in Your Royal name: for which I kiss the Royal feet of Your Caesarean Majesty a hundred thousand times.[31]

On the arrival of this decree, I halted my journey, and this was of no little benefit to my health, for I had not slept for sixty days and was exhausted, so that to travel at such a time was to endanger my life. But I had disregarded all that, holding it better to die in this undertaking than, for the sake of preserving my life, to be the cause of many disturbances and uprisings, and further infamous deaths. I sent at once Diego de Ocampo,[32] alcalde mayor, with the aforementioned decree, to follow Pedro de Alvarado and to give him a letter from me ordering him on no account to approach the place where the men of the adelantado were, so as to avoid a disturbance. I ordered the alcalde mayor to notify the adelantado of the contents of the decree and to inform me at once of his reply. He then departed in all haste to the province of the Guatescas, through which Pedro de Alvarado had passed but had now moved on into the interior of the province. When Alvarado learnt that the alcalde mayor was coming in my place, he at once informed him that he had received news of a captain of Francisco de Garay's, called Gonzalo Dovalle,[33] who, with twenty-two horsemen, was ravaging several villages in that province and stirring up the people. Pedro de Alvarado had also been warned that Gonzalo Dovalle had placed spies on the road along which he was to pass. This had greatly angered him, and he now believed that Gonzalo Dovalle intended to attack him, so he alerted his men until they

reached a village which they called Las Lajas,[34] where he found
Gonzalo Dovalle and all his company. As soon as Alvarado arrived
he spoke with the captain and told him that he had heard what he
was up to and was surprised at him, because the intention of the
governor and his captain was not, nor ever had been, to do him any
harm; on the contrary, he had given orders that they should be attended to and given all they required; but that as the situation had
now changed, he asked him as a favor, in order to ensure that there
would be no disturbances or harm caused between them, not to take
it ill if the arms and horses of his men were confiscated until some
agreement could be reached in these matters. Gonzalo Dovalle excused himself, saying that things had not happened as Alvarado had
been informed, but that, even so, he would agree to do as he asked.
And so the two captains and their men were united, eating and living together in harmony without any ill will or quarrels. As soon as
Ocampo, the alcalde mayor, learnt of this, he sent a secretary of
mine who was with him, called Francisco de Orduña,[35] to the captains Pedro de Alvarado and Gonzalo Dovalle with an order to return to each man his horse and arms, and to tell them that it was my
intention to help them and to attend to their needs as long as they
did not cause trouble or disturbances in the land. He likewise sent
another order to Alvarado, telling him to help them but not to attempt to touch anything of theirs or to annoy them; and he complied with this request.

Most Powerful Lord, at the same time, the ships of the
aforementioned adelantado were lying at the mouth of the Pánuco
River, as if threatening the inhabitants of the town of Santisteban,
which I had founded some three leagues upriver, and where the
ships which come to that port normally anchor. For this reason
Pedro de Vallejo, my lieutenant in that town, in order to avert the
danger he thought would follow any disturbance caused by those
ships, required the captains and masters of them to sail up to the
town and anchor there peacefully, without causing any damage or
unrest in the land, and said that if they brought any decrees from

Your Majesty to settle or explore that land, or for any other purpose, they were to show them; and they insisted that, once they had been shown, Your Majesty's orders would be obeyed in all respects. The captains and masters answered this request in a manner which meant, in effect, that they totally refused to comply with the lieutenant's instructions; he was then obliged to send them another order, demanding that they comply with the terms of the first or incur certain penalties. To this they replied as before. And so it was that two masters of those ships, whose names were Castromocho and Martín de San Juan, from Guipúzcoa, seeing that the presence of the masters and captains of these ships at the mouth of the river for two months or more was causing a disturbance both among the Spaniards living there and among the natives of that province, sent messengers in secret to Lieutenant Vallejo informing him that they wished for peace and obedience to commands of justice. They, therefore, urged him to go to their two ships, where they would welcome him and do whatever he ordered them, adding that they had a scheme for persuading the other ships to surrender peacefully and obey his commands.

For this purpose the lieutenant decided to visit those ships accompanied only by five men. When he arrived he was well received by the masters and sent word to Captain Juan de Grijalva, who was the commander of the fleet and lived aboard the flagship at that time, summoning him to obey the orders which he had already been given. The captain not only refused to obey but ordered the other ships to join him and to surround and open fire on the two mentioned above until they were sunk. Because this order was made in public so that all present heard it, the lieutenant, in his defense, ordered the guns on board the two ships which had obeyed him to be made ready. The captains and masters of the ships with Juan de Grijalva refused to obey his commands and so he sent a notary called Vicente López to speak to the lieutenant. Once he had delivered his message, the lieutenant replied justifying his orders and explaining that he had come there solely with peaceful intent and to prevent the unrest and other disturbances that had been caused by those ships remaining outside the port where it was customary to anchor, like pirates preparing to make a raid on His Majesty's lands, all of which looked very bad. He said other things to the same effect, and so persuasive was he that the notary returned to Grijalva with his reply, and telling him all the lieutenant had said, persuaded the captain to obey, for it was clear that the lieutenant was the officer of justice in that province under Your Majesty, and Captain Grijalva knew that neither the adelantado Francisco de Garay nor he himself had presented any Royal warrants which the lieutenant and the inhabitants of the town of Santisteban were bound to obey, and that to have his ships lying like pirates off Your Caesarean Majesty's coast was a most ugly thing. Captain Grijalva and the masters and captains of the ships were moved by these arguments to obey the lieutenant, and they sailed upriver to where ships usually anchor. As soon as they reached port Juan de Grijalva was arrested for his refusal to obey the lieutenant's commands. When his imprisonment was made known to my alcalde mayor, he at once gave orders that Grijalva should be freed and well treated, together with all the others who had come in those ships, and that nothing of theirs was to be touched; and so it was done.

The alcalde mayor likewise wrote to Francisco de Garay, who was in another harbor ten or twelve leagues from there, informing him that I could not go to see him myself but was sending the same alcalde mayor with my authority, so that between them they might reach some agreement as to what was to be done, and examine each other's decrees so as to conclude this matter as was most befitting to Your Majesty's service. When Francisco de Garay saw the alcalde mayor's letter he went to meet him and was very well received, and he and all his people were provided with all they required. When they were together they discussed the matter, examined their documents, and reached an agreement: the alcalde mayor showed the adelantado the decree with which Your Majesty so graciously favored me and required him to obey it, which he did, saying that in compliance with it he wished to return to the ships with his men, and go and settle in some other land beyond that mentioned in Your Majesty's decree. As he knew that I wished to help him, he asked the alcalde mayor to collect all his people, for many of them wanted to remain behind and others had deserted, and to provide both ships and men with the provisions they needed. The alcalde mayor at once saw to all that he asked, and it was immediately announced in that port, where most of the men from both parties were to be found, that everyone who had come in the fleet of the adelantado Francisco de Garay should rejoin him under pain, if he were a horseman, of losing his arms and his horse and of being seized and returned to the adelantado, and, if he were a foot soldier, of receiving a hundred lashes and being likewise seized.

Francisco de Garay also asked the alcalde mayor to have the arms and horses, which some of his men had sold in the port of Santisteban, and in the harbor where they were and in other places in the neighborhood, returned to him, for without arms and horses his men would be of no use. The alcalde mayor did all he could to discover where those arms and horses might be, and ordered all those who had bought them to return them all to the adelantado. The alcalde mayor also placed alguaciles on the roads to stop all those trying to escape; and many were taken prisoner in this way. He also sent the alguacil mayor[36] and a secretary of mine to the town of Santisteban to make the same searches and proclamations for the return of the deserters, to collect all the provisions they could find to equip Garay's ships, and also to recover the horses and arms which had been sold; all of which was done with the greatest diligence. The adelantado then went to the harbor to embark, and the alcalde mayor remained where he was with his people, so as not to make too great demands on the harbor and so as to be better able to provide for themselves. He remained there six or seven days to ensure that all that had been arranged by his and my orders was carried out. The alcalde mayor wrote to Garay asking him if there was anything else he required, because he was short of supplies and was returning to México City, where I reside. The adelantado then sent a messenger to say that he was unable to leave because he had lost six of his ships and the rest were not fit to sail, and that he was preparing a statement to prove to me that, as he had said, he was not in a position to be able to leave. He also informed me that his people had appealed against the orders of my alcalde mayor, and had given sixteen or seventeen reasons why they were not bound to obey them. One of these reasons was that certain of the people in his company had died of hunger; others, which were not very polite, were directed against him personally. Moreover, he said that all his efforts to return his men were insufficient, and those who were there at dusk were gone at dawn, for if they were captured and handed over to him one day, they went on the following day as soon as they were set free; between dusk and dawn he had lost two hundred men. He therefore begged the alcalde mayor most earnestly not to depart until he arrived, because he wished to come and see me here in this city, and if the alcalde mayor left him there he would drown himself in despair. When the alcalde mayor read his letter he decided to wait for him. He arrived two days later, and the alcalde mayor sent a messenger to inform me that the adelantado was coming to see me, and that they would proceed slowly to a town called Cicoaque, which is on the borders of these provinces, and there await my reply. The adelantado also wrote to me giving me an account[37] of the poor condition of his ships and the ill will that his men had shown him; therefore, because he believed that I would be able to remedy this and also provide him with some of my men, and with everything else he might need, and because he recognized that no one else could help him, he had resolved to come to see me. He also offered me his eldest son with all he possessed, hoping that I would make him my son-in-law, by marriage to a young daughter of mine.[38]

Meanwhile, as they were about to depart for this city, the alcalde mayor noticed that some highly untrustworthy persons had sailed with Francisco de Garay, friends and servants of Diego

Velázquez, who had shown themselves to be thoroughly hostile to my interests; and, seeing that if they remained in that province their presence would cause disturbances and unrest, he, by virtue of a certain Royal decree which Your Majesty sent me so that I might expel all such troublemakers from the land, ordered them to depart. They were Gonzalo de Figueroa, Alonso de Mendoza, Antonio de la Cerda, Juan de Ávila, Lorenzo de Ulloa, Taborda, Juan de Grijalva, Juan de Medina and others. Once this had been done, they went to the town of Cicoaque, where they found my reply to their letters, in which I said that I would be much pleased by the arrival of the adelantado, and that when he reached this city I would very willingly make arrangements concerning all he had written, and ensure that his fleet was as well equipped as he could wish. I likewise provided for his needs on the journey and ordered all the lords of the villages along his route to give him all that he required.

When Francisco de Garay arrived in this city I welcomed him as was fitting, with all goodwill and as many demonstrations as I was able; indeed, I received him as I would my own brother, for I was truly sorry at the loss of his ships and the desertion of his men, and I offered him my assistance, for I intended to do all that I could for him. As he was most eager to put into effect what he had written to me concerning the proposed marriage, he entreated me again with such persistence that to please him I agreed to do everything he asked. So with mutual consent we drew up upon oath certain agreements which set out the obligations of both parties and arranged the marriage, provided that Your Majesty, after learning of our contract, should give Your approval. In this manner, in addition to our long-standing friendship, we were bound by the contracts and agreements we had made on behalf of our children. We were now of one mind and purpose and everything in the agreements we had drawn up was pleasing to us both, but especially to the adelantado.

Most Powerful Lord, I have already described to Your Caesarean Majesty the great efforts of my alcalde mayor to make the adelantado's men, who were scattered throughout the land, return to him, and the steps he took to this end; these, although many, were not sufficient to remedy the dissatisfaction they all felt against Francisco de Garay: on the contrary, believing that they would be obliged to go with him in accordance with the orders which had been made public, they went inland in bands of three and six in several different directions. Hidden in this fashion, so that they could not be captured and taken back, they were the chief cause of rebellion among the natives of that province, who saw the Spaniards scattered throughout the land, creating disorder and other disturbances among them, taking their women and supplies by force. This led to a general uprising, for they believed, as the adelantado had made known through an interpreter when he first arrived, that there was dissension among the Spanish commanders, as I have already related to Your Majesty. And it happened that these Indians were so cunning that, having first been informed when and in what places those Spaniards could be found, they fell on them by day and night in the villages among which they were scattered, and taking them unawares and unarmed they killed a great number of them. Their daring flourished so, that they approached the town of Santisteban del Puerto, which I had founded in Your Majesty's name, where they attacked so fiercely that they placed the inhabitants in great difficulties, so that they gave themselves up for lost, and indeed would have been, had they not been prepared, and all together in a place where they could fortify themselves and resist the enemy; so much so indeed that many times they sallied out and fought with them in the field and finally routed them.

When matters were in this state, I received news of what had happened from a messenger who had escaped on foot from those battles. He told me that all the natives in the province of Pánuco were in revolt, and that many of the Spaniards from the adelantado's company who had remained there had been killed, and also some of the citizens of the town which I founded in Your Majesty's name. I feared the disaster was so great that not a single Castilian had escaped alive. Our Lord God knows how much I was grieved at this, and also because I knew that no such occurrence can happen in these parts without it causing much hardship and endangering our hold on them. The adelantado was so stricken by this news, because he believed he was the cause of it and because he had left one of his sons and all he had brought with him in that province, that he fell ill of his grief, and of this sickness passed from this life within the space of three days.[39]

That Your Excellency may be informed in more detail of what happened after I received this first news, I shall add that the Spaniard who brought me word of the rising in Pánuco could tell me no more than that he had been surprised, together with three horsemen and a foot soldier, by some of the inhabitants of a village called Tacetuco,[40] who had fought with them and killed the foot soldier, two of the horsemen and the horse of the third; he and the surviving horseman had managed to escape because it was dark by then. They had seen a house in the village where they were to have been awaited by the lieutenant with fifteen horsemen and forty foot soldiers, but this house had been burnt, and he believed by what he had seen that they had all been killed.

I waited six or seven days to see if any further news would arrive, and during this time a messenger came from the aforementioned lieutenant, who was then in a village called Teneztequipa,[41] which is subject to this city and lies on the border of that province, with a letter informing me how he had waited in the village of Tacetuco with fifteen horsemen and forty foot soldiers for the reinforcements which were to join him there because he intended to cross the river and pacify certain villages which were still in revolt. Shortly before dawn their quarters had been surrounded by a large number of people and set on fire; and, although they mounted in great haste, they were yet taken unawares, for they had believed those people to be as subdued as always. The fighting was so fierce that all had perished save he and two other horsemen who had succeeded in escaping, although his own horse was killed and one of his men had taken him up behind. They had made good their escape because after two leagues they came upon an alcalde from the town with some men, who came to their assistance; but they could not withstand the enemy for long, and all fled together from that province. He had no news of the people who had remained in the town nor of any of Francisco de Garay's men, who were scattered in several places, but he did not think that there were any left alive. For, as I have already informed Your Majesty, after the adelantado had come here with his people, and had told the natives of that province that I was no longer to have anything to do with them, as he was the governor they must now obey, and said that if they joined him, together they would drive out all the Spaniards I had in that town and any more I might send, the natives rebelled and were of a mind never to serve a Spaniard again, even killing some they found alone on the roads. The lieutenant believed, therefore, that this was a concerted effort by all the Indians, and that just as they had fallen on him and his men so they had fallen on the people in the town and those scattered throughout the various villages, all of whom were quite unprepared for such an uprising, as the Indians had previously served them without complaint.

Having thus been better informed by this news of the rebellion in that province and of the death of those Spaniards, I at once dispatched with the greatest haste fifty horsemen, and a hundred crossbowmen and harquebusiers on foot, and four pieces of artillery with a large store of powder and shot, under a Spanish captain, together with two native chieftains from this city with fifteen thousand men each. I ordered this captain to go as swiftly as possible to that province and to stop nowhere unless it were absolutely necessary, until he had reached the town of Santisteban del Puerto, and discovered what had become of the settlers and other people who had remained there, for it was possible they were besieged somewhere, and if this was so, he was to help them. So he departed and went with all haste and entered that province; and they fought with him in two places, but Our Lord God granted him victory, and he continued on his way until he reached the town, where he found twenty-two horsemen and a hundred foot soldiers, who were besieged there and had been attacked six or seven times, but had managed, although with great difficulty, to defend themselves by means of some guns which they had there. But they could not have resisted much longer, and if the captain I sent had arrived three days later, they would all have perished; for they were all dying of hunger and had already sent one of Francisco de Garay's brigantines to the town of Vera Cruz to inform me of all that was happening, because they could not send a message any other way, and also to return with provisions, which afterwards it did, although they had by that time been relieved by the forces I sent.

It was there they learnt how the men whom Francisco de Garay had left in a village called Tamiquil,[42] some hundred foot soldiers and horsemen, had all been killed; no one had escaped except an Indian from the island of Jamaica, who escaped through the forests and from whom we heard how they had been attacked by night. It was estimated that 210 of the adelantado's men had died and forty-three of the settlers whom I had left in Santisteban and who were at the time in the villages which they held as *encomiendas*.[43] It is also thought that even more of the adelantado's men may have perished, because there is no record of them all. The men whom the captain took with him, together with those of the lieutenant and the alcalde and the people who were found in the town, now numbered some eighty horse and were divided into three companies. They made war on that province in such a manner that they captured some four hundred lords and chieftains besides other common people, all of whom, I mean the chieftains, were burnt in punishment, for they confessed to being the instigators of the war, and each one to having killed, or had a part in killing, Spaniards.[44] Once this was done, the other prisoners were released and all the other natives returned with them to their villages. The captain, in Your Majesty's name, appointed as new lords in those villages those entitled to succeed according to their custom. At this time I received letters from the aforementioned captain and from others who were with him, telling me how already, praise be to Our Lord, the whole province was quite safe and peaceful and the natives serve very well; and I believe there will be peace throughout the year once the ill feeling has passed.

I assure Your Caesarean Majesty that these people are so turbulent that at any novelty or opportunity for sedition they rebel, and so it has always been, for it was their custom to rise up against their lords and they never let an occasion for rebellion pass without taking advantage of it.

Most Catholic Lord, in previous chapters, I told how at the time of my hearing of the arrival of Francisco de Garay at the Pánuco River I had a fleet ready to sail to the cape or point of Las Hibueras and gave the reasons which had moved me to do this. On the arrival of the adelantado, however, I canceled my plans, for I believed that he wished to take possession of the land by his own authority, and if he did so I would need all my people to resist him. Having brought the affair with the adelantado to a conclusion, it seemed to me that Your Majesty would be well served by such an undertaking, although it would cost me a considerable amount, in pay for the sailors, provisions for the ships and men who were to sail in them. I therefore pursued my original plan. I purchased five more large ships and a brigantine and collected four hundred men, artillery, munitions, arms and other provisions and foodstuffs. In addition to this I sent two servants of mine with eight thousand *pesos de oro* to the island of Cuba to buy horses and provisions, not only for this first voyage but to have them ready to load onto the ships when they returned, so that nothing for which I sent them should be left undone because of a lack of supplies. I also did not wish them to annoy the natives by demanding provisions, for it would be better to give them some of our own than to take any from them.

With these orders they left the port of San Juan de Chalchiqueca[45] on the eleventh day of January in the year 1524 bound for Havana, which is the northernmost point of the island of Cuba,

18. The aftermath of the fall of Tenochtitlan. Folio 170 recto of Codex Vindobonensis S.N. 1600. *Courtesy of the Österreichische Nationbibliothek.*

where they are to furnish themselves with all they lack, especially horses, and gather together the ships, whence, with God's blessing, they will continue their journey to the aforementioned land of Las Hibueras. On reaching the first harbor, they are to land, together with all the men, horses, supplies and everything they have on their ships, and in the place they think most suitable they are to fortify themselves with their artillery, of which they have many good pieces, and there found their town. When they have done this they are then to send three of the larger ships to the port of Trinidad on the island of Cuba, because it is on the most convenient course for them, and because one of those servants of mine has gone there to prepare all the things that the captain may require. The other smaller ships and the brigantine, with the chief pilot and a cousin of mine called Diego de Hutado as their captain, are to sail along the coast from the bay of La Ascensión in search of that strait[46] which is thought to be there, and once they have seen everything they are to return to wherever the captain Cristóbal de Olid may be, whence they are to send one of those ships with an account of what they have found and of all that Cristóbal de Olid has discovered about the land and what has happened there, so that I may send a full report of it to Your Caesarean Majesty.

I also reported that I had got ready certain people to go with Pedro de Alvarado to those cities of Uclaclán[47] and Guatemala which I have mentioned in previous chapters, and to other provinces beyond, of which I have also heard, and how this expedition also had been interrupted by the arrival of Francisco de Garay. And because I had already spent much on horses, arms, artillery and munitions, as well as money given as subsidies to the men; because I believe that Our Lord God and Your Sacred Majesty will benefit greatly from this, and because, according to my information, I may expect to discover many rich and strange lands with many very different peoples, I again resolved to continue with my original plan. In addition to what I had already provided, I again fitted out

Pedro de Alvarado and dispatched him from this city on the sixth
day of December in the year 1523. He took with him 120 horsemen, and with spare mounts, a total of 160 horses, together with
three hundred foot soldiers, 130 of whom are crossbowmen and
harquebusiers. He has four pieces of artillery with good supplies of
powder and ammunition. He is also accompanied by some chieftains from this city and from other cities in the vicinity and with
them some of their people, although not many, because the journey
will be so long.

I have received news of how they reached the province of
Tecuantepeque[48] on the twelfth of January and are going well.
May it please Our Lord to guide both expeditions, for I firmly believe that as they are all engaged in His service and in the Royal
name of Your Caesarean Majesty they cannot fail to achieve a great
and prosperous result.

I also instructed Pedro de Alvarado to have special care to
send me a long and detailed account of all that happens to him so
that I may send it to Your Highness. And I am certain, according to
the information and maps I have of that land, that Pedro de Alvarado and Cristóbal de Olid must meet, if no strait separates them.

I would have dispatched many such expeditions and discovered much of what is unknown about this land had I not been hampered by the disturbances caused by the fleets which have come
here. I assure Your Holy Majesty that You have been very ill-
served by them, not only in that many lands have still not been
discovered, but also because a great fortune in gold and pearls has
not been collected for Your Royal treasury. From now on, however, if no more of them arrive, I shall endeavor to restore all that
has been lost, and in this I shall spare neither myself nor my fortune
in doing so; for I assure Your Sacred and Caesarean Majesty that, in
addition to having spent all I own, I owe much, which I have taken
from Your Majesty's revenues for expenses, which, as Your Majesty may reckon from the accounts, amounts to more than sixty

thousand *pesos de oro*, besides a further twelve thousand which I have borrowed from various people to meet the cost of my household.

I said in previous chapters that some of the provinces which were in the neighborhood of Espíritu Santo and served the town had rebelled and even killed several Spaniards; so, to bring these back to the Royal service of Your Majesty, and also to win over other neighboring provinces, because the men of that town are not sufficient to retain what has been won and to conquer those others, I sent a captain with thirty horsemen and a hundred foot soldiers, some of whom were crossbowmen and harquebusiers, with two pieces of artillery and a good supply of powder and shot. They departed on the eighth of December of the year 1523. I have as yet received no word from them, but I believe they will be very successful and that Our Lord God and Your Majesty will be well served by this expedition which, it is hoped, will achieve notable discoveries. It is a strip of land on the north coast, between the regions of exploration of Pedro de Alvarado and Cristóbal de Olid, which until now has been peaceful. Once this small strip is conquered and pacified, Your Holy Majesty will have on the north coast land more than four hundred leagues in unbroken extent subject to Your Royal service; and along the coast of the Southern Sea, more than five hundred leagues.

In the whole territory, from one sea to the other, the natives serve without complaint, save for two provinces which lie between those of Teguantepeque, Chinanta, Guaxaca and Guazacualco,[49] in the middle of all four; the people of these two provinces are called Zapotecas and Mixes.[50] Their land is so rocky that it cannot be crossed even on foot, for I have twice sent people to conquer them, who were unable to do so because of the roughness of the terrain, and because their warriors are very fierce and well armed. They fight with lances twenty-five or thirty spans in length, very heavy and well made, and with heads made of flint. With these they have defended themselves and killed some of the Spaniards who have gone there. They have done, and are doing, much harm to their neighbors who are Your Majesty's vassals, by raiding them at night, burning their villages and killing many of them. So much damage have they done that many of the villages near to them have rebelled and joined forces with them. To prevent this from spreading, although at present I am rather short of men, I collected 150 foot soldiers—horses are no use there—most of whom were crossbowmen and harquebusiers, and four pieces of artillery with all the necessary munitions both for the guns and the foot soldiers. I appointed Rodrigo Rangel, alcalde of this city, as their captain; a year ago he had marched against them, but as it was the rainy season he was unable to achieve anything and returned after two months. This captain and his men left the city on the fifth of February of this year, and I believe that, God willing, as they are well equipped, are going in a good season, and are accompanied by many skillful warriors from this city and thereabouts, they will bring this venture to a conclusion, from which no little benefit will redound to Your Highness's Imperial Crown, for at the moment not only do they not serve, but they cause much harm to those who do; also the land is very rich in mines.

When these people have been conquered, the men who are going there say they will lay waste the country and enslave the inhabitants for having been so rebellious, because many times they were required, and once even offered themselves, to become Your Majesty's vassals, and also for having killed Spaniards and done so much harm. I ordered that those who were taken alive should be branded with Your Highness's mark, and that once those belonging to Your Majesty had been set aside the rest should be distributed amongst the men on the expedition.

Most Excellent Lord, I may assure Your Royal Excellency that the least of these expeditions which have been dispatched has cost me more than five thousand *pesos de oro* of my own, and those led by Pedro de Alvarado and Cristóbal de Olid have cost more than fifty thousand in cash, besides other expenses of my estate which have not been accounted for or recorded. But as it is all in the service of Your Caesarean Majesty, even were it to cost me my life in addition, I should count it a greater favor. Should such an occasion arise I shall not hesitate to put it at risk.

In the last account as in this I have mentioned to Your Majesty that I started to build four ships on the Southern Sea, and as they were begun a long while ago, it will seem to Your Royal Highness that I have been somewhat negligent in not having completed them yet. I will, therefore, explain to Your Sacred Majesty the reason; it is that the Southern Sea, or at least the part where these ships are being built, is two hundred leagues or more from those ports on the Northern Sea where all material arriving in New Spain is unloaded, and there are very rocky mountain passes and wide and deep rivers, across which all the things needed for those ships must be brought; they are, therefore, transported with great difficulty, for there is no other place where they can be obtained. In addition to this, when I had collected in a house in the harbor where the ships are being built all the equipment they required—sails, cables, rigging, nails, anchors, pitch, tallow, tow, bitumen, oil and other things—a fire broke out one night and everything was destroyed, except for the anchors, which could not burn. I have now begun again, because four months ago a ship came from Castile bringing all the things I required for those ships, since, fearing the possibility of what in fact happened, I had provided for it and asked for the materials to be sent. And I assure Your Caesarean Majesty that these ships have cost me so far, and they have not even been launched yet, more than eight thousand *pesos de oro*, besides additional expenditure, but now, praised be Our Lord, they are at such a stage that by next Whitsun or St. John's day in June, they will be ready to sail if I can find some bitumen, because, since all I had was burnt, I have been unable to acquire more; but I hope that some will soon arrive from Spain, because I have already ordered it. I hold these ships of more importance than I can express, because I am certain that if it so please Our Lord God, they will gain for

Your Caesarean Majesty more realms and dominions than those of which our country now knows. May it please Him to guide them as He wills, and as may so greatly benefit Your Caesarean Majesty, for I am convinced that if I do this there will then be nothing wanting to make Your Excellency monarch of the whole world.

After it had pleased Our Lord God that we should capture this great city of Temixtitan, it did not seem to me a good plan to reside there for the present, on account of several disadvantages, so I brought all my men to a town I have already mentioned, called Cuyoacán, which lies on the shores of this lake. As I always wished the great city to be rebuilt because of its magnificence and marvelous position, I strove to collect together all the inhabitants who, since the war, had fled to other parts and, although I held, and indeed still hold, the lord of it a prisoner, I charged a captain general whom I had known in the time of Mutezuma with the task of repopulating it. And so that he should have more authority I gave back to him the title he held when his lord was in power, which was that of *Ciguacoatl*, which means lieutenant of the king.[51] I likewise appointed chieftains whom I had known previously to the offices in the government of this city which they had once held. And to this *Ciguacoatl* and the others I gave such lands and people as were necessary for their sustenance, although not as much as they had owned before, nor enough to make them dangerous at any time. I have always tried to honor and favor them, and they have done so well that now there are some thirty thousand people living in the city, and the markets and commerce are organized as before.

I have given them such liberties and exemptions that the population grows each day, for they live very comfortably and many of the artisans live by working among the Spaniards: these are carpenters, masons, stonecutters, silversmiths and others. The merchants carry on their businesses in full confidence, and the other people live either by fishing, which is a flourishing trade in this city,[52] or by agriculture, for many of them have their own plantations where they grow all the vegetables grown in Spain of which we have been able to obtain seeds. I assure Your Caesarean Majesty that if they could but be given plants and seeds from Spain, and if Your Highness were pleased to command them to be sent to us, as I requested in my earlier report, there would in a very short time be a great abundance of produce, for these Indians are much given to cultivating the soil and planting orchards; and from this I am sure that Your Highness's Imperial Crown will derive no little profit, for it will be the cause of maintaining these parts, and Your Sacred Majesty shall have more revenues and dominions in them than in any which Your Highness now owns in the name of God, Our Lord. Your Highness may be certain therefore that I shall not be found wanting, but shall work toward this end with all my strength and capacity.[53]

After this city had been taken I immediately set about building a fortress in the water in a part of the city where the brigantines might be safely guarded and yet able to attack the whole city should the need arise, and so that I might command the entrance and exits to the city; and so it was done. It is constructed in such a manner that, although I have seen many arsenals and forts, I have seen none to equal it; and many who have seen more than I agree with me. The fashion in which it is built is that the part which lies toward the lake has two very strong towers with embrasures where necessary. Both of these towers jut out beyond the curtain wall and are connected to it by a wall also with embrasures. Extending back from these two towers is a building of three naves, where the brigantines are kept, with gates, between the two towers, opening onto the lake. This building is likewise provided with embrasures, and at the end facing the city is another very large tower with many rooms up and down for defending or attacking the city. I am sending Your Holy Majesty a plan of it so that this may be more clearly understood, and shall, therefore, particularize no further, but, so long as we hold it and keep there as many ships and guns as we now have, it lies with us to decide whether there is peace or war.[54]

Once this building was completed I considered that we were

now secure enough to carry out my plan, which was to settle inside the city, and so I moved in with all my people, and the building sites were distributed among the settlers. In the name of Your Royal Highness I gave to each of those who had taken part in the conquest an additional plot in payment for their labors, as well as the one to which they were entitled as settlers who have to give service according to the order of these parts. They have worked so rapidly that many of the settlers' houses are already finished and others well under way. And because there is an abundance of stone, lime, wood and of the bricks which the natives make, they are such fine and large houses that Your Sacred Majesty may be certain that in five years this city will be the most noble and populous in the known world, and it will have the finest buildings.

The district where the Spaniards have built is separate from that of the natives and divided from it by a stretch of water, although there are wooden bridges on all the roads joining the two districts.[55] There are two large native markets, one in their quarter and one among the Spaniards, where every kind of food found in the land may be bought, for they come from all over the country to sell it.[56] There is now no scarcity of anything there used to be in the days of the city's prosperity. It is true, however, that there are now no gold or silver ornaments, no featherwork nor any rich thing as there used to be; a few small pieces of gold and silver may sometimes be found, but not as before.

Owing to the differences which Diego Velázquez has had with me, and the ill will which he has induced against me in Juan de Fonseca, bishop of Burgos, on whose orders all the officials of the Casa de la Contratación in Seville acted, especially Juan López de Recalde, the contador, on whom all depended in the bishop's time, I have been denied the arms and artillery which I required, although I sent the money for them many times. Yet, since nothing so sharpens a man's wits as necessity, and since my need was so extreme and there was no hope of improvement, for they would not permit Your Holy Majesty to be informed, I sought a means whereby I might prevent the loss of all that had been won by such hardships and danger, for such a loss would have been a grave disservice to Our Lord God and to Your Caesarean Majesty, and would have placed us all in great peril. So I hastened to find copper in some of the provinces in these parts, and offered a good price so that it might be found the sooner. As soon as a sufficient quantity was brought to me I set a gunsmith, who was fortunately found here, to make two medium-sized culverins, which turned out so well that for their size there could be none better. Besides the copper, however, I needed tin, for they could not be made without it, and for making the culverins I had acquired some with extreme difficulty, by buying at great expense all the plates and other articles made of it which I could find, but no more was to be had at any price. I began, therefore, to enquire throughout the land if there was any to be found, and it so pleased Our Lord, who has always troubled to provide us with what we require in the greatest difficulties, that I found among the natives of a province called Tachco a few small pieces of it like very thin coins, and, continuing my investigation, I discovered that in the aforementioned province, and in others, too, it was indeed used as money;[57] and finally I learnt that it was mined in the same province of Tachco, which is twenty-six leagues from this city. Once I had learnt the whereabouts of these mines, I sent some Spaniards there with tools and they brought me samples of it. I ordered them to extract from then on all that was necessary and this they will continue to do, although with some difficulty. While searching for these metals a supply of iron was found, in large quantities, according to what I was told by those who claim to know about these things.

Since finding this tin I have been making daily, and continue to make, a few guns; so far five pieces have been completed: two medium-sized culverins, two slightly smaller ones, and a serpentine. I also have two sakers which I brought with me when I came first, and another medium-sized culverin, which I purchased from the property of the adelantado Juan Ponce de León.[58] From the ships which have arrived, I have in all thirty-five pieces of bronze both large and small from falconets upwards, and in cast iron some seventy pieces, lombards, small-bore culverins and other cannon.[59] Thus, praised be Our Lord, we are now able to defend ourselves. As to munitions, God likewise provided for us, for we found so much saltpeter and of such good quality that it sufficed for other needs as well, for we had vessels in which to bake it, although much was used in our many expeditions. As for the sulphur, I have already written to Your Majesty about a mountain in this province from which much smoke arises. A Spaniard descended into the mouth of it some seventy or eighty fathoms on the end of a rope and brought some out which has lasted until now.[60] But in future we will not have to go to such trouble—for it is dangerous—because I shall always write to Spain for it, now Your Majesty has been pleased that no bishop shall prevent it reaching us.

Having established peace in the town of Santisteban, which was founded by the Pánuco River, and having brought to an end the conquest of the province of Tututepeque, and dispatched the captain who went to Impilcingo and Colimán, all of which I mentioned in the previous chapters, and before coming to this city, I went to the town of Vera Cruz and to that of Medellín, to visit them and to provide for certain things which were required in those ports. I discovered that because there is no Spanish settlement closer to the port of San Juan de Chalchiquecan than the town of Vera Cruz, all the ships went there to unload, since San Juan is not very safe and many ships were lost on account of the north winds which blow along that coast.

I went, therefore, to the aforementioned port of San Juan to look for a place close by where I might found a town; but despite our efforts at that time we could find nothing save hills of drifting sand. At last, however, after some while we came across a good site two leagues from that port, with all that was required for building a town; there is an abundance of wood and water and grazing land, although there is no timber or stone, nor any other building material that is not a long way from there. An inlet was discovered near this place, up which I sent a canoe to find out if it joined the sea, and if the open boats would be able to row up it to the town. It was found to lead to a river which flowed into the sea; and at the mouth of the river the water was found to be a fathom or more in depth, so that by clearing the inlet, for at the moment it is blocked with tree trunks, the boats might come right up to the houses in the town to unload. Seeing how well placed this site was and the great need to ensure the safety of the ships, I ordered the town of Medellín, which lay twenty leagues inland in the province of Tatalptetelco, to be moved there; and so it was done. Nearly all the settlers have already moved and have built their houses there, and orders have been given to clear the inlet and to build in that town a customs-house. Thus, although the ships take some time to unload, for their cargo has to be conveyed two leagues upstream by boat, they now have a safe anchorage. I am certain that the town will become, after this city, the best in New Spain, for already some ships have unloaded there and their merchandise has been carried in the boats, and even in some brigantines, up to the town. In future the ships will be safe, for the port is a good one and I am working to arrange matters so that they may unload without difficulty. Likewise the roads between that town and this city are being made with all haste, so that the merchandise will be more speedily delivered, because it is a better road and will cut the journey by a day.[61]

Most Powerful Lord, in past chapters I have told Your Highness to what places I have sent expeditions both by land and sea, in the belief that, guided by Our Lord, they will prove of great service to Your Majesty; and as I always take care to think of every possible means whereby I may fulfill my desire to advance the Royal service of Your Majesty, I saw that nothing now remained save to investigate the unexplored coast between the Pánuco River and the coast of Florida, which was discovered by the adelantado Juan Ponce de León, and from there to continue up this same Florida coast northwards to Los Bacallaos, for it is believed that there is on that coast a strait leading to the Southern Sea. If it is found, it will, according to a chart I have, come out very close to the archipelago which Magellan discovered by Your Highness's command. And if Our Lord God be pleased that we find this strait, it will prove a very good and very short route from the Spice Islands to Your Majesty's realms, for it will be two-thirds shorter than the one now sailed, and will be without hazard or peril for the ships, for they will always come and go through the realms and dominions of Your Majesty, so that whenever they are in need they may repair without fear or danger to one of Your Highness's ports.[62]

I have considered the great service which such an undertaking would render to Your Majesty, although I am penniless and heavily in debt, on account of what I owe and have spent on the expeditions I have sent by land and sea, and through the cost of supplying all the munitions and artillery in this city and elsewhere, and many other expenses which occur each day; for I provide everything at my own expense, and all the things which we require are so dear and at such excessive prices that, although the land is rich, the profit I may gain from it does not suffice to cover the great outlays that I have. Yet with regard to all that I have said in this chapter, setting aside all my personal difficulties, and though I assure Your Majesty that I have had to borrow all the money for it, I have determined to send three caravels and two brigantines in this quest (although I believe it will cost me more than ten thousand *pesos de oro*) and add this service to the others I have performed. For I hold this to be the most important of them if, as I say, the strait is found, and, even if it is not, many great and rich lands must surely be discovered, where Your Caesarean Majesty may be served and the realms and dominions of Your Royal Crown much increased. Should there, however, prove to be no such strait, then it will be most useful for Your Highness that it be known, for some other means may be found for Your Caesarean Majesty to benefit from the Spice Islands and all the others which are adjacent to them. In this I offer myself to Your Highness's service and will be greatly pleased if Your Majesty choose to command me, in default of that strait, to find some such means whereby Your Majesty would be well served and at less cost. May Our Lord grant, however, that the fleet succeed in its purpose, which is to discover the strait, because that would be best; and I am sure it will, because nothing can eclipse Your Majesty's Royal good fortune, and diligence, careful preparation and determination will not be found wanting on my part to carry it out.

Likewise I intend to send the vessels which I have built on the Southern Sea. If Our Lord so wishes these will sail at the end of July of this year, 1524, down the same coast in search of that strait, for, if it exists, it cannot escape those who go by the Southern Sea and those who go by the Northern, because those who go in the south will follow the coast until they find it or reach the land discovered by Magellan, and the others on the north until, as I have said, they reach Los Bacallaos. Thus on the one coast or the other they cannot fail to discover it. I assure Your Majesty that according to the information I have received of lands up the coast of the Southern Sea, I would have profited considerably, and served Your Majesty too, by sending these ships there, but as I have been told of the great desire which Your Majesty has to discover this strait and the great service which its discovery would render to Your Royal Crown, I lay aside all those other interests and advantages, of which I have heard many tales, in order to follow this course. May Our Lord guide it as He wills, and may Your Majesty's desire be satisfied, and likewise my desire to serve.

The officials[63] that Your Majesty sent to take charge of Your Royal revenues and property have arrived and have begun to audit the accounts with those who previously had this charge, and whom I had appointed in Your Highness's name. As these officials will send Your Majesty an account of all the provisions which have been made until now, I will make no detailed report of them, but refer myself to their account, which I believe will demonstrate to Your Highness the vigilance and solicitude that I have shown in everything touching Your Royal service. And although I have been greatly occupied in the wars and the pacification of this land, as their outcome clearly shows, I have not for all that neglected to take special care to preserve and collect all that has been possible of what belongs to Your Majesty.

From the account which the aforementioned officials are sending to Your Caesarean Majesty it will appear, and Your Majesty will see, that I have spent some 62,000 *pesos de oro* of Your Royal revenues on the pacification of these parts and the expansion of the dominions that Your Caesarean Majesty holds in them. It is well that Your Highness should know that I could not do otherwise, for I only began to spend them after I had nothing left of my own to spend and was even in debt by more than thirty thousand *pesos de oro* which I borrowed from several people. As there was nothing else to be done, and I could not otherwise meet the requirements of Your Highness's Royal service and of my desire, I was obliged to spend it; but I do not believe that the profit it has yielded and will yield can be less than a thousand per cent. Although Your Highness's officials are agreed that it was spent in Your Majesty's service, they will not enter it in the accounts because they say they have neither the commission nor the authority to do this. I therefore beseech Your Majesty, if it seems well spent, to order it to be entered in the accounts and also to command that I be refunded some fifty thousand *pesos de oro* which I have spent out of my estate and have borrowed from friends, for if this is not returned to me I shall be unable to repay my creditors and will find myself in great need. I cannot think that Your Catholic Majesty will permit this, but, rather, in addition to paying me, will grant me many great favors; for besides the fact that Your Highness is so Catholic and so Christian a Prince, my services, for their part, are not undeserving of it, as their fruits will bear witness.

From these officials and from other persons in their company and also from letters written to me from Spain, I have learnt that the things which I sent Your Caesarean Majesty with Antonio de Quiñones and Alonso de Ávila, representatives of New Spain, never reached Your Royal presence, because they were seized by the French, on account of the insufficient protection which the Casa de la Contratación in Seville sent to accompany them from the Azores.[64] I was much grieved at their loss, for they were all so rich and strange that I greatly desired Your Majesty to see them, for, besides the benefit which Your Highness would have gained from them, my services would be more manifest. I am not altogether sorry, however, that they were lost, for Your Majesty would have had little need of them, and I shall endeavor to send others, richer and more wonderful, according to the news that I have of some provinces which I have lately sent to conquer, and others to which I will send as soon as I have the men. Moreover, the French, and other rulers to whom those things will become known, will see thereby the reason why they must subject themselves to the Imperial Crown of Your Caesarean Majesty, for, in addition to the many great realms and dominions which Your Highness has in those parts, I, the least of Your vassals, am able to perform so many and such great services in respect of these several and distant lands. For the first of my offerings, I now send with Diego de Soto, a servant of mine, certain small things which, although they were rejected before as being unworthy to accompany the others, have some value, and also some which I have acquired since then. With these I am also sending a culverin cast from twenty-four hundredweight and fifty pounds of silver, and I also believe there was some gold in it, for it had to be cast twice. It was very costly, for the metal was worth 24,500 *pesos de oro* at five *pesos* a mark; and there were other expenses, such as the casting, engraving and the transport to the harbor, which cost me another three thousand *pesos de oro*.[65] But as it was a rich and magnificent sight, and worthy to go before so High and Excellent a Prince, I determined to finish it and spend the money. I beseech Your Caesarean Majesty to accept my small service, bearing in account the extent of my wish to do still greater ones if fortune permits. For although I am in debt, as I have mentioned to Your Highness above, I was willing to contract further debts, in the desire that Your Majesty might know of my great desire to serve, because I have had the ill fortune to be so opposed before Your Highness that I have been denied the opportunity to demonstrate this desire.

Likewise I am sending to Your Sacred Majesty sixty thousand *pesos de oro* belonging to Your Royal revenues, as Your Highness will see from the accounts which the officials and I are sending; and we venture to send such a sum all together at one time both because of the great need we here feel that Your Majesty must have of it, on account of the wars and other things, and so that Your Majesty should not be too sorry at the past loss. Henceforth I shall send all I am able to acquire at every opportunity, and Your Sacred Majesty may be assured that as things are developing at present, and Your Highness's realms and dominions are extended, You will draw from them surer revenues and at less expense than from any of Your other realms, provided we are not further hindered by disturbances such as have arisen in the past. I say this because two days ago there arrived at the port of San Juan, Gonzalo de Salazar, Your Highness's factor, who told me that he had heard, while he had put in at the island of Cuba, that Diego Velázquez, the admiral's lieutenant there, had reached an understanding with the captain Cristóbal de Olid, whom I, in Your Majesty's name, had sent to Las Hibueras, that he would rebel and seize the land for Diego Velázquez. This seemed such an ugly business and such a great disservice to Your Majesty that I can scarcely believe it; on the other hand, knowing the cunning which Diego Velázquez has always practiced against me to harm me and hinder my services, I do believe it. For when he can do nothing else, he tries to prevent men from coming to these parts, and, as he rules in that island, he seizes all those who go from here to Cuba and oppresses them, robbing them of much of what they own and afterwards bargaining with them for their freedom, so that they, to be rid of him, do and say whatever he wishes. I shall discover the truth, and if it is so then I am of a mind to send for the aforementioned Diego Velázquez and arrest him and send him to Your Majesty; for by cutting out the root of all these evils, which he is, all the branches will wither and I may more freely carry out those services which I have begun and those which I am planning.[66]

Each time I have written to Your Sacred Majesty I have told Your Highness of the readiness displayed by some of the natives of these parts to be converted to Our Holy Catholic Faith and to become Christians; and for this purpose I have begged Your Caesarean Majesty to send religious persons of a goodly life and character. Until now, however, very few—I may say hardly any—have arrived, and because it is certain that they would reap great profit, I would once again remind Your Highness and beseech You to send them with all haste, because Our Lord God will be greatly served thereby, and the desire which Your Highness, as a Catholic, has in this matter shall be fulfilled.[67] The representatives, Antonio de Quiñones and Alonso de Ávila, the municipal councils of the towns of this New Spain and I sent to Your Majesty asking You to provide us with bishops or other dignitaries to administer the divine offices, because at that time it seemed to us the best way; but now, considering the matter more fully, it appears to me that Your Holy Majesty should provide other means whereby the natives of these parts may be more speedily converted and instructed in Our Holy Catholic Faith. And it seems to me that the manner in which this should be done is that Your Holy Majesty should send to these parts many religious persons, as I have already said, who would be most zealous in the conversion of these people, and that they should build houses and monasteries in the provinces which we think most appropriate; they should receive some of the tithes for the construction of their houses and their sustenance, the rest being set aside for churches and their ornaments in the towns where Spaniards are settled, and for their clergy. These tithes should be collected by Your Majesty's officials, who should keep account of them and distribute them to these monasteries and churches; this sum will be more than sufficient so that Your Majesty may benefit from the remainder.

I therefore ask Your Highness to beseech His Holiness to concede to Your Majesty the tithes for this purpose, informing him of the great service that will be rendered to Our Lord God by the conversion of these people and telling him that this cannot be achieved by any other means. Because if we have bishops and other dignitaries, they will only follow the customs which, for our sins, they pursue these days, of squandering the goods of the Church on pomp and ceremony, and other vices, and leaving entailed estates to their sons or kinsmen. And the evil here would be still greater, for the natives of these parts had in their time religious persons administering their rites and ceremonies who were so severe in the observance of both chastity and honesty that if any one of them was held by anyone to have transgressed he was put to death. If these people were now to see the affairs of the Church and the service of God in the hands of canons or other dignitaries, and saw them indulge in the vices and profanities now common in Spain, knowing that such men were the ministers of God, it would bring our Faith into much contempt, and they would hold it a mockery; this would cause such harm that I believe any further preaching would be of no avail. Seeing that so much depends on this, and that Your Majesty's prime intent is, and should be, to see these people converted, which intent we who reside here in Your Royal name must diligently pursue, and, as Christians, we must have particular care of these people, I have sought to advise Your Caesarean Majesty of this, and have offered my opinion, which I beseech Your Highness to accept, as coming from one of Your subjects and vassals, who has worked and will work with all his bodily powers to extend Your Majesty's realms and dominions in these parts, and to publish Your Royal fame and great power among these people, and likewise desires and will labor in spirit that Your Highness may command Our Holy Faith to be sown amongst them, earning thereby the blessing of everlasting life.

As we have no bishop for the conferment of holy orders and the consecration of churches, ornaments, holy oil, water and other things, and it would be difficult to send for them elsewhere, Your Majesty should likewise beseech His Holiness to grant these powers to the two principal persons in the religious orders that are to come here, and that they should be his delegates, one from the Order of St. Francis and the other from the Order of St. Dominic.[68] They should bring the most extensive powers Your Majesty is able to obtain, for, because these lands are so far from the Church of Rome, and we, the Christians who now reside here and shall do so in the future, are so far from the proper remedies of our consciences and, as we are human, so subject to sin, it is essential that His Holiness should be generous with us and grant to these persons most extensive powers, to be handed down to persons actually in residence here whether it be given to the general of each order or to his provincials.

The collection of tithes in these parts has been leased out in some of the towns and in others is under offer. They commence from the year 1523, because it did not seem to me that they should be levied before, as they were insignificant in themselves, and because at that time all those who had any produce, as it was in time of war, spent more on keeping it than the profits they gained therefrom. Whatever else Your Majesty may command will be done as You so please.

The tithes for this city between the years of 1523 and 1524 amount to 5,550 *pesos de oro*, and the towns of Medellín and Vera Cruz are expected to bring in some thousand *pesos de oro;* but their collection has not yet been auctioned, and I hope that there will be even more. I do not know what the estimates are in the other towns because, as they are far away, I have had no reply from them yet. The money will be used to build churches, pay the clergy and the sacristans, purchase ornaments and provide for all other such expenses. Your Majesty's contador and treasurer will keep the accounts, for everything will be handed over to the treasurer and nothing spent without an order of payment from the contador and myself.

Most Catholic Lord, I have been informed by the ships which have recently arrived from the Islands that the judges and officials of Your Majesty who reside in Hispaniola have ordered, and have had it publicly announced there and in all the other Islands, that no mares or any other breeding animals may be shipped to New Spain under pain of death. This they have done, so that we shall always have to buy our horses and cattle from them, for which they charge excessive prices. This they should not do, because it is notorious what great disservice is done to Your Majesty in preventing this land from being pacified and settled; they know themselves that we need these animals which they deny us to preserve what we have gained and to gain more; and, furthermore, because those Islands have received much enrichment and many advantages from New Spain. I therefore beseech Your Majesty to send a Royal warrant to the Islands granting to all who wish to export animals from them the right to do so without fear of punishment, for not only do they have no need of what they deny us, but Your Majesty is ill-served by it, because we here shall be able to make no new conquests nor even hold what we have already conquered. I might have gotten back at them for this in such a way that they would have been glad to revoke their mandates, by publishing one myself that nothing sent from the Islands except the animals they deny us might be unloaded in this land; they would then be glad to allow them to be exported in order to receive the imports, for their only means of supply is by trading with this land. Before such trading began there was not a thousand *pesos de oro* between all the settlers of the Islands, and now they have more than they have ever had in their lives. Yet in order to give no further opportunity to the tongues of those who have slandered me already, I have refrained from such action until Your Majesty be informed, so that Your Highness may provide as most benefits Your Royal service.

I have also informed Your Caesarean Majesty of the need we have of plants of every sort, for this land is well suited to all kinds of agriculture. And because until now nothing has been sent, I once again beseech Your Majesty, as it will be a great service, to send a warrant to the Casa de la Contratación in Seville that every ship shall bring a certain number of plants and shall be forbidden to sail without them, for they would be most advantageous for the colonization and prosperity of this land.

As it is my duty to make the best arrangements I am able for the colonization of this land, and so that the natives and the Spanish settlers may maintain themselves and prosper, and Our Holy Catholic Faith take root; and as Your Majesty graciously entrusted me with these matters, and Our Lord God was pleased to provide the means by which I might come to the notice of Your Majesty and under Your Highness's Imperial Yoke, I issued certain ordinances[69] which I had publicly announced, of which, as I am sending a copy of them to Your Majesty, I shall say nothing, but that by all I have seen up until now it would be most expedient for these ordinances to be obeyed. Some of the Spaniards who reside in these parts are not entirely satisfied with some of them, especially those which oblige them to settle on the land, for most of them expect to do with these lands as was done in the Islands when they were colonized, that is, to harvest, destroy and then abandon them. And because it seems to me that it would be unpardonable for those of us who have had experience in the past not to do better for the present and the future, by taking measures against those things which are well known to have caused the ruin of the Islands, especially, as I have written to Your Majesty many times, because this land is of such magnificence and nobility, that God, Our Lord, may be so well served, and Your Majesty's Royal revenues much increased, I beseech Your Majesty to have these ordinances examined and, if it so pleases Your Highness, to command me as to what principle I am to follow in the enforcement of these ordinances, and also as to which are of most service to Your Majesty. I shall always take care to add whatever seems to me most fitting, for the great size and diversity of the lands which are being discovered each day and the many new things which we have learnt from these discoveries make it necessary that for new circumstances there be new consideration and decisions; should it appear in anything I now say or might in future say to Your Majesty that I contradict what I have said in the past, Your Highness may be assured that it is because a new fact elicits a new opinion.

Most Invincible Caesar, may Our Lord God watch over the Imperial Person of Your Majesty, and may He keep and preserve You in His Holy service for very many years, with the increase of greater realms and dominions and whatever else Your Majesty may desire. From the great city of Temixtitan in New Spain on the fifteenth day of October in the year 1524. From Your Sacred Majesty's most humble servant and vassal who kisses the Royal feet and hands of Your Majesty—HERNANDO CORTÉS.[70]

The Fifth Letter

SACRED CATHOLIC AND CAESAREAN MAJESTY:

On the twenty-third day of the month of October of last year, 1525, I dispatched a vessel to Hispaniola from the town of Trujillo, which is the port at the cape of Honduras, and with a servant of mine who went in her, as she had orders to sail to the Kingdom of Spain, I wrote to Your Majesty[1] concerning certain events which took place in that gulf they call Las Hibueras,[2] between the two captains[3] whom I had sent there and another called Gil González, and also about my own arrival there later. And I was unable, at the time when I dispatched the aforementioned ship and my messenger, to give Your Majesty any account of my journey and of the things which befell me from the time I left this great city of Temixtitan until I met with the people of those parts, and they are things that Your Highness should know about; if only to persist in my custom of faithfully informing Your Majesty of all my deeds, I shall therefore relate these events briefly, as best I am able, for were I to attempt to describe them exactly as they happened I am certain that I would prove unequal to the task and that my narrative would not be understood; consequently, I will relate only the principal and most notable things which befell me on that journey, although of many that I shall omit as unimportant, any one would provide material for a lengthy account.

Having taken measures concerning Cristóbal de Olid, as I

338

informed Your Majesty, it seemed to me that I had for a long time now lain idle and attempted no new thing in Your Majesty's service on account of the wound in my arm; and although that was not yet healed, I determined to engage in some undertaking, and so I departed from this great city of Temixtitan on the twelfth day of October of the year 1524[4] with a few horsemen and foot soldiers, men of my own household and my friends and relations; and with them came Gonzalo de Salazar and Peralmíndez Chirinos, factor and veedor for Your Majesty.[5] Likewise I took with me all the principal natives[6] of this land and left the care of justice and government to Your Majesty's treasurer and contador, and also to the licenciado Alonso de Zuazo. I left in the city all the necessary artillery, munitions and soldiers; I likewise had the fortress provided with cannon and the brigantines made ready. I also appointed a warden to defend the city and to take the offensive against anyone as he so desired.[7]

With this intent I set out from the city of Temixtitan and reached the town of Espíritu Santo, which lies in the province of Cazacoalco,[8] 110 leagues from this city. And whilst settling certain matters in the town I sent to the provinces of Tabasco and Xicalango[9] to inform their lords of my journey to those parts, commanding them to come and speak to me or to send such persons as should be able faithfully to transmit my orders so that I might give them their instructions. This they did, receiving my messengers with due honor and sending back with them seven or eight men of rank with the authority such as they are accustomed to send at such times. While asking them about certain things I wished to know concerning the land, they told me that on the coast, beyond that land which is called Yucatán, toward the bay named Asunción,[10] there were certain Spaniards who did them much harm, for besides burning many villages and killing some of the inhabitants, as a result of which many of them had abandoned those places and fled to the hills, they had most severely harmed the merchants and traders; for, because of them the trade which had once flourished along that coast had now ceased. As eyewitnesses they gave me an account of almost all the villages on that coast as far as the place where Your Majesty's governor Pedrarias de Ávila resides.[11]

They drew on a cloth a map of the whole country[12] from which it seemed that I would be able to cover the greater part of it, especially the place where they indicated that I might find the Spaniards. Having thus received such welcome news about the road I was to take to accomplish my aims and bring the inhabitants of those lands to the understanding of Our Holy Faith and Your Majesty's service, and seeing that I must needs, on so long a journey, make my way through many diverse provinces and peoples; eager furthermore to discover if those Spaniards were some of those I had sent under the captains Cristóbal de Olid or Pedro de Alvarado or Francisco de las Casas; and to settle these matters aright, it seemed to me that it would benefit Your Majesty's service if I were to go there myself, for I would see and discover many lands and provinces hitherto unknown and might be able to pacify many of them, as indeed was afterwards done. Having therefore foreseen the benefits that would accrue from my journey and ignoring all the hardships, dangers and expenses which then presented themselves or might be imagined, I determined to proceed along that road as I had indeed intended to do before leaving this city.[13]

Before reaching the town of Espíritu Santo, I had, on two or three stops along the route, received letters from Temixtitan sent by those whom I had appointed as my lieutenants as well as from other persons; likewise Your Majesty's officials who were in my company also received some. These letters informed me that between the treasurer and contador there was not that accord necessary for the execution of those offices and duties with which I, in Your Majesty's name, had entrusted them. I had dealt with this matter as I deemed fit, which was to write them most stern letters reproving them for their conduct and warning them that if they did

§ Siguese la sesta rrela çon q̄l dho capitan general hernando
cortes escriuio a su magestad quādo entro mas d̄ seys çien
tas leguas de la çibdad d̄ temjxtitan por la tierra a dentro
a donde sufrio grandes trabajos y se puso a grandes peli-
gros y se creyo q̄ dixo ser muerto y le sa q̄ncaro su casa en
temjxtitan §

.S.C.C.M. non es aceptio persenarum apud
deum q̄ secclaw y el libre hy el secour

§ parta fo prim̄ y el bexal el acendado y el que
no tiene un mca d̄ bed it. Vol. an ele
ubeyne. A tres dias del mes d̄ otubre del año d̄ poz
mjee. d̄ çinquen vs A veynte d̄ anco d̄o y aqa por un
vn navio para la yslo espanola d̄s d̄ la villa rrea de
d̄ truxillo del ynerto y le vo d̄ son guias con bu guarda
njo q̄ enel An bie q̄ abian d̄ passar. A nessos rreynos coqth
a V. magestad aegunas cosas d̄ las que An a q̄l q̄ ece man
gol fo de las hi guerad a bian passad ansi. Antre los capitans
q̄ yo An bie. y el capitan gil gonçalez como despues q̄ yo bj ne
el porque al tienpo q̄ des paxe. A si d̄ un nabio. A mensajero no
yn de par a b̄ magestad menta d̄ q̄ mj çe mjno d̄ cosas q̄ enel
melcac aclo des pues que parti. desta gran ab as d̄ temjx
titan. Hasta topar conlas gentes d̄ a quellas pantes me
pareçio que es bien q̄ V. al si tro las sepa. al co menos por
no ver dezyo. al estilo que tengo que es no d̄ xar Casa que A
V. magestad no manjfieste las rrelacate Aln su ma co mejor
q̄ yo pudiere. por que d̄zir las Como passaron nj yo las sa
bria si nj sacar nj por lo q̄ yo d̄ xese alla se podrian conpre
hender pero d̄ re las Cosas notables y mas prin a y alco que
enel d̄o Camjno me acaeçieron abn q̄ antes q̄ pasan por d̄
cesorias q̄ Cada vna dellas podra ser ma teria d̄ carga escritura

§ segundo

§ D̄ asa or sen para An lo d̄ d̄ ponal d̄ olis como ate mo es
crib por que me pareçio q̄ ya abia mucho tienpo q̄ mj d̄ ck forta

not make their peace and from thenceforth behave very differently, I would take measures which would please neither of them and even report the affair to Your Majesty. After this, while still in the town of Espíritu Santo, preparing to embark on my journey, I received further letters from them and from others as well, from which I learnt how their disputes still persisted and indeed were aggravated, and that once in council they had drawn swords against each other, which had caused such a scandal and uproar that not only had the Spaniards taken up arms and split into factions, but the natives of the city had also been about to take up arms, saying that this disturbance was directed against them. Seeing, therefore, that my threats and warnings were of no avail, and that I could not go myself unless I abandoned my journey, it seemed to me that the best remedy was to send the factor and veedor who were with me at that time; I gave them powers equal to those held by the treasurer and contador, so that they should discover who was guilty and restore order. In addition to this, I gave them secret orders[14] whereby they might, if reason failed, suspend them from office, and conjointly with the licenciado Alonso de Zuazo govern in their stead, and punish the guilty. When this had been arranged the aforementioned factor and veedor departed, and I was quite certain that their arrival in the city would be effective and would soon finally settle those disputes; and with this my mind was somewhat put at ease.

When they had left for Temixtitan I mustered the men left to me for my journey; and I counted ninety-three horsemen, who had between them some 150 horses, and some thirty foot soldiers.[15] At that time there was a large caravel anchored in the harbor which had been sent to me from the town of Medellín with supplies; this I now loaded with the supplies I had brought and four pieces of artillery, crossbows, harquebuses and other munitions, and told them to proceed to the Tabasco River and there await my orders. I then wrote to a servant of mine who lives in the town of Medellín, telling him to load two large caravels and a large boat with provisions and to send them to me. I also wrote to Rodrigo de Paz, in whose charge I had left my house and property in this city, asking him to try to send immediately five or six thousand pesos de oro with which to purchase these supplies; and I even wrote to the treasurer asking him to lend me the sum, for I had no money left. Thus everything was settled and the two caravels sailed, as I had commanded, to the Tabasco River, although they were not much use, for my road lay inland, and to send for the provisions and other things from the coast was most difficult, for very extensive marshes lay in between.

Having thus arranged for those provisions to be sent by sea, I set out by a coast road to the province of Copilco,[16] which is some thirty-five leagues from the town of Espíritu Santo; to reach this province we crossed, besides many marshes and small rivers over all of which were bridges, three large rivers, one of which flowed by a town called Tumalán,[17] which is nine leagues from Espíritu Santo; another is called Agualulco[18] and is nine leagues further on; these two we crossed in canoes, the horses being led by the bridle and swimming across. The third,[19] however, was too wide for the horses to swim, and so, half a league inland from the sea, a wooden bridge was constructed, over which the horses and men passed, and it was a most noteworthy sight, for the river was 934 paces across.

This province of Copilco abounds in that fruit which is called cacao, and in other produce of the land, and there is much fishing. There are ten or twelve good towns—I mean provincial capitals—without counting the hamlets. The land is very low-lying, with so many marshes that in wintertime it is impossible to travel except by canoe, and although I passed through it in the dry season, in the course of the journey, which lasted some twenty leagues, I had to construct more than fifty bridges without which the people could not have crossed. The natives are mostly peaceful, although somewhat timorous on account of the few dealings they have had with the Spaniards. My arrival made them more confident, and they served with a goodwill not only me and the Spaniards in my company but also those with whom they were deposited.[20]

According to the map which the people of Tabasco and Xicalango had given me, I was to proceed from the province of Cupilcon to another called Zagoatan; but as the natives of Cupilcon travel only by water, they did not know which road I should take overland, although they indicated to me in which direction the aforementioned province lay. Thus I was obliged to send out some Spaniards and Indians to find a way, and once found to open it up for us for some very dense forests lay across our path. And it pleased Our Lord that they should find such a road, although with difficulty, for besides the mountains there were some very hazardous marshes over all or most of which we had to build bridges. Also, we had to cross a very fast-flowing river called the Guezalapa,[21] which is one of the tributaries that flow into the Tabasco River. From there I dispatched two Spaniards to the lords of Tabasco and Cunoapá, asking them to send up that river fifteen or twenty canoes laden with provisions from the caravels anchored there, and so as to help me cross the river. I requested them, moreover, to take the provisions to the principal town of Zagoatan,[22] which, it appeared, was twelve leagues upstream from that place where I crossed. And they did all this very well as I had asked them to do.

After having found a road to the Çalapa River which we had to cross, I set out from the last village in this province of Copilco, which is called Anaxuxuca,[23] and slept that night in a deserted place amongst some lakes. The following day I arrived early at the river but found no canoes with which to cross, as those which I had asked the lords of Tabasco to send had not arrived. I discovered that the scouts who had gone on ahead were opening a way upriver from the other side, for, as they had been informed that the river passed through the middle of the most important town in the aforementioned province of Zagoatan, they were following it so as not to lose their way. One of them had taken a canoe in order to reach the town sooner and found the inhabitants greatly disturbed. He spoke to them through an interpreter, reassuring them somewhat, and then sent the canoe back downstream with some Indians to inform me of what had passed between him and the natives of that town and to say that he was coming back with some of them, opening a road along which I could travel until he met with those who were working from this end. This greatly pleased me not only because those people had been somewhat pacified but because the road which I had considered doubtful or at least dangerous was now assured. Then with that canoe and some wooden rafts which I had built I began to move the baggage across the river, which is fairly deep.[24] While thus occupied, the Spaniards whom I had sent to Tabasco returned with twenty canoes laden with provisions from the caravel which I had sent from Coazacoalco. They told me that the two other caravels and the boat had not arrived at Tabasco but were still in Coazacoalco and would come very shortly. In these canoes came some two hundred Indians from Tabasco and Cunoapá, and in those canoes we crossed the river without further risk save that one Negro slave was drowned, and we lost two loads of iron tools of which afterwards we stood in some need.

That night I slept on the other side of the river with all my people, and the next day followed on the trail of those who were opening the road upstream, with no guide but the bank of the river itself. We journeyed six leagues and slept that night in a forest, where it rained heavily. When it was already dark the Spaniard who had gone up the river as far as the town of Zagoatan returned with some seventy Indians from that town and told me how he had opened a road to one side but that in order to take it we had to retrace our steps two leagues.[25] This I did, although I ordered that those who were opening a road along the riverbank and who had already gone three leagues beyond the place where I had slept should continue; and a league and a half farther on they came upon the farms outside the town. In this manner two roads were opened where there was none before.

I followed the road which the natives had opened, and, although it was a difficult one on account of some marshes and the rain which fell heavily that day, I reached a quarter of the town which, although it was the smallest, was very fine and had more than two hundred houses in it.[26] We were unable to reach the other quarters because they were separated from us by rivers which ran between them and could only be crossed by swimming. They were all deserted, however, and when we arrived the Indians who had come with the Spaniard to see me had all fled, although I had spoken kindly to them and had given them some trifles which I had with me, thanking them for the trouble they had taken in opening the road for me. I had then told them that I had come to these parts by Your Majesty's commands to teach them that they must worship and believe in only one God, creator and maker of all things, and must acknowledge Your Highness as sovereign and lord of the land, and all those other things which they have to be told concerning this matter. I waited three or four days, believing they had fled in fear and would return and speak to me, but no one at all appeared. Thereupon, in order to speak with them, so I might bring them peaceably to Your Majesty's service and then discover from them which road I was to take, as there was not a single road to be found anywhere in the whole country nor any evidence to show that it had been trod by human feet, because the Indians travel only by canoes on account of those great rivers and marshes, I decided to send two companies of Spaniards and some of the natives of this city of Temixtitan and thereabouts, to seek out the natives of this province and to bring me some for the purposes above-mentioned.

Thus with those canoes which had come upriver from Tabasco, and with others which were found in the town, my men explored many of those rivers and marshes, for it was impossible to go on foot. But they encountered no more than two Indians and a few women, from whom I tried to discover the whereabouts of the lord and people of that land, but they told me nothing save that they had dispersed through the forests and through those marshes

and rivers. I also inquired of them about the road to the province of
Chilapan,[27] which, according to my map, should have followed the
same route, but they would not tell me, saying that they did not
travel by land but by the rivers and marshes in their canoes, and
therefore could reach that place by no other way. All they could do
was to point to a range of mountains,[28] which appeared to be about
ten leagues away, saying that the principal town of Chilapan stood
near there on the banks of a very large river, which lower down
flowed into that of Zagoatan and thence into the Tabasco. They
said also that upstream there was another town called Ocumba,[29]
but they were likewise unable to show me the way overland.

　　I stayed in that town twenty days searching incessantly for a
road which led somewhere, but nowhere did I find one small or
large; on the contrary, in whichever direction we went out round
the town there were such extensive and dangerous marshes that it
seemed impossible that we might ever cross them. Seeing, however,
that we were very short of supplies, we entrusted ourselves to Our
Lord and built a bridge over an impassable marsh. It was three hundred paces long and built of many timbers thirty-five or forty feet
in length with others laid across them. And so we crossed and continued our search for that land in the direction in which they had
told us the town of Chilapan stood. I also sent a company of horse
with some crossbowmen in search of that other town of Ocumba.
They found it that same day and reached it in two canoes and by
swimming, but the inhabitants all fled, and they were able to capture only two men and some women, though they found many
provisions and came out to meet me on the road with them. That
night I slept in the open. And it pleased God that the land here was
somewhat more open and dry and with many less marshes than before. The Indians who had been captured in Ocumba led us to Chilapan, which we reached very late the following day, and found it
burnt and its inhabitants gone.

　　This town of Chilapan is most pleasantly situated and very
large. There were many fruit trees of the kind which grow here

and many fields full of maize which, though not yet ripe, was of great help to us in our need. I remained in this town for two days, collecting provisions and making sorties to search for the inhabitants of the town and pacify them, and also to discover from them the road ahead, but we found no more than the two we captured when first entering the town. From these I learnt the road I had to take to Tepetitán, or Tamacastepeque, as it is also called.[30] And so, partly by guesswork and with no road to follow, they led us to that town, which we reached in two days. On the journey we crossed a very large river called Chilapan, from which that town takes its name. We crossed with great difficulty, for it was very wide and fast-flowing, and as we had no canoes everything was taken across on rafts. Another slave was drowned here, and the Spaniards lost much of their baggage.

After having crossed this river at a place a league and a half from the town of Chilapan, we traveled six or seven leagues to that of Tepetitán over many great marshes where the horses were in water never less than up to their knees, and often up to their ears. Over one that was especially bad we built a bridge, and two or three Spaniards were nearly drowned. After two days of these hardships we reached that town, which we likewise found deserted and burnt; this greatly increased our troubles. We found some fruit that grows there and some fields of green maize which was somewhat riper than in the last town. We also discovered in some of the burnt houses granaries of dried maize which, although there was little of it, was a great help to us in our extreme need.

In this town of Tepetitán, which stands close to the foothills of a great range of mountains, I remained six days, making some sorties into the countryside roundabout in the hope of finding some of the natives, so that I might speak to them and persuade them to return to their town, and also so I might discover the road ahead; but all we could find was one man and a few women. From these I learnt that the lord and the people of that town had been induced

by those of Zagoatán to burn their houses, and had fled to the forests. He said that he did not know the road to Ystapan,[31] which,
according to my map, was where I had to go to next, for there was
no overland route, but he would guide me roughly in the direction
in which he knew it to be.

      With this guide I dispatched some thirty horsemen and an-
other thirty foot soldiers and commanded them to proceed until
they reached that town and then to write me an account of the
way, for I would not leave Tepetitán until I had received their letters. And so they left, but as two days went by without my receiving any letters or otherwise hearing from them, I was forced by the
extreme need in which we found ourselves to leave and follow their
trail, with no other guide; and it was by no means an easy task to
follow the trail they had left through the marshes,[32] for I assure
Your Majesty that even in the shallowest part of the marsh the
horses sank in up to their girths, although they were not being
ridden but led by the bridles. I proceeded in this fashion for two
days, with no news of the people who had gone ahead and greatly
perplexed as to what I should do, for it was impossible to turn back
and yet I knew nothing of what lay ahead. However, it pleased
God, who comes to succor us in our greatest afflictions, that, while
we were resting in a field and greatly distressed thinking that we
were all soon to perish utterly, two Indians, natives of Temixtitan,
arrived with a letter from those Spaniards who had gone on ahead,
in which they informed me how they had reached the town of Ystapan, and how on their arrival the Indians had sent their women and
possessions across a great river[33] which ran close by there; the men
had remained behind thinking that the Spaniards would be unable
to cross a great marsh which lay outside the town. When they saw,
however, that the men were swimming across holding on to the
saddletrees of the horses, they set fire to the town and fled across
the river in their many canoes or by swimming, many drowning in
their haste. The Spaniards, however, crossed so swiftly that they

prevented the town from being completely destroyed and captured seven or eight persons, one of whom seemed to be a chieftain; these they were holding until I arrived.

I cannot describe to Your Majesty the joy caused among the men by the receipt of this letter, for, as I have said above, we had almost abandoned hope. The following day I continued on my way, and, guided now by the Indians who had brought the letter, I reached the town that evening, where I found the Spaniards who had gone on ahead in high spirits, because they had found much maize, though not yet ripe and *yucas* and *ajíes*,[34] which is what the natives of the islands live on and makes a fair meal. When I arrived I had those natives who had been captured brought before me, and asked them through the interpreter why they had all burnt down their own homes and towns and abandoned them, for I had done them no harm whatsoever but on the contrary had given gifts to those who waited behind for me. They replied that the lord of Zagoatan had come there in a canoe and had greatly frightened them, making them abandon and burn their town. I then had brought before that chieftain all those Indians, both men and women, who had been captured in Zagoatan, Chilapan and Tepeti-tán and told him how the lord of Zagoatan was an evil man and had deceived them; he had only to ask those before him to know that neither I nor any of my company had done them harm or ill-treated them. These then confirmed my report; and afterwards they all wept saying they had been deceived, and showing themselves most sorry for what they had done. To assure them further I permitted all the Indians whom I had brought from those other villages to return to their homes, and I gave them some small things, and letters for each village, which I told them to keep by them in these villages and show to the Spaniards who passed by there, for with them they would be safe. I also told them to inform their chieftains of the mistake they had made in burning and deserting their towns and homes; thenceforth they were not to do it again, for they might live there in safety, and no harm would be done them. With

this they departed very reassured and contented, and as this was
done in the presence of the people of Ystapan, it greatly helped to
assure them also.

After having done this, I spoke to that Indian who appeared
to be a chieftain and told him that he had seen how I did no harm to
anyone and that my coming to these parts was not to annoy them,
but, on the contrary, to instruct them in many things concerning
both the security of their persons and belongings and the salvation
of their souls. I greatly entreated him, therefore, to send two or
three of those who were there with him, to whom I would add as
many natives of Temixtitan, to find the lord of that place and tell
him that he need have no fear, but that rather he would gain much
by his return. He replied that it would greatly please him to do so,
and I dispatched them at once together with some Indians from
Mexico. On the following morning the messengers returned with
their chieftain and some forty followers, and he told me that he had
deserted and burnt his town on the orders of the lord of Zagoatan, who, furthermore, had told him not to await my arrival
because I would kill them all. But he had learnt from those messengers that he had been deceived and lied to, and he regretted what he
had done and begged me to forgive him, promising thenceforth to
do all that I told him. He then asked me to return to him certain
women whom the Spaniards had taken when they were there, and I
found some twenty and gave them to him with which he was most
content.

It happened, however, that a Spaniard found an Indian of his
company, a native of Mexico, eating a piece of flesh of the body of
an Indian he had killed when entering that town, and this Spaniard
came to tell me of it, and I had the Indian burnt in the presence of
that lord, telling him that the reason for such a punishment, namely,
that he had killed and eaten one of his fellow men, which was forbidden by Your Majesty, and which I, in Your Royal name, had
required and commanded them not to do. And so I had had him
burnt, for I wished to see no one killed, on the contrary, I had come

by Your Majesty's command to protect and defend both their persons and their property and to teach them how they were to believe in and worship the One God, who is in heaven, Maker and Creator of all things, and by whose will all living creatures are governed; and to turn aside from their idols and the rites which they had practiced hitherto, for they were all lies and deceits which the Devil, the enemy of mankind, had devised to snare them and lead them to eternal damnation, whereby they would suffer the most great and terrible torments, and to lead them away from the knowledge of God, so that they should not be saved nor enjoy the blessed glory which God has promised and set aside for those who believe in Him, and which the Devil himself had lost through pride and wickedness. Likewise I said I had come to tell them of Your Majesty whom Divine Providence has decreed that the whole world shall serve and obey; and that they also must submit and place themselves under the Imperial Yoke and to do all that we, Your Majesty's ministers in these parts, might command. If they did this, they would be very well treated and maintained in justice and their persons and property protected, but if not, I would take action against them and punish them in accordance with the law. I also told them many other things touching this matter but will not mention them to Your Majesty as they are very lengthy.

That lord was much delighted by all this and sent some of the people who had accompanied him to bring provisions. I gave him some small things from Spain, which he prized highly; and he remained in my company very contentedly all the time I was there. He ordered a road to be opened to another town that is five leagues upstream from this one and is called Tatahuitalpan;[35] and because a deep river crossed our route he had a very good bridge built by which we crossed, and he also had some dangerous marshes filled in. He likewise gave me three canoes in which I sent three Spaniards downriver to the Tabasco River (because this is one of its main tributaries), where the two caravels were awaiting my instructions. With these Spaniards I sent orders that they should proceed along the coast, doubling the cape which is called Yucatán, until they reached the bay of Asunción, where they would find me or receive further instructions. I also told the Spaniards to use their three canoes and all the others they could find in Tabasco and Xicalango to bring all the provisions they would hold up a waterway[36] to the province of Acalan, some forty leagues from this town of Yzatpan, where I would wait for them.

When these Spaniards had gone and the road was completed I asked the lord of Yztapan to give me three or four more canoes, to convey half a dozen Spaniards, together with a chieftain and some of his own people, up the river, to reassure the villages and prevent the inhabitants from abandoning and setting fire to them. This he did with every appearance of goodwill, and the result was most beneficial, for they quietened the natives of four or five villages up the river, as I will hereafter relate to Your Majesty.

This town of Yztapan is a very large one, standing on the banks of a very beautiful river. It is a very suitable site for Spaniards to settle: it has excellent grazing land along the riverbank; it also has very good arable land, and the countryside roundabout is good and inhabited.

Having remained in this town of Ystapan [sic] for eight days and attended to the matters mentioned in the previous chapters, I departed, and reached the village of Tatahuitalpan—which is a small one—that same day; I found that it had been burnt and abandoned. I arrived before the Spaniards who had gone in the canoe because they had been delayed by the currents and the great bends in the river. When they did arrive I sent them across to the far bank with some men, to search for the inhabitants of that town and to reassure them as had been done before. About half a league from the river they came across some twenty men in a house containing idols which were highly decorated. These men were then brought before me, and from them I learnt that all the people had fled in terror, leaving them behind to die with their gods, for they had no wish to flee. While we were thus discoursing, certain of our Indians passed by carrying things they had taken from those idols; and when the villagers saw this they cried that their gods were dead. On hearing this, I spoke to them telling them to observe how vain and foolish was their belief, for they placed their trust in idols which could not even defend themselves and were so easily overthrown.

They replied that they had been brought up in that belief by their fathers, and that they would persist in it until they knew of something better. I had not the time to tell them anything more than what I had told the people of Yztapan, but two Franciscan friars[37] in my company told them many things concerning this matter. I asked that some of them should go and find the people and the lord of the town and reassure them. The lord of Yztapan likewise spoke to them, telling them how well I had treated both him and his people. Whereupon they pointed to one of their number, saying that he was their lord. This man then dispatched two of them to command the villagers to return, which they never did.

Seeing that they were not coming, I asked the man they had called their lord to show me the road to Zaguatecpan,[38] which lay upstream and through which, according to my map, I had next to pass. He said that they knew of no road by land, for they only traveled by water. They would nevertheless show me the direction through the forests, although they could not be certain of it. I asked them to show me the situation in which the town stood, and noted it as best I could. I then sent the Spaniards who were in the canoes, together with the lord of Yztapan, upriver to Zaguatecpan. There they were to reassure the people of that town as well as those of another called Ozumazintlan,[39] which they would reach first. If I arrived first, I would wait for them; but if not, they should wait for me.

When they had left I set out overland with those guides. On leaving the town, we came across a great marsh which lasted for half a league or more, and our Indian friends laid down quantities of branches and reeds over which we passed. After this we reached a deep stretch of water over which we had to construct a bridge for

transporting the luggage and the horses' saddles; the horses themselves swam across. When we had crossed this we came to another
which was part marsh and lasted for a good league, where the
horses sank in up to their knees and often to the girths; but as the
ground underneath was fairly firm we crossed without accident
and soon reached the forest. Here we spent two days opening a
road in the direction indicated by the guides, until at last they declared they were lost and did not know where to go. This forest
was so dense that we could only see a pace in front of us or, looking
up, the clear sky above us; and so thick and high were the trees that
even those who climbed them could not see even a stone's throw
distant.

When the people who had gone ahead with the guides to
open a road informed me that they had lost their way, I ordered
them to stop while I went ahead to them on foot; and when I saw
how lost they were I ordered them to return to a small marsh we
had passed on our journey and where, on account of the water,
there was some grass for the horses, who had not eaten for the past
two days. We camped there that night in much distress through
hunger, which was further increased by the little hope we had of
reaching a village; so much so indeed that my men had almost despaired and were more dead than alive. I took out a ship's compass
which I always carried with me and on which I had often been
forced to rely, although never had we been in such difficulties as
then; and by recalling the situation in which the Indians had said we
would find the town, I calculated that by marching in a northeast-
erly direction from where we were we would arrive at the village
or near it. I therefore ordered those who were cutting the road to
take the compass and to follow that course without ever departing
from it. This they did, and it pleased Our Lord that they followed
it so surely that at the hour of vespers they came out right in front
of some idol houses in the middle of the town. All the men were so
delighted at this that without thinking they all rushed forward, not
noticing the large marsh that lay between them and the town,

where many of the horses sank, some of which were not recovered until the following day, although, thanks to God, none of them was lost. Those of us who followed behind avoided the marsh in another place, although not without much difficulty.

We found that village of Zaguatecpan burnt, including the temples and houses of the idols. We found no one there nor any news of the canoes which had gone up the river. But there was an abundance of maize which was riper than any we had previously seen, and also yuca and ajíes and good pasture for the horses, because on the banks of the river, which are very beautiful, we found some excellent grass. Thus refreshed we forgot some of our past hardships, although I was much distressed to hear no news of the canoes I had sent upriver. Walking about the village, however, I came upon a crossbow bolt fixed in the ground, by which I knew the canoes to have passed that way, for all the people in them were crossbowmen; this distressed me still further, for I thought they must have fought with the Indians and all been killed, as they did not appear. A few small canoes had been found in the village, and in these I sent some of my men across the river, where they found many plantations. Crossing these, they came to a great lake where they found all the inhabitants of the village, either in canoes or on small islands. When they saw the Christians they approached without fear and said things which the Spaniards could not understand. They brought thirty or forty of them to me, however, who, after I had spoken to them, told me that they had been induced by the lord of Zaguatan [sic] to burn their village and had fled in terror of us to those lakes where they now were. But, later, certain Christians of my company had come that way in canoes, accompanied by some of the natives of Yztapan, from whom they had learnt of the good treatment which I accorded to all, and now their fears had been allayed. The Christians had remained there two days waiting for me but, as I did not come, had proceeded upstream to another village, called Penecte,[40] and a brother of the lord of Çaguatepan had accompanied them with four canoes full of people to help if they were attacked by the inhabitants of that town; furthermore, they had given them all the provisions they required.

I was greatly pleased to hear this, and because they had come fearlessly to me themselves I believed all they said. I asked them straightaway to send a canoe in search of those Spaniards and to take a letter from me to them, ordering them to return to me at once. This they did most diligently, for on the following day, at the hour of vespers, they returned together with the Indians who had carried my letter to them and another four canoes loaded with people and supplies from the village whence they came. They informed me that after leaving me they proceeded upriver until they reached the village before this one, which is called Ozumazintlan, and they found it burnt and the inhabitants gone. But when the people of Iztapan, who accompanied the Spaniards, arrived, they sought them out so that many returned and gave the Spaniards provisions and everything else they required. Then they had gone to Çaguatepan, which they likewise found abandoned and the inhabitants fled to the far side of the river. When, however, the people of Yztapan spoke to them, they had all taken heart and welcomed the Spaniards, giving them very fully of everything they asked for. There they had waited for me two days, but seeing that I did not come, and thinking that as I had taken so long, I must have come out farther upriver, they went on to the town of Petenete [sic], six leagues from there, led by some people of the village and a brother of the chief. This town they also found deserted, but not burnt; the inhabitants had fled to the other side of the river. But the people of Yztapan and of Çaguatepan had allayed their fears, and now they were coming to see me in four canoes bringing gifts of maize, honey, cacao and even a little gold.

They had sent messengers to three other towns they had been told lay upstream; these were called Coazacoalco, Tenango and Teutitan,[41] and they thought that they would come to speak to me on the following day. And so they did, for the next day seven or eight canoes came to me down the river, and in them were people from all those towns bringing me some supplies and a little gold. I spoke to them all at great length to make them understand how they were to believe in God and serve Your Majesty; and they all offered themselves as Your Highness's vassals and subjects and promised always to do as they were commanded. The people of the village of Çaguatepan then brought some of their idols and broke and burnt them in my presence. The chief of the town, whom I had not seen before, afterwards came and gave me a little gold; and I gave them all some few things, by which they were most pleased and assured.

When I enquired about the road to Acalan[42] they began to argue among themselves. The people of Çaguatepan said that it lay through those towns upstream, and before the inhabitants of these arrived, they told me they had hewn out six leagues of road and built a bridge over a river we would have to cross. The others, when they arrived, however, said that this route was a very long way round and passed through barren and deserted country, and that the shortest way to Acalan was to cross the river at this town, where I would find a path much used by traders, along which they would lead me to Acalan. Finally, they decided among themselves that this was indeed the best route. I had previously sent a Spaniard, together with some natives, in a canoe from Çaguatepan to the province of Acalan to inform the people there of my arrival and to assure them that they had no cause for fear; and, moreover, to discover if the Spaniards who were to have brought the supplies from the brigantines had arrived. I now sent another four Spaniards,[43] accompanied by those who claimed to know the way, to examine it and inform me if there was any obstacle or hindrance on it; and I said that I would await their report.

I was, however, forced to leave before they wrote, for I was afraid that the provisions we had collected for the journey would soon be exhausted, and I had been told that we would have to travel five or six days through barren countryside. I began to cross the river with the aid of a large number of canoes, but, as it was wide and fast-flowing, we only reached the other side after much effort. One horse was drowned and some items of baggage belonging to the Spaniards were lost. Once over, I sent a company of foot soldiers on ahead with the guides to open a road, and I, with the other people, followed behind. After having marched for three days through dense forest along a very narrow track, we reached a great lagoon more than five hundred paces wide,[44] and though I searched up and down for a way across I could find none. Moreover, the guides told me that it was a useless search unless I marched for twenty days toward the mountain.

This lagoon placed me in so great a quandary that I am at loss to describe it, for the crossing seemed to be beyond our means, as it was so very wide and we had no canoes, and even if we had had them for the men and baggage, the horses would have been unable to cross, for in their path lay great marshes and the roots of trees; to send them across by any other means was unthinkable. To turn back was likewise impossible, for it meant certain death for all, not only because of the bad roads we would have to travel, and the great rains which had fallen, swelling the rivers so that by now all our bridges would have been swept away (and to rebuild would have been impossible, as all our people were exhausted), but also because we had consumed all our provisions and could find nothing else to eat. There was a large number of us, there being besides the Spaniards and the horses some three thousand natives in my company. To advance was, as I have told Your Majesty, so difficult that no human intelligence could have devised a solution if God, who is the true remedy and succor to all who are afflicted and in need, had not provided it. Thus I found a tiny canoe in which the Spaniards whom I had sent ahead to examine the road had crossed, and with this I had the lagoon sounded, finding it to be in all places four fathoms in depth. I therefore had some lances bound together with which to test the bottom and found that, in addition to the water, here was another two fathoms of mud, thus there were six fathoms in all.

I determined, therefore, that as there was no other solution I would build a bridge, and at once set about having some timbers cut, from nine to ten fathoms in length depending on how far they were to emerge above water. This I entrusted to the Indian chieftains who were with me, telling them to divide the work up among their people. Then the Spaniards and I, on rafts and in that canoe and two others which we had found afterwards, began to sink these posts into the bed of the lagoon.[45] No one believed that such a task could ever be accomplished, and some even whispered that it would be better to return before everyone was too exhausted and weak with hunger to be able to; for in the end the project would have to be abandoned anyway, and we would be forced to return. Indeed, there was so much whispering among the Spaniards that they almost dared to approach me openly. When I saw how discouraged they were, and truly they had cause to be, for the work we had undertaken was of such a formidable nature and they were demoralized and lethargic, having eaten nothing but the roots of plants, I told them that they should no longer assist in the building of the bridge, but that I would complete it with the Indians alone. I then called all those chieftains and told them to take account of what difficulties we were in, and that we must needs cross that lagoon or perish; I therefore beseeched them to urge their people on to finish the bridge, for beyond lay the province of Acalan, where there was an abundance of food and we all might rest. Besides the provisions to be found on the land, they well knew that I had ordered supplies from the ships to be brought thither in canoes, so that once we arrived we should not want for anything. I promised them, furthermore, that when I returned to this city I would, in Your Majesty's name, reward them most richly. They then agreed to do their best, and at once began to divide the task between them; and so hard did they work, and so skillfully, that in four days they had finished the bridge, over which all the horses and men crossed, and which I am certain will stand for ten years if no one destroys it. Indeed, unless it were burnt, it would prove most difficult to destroy, for it is made of more than a thousand timbers, of which the smallest is almost as thick as a man's body, from nine to ten fathoms in length, not to mention an immense quantity of lighter timber. I assure Your Majesty that I do not believe there is any man capable of describing adequately the mastery with which the chieftains of Temixtitan and the Indians built that bridge; truly it was the most remarkable feat ever seen.

When all the men and horses had finally crossed this lagoon, we came upon a great marsh which lasted for two crossbowshots, the most frightful thing the men had ever seen, where the unsaddled horses sank in up to their girths until nothing else could be seen; and in struggling to get out they only sank in deeper, so that we lost all hope of being able to bring a single horse out safely. But still we determined to attempt it, and by placing bundles of reeds and twigs beneath them to support them and prevent them from sinking, they were somewhat better off. While we were thus moving back and forth between the horses, a narrow channel of mud and water was revealed along which the horses were able to swim a little. Thus it pleased Our Lord that they should all emerge without loss, though so exhausted they could barely stand up. We all offered many thanks to God for so favoring us. While thus engaged, the Spaniards whom I had sent on to Acalan arrived, bringing some eighty of the natives of that province, all laden with supplies of maize and edible fowl.[46] God alone knows how much joy this brought us, especially as they informed us that the people of that province were all peaceful and secure and had no intention of fleeing before us. With those Indians of Acalan came also two persons of rank who said that they had come on behalf of the lord of the province, who was called Apaspolon,[47] to inform me that he welcomed my arrival. For some while he had heard news of me from the traders of Tabasco and Xicalango and would be glad to meet me; he also sent a little gold with his messengers, whom I received with as much joy as I was able, thanking their lord for the goodwill he had shown to Your Majesty's service. I then gave them a few small gifts, with which they were delighted, and sent them back with the Spaniards who had brought them. They were full of admiration for the bridge, and this greatly helped to secure their allegiance, for their country lies among lakes and marshes and they might well have fled and hid among them, but when they saw that bridge, they believed that nothing was impossible for us.

Also at this time there arrived a messenger from the town of Santisteban del Puerto, on the Pánuco River, carrying a letter from the justices of those parts. With him came four or five Indians with letters from this city of Temixtitan, and also from Medellín and Espíritu Santo, and I was greatly pleased to hear that all was well, though I received no news of the factor and veedor Gonzalo de Salazar and Peralmíndez Chirino (whom, as I said above, I had sent from the town of Espíritu Santo to settle the differences between the treasurer and the contador) because they had not yet reached the city.

The day after the Indians and Spaniards who were going ahead to Acalan had left, I set out with the rest of my company in that same direction. I slept one night in the forest, and a little after noon on the following day reached the fields and farms of the province of Acalan. In front of us, however, lay a large marsh, which forced us to make a detour of rather more than a league, leading our horses by the bridles with some difficulty. Close to the hour of vespers we reached the first village, which is called Tiçatepal,[48] where we found the inhabitants very comfortable and secure in their houses. They also had plentiful supplies, sufficient both for the men and horses, so that our past hunger was soon satisfied.

Here we rested six days, and a youth of good appearance and well attended came to see me, saying that he was the son of the lord of that land; he brought us some gold and fowl, offering his person and his land in Your Majesty's service, for his father now was dead. I made as though I was much distressed by the death of his father, although I could see he was not telling the truth. I gave him a necklace of Flemish beads that I was wearing, and he valued them highly; then I bade him depart with God's blessing, but he remained with me two days of his own will.

One of the natives of that town, who claimed to be its ruler, told me that close by lay another town, which was also his possession, where there were better lodgings and more abundant provisions, for the place was larger and had more inhabitants. He suggested, therefore, that I should go there because I would be more comfortable. I readily agreed and sent him to cut a road and prepare for our arrival. This he did very well, and so we went to that town, which is five leagues from the other; here we also found the people unafraid and in their houses, and a certain quarter cleaned and prepared for our lodgings.

This is a most beautiful town and is called by the inhabitants Teutiacar.[49] It has very fine temples, and two in particular where we took up residence, throwing out the idols at which the natives showed no great distress, for I had already spoken to them explaining the error of their ways and how there was only one God, Maker of all things, and all else I could say touching this matter, though I afterwards spoke at greater length to the chieftain and all the assembled people. I learnt from them that the larger of these two temples or idol houses was dedicated to a goddess in whom they had great faith. To her they sacrificed only beautiful virgins, and if they were not so, the goddess became angry with them. For this reason they took great pains to seek out only such as would satisfy her; those of a right disposition they reared from childhood for this purpose. On this matter I also spoke as I saw fitting, and it seemed they received my words tolerably well.

The lord of this town proved to be very friendly and spoke at length with me, giving me a very long account of the Spaniards I was seeking and of the road I was to take. He also told me, in the greatest secrecy, begging me to tell no one that it was he who had so informed me, that Apaspolon, lord of all that province, was alive, but had had it put about that he was dead; the youth who had come to see me was indeed his son, but had been sent to lead me aside from the direct route so that I should not pass through his lands and his towns. He told me this because he wished me well, and because he had been well treated at my hands, but he entreated me to reveal the secret to no one, for should he be discovered, Apaspolon would kill him and burn all his lands. I thanked him greatly and paid him for his goodwill with a few small gifts, and promised to keep his secret as he had requested, promising him that in due time he would be well rewarded by me in Your Majesty's name.

Then I called that lord's son who had come to see me and told him that I was very surprised at him and at his father's having refused to come and visit me, knowing that I wished to meet him on good terms, and pay him respect and give him some presents, because I desired to repay him for all the favors that I had received in this land. I said also that I knew for certain that his father was alive, and I entreated him to go and try to persuade him to come to see me, for he might be assured that he would benefit greatly thereby. He then replied that it was true his father was still alive; if he had denied it, it was only because he had been commanded to do so. He would go now and do everything in his power to bring him to me; he believed he might succeed, because his father would like to see me now that he knew I came to do no harm but rather to give his people such things as I had with me, although he was somewhat ashamed of appearing before me, as he had previously refused. I begged the youth to do all in his power to bring his father to me, and this he did, for on the following day they both arrived and I received them warmly. Apaspolon excused himself, saying that he was afraid until he had learnt my intentions, but now that he knew them, he greatly desired to see me. It was true he had ordered me to be led away from his towns and villages, but now that he knew my intentions he asked me to go to his capital, since there he was better able to provide me with all I required. He then ordered a broad road to be cut to the town, and on the following day we departed together, and I gave him one of my horses and he rode it most hap-

pily until we reached a village called Izancanac,[50] which is very
large and full of temples, and stands on the banks of a great lagoon
which reaches as far as the point of Términos, between Xicalango
and Tabasco. Some of the people had fled, but some were in their
houses. There we found abundant supplies, and Apaspolon stayed
with me in my quarters, although he had a house of his own nearby
where his household was. While I was there he gave me a long account of the Spaniards I had come to find and drew a map on a
piece of cloth of the road I was to take. He also gave me some gold
and a few women, though I had not asked him for anything; indeed
I have never asked anything of the lords of these parts if they did
not wish to give anything of their own accord.

      We had now to cross that lagoon before which lay a great
marsh. Apaspolon ordered a bridge to be built across the marsh, and
for the lagoon he gave us as many canoes as we required and guides
for the journey. He also gave me a canoe and guides for the Spaniard who had brought me the letters from the town of Santisteban
del Puerto, and also for the Indians from México and the provinces
of Xicalango and Tabasco. I then gave this Spaniard letters for the
colonies, the lieutenants I had left in the great city, for the ships at
Tabasco, and for the Spaniards who were to bring the provisions,
instructing each of them as to what they were to do. Once this
matter had been dispatched, I gave Apaspolon certain trifles which
he fancied, and leaving him very contented and all his people very
secure I left that province of Acalan on the first Sunday in Lent in
the year 1525. That day we achieved nothing but the crossing of
the lagoon, which was no mean task. I gave this lord a letter because
he asked it of me, so that should any Spaniards come to his land
they would know that I had passed that way and that he was my
friend.

      Here in this province there occurred an incident of which
Your Majesty should know: an honored citizen of this city of Temixtitan, who was called Messicalçingo, and was later baptized Cristóbal, came very secretly to me one night with a certain drawing on

a piece of the paper used in these parts. And explaining to me what it meant, he said that Guatimuçin (the former lord of Temixtitan whom I had held prisoner since our capture of the city, as he was a man who could cause great trouble, and took with me on my journey together with the other lords whom I held to be the key to peace or revolution in these parts) and Guanacacin, lord of Tesuico, and Tetepanquezal, lord of Tacuba,[51] and a certain Tacitecle, who was at the time in México City in the Tlatelulco district, had often told him, Mexicalçingo, now christened Cristóbal, how they had been deprived of their lands and their power and were now ruled by Spaniards, and that it would be a good plan to seek some means whereby they might regain their lost possessions and power. They had spoken together many times on the journey, and it seemed to them that the best solution was to arrange to kill me and all my company, after which they would rouse the people of this land and fall on Cristóbal de Olid and kill him and his men also. When this had been done, they would send their messengers to Temixtitan to incite the people to kill all the Spaniards in the city, which they believed could easily be done because the men there had recently arrived and were not prepared by the experience of the war. Once they had accomplished this, they would raise the whole land behind them and kill all the Spaniards wherever they might be. This done, they would place strong garrisons in all the seaports so that no ship which arrived could escape them and return to Castile with the news. In this way they would be lords as they were before; they had already divided up the land among themselves and had made this Mexicalcingo the lord of a certain province.

When I had heard all about this treachery from Cristóbal at such length, I gave thanks to the Lord for having revealed to me so foul a plot against me and the other Spaniards. Immediately at dawn I seized all those lords and had them imprisoned separately. I then asked each of them about their plot, pretending to each that one of the others had revealed it to me, for as they could not speak to each other they did not know they were being deceived. They were thus

forced to confess that it was true that Guatimuçin and Tetepanquezal had planned it, and that the others knew of it but had never
agreed to participate in it. These two were hanged, therefore, but I
released the others, for apparently they had done nothing more
than listen to them, although that in itself was sufficient for me to
put them to death. I have left their cases open so that they may be
punished if they ever relapse, but they are so frightened that I do
not think they will, for as they have never discovered from whom I
learnt of their plot, they believe it was done by some magic art, and
that nothing can be concealed from me. Having observed that in
order to be certain of my road I have often taken out a ship's chart
and a compass, especially when cutting the Çagoatezpan [sic] road
which came through so accurately, they told many of the Spaniards
that it was there that I had learnt their secret. Some of them have
even come to me and, eager to show me their good intentions, have
begged me to look into the glass of it and the chart, because I would
see there that they spoke the truth, since through those objects I
knew everything else. I encouraged this belief, giving them to
understand that the compass and the chart did indeed reveal all
things to me.[52]

This province of Acalan is very large and well populated. It
has many towns, some of which were visited by the Spaniards in
my company. It is rich in honey and other foodstuffs; there are
numerous merchants and traders who travel to many places and are
rich in slaves and other things with which they barter in this land.
The province is completely surrounded by lagoons and estuaries, all
of which stretch as far as the bay or harbor called Los Términos,
by which they have great commerce with Xicalango and Tabasco,
and it has even been said, although the truth of it is not yet known,
that they pass through there to the other sea, thus making the land
called Yucatán an island.[53] I will endeavor to discover the truth of
this, so as to render Your Majesty a trustworthy account. I was
informed there is no other chieftain in the land except the most
prosperous of the merchants, and the one who does most trading by

sea, who is in fact Apaspolon, of whom I have already made mention to Your Majesty; the reason for his prosperity is that he carries his trade to distant places, as far as the town of Nito, where, as I will hereafter relate, I found certain Spaniards of the company of Gil González de Ávila, and where he had a whole district peopled by his agents in the charge of one of his brothers. The chief articles of trade in those parts are cacao, cotton materials, dyes, a certain kind of ink with which they stain their bodies to protect them against the heat and the cold, torches for light, pine resin for censing their idols, slaves and certain colored beads made from shells, which they hold most precious for decorating their bodies during their feasts and celebrations. They also trade in a little gold, but it is mixed with copper or other metals.[54]

To this Apaspolon and to many honored citizens of his province I spoke concerning their idols as I had done to others on my journey, and about what they must believe and do in order to obtain salvation. Likewise I told them what they were bound to do in Your Majesty's service. They seemed to be satisfied by what I said and burnt many of their idols in my presence, saying that thenceforth they would honor them no more and promising to be always obedient to whatever I might command them in Your Majesty's name. And so I took my leave of them and departed as I said above.[55]

Three days before I left this province of Acalan I sent four Spaniards with two guides given me by Apaspolon to examine the road I had to take to the province of Mazatlan,[56] which in their language is called Quiatleo, for I had been told that the land thereabouts was uninhabited, and that I would have to spend four days in the forest before reaching the aforementioned province. I sent them therefore to explore the road and see if there were any rivers or marshes to cross. I also ordered all my men to take provisions for six days, so that we should not find ourselves in such straits as before. They supplied themselves very fully, for there was an abundance of everything, and five leagues beyond the lagoon which we

had crossed I met the four Spaniards who had, with the help of two
guides, been to explore the road, and they told me that it was an
excellent one, and although it led through thick forest, it was very
flat without rivers or marshes to hinder our passage. They had even
reached some fields in the province of Mazatlan, and had seen some
people there, though they themselves had returned unseen and un-
heard. I was greatly pleased by this news, and ordered that henceforth six foot soldiers and some of our Indian allies should travel
one league in front of those who were opening up the road, so that
if they came across any travelers, they might seize them, thus permitting us to reach the province without being observed and prevent the inhabitants from deserting and burning their villages as
those before them had done. That same day, close to a lake, these
men found two Indians, natives of the province of Acalan, who said
they were coming from Mazatlan, where they had been trading salt
for cloth. This appeared, in part, to be true, for they were indeed
laden with cloth. They were then brought before me, and I asked
them if those of that province had any notice of our coming, and
they replied that they had not but were all very peaceful. I told
them that they must return with me, but not to be distressed on
that account, for they would lose none of the goods they were
carrying, but, on the contrary, I would give them more, and once
we arrived in Mazatlan they would be permitted to return, for I
was a firm friend of all the people of Acalan, because they and their
lord had received me most kindly. They did this with great goodwill, returning and even leading us by another road, for the one the
Spaniards had been cutting led only to some fields, whereas theirs
went straight to the villages.

That night we slept in the forest, and on the following day
the Spaniards whom I had sent ahead as scouts came across four
Indians from Mazatlan with their bows and arrows who, it seemed,
had been posted on the road as sentries, and when my men came
upon them they fired their arrows, wounding one of my Indians.
As the forest was very thick, the Spaniards were only able to cap-

ture one of them, who was handed over to three of my Indians while the Spaniards proceeded up the road ahead, believing that there were more of them. But as soon as my men had gone, the fugitives, who, it appeared, had hidden there close by in the forest, returned and fell upon our Indian friends who were holding their companion, and fighting with them managed to free him. Our Indians, however, pursued them through the forest and, catching up with them, fought and wounded one in the arm with a great blow from a sword. They took this one prisoner, but the others, hearing our men nearby, fled. I asked this Indian if they knew of my coming, and he replied that they did not; I then questioned him as to why they were there on the road as sentries. He answered that it was their custom, since they were at war with many of their neighbors, and, in order to protect the workmen in the fields, their lord had ordered sentries to be always on the roads so they should not be taken unawares.

I hastened on, because I had learnt from the Indian that we were close to the town, and I wished to arrive before the Indians who had escaped had time to raise the alarm; and I ordered those of my men who were going ahead to halt when they reached the fields and remain hidden in the forest until I arrived. When I arrived it was already late, and I advanced with all speed, hoping to reach the town that night; but, seeing that our baggage train had been broken up somewhat, I sent a captain with twenty horse to wait in the fields, collect the Indian bearers when they arrived and pass the night there with them; once he had collected them all he was to follow after me. I took a path which, although quite straight, led through very dense forest. I went on foot leading my horse by the bridle, and all those who followed me did likewise. We proceeded in this fashion until just before nightfall, when we came upon a marsh which we were unable to cross without some preparation. I gave orders, which were passed down the line from one man to another, that we were to turn back to a small clearing we had passed. We slept there that night, although there was no water to drink either for us or the horses.

The following morning I had a path across the marsh covered with twigs, and we led the horses across, although not without difficulty, and three leagues from the place where we had slept we sighted a town[57] on a hill and, thinking that we had not been seen, approached with great caution. It was so well fortified, however, that we could find no way in, and when at last we found a way, we discovered it had been abandoned, though it was well stocked with supplies of maize, birds, honey, beans and other produce of the land, for as they were taken by surprise they had no time to remove their provisions which, as it was a frontier town, were plentiful.

This town stands upon a high rock: on one side it is skirted by a great lake and on the other by a deep stream which runs into the lake. There is only one level entrance, the whole town being surrounded by a deep moat behind which is a wooden palisade as high as a man's breast. Behind this palisade lies a wall of very heavy boards, some twelve feet tall, with embrasures through which to shoot their arrows; the lookout posts rise another eight feet above the wall, which likewise has large towers with many stones to hurl down on the enemy. There are also embrasures in the upper parts of all the houses, facing outwards, and likewise embrasures and traverses facing the streets; indeed, it was so well planned with regard to the manner of weapons they use, they could not be better defended.

I sent certain of my men to find the inhabitants of the town, and they captured two or three Indians, whom I sent, together with one of those merchants from Acalan whom I had taken on the road, to find their lord and tell him not to be afraid, and to return to his town. I had not come to do harm but, on the contrary, would assist him in those wars of his and would leave his land secure and at peace. After two days the messengers returned, bringing with them an uncle of the lord of the country, who in fact governed it, as the chieftain was a boy and, they said, had not come because he was afraid. I spoke then to this uncle and reassured him, whereupon he went with me as far as another town in the same province, which is called Tiac[58] and lies seven leagues farther on. The inhabitants of this place are at war with those of the first town; and it is much larger and well fortified, although not so strong, for it stands on the plain, but it has its earthworks and walls and watchtowers which are very strong. Each of the three districts of the town is fortified separately and the whole town is encircled by a wall.

I had sent on to this town two captains of horse and one of foot, and they found it abandoned, though well provided with supplies; close to the town they took seven or eight men, some of whom they released so they might go and speak to their lord and reassure the people. They did so well that even before I arrived messengers had come from the lord bringing provisions and clothing. After I arrived they came twice more, to bring us food and speak to us on behalf of the lord of this town and of five or six others which are in this province, each of which is independent. They all offered themselves as Your Majesty's vassals and as our allies, although I could never persuade the lords themselves to come and see me. As I could delay no longer, I sent these messengers to say that I thanked them for their goodwill and received them in Your Highness's name, and I asked them to give me guides for the road ahead. This they did willingly and gave me a guide who was very familiar with the road to where the Spaniards were and had seen them himself. With this I left the town of Tiac and went to spend that night in another which is called Yasuncabil [59] and is the last in that province; this was likewise deserted and fortified in the same fashion as the others. The lord here had a very attractive house, although it was made of straw.

In this town we provided ourselves with all we might require on the journey, for the guide told us that we would have to spend five days in uninhabited country before we reached the province of Tayça, through which we had to pass, and so it turned out.

Here in this province of Mataçlan [sic] or Guiache [sic] I dismissed the two merchants I had taken on the road and the guides whom I had brought from Acalan, and I gave them for themselves and for their chieftains some of the things I had, with which they were greatly pleased. I also sent back to his home the lord of the first town, who had accompanied me, and I returned to him certain women whom my men had captured in the forest, and gave him one or two little things with which he was most pleased.

After leaving this province of Macalan [sic], I took the road to Tayça, and four leagues farther on I slept in the barren countryside through which the road now ran; and there were great forests and mountains with a difficult pass which, as all the rocks and stones were of a very fine alabaster, I named the Alabaster Pass.[60] On the fifth day the scouts who had gone ahead with the guides came upon a very large lake which seemed to be an arm of the sea, and still I believe it to be, for although its waters are fresh it is so very large and deep.[61] On a small island they saw a town which the guide said was the capital of the province of Tayça, but that there was no way of reaching it save in canoes. When they heard this the Spaniards remained, taking turns on guard by the shore, and sent back one of their number to report to me. I halted all my people and went ahead on foot to view that lake and see how it was situated; and when I arrived I found that the scouts had caught an Indian, a native of that town, who had come in a small canoe with all his weapons to reconnoiter and see if there were any people; and although he was unprepared for what befell him, he would have escaped my men had not a dog, which they had, caught him before he could throw himself into the water.

From this Indian I learnt that nothing was known of my arrival. I then asked him if there was a road to the town, to which he replied that there was none, but he said that close by on the far side of a small arm of the lake there were some fields and a few houses where, if we approached without being seen, we might find some canoes. I at once sent orders to my people to follow behind me, and, taking ten or twelve crossbowmen, I went on foot where that Indian led. We crossed a big marsh where we sank in up to our belts and at times farther; and at last we came to some plantations. But because of the bad road and because we were not always able to conceal ourselves, our advance could not fail to be noticed, and we arrived just in time to see the Indians taking to their canoes and fleeing across the lagoon. I followed swiftly along the bank of that lagoon for two-thirds of a league, all of which was cultivated, but everywhere we had been observed and the people were fleeing. As it was already late, and to continue any farther was of no use, I collected my people and encamped them there in those fields, taking all precautions I could, for the guide from Mazatlan said they were a numerous people and most skilled in war, for which reason they were feared by the neighboring provinces. This guide then told me he wished to take the small canoe in which the Indian had come, and go to that town on the island which lay some two leagues away. He would then speak to the lord, whom he knew well and who was called Canec. He would tell them of my intentions and the cause of my arrival in these lands, as he had accompanied me and knew them and understood them himself. He said he thought that this lord would believe him, for he had often lodged at his house and knew him very well.

I at once gave him the canoe and the Indian who had come in it and thanked him for his offer, promising him that if he succeeded I would reward him most generously. So he departed, returning about midnight with two respected inhabitants of the town who claimed to have been sent by their lord to see me and ascertain whether my messenger had spoken the truth, and to discover what I wanted of him. I welcomed them, gave them a few small gifts and told them that I had come to these lands on Your Majesty's commands to see them, and speak to the lords and natives thereof on matters touching Your Royal service and their advantage. I told them to bid their lord set aside all fear and come to my camp, and that for greater security I would give them a Spaniard who would go with them and remain as a hostage while their lord was with me; and with this they departed, together with the guide and a Spaniard. On the following morning the lord arrived, accompanied by some thirty men in five or six canoes; and with them they brought the Spaniard I had given as a hostage. He seemed very happy to meet me and I, for my part, received him well, and, because it was the hour of Mass, I ordered that it should be sung, and performed with great solemnity and be accompanied by flageolets and sackbuts. To this he listened with great attention and watched all the ceremonies most carefully. When the Mass was ended one of those friars who accompanied me preached him a sermon, through the interpreter so that he would fully understand, about the articles of our Faith, and giving him to understand with many arguments that there is only one God, and that his own religion was an error. He said he was, and appeared to be, greatly pleased by what he had heard, and said he would at once destroy his idols and believe in that God of which we had spoken. He greatly desired to know how to serve and honor Him, and that if I wished to go to his town I would see him burn those idols in my presence; furthermore, he wished me to leave in his town that cross which he had been told I left in all the villages through which I passed.

When this sermon was over, I spoke to him again, telling him of Your Majesty's greatness and how he and I and all the world were Your subjects and vassals and obliged to serve You and that Your Majesty granted to those who did so great favors, which I in Your Royal name had already dispensed in these parts to all who had offered themselves in Your Royal service and placed themselves under Your Royal Yoke and I promised him the same if he did likewise.

He answered that until then he had served no overlord nor knew of any whom he ought to serve, although it was true that five or six years ago people of Tabasco had passed that way and told him how a captain with certain people of our nation had entered their land and three times defeated them in battle, and afterwards had told them that they were to be vassals of a great lord, and all the other things which I was now telling him. He therefore wished to know if this great lord of whom I spoke were indeed the same. I replied that I was the captain of whom the people of Tabasco had spoken, and that if he wished to learn the truth he had only to ask the interpreter with whom he was speaking, Marina,[62] who traveled always in my company after she had been given me as a present with twenty other women. She then told him that what I had said was true and spoke to him of how I had conquered México and of all the other lands which I held subject and had placed beneath Your Majesty's command. He appeared very pleased to learn of this and said that he also wished to be Your Majesty's subject and vassal, and that he considered himself most fortunate to be under the sway of a prince so powerful as I told him Your Highness is.

He ordered birds and honey to be brought and a little gold and certain beads of colored shells which they prize highly and gave them to me.[63] I likewise gave him certain things of mine which greatly pleased him, and afterwards he ate with me most agreeably. After we had eaten I told him how I was going in search of those Spaniards who were by the coast, because they were of my company and I had sent them, but a long while had passed and I had heard nothing of them. For this reason I had come to look for them, and I asked him to tell me if he had received any news of them. He replied that he had heard much of them, for very close to where they now were, lived certain of his vassals who cultivated for him peanuts, in which this land was very rich; and from these and from the many traders who traveled between his lands and the coast he continually received news of them. He said he would give me a guide to lead me to them, but he also warned that the road was a hard one over steep and rocky mountains, and that it would be less fatiguing for me to travel by sea.[64] I replied saying that we were obliged to go by land, for we could never find sufficient ships for all the men in my company and for the horses and the baggage. I asked him, therefore, to show us how we could cross that lake; he answered that by going on some three leagues I would reach a place where the lake gave way to dry land, and to reach the coast I could follow the road which led directly from opposite his town. He asked me, since my men were going in that direction, to come with him in a canoe, and visit his town and his house, where I would see him burn his idols and might order a cross to be made for him. I, therefore, in order to please him, though much against the wishes of my men, boarded one of his canoes with more than twenty men, most of whom were crossbowmen, and went to his town, where we passed all that day in recreation. When it was almost dark I took my leave of him, boarded a canoe with a guide he had given me and came to spend the night on land, where I found that many of my people had come down to the lake shore; and so we slept there that night. I left in this town, or rather in those fields, a horse which had got a stake lodged in its foot and could not walk. The lord of the town promised to cure it, but I do not know what he will do.[65]

The following day, after having mustered my men, I departed along the road indicated by the guides, and after about half a league we came upon some flat pasture land; after that we went through a small forest which lasted about a league and a half and then came out again onto some very beautiful plains. When we reached them I sent ahead some horsemen and foot soldiers to seize anyone they found in the open, for our guides had told us that we would reach a town that night. On these plains we found many fallow deer, and we speared eighteen of them from horseback. But because of the sun and the horses' lack of exercise for some days past, there having been little opportunity for galloping on our journey through the forest, two of them died and many were in grave danger of doing so.

Our hunting done, we continued on our journey, and after a little while came upon some of the scouts whom I had sent on ahead resting, with four Indian hunters whom they had captured, together with a dead lion and some iguanas, which are large lizards found in the Islands. I inquired of these Indians whether they had received news of me in their town. They replied that they had not and pointed out to me where it lay, which seemed to be barely a league away. I made all haste to reach there, thinking that I should find no obstacle in my path, but when I thought I was about to enter the town, and could see the people quite clearly, I came upon a very deep river. Seeing this, I halted and called out to the Indians; and two of them came in a canoe, bringing as many as a dozen hens. When they drew near where I was, with my horse up to its girth in the water, they stopped and, although I spent a long time in talking and reassuring them, they would come no closer, but, on the contrary, began to return to the town. Thereupon a Spaniard who was on horseback close to me jumped into the water and began to swim after them. They then abandoned their canoes in terror, but some foot soldiers soon swam up and seized them.

By now all the people whom we had seen in the town had left it, and I asked those Indians where we might cross over to the town; they showed me a road leading to a place about a league upstream where there was a passage over dry land. By this route we arrived in the town and passed the night there, having covered that day a good eight leagues. This town is called Checan,[66] and its chief, Amohan. I remained here four days, acquiring provisions for six days, which, so the guides told me, I would spend crossing uninhabited country. I was also waiting for the lord of the town, hoping that he would come, as I had sent those Indians to reassure him; but neither he nor they returned. When these four days had passed and I had gathered in all the stores that could be found, I departed and traveled that day over very good ground, level and green, with no forests, only a few small woods. After six leagues we came upon a large house at the foot of some hills, close to a river, with two or three small ones close by, and some cultivation roundabout. The guides told me that this house belonged to Amohan, chief of Checan, and that he had it there as an inn, for many merchants passed that way.

I stayed there for one day after that on which I arrived, as it was a feast day, and also the delay gave those who had gone ahead time to open up a road. We had some fine fishing in that river and caught a great quantity of shad, which we pulled ashore without so much as a single one escaping our nets.

On the next day I departed, following a most difficult road for almost seven leagues and came out at last to some beautiful open country with no forest but only a few groups of pine trees. This open country lasted for a further two leagues, in which space we killed seven deer and ate by a cool stream that ran along the far side of this plain. After we had eaten we began to ascend a narrow pass, not high, but so steep that the horses, although led by the bridle, could barely climb it. On the descent the ground was flat for about half a league; we then began to climb another pass, which in all lasted for some two and a half leagues up and down, and was so steep and rough that there was not a single horse which did not lose a shoe. I spent that night at the foot, in a ditch, and had to wait almost until the hour of vespers on the following day for the horses to be shod. But although there were two blacksmiths and more than ten others helping to drive in the nails, the horses could not all be shod that day. I therefore went to spend the night three leagues farther on, leaving many of the Spaniards both to attend to the shoeing of their horses and to wait for the baggage which, on account of the bad road and the great rains, had not yet arrived.

On the following day I left that place, for the guides told me that close by was a small village called Asuncapin,⁶⁷ belonging to the lord of Taica [sic], and that we would arrive there well before dark. After having traveled five or six leagues, we reached the aforementioned village and found it abandoned. I camped there for two days to wait for the baggage and gather some provisions. I then departed and went to spend the night in another village, called Taxuytel,⁶⁸ which is five leagues from the other and belongs to Amohan, chief of Checan. Here then were many peanuts but only a little maize, which was green.

I was informed by the guides and the headman in the village, whom we came upon together with his wife and son before they could escape, that we would have to cross some very high and very steep mountains, all totally without habitation, before reaching the next village, which belonged to Canec, the lord of Taica, and was called Tenciz. We did not remain long at this place but set out again on the day after our arrival. After crossing six leagues of flat ground, we began to climb a pass which is the most remarkable sight in the world to see, and the most perilous to cross, for even though I attempt to describe for Your Majesty the cragginess and extreme harshness of these mountains, not even one who is more skilled at writing than I could adequately express it, nor could one who heard of it understand it fully, unless he had himself seen it with his own eyes and had himself experienced the crossing of it. Let it suffice for Your Majesty to know that we spent twelve days covering the eight leagues of the pass, that is, until the end of our train was over, and that we lost sixty-eight of our horses, which either fell over the cliff or were hamstrung; and the remainder were so injured and in such a sorry state that we did not expect any of them to be any use again. Thus sixty-eight horses died from their injuries or exhaustion in that pass, and those who escaped were not fully recovered for more than three months.

All the time we were crossing the pass it rained without cease, all day and all night long, but those mountains were such that they did not retain water, and consequently we suffered greatly from thirst, most of our horses dying because of it. And were it not for the water we collected in pots and other vessels while encamped in the huts and shacks we built to shelter us, as it rained enough to provide water for us and the horses, no man or horse would have escaped from those mountains.

During this crossing a nephew[69] of mine fell and broke his leg in three or four places, which, in addition to the pain he was forced to endure, increased our burden, for it was difficult to carry him across that pass.

To relieve our difficulties we found, a league before we

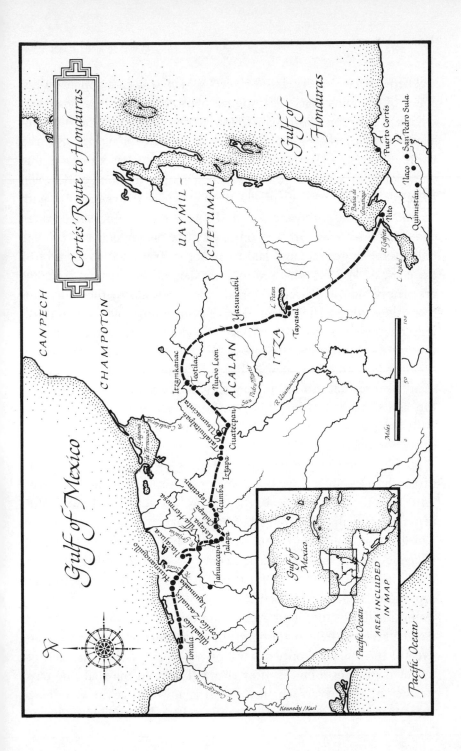

Cortés' Route to Honduras

Gulf of Mexico

Gulf of Honduras

CANPECH

CHAMPOTON

UAYMIL

CHETUMAL

ITZA

ACALAN

San Pedro Mártir

R. Usumacinta

R. Candelaria

Términos

R. Grijalva

R. Coatzacoalcos

Iztapa

Tonalá

Cupilco-Zaquala

Ciuatán

Copilco-Acuala

Iquinuapa

Aguapa

Izancanac

Tuztlan

Nuevo León

Yasuncabil

Tayasal

L. Petén

Tatahuitalpan

Usumacinta

Ciuatecpan

Iztapa

Acumba

Zaguatán

Tepetitan

Villa Hermosa

Jalapa

Jahuacapa

Tacahuela

Tuitin

Huimanguillo

El Golfete

L. Izabal

Nito

Bahía de Amatique

Puerto Cortés

San Pedro Sula

Naco

Quimistán

Gibustán

Miles

0   50   100

N

AREA INCLUDED
IN MAP

Gulf of Mexico

Pacific Ocean

Pacific Ocean

Kennedy/Karl

reached Tenciz, a very large river[70] which was so swollen on account of the rains that it was impossible to cross; but the Spaniards who had gone on ahead had found a ford upstream, the most remarkable that has ever been heard of or could be imagined. For the river, at that place, spreads out for more than two-thirds of a league on account of some large rocks which hinder its course. Between these rocks are narrow channels through which the river flows with the most terrible force and speed. There is a large number of these channels, since they are the only way the water can escape. We felled some large trees and laid them across from one to another of these rocks. We then crossed in great danger, holding fast to some creepers which had been fastened from one side to the other, for from the slightest slip it would have been impossible to avoid falling. There were more than twenty of these channels, so that it took us two days altogether to cross. The horses swam across lower down, where the current was less fierce, but some of them took as many as three days to reach Tenciz, which was only a league away, for, as I have said before, they suffered so much in the mountain crossing that we had almost to carry them on our shoulders, as they could not walk.

I arrived at the village of Tenciz on Easter Saturday, the fifteenth of ———, 1525,[71] but many of my people did not arrive until three days later, that is, those who had horses and had waited behind for them. Two days before my arrival the Spaniards who had gone on ahead had found three or four of the houses in the village occupied and had taken twenty or so of the inhabitants, for they knew nothing of my approach. I asked them if they had any provisions, and they replied that they had not nor could any be found in all the land. This greatly increased our misfortunes, as for ten days we had eaten nothing but palm nuts and palmettos, and even of these we had only a few, for we no longer had the strength to cut them. But a chieftain of that village told me that one day's journey up that river, which we must again cross at the same place, there was a well-populated province called Tahuytal,[72] where we would find an abundance of maize, cacao, and hens, and that he would give me a guide to lead us there. I immediately detailed a captain to go there with thirty foot soldiers and more than a thousand of the Indians who were with me. And it pleased Our Lord that they should find the place abandoned and a great abundance of maize, with which we furnished ourselves, although with difficulty on account of the distance.

From these farms I sent, with a native guide, certain Spanish crossbowmen to explore the road we had to travel to a province which is called Acuculin,[73] until they reached a village which is ten leagues from where I was and six from the capital of that province, whose lord is named Acahuilguin. They arrived unnoticed, and, after having seized seven men and one woman from a house, returned to tell me that the road, as far as they had gone, was somewhat difficult but had seemed very good in comparison with those we had previously traveled.

From these Indians they brought, I inquired of the Christians for whom I was looking; among them was one who was a native of Aculan [sic] who said he was a merchant and that the center of his trade was in the same town where the Spaniards lived. This place was called Nito,[74] where there was extensive trade with all parts of the county and the merchants from Aculan had had a district of their own where there lived a brother of their chief Apaspolon. The Christians had fallen upon the town one night and seized their merchandise, of which there were great quantities, since there were merchants in the town from many places. From then on, which must have been about a year, they had gone to other provinces and he, and certain other merchants of Aculan, has asked permission of Acahuilguin, lord of Acuculin, to settle in his land. They had built, in a place he assigned to them, a small town where they lived, and where they carried on their trade, although the business had much declined since the arrival of the Spaniards, for the only road lay through Nito and no one dared take it. He said, however, that he would lead me to where they were, although be-

fore reaching them I would have to cross a great inlet from the sea
and many difficult mountains, which would mean a ten-day journey. I was greatly pleased to have such a good guide and treated
him well; and the guides from Mazatlan and Tayça told him how
they likewise had been well treated by me, and how I was a good
friend of Apaspolon, his lord. This seemed to reassure him so much
that I released both him and his companions; and I trusted so far in
them that I also dismissed the other guides, to whom I gave some
small trifles for themselves and their lords and thanked them for
their services, whereupon they left most contented.

I then sent four of those from Acuculin, together with another two from Tenciz, to speak to the lord of Acuculin and assure
him that he had no cause to hide from me. Behind them I sent
others to open up a road, but I myself was delayed two days by our
need to obtain provisions, though our need to rest was considerable, especially for the health of the horses. Finally, however, we
set out, leading most of our horses by the bridle; the following
morning we discovered that the man who was to be our guide and
all those who were with him had gone. God alone knows how
much I regretted having dismissed the others. I continued my journey, however, and spent the night in a forest five leagues farther on,
where we went over many bad stretches and a horse, which was the
only one unhurt, was hamstrung and even now has not recovered.
On the following day I traveled six leagues and crossed two rivers,
one of them by means of a fallen tree which enabled the men to
reach the other side in safety; the horses were forced to swim across
and two mares drowned. The other river we crossed in canoes, the
horses again swimming.

I spent that night in a small village of some fifteen houses, all
of which were new; and I learnt that they belonged to the merchants of Acalan who had fled from that town where the Christians
now were. I remained there a day to collect my men and the baggage which had remained behind, and then sent out two companies
of horsemen and one of foot soldiers to the town of Acuculin, from

where they wrote to me that they had found it deserted; but in a large house belonging to the lord of the town they had found two men who said they were waiting there by command of the lord, so that they might advise him of my arrival, for he had heard of my coming from those messengers whom I had sent from Tenciz and would be greatly pleased to see me and would come as soon as he knew I had arrived. One of these Indians had then left to tell his lord and to fetch some provisions while the other remained behind. They wrote to me also that they had found cacao on the trees but no maize, although there was some reasonable grazing for the horses.

When I arrived in Acuculin I asked if the lord had come or the messenger returned, and they replied that they had not, so I spoke to the Indian who had stayed and asked him why this was so. He replied that he did not know and was himself much surprised by it, but it was possible the lord had delayed until receiving news of my arrival, and now that he had done so he would come.

I waited two days, but as he did not appear I spoke again to the Indian, and he said that he did not know why the lord had not come, but that if I gave him some Spaniards to accompany him, he knew where he was and would go and call him. He departed with ten Spaniards and led them for a good five leagues through the forests to some huts which, the Spaniards said, had recently been occupied. That night the guide left them and they returned.

As I was now without any guide at all, which was cause enough to increase our hardships twofold, I sent groups of people, both Spaniards and Indians alike, throughout the entire province, and they explored every part of it for some eight days or more, but they could find no one save for a few women, who were of little use to us as they neither knew the road, nor could tell us anything of the lord or the inhabitants of the province. One of them, however, said that she knew of a town, two days' march away, called Chianteca, where we would find people who could tell us of the Spaniards for whom we were looking, for in that village there were many merchants who traded in many parts. I then sent some people, with this woman as a guide, but although the village was a good two days' journey from where I was encamped and the road was bad and led through deserted country, the natives had been warned of my coming and no guide could be found.

It pleased Our Lord that when we had almost given up all hope, on finding ourselves with no guide and unable to use the compass, for we were among the rockiest and steepest mountains I have ever seen with no road to lead us out save the one we had come on, we found in the forest a lad of about fifteen, who, when asked, said he would lead us to some farms in Tanyha,[75] another province through which I had to pass, according to my map. He said that those farms were two days' journey from the place where we were then encamped. With this guide I departed, and in two days arrived at those farms where the scouts whom I sent ahead captured an old Indian who guided us to the villages of Tanyha, which are another two days' journey farther on. In these villages we took four Indians, and when I questioned them they gave me some definite news of the Spaniards whom I sought, saying that they had seen them, and that they were but two days' march from there in the town called Nito, which I had on my map. As it was a center of much trade, news of it was known in many places, as they had told me in the province of Aculan, which I have already mentioned to Your Majesty. They also brought me two women, natives of Nito, who gave me a more complete account, for they told me that they were in the town when it was taken by the Christians, who fell upon it at night, and they had been captured together with many others and had served certain of the Christians whom they mentioned by name.

I cannot describe to Your Majesty the great joy which I and all my company felt on hearing this news in Tanyha and knowing that we were now so close to the end of our so perilous journey. For, even on the last four days' journey from Acuculin, we had undergone innumerable hardships because there were no roads and

we had to cross steep and precipitous mountain passes where some
of our remaining horses fell to their deaths, and a cousin of mine,
called Juan de Avalos,[76] fell down a cliff with his horse and broke
his arm; and had it not been for the plates of the armor he was
wearing, which protected him from the rocks, he would have been
dashed to pieces; and, even so, we had great trouble in bringing him
up again. There were many other misfortunes besides, which
would take too long to recount, but most of all we suffered from
hunger, for although I still had some of the pigs which I had
brought from México, we had eaten no bread for eight days, when
we arrived in Tanyha. Our only food had been palmettos cooked
with the meat and without salt, which had long been exhausted;
with this and some palm kernels we survived. Neither did we find
anything to eat in these villages in Tanyha, for, as they were so close
to the Spaniards, the inhabitants had abandoned them some time
before for fear of an attack, although had they but known the condition in which I afterwards found the Spaniards, they need have
feared nothing on their account. The news that we were now so
close to them made us forget all our past troubles and hardened us
to bear the present ones which were no less great, especially that of
hunger, which was the worst, because even those palmettos, without salt, were not sufficient, for they had to be cut with great difficulty from some very thick and tall palms, and it took two men a
whole day to cut what they could eat in half an hour.

Those Indians who had given me the news of the Spaniards
now told me that I would have to travel for two days over a bad
road before reaching Nito, and that before the town there was a
great river[77] which could only be crossed in canoes, as it was too
wide to swim.

I immediately sent fifteen Spaniards on foot with one of
those guides to explore the road and the river;[78] I also ordered them
to see if they could, without being discovered, obtain some information about these Spaniards so that I might learn to what company they belonged—whether to that I had sent under Cristóbal de

Olid, or Francisco de las Casas, or under Gil González de Ávila.[79] So they departed, and the Indian guided them to that river, where they took a canoe belonging to some merchants and then hid themselves for two days. At the end of this time four Spaniards came from the town, which was on the far side of the river, in a canoe to fish. These they seized without anyone escaping and without being observed from the town. When they were brought before me, I learnt that the people there were of the company of Gil González de Ávila, and that they were all sick, and half-dead with hunger.

I then sent two of my servants in that same canoe to the town with a letter informing the Spaniards of my arrival and saying that I intended to cross that river, for which purpose I begged them to send me all the boats and canoes they had. I then set out with all my company to the river and was three days in reaching it. When I arrived, one Diego Nieto, who said he was in charge in the town, came bringing me a boat and a canoe in which I, with ten or twelve men, crossed over that night to the town, although in extreme peril, for a strong wind caught us, and, as the river is very wide at its mouth there, we were in danger of being lost, but it pleased Our Lord to bring us safely to land. On the following day I had a boat which was there made ready and ordered more canoes to be found and lashed together in pairs; in this fashion all the men and horses crossed in five or six days.

The Spaniards I found there were some sixty men and twenty women whom the captain Gil González de Ávila had left behind. I found them in such a plight that it moved us to the greatest pity simply to see them and to see the joy with which they greeted my arrival, for, truly, had I not come, not one of them would have lived long, for in addition to being few and unarmed and without horses, they were very ill and wounded, and dying of hunger, because they had exhausted the provisions they had brought with them from the Islands and those that they had found in the town when they occupied it. Furthermore, they had no means of obtaining more, for they were not in a condition to scour the countryside looking for it. And even if they had had any, the town was situated in such a place that there was no way out, or rather they failed to find the one which we later discovered after much difficulty; and, moreover, they had never traveled more than half a league inland from the town.

When I saw the great straits these people were in, I determined to find them some support until I could procure means to send them back to the Islands where they might recover, for there were not eight among them fit enough to remain in the country as settlers. I therefore sent some of my people in the two boats that were there and in five or six canoes by sea to many different places. The first expedition went to the mouth of a river which is called Yasa[80] and lies in the direction of the road along which we had come, ten leagues[81] from this town of Nito, for there, I had heard, were many villages and abundant provisions. When they arrived at the river they sailed up it for six leagues and reached some quite large fields, but the natives observed their approach and, storing up all the provisions they had in some nearby houses, fled into the forest with their women and children and all their belongings. When the Spaniards reached those houses it began to rain so heavily that they were forced to take shelter in a large house which was there, and, as they were wet through, they thoughtlessly all took off their armor, and many even their clothes as well to dry them and warm themselves before the fires they had made. While they were thus unprepared the Indians fell upon them, and as they took them by surprise wounded many of them in such a manner that they were forced to re-embark and return to me as empty-handed as they had left. When they arrived, God knows how sorry I was, both to see them wounded, some of them seriously, and at the advantage the Indians had taken of them, not to mention their failure to bring any of the things we so desperately needed.

I immediately sent out another expedition in the same boats and canoes but under a different captain and with more men, drawn both from the Spaniards and the Méxicans who had accompanied me. But because there was not room in the boats for all the people, I ordered some of them to cross to the other side of that great river which skirts this town and then proceed along the coast while the boats and canoes were to follow close inshore so as to help them across the many rivers and inlets. So they departed and came to the mouth of the aforementioned river where the other Spaniards had been wounded, but then they returned without any supplies and having done nothing save capture four Indians who were paddling a canoe at sea. When they were asked the reason for their failure they answered that with the heavy rains the river had swollen and was flowing so furiously that they had been unable to proceed up it for more than a league, but, believing that it would subside, they had waited eight days without the means to kindle a fire or any provisions except for the fruit from the trees in the forest, and some of them returned in such a condition that it was no easy task to save their lives.

I now found myself in such need that if it had not been for some few pigs left over from the journey which were most strictly rationed and eaten without bread or salt, we should all have ended our days there. I questioned those Indians we had captured in the canoe, through the interpreter, as to whether they knew of any place where we might go to find provisions, promising them that if they led me to such a place I would set them at liberty and give them many gifts besides. One of them said that he was a merchant, and the others his slaves, and that he had gone that way many times in his ships to trade and knew of a bay that reached from there to a great river, which all the merchants crossed whenever bad weather prevented them from navigating on the open sea. Beside that river there were many large settlements with very rich people, well supplied with provisions. He said that he would guide us to certain villages where we might have all that we required; but, in order to assure me that he spoke the truth, he offered to be put in chains so that should he have lied I might punish him as he deserved. I at once had the boats and canoes made ready and manned them with all the able men left in my company and dispatched them with that guide. After ten days they returned just as they had left, saying that the guide had led them into some marshes where the boats and canoes were unable to maneuver, and although they had done everything in their power they had failed to find a way. I then asked the guide why he had deceived me, and he replied that he had not done so, but that those Spaniards with whom he had been sent had refused to go on, even though they were very close to reaching the sea where the river entered;[82] and, indeed, many of the Spaniards confessed that they had heard the sound of the sea very clearly, and therefore it could not have been far away.

I cannot describe what I felt on finding myself so helpless and almost beyond hope, believing that not one of us could escape alive but must all die of hunger. While thus perplexed, Our Lord God, who always undertakes to aid us in such necessities and, unworthy though I am, has so often assisted and succored me because I am engaged in the Royal service of Your Majesty, sent thither a ship from the Islands, not in the least expecting to find me there. In her came thirty men, not counting the sailors, and also thirteen horses and some seventy pigs, twelve casks of salted meat, and some thirty loads of bread of the kind used in the Islands. We all gave many thanks to Our Lord for having thus saved us in the hour of our need and I bought all those provisions and the ship herself, which cost me four thousand *pesos*.[83] I had already made great haste to repair a caravel which the Spaniards in Nito had allowed to fall almost into pieces, and had also begun to build a brigantine from the remains of others which had been wrecked thereabouts. By the time the ship arrived from the Islands the caravel was almost ready, but I doubt if we would ever have completed the brigantine had that ship not come, for it brought a man who, though not a ship's carpenter by trade, had considerable aptitude for our task. Later, in exploring the surrounding countryside, we discovered a track which led across some very steep mountains to a town called Leguela, eighteen leagues from Nito. There were abundant provisions there, but, as it was so far and the road was so bad, it was impossible to transport them.

From certain Indians whom we captured in Leguela I learnt that it was at Naco,[84] where Francisco de las Casas and Cristóbal de Olid and Gil González de Ávila had been and where Cristóbal de Olid had died (of which event I have prepared a report for Your Majesty and will speak hereafter). This was confirmed by the Spaniards I found in Leguela [Nito], and I immediately ordered a road to be opened and sent out a captain with all the horsemen, keeping by me only the sick, the servants of my household, and such persons as wished to remain with me and leave by sea. I instructed that captain to go to Naco and attempt to pacify the people of that province, who had been somewhat disturbed by the presence of those Spanish captains; as soon as he arrived he was to send ten or twelve horsemen and as many crossbowmen to the bay of San Andrés, which is twenty leagues from that town. Meanwhile I would take all the sick and the others who had remained behind in the ships to the afore-mentioned bay, and if I arrived first, I would wait for them; but if they did, then they were to wait for me, so that I might tell them what they were to do.

After these people had left and the brigantine had been completed, I was about to embark with the rest of my company when I discovered that although we had some supplies of meat, we had none of bread, and as we had so many sick, it would be unwise to put to sea in such condition, for if we were delayed by the weather, we should starve to death instead of finding a remedy for our hardships. While seeking a solution to this problem, one who had been left as captain of those Spaniards in Nito told me that they had been two hundred strong when they had arrived with Gil González and had come in four ships and a very good brigantine. With the brigantine and the ships' boats they had sailed up that river and had found two large lagoons of fresh water, on the shores of which were many villages well supplied with provisions. They had sailed to the end of the lagoons, some fourteen leagues upstream, where the river became so narrow and the current so fierce that although they had attempted to continue, they could make no more than four leagues in six days, although the river was still navigable. They had therefore been unable to explore that river adequately, but he believed that there were good supplies of maize to be found. But he said that I had too few people to go there with, for when they had gone, eighty of his men had taken a town by surprise, and although they had captured it, the Indians had returned, wounding several of them and driving them back into the ships.

Seeing, however, the extremity we were in and that it was more dangerous to put to sea without supplies than to go and find them on land, I decided to ignore the danger and go up that river; for apart from our having no alternative but to find food for those wretched people, it seemed that Our Lord God might permit me to discover something whereby I might render Your Majesty a service. I therefore counted the people well enough to accompany me and found some forty Spaniards who, though not altogether fit, would serve to guard the ships while I loaded. With these forty Spaniards and some fifty Indians who still remained out of those I had brought from México, I set out in the brigantine, two open boats and four canoes, leaving in that village one of my stewards to care for the sick whom I left in his charge. In this fashion I pursued my course upstream with great difficulty on account of the rapid currents, and in one day and two nights reached the first of the two lagoons, which was three leagues from our starting point and about twelve leagues round, and which has no villages on its shores, being surrounded by marshland. I spent one day crossing this lake and then came to a place where the river narrowed again. I sailed up it, and on the following morning reached the second lagoon, which is the most wonderful thing in the world to behold, for between the highest and the steepest mountains imaginable lay an inland sea so large that it must measure more than thirty leagues around. I sailed along one shore of it until, when it was almost night, we came upon a path which, after two-thirds of a league, led to a village, but the inhabitants seemed to have been warned of our arrival, for it was abandoned and empty of all provisions. In the fields, however, we found much green maize, which we ate that night and on the following morning; seeing that we would not find there the provisions we sought, we loaded up that green maize and returned to the boats, without having encountered or even seen any natives of that land.[85]

I then sailed to the far side of the lagoon, but the crossing was made difficult by contrary winds and we lost a canoe, although the people were saved by the boats and only one Indian was drowned. It was late in the evening when we reached the shore, and so we were unable to land until the following morning, when we left the brigantine anchored in the lagoon and sailed up a small river in the boats and canoes. I then saw a road and landed with thirty men and all the Indians and sent the boats and canoes back to join the brigantine. I followed that road, and after a quarter of a league came upon a village which seemed to have been deserted a long while before, for the houses were overgrown with grass, although there were good plantations of peanuts and other fruit trees. I explored the village for a road leading to some other place, but when at last I found one, it was so choked with undergrowth that it appeared not to have been used for a long time. But as I could find no other, I determined to follow it and traveled five leagues that day through some forests so dense we had to climb the path through them on our hands and knees.[86] At last we came upon some maize plantations and in a small hut which was close by we captured three women and a man, doubtless the owner of the plantation. They guided us to other plantations where another two women were captured who, in turn, led us along a road to a very large plantation in the midst of which were some forty small houses which seemed to have been recently built. It would appear, however, that the inhabitants had been warned of our arrival, for they had all fled to the forests; but as we came upon them by surprise, they had no time to gather up all their possessions and so there was something left for us, especially hens, pigeons, partridges and pheasants, which they had in cages; but we found neither dried maize nor salt. I passed the night in this place, and found some green maize which we ate with the birds, and this satisfied our hunger.

When we had been in this village a little over two hours, two of the Indian inhabitants returned and were very much alarmed to find such guests in their houses. They were seized by the sentries, and, when asked if they knew of any town nearby, replied that they did and that they would lead me there the next day, but that we would not arrive before dusk. On the following morning we departed with those guides, and they led us by a road worse than that of the day before, for in addition to being equally as overgrown we had, every crossbowshot, to cross one of the rivers which empty into the lake. This great quantity of water flowing from the surrounding mountains is what causes those lagoons and marshes to be formed and that river to flow so fiercely into the sea, as I have already described to Your Majesty.

Continuing on our way, we traveled seven leagues in this fashion without reaching a village, crossing forty-five large rivers and countless streams. We captured three women during the course of the day who were coming with loads of maize from that same town to which our guide was leading us, and they assured us that the guide was not deceiving us. At sunset, or just after, we heard a noise of people and drums, and when I asked those women what it was, they replied that it was a celebration they were holding that day. I then ordered all my men to hide in the forest as quickly as possible and sent some of my scouts right up to the edge of the town, and others I placed on the road to seize any Indian who might pass that way; thus we spent the night in a torrent of rain amid the most unbelievable plague of mosquitoes. Indeed, so rough was the road and so dark and stormy the night that two or three times, when I attempted to find the town, I failed even to find the road, although we were so close we could almost hear the Indians talking. Thus I was forced to wait until dawn, and we were awake so early that we surprised them all while they still slept. I had given orders that no one should enter a house or utter a sound, but that we should surround the main houses, especially the one belonging to the chieftain, and a large hall in which our guides had told us all the warriors slept.

God and our good fortune so willed it that the first house we came upon was indeed that of the warriors; and, as it was now light and everything was plainly visible, one of my company, seeing so many men in arms and seeing how few we were to attack, even though our opponents were asleep, thought it expedient to call for help and so began to shout with all his might, "Santiago! Santiago!" which awoke the Indians. Some of them took up their weapons, others did not; and, as the house had no walls on any side, the roof being supported only by posts, they leapt out anywhere they wished, for we were unable to surround the place completely. I assure Your Majesty that had that man not shouted, not one of them would have escaped us, which would have been the finest exploit ever achieved in these lands, and might even have allowed us to pacify them all, by releasing them and explaining the reason of my coming and how we meant them no harm but rather were setting them free after we had captured them, and this might have benefited us greatly; but instead the contrary happened. We succeeded in capturing only some fifteen men and twenty women; some ten or twelve more who would not be taken were killed, among whom, unbeknown to us, was the lord of the village, who was later identified by the captives. Neither did we find anything to our advantage, for although there was some green maize, it was not the kind of provisions we were looking for. I remained in this village two days to allow my men to rest; and I asked the Indians we had captured if they knew of any town or village where I might find supplies of dried maize. They replied that they knew of one such town which was called Chacujal,[87] which was very large and very old and well stocked with all kinds of provisions.

After two days I departed, led by those Indians toward the

town of which they had spoken; and that day we traveled a good six leagues, likewise over a bad road and across many rivers, and reached some extensive cultivation which the guides said belonged to the town we were bound for. We then went round them for about two leagues through the forest, so as not to be observed, and captured eight Indians, woodcutters and other laborers, who were hunting in the forest and coming unsuspectingly toward us; and as I always had scouts posted out ahead not one of them escaped us. As it was almost sunset the guides now told me to halt, as we were very close to the town. I did so and remained in the forest for three hours after nightfall. Then I began to proceed and crossed a river whose waters came up to our chests, and the current was so strong that we would have found ourselves in great danger had not we all held on to each other and thus crossed safely. Once on the far bank, the guides told me that the town was now at hand. I halted my men and, taking two companies, went forward until I could see the houses; and all was quiet and the natives seemed unaware of our arrival. I then returned to my people and ordered them to take some rest, placing six men on either side of the road within sight of the village. No sooner had I lain down on some straw than one of the scouts came up to me and said that a host of armed men were coming down the road, but that they were talking together and in other ways behaving as though they knew nothing of our presence.

I alerted my men as quietly as I could, but as the distance between us and the town was so short they discovered our scouts, and immediately let fly a shower of arrows and sent word round the town; then they retreated, fighting with us all the way, until we entered the town when, as it was dark, they disappeared down the streets. Because it was dark and I thought they might be preparing an ambush, I would not allow my men to disband, but, keeping them well together, I marched to a great square where they had their temples and shrines. When we saw these temples and the buildings roundabout in the same manner as those of Culua, our fears were much increased, for since leaving Acalan we had seen nothing of this kind. Many among my company were of the opinion that we should leave the town and cross the river that same night before the Indians discovered how few we were and cut off our retreat. And truly it was not bad advice, for what we had seen of the village gave us every reason to fear. We remained, however, gathered together in that square for a long time, and never once did we hear a sound of people; and it seemed to me that we ought not to depart in that fashion, for perhaps the Indians, seeing that we remained, would be more frightened, whereas if they saw us retreat they might discover our weakness, which would place us in grave danger. It pleased Our Lord that it should so happen, for after having been in that square a long while I collected my people together in one of those great rooms and sent others out into the town to report if they saw or heard anything in the village. But they did not hear a sound; on the contrary, they had gone into many houses where fires were burning and had found a great quantity of provisions with which they returned most cheerful and delighted. We remained there that night keeping the best watch we could.

As soon as it was light we explored the whole town, which was very well laid out and the houses were very good and built close together. We found in all of them a large quantity of cotton, some of which was woven, some unwoven, and good-quality garments of the kind they use; we also found an abundance of dried maize, cacao, beans, peppers and salt, and many hens and pheasants in cages, and partridges and dogs[88] that they breed for food, which are quite tasty, and all kinds of provisions. So much indeed that had ships been available we could have loaded them with enough for a considerable time. But to take advantage of them we had to carry them twenty leagues on our shoulders, and we were in such a condition that had we not rested there for a few days it would have been all we could do to return to the boats, without carrying extra burden.

That same day I sent for a native of the town whom we had captured in those plantations and who seemed to be a person of

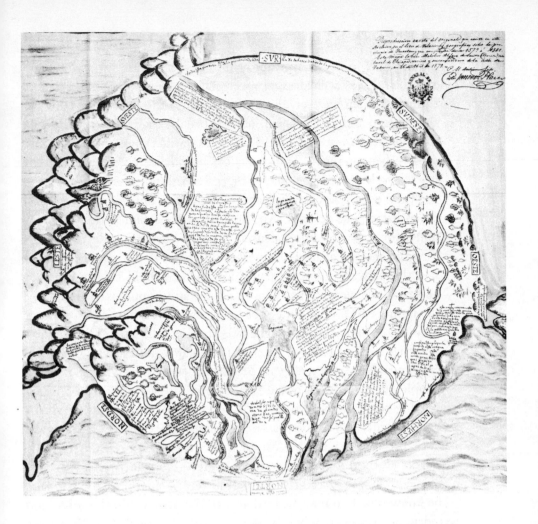

20. Map of Tabasco attributed to Melchior de Alfaro Santa Cruz. This map
accompanied Alfaro's report, one of the two now extant, of the province of
Tabasco made in 1579. The circular form suggests that the mapmaker was
influenced by what appears to have been a Maya convention (c.f. the circular map in the Book of Chilam Balam of Chumayel). For further details
see, Ralph R. Roys, *The Indian Background of Colonial Yucatán*, Carnegie
Institute of Washington Publication No. 548, p. 184. Reproduced from Alfred Percival Maudslay's translation of Bernal Díaz del Castillo's *True
History of the Conquest of New Spain*, London, 1908–1916. *Courtesy of
the British Museum.*

importance, for when we caught him he was hunting with bow and arrow and was well dressed after their fashion, and spoke to him through the interpreter, telling him to find the lord and people of that village and say to them, on my behalf, that I had come to do them no harm but rather to speak to them of things which would greatly benefit them. The chief, or some respected citizen, of the town should therefore come to me, to learn the cause of my arrival, for they could be certain that much good would come of it, and much harm if he refused. And so I dispatched him with a letter of mine, for they are much assured in these parts by such things, although this was against the wishes of some of my company, who said that it was unwise to send him, for he would inform them of how few we were. The town was large and populous, to judge by the number of houses, and once they discovered how few we were they might join forces with the neighboring villages and attack us. I saw that they were right; yet, as I wished to find a way of equipping ourselves with sufficient provisions, and believed that if those people came to me in peace they might provide a means of transporting some of the provisions, I set aside all that might befall us; because truly the risk we ran of dying of hunger if we did not take back provisions was as great as that which could ensue from an attack by the Indians. I persisted, therefore, in dispatching the Indian, and it was agreed that he would return the following day, for he knew where to find the lord and all the people. On the following morning, however, when he should have returned, two Spaniards walking round the outside of the town and exploring the countryside discovered my letter fixed to a pole beside the road, by which we were certain we would receive no reply; and indeed neither that Indian nor any other person ever came, although we spent eighteen days in that town, resting and seeking for a means by which to transport those provisions.

Thinking on this matter, it seemed to me most expedient to follow the river downstream from the town to see if it flowed into the river which flows into those lakes where I had left the brigantine, the boats and the canoes. I asked those Indians whom we held prisoner, and they replied that it did, although we did not understand them very well, nor they us, for their language is different from the others we have heard so far.[89] Using signs and a few words I understood of their language, I asked that two of them should accompany ten Spaniards and show them where that river joined the main one. They replied that it was very close and that they would return that same day. And so it pleased Our Lord that after walking for two leagues through some very attractive plantations of peanuts and other fruit trees they came upon the main river which the guides said was the one which flowed to the lake where I had left the boats; and they told us its name, which is Apolochic.[90] I then asked them how many days it would take by canoe to reach the lakes, and they replied five; so I sent two Spaniards with one of those guides who was to lead them by a short cut to the brigantine. I ordered them to bring the brigantine, boats and canoes to the mouth of that great river and to attempt to come upstream in a boat and a canoe to the point where the other river joined it.

When they had departed I ordered four large rafts to be built of timbers and large canoes. Each one carried about sixty-five bushels of dried maize and ten men as well as quantities of beans, peppers and cacao with which the Spaniards loaded them. When after eight days these rafts were at last completed and the provisions stowed on board, the Spaniards whom I had sent to the brigantine arrived and told me that six days previously they had begun to go up the river but had been unable to bring the boat to the agreed place; instead they had left it five leagues downstream with ten Spaniards guarding it. Likewise they had been unable to make much progress with the canoe, for they were very tired from rowing, but they had hidden it only a league away. As they were coming up the river they had been attacked by some Indians, and they believed that although they were few they would gather forces to await our return. I at once dispatched some men to bring the canoe up to where the rafts were, and, having loaded it with provisions, I sent aboard those who were required to guide us with some long poles to keep us clear of the trees in the river which were most dangerous. I sent the rest of my people under a captain back down the road along which we had come, with orders that if he arrived ahead of me, he was to wait where he had disembarked and I would meet him there; if, however, I arrived first, I would wait for him. I then boarded that canoe escorting the rafts with only two crossbowmen, as there were no others.

Although the journey was most dangerous on account of the fast current and ferocity of the river, and also because we were certain the Indians would attack us on the way, I determined to go myself with the rafts to ensure that every care was taken. Therefore, commending myself to God, I allowed myself to be carried off down river, and we were swept along at such a speed that within three hours we reached the place where the boat had been left. We had hoped to unload some of our cargo onto her so as to lighten the rafts, but the current was so strong that they were unable to stop. I boarded the boat and ordered that the canoe, well provided with oarsmen, should always keep ahead of the rafts to discover if there were any Indians in canoes and give warning of any dangerous places. I remained behind in the boat, waiting for all the rafts to pass, for should anything occur I would be of more help to them coming downstream than going upstream.

Just before sunset one of the rafts struck a submerged log which somewhat unbalanced it; the fury of the waters soon righted it, however, but not before it had lost half its cargo. After we had traveled some three hours into the night, I heard some Indians raise a great cry ahead of us, but as I dared not leave the rafts I did not go forward to discover the cause of it, and after a while it ceased and all was silent for a time. A little later, however, I heard it again; this time it seemed much closer, but again it stopped and I was unable to discover what it was, because the canoe and the three rafts went ahead while I followed behind with the damaged raft, which was slower. For a long time we had no more cries and so dropped our guard somewhat; I took off my helmet and rested my head in my hands, for I had a high fever.

Suddenly, at a bend in the river, we were caught by the current with such force that the boat and the raft were driven ashore, at the very place, it seemed, from where the shouting had come, for the Indians who had been brought up beside this river knew it well and knew that the current would force us into the bank at that point. Many of them were waiting there for us, and when the rafts and canoe reached them they shot at them with arrows, wounding nearly everyone on board, but as they knew we were following behind they did not attack them as fiercely as they later attacked us. The people in the canoe could not come up against the current and so were unable to warn us. When we struck the shore the Indians let forth a tremendous cry and assailed us with so many arrows and stones that they wounded us all; I was struck on the head, which was the only part of me unprotected by armor. It pleased Our Lord, however, that this should occur at a place where the river-banks were very high and the water deep, and for this reason we were not captured, because those who attempted to leap down onto the boat and canoes missed us in the dark, and fell into the water, and few, I believe, can have escaped with their lives. So rapidly were we carried past them on the current that very soon after we could no longer hear their shouts. And so we traveled almost all that night without further encounter, though from time to time we heard them calling out from the distance or from the banks of the river; for both sides are inhabited and lined with beautiful plantations of cacao and other fruit trees. At dawn we found ourselves five leagues from the mouth of that river which flows into the lake where the brigantine was awaiting us. And we arrived there that day almost at noon, so that in a single day and night we had traveled twenty leagues down that river.

When we came to unload the provisions from the rafts onto the brigantine, most of them were discovered to be wet, and seeing that if they were not dried all would be lost and our efforts wasted (and we had no other food supplies), I had all the maize that was dry taken out and stowed in the brigantine; the wet maize was then thrown into the two boats and the two canoes. I then ordered it to be taken as swiftly as possible to the town to be dried, for, because of the swamps, there was no place on the lagoon where this could be done. Thus they departed, and I told them to return straightaway with the boats and canoes to help me embark my people, for the brigantine and the one remaining canoe were not sufficient for the purpose. I then set sail and proceeded to the place where I was to await the people who were coming overland; and after three days they arrived, all very well, save for one Spaniard who, they said, had eaten a certain plant by the road and died almost instantly. They also brought with them an Indian whom they had surprised and captured in the town where I had left them; and as he was different from the other Indians of that land, both in dress and language, I spoke to him by signs and with the help of one among the prisoners who understood his language. Thus I learnt that he was a native of Teculutlan, and when I heard the name of this town it seemed to me that I had heard it before; and, indeed, when I returned to the town and looked up certain notes of mine, I discovered the name written there, whereby it seemed that overland from where I was to the Southern Sea was no more than seventy-eight leagues. For also in those notes it appeared that Spaniards of Pedro de Alvarado's[91] company had been in Teculutlan, a fact which the Indian confirmed. And I rejoiced greatly to know of the short distance which separated us.

Now that all my men were together and the boats still had not arrived, we soon finished the few dry provisions which remained, and then boarded the brigantine, although with great difficulty, for there was not enough room, thinking to cross the lake to the town where we had first landed, for the maize had been ripening then, and as twenty-five days had passed we expected to find much of it now ripe enough for us to make use of it. One morning, however, while sailing in the middle of the lake, we saw the boats

approaching, and so we all landed together. All my people, Spaniards as well as our Indian friends, and some forty-five Indian prisoners, went together to the town and found a very good crop of
maize, much of which was ripe. They encountered no opposition;
and Christians and Indians alike made three journeys each that day,
for the fields lay close by. When the brigantine and the boats were
loaded I returned with them to Nito, leaving my people transporting maize. Straightaway I sent back the two boats together with a
third that had come ashore there from a ship, which had been lost on
the coast coming to New Spain, and four canoes, in which all my
people returned, bringing an abundant supply of maize. This was
such a relief to us that it well repaid our labors, for had we not had
it we should all have perished of hunger with no hope of relief.

I then had all those provisions stowed aboard the ships, and
embarked the remainder of my company and all the people of that
town who had followed Gil González and set sail on the ———— of
————[92] for the harbor in the bay of San Andrés. I first anchored
off a headland and set ashore all those who were still able to walk,
together with two horses that I had with me in the ship, and ordered them to proceed overland to the aforementioned harbor,
where they were to meet or await the others who were on their
way from Naco; for our ships were dangerously overloaded,
whereas that road was well traveled and presented few difficulties. I
sent also a boat down the coast to help them cross several rivers
which lay in their path. When I myself arrived in San Andrés I
discovered that the people who had come from Naco had preceded
me by two days. From them I learnt that all the others were well
and had an abundance of maize and peppers and many fruits of that
country, but they had no meat or salt nor had they tasted any for
two months. I remained in that harbor twenty days organizing what
the people in Naco had to do, and looking for a place to settle on
that bay, for the harbor is the best we have discovered on this mainland; that is to say between the Gulf of Pearls and Florida.

It pleased Our Lord that we should find a good and most

suitable site and when I sent certain of my men to explore some streams, though they had little equipment, they found good samples of gold, at distances of one and two leagues from the town. For this reason and also because the harbor is such a fine one, the surrounding countryside so fertile and so well inhabited, it seemed to me that Your Majesty would be well served if I were to found a town there. I therefore sent to Naco, where the remainder of the people were, to ask if any of them wished to become settlers, and as the land is good, nearly fifty, for the most part those who had been in my company, came forward, and so in Your Majesty's name I founded a town there. As the day on which we cleared the ground was the day of the Nativity[93] of Our Lady, I called the town by that name and appointed alcaldes and regidores and left there priests and church ornaments and other things necessary for the Mass. I also left them skilled craftsmen, such as a blacksmith with a very good forge, a carpenter, a calker, a barber and a tailor. The settlers had between them twenty horsemen and some crossbowmen; and I also provided them with certain pieces of artillery and some powder.

When I arrived in that harbor and learnt from those Spaniards who had come from Naco how the inhabitants of that and all the neighboring towns had left their homes and fled to the mountains and forest, and, although several of them had been invited to, now they were afraid to return on account of the harm they had received at the hands of Gil González and Cristóbal de Olid, I wrote to the captain who was there asking him to do all in his power to secure some of these Indians and to send them to me that I might reassure them. He did this, sending me certain persons whom he had captured on an expedition. I spoke to them and greatly assured them and made some of the principal persons from México speak to them; they told them who I was and all I had done in their land, of the good treatment all received from me once they had become my friends, and of how they were protected and governed in justice: they, their property and their women and children.

They told them also of the punishments received by all those who rebelled against Your Majesty's service and many other things besides, which seemed to reassure them somewhat. They answered, however, that they were afraid what they had been told was not the truth, for those other captains before me had said the same things, and more, but afterwards it was discovered to be false, for the women they had given them to make bread were not returned, neither were the men who had carried their baggage. They were afraid that I would do likewise. Nevertheless, they were somewhat reassured by what the Mexicans, and the interpreter who was beside me, had told them, and by seeing how well treated and cheerful they were in our company.

I then sent them away to speak to the lords and peoples of the villages, and after a few days the captain wrote to me saying that some of the people from the surrounding villages had returned peacefully to their homes, especially to the principal ones, which are Naco itself, where they are quartered, Quimistlan, Zula and Cholome,⁹⁴ the smallest of which has more than two thousand houses, besides a number of dependent hamlets; these had said that soon the whole land would be at peace, for they had sent out messengers reassuring the others and informing them who I was and of all they had been told them by the people of Mexico. They were also anxious for me to visit them, for by so doing the people would be more easily reassured. This I would most willingly have done were it not that I had to continue my journey so as to set in order certain matters which I will relate to Your Majesty in the following chapter.

Invincible Caesar, on my arrival at the town of Nito, where I found the people of Gil González de Ávila in such a state, I learnt from them that Francisco de las Casas, whom I had sent to find Cristóbal de Olid, as I have already informed Your Majesty, had left, sixty leagues down the coast in a bay which the pilots call Las Honduras, certain Spaniards who no doubt had settled there. As soon as I arrived in this town in the bay of San Andrés where in

Your Majesty's name I founded the town called Natividad de Nuestra Señora, and while I remained there to arrange the building and settlement of it, likewise to give orders to the captain and people in Naco concerning what action they were to take to pacify and secure those villages, I sent the ship which I had purchased to the aforementioned bay of Honduras to get news of the people there and to return with it. When I had completed my tasks, the ship returned bringing with it a representative of the town and a regidor, who entreated me to go and relieve them, for they were in extreme need because the captain whom Francisco de las Casas had appointed over them and an alcalde who had been appointed likewise had seized a ship then lying in the harbor, and of 110 men had persuaded fifty to follow them. The others had had nearly all their belongings taken from them and were left without weapons or any iron tools and were constantly afraid that either the Indians would kill them or they would die of hunger, as they had no means of obtaining food. A ship from the island of Hispaniola owned by a man called *bachiller* Pedro Moreno[95] had landed there, but although they had begged him to provide them with food he had refused to do so, as I heard at greater length when I reached that town.

To remedy this I once again embarked with all those sick people, though by that time some of them had died, intending to send them from that place to the Islands and to New Spain, as afterwards I did. I took some of my servants with me, and ordered twenty horsemen and ten crossbowmen to go overland, as I had been informed that the road was a good one, although they would have several rivers to cross. It took me nine days to arrive owing to contrary weather, but as soon as we had cast anchor in the bay of Las Honduras, I got into a boat with two Franciscan friars who always traveled with me and about ten of my servants, and went ashore to find the people of the town waiting for us on the beach. As I drew near, however, they all rushed into the water and lifted me out of the boat onto their shoulders to show how delighted they were at my arrival; and so together we walked to the church which they had there. After having given thanks to Our Lord they begged me to be seated, for they wished to give me an account of all that had happened. They were afraid that, on account of an unfavorable report made to me, I might be angry with them, and they wished me to know the truth before I judged them on such evidence. I did as they bade me, and a priest who was there stood up and spoke on their behalf as follows:

"Sir, you well know how you sent all, or nearly all of us who are here present, from New Spain under Cristóbal de Olid, your captain, to settle these parts in His Majesty's name, and that you ordered us all to obey the aforementioned Cristóbal de Olid in all that he commanded, as we would yourself. And so we departed with him for the island of Cuba, where we were to take on board certain provisions and horses which we required. Having arrived at Havana, which is a harbor of that island, Cristóbal de Olid exchanged letters with Diego Velázquez and His Majesty's officials residing there, and they sent him some men. When we had furnished ourselves with all we needed, which was provided most fully by your servant Alonso de Contreras, we departed and continued on our way. Omitting some incidents that befell us on our journey which would be too long to tell, we reached this coast fourteen leagues beyond the port of Caballos, and as soon as we had landed Cristóbal de Olid took possession of it on your behalf in His Majesty's name and founded there a town with the alcaldes and regidores, who had previously been appointed to their offices. He likewise carried out certain other official duties relating to the foundation and settlement of this town, while acting always on your behalf and as your captain and lieutenant. Some days later, however, he made common cause with the servants of Diego Velázquez[96] who had accompanied him and made certain pronouncements which clearly showed that he had ceased to recognize your authority; and although most of us thought this ill done, we dared not reprove his conduct, for he threatened us with the gallows. Rather than opposing him, therefore, we acquiesced in all he did, and we were even joined in this by certain servants and relatives of yours who likewise dared not and could not do otherwise. After this had been done he learnt, from six messengers whom he captured, that certain of Gil González's people were coming to see him. He went out to meet them by a river crossing they were bound to pass; and there he waited several days in the hope of capturing them. As they did not come, however, he left a captain on guard and returned to the town, where he began to fit out his two caravels and arm them with guns and munitions, preparing to attack a town of Spaniards which the captain Gil González had settled farther up the coast. While thus engaged in preparing his offensive, Francisco de las Casas arrived with two ships, and as soon as Cristóbal de Olid knew who it was, he ordered the guns of his ships to fire on him. Francisco de las Casas then hoisted flags of peace and called out that he had been sent by you, but the bombardment did not cease, and suddenly a volley of ten or twelve shots was fired, one of which went straight through one side of the ship and out of the other. Francisco de las Casas now realized his hostile intent and was able to confirm the suspicions already entertained against Olid, so he manned and lowered his boats and opened fire upon the two caravels in the harbor, which he soon captured with all the ordnance aboard, their crews fleeing to safety ashore.

"As soon as Cristóbal de Olid saw that his ships had been taken, he began to discuss terms with him, not intending to achieve anything, but simply to delay him until the people who were waiting for Gil González had returned, hoping thereby to deceive Las Casas, and indeed Las Casas did all he asked with great goodwill. Thus they began discussing terms without ever reaching any conclusion, until a storm blew up, and as there was no harbor but only the rocky coast it drove Las Casas's ships against the shore; some thirty men were drowned, and all they possessed was lost. Las Casas himself and all the others who escaped were naked and so battered by the sea that Cristóbal de Olid captured them all, and before they entered the town made them swear upon the Gospels that they would obey and serve him as their captain and would never act against him.

"At this time news arrived that Olid's captain had seized fifty-seven men who were under the command of the alcalde mayor of the aforementioned Gil González de Ávila, but that afterwards he had released them, and each party had gone their separate ways. Olid was greatly angered by this and promptly marched inland to that town of Naco, where he had been previously, taking with him Las Casas and some of the others who had been captured with him, and leaving the rest of the prisoners behind in that town with a lieutenant and an alcalde. Many times Las Casas, in the presence of all, begged Olid to allow him to return to you and give an account of what had happened, or if not, to guard him well and not to trust him. Despite this, however, Olid refused to let him go.

"Some days later Cristóbal de Olid learnt that the captain Gil González de Ávila was encamped with a few people at a town called Choluma [sic] and sent some of his men against him. They fell on Gil González by night, capturing him and all his men; thus Cristóbal de Olid held both these captains for some time, and although they constantly demanded their release he would not grant it them. He also made all the people of Gil González swear to hold him as their captain, as he had those of Las Casas. Many times after the capture of Gil González, Francisco de las Casas, in everyone's presence, asked Olid to release them, and if he refused, to guard them closely, for they meant to kill him, but he would not. His tyranny became so intolerable, however, that one night, when all three were in a room with many others discussing certain things, Francisco de las Casas seized him by the beard, and with the penknife, for he had no other weapon, with which he had been cutting his nails as he walked about, stabbed him, crying, 'We can suffer this tyrant no longer.' Gil González and certain other servants of yours then disarmed the guards, and inflicted more blows on Olid; the captain of the guard, the ensign [alférez], the captain who had been sent against González and others who came to his assistance were soon captured and disarmed, without any being killed; Cristóbal de Olid, however, escaped in the confusion and hid. Within two hours the two captains had pacified the people and imprisoned the more important among his followers; they then proclaimed publicly that whosoever knew of the whereabouts of Cristóbal de Olid should reveal it immediately on pain of death. They soon discovered where he was and placed him under heavy guard. On the following morning he was tried and both captains sentenced him to death, which sentence was duly executed by cutting off his head; everyone was greatly pleased to be so liberated.

"It was then proclaimed that all those who wished to remain and settle in that land should say so, and that those who wished to leave should do likewise. One hundred and ten men declared that they wished to stay, and all the rest, among whom were twenty horsemen, said that they wished to go with Francisco de las Casas and Gil González, who were returning to you and we in this town are of that one hundred and ten. Then Francisco de las Casas gave us all that we required, appointed a captain over us and directed us to this coast where we were to settle on behalf of Your Honor and in the name of His Majesty: he likewise appointed alcaldes, regidores, a notary, a representative of the town council, and an alguacil, and ordered us to call the town Trujillo.[97] He also promised us, and pledged himself as a gentleman of honor, that very shortly he would obtain from Your Honor more men, horses, arms, supplies and everything else that was necessary for pacifying the land; he gave us an Indian girl and a Christian as our interpreters. So we left him to go and do as he had commanded us; and he dispatched a ship to inform you of all that had happened, for the news would arrive sooner by sea and you would; therefore, send us help more swiftly. When we reached the port of San Andrés, which is also called Los Caballos,[98] we found there a caravel which had come from the Islands, and because that port did not seem to us a suitable place to build a town, and we had a report of this harbor, we chartered that caravel to

transport our baggage, and the captain went aboard with everything we possessed and some forty men, while all the horsemen and
the rest of the people went by land with hardly more than the shirts
on our backs, so as not to be encumbered lest anything befall us on
our journey. The captain delegated his powers to an alcalde—the
same one who is here with us now, for the other departed with him
in the caravel, commanding us to obey him in his absence. And so
we parted from each other to meet again at this port; on the road
we had some skirmishes with the natives, who killed two Spaniards
and a few of the Indians in our service.

"When at last we reached this harbor, exhausted and with
our horses unshod, but cheerful, expecting to see our captain and
baggage and arms, we were dismayed to find nothing there at all,
for we ourselves had no clothes or arms or horseshoes, for they had
all been taken by the captain in the caravel, and we were greatly
perplexed, not knowing what to do. Finally we decided to wait
until Your Honor sent help, which we were certain would come,
and set about founding the town. We took possession of the land
on your behalf and in His Majesty's name, and confirmed it with a
deed, drawn up before the notary of the municipal council, as you
shall see. Five or six days later, at dawn, a caravel appeared anchored at sea some two leagues from this port, and the alguacil
went out in a canoe to discover whose it was. He returned with the
news that it belonged to a bachiller Pedro Moreno of the island of
Hispaniola, who had come by command of the judges who reside
on that island to inquire into certain matters between Cristóbal de
Olid and Gil González. He carried many arms and provisions in
that caravel, all of which belonged to His Majesty.

"We were all greatly pleased by this news and offered many
thanks to Our Lord, believing that our hardships were at an end.
Then the alcalde and the regidores and some of the other settlers
went to ask him to supply us, and explain to him our shortages, but
on their arrival he armed the men and would allow no one to board
the caravel; after much discussion, however, he allowed four or five

without arms to go on board. There they told him how they had come to settle at your orders in His Majesty's name, and, because our captain had left in a caravel with all our belongings, we were in need of provisions, arms, horseshoes, garments and other things. They believed that God had brought him there for our relief, and, as all he carried belonged to His Majesty, they begged and entreated him to provide for us, for by so doing he would serve His Majesty, besides which we undertook to pay for all he gave us. To this he replied that he had not come to provide for our needs and would give us nothing unless we paid him at once in gold or slaves.

"Two merchants who were on board and one Gaspar Troche, of the island of San Juan, told him to give us all we asked for, offering to stand security themselves for any sum up to five or six thousand *castellanos*, to be paid within any period he should decide upon, for he knew that they had sufficient means to repay. They did this, they said, because they wished to serve His Majesty and because they were certain that Your Honor would repay them, as well as thank them. But still he refused absolutely to give us anything whatever; indeed, he said he wished to depart and told us to do likewise. He threw us off his ship and sent after us one Juan Ruano whom he had with him and who had been the principal instigator of Cristóbal de Olid's treachery. This man then spoke secretly with the alcalde and the regidores and with certain others among us, saying that if we did as he asked, he would make the bachiller give us all we required and would even arrange matters with the judges in Hispaniola so that we should not have to repay any of it. He would return to Hispaniola and ensure that the judges provided us with men, horses, arms, provisions and all else we might require; the bachiller would soon return with all this and powers from the judges to become our captain.

"When asked what it was we had to do, he replied that before anything else we were to depose from their Royal offices the alcalde, regidores, the treasurers [*sic*], the contador and the veedor who had been appointed by Your Honor and to request the bachiller

Moreno to appoint him, Ruano, as our captain, and we should agree
to pledge our allegiance to the judges and not to you. We were all
to sign a petition to this end, and swear to obey and hold as captain
the aforementioned Juan Ruano, and promise that if any of your
men came with orders we were not only to disobey them, but also,
if they attempted to impose your orders, to resist them by force of
arms. We replied that we could not do this, for we had sworn otherwise and owed our allegiance to His Majesty, and to Your Honor
in His name, as his captain and governor, and would not do as he
asked. Juan Ruano then told us that we must either do as he said or
die, for certainly Moreno would not give us so much as a jug of
water if we refused but would sail away and leave us to our fate;
therefore we were to consider carefully our decision. So we met
again together and compelled by great necessity decided to do as he
wished rather than die of hunger or, as we were unarmed, be killed
by the Indians. We told Juan Ruano, therefore, that we would do
as he requested us, and with this he returned to the caravel. The
bachiller Moreno then came ashore with a large number of armed
men, and Juan Ruano drew up the petition asking him to be our
captain, and all, or nearly all, of us signed it and gave him our oaths.
The alcalde, the regidores, the treasurer, the contador and the
veedor all quit their offices, the name of the town was changed to
La Ascensión, and certain documents were drawn up saying how
we henceforth owed allegiance to the judges and not to you.

"Then he brought us all we had asked for, and sent an expedition into the surrounding country which returned with certain
people whom he had branded as slaves and carried away with him.
But he refused to give a fifth to His Majesty and ordered that in
future there would be no treasurer or contador or veedor of the
Royal rights, but that Juan Ruano, whom he left as our captain,
would collect it all himself without any other record, account
or audit. This done he departed, leaving as our captain the aforementioned Juan Ruano with certain requerimientos, in case any people should come here from Your Honor. He promised to return

soon in such force that no one would be able to resist him. After he had gone, however, we, seeing that what had been done was contrary to His Majesty's service and likely to give rise to greater disturbances than those past, seized Juan Ruano and dispatched him to the Islands, and the alcalde and regidores took up their offices as before. Thus we have been and still are loyal to Your Honor in His Majesty's name, and we beg you to forgive us the things done under Cristóbal de Olid, for in that matter, as in this, we were compelled by force."

I answered them saying that I forgave them in Your Majesty's name for all that had occurred in the time of Cristóbal de Olid, and absolved them of blame for what had happened since, because they had been constrained by necessity. I urged them to make sure they were not responsible for such disturbances and scandal in the future, because such things were the cause of great disservice to Your Majesty and they would be punished for them. But that they might more surely believe that I had forgotten what had happened and had wiped it from my memory, I said I would, in Your Majesty's name, help and favor them all I could as long as they did all they were required to as loyal vassals of Your Majesty; I, in Your Royal name, then confirmed in their offices the alcaldes and regidores whom Francisco de las Casas, as my lieutenant, had appointed. This pleased them greatly, and they were much relieved to find that their past offenses were not to be held against them. Because they assured me that Moreno would return very shortly with many people and dispatches from those judges who reside on Hispaniola, I did not at that moment wish to leave the port and proceed inland. The Spaniards, however, told me that there were certain native towns, some six or seven leagues from this town, with whom they had had some skirmishes while searching for food, but that some of them, if there were an interpreter by whom we could make ourselves understood, appeared ready to make peace, and had conveyed their goodwill by means of signs, although they had received no good at the hands of the Spaniards who had attacked them and carried off some women and boys which Moreno had had branded as slaves and taken away in his ship; and God alone knows how much this news distressed me, for I realized the great harm that would follow such a deed.

In the ships I sent to the Islands, I sent a letter to those judges in which I set down at length all that the bachiller Pedro Moreno had done in this town, and with it a requirement on Your Majesty's behalf that the aforementioned Pedro Moreno should be sent to me under heavy guard, and with him all the natives of this land he had taken as slaves, for he had taken them in defiance of all the laws, as they would see in my letter. I do not know what they will do about this matter, but I will inform Your Majesty as soon as I receive their reply.

Two days after my arrival in this town of Trujillo I sent a Spaniard who understands the language together with three Indians from Culua to those towns which the Spaniards had mentioned; and I told this Spaniard and the three Indians everything they were to say to the chiefs and people of those towns, and to impress upon them that it was I myself who had come to these parts, for the numerous native merchants have carried news of me and of my doings in México along the trade routes to many lands. The first towns they went to were called Chapagua and Papayeca, which are seven leagues from the town and two leagues from each other. They are both very important towns, as it appeared later, for Papayeca has eighteen villages subject to it and Chapagua has ten.

And it pleased Our Lord, who we know by daily experience has especial care of Your Majesty's affairs, that they listened to our embassy with great attention and sent back with those messengers others of their own to satisfy themselves that what they said was true. When they arrived I welcomed them, and after giving them a few small things, spoke to them through my interpreter, for their language is almost the same as that of Culua, except for a few words and slight differences in pronunciation.[99] I again affirmed all that had been said and added many other things which I thought would inspire their confidence, entreating them to persuade their lords to come and see me. With this they departed, greatly pleased. Five days later there came, on behalf of the people of Chapagua, a chieftain called Montamal, lord, it appeared, of one of the subject villages called Telica. On behalf of the people of Papayeca there came the lord of another subject village who was called Çecoatl, and his village Coabata. They brought some maize, hens and some fruit, and said that they had come on behalf of their lords and that I should tell them what I wanted and why I had come to their land. The lords, they said, had not come themselves for fear of being carried away in the ships, as had happened to certain of their people when the first Christians who landed there had caught them. I told them how much that action had distressed me and said they might be sure that no such injury would be done them in future, and I would send in search of those who had been taken away and have them returned. I pray to God those lawyers do not make me break my word, for I am rather afraid that they will not send back those Indians, but rather seek to exculpate the bachiller Moreno who took them, for I do not believe that he did anything here which was not by their instruction and command.

In reply to what those messengers asked me about the cause of my arrival in their land, I told them that I believed they already knew how eight years previously I had come to the province of Culua, and Mutezuma, who at that time was lord of the great city of Temixtitan and of the whole country, having been told by me how I had been sent by Your Majesty, to whom the whole world is subject, to see and to explore those lands in Your Excellency's Royal name, had received me very well and acknowledged the allegiance that he owed to Your Highness; and all the other lords in that country had done likewise. And I told him of everything else that had happened to me here. I had been commanded by Your Majesty to see and examine the whole land without omitting a single thing, and to found there towns of Christians to instruct them in the mode of life they were to follow for the preservation of their persons and their property, as well as for the salvation of their souls. This was the reason for my coming and they might be certain that they would receive no harm but would profit greatly by it, for those who obeyed Your Majesty's Royal commands would always be well treated and maintained in justice, and those who were rebellious would be punished. I also told them many other things to the same purpose, but I shall not relate them here so as not to tax Your Majesty with lengthy writings and because they are of no great importance.

To these messengers I gave a few small things which they prize highly, although among us they are regarded as of little value, and thus they departed very happily. And because I asked them to, they returned later with provisions and people to clear the site of the town, as it was extensively wooded. Although the chiefs still did not come to see me, I pretended it was a matter of no consequence, and asked them to send messengers into the surrounding villages to tell them all I had said, and to request them on my behalf to come and help in building that town; and they agreed to do so. Within a few days fifteen or sixteen villages or, rather, independent towns had come, with a display of great goodwill, to offer themselves as Your Majesty's vassals; furthermore, they brought people to help us build the town and provisions on which we lived until assistance arrived from the ships which I had sent to the Islands.

At this time I dispatched the three ships that I had and another which arrived later which I also purchased, and in them I sent all the sick who were still alive. One was bound for the ports of New Spain, and in her was a long letter which I had written to the officers of Your Majesty whom I had left in my place, as well as to the various municipal councils telling them of what I had done there and how I was obliged to remain a while longer in those parts. I requested them to give all their attention to the responsibilities and duties which I had asked them to perform and gave them my advice about what to do in certain matters. I commanded this vessel to return by the island of Cozumel, which lay on the route, and to pick up some Spaniards, more than sixty in number, who had been abandoned there by a certain Valenzuela, who had seized a ship and sacked the town on the island which was the first colony Cristóbal de Olid had founded. The other ship, which I had just purchased in an inlet close to the town, I sent to the town of Trinidad on the island of Cuba to load up with meat, horses and men, and to return with as much haste as possible. A third was sent to Jamaica for the same purpose. The large caravel or brigantine which I had had built was sent to Hispaniola with a servant of mine who was carrying letters for Your Majesty and for the judges residing in that island. It was later discovered, however, that none of these ships reached its destination. The one bound for Cuba was carried to Guaniguanico, and the crew had to travel fifty leagues overland to Havana to find their cargo. When this ship, which was the first to do so, returned, I learnt how the one I had sent to New Spain had picked up the people stranded on Cozumel but had then been wrecked on a headland on the island of Cuba called San Antón, or Corrientes; everything on board was lost, and a cousin of mine, called Juan de Avalos, who was in command of the vessel, drowned, together with the two Franciscan friars[100] who had accompanied me and some thirty more people whose names have been given me. Those who reached the shore had wandered through the forests not knowing where they were or where to go, and almost all had died of hunger. Of some eighty persons only fifteen remained alive, and these by good fortune reached that port of Guaniguanico where my other ship was anchored. Close by was a plantation belonging to a citizen of Havana where my ship was taking on a cargo, for there was an abundance of provisions; there those who were still alive were able to recover. God knows my grief at this loss, for besides having lost thereby relations and servants, many breastplates, harquebuses, crossbows and other weapons, my dispatches failed to arrive, which caused me even greater sorrow, as I shall relate to Your Majesty hereafter.

The ships bound for Jamaica and Hispaniola both arrived at

Trinidad in Cuba, where they met the licenciado Alonso de Zuazo, whom I had left as chief justice and one of those charged with the government of New Spain during my absence. They also found a ship in that port which those lawyers in Hispaniola were going to send to New Spain to ascertain the truth of the rumors that were circulating to the effect that I was dead.[101] When the ship's master heard that I was still alive he changed course, for he was carrying thirty-two horses, certain pieces of harness and provisions which he hoped to sell where I was at a better price; in this ship the afore-mentioned Alonso de Zuazo sent me letters telling how in New Spain there had been great feuds and disputes amongst Your Majesty's officials, and that it had been put about that I was dead. Two of them had publicly proclaimed themselves governors and had had themselves sworn in as such. They had then seized Zuazo and two other officials and also Rodrigo de Paz, in whose care I had left my house and property. This they had looted; they had deposed all the justices whom I had appointed and replaced them with others of their own making; and many other things they had done, which, as they are lengthy to relate and because I am sending the original letter to Your Majesty, I will not set down here.

Your Majesty may well imagine how much this news distressed me, particularly to learn how they repaid my services, looting my house which would have been ill done even though I were dead; for though they may say, by way of an excuse, that I owed Your Majesty some sixty thousand *pesos de oro*, they know full well that rather than my being in debt, I am owed 150,000 *pesos* which I have spent, and not extravagantly, in Your Majesty's service.

I immediately set about to right this situation; on the one hand it seemed to me that I should depart in that same ship in person and punish this great outrage, for now all those hereabouts who are given some office in my absence think that if they don't thumb their noses at me they're not worthy of the honor. Indeed, another captain whom Pedro Arias sent to Nicaragua has likewise rebelled against his allegiance, as I will later inform Your Majesty at greater length.[102] On the other hand, I was very sorry to have to leave that land in its present circumstances, for that would mean losing it altogether, and I am certain that Your Majesty will benefit greatly from it and that it will be another Culua. For I have received news of very large and wealthy provinces with powerful lords richly attended, especially one they call Hueytapalan, or, in another language, Xucutaco, which I have known of for six years and, having made inquiries about it throughout my journey, have discovered at last that it is eight or ten days' march from that town of Trujillo; that is to say, some fifty or sixty leagues. And such wonderful news has been received of it that I marvel at what is said, for even if two-thirds of it prove false it must exceed Mexico in riches and equal it in the great size of the towns, the multitude of people and the government thereof. While thus perplexed, I reasoned that nothing could be well done or directed save by the hands of the Creator and Mover of all things, and I therefore had Masses said and ordered processions and sacrifices, beseeching God to guide me in the path where I might serve Him best.

After we had practiced these devotions for a few days, it seemed to me that after all I must abandon everything else and go and put a stop to those troubles. I left there as my lieutenant in that town a cousin of mine, called Hernando de Saavedra, brother of Juan de Avalos who was drowned in the ship bound for this great city, with some thirty-five horsemen and fifty foot soldiers under his command. After having given him instructions,[103] as best I could arrange about what he was to do, and having also spoken to some of the native lords of that country who had already come to see me, I embarked on the aforementioned ship with my household servants, at the same time giving orders to the people in Naco to go overland by the road along the south coast which Francisco de las Casas had taken to the place where Pedro de Alvarado had settled, for the road from then on was certain and safe, and they would be in sufficient numbers to go where they wished without fear of attack. I

likewise sent instructions to that other town, La Natividad de Nuestra Señora, and embarked in fine weather. But as we were about to
set sail, riding on one anchor, a dead calm descended, so that we
were unable to leave harbor. On the following morning news
reached me on board ship that it was being whispered among the
people I had left on land that they expected some disturbance in my
absence; for this reason and also because the weather was unfavorable I landed again, made inquiries and by punishing certain of the
ringleaders restored the peace. I stayed two days on shore because
the weather prevented us from leaving port, but on the third the
weather was favorable and we put to sea. We had gone no more
than two leagues, however, and were doubling a long headland
which forms one of the arms of the bay, when our main yard broke
and we were forced to return to port to have it replaced. Three
more days were spent on these repairs, but at last I set sail again
with a fair wind and ran before it two days and nights during
which time we covered fifty leagues or more, but then a fearful
northerly gale caught us and broke our foremast off short at the
cap, and we were forced to put back into port, which we managed
only with the greatest difficulty. When we arrived we thanked
God greatly, for we thought we were lost and I and all the people
were so battered by the sea that we had to take some rest; and
therefore while waiting for the weather to improve and the ship to
be repaired, I came ashore with all my people. Seeing that I had
now put to sea three times with good weather, and each time had
been forced to return, I considered that God did not wish me to
abandon that land, and my view was confirmed by the fact that
some of the Indians who had been at peace were now in revolt.

I again commended the matter to God, ordered processions
and had Masses said, and it seemed to me that if I were to send this
ship, in which I was to have sailed for New Spain, to convey letters
of authority to my cousin Francisco de las Casas and letters to the
councils and officials of Your Majesty, reproving them for their
misdemeanors, together with some of the Indian chieftains who

were with me to persuade the people there that I was not dead as they had been told, that then peace would be restored and the troubles which had begun soon brought to an end. I arranged everything accordingly, although I would have made many more provisions than in fact I did, had I known at the time of the loss of the first ship which I had equipped very fully and which I was certain had arrived many days previously, and with it the loss of my dispatches concerning the Southern Sea.

After having dispatched this ship to New Spain I was unable to go inland myself because I had not recovered from the results of the storm at sea, and indeed I am not fully recovered even now, and also because I was awaiting the return of the ships from the Islands and engaged in settling certain other matters. I sent my lieutenant with thirty horsemen and as many foot soldiers and ordered him to explore the hinterland. They traveled some thirty-five leagues up a most beautiful valley with many large towns rich in everything that grows in this land and well provided for the breeding of all kinds of herds and for the cultivation of any crop grown in Spain. They had no hostile encounter with the natives but spoke to them through the interpreter and the Indians of those parts who were already our friends, and persuaded them to remain in peace, with the result that more than twenty chiefs of important towns came before me and willingly offered themselves as Your Highness's subjects, promising to be obedient to Your Royal commands, which they have been up until now. From that day until the day of my departure there were always some of them in my company, and almost every day some went away and were replaced by others who brought provisions and served in every way that was asked of them. I pray God that they continue so and are guided to the ends which Your Majesty desires. And I have every faith that it will be so, for no bad end can come of such a good beginning unless it be through the fault of us who are in command.

The provinces of Papayeca and Chapagua, which, as I have

said, were the first to offer themselves in Your Majesty's service and as our friends, were also those who had rebelled when I embarked, and now that I had returned they were somewhat afraid, but I sent certain messengers to reassure them. Some of the natives of Chapagua came to see me but never the chiefs, and their villages were always empty of their women and children and their belongings. Several men came to serve us in the town, and I required them many times to return to their villages, but they would not, always promising to do so on the following day. I managed to lay hands on three of their lords, whose names were Chicohuytl, Poto and Mendoreto; once I had seized them I gave them a certain period within which they were to command their people to return from the mountains; otherwise they would be punished as rebels. Thus they returned and I released those lords, since which time they have been very quiet and secure and they serve us very well.

The natives of Papayeca never appeared, least of all the lords, who hid in the mountains with all their people, leaving the villages deserted. Although they were required to return many times, they would not obey, so I sent a captain with horsemen and foot soldiers together with many of the native Indians. One night they fell upon one of the two lords of the province, whose name was Pizacura, and demanded of him why he had been disobedient and rebellious. He replied that he would have returned to his village were it not for his companion, Maçatel, who had more influence in the community and had refused his consent; but he said that if they let him go he would spy on [Maçatel] so that they might capture him; and if then they hanged him all the people would return peacefully to their villages, for with no opposition he could easily persuade them. So he was released, which was the cause of much greater harm as it later turned out. Certain of our Indian friends spied on Maçatl [sic] and led the Spaniards to him. He was captured, and, having been told what his companion Pizacura had said of him, he was ordered to bring his people down from the mountains and back into their village within a certain time, but we were unable to make him do this. He was therefore tried, sentenced to death and executed.

This has been a great example to the others, for afterwards the inhabitants of some villages who were also somewhat rebellious returned to their homes, and there is no village where the women and children are not returned and living without fear, except that of Papayeca, which I have been unable to reassure. After Pizacura had been released, the inhabitants of that province were tried and war was declared against them as a result of which some hundred persons were seized and enslaved. Among these was Pizacura himself, whom I did not sentence to death, although I might have done on the findings of his trial. I instead brought him with me to this great city together with two other lords from other towns which were somewhat rebellious, so that they might see the things of New Spain. I would then send them back so that they might spread the news of how the natives are treated here and how they serve, and then do likewise themselves. Pizacura, however, fell ill and died, but the other two are well and I will send them back when there is an opportunity. With the capture of this Pizacura and of another youth who seemed to be the rightful ruler, together with the punishment inflicted on those other hundred or so people who were enslaved, the whole province was made secure, and when I left there all the villages were inhabited and very peaceful, having been distributed among the Spaniards, whom they appeared to serve willingly.

At this time there arrived in Trujillo a captain with some twenty men, some of whom had been among those I had left at Naco under Gonzalo de Sandoval, and some were from the company of Francisco Hernández,[104] the captain whom Pedro Arias de Ávila, Your Majesty's governor, had sent to the province of Nicaragua. From them I learnt how a captain of Francisco Hernández's had arrived in Naco with some forty men, both foot and horse; he had come to the bay of San Andrés to look for the bachiller Pedro

Moreno, whom the judges in Hispaniola had sent out to these parts, as I have related to Your Majesty, and who, it seemed, had written to Francisco Hernández, urging him to rebel against the governor's authority, just as he had done with the people left by Gil González and Francisco de las Casas. That captain had come, therefore, to speak to him on behalf of Francisco Hernández as how best to throw off his allegiance to the governor and grant it instead to those judges in Hispaniola, or so it appeared from certain letters which he carried on him.

I now sent them back, and with them sent letters to Francisco Hernández himself, and an open letter to all his people, and wrote individually to certain of the captains in his company whom I knew reproaching them for their evil doings and for having been deceived by that bachiller, and assuring them that Your Majesty would be little pleased with them, and other things which I thought might dissuade them from the mistaken course on which they were bent. One of the reasons they gave in support of their behavior was that they were so far distant from Pedro Arias de Ávila that it was costly, troublesome and sometimes even impossible for them to be provided with all they required; furthermore, they were always in need of equipment and provisions from Spain, and these could be more easily obtained through those ports which I had settled in Your Majesty's name. The bachiller Moreno had written to them saying that he had settled all that land on behalf of the judges and would soon return with many men and provisions. I wrote that I would order those towns to provide them with all they required and to trade and maintain friendly relations with them, since we were all of us Your Majesty's vassals and engaged in Your Royal service, but that my offer was made only on the condition of their remaining obedient to their governor, as they are bound to, and not otherwise. Because they said that what they most needed at present were shoes for their horses and tools for working in the mines, I sent them two of my mules loaded with these things. When they reached the settlement of Gonzalo de Sandoval he gave them another two mules, which I had there, likewise loaded with horse-shoes and tools.

After these had departed, certain natives from the province of Huilacho,[105] which lies sixty-five leagues from the town of Trujillo, who some time before had sent messengers offering themselves as Your Majesty's vassals, came to see me saying that twenty horsemen and forty foot soldiers, together with many Indian allies from other provinces, had come and were subjecting them to grave indignities and injuries, taking away their women and children and stealing their property. They begged me to put an end to these evils, for, when they had offered themselves as my friends, I had promised to uphold and defend them against whosoever might do them harm. Afterwards my cousin Hernando de Saavedra, whom I had left as lieutenant in those parts and who at that time was pacifying the province of Papayeca, sent me two of the men about whom the Indians had complained. They had been sent by their captain to find the town of Trujillo, for the Indians had told them it was close by and they might go without fear because all the land was at peace. From them I learnt that the people who had offended the Indians were of the same Francisco Hernández and that their captain was one Gabriel de Rojas. I then dispatched, together with these two men and the Indians who had come to complain, an alguacil with orders of mine for Gabriel de Rojas, telling him to leave the province at once and to return to the natives the women and children and other property he had taken from them; besides this, I also sent him a letter saying that if he needed anything to let me know, for I would willingly supply him as best I was able.

When he saw my letter and my command, he at once did as I bade him, and the natives of that province were most contented, although they returned later to tell me that after the departure of the alguacil they had again been robbed. With this captain I once again sent letters to Francisco Hernández, offering all that I had of which he and his people were in need; for I believed that Your Majesty would be served thereby, and bidding him remain loyal to his governor. I do not know what has happened since then, although I learnt from the alguacil whom I sent, and from those who went with him, that when they were together a letter from Francisco Hernández had arrived for Gabriel de Rojas, entreating him to return with all possible haste, as there was great discord among his men, and that two of his captains, one of whom was called Soto and the other Andrés Garabito, had rebelled because they said they knew that he intended to throw off his allegiance to his governor. Thus affairs remained in such a manner that only harm could follow to both the Spaniards and the natives. Your Majesty may judge how much harm results from these commotions, and how necessary it is to punish those who are the cause of them.

I wished to go myself to Nicaragua, believing that I might be able to find some remedy for these evils, which indeed would be a great service to Your Majesty. I was making preparations for the journey, and even opening a road through some high mountains I had to pass, when there arrived in the port of the town of Trujillo the ship which I had sent to New Spain, and in her a cousin of mine, called Diego Altamirano,[106] a friar of the Order of St. Francis, from whom I learnt, by the letters he brought me, of the many disturbances, quarrels and feuds which had broken out amongst Your Majesty's officials whom I had left there in my place, and of the urgent need for me to go there in person and resolve them. I therefore abandoned my journey to Nicaragua and my return by way of the south coast, which I am certain would have greatly served both God and Your Majesty, owing to the many large provinces that are on the way; for although some of them are at peace, they would have been more confirmed in Your Majesty's service by my having passed through them, especially those of Utlatan and Guatemala, where Pedro de Alvarado has always resided, which, after having rebelled on account of certain ill treatment they received, have never again been pacified. On the contrary, they have done, and continue to do, much harm to the Spaniards and to our Indian allies who live thereabouts, for the country is very difficult and thickly populated; and the people are very fierce and brave in war, devising all kinds of methods of attack and defense, digging pits and using other devices to kill the horses which have had much success.

Although Pedro de Alvarado makes constant war against them with more than two hundred horsemen, five hundred foot soldiers and more than five thousand, and at times as many as ten thousand, of our Indian allies, he has been unable to subject them to Your Majesty's service; rather each day they grow stronger through the people who come to join them. I believe, however, that if I were to go that way I might, if God so willed it, win them over by kindness or some other such means, for some of the provinces rebelled because of the bad treatment they received in my absence, and a hundred or so horsemen and three hundred foot soldiers, commanded by the veedor who governed at that time, were sent against them together with many pieces of artillery and a great number of our Indian allies; but they repulsed them and killed ten or twelve Spaniards and many Indians and the situation remained unchanged. But when I arrived I needed only to send them a messenger announcing my arrival, and all the principal chieftains of the province, which is called Coatlan, came to me and explained the cause of their rebellion, which was most justified, for the Spaniard to whom they had been entrusted had burnt eight principal lords, five of whom died immediately, and the others a few days later; and although they had demanded justice, it had not been given them. I then consoled them so that they were contented and are now peaceful and serve as they did before I left, their being now no danger of further wars. I believe that the rebellious villages in the province of Coazacoalco likewise became peaceful in a similar way when they heard the news of my arrival, without my having to send a messenger to them.

Most Catholic Lord, I have already written to Your Majesty concerning certain small islands, called Los Guanajos, that lie at the entrance to the bay of Las Honduras, some of which are now deserted on account of the many expeditions sent there from the Islands to take the natives as slaves. Some of them, however, still have a few inhabitants, and I learnt that another expedition was being fitted out in Cuba and Jamaica to complete this devastation. To prevent this calamity I sent a caravel to search among the Islands for the fleet and to require it on Your Majesty's behalf neither to land nor in any way to harm the natives; for I thought to pacify them and bring them to Your Majesty's service, because I had learnt something of them from those who had come to live on the mainland. At an island called Huitila,[107] this caravel came upon one from the expedition and brought the captain, one Rodrigo de Merlo, and all the natives he had captured in those islands to me. I ordered the natives to be returned to their homes but took no action against the captain, because he showed me a license he had given him by the governor of Cuba, a right which had been conceded to him by the judges who reside in Hispaniola. I, therefore, dismissed him with no other punishment than that of freeing the Indians he had captured, but he and his people all settled in those towns I had founded on the coast because they thought the land was good.

When the lords of those islands knew of the favor which I had done them and heard from those of the mainland of how well I treated them, they came to thank me for my kindness and to offer themselves as Your Majesty's vassals, asking me to command them how they might serve. I commanded them, in Your Majesty's name, to cultivate their fields for the present, for truly they can serve in no other way. Thus they departed, and they carried to each island a written command of mine to be shown to any Spaniard who might come that way; this I assured them in Your Majesty's name would protect them from all harm. They also asked me to send a Spaniard to each island with them and, although, because I was on the point of leaving, I could not attend to it myself, I left orders for the lieutenant Hernando de Saavedra to do so in my stead.

I then boarded the ship which had brought me the news of the situation in New Spain, taking in her and in two others which were there only some twenty people of my company, together with our horses, because the rest of them had decided to settle in those towns along the coast and the others were waiting for me on the road, thinking that I intended to travel overland. To these I sent orders to continue their journey and informed them of my departure and the reason for it. They have not arrived yet, but I have news that they are coming.

Having thus arranged all matters concerning those towns which I founded in Your Majesty's name, although much grieved that I was unable to leave them in the condition I hoped, and that was proper, I set sail on the twenty-fifth day of April, 1526, with those three ships, and the weather was so favorable that within four days I found myself 150 leagues from the port of Chalchicueca, but there I encountered a wind so strong that I could proceed no farther. Thinking that it would soon abate, I remained at sea for one day and night, but the weather was so bad that the ships were beginning to break up and I was forced to make for the island of Cuba. Six days later I put into the port of Havana, where I landed and was welcomed by the inhabitants, for there were among them many who had been my friends when I lived there. Because my ships had been badly damaged at sea, it was necessary to repair them, which delayed me there ten days, and to hasten my return I even purchased another ship which was being careened there, and left mine behind because she was leaking badly.

The day after my arrival in Havana a ship from New Spain entered that port, and on the second day another, and on the third day yet another. From these I learnt how all the land was at peace and most tranquil and secure now that the factor and veedor were dead, although there had been some disturbances for which those responsible had been punished. This cheered me greatly, for I had feared some unrest during the delay in my arrival, which I greatly regretted.

From there I wrote, though briefly, to Your Majesty, and departed on the sixteenth of May, taking with me some thirty natives of this land who had stowed away in those ships. A week later

I reached the port of Chalchicueca but was unable to enter because of a change of wind and stood two leagues out to sea. When it was almost dark I landed in the boat from my ship and a brigantine we found abandoned and proceeded on foot to the town of Medellín, four leagues from where I had disembarked; and without being observed by anyone in the town I went to the church to give thanks to Our Lord. I was soon discovered, however, and the people greeted me and I them. That same night I sent messengers to this city as well as to all the other towns in the land advising them of my return and providing for certain things which I considered necessary for the service of Your Holy Majesty and the good of the land.[108] I remained eleven days in that town to recover from the hardships of the journey, during which time I was visited by the chiefs of many towns and other natives of these parts who showed great joy at my return. From there I set out for this city and was a fortnight on the road, and at every point of the journey I was welcomed by many natives, some of whom had come from more than eighty leagues away, for, as they were expecting me, they had placed their couriers on the road to inform them of my arrival. So within a short while large numbers of them had come from many places far and wide to see me, and they all wept and recounted in such vivid and pitiful words the sufferings they had endured in my absence through the ill treatment they had received that they broke the hearts of all who heard them. And although it would be difficult to give Your Majesty an account of all the things they said, I might describe a few which are worthy of note but will leave them to be told *de ore proprio.*

When I arrived in this city the Spaniards and the natives had gathered there from every region of the land, and they welcomed me with such rejoicing as if I had been their own father. Your Majesty's treasurer and contador rode out to meet me with a large force of horsemen and foot soldiers, all in fine array and all showing the same welcome as the others. I then went directly to the monastery of St. Francis to give thanks to Our Lord for having saved me from so many dangers and hardships and brought me to such peace and rest, and for having allowed me to see the land which was once so torn by civil strife now living quietly in harmony.

I remained six days with the friars giving account of my sins to God, and two days before I departed there arrived a messenger from Medellín who informed me of how certain ships had arrived in the port and how in one of them there was said to be a judge of inquiry[109] sent by Your Majesty. Nothing further was known, but I thought that it must be that Your Catholic Majesty, hearing of the civil disturbances into which Your Highness's officials had plunged the land that I had left in their charge and not being certain of my return, had ordered an inquiry into the situation. God knows how glad I was of this, for it would have greatly distressed me to be judge of this matter because as I had been injured and robbed by these tyrants it seemed to me that any decision I might make would be attributed by malicious people to personal revenge, which is the thing I abhor above all others; although to judge by their deeds, I could never have been so harsh that it would not have been less than they deserved. When I received this news I sent a messenger with all haste to the port to learn for certain, and I sent orders to the lieutenant and justices of that town of Medellín that no matter for what reason that judge came, coming as he did from Your Majesty, he was to be well received and attended, and lodged in a house that I have there, where I ordered that he and all his people were to be given every service they required; although, as it afterwards appeared, he refused to accept anything.

The day following the departure of my messenger, which was the feast of St. John, another messenger arrived while I was engaged in celebrations consisting of bullfights, jousting with wooden lances and other sports, bringing me a letter from the aforementioned judge and another from Your Sacred Majesty which informed of why he had come and how Your Sacred Majesty had ordered an inquiry into the manner in which I have governed this country since I have been here; and truly I was much pleased by the immense favor Your Sacred Majesty was bestowing on me in wishing to be informed of my services and errors, and also by the benevolence with which Your Highness informed me of Your Royal will to grant me favors. For both these I kiss a hundred thousand times the Royal feet of Your Catholic Majesty, and do pray that Our Lord may permit me to repay some small part of so singular a favor and that Your Catholic Majesty may recognize my desire to do so, for recognition alone could be no small payment, in my opinion.

In the letter which Luis Ponce, the judge of inquiry, himself wrote to me, he informed me that he was about to leave for this city, and because there are two principal roads leading to it and he did not say by which he would come, I sent servants of mine along both of them to attend and escort him. But the aforementioned Ponce de León was in such a haste that, although I had dispatched them as swiftly as possible, they met him when he was less than twenty leagues from the city; and although my messengers say that he received them with due courtesy he would accept no service from them. I was sorry at this, for they said he greatly needed their assistance on account of his hurried journey, but I was also glad, for it seemed to me that he had acted as a just man who wished to fulfill his office with total rectitude, and as he had come to inquire into my government did not wish to give rise to suspicion against himself in any way. He came within two leagues of the city and spent the night there. I had everything prepared to welcome him in the morning, but he sent word that I should not ride out to him, for he wished to remain there until after lunch; he asked me, however, to send him a chaplain to say Mass, which I did. But fearing that this might be—as indeed it was—a means of avoiding a public reception, I made preparations nonetheless. Even so, he rose so early that, although I made all haste, he was already inside the city when I met him. We then went to the monastery of St. Francis and heard Mass, after which I told him that, if he wished, he might present his credentials there, for all the members of the municipal council were there with me, and also Your Majesty's treasurer and contador. But he declined, saying he would present them the following day.

Thus it was that on the following morning we all gathered in the principal church of the city, the town council also being present together with the aforementioned officials and myself; and when he presented his credentials to us we took and kissed them and held them over our heads as letters from our king and rightful lord, which we swore to obey and comply with in all particulars as Your Sacred Majesty had by them commanded us. All the municipal officials handed him their rods of office, and all the other ceremonies were duly performed as Your Catholic Majesty will see from the account made by the notary of the municipal council in whose presence all was done. My residencia was then publicly proclaimed [110] in the main square of this city, but in the seventeen days I was there I was not asked a single question. During this time the aforementioned Luis Ponce, the judge of inquiry, was taken ill together with all those who had come with him, and it was Our Lord's will that he and some thirty of his companions should die of this sickness among whom were two friars of the order of St. Dominic; and even now many people are still sick and in grave danger of death, for it seems to have been some kind of plague which they brought with them.[111] Some of the people here have caught it too, and two of them died of it, while many have not yet recovered.

Immediately after Luis Ponce had passed from this life and was buried with all the honor and solemnity due to a person sent by Your Majesty, the municipal council of this city and the representatives of all the towns who had gathered here asked and requested me on Your Catholic Majesty's behalf again to take charge of the government and administration of justice which had previously been granted to me by Your Majesty's command and by Your Royal provisions, giving me their reasons for it and showing me what evils would result if I refused, as Your Holy Majesty may see from the copy which I have sent. I sought to excuse myself, as likewise appears in the aforementioned copy, but again they requested it of me several times, showing me still greater evils which might ensue if I persisted in my refusal.[112] And I have firmly withstood their pleas until now, even though I can indeed see that some evil will come of it. But I wish Your Majesty to be certain of my honesty and fidelity in Your Royal service, for this I hold above all else and without Your trust in me all the goods of this world are of no value to me and I would not live. I have therefore put aside everything else to this end, and have maintained with all my powers in the office one Marcos de Aguilar, whom the aforementioned Luis Ponce had as his alcalde mayor, and I have asked and requested him to proceed with the inquiry into my administration; but this he has refused to do, saying that he does not have the authority. This has caused me considerable distress, for I desire nothing so much, and with good reason, as to see Your Holy Majesty truly informed of all my services and mistakes, because I most firmly believe that Your Caesarean Majesty will repay me with great and substantial favors, having regard not to the small extent of my capabilities but to the generosity with which Your Excellency is bound to reward him who serves so well and faithfully as I have done. I, therefore, do humbly beseech You with all the earnestness of which I am capable, not to allow this matter to remain in obscurity but to have the good and the bad of my services made public; for, as it is a matter of my honor, which I have sought through many hardships and by exposing my person to great dangers, I pray that neither God nor Your Majesty, out of reverence for Him, may permit the tongues of wicked, envious or malicious people to rob me of it. I ask of Your Sacred Majesty no other reward for my services; and may God grant that I shall not live without it.

Most Catholic Prince, it seems from what I have heard that from the time I first entered into this negotiation I have had many, various and powerful rivals and enemies; yet their malice and evil designs have never prevailed against the renown of my services and fidelity. Having now despaired of just success, they have contrived two schemes, by means of which it appears they have put a cloud of darkness before the eyes of Your Highness, whereby they have turned You aside from the Holy and Catholic purpose, for which Your Excellency is renowned, in rewarding and recompensing me for my services. One of their schemes is to accuse me before Your Highness on a charge of *crimine lesae majestatis*, of saying that I am not bound to obey Your Royal commands, and do not hold this land in Your Royal name, but in a tyrannous and unspeakable manner, giving in proof of their assertions depraved and diabolical statements which are entirely false. If these people were to look upon my actual achievements impartially, they would judge them quite differently; for until now there has not been, nor shall there ever be whilst I live, a single letter or command from Your Majesty which has not been, is not, or will not be obeyed and fulfilled in every detail. Now the iniquity of those who have said this will become manifest and clear; for if there were any truth in what they say, I would not have traveled six hundred leagues from this city, by dangerous roads and through uninhabited lands, leaving this country in the hands of Your Majesty's officials who were expected to be the persons most zealous in Your Majesty's service, although their deeds did not merit the trust I placed in them.

They also attack me by saying that I have kept the greater part of the natives of this land to myself as my slaves, and from them I have obtained a great quantity of gold and silver which I have stowed away; that I have spent unnecessarily more than seventy thousand *pesos de oro* from Your Catholic Majesty's revenue; and that I have not sent to Your Excellency all that is owed to the Royal revenue, keeping it under false pretenses, though what these can be, I cannot imagine. I believe that these people have given coloring to a current rumor, but it cannot, I am sure, be such that the first use of the touchstone will not show their metal to be false. As to their saying that I hold a large part of the land, I confess that it is true, and likewise it is true that I have received a large quantity of gold; but I maintain that it is not enough to prevent me from being poor and in debt for more than 500,000 *pesos de oro*, without pos-

sessing a single *castellano* with which to pay it. For though I have
gained much, I have spent more, and not in purchasing estates or
other lands for myself, but in extending throughout these parts the
sovereignty and Royal patrimony of Your Highness, by conquering for Your Excellency many realms and dominions which were
won only at great risk to my person and after many hardships and
dangers. This they, with their poisoned tongues, can never conceal
or deny, for on examining my books they will find there more than
300,000 *pesos de oro* of my own which have been spent on these
conquests; once these were exhausted I spent sixty thousand *pesos
de oro* of Your Majesty's, not, however, on my own private expenses, for they never passed through my hands, but in paying on
my instructions for the costs of the conquest, and whether they
have been well spent or not may be judged from the results which
are plain for all to see.

As to what they say about my not sending the revenues to
Your Majesty, this is quite plainly the contrary to the truth, for in
the short while that I have been in this land, I believe more wealth
has been remitted to Your Majesty than from all the Islands and the
mainland which was discovered and settled more than thirty years
ago, at great expense to the Catholic Monarchs, your grandparents,
which has not been the case in this land. Not only have I sent to
Your Majesty all that is Yours by law but also some considerable
amount of my own and of those who have helped me, taking no
account of all that we have spent in Your Royal service. When I
sent my first account to Your Majesty with Alonso Hernández
Puerto Carrero and Francisco de Montejo, I did not merely send
the fifth which belonged to Your Majesty of what had been taken
up until then, but the whole amount that had been acquired, for it
seemed proper, as it was the first spoils of our conquest. The fifth
part which was Your Majesty's of all the gold that was captured in
the city while Mutezuma still lived, that is, what we had melted
down, amounted to some thirty thousand *castellanos*, and although
the jewelry had also to be divided up amongst us all, they and I,

most willingly, agreed that the whole should be sent to Your Majesty, and this amounted to more than 500,000 *pesos de oro*. All of this, however, was taken from us when we were driven from the city as a result of the rebellion caused by Narváez's arrival in this land which, though a punishment for my sins, was not due to my negligence.

When this city was later reconquered and subjected to Your Highness's Royal service, the same was done again: after the Royal fifth had been taken from the gold that was melted down, we agreed that all the jewelry pertaining to my companions and myself should be sent to Your Highness, and their worth was no less than that of those which we had captured the first time. With all haste and every care I dispatched them, together with three thousand *pesos* in gold bars, in the charge of Julián Alderete, who at that time was Your Majesty's treasurer; but they were seized by the French. Neither was I to blame for this, but rather those who failed to provide a fleet to escort the vessel from the Azores as they should have for such an important shipment.[113]

When I left this city for the gulf of Las Hibueras I likewise sent to Your Excellency sixty thousand *pesos de oro* with Diego de Ocampo and Francisco de Montejo, and if more was not sent then it was because it seemed to me, and also to the officials of Your Catholic Majesty, that by sending so much together at one time we were exceeding and contravening the orders laid down by Your Majesty concerning the shipment of gold from these parts. Knowing, however, Your Sacred Majesty's urgent needs, we dared to send such a sum, and with it I also sent to Your Highness, by Diego de Soto, a servant of mine, all that I owned, leaving me not a single *peso de oro*. This was in the form of a silver fieldpiece which cost me, with the metal and casting and other expenses, more than 35,000 *pesos de oro*; in addition there were certain ornaments of gold and precious stones which I sent not because of their value, although that was not insignificant to me, but because the French had taken the first ones I sent and I was grieved to think that Your Holy Majesty had not seen them. I therefore sent all I possessed, although that was trifling compared with the first consignments, so that a sample might be seen. Thus have I served Your Catholic Majesty with pure zeal and good intent, offering all I possess, and I cannot understand what reason there is to believe that I have held back anything which belongs to Your Highness. My officers have also informed me that during my absence they have sent certain quantities of gold, so that the shipments have continued to be sent whenever an opportunity has arisen.

Most Powerful Lord, I have also been told that Your Sacred Majesty has been informed that I have an income of two hundred millions from the provinces allotted to me; and because my desire is and has been none other than that Your Catholic Majesty should know for certain of my devotion in Your Royal service, and should be entirely certain that I have always told, and will always tell, the truth, I cannot better show it than by offering this great income to Your Majesty's service. There could be no better opportunity for me to persuade Your Majesty of the falsity of the suspicions which Your Majesty is so openly said to hold of me. I therefore beseech Your Majesty to accept all I possess in these kingdoms, leaving me, as a favor, only twenty millions; thus Your Majesty will receive a hundred and eighty millions, and I shall serve at Court, where I think no one will surpass me in my devotion, or overshadow my services to Your Majesty. And even in matters concerning this country, I shall be of great service to Your Majesty, for as an eyewitness I shall be able to advise Your Highness as to what must be done here to advance Your Royal service and prevent Your Majesty from being deceived by false reports. Moreover, I assure Your Holy Majesty that I shall render no less service by advising what action should be taken so that these parts may be preserved and the natives thereof brought to the knowledge of our Faith, and so that Your Majesty's substantial revenues may be increased rather than diminished, as has happened on the Islands and the mainland through bad government. If the Catholic Monarchs, parents and grandparents of Your Highness, had been advised by people zealous in Their service and not with their own personal interest at heart, as in fact all those who have informed Their Highnesses and Your Majesty of the things of these parts have had, what might not have been gained by their having been won and held up to now, even in spite of difficulties and obstacles which have reduced the opportunities for profit?

Two things make me desire that Your Holy Majesty should honor me by permitting me to serve in Your Royal presence. The most important is to convince Your Majesty, and indeed the whole world, of my loyalty and devotion in Your Royal service, for this is more dear to me than any other benefit that may be granted me in this life, because it is in order to gain the reputation of a servant of Your Majesty and of the Royal and Imperial Crown that I have exposed myself to such dangers and suffered such unprecedented hardships, and not through a thirst for riches; for had that been my motive, I indeed have had plenty for a poor squire like myself and would not have lavished such wealth to achieve my other ambition which I hold as the principal aim of my life. My sins, however, have kept me from it, and I do not believe I can really satisfy Your Majesty of my loyalty and devotion unless this so great favor is granted me. Lest Your Majesty think I ask too much, I say that I will consider it no small mercy if Your Majesty should grant me but ten millions in those realms, leaving all else I possess here, although it is barely enough for me to appear at Court without shame. As I have had charge of the government of these parts in Your Majesty's Royal name, and have so much increased the Royal dominion and patrimony and have placed beneath the Royal Yoke so many provinces with so many and such noble towns and cities, I have put an end to many idolatries and offenses against our Creator, bringing many of the natives to the knowledge of God and planting in these lands Our Holy Catholic Faith, so that if there is no intervention from those who think ill of such things and whose zeal is directed toward different ends, there will, in a very short time, arise in these parts a new Church, where God, Our Lord, may be better served and worshipped than in all the rest of the world.[114] I therefore entreat Your Majesty to satisfy my desire, which is to be admitted to the Royal presence where Your Highness will be very well served by me and convinced of my loyalty.

The other reason for my wishing to appear before Your Majesty is that I am most certain that I will be able to inform Your Catholic Majesty of everything concerning this land and the Islands, too, so that they may be provided for in a manner that will greatly advance the service of Our Lord God and Your Majesty. For there my words would be given greater credit than letters I write from here; since everything I say here will be attributed, as it has been before, to a desire for gain, and not to the zeal which, as Your Holy Majesty's vassal, I owe to Your Royal service. So great is my desire to kiss Your Majesty's Royal feet and to serve in Your Royal presence that I am unable to express it; but if Your Highness is not pleased to grant me this favor or finds it inopportune to maintain me in those kingdoms so that I may serve as I desire, I beg Your Highness to permit me to retain all that I now possess in this land or what my representatives will ask of Your Majesty in my name, granting it to me in perpetuity for myself and my heirs, so that I shall not arrive in Spain begging for alms. I shall consider it a most signal favor if Your Majesty would grant me permission to go and fulfill what I so fervently desire, for I know and trust in the Catholic conscience of Your Holy Majesty that once my services have been made manifest and the purity of the intention with which they were performed Your Majesty will not allow me to live in poverty. The arrival of this judge of inquiry seemed to me to offer a good opportunity for the achievement of my desire, and I even began to make preparations, but two things prevent me: the first was that I found myself without money for the journey because my house had been pillaged and property stolen, as I believe I have already informed Your Majesty; the second was the fear that during my absence there would be a rebellion or other disturbances among the natives, or even among the Spaniards, for to judge by what has happened in the past one can easily foresee the possibility.

Most Catholic Lord, while I was engaged in writing this dispatch a messenger came to me from the Southern Sea bearing a letter which informed me of how there had arrived on those shores, close to a village called Tecoantepeque, a ship, which it seemed, from another letter that he brought from the captain of the vessel and which I have sent to Your Majesty, belonged to the fleet that Your Sacred Majesty sent to the islands of Maluco under Captain Loaisa. Your Majesty will read in this captain's letter of the incidents of his journey; I, therefore, will give no account of them to Your Highness, save to inform Your Excellency of the provisions I made in this case. I at once dispatched a reliable person with all speed to the place where the aforementioned vessel had landed to provide the captain with everything he might require should he wish to return, and to learn from him all the details of his voyage so that I might send a very full and particular account to Your Highness by the shortest possible route. In case this ship was in need of repair, I also sent a pilot to bring her to the port of Zacatula, where I have three ships prepared to embark on a voyage of exploration along those coasts, so that she might be refitted for Your Majesty's service and the success of her voyage. As soon as I receive any information from this ship I will immediately forward it so that Your Majesty may be fully informed and command me as to what most benefits Your Royal service.[115]

My ships, as I have already informed Your Majesty, are ready to start on their voyage, for as soon as I arrived in this city I began to make preparations for their departure. They would have sailed already but that they were waiting for certain arms, artillery and ammunition which were being brought from Spain for their defense. And I pray to Our Lord that by this journey I shall render a great service to Your Majesty's good fortune, for even if no passage is found I hope to discover a route to the Spice Islands so that Your Majesty may be informed every year of what is done there. If

Your Majesty chooses to grant me the favors[116] which I asked for concerning that discovery, I will undertake to discover a route to the Spice Islands and many others, if there be any between Maluco, Malaca and China, and so arrange matters that the spices shall no longer be obtained by trade, as the king of Portugal has them now, but as Your Majesty's rightful property; and the natives of those islands shall serve and recognize Your Highness as their rightful king and lord.[117] For I pledge myself, if the aforementioned additions are made to me, to go in person or to send thither such a fleet as will subdue those islands, and to settle them with Spaniards and to build fortresses so well equipped with artillery and other means for their defense that no prince of those parts or any other will be able to invade them. If, therefore, it pleases Your Majesty that I should undertake this enterprise, concede me all that I have asked, because I believe that Your Highness will be rendered a great service thereby, and if this should prove not to be so, Your Majesty may punish me as one who does not tell his king the truth.

Since my return I have also ordered expeditions to be sent overland and by sea to settle by the river of Tabasco, which is also called Grijalba, and to conquer many provinces thereabouts which will be a great service both to Your Majesty and Our Lord God; and the ships which trade in these parts will derive much benefit by having this port settled with Spaniards and these coasts subdued, for many ships have run aground there and the natives, who are still unconquered, have killed their crews.

I am also sending to the province of the Zapotecas, of which Your Majesty has already been informed, three captains to invade it in three different directions, so as to conquer it as swiftly as possible. This will most certainly be very beneficial, not only because of the harm which the natives of that province do to others who have been pacified, but also because they occupy the richest mining lands to be found in New Spain, from which, once they have been conquered, Your Majesty will derive great profits.

I have likewise prepared an expedition (and gathered together a great many of the people for it) to found a colony along the river of Las Palmas, which is on the north coast below the Pánuco and in the direction of Florida, for I have been informed that it is a very rich land with a harbor, and I do not think Our Lord God and Your Majesty will be less served there than in all the other parts, because I have indeed received good news of that country.

Between the north coast and the province of Mychuacan there is a certain tribe called the Chichimeca.[118] They are a very barbarous people and not so intelligent as those of the other provinces. I am likewise now sending sixty horsemen and two hundred foot soldiers together with many of our native allies to investigate that province and its inhabitants. I have given my men instruction that if they discover in these people some aptitude or ability to live as the others do and to be instructed in the knowledge of Our Holy Faith and to recognize the service which they owe to Your Majesty, they are to make every effort to pacify them and bring them under Your Majesty's Yoke; they are also to settle among them in whichever place seems most convenient. If, however, they find that they are not as I have said above and refuse to be obedient, the Spaniards are to make war on them and reduce them to slavery; so that there may be no part remaining of all this land which does not serve and acknowledge Your Majesty. By making slaves of this barbarous people, who are almost savages, Your Majesty will be served and the Spaniards will benefit greatly, as they will work in the gold mines, and perhaps by living among us some of them may even be saved.

It is known that among these people there is a certain part where there are many towns, whose inhabitants live in the same manner as the people here. Some of these towns have even been visited by Spaniards, and I am certain that land will soon be settled, for we have heard that it is very rich in silver.

Most Powerful Lord, two months before I left this city for the gulf of Las Hibueras I sent a captain to the town of Colimán,[119] which is by the Southern Sea, 140 leagues from this city. I commanded him to proceed down the coast from that town for 150 or two hundred leagues for the sole purpose of exploring the coast, and also to discover if there were any harbors. This captain did as I commanded him, traveling some 130 leagues down the coast from Coliman and sometimes as many as twenty or thirty leagues inland and bringing me an account of many harbors which he found on the coast. This was of no small advantage because we have found few of them in all the lands we have discovered up until now. He also found many large towns and warlike tribes with whom he had several encounters and succeeded in pacifying some of them, but he was unable to proceed further because his men were few and he could find no pasture for the horses. In his account he brought news of a very large river which the natives had said was ten days' march from the place where he had halted, and of the people who dwelt along its banks they told him many strange and wonderful things. I am now sending him back with more people and arms so that he may explore that river, which, to judge by the reports of its width and great size, will most probably turn out to be a strait. As soon as he returns I will immediately send an account to Your Majesty of all that he knows of it.

All these above-mentioned captains are now about to start on their expeditions; may Our Lord be pleased to guide them as He sees fit. I can only say, for my part, that even though I fall still further from Your Majesty's favor, I shall not cease to give my services, for it is not possible that Your Majesty should fail to recognize my services in time; but, even should this happen, I will be content with doing my duty and knowing that all the world knows of my services and the loyalty with which I perform them, and I want no other inheritance for my children save this.[120]

Notes

(The spelling of words in Nahuatl generally follows that of Sahagún; such words have not been accented except when they appear so in quotation or are of post-conquest origin. The problems of stress and accent in classical Nahuatl are many and controversial. Generally, however, the stress is taken on the penultimate syllable of most words of more than one syllable. [See Bright, "Accent in Classical Aztec" and S. Newman, "Classical Nahuatl," p. 183, for an outline of the problem.] The spelling of modern place names is that used by the United States Board on Geographic Names.)

Notes to the First Letter

1. On the death of Christopher Columbus his son Diego succeeded to the hereditary title of Grand Admiral which had been granted to his father by Ferdinand and Isabel. In 1511 Don Diego appointed Diego Velázquez, former member of his uncle's household and one of the richest men in Hispaniola, to conquer Cuba. Velázquez, with Pánfilo de Narváez as his lieutenant and a force of some 330 men, soon overran the island. Only one chieftain seems to have offered any serious resistance to the Spaniards. When he was finally caught he was sentenced to be burned to death and according to Las Casas's version of the story (bk. III, chaps. 21–25) refused baptism for fear of having to spend eternity in the company of Spaniards.

2. Cozumel or Ah-cuzamil-peten, "The Swallow Island," was discovered by Grijalva (Grijalba) on the day of the feast of the Intervention of the Holy Cross and given the name Santa Cruz.

   The name Yucatán is probably derived from a Spanish corruption of *Ci uthan*, meaning "they say so": many place names in Central and South America have similar etymologies. The correct Mayan name for the peninsula was *uluumil cutz yetel ceh*, or "Land of Turkeys and Deer," per-

449

haps analogous with the Biblical "Land of Milk and Honey." It was also called Peten, which may mean either an island or a province. For a long time the Spaniards believed Yucatán to be an island and christened it Isla de Santa Maria de los Remedios, because Alaminos, after a hurried reconnaissance, assumed the Laguna de Terminos to be a strait separating the peninsula from the mainland. The first known map to show it as part of the mainland dates from as late as 1527 (Diego de Landa's *Relación de las Cosas de Yucatan*, pp. 4 ff.).

3. Santiago was at that time the capital of the island.

4. For an account of this ill-fated expedition see H. R. Wagner, *The Discovery of Yucatan by Francisco Hernández de Córdoba*, a translation of the relevant documents with an introduction and notes. See also the same writer's discussion of the available material in "The Discovery of Yucatan by Francisco Hernández de Córdoba."

5. Antón de Alaminos was Columbus's pilot on his last voyage in 1502. He sailed with Ponce de León (see the Third Letter, n. 68) to Florida and with Córdoba, Grijalva and Cortés to Yucatán.

6. Campoche, or Campeche, is here confused with Catoche, where they landed on May 5. Campeche lies farther to the west on the bay of the same name. Its Mayan name is supposed to have been Kimpech or Kinpech, but this word appears nowhere in any extant document. The name Catoche, or Catoch, is given various etymologies. Jean Genet in his edition of Landa suggests that the Spaniards turned *ecab c'otoch*, meaning "these are our houses," into El Cabo de Catoch, Cape Catoch. (See also Bernal Díaz, chap. 2.) Crosses were found in Catoche which gave rise to a belief that St. Thomas had reached America before the Spaniards. Bernal Díaz (chap. 3) speaks of crosses in Campeche, and Torquemada (bk. XV, chap. 49), Oviedo (bk. XVII, chap. 7) and Gómara (p. 305) all mention crosses, although Oviedo denies that they had any connection with Christianity (see also the Second Letter, n. 41). Crosses seem to have been associated with the gods of rain, and after the arrival of the Spaniards sacrificial victims to these gods were in some cases crucified before having their hearts removed (Landa, *op. cit.*, p. 116).

7. The town was called Champoton and the chieftain Machocobon. Champoton is variously called Chanpoton, Potonchan (there was also a town on the Tabasco River with this name) and *Chakan Putun*, "the savannah of the Putuns." Machocobon is written Mochkonoli and Mochcouoh by Landa. Tozzer believes it to be the Yucatán patronymic *Couol*, giving *Moch* or *Mochan Couoh* (Landa, *op. cit.*, p. 11).

8. In 1516 Cardinal Jiménez de Cisneros, under pressure from Las Casas and other ecclesiastical reformers, sent three Hieronymite Fathers, Luis de

Figueroa, Bernardino de Manzanedo and Alonso de Santo Domingo, to carry out a full investigation of the Indian problem. Under Las Casas's direction they were to attempt to implement a plan for a cessation of the *encomienda* system (see n. 40) and the redistribution of the Indians; they were also instructed to investigate the possibility of Indian self-government. Should this fail, Cisneros added an afterword to his instructions outlining an alternative which was in effect a complete reversal of Las Casas's scheme: certain changes would be made to the existing regulations (The Laws of Burgos) in an attempt to ameliorate the lot of the Indians without angering the colonists. The Hieronymites were, it seems, practically royal governors, although Las Casas—who soon fell out with them—denies this, for Alonso de Zuazo, the *juez de residencia* who accompanied them, was ordered to consult with them on everything (L. B. Simpson, *The Encomienda in New Spain*. Appendix I of this book is an English translation of Cisneros's instructions and Giménez Fernández, *Bartolomé de Las Casas*, I: 149–218).

9. The *Siete Partidas* of Alfonso X, the great thirteenth-century law codes of Castile, grant to the king a fifth of all captured spoils. The captain was to be given a seventh if he were a "natural lord" (*Señor por naturaleza de linaje*) but otherwise a tenth (pt. II, tit. 24, ley 4). Cortés, however, agreed with his men to take a fifth (Bernal Díaz, chap. 105). This was considered to be an infringement on the rights of the Crown and charged against Cortés in his *residencia*.

10. Gonzalo de Guzmán was a royal treasurer.

11. Grijalva's expedition consisted of four caravels. The three other captains were Francisco de Montejo, Pedro de Alvarado and Alonso de Ávila. They set sail on May 1, 1517. (See Oviedo, bk. XVII, chap. 8; and Juan Díaz, Grijalva's chaplain, *Itinerario de larmata del Re Catholico verso la Isola di Iuchathan del Anno M.D. XVIII*, an Italian translation of a Spanish original now lost, in *CDHM*, vol. I. Translated by Patricia de Fuentes in *The Conquistadors*, New York, 1963, pp. 5–16.) Bernal Díaz (chap. 8) gives April 8. Grijalva came from the same town (Cuéllar) as Velázquez, and according to Gómara was his nephew, although Las Casas, who seems to have known Grijalva well, makes no mention of this (see bk. III, chap. 98).

12. The Spaniards found a stone temple which Juan Díaz says consisted of two towers: a large solid base 180 feet round and eighteen steps high surmounted by a turret the size of two men. Cozumel was a traditional place of pilgrimage, and this temple housed a famous idol which was reputed to answer the questions put to it. Herrera (dec. IV, bk. 10, chap. IV) and Gómara (p. 305) say that it was hollow, allowing a priest to conceal himself inside it.

13. They arrived on Thursday, the thirteenth, the feast of the Ascension.

14. Vicente Yáñez Pinzón was one of the three Pinzón brothers who sailed with Columbus's first expedition in 1492. Punta de las Veras was discovered in January, 1500.

15. Two Indians had been captured on the previous expedition. They were christened Julian and Melchior and served the Spaniards as interpreters.

16. Tabasco.

17. Pedro de Alvarado (see the Second Letter, n. 78) was in command. A list of his cargo is provided by Gómara (pp. 298–299), who estimates its value at between fifteen thousand and twenty thousand *pesos de oro*. Grijalva's refusal to settle seems to have caused some dissatisfaction amongst his troops. Cervantes de Salazar (bk. II, chap. 10), while suggesting that Grijalva was looking to his own ends by returning to Cuba, intimates that he was expecting the ship sent by Velázquez under Cristóbal de Olid to bring not only reinforcements but also the governor's permission to settle.

18. The *maravedí* was the basic unit of Spanish currency at this time: 450 *maravedís* of gold and silver, equivalent to 42.29 grams of pure silver, made a *castellano* or *peso de oro*. This was divided into eight *reales* (or *tomines*), eleven of which made a *ducado* or ducat. The ducat, modeled on the Venetian coin, was also called an *excelente de Granada*. It was 23¾ carats fine and was tariffed at 375 *maravedís*. In 1537 the *escudo* (22 carats fine and tariffed at 350 *maravedís*) was substituted for the ducat, though the latter continued to be used as a unit of account. In 1548 an increased vellon circulation was authorized, and in 1552 the silver content of the vellon was reduced from 7 to 5½ grains fine. In the 1520s copper began to be added to the *peso de oro* in America, producing the *oro de tepuzque*. This was done in an attempt to combat the inflated prices charged by Spanish merchants. Ultimately, the coin's value dropped to 272 *maravedís* (John Lynch, *Spain under the Hapsburgs*, appendix I. Felipe Mateu y Llopes, *La moneda española*, pp. 231–274).

An *arroba* is equivalent to approximately 14.76 liters, but this may vary regionally and according to the liquid.

19. Cortés's Christian name is commonly spelled Hernán today, but Fernando and Hernando were the forms most used during his lifetime.

20. Gómara (p. 300) says that Velázquez asked Cortés to help him equip the fleet because he had "two thousand *castellanos* in company with Andrés de Duero." Las Casas (bk. III, chap. 114) pours scorn on this idea, pointing out that two thousand *pesos* would not have gone very far, and in any case were nothing to a man who had spent twenty thousand and more on the expedition. Cortés may have borrowed an additional sum, but it seems likely that, apart from Cortés and Velázquez, several other wealthy settlers

were involved and contributed to the cost of the fleet. Velázquez's agent, Benito Martín, claimed that seven ships were provided and equipped by his master; the remaining four were probably those provided by Cortés and his partners. (Martín's statement is in Alamán, *Disertaciones*, vol. I, appendix II, p. 27.)

21. The Spanish is *procurador*. He had no special powers except those of representation, and the word is generally used by Cortés simply to mean an agent or deputy.

22. This caravel belonged to Valdivia, who, in 1511, had been sent to Santo Domingo to inform the governor of the quarrel between Balboa and Nicuesa. The ship was wrecked on some islands called Las Vivoras. Those who escaped the wreck were caught on landing and later sacrificed; only two, Gerónimo de Aguilar and Gonzalo Guerrero escaped. They fled into the interior where they were recaptured but allowed to live. Guerrero became an Indian to all intents and purposes, and according to Bernal Díaz (chap. 27) rose to a position of tribal importance. He was even rumored to have urged the Indians to resist the Spaniards. Cervantes de Salazar gives the most full, but also possibly the most fanciful, account of the wreck (bk. II, chaps. 25–29), an English translation of which is given in appendix D of Landa.

23. The brigantine and the *batel* (a small open boat) were under the command of Diego de Ordaz. The text of Cortés's letter is given by Bernal Díaz (chap. 27). Herrera and Landa both give their own versions, and Cervantes de Salazar (bk. 11, chap. 25) says that there were two letters. The second "in a round hand" was sent by the captains who feared that Aguilar might no longer be able to read easily.

24. Aguilar, who was in orders, had been enslaved in an Indian village some two days' journey from the coast, according to Cervantes de Salazar (bk. II, chap. 28). His resistance to the temptations offered him by his captors won him a certain respect which helped to keep him alive. He spoke Chontal Maya and was to prove invaluable to Cortés as an interpreter.

25. Guerrero, the only other survivor of the wreck, is said by Bernal Díaz (chap. 27) to have lived five leagues from Aguilar, who went to see him. But he is wrong, for Landa says that he lived at Chetumal, more than eighty leagues away, and Cervantes de Salazar confirms this (bk. II, chap. 27). Guerrero was finally shot dead by a harquebus (Landa, p. 8, n. 36).

26. Potonchan; it was renamed Santa Maria de la Victoria by the Spaniards, but it is more often referred to by its original name.

27. Diego de Godoy. The document he was witnessing was the *requerimiento*. In 1513 King Ferdinand ordered a committee of theologians to meet

in the Dominican monastery of San Pablo at Valladolid, with the aim of examining the Spanish claims in America and of establishing the legal status of the American Indian. Before this committee the lawyer Martín Fernández de Enciso read a memorial expounding the thesis that the Indies had, by the papal donation of 1493, been given to Spain as incontestably as the promised land of Canaan had been given to the Jews; the Spaniards, therefore, would commit no sin by treating the Indians as Joshua had treated the people of Jericho. Enciso's interpretation of the Book of Joshua was highly dubious and his analogy hardly justified, for, as Las Casas later pointed out, there was no need to evoke the harsh laws of Moses when Christ had taught otherwise. Nonetheless, the theologians of San Pablo accepted his theories after some debate, with the proviso that any Indian who willingly made over his land to the Crown might continue to live there as a vassal. Ferdinand accepted this ruling but ordered that a formal proclamation should be drawn up and a copy given to every conquistador. It is almost certain that Palacios Rubios, one of the greatest of Spanish jurists, was the author of this proclamation, the *requerimiento* or requirement, which was to be read, with or without interpreters, to the Indians before any attack might legally be made on them. It begins with a brief history of the world since the creation, and then proceeds to describe the establishment of the papacy and the donation of America to Spain by Alexander VI. The middle section, which gives the document its name, requires the Indians to recognize the sovereignty of the Catholic Church, and in its place the secular authority of the Spanish Crown. The other demand is that they permit the faith to be preached to them. This is then followed by a description of what will befall them if they fail to comply with these requests. The Spaniards will enter their lands by force and will make slaves of their wives and children. In addition to this, "We [the Spaniards] will do all the harm and damage that we can, as to vassals who do not obey and refuse to receive their lord and resist and contradict him; and we protest that the deaths and losses which shall accrue from this are your fault and not that of Their Highnesses nor ours, nor of the knights who come with us." When the *requerimiento* had been read it was witnessed by a notary; the way was now morally clear for the attack. This document received a mixed reception. Las Casas said he did not know whether to weep or to laugh. But it seems to have been taken seriously enough by Crown officials (the fact that he had not read it at Cholula was charged against Cortés in his *residencia*) if not by the conquistadors themselves. Las Casas spoke contemptuously of it being "read to the trees," in many cases no less than the truth, and Oviedo describes an attempt to have it read to a deserted village. (Lewis Hanke has collected instances of such readings in "A aplicaçao do requerimiento na America Espanhola.") On one occasion Oviedo confronted Palacios Rubios himself, asking if such readings were sufficient to satisfy a man's conscience. He replied that they were if carried out in the correct manner. (Lewis Hanke, *The Spanish Struggle for Justice in the Conquest of America*, pp. 31–36. See also the same writer's "The Requerimiento and its Interpreters." The Spanish text of the *requerimiento* may be found in *DIU*, 20:311–314. An English translation is given in Charles Gibson, *The Spanish Tradition in America*, pp. 58–60.)

28. The battle of Cintla, as it was called, took place on March 25. Bernal Díaz (chap. 33) says that there were thirteen horsemen and lists their names. Cortés always underestimates the number of the dead and wounded; according to Cervantes de Salazar (bk. II, chap. 33) sixty men were wounded on this occasion.

29. Gómara (p. 309) says that St. James, the patron saint of Spain, and St. Peter, Cortés's own patron, appeared on the battlefield. Bernal Díaz (chap. 34) says that he, poor sinner, failed to see them, adding, however, that what he did see was "Francisco de Morla on a chestnut horse riding beside Cortés." (An interesting discussion of this vision and a comparison between the versions of Bernal Díaz and Gómara is given by Robert Moorman Denhardt in "The equine strategy of Cortés.") Cervantes de Salazar (bk. II, chap. 33) tells a fanciful story of an unknown horseman who swept the Indians before him. He and Gómara are drawing on an old tradition. St. James (Santiago) is first described as a warrior in the *Historia Silense* (p. 76). He made his most famous appearance mounted on a white charger at the mythical battle of Clavijo. He is often depicted as the Moor-Slayer (Matamoros) on the tympana of Spanish churches, and his name gave rise to the famous battle cry "¡Santiago y cierra España!" generally shortened to "¡Señor Santiago!" or simply "¡Santiago!"

30. According to Bernal Díaz (chap. 38), the fleet dropped anchor at San Juan de Ulúa on Holy Thursday (April 21) and disembarked the following day. One of the two chieftains (*principales*) mentioned by Cortés was the person called Tendile by Bernal Díaz, the name by which he is now most commonly known. Sahagún (bk. XII, chap. 2, p. 5), however, calls him Tentlil and mentions four other chieftains. Pinotl, "high steward" (*calpixqui*) of Cuetlaxtlan; Yaotzin, high steward of Mictlanquahtla; Teociniacatl, steward of Teociniocan; and Cuitlalpitoc, called "a servant of one of these *calpisques*" in the Spanish text and "only a servant" (*çan tetlan nenqui*) in the Nahuatl. Tentlil is referred to as a *cacique;* this word, which acquired a more specific meaning in colonial times, is used frequently by the chroniclers, though less often by Cortés, who first brought it from the Antilles. It is of Arawak origin and was, of course, unknown to the mainland Amerindian. According to Ixtlilxóchitl (I: 339), Tentlil was Motecuçoma's governor of Cotozta (Cotaxtla) or Cuetlachtlan.

31. It is uncertain how many ships there were in this fleet and how many men sailed in them. Gómara (p. 301) puts the number of men at 550, fifty of whom were sailors. Bernal Díaz (chap. 26) says that there were 508 soldiers and one hundred sailors. He also mentions eleven ships and one brigantine. According to Peter Martyr (*De Orbe Novo*, fol. LIX r., *trans.* II: 26), there were five hundred soldiers, ten caravels and three brigantines. Whatever the exact figure may have been, it was certainly something more than that given by Cortés.

32. There is some doubt as to where the municipal council of Vera Cruz first came into being. Bernal Díaz (chap. 42) says, "Then we decided to build, found and settle in a town which we called La Villa Rica de La Vera Cruz because we arrived on the Thursday of the Last Supper and went ashore on Good Friday." This refers to San Juan de Ulúa, but later, in chap. 48, he says that they decided to found the town on some plains half a league from a village called Quiauiztlan. It seems probable that Cortés threw over Velázquez's authority at San Juan de Ulúa and then searched for a suitable place to build a town. Gómara (p. 21) says that he "called it La Villarica de la Vera Cruz as he had decided when in San Juan de Ulúa he appointed the town council" (see also Torquemada, bk. IV, chap. 23).

33. Velázquez's instructions may be found in *Cedulario*, pp. 9–33.

34. There are no lions or tigers in Mexico, but the Spaniards no doubt had only vague ideas of what they looked like anyway, and easily confused them with pumas and jaguars. The mountains are those of the Sierra Madre: the highest peak is the Citlaltepetl, or Orizaba volcano, at 18,700 feet.

35. These were disks of obsidian, a hard volcanic rock with a vitreous sheen, put to many uses by the Amerindians. This type of ornament was commonly referred to as "the mirror of the Incas." The people described here are the Totonaque (Totonaca). They were a nomadic tribe from the north who, according to Torquemada (bk. III, chap. 18), originated from a place called Chicomoztoc ("Seven Caves"), together with the Xalpenaca, who belonged to the same ethnic group. The Totonaque spent some time in Teotihuacan and claimed to have built the great temples of the Sun and Moon. They finally settled in what is now the state of Veracruz, developing a high level of urban culture, but were overrun by the Mexica in the mid-fourteenth century.

Sahagún describes the Totonaque as being "quite elegant."

"The men clothed themselves; they wore capes, breech clouts, sandals, arm-bands, necklaces, quetzal feather devices; they bore fans; they had trinkets. They cut their hair, arranged their hair-dress well, looked at themselves in mirrors. The women wore skirts, embroidered shifts."

They spoke a "barbarous tongue," though Nahuatl seems to have been widely used and also Otomi. (Sahagún, bk. X, chap. 29, pp. 184–185. See also *Huastecos, Totonacos y sus Vecinos,* Ignacio Bernal and Hurtado Dávalos, eds.)

36. Thus in Alcalá. Gayangos (p. 23) reads *potuyuca,* which is certainly what appears in the Vienna Codex. *Yuca* is the Adam's-needle, a farinaceous plant eaten like a potato. I do not know if bread was made from it in the Antilles, but it was evidently not used for that purpose by the Totonague. Sahagún says that the maize cake, the *tortilla,* was a Totonac specialty. It was cooked on a pottery griddle and dipped in chili.

37. Human sacrifice originated among the Mexica, but by the time the Spaniards arrived it had become a common practice throughout Mesoamerica. The Codex Telleriano-Remensis states that the first sacrificial victims were the *Tzinacantepeca* who rebelled against Mexico in 1483: previously only birds and small animals had been sacrificed. Methods varied, but the most common was the plucking out of the victim's heart as mentioned here. The victim was first dressed in the attributes of the god to whom he was to be dedicated. He was then led, or dragged by the hair if he proved unwilling, to the top of the *teucalli,* or temple, whereupon he was seized by five priests and stretched over the *techcatl,* an oblong block of stone about two and a half feet high by one and a half feet wide. Two priests held him down by his arms and two by his legs while the fifth forced back his head with a wooden yoke that choked off his screams. The officiating priest plunged a stone knife, generally made of obsidian, upwards and behind the sternum. The heart was then plucked out and placed in a wooden dish called the *cuauhxicalli,* or "eagle dish," the idea being originally that as the eagle is nourished by the tuna fruit so the sun is nourished by the human heart, which thus received the name *cuauhnochtli,* or "eagles' food." The body was thrown down the temple steps, then flayed and cut up: the skull went to the skull rack, the thigh to the emperor and the remainder was eaten with great solemnity by the victim's captor (*Codex Mendoza,* 1: 17, 38). Other methods were decapitation and a ceremonial combat between a warrior armed with a *macuahuitl,* a club set with obsidian blades (see the Second Letter, n. 15) and his victim, who was tied to a broad flat stone and given a *macuahuitl* set only with feathers. Landa describes a sacrifice in which the victim was bound to a wooden frame and shot full of arrows, but according to Herrera (dec. IV, bk. X, chap. 4), this was reserved for those guilty of serious crimes. Among the Mexica, children were sacrificed to the *Tlaloque,* the rain gods who were local rather than national. The victims were purchased from their parents, who if they refused were themselves sacrificed for insubordination (see George C. Vaillant, "Human sacrifice in ancient Mexico").

38. There is little evidence to support this accusation. Bernal Díaz (chap. 3), records finding obscene images at Cozumel. Oviedo (bk. V, chap. 3) speaks of homosexual slaves in Panama and in Yucatan (bk. XVII, chap. 17) and Torquemada (bk. XII, chap. 11), mentions instances of homosexuality in Guatemala. It seems, however, to have been severely punished in most areas. The lord of the Xius was said to have thrown all offenders into a furnace (Landa, p. 124, n. 576).

39. The conspirators had intended to steal a ship and return to Cuba so that Velázquez might be warned in time to prevent Puertocarrero and Montejo from reaching Spain. Bernardino de Coria revealed the plot to Cortés, who promptly hung two of the conspirators, Juan Escudero and Diego Cermeño (Bernal Díaz calls them Pedro and Juan) and cut the feet off a third, the pilot Gonzalo de Umbría [Ungría]. Two sailors were flogged, but Juan Díaz, who had been Grijalva's chaplain, was in orders and could not be touched. This is Díaz's version (chap. 57) but the others differ only slightly (see Torquemada, bk. IV, chap. 25; Cervantes de Salazar, bk. 111, chap. 21; and Oviedo, bk. XXXIII, chap. 2).

40. Diego Velázquez was responsible for distributing the Indians to the settlers to be held in *encomienda*. This system of enforced labor first came into being as a means to evade the laws against slavery. It was essentially a compromise by the Crown, which was torn between its Christian conscience on the one hand and economic pressures on the other. The *encomienda* consisted of a group of villages *encomendados*, or entrusted, to individual Spaniards who undertook the obligations of military service, cared for the welfare and religious tutelage of their charges and maintained the local clergy. Villages not assigned to an *encomendero* were made over to the Crown. In the early days of Spanish colonialism the terms *encomienda* and *repartimiento* were used synonymously; later, however, when the *encomenderos* were forbidden to exact labor from their Indians, the *repartimiento* came into force as a distinct system whereby every village supplied to the settlers a certain number of laborers each week. They worked for a fixed wage and were supervised by a magistrate especially appointed for the task (see L. B. Simpson, *op. cit.*, and F. A. Kirkpatrick, "Repartimiento-Encomienda").

41. There are two extant copies of this list. The one I have translated is from the Vienna Codex. The other, entitled *Manuel del Tesorero*, is in the Archivo de Indias at Seville. The variations between the copies are only slight and would appear to be due to copyists' errors. They have not been recorded here but may be found in *CDHE*, I: 461–472, and, in translation, in Marshall H. Saville, *The Goldsmith's Art in Ancient Mexico*, pp. 21–31.

42. *Antiparas.* Saville translates as "leggings."

43. A small copper coin.

44. *Guariques.* See Oviedo, bk. XVII, chap. 13. They appear to have been circular earrings.

45. A measure of weight usually calculated at one half drachm or 179 centigrams, although in the sixteenth century there were considerable regional differences.

46. Not in the Vienna Codex.

47. Not in the Vienna Codex.

48. In place of the above two paragraphs the *Manuel del Tesorero* has: "Of all the aforementioned things, as they have come to us, we are sending with Domingo de Ochandiano, by virtue of a letter, about which His Majesty commanded us to write, dated in Molina del Rey on the fifth of December, 1519: and the aforementioned Domingo brought a decree from His Majesty in which he ordered that the abovementioned things should be entrusted to Luis Veret, Keeper of the Jewels of Their Majesties, together with a receipt from the abovementioned Luis Veret, which is in the power of the aforementioned treasurer."

Notes to the Second Letter

1. Culhuacan was one of the city-states which sprang up in the Mexican valley after the collapse of the Toltec empire about the middle of the twelfth century A.D. The city was supposedly founded by Mixcoatl, the chieftain who first brought the Tolteca to the central plateau, in A.D. 900. The capital, however, was soon moved to Tula, but when, in 1168, this fell to nomadic invaders from the north, Culhuacan claimed the position of ancestral capital, tracing its descent back to Quetzalcoatl himself as lord of Tula; and, although this claim was quite unfounded, it gave Culhuacan enormous prestige. In 1375 the Mexica, in an attempt to establish a dynastic link with the earlier cultures, elected Acamapichtli, son of the ruler of Culhuacan, as their king. From then on they chose to style themselves the Culhua-Mexica. Cortés, however, calls them "Culuans" and "Mexicans" indiscriminately. (Robert H. Barlow, "Some Remarks on the term 'Aztec Empire,'" pp. 346–349. R. C. Padden, *The Hummingbird and the Hawk,* pp. 5 ff. See also E. R. Wolf, *Sons of the Shaking Earth,* pp. 21–129, for an account of Mesoamerican prehistory. For the later period see Friedrich Katz, "The Evolution of Aztec Society," a summary in English of the same author's *Die Sozialökonomischen Verhältnisse bei den Azteken im 15. und 16. Jahrhundert.*)

2. Tenochtitlan: the origin of the name is still a matter for dispute. One interpretation is *tetl,* "stone or rock," *nochtli,* "prickly pear (growing)"

and *titlan*, "near": "Near the prickly pear growing on a rock." Cooper Clark suggests *Tenoch*, the name of the founder of the city, and *titlan*, "in the place of": "In the place of Tenoch" (*Codex Mendoza*, II:1). The glyph is a stone and prickly pear (see George Kubler, "The name 'Tenoch-titlan' ").

A mythogenetic legend tells of how Huitzilopochtli (see n. 66) came to a priest in a vision and commanded him to found a city where an eagle was found nesting in a *tunal* (Padden, *op. cit.*, pp. 61–62). Tenochtitlan was in fact a dual city, originally founded (in 1344 or 1345) as part of the older city of Tlatelolco, which has probably been in existence since the early Militarist period. As the two communities expanded, the boundaries between them disappeared, although Tlatelolco remained independent until an effort by the chieftain Moquihuix, in 1473, to gain control of Tenochtitlan was crushed by Axayacatl. Tlatelolco was then reduced to the status of a vassal state. The Tenocha "Prince of the House" became the ruler of the city and the famous marketplace was divided up among the Tenocha lords who each received a 20 per cent tax from the commerce done in their particular area (Robert H. Barlow, ed., *Anales de Tlatelolco*, pp. 3, 59; Wolf, *op. cit.*, p. 131. *Códice chimalpopoca*, pp. 55–56).

3. Motecuçoma II, surnamed Xocoyotzin, the Younger, the son of Axayacatl, was the ninth *Uei Tlatoani* of Mexico. He succeeded to the throne in 1503, and his brother Macuilmalinaltzin, a rival for the kingship, was chosen to be his successor. Motecuçoma, who was a priest of Huitzilopochtli, greatly extended the Mexica empire at the same time as he increased the power of the priesthood and brought about the rigid centralization of government that may have contributed to Cortés's success. The nature and extent of his achievements must, however, of necessity remain hypothetical. His name divides into *Mo*, "he" (reverential); *Tec* (*utli*), "a lord"; and *çoma*, "he is courageous," the ideograph for which is a wig (*tzontli*). His name may therefore be rendered as "Courageous Lord." *Xiuhuitzolli*, a turquoise diadem (the ruler's insignia) on a wig was his personal ideograph. He was the only Mexica ruler or *Uei Tlatoani* ("Great Speaker King") to bear the title *Tlacatectli* or "Master Judge" (see *Codex Mendoza*, I:42). I have chosen the spelling Motecuçoma, used by Sahagún in the Nahuatl version of his work, for this is probably the closest we can come to a correct phonetic transcription. In the text I have followed Cortés's orthography. Moctezuma is the common modern Spanish form, which in English has become Montezuma.

4. Accounts of the grounding of the ships vary. Bernal Díaz (chap. 58) says that it was done by consent of Cortés's supporters; Cervantes de Salazar (bk. III, chap. 22) says that he persuaded the pilots and masters to declare

the ships unseaworthy. Five were grounded first and later four. Cortés then offered the remaining one to anybody who might still wish to return; no one accepted and it too was grounded. He did not burn his ships, a myth which seems to have originated in 1546 from another of Cervantes de Salazar's works (the dedication to Cortés of the "Diálogo de la dignidad del hombre," in *Obras que Francisco Cervantes de Salazar a hecho, glosado y traducido*, fol. 4), though he may have burned them later when all the tackle had been removed.

5. Juan de Escalante, *alguacil mayor* and lieutenant of Vera Cruz.

6. Nautla (Veracruz).

7. The Pánuco. Cortés also refers to the local chieftain as Pánuco.

8. Xicochimalco.

9. Ixhuacan.

10. Puerto de la Leña.

11. Most likely the modern Zautla. Gómara (p. 326) refers to it as Zaclotan and says that some Portuguese members of the expedition called it Castilblanco because it reminded them of a Portuguese town of that name. According to Wagner (p. 489, n. 17), by 1570 the name Castilblanco had been transferred to Ixtacamaxtitlan (see Bernal Díaz, chap. 61, and Cervantes de Salazar, bk. III, chap. 26). The chieftain's name was Olintetl, and he was so enormous the Spaniards dubbed him "The Shaker."

12. Ixtacamaxtitlan (Puebla).

13. Tlaxcala (probably "Land of Bread") was a province founded on the remains of the old Olmec civilization sometime in the thirteenth century A.D. The Tlaxcalteca were composed of three main ethnic groups, speaking Nahuatl, Otomi and Pinome. The Nahuas, however, soon established themselves as the dominant race, while the Otomis were ranged along the frontiers, much like march warriors. They were respected for their valor, much prized as captives by the Mexica but regarded as barbarians. The Pinomes probably became assimilated with the Otomis; they were the most backward of the three groups, and their name became a synonym for savage. Tlaxcala was divided into four confederated states, Tepeticpac, Ocotelolco, Tizatlan and Quiahuixtlan, each ruled by a *Tlatoani* (pl., *Tlatoque*) or "speaker." Matters of national importance were decided in conference, but in all other affairs the four states were autonomous. Most Amerindian states were organized on similar lines, a fact which the Spaniards, with their European notions of kingship, failed to understand for some time. When at last they did realize, the divided Indian state became a common feature of colonial rule (Charles Gibson, *Tlaxcala in the Sixteenth Century*, pp. 89 ff.).

The relationship between the emergent Mexica empire and Tlaxcala was at first quite amicable. But Tlaxcala was wealthy—her riches derived from an extensive mercantile network that reached from coast to coast—and the Mexica soon began to make efforts to avail themselves of these resources by conquest. The Tlaxcalteca resisted, and despite their ever-diminishing power managed to remain independent, though hemmed in on all sides by dependencies of the empire. Finally, together with Cholula and Huexotzinco, Tlaxcala reached an agreement with Mexico whereby, on certain prearranged occasions, they fought staged battles known as *Xochiyaoyotl*, or "Flower Wars," with each other. The purpose of these wars was to provide sacrificial victims for the altars of the victors. They also served as a proving ground for young warriors and enabled the Mexica, who invited the chieftains of the "Enemies of the House," as they were called, to witness these sacrifices, to apply diplomatic pressure upon a people they had failed to defeat in war. An appearance of open hostility was maintained for the benefit of the common people, and neither side would have passed over an opportunity such as Cortés offered to overthrow the other.

Main sources for the history of preconquest Tlaxcala are Diego Muñoz Camargo, *Historia de Tlaxcala* (title varies) and the work of Tadeo de Niza, now lost, but used extensively by Ixtlilxóchitl for vol. II, chap. LXXXIII *et seq.* of the *Historia Chichimeca*. A complete bibliography may be found in Gibson, *op. cit.*, pp. 235-291.

14. Lorenzana in his edition of Cortés (pp. V–VIII) locates this wall at a place five or six leagues from Ixtacamaxtitlan, next to a hill called Atotonilco. Traces of it have been found at Peñon (Mitra) between Tlaxco and Terrenate (Gibson, *op. cit.*, pp. 7 ff.). It probably reached between these two points, a distance of some five miles. There were also similar border fortifications at Hueyotlipan and Cacaxtla, in the northwest and southeast respectively.

15. The javelin, or *tlacochtli*, was the most important of these weapons. It was made of cane wood with a flint or obsidian head and thrown by means of the *atlatl*, or throwing stick. Bows and arrows, slings and spears were also common; poisoned arrows, however, seem never to have been used by the Mexica. For fighting at close quarters, the Mexica warrior carried a *macuahuitl*. This was essentially a club three and a half to four feet long and four to five inches wide. It was set with rows of obsidian fragments so sharp that a member of Cortés's army is said to have had his horse decapitated by a single blow. Obsidian is very brittle, however, and was useless against Spanish armor, as the blades broke off after a few blows. Shields were made of bark or netted canes covered with cotton cloth and feathers (see Oviedo, bk. XLII, chap. 3). According to the

Anonymous Conqueror they were so strong that only a crossbow bolt could penetrate them (translated by Patricia de Fuentes in *The Conquistadors*, p. 169). They wore a quilted cotton armor called *Ichcahuipilli*, which varied in length from a jacket to the full body covering mentioned by Alvarado in his second letter to Cortés from Guatemala (in De Fuentes, *op cit.*, p. 193). It consisted of cotton lengths soaked in brine and wound tightly around the body twenty times or more; the Spaniards found this so effective that they adopted it as both lighter and cooler than steel armor. (A. F. Bandelier, "Art of War and Mode of Warfare of the Ancient Mexicans"; George Vaillant, *The Aztecs of Mexico*, pp. 219–220. See also Alberto Mario Salas, *Las Armas de la Conquista*, which examines in detail the weaponry of both the Spaniards and the Mexica.)

16. Xicotencatl, the Younger. His father, who bore the same name, was lord of Titzatlan.

17. The reference is to a semimythical hero of the war against Granada who seemed the epitome of reckless bravery, leading raids far into enemy territory with little hope of return. He is also the eponymous hero of a play by Lope de Vega.

18. Maxixcatzin, lord of Ocotelulco. Cortés seems to have had dealings with none of the other *Tlatoque* except Xicotencatl, the Elder. He never mentions the other two, Citlalpopoca and Tlehuexolotzin. Maxixcatzin may have had more influence than his corulers, but he was not "lord" of Tlaxcala.

19. Salt was an important article of commerce on the central plateau, and it came largely from saltpeter mined near Ixtapaluca and Ixtapalapa. Gold, silver, precious stones, feathers and other items were also scarce, although as Gibson suggests (*op. cit.*, p. 15) the province's economic plight may have been exaggerated later (see also Muñoz Camargo, *op. cit.*, p. 111).

20. The bread is the tortilla, the fowl turkeys. Some geese and ducks were also reared domestically but most were hunted wild. Fishing was done with pole and landing nets as well as hooks and lines. Hooks seem to have been used by the Mexica before the arrival of the Spaniards, for Grijalva saw the Maya on Cozumel fishing with gold hooks, and the Maya imported all their metal from Mexico (Sigvald Linné, "Hunting and Fishing in the Valley of Mexico in the middle of the 16th century").

21. Trade was done exclusively by means of barter. There was no money as such, though the cacao bean was used for balancing an exchange. Quills of gold dust and crescent-shaped knives were also used, and among the Maya red shells or beads and copper bells were common (Landa, *op. cit.*, p. 95; Vaillant, *op. cit.*, pp. 138–139. For trade in Mesoamerica see *Trade and Market in the Early Empires*, Karl Polanyi *et al.*, eds., pp. 114–153).

22. Cholula (Puebla).

23. They were more likely to have been awaiting sacrifice. Mexico was a society without prisons. Theft was punished either by slavery until restitution was made or a fine of twice the amount stolen. Highway robbery, theft in the marketplace, theft of gold, silver and jade, as substances used in religious ornamentation, were all punished by death. Theft of corn was likewise a capital offense, though a hungry traveler was permitted to pluck a few ears. Practically every crime that in modern jurisprudence constitutes a felony was made capital and often punished by sacrifice. (Vaillant, *op. cit.*, pp. 130–134; R. B. Gaither, "Government and Jurisprudence of the Mexicans before the Spanish Conquest.")

24. Huexotzinco.

25. "Every kingdom divided against itself is brought to desolation." Matt. 12:25.

26. This is Doña Marina. She was, according to Bernal Díaz (chap. 37), the daughter of a chieftain in Vera Cruz and was sold into captivity when her mother remarried in order to leave the succession free for a stepbrother whom Bernal Díaz calls the cacique Lazarus. The place of her origin is uncertain. Bernal Díaz says that she was born in Painala (or Paynala), but there seems to be little evidence for this. The traditional place of her birth is supposed to be Jaltipan (Wagner, pp. 69 ff.), but Juan Xaramillo, the husband to whom she was later married by Cortés, stated that she was the daughter of a chieftain of Oluta in Vera Cruz (in Cuevas, appendix IV). Orozco y Berra (IV: 111 ff.) weighs the evidence and comes to the same conclusion, although he admits the possibility of Jaltipan.

She was given to Cortés with some Indian women after the battle of Cintla, and given by him to Puertocarrero. She returned to Cortés when Puertocarrero was sent to Spain, and acted as his mistress and translator during the conquest. She spoke Nahuatl as her mother tongue and had learned Chontal Maya, the dialect spoken in Tabasco, while in captivity. She translated into Maya for Aguilar, who then translated into Spanish, though later she seems to have acquired enough knowledge of Spanish to translate directly.

There is some dispute over the origin of her name. The explanation provided by José Ramírez is perhaps the most convincing. He suggests that her Nahuatl name was *Malinal* (or *Malinalli*), the name of the twelfth day in the Mexican month. "Malinche"—the term by which she, and often Cortés also, were popularly referred—was a Spanish corruption of the reverential form of this name (*Malinaltzin*), and she was christened Marina, as this was the closest Spanish equivalent (*Archives Paleographiques de l'Orient et de l'Amérique*, I:220. Quoted by Orozco y Berra, *loc. cit.*).

Marina's relations with Cortés have been the subject of a good deal of romanticization (analyzed by Jaime Delgado, "Hernán Cortés en la poesia española de los siglos XVIII y XIX"), but it seems that far from being an obviously devoted couple some of Cortés's soldiers took Marina to be Aguilar's wife (she must certainly have spent much of her time with him), a mistake repeated by Muñoz Camargo (p. 181). She bore Cortés a son, Martín, who seems to have been a favorite child. He was legitimatized by Clement VII in 1529 and left one thousand gold ducats a year for life in his father's will (*The last Will and Testament of Hernando Cortés*, pp. 10, 35).

27. Cortés has been accused, notably by Las Casas (*Brevissima Relación de la Destrucción de las Indias* (fol. ci v.), of slaughtering the population of Cholula in order to terrorize the Mexica capital into surrender.

According to Las Casas, it was a matter of policy: a massacre greatly reduced the Indians' determination to resist. There may be some justification in this, for Cortés's agent at his residencia—Cortés himself was away in Spain at the time—admitted that the purpose of the massacre was to "give the law" and make Cortés feared (quoted by Wagner, p. 174). Cortés's tale of a plot, though substantiated by Bernal Díaz (chap. 83) and later Spanish chronicles, sounds like an excuse. Cholula was a religious center and its people were mostly merchants. This does not of course mean that they were incapable of attempting to wipe out the Spaniards, but it seems unlikely that Motecuçoma would have chosen such a place for an ambush: furthermore, the Chololteca had only recently been incorporated into the empire, and it is doubtful therefore that the Mexica would have trusted them very far. Cortés claims that Motecuçoma had a huge army standing by but makes no mention of it after the massacre. Vázquez de Tapia gave a substantially different version of the events at Cortés's residencia (*Sumario*, 1:58–59).

"The witness does not know for what reason the aforementioned Don Fernando Cortés called together the principal persons of the town saying that he wished to leave but wanted to speak with them first. These principal persons then came and he told them to bring bearers, and they brought many, some four or five thousand Indians, in the opinion of this witness. He then put them into the principal mosque [temple], into some courtyards and enclosures that were there. He then ordered the Spaniards who were with him to kill them, and thus they killed them and once they were all dead, he went out into the city with all his people." Vázquez de Tapia, though a witness, was not likely to have been party to Cortés's plans; but then, on the other hand, neither was Bernal Díaz, who gives a very full account of the plot (*loc. cit.*) and has some harsh words for Las Casas. He claims that Motolinía excused the massacre on the grounds that it dissuaded the Indians from their idolatry. This may be true, but his statement that a Franciscan enquiry held at Cholula after the conquest established that there was a plot is more questionable, and such an inquiry is mentioned neither by Motolinía, Sahagún nor any other Franciscan (Wagner, p. 177). Orozco y Berra (IV:252) thinks that the plot was fabricated by the Tlaxcalteca, possibly with the help of Doña Marina, in order to be able to pay off an old enemy. This is possible, but the most convincing explanations seem to be those of Las Casas and Wagner (p. 173), who suggest that Cortés was securing his lines of communication with the coast. This would explain why he went there in the first place, for the reasons he gives himself are not very satisfactory.

The number of the dead is given by Cortés as three thousand in two hours. Vázquez de Tapia puts it as high as twenty thousand. It was probably somewhere between five thousand and ten thousand.

28. Cholula had once been an "Enemy of the House" and an ally of Tlaxcala. A quarrel between the two areas, skillfully exacerbated by Mexica diplomacy, led to a war in which the Chololteca were forced to seek Mexica aid. This lost them their independence.

29. There is no such word. Cortés was probably given *pinole*, which is toasted ground maize with pepper and cacao (chocolate) added. This mixture might have been referred to by the Spaniards as *pan y cacao* and corrupted into *panicap*. Gayangos suggests (p. 76) *atole*, a kind of corn gruel.

30. Acatzingo and Izucar (Puebla).

31. Popocatepetl ("Smoking Mountain") and Iztaccihuatl ("White Woman") were venerated as man and wife. The volcano is 17,887 feet high. It erupted in 1347 and 1354 and was active from 1519 until 1530. It erupted again in 1665 but has remained dormant ever since. The first person to attempt an ascent, as mentioned here by Cortés, was Diego de Ordaz, for which he was granted a smoking volcano in his arms. The first scientific exploration was undertaken by William and Frederic Glennie in 1827. Although no true concept of retribution after death seems to have existed among the Amerindians, the crater of Popocatepetl was said to contain the spirits of evil rulers.

32. Calpan (?). Antonio Carrión gives Cortés's route from Cholula to Amecameca as Izcalpan (Calpan), Papaxtla, Xalitzintla, Zacatzinco, Zacatelolotl, Tepetolonco, Tepechco, Apatlaco and Amecamecan (Amecameca) (*Historia de la Ciudad de Puebla*, I:45).

33. Amecameca.

34. Ayotzinco.

35. This was Cacamatzin, a nephew of Motecuçoma and lord of Texcoco.

36. Mizquic.

37. Cuitlahuac. The modern town of Tlahuac occupies the same site, although the Chalco lake has since been drained.

38. Itztapalapa. The brother of Motecuçoma to whom Cortés refers was Cuitlahuac, eleventh son of Axayacatl. On Motecuçoma's death, he succeeded his brother but died of smallpox eighty days later.

39. Coyoacan.

40. Mexicactzingo and Huitzilopochco (now called Churubusco). Orozco y Berra (IV: 270) suggests that Niciaca might be a corruption of Coyouhuacan (Coyoacan).

41. Potonchan.

42. Both this speech and the one that follows (pp. 85–86, 98–99) would seem to be apocryphal. Motecuçoma could never have held the views with which Cortés accredits him. Eulalia Guzmán (*Relaciones de Hernán Cortés*, I: 279 ff.) has pointed out the Biblical tone of both these passages and how their phraseology reflects the language of the *Siete Partidas*. Cortés is casting Motecuçoma into the role of a sixteenth-century Spaniard welcoming his "natural lord," who in this case has been accredited with a vaguely Messianic past. Indeed the whole setting has a mythopoeic ring: Motecuçoma is made to raise his garments and to declare, "See that I am flesh and blood like you and all other men, and I am mortal and substantial," words reminiscent of those of Jesus to his disciples, "A spirit hath not flesh and bones as ye see me have" and of Paul and Barnabas to Lystra, "We also are men of like passions with you." (J. H. Elliott, "The Mental World of Hernán Cortés," pp. 51–53). There is evidence, however, that Motecuçoma did believe himself to be the living incarnation of Huitzilopochtli (see Durán, chaps. LIII–LIV; and Sahagún, bk. IV, chap. 10), and certainly such an identification would not have been alien to Mexica religious thought. Despite the absurdity of attributing such words and gestures to an Amerindian, it seems likely that Cortés's account of the events is based on partially understood information about the native mythologies. A number of modern commentators seem to believe the thesis of Motecuçoma's speeches, namely, that the Mexica lived in fear of a vengeful Messiah, who would one day return from the east, and mistook Cortés for his captain. Later this Messiah, who in the words attributed to Motecuçoma is only a legendary tribal chieftain, becomes Quetzalcoatl, the "Plumed Serpent" lord of Tula, whose story as told by Sahagún bears some resemblance to the Cortés-Motecuçoma version of Mexica prehistory. There is, however, no preconquest tradition which places Quetzalcoatl in this role, and it seems possible therefore that it was elaborated by Sahagún and Motolinía from informants who themselves had partially lost contact with their traditional tribal histories.

The identification of Cortés with Quetzalcoatl is also the work of Sahagún (see bk. XII, chap. 4, pp. 11 ff.). Don Antonio de Mendoza, first viceroy of New Spain, however, said that Cortés was mistaken for Huitzilopochtli (Elliott, *op. cit.*, p. 53), traditionally associated with the south, and about whom no Messianic legend is known to exist. It is possible that Mendoza was told this by Cortés himself, and "Uchilobos" was the only Mexica deity Cortés could name.

Cortés may have picked up a local legend and embellished it in an attempt to prove that Motecuçoma was himself an usurper and therefore had no right to the lands he ruled (cf. the Third Letter, n. 3). A like strategy was used in Peru in the 1570s to discredit the Incas. The viceroy Francisco de Toledo collected together an immense body of information to prove that the Incaic dynasties were of recent foundation, and their scions not, therefore, "natural lords." (Lewis Hanke, "Viceroy Francisco de Toledo and the Just Titles of Spain in the Inca Empire." See also Robert S. Chamberlain, "The Concept of the 'Señor Natural' as Revealed by Castilian Law and Administrative Documents.")

Where Cortés first heard the story is uncertain. Cervantes de Salazar (bk. 111, chap. 49) and Bernal Díaz (chap. 79) both say that it was in Tlaxcala but both are very vague (see also Muñoz Camargo, pp. 184–185). Professor Guzmán says that a similar legend was common in the Antilles. But perhaps the first contact was made in Yucatán, where a foliated cross appears on a number of Mayan buildings and seems to have been associated with Quetzalcoatl, called Kukulcan in Maya. (The cult, however, appears to have been imported from Mexico, whose priests are often shown wearing white robes, see George C. Vaillant, "A bearded mystery.")

If it is unlikely that Motecuçoma took the Spaniards to be the vicars-on-earth of the "Plumed Serpent," it is even more unlikely that it would have in any way affected his attitude toward Cortés. Besides the improbability of any leader acting on a prophecy, Quetzalcoatl's cult was largely confined to the lowland regions beyond Popocatepetl and Iztaccihuatl and appears to have held little sway in central Mexico itself (*Códice Borgia*, 1: 67). Its cult center was Cholula, which, when it came under Mexica rule, was granted no special respect and even forced to venerate Huitzilopochtli. Nor, it might be added, did Cholula accord to Cortés the welcome he might be expected to receive as Quetzalcoatl's lieutenant. Motecuçoma was himself a priest of Huitzilopochtli; and, secure in the power of the tutelary deity of his race, it does not seem likely that he would have resigned his powers to the supposed avatars of an apotheosized Toltec chieftain.

The attitude of the Mexica toward the Spaniards can best be explained by the traditional immunity from harm enjoyed by all ambassadors—and Cortés claimed to be an ambassador albeit without an embassy. It is also possible that once Motecuçoma had realized Cortés's intentions, he deliberately drew him inland, not understanding that the sea could be a supply route for the Spaniards: a perhaps similar and equally disastrous tactic was employed by Atahualpa against Pizarro (cf. George Kubler, "The behaviour of Atahualpa." In *HAHR*, 25: pp. 413–427). Motecuçoma may well have underestimated the Spanish powers of diplomacy and the state of unrest within his own empire. It was unfortunate for him, as for Atahualpa, that the Spaniards were in a position to play one Indian against another.

43. As Cortés implies, this was a ruse to imprison Motecuçoma. Juan Alvarez testified that Escalante (the captain mentioned by Cortés) had gone to Nautla with a force of Spaniards and Totonaque to look for gold. The Indians refused to give them any, and a fight ensued in which the Spaniards were defeated, losing two of their men. Bernal Díaz (chap. 94) says that Escalante and six other Spaniards were killed. Gómara (pp. 353–354) says that it was not Escalante but Pedro de Ircio who was killed. He also says that the expedition was sent to prevent Francisco de Garay from settling on the coast (see Wagner, pp. 208–209).

Cuauhpopoca ("Bright Eagle") was lord of Coyoacan: Ixtlilxóchitl (vol. II:378) claims that he was also governor of the north coast. Eulalia Guzmán, however, thinks that this is probably a confusion with Cohuatlpopoca. According to one report, Cuauhpopoca was tied to a stake and shot full of arrows by the Tlaxcalteca and not burned as Cortés claims.

44. These provinces were all tributary towns in the Mixtec-Zapotec region. Cuçula might be Sosola, of which there are three—San Juan, San Mateo and San Jerónimo Sosola. The town appears in the Codex Mendoza as Çoçolan.

45. Tamazulapa. There are three towns with this name in the same area.

46. Malinaltepec. There were several towns with this name, and it is impossible to say exactly which one is referred to here, but it is probably San Miguel de Malinaltepec.

47. Land of the *Tenimes* or barbarians. The capital of the province was Chinantla, and the language spoken Chinanteca (Eulalia Guzmán, *op. cit.*, 1: 259). Although Cortés only mentions "Tenis" as speaking a language other than Nahuatl, all the towns mentioned here must also have used Mixtec or Zapotec dialects.

48. Tuxtepec.

49. The river is the Coatzacoalcos. "Sanmin" is presumably a contraction of San Martín, the name given to a small range of mountains beside the Gulf of Mexico. Mazamalco is a corruption of Coatzacualco (Coatzacoalcos).

50. Chalchiuhcueyecan is the Nahuatl name for the coastal area near the port of San Juan de Ulúa.

51. Coatzacoalcos.

52. Tochintecuhtli, Tochinteuctli or Tuchinteuhctli, "Lord Rabbit" (Eulalia Guzmán, *op. cit.*, p. 262, n. 106).

53. Tetzcoco, Tezcoco, or Texcoco, as it is called today, was the capital of Alcolhuacan and one of the city-states that made up the Triple Alliance of the Mexican valley. Texcoco was founded in the twelfth century by Chichimeca tribes on what is possibly the site of an earlier Toltec settlement. Three other tribes occupied this same area: the Otomi, Tepaneca and the Alcolhua. They were either late-comers granted lands by Xolotl, the Chichimeca chieftain (see Ixtlilxóchitl, vol. II, chap. V, *Códice Xolotl*, pp. 17–119 *passim*), or the autochthonal inhabitants driven to take refuge in and around the lake by invaders from the north. (Chichimeca means, "Sons-of-Dogs"[?]; like Tenime and Pinome it was a term of genetic abuse.) Xolotl first set up his capital at Tenayocan; Quinatzin, his great-grandson, later moved it to Texcoco and married a Culhuan princess in an attempt to assimilate the heritage of Tula. The Chichimeca later came to identify themselves with the Acolhua, changing the name of their kingdom to Acolhuacan. Texcoco flourished under Neçaualcoyotl in the mid-fifteenth century, but was soon subordinated to the rising power of Tenochtitlan, with Neçaualcoyotl being forced to fight a mock battle and set fire to the main temple of the city. Texcoco remained an active member of the Triple Alliance until the arrival of the Spaniards activated political rivalries among members of the ruling family. The city was said to have been the cultural center of Anahuac and it possessed extensive archives which were destroyed by the Tlaxcalteca during the siege of Tenochtitlan.

54. Acolman and Otumba.

55. Cacamatzin. When Neçahualpiltzintli died in 1516, his son Cacama (the *tzin* is an honorific) was chosen to succeed him. In 1518 his brother Ixtlilxochitl broke away and established a separate kingdom with his capital at Otumba. It was Ixtlilxochitl, together with another brother, Coanacochtzin, who was responsible for Cacama's capture. The description given by Cortés, however, sounds too contrived. It is more likely that Cacama was in Tenochtitlan when Cortés seized Motecuçoma and was imprisoned along with him.

56. Cuicuitzcatzin ("Swallow") was one of Cacama's younger brothers, not his son (see the Third Letter, n. 11).

57. Bernal Díaz (chap. 104) says that the sum was estimated at 600,000 *pesos*, without the jewels. Once the royal fifth and Cortés's fifth had been ex-

tracted, the remainder was divided among the troops, though Cortés makes no mention of this. Gómara (p. 357), who also speaks of a division, puts the sum at something over 160,000 *pesos*.

58. The blowgun is still in common use today. It measures between four to six feet in length and fires a clay pellet. It is quite effective against small birds but useless for anything larger.

59. MS. reads, *y dióme unas turquesas de oro*. *Turquesa*, in this context, is evidently a bullet mold and not, as all other translators have rendered it, a turquoise. It is unlikely, however, that Cortés would ever have requested such a thing as a gold bullet mold from Motecuçoma and the text is perhaps corrupt. Gómara's version of this passage (in González de Barcía's edition, *Historiadores Primitivos de las Indias Occidentales*, II:94) reads, *La Red para Bodoques, i Turquesas era de Oro i algunos de Plata*: this translates as, "the bag for the bullets and the bullet molds was of gold and some were of silver," and this is probably what Cortés intended.

60. On the eve of the conquest Motecuçoma's empire included the modern states of Puebla and Morelos, most of Guerrero, Mexico, Hidalgo and Veracruz, and a fair portion of Oaxaca. This "empire" was the creation of a Triple Alliance among the city-states of Tlacopan (Tacuba), Texcoco and Tenochtitlan, built around the Mexican valley lake system. The tribes who occupied these cities were respectively the Tepaneca, the Acolhua and the Mexica. By the time the Spaniards arrived, however, Tenochtitlan had wrested effective control of the empire from its neighbors. Cortés is here referring to Anahuac (*Atl-Nahuac* or "Near-the-Water"), a name which was originally given to the coastal regions and the lands around the lake system, but later seems to have become a metonym for all Mexico. (For the geography of the empire see Robert H. Barlow, *The Extent of the Empire of the Culhua Mexica*.)

61. The lakes are those of Chalco and Texcoco. The first is of fresh water, the second of salt.

62. This was the marketplace in Tlatelolco. As already noted (see n. 2), it was divided up among the Tenocha lords, who each collected a 20 per cent sales tax from all business done within their allotted areas. (For a description of the place, see Vaillant, *op. cit.*, pp. 234 ff., and the Anonymous Conqueror, *op. cit.*, pp. 178–179.)

63. These were called *itzcuintlis* and are now extinct. They were an important article of trade sold mainly in Acolman and were still available as late as 1580 (Durán, chap. XCVIII). They appear frequently on pottery from western Mexico, and seem to have resembled the Chihuahua.

64. Called *tameme* in Nahuatl. The amount they could carry and the distance they could travel was fixed by law.

65. The maguey (*metl* in Nahuatl) is the American aloe or *Agave Americana*. The "wine" referred to here is pulque, a powerful syrupy liquor still popular today.

66. A useful account of Mexica religious practices is given by Alfonso Caso in *The Aztecs, People of the Sun*.

   The chief gods of the city were Huitzilopochtli and Tlaloc: of these two Huitzilopochtli was by far the most important. His name means "Hummingbird of the South" (from *Huitzilin*, "hummingbird," and *opochtli*, meaning literally "on the left"), and, although he is generally referred to simply as the war god, he was—or at least had become by the time the Spaniards arrived—the tutelary deity of the Mexica. There is no wholly convincing analysis of his place in the Mexica pantheon, but an interesting intepretation is given by Padden (*op. cit.*). The temple described here, the great *teucalli* of Tenochtitlan, was a truncated pyramid built in tiers of stone laid against an artificial mound. The temple was so constructed that a man standing at the base was unable to see to the top; when the sacrificial victim began to ascend he seemed to be climbing into the sky. The tiers of the temple were equated with the tiers of the universe, and the temple itself with the navel of the world, the Mountain of Snakes where Huitzilopochtli was said to have sprung from the womb of his mother (E. R. Wolf, *op. cit.*, p. 83).

67. The lords of subject provinces were forced to spend a certain part of each year in the capital. They were all hostages, and six hundred of them formed Motecuçoma's personal guard of honor. In this manner the *Uei Tlatoani* was able to keep a firm measure of control over the more distant provinces of the empire.

68. Probably the *Matricula de Tributos*. See the *Codex Mendoza*, which is, in part, a copy of the *Matricula*. The bibliography of the manuscript is dealt with in the introduction to Robert H. Barlow's *The Extent of the Empire of the Culhua Mexica*, pp. 4 ff.

69. The date of Narváez's arrival is uncertain. If Cortés is to be believed, it was sometime in May, but in a complaint made against Narváez and Velázquez by four of Cortés's own men he is said to have arrived in April (in *La Noche Triste*, G. R. G. Conway, ed., pp. 40 ff. *passim*).

70. Coatzacoalcos. The captain was Juan Velázquez de León. The single ship mentioned earlier was presumably that of Lucas Vázquez de Ayllón.

71. Paper was made from the pulp of a species of fig tree (*Ficus Petiolaris*). When this had been beaten flat and dried it was covered with a paste and dusted with a white powder. The result was a thin, hard board that folded to make a screen. Bark and deerskin were also used (V. W. von Hagen, *The Aztec and Maya Papermakers*).

72. Bartolomé de Olmedo, a member of the order of Merced. He was an able diplomat, much praised by Bernal Díaz, who often prevented Cortés from enraging friendly tribes by overturning idols and attempting forced conversion. He died late in 1524 or early in 1525 (see José Castro Seone, "El P. Bartolomé de Olmedo, Capellán del Ejército de Cortés"). Cortés's account of the campaign against Narváez is naturally biased; he gives only the minimum of details and these are not always accurate. The matter is too complicated to be examined here, but a very full account may be found in Wagner, chap. XVIII.

73. The friar was Juan Ruiz de Guevara; the two lay brothers were the notary Alonso de Vergara and someone Bernal Díaz (chap. 111) calls Amaya. They went to Vera Cruz to present their credentials to Sandoval, who promptly arrested them and had them carried to Mexico in hammocks.

74. Velázquez de León had previously been imprisoned by Cortés (Bernal Díaz, chap. 93).

75. Lucas Vázquez de Ayllón was an *oidor* of the *Audiencia* in Santo Domingo.

76. According to Bernal Díaz (chap. 112), Cortés sent no letters with Guevara. He did, however, send some Indian messengers begging Narváez to keep the peace, while Cortés's army was busy trying to bribe Narváez's captains.

77. Ayllón finally succeeded in making the captain take him to Hispaniola. The other ship, with his *alguacil* and secretary on board, reached Santo Domingo some months later. According to Gómara (p. 179), Ayllón was drowned while on a slaving expedition in 1524, "without ever having done anything worthy of recall."

78. Pedro de Alvarado was left in charge. He was born in Badajoz in 1485 and first went to the Indies in 1510 with his brothers Jorge, Gonzalo, Gómez and Juan, all of whom participated in the conquest, although without distinguishing themselves in any way. Alvarado spent eight years in Santo Domingo, then joined Grijalva's expedition in 1518. The following year he sailed with Cortés, whom he served as second-in-command until the massacre in Tenochtitlan. He was said to have been brave but rash, a judgment which the events bear out. He had blond hair, which earned him the name of *Tonatiuh* ("the Sun"). After having conquered Guatemala in 1524, he made an abortive attempt to participate in the conquest of Peru. He was crushed by a falling horse in the Nochiztlan Mountains in 1541 and died shortly after in Guadalajara. (For an account of Alvarado's career see J. E. Kelly, *Pedro de Alvarado, Conquistador*.)

Cortés's figures for the number of men left behind in Tenochtitlan are obviously incorrect. Three witnesses later testified at an inquiry into the affair that they did not exceed 120, most of whom were disabled or could not be trusted. (The witnesses were Juan Álvarez, Diego de Ávila and Diego Holguín. Their statements may be found in Polavieja, pp. 150–256. See also Wagner, p. 505, n. 19.)

79. Presumably the one whom Bernal Díaz (chap. 119) calls Juan de León. He says also (loc. cit.) that Andrés de Duero and Amador de Lares had plotted with Cortés in Cuba to usurp Velázquez's authority and split the profits of the expedition between them. Andrés de Duero seems to have been in contact with Cortés from the moment Narváez arrived on the mainland.

80. This plot sounds like a fabrication. Cortés does not give enough details, and, furthermore, Rodrigo Álvarez Chico and the notary Pedro Hernández appear to have gone to Narváez with Cortés's mandate before the consultations with Andrés de Duero and the two priests, which probably took place in Tepaniquita (Tampaniquita, in Bernal Díaz, chap. 115), some nine leagues from Cempoal. By reordering the sequence of events Cortés has succeeded in making his attack on Narváez seem inevitable. In fact, we know that he had won over many of Narváez's men and must now have felt strong enough to defeat him. According to Bernal Díaz (loc. cit.), the messenger mentioned by Cortés was Juan Velázquez.

81. Narváez had founded the town of San Salvador on the site of the present-day city of Veracruz. The alcaldes were Francisco Verdugo and Juan Yuste; the regidores, Juan de Gamarra, Jerónimo Martínez de Salvatierra, Diego Velázquez and Pedro Velázquez.

82. There seems to have been some truth in this. Seven witnesses testified before the Audiencia in Santo Domingo that Cuba had been emptied in order to provide Narváez with soldiers. Only the infirm and the old remained behind. While it seems that some of them went willingly, some even to join Cortés, many of them were threatened or cajoled. It is also possible that there is some truth in Cortés's reiterated accusation that Velázquez misused his power over the repartimiento (Polavieja, pp. 29–53, Wagner, pp. 267–268).

83. Pentecost fell that year on May 27. Cortés's dates, however, are unreliable, and the attack may have taken place any time between that date and June 18 (see Eulalia Guzmán, op. cit., p. 381, n. 373). Velázquez de León is said to have bribed Rodrigo Martínez, the captain of artillery, to plug the touchholes of the cannon with wax. But this may have been done because of the rain—or not done at all, as Cortés succeeded in using them. Andrés de Tapia (in De Fuentes, op. cit., p. 47) says that Cortés had managed to have the cinch straps on Narváez's horses cut, thus

converting the horsemen into foot soldiers. Sandoval had been given orders to kill Narváez if he resisted; he was finally captured by Pedro Sánchez Farfán, after having one eye thrust out with a pike (on Narváez's character see Frank Goodwyn, "Pánfilo de Narváez, a character study of the first Spanish leader to land an expedition in Texas").

84. According to Bernal Díaz (chap. 124), Diego de Ordaz was sent to Guazaqualco (Coatzacoalcos) and Juan Velázquez to the Pánuco River. Two ships were also sent to Jamaica for horses, goats, pigs, sheep and chickens to breed in Coatzacoalcos. He claims that there were only 120 men in each expedition, and that twenty of these were Cortés's own. He states, however, that news of Alvarado's predicament reached Cempoal before they departed. Cortés then offered Narváez's men rich rewards if they would accompany him with a good will; they agreed, but Bernal Díaz remarks that "had they known the forces of Mexico not one of them would have come."

85. The details of Alvarado's massacre of the Mexica nobility are too conflicting to give any clear picture of what happened. All we can be certain of is that some time during the feast of *Toxcatl* a large number of the Mexica nobles were murdered in the precincts of the great *teucalli*, probably because Alvarado, who was in charge during Cortés's absence, suspected them of plotting to kill him and his men at the height of the celebrations. According to James Cooper Clark (*Codex Mendoza*, 1: 24) *Toxcatl* took place on May 6. Other native accounts say that the feast lasted for ten days; as Alvarado must have struck either on the first or second day, this means that the massacre took place some time around May 7. It seems likely that either Motecuçoma persuaded Cortés to allow *Toxcatl* to be performed as usual or that the Mexica went ahead regardless. Sahagún (bk. XII, chap. 19, p. 49) says that Alvarado asked Motecuçoma to celebrate the feast because he wanted to see it. This is repeated by the *Codex Ramirez* (p. 88) but in language so similar to Sahagún's that it is evident both works are employing the same source. If Sahagún's informant is right, then Alvarado must have planned the massacre. The *Codex Ramirez* says that Cortés "ordered it to be done before leaving." It seems an unlikely time to choose. Cortés may have believed that he could crush any resistance once he wiped out the Tenocha lords, but, if he had such a plan in mind, he would surely have acted before leaving Tenochtitlan, rather than entrust the work to Alvarado, whose force was pitifully small (see n. 78).

Some time before the beginning of the feast Alvarado began to hear rumors of a plot, rumors no doubt brought to him if not actually invented by the Tlaxcalteca, who hated *Toxcatl*, which usually meant the slaughter of large numbers of their countrymen captured in the "Flower Wars."

Alvarado said at his residencia that he had been refused supplies by the Mexica, who had also killed one of his Indian women; and when he went to the temple enclosure he had seen a number of staves, and had been told by the Indians that they were to be used for impaling the Spaniards. As these details are not mentioned by the other witnesses, I suspect that Alvarado is repeating what the Tlaxcalteca said they had seen (see *Proceso de Residencia contra Pedro de Alvarado*, pp. 3–4, 36–38). He did, however, go to the temple, where he found two Indians squatting before the statue of Huitzilopochtli and "another idol," undoubtedly Titlacaua (or Tezcatlipoca), in whose honor the festival was being held. Alvarado assumed these to be possible sacrificial victims and had them carried back to his quarters. Under torture they admitted the existence of a plot but gave no details except that it would come within ten days (*i.e.*, at the height of the feast). He then applied the same treatment to a Texcocan and received the same answer. Taking half his men, he marched at once to the temple. The resulting massacre is described by Sahagún's informant:

"They surrounded those who danced whereupon they went among the drums. Then they struck the arms of the one who beat the drums; they severed both his hands. . . . Of some they slashed open the back, and then their entrails gushed out. Of some they split the head. . . . Of some they hit the shoulder; they split open and cut their bodies to pieces. Some they struck in the shank, some on the thighs. Of some they struck the belly, and their entrails streamed forth. And when one in vain would run, he would only drag his entrails like something raw as he tried to flee" (bk. XII, chap. 20, pp. 53–54).

The Spaniards then plundered the dead and retreated to their quarters. The Mexica were not slow in responding; they launched a furious attack against Axayacatl's palace, to which Alvarado replied by forcing either Motecuçoma or Itzquauhtzin, ruler of Tlatelolco, or both, onto the roof to order off their people. Sahagún (bk. XII, chap. 21, p. 55) has only Itzquauhtzin on the roof, the *Codex Ramirez* has "Motecuçoma . . . with a chieftain from among the prisoners." Both say that the Mexica responded with loud cries of abuse. This seems unlikely. Two witnesses at Alvarado's residencia, Nuño Pinto and Alvaro Lopes [*sic*], said that the fighting lasted two days or less (*Proceso de Residencia*, pp. 131, 134). If this was so, only Motecuçoma was powerful enough to have stopped it.

86. Texcoco.

87. On his return Cortés refused to see Motecuçoma because of his alleged complicity with Narváez. According to Clavigero (*Historia Antigua de México*, p. 154), when Cortés did finally see Motecuçoma it was only to order him "with loud threats" to open the market. Motecuçoma is said to have replied that the only people who had sufficient authority to carry out

such an order were all in prison with him; he suggested therefore that Cortés release his brother Cuitlahuac. Cortés did so, but as soon as Cuitlahuac was free he launched an attack against the Spaniards. This sounds an unlikely story, but it is certain that Cuitlahuac was in command of the Mexica forces during the siege and was elected *Uei Tlatoani* on his brother's death. Cortés, who appears to have had only an uncertain understanding of Mexica government, may have believed that no one would dare attempt to usurp Motecuçoma's power, and that as long as he held him the Mexica would be incapable of action.

88. The chieftains of Tenochtitlan, Texcoco and Tacuba were probably all seized by Cortés soon after his arrival in the Mexica capital; with them were all of Motecuçoma's family.

89. There are two versions of Motecuçoma's death. The first, that given by Cortés, is corroborated by most of the Spanish writers. Bernal Díaz (chap. 126) and Vázquez de Tapia, both witnesses, say that there were a large number of Spanish soldiers on the roof guarding the *Uei Tlatoani;* if this was so, it is possible that the Mexica were aiming at them rather than at Motecuçoma. Gómara (p. 365) suggests that the Mexica did not see him, and Juan Cano told Oviedo (bk. XXXIII, chap. 54) that "Motezuma died from a stone which those outside threw at him, which they would not have done had not a buckler been placed in front of him, for once they had seen him they would not have thrown." Bernal Díaz says that Motecuçoma died because he refused to eat or to have his wound attended, a story repeated by Herrera (dec. 11, bk. X, chap. 10). If the Mexica did attack him on the roof, this might be true. Bernal Díaz then goes on to say that Cortés and the other soldiers wept at Motecuçoma's death as though they had lost a father, which seems somewhat unlikely.

The second theory is that Motecuçoma was stabbed to death shortly before the Spaniards fled the city. This idea is advanced by most of the native writers, though some of them agree that Motecuçoma had been discredited and would therefore be open to attack if he appeared in public. The *Anales Tolteca-Chichimeca* (quoted by Orozco y Berra, IV: 425) even say that it was Cuauhtemoc who threw the stone. Durán (chap. LXXVI) also mentioned the wound but says that when Motecuçoma was found it was almost healed, and that he had been stabbed five times in the chest. Ixtlilxóchitl (I:341), who is largely pro-Spanish, repeats the Spanish version of the killing but adds, "his vassals say that the Spaniards killed him by stabbing him in the bowels." The *Codex Ramirez* (p. 144) also says that he was killed by a sword thrust in the bowels. Torquemada (bk. IV, chap. 70), following Sahagún, says that Motecuçoma and Itzquauhtzin, lord of Tlatelolco, were found garroted. There is little evidence to support this: garroting was for formal executions, not assassination.

In addition to the murder of the *Uei Tlatoani*, Cortés is also accused of having killed the lords of several of the neighboring towns. Though both the Spanish and the native sources agree that these lords were imprisoned —Cortés himself admits it—the Spaniards claim that they were killed by their own people during the *noche triste*. Alvarado Tezozomoc says that besides Motecuçoma the Spaniards killed "Itzcuauhtzin, the *Cuauílatoani* of Tlatilolco and Cacamatzin lord of Texcoco" (*Crónica Mexicayotl*, p. 149). Ixtlilxóchitl (II:396) says that Cacama fought so hard he had to be stabbed forty-seven times. Durán (*loc. cit.*) says that "many chieftains and lords who had been imprisoned with him were all stabbed to death when they [the Spaniards] fled their quarters." It seems likely that they were all in fact murdered by Cortés, either in the belief that this would paralyze the Mexica offensive, or in the hope that the people would be too occupied with the funeral rites to prevent his leaving. The murders were undoubtedly done in secret, and knowledge of them withheld from the common soldiery. The bodies do not seem to have been discovered until the day after the noche triste. According to Sahagún, "When four days had passed since all [the chieftains] had been hurled from the [pyramid] temple, [the Spaniards] came out and cast forth [the bodies of] Motecuçomatzin and Itzquauhtazin, who had died, at the water's edge at a place called Teoayoc. For here was a carved stone image of tortoise; like a tortoise was the representation in stone.

"And when they were seen and recognized as being Motecuçomatzin and Itzquauhtzin, they took up Motecuçomatzin in their arms and carried him there to a place called Copulco" (bk. XII, chap. 23, p. 63).

Motecuçoma was buried in Tenochtitlan and Itzquauhtzin in Tlatelolco; what happened to the bodies of the others is not recorded. (See also Orozco y Berra, IV: 437–443, who quotes at length from the authorities mentioned above.)

90. This was possibly not, as Cortés suggests, the temple of Huitzilopochtli but the *Yopico*, dedicated to Xipe Totec, the "Flayed God," which lay closer to the palace of Axayacatl. The Indians on top of this "tower" seem to have been directing the attack. The position was obviously a vital one, and Cortés employed a large number of his men against it, despite his claims to have taken it almost singlehanded.

91. This must have been the Ciuacoatl, or "Serpent Woman." She was the mythical mother of Huitzilopochtli and cared for all women who died in childbirth. Huitzilopochtli's high priest assumed her name, although the office was always held by a man (see also the Fourth Letter, n. 51).

92. Gómara (p. 368) says that the retreat from Tenochtitlan, the famous noche triste, took place on the night of July 10. Bernal Díaz agrees (chap. 128) but may be cribbing from Gómara. If Cortés's record is accurate,

however, they held out for six days after St. John the Baptist's day, which means they left the city on June 30. According to Sahagún (bk. XII, chap. 24, p. 65), a woman going for water was the first to raise the alarm, which was then taken up by a sentry on the *tecpan*, or clan building.

93. Bernal Díaz (chap. 128) says that the church of Santa Maria de los Remedios was built on the same site. Sahagún calls the place Otonteocalco in Spanish, and Otoncalpolco in Nahuatl (Eulalia Guzmán, *op. cit.*, p. 469, n. 468). For Cortés's route see endpaper map. My authority for the place names is bk. XII, chaps. 24–27, pp. 65–77 of Sahagún and pp. 469 ff. of Guzmán.

94. The Spaniards were hindered in their retreat by the gold they were carrying; but it seems that the majority of the men killed were Narváez's, who were lacking in experience. The number of the dead given here by Cortés is obviously false. Six or seven hundred is a fair estimate, but all the authorities disagree. A useful table of their opinions is given by Wagner (p. 300). According to Bernal Díaz (chap. 128), the Tlaxcalteca *tamemes* carrying the gold escaped alive.

Among the dead was a daughter of Motecuçoma who had been baptized and christened Doña Ana. She is supposed to have been pregnant by Cortés when she died. At least two other daughters of Motecuçoma survived and were christened Isabel and Marina. Isabel, the eldest, was married to Alonso de Grado and given, as was her right, Tacuba and its dependencies; Marina was married to Juan Paz, an hidalgo, according to Cortés, and given Ecatepec and its dependencies (*Donación de Tierras a las Hijas de Moctezuma*, in Sanchez Barba, pp. 358–362). Cortés also mentions a third daughter called Maria but says nothing about her being given either a husband or lands. Perhaps she was his child rather than Motecuçoma's, for he left ten thousand *ducados* in his will to a daughter of that name (*Last Will and Testament of Hernando Cortés*, pp. 11, 37).

95. Teocalhueyacan.

96. The lakes are Zumpango, Xaltocan and San Cristóbal. The town is Tepotzotlan.

97. The village of Citlaltepec.

98. Xoloc. In plate 23 of the *Lienzo de Tlaxcala* it appears as Aychqualco.

99. Aztaquemecan.

100. Çacamulco.

101. This was the battle of Otumba (see Bernal Díaz, chap. 128). The Indians were Otomis subject to Texcoco.

102. Apan (?).

103. Hueyotlipan. Cortés received a mixed welcome in Tlaxcala. Xicotencatl was openly hostile and kept his men constantly on the alert. Maxixcatzin, however, is supposed to have insisted on maintaining the alliance on condition that Cortés promised the Tlaxcalteca a share in the spoils, the city of Cholula and the provinces of Huexotzinco and Tepeaca (Muñoz Camargo, p. 236). Wagner (p. 311), quoting from another source, gives two other conditions: command of a fortress in Tenochtitlan and perpetual freedom from tribute. Much has been made of these promises and Cortés's failure to keep them, yet it is not certain that they were in fact ever made, although Maxixcatzin was in a position to bargain and it would be reasonable to suppose that he did. Ixtlilxóchitl says that Cortés promised to confirm the power of the Tlaxcalteca *Tlatoque* in return for aid and Bernal Díaz mentions promises of repayment but nowhere specifies what sort. In 1565 an inquiry was conducted, on Tlaxcalteca initiative, into the affair. Living conquistadors were called as witnesses, but only a very few claimed to have heard Cortés actually make any promises. The rest denied all knowledge of them or admitted to having heard rumors but were unable to say just what Cortés was alleged to have promised. On the evidence of this inquiry, however, Tlaxcala was, in 1585, granted exemption from the obligation to pay tribute, a concession which lasted more or less throughout the colonial period, though in practice it was frequently overruled. (A list of the royal decrees granting privileges to Tlaxcala may be found in Gibson, *op. cit.*, appendix VII.) Cervantes de Salazar (bk. V, chaps. VI, VIII) says that the Mexica sent ambassadors to the Tlaxcalteca pleading for a united front against the Spaniards. But the Tlaxcalteca knew only too well that such an alliance would mean the loss of their independence, for, if the Spaniards were defeated, the Mexica would not be slow in taking their revenge on an old and troublesome enemy. The plea, however, divided the Tlacalteca camp. Xicotencatl was knocked down the steps of the council chamber, and the ambassadors were dismissed, "very confused about what had happened and not daring to ask for a reply" (Cervantes de Salazar, chap. VIII).

104. Juan de Alcántara (Bernal Díaz, chap. 129).

105. Cortés was wounded in the head a second time on his journey to Honduras. His skull, at present in the Hospital de Jesús in Mexico City, shows evidence of severe fractures down the left side.

106. Near Zautla. See Bernal Díaz (chap. 134), according to whom, the Spaniards were Juan de Alcántara and two others from Vera Cruz.

107. None of the tribes with whom Cortés came in contact were truly cannibalistic. Certain portions of the sacrificial victims were eaten, but this was a symbolic ritual. The reiterated accusations made by Cortés and

other Spaniards seem partly an excuse for taking slaves, partly a preconceived idea of native customs acquired in the Antilles, whose inhabitants were often cannibals.

Bernal Díaz (chap. 135) is bitter about the division of the slaves: Cortés as usual seems to have taken the best cut for himself. The soldiers also complained about Cortés's fifth: "They swore to God that such a thing had never been done before, having two kings in the lands of our King and Lord, and taking two-fifths."

108. According to Bernal Díaz (chap. 136), Andrés de Duero and several other captains now returned to Cuba with some gold and jewelry with which to buy supplies. Solís went to Jamaica for horses, and Francisco de Álvarez Chico and Alonso de Ávila were sent to Santo Domingo on some unspecified business. Diego de Ordaz returned to Castile. The Garay expedition consisted of three ships, one of which sunk. The men from the other two, under Diego de Camargo and Miguel Díaz de Auz, joined Cortés in Tepeaca (Bernal Díaz, chap. 133). Two ships from Velázquez also arrived about this time, carrying provisions for Narváez. The first was under the command of Pedro Barba; the second under Rodrigo Morejón de Lobera: these likewise joined Cortés. Bernal Díaz also says that a ship arrived from Castile, sailing by way of the Canaries to circumvent the embargo on ships going to New Spain. She belonged to Juan de Burgos and was well stocked with arms and powder. In all, these reinforcements amounted to approximately 171 men, fifty horses and a good supply of equipment.

109. Huaquechula (Puebla).

110. They were under the command of Cristóbal de Olid. According to Bernal Díaz (chap. 132), Olid was accompanied by over three hundred soldiers "and all the best horses we had." The majority of the officers in the army seem to have been Narváez's men, and it was they who persuaded Olid not to go to Huaquechula. Díaz also denies that Cortés was present during the battle.

111. Toribio de Motolinía spells it Acapetlahuacan (*Memoriales*, p. 205). It is probably Ocuituco.

112. Izúcar.

113. Oaxaca. The present-day state is much larger than the area referred to by Cortés, which is the Mixtec province of what is today Coaixtlahuaca. According to the *Codex Mendoza* (III, fol. 43 r. v.), there were only eleven tax-collecting stations in the area.

114. Cuitlahuac, ruler of Ixtapalapa. His reign lasted only eighty days. He died of smallpox on November 25, 1520 (see n. 38).

115. Chimalpopoca. He was not Motecuçoma's heir, since the succession was not decided by primogeniture but by election. Motecuçoma must also have had many more sons than two (Sahagún, bk. XII, chap. 24, p. 66).

116. Rodrigo Rangel was in command at Vera Cruz.

117. According to Torquemada (bk. IV, chap. 4), Grijalva was the first to use this name.

118. The Vienna Codex has no signature. Fernán Cortés appears in Lorenzana and most subsequent editions.

119. This note appears at the end of the first printed edition (Seville, 1522). It was not written by Cortés. According to González de Barcia, Cromberger was the author (*Historiadores Primitivos de las Indias Occidentales*, I: 62). If this is so, he must have had access to a letter written by Cortés in August, 1521, which reached Spain in March, 1522. This letter is now lost, but it must have contained a brief notice of the fall of Mexico.

Notes to the Third Letter

1. Jalacingo (Veracruz).

2. Francisco de Orozco.

3. The text of these ordinances (*Ordenanzas Militares dadas por Hernando Cortés in Tlaxcallan*) may be found in Sanchez Barba, pp. 336–341. They are discussed by C. Harvey Gardiner in *The Constant Captain*, pp. 66–71.

The speech made by Cortés on this occasion, or rather his account of it, is intended to persuade the emperor that in attempting to take Tenochtitlan by force, he is acting both in the best interests of the Crown and in accordance with the law. The Mexica, he argues, are not free citizens but rebellious vassals and must be punished as such. The reference here is to the donation of Motecuçoma (see the Second Letter, n. 42). This is almost certainly a creation of Cortés, but it was no doubt accepted by the Crown; and later writers such as Fernández del Pulgar who sought to justify the conquest used it as the basis for their arguments (*Historia Verdadera de la Conquista de la Nueva España*). Without it, Cortés's action could only have been seen as a flagrant act of aggression. Cortés gives a further list of reasons for attacking the city: the Spaniards are fighting for their Faith against a barbarian, that is to say non-Christian, people; they are fighting for their king and to defend themselves. All these are "just" causes and appear in one form or another in the *Siete Partidas* (cf. part. II, tit. 23, leyes I–II. See Silvio Zavala, *La "Utopía" de Tomás Moro en la Nueva España y otros estudios*, pp. 49–50). *Ordenanzas Militares y Civiles*, pp. 13–23.

4. Texmelucan.

5. Coatepec.

6. Coanacochtzin.

7. Coatlinchán and Huexotla (both in the state of Mexico).

8. Tenango.

9. From early January, 1521, until the end of May, Cortés slowly encircled the Mexica capital. Once the highly successful Tepeaca campaign had secured the vital lines of communication with the coast, Cortés suppressed, or forced into alliance, every city to which the Mexica might have turned for support. Texcoco was chosen as the base for these operations probably because of its proximity to Tlaxcala, its size—sufficient to support a large army—and the sparsity of the population on the eastern shores of the lake system. Within five months of establishing himself in Texcoco Cortés had brought the cities around the lakes under Spanish control, and the way was now clear for an offensive against Tenochtitlan itself (C. Harvey Gardiner, *Naval Power in the Conquest of Mexico*, pp. 190 ff. See also Lúcas Alamán, *Disertaciones*, I: 126 ff.).

10. Ahuaxpitzactzin, Cuicuitzcatzin.

11. According to Ixtlilxóchitl (II:414–415) Tecocoltzin, christened Fernando Cortés, and a favorite of the conqueror's, was the first to ascend the throne. Bernal Díaz (chap. 137) says that he was instated the day after their arrival in the city, but is clearly confusing him with Don Fernando Ahuaxpitzactzin. Sahagún (bk. 8, chap. 3, p. 10) lists the last kings of Texcoco as Cacamatzin, Coanacochtzin, Tecocoltzin and Ixtlilxochitl: Ahuaxpitzactzin and Cuicuitzcatzin, puppet rulers of the Spaniards, are omitted for patriotic reasons. The two Spaniards left as guardians for Don Fernando (Ahuaxpitzactzin) were Antonio de Villarroel, who later changed his name to Serrano de Cardona, and Pedro Sánchez Farfán (Bernal Díaz, *loc. cit.;* Orozco y Berra, IV: 517–518).

12. Bernal Díaz (chap. 147) says that a ship belonging to Juan de Burgos arrived about this time. In chap. 136, however, he says that Juan de Burgos arrived while Cortés was still in Tlaxcala, sometime in late December or early January (see n. 96). But in a statement made after his death the date is given as early as July (Wagner, p. 515, n. 36). Herrera (dec. 111, bk. I, chap. V) also makes a reference to this ship but gives no more details than Cortés. The only other vessels to land at Vera Cruz arrived in late February, by which time the brigantines had already reached Texcoco.

13. Huaquechula (Puebla).

14. Zultepec.

15. The village was Calpulalpan, called Pueblo Morisco by the Spaniards. Juan Yuste came over with Narváez and had been made alcalde of San Salvador. He was a member of Francisco de Morla's party, which was ambushed and defeated in the manner described.

16. Ayotecatl, Teuctepil and Chichimecatlecle.

17. Martín López, the shipwright, seems to have been given orders to begin the construction of the brigantines in September, 1520. He left Tepeaca with three assistants, two of whom have tentatively been identified as Juan Martín Narices and one of the two Mafla brothers, either Pedro or Miguel; a number of other Spanish artisans joined him later. The brigantines were completed by February, 1521, and were then tested in the Zahuapan River, which had been dammed for this purpose, and immediately after were transported to Texcoco. The caravan first moved to Hueyotlipan, where it waited eight days for an escort sent by Cortés under Sandoval. When Sandoval finally arrived they moved on, taking three days to reach Texcoco (Gardiner, *Naval Power*, pp. 86 ff.). The route taken by the brigantines is discussed by Orozco y Berra and José María Luis Mora, see Lúcas Alamán *et al.*, eds., *Diccionario Universal de Historia y de Geografía*, V: 818, 856. See also the study of López by Guillermo Porras Muñoz, "Martín López: Carpintero de Ribera."

18. Xaltocan.

19. Cuauhtitlan.

20. Tenayucan or Tenayocan, now called Tenayucan.

21. Azcapotzalco.

22. Tlacopan. Capital of the Tepaneca tribe. Tacuba, as it is called today, was the least powerful of the cities of the Triple Alliance, receiving only half the amount paid in yearly tributes to Texcoco and Tenochtitlan. The city's territorial dominion reached as far as the Tarascan frontier, roughly between the present-day states of Mexico and Michoacán.

23. Acolman. According to Wagner (p. 341), he reached Texcoco about February 18.

24. Huaxtepec, now Oaxtepec (Morelos).

25. Ayachipichtlan, now Yecapixtla.

26. According to Bernal Díaz (chap. 142), Sandoval reached Chalco on March 12. After his return to Texcoco there was a branding of the slaves captured in the raid. Cortés's dealing with his men, according to Bernal Díaz (chap. 143), was even more unjust than it had been in Tepeaca.

27. The ships, two caravels and a *nao* of 150 tons, belonged to Rodrigo Bastidas. The nao was called the *Maria;* she reached Vera Cruz on February 24 carrying, among others, a friar called Pedro Melgarejo de Urrea. He was a Franciscan from Seville, and his reputation in Mexico was not a good one. Bernal Díaz (chap. 143) speaks of him in an unflattering tone: "There came a friar of St. Francis, who was called Pedro Melgarejo de Urrea, a native of Seville, who brought some bulls of our Lord St. Peter, and with these we might absolve ourselves if we had anything owing on account of the wars in which we were engaged; thus within a few months this friar returned rich and comfortably off to Castile." (These bulls were the *Bulas de Cruzada* by which a soldier might gain a dispensation for sins committed during the wars.) Despite this, Melgarejo soon became a firm friend of Cortés, but later fell out with him because he failed to deliver ten thousand *pesos* with which he had been entrusted for Martín Cortés, the conqueror's father. On his return to Spain, Melgarejo was made *Predicador de su Majestad y Consejero de Indias* ("Preacher to His Majesty and Counsellor on the Indies") and, in 1520, Bishop of Dulcigno. Furthermore, Grijalva has this to say of him: "Father Melgarejo showed such courage and zeal in this enterprise [the conquest] that he was present at every battle with a crucifix in his hands. . . . This Religious preached to the army on numerous occasions, which was no small task, for the most difficult thing in this enterprise was to calm and control our men, for many were the opportunities for them to be covetous, cruel to the Indians and disobedient to their captain. The spirit and fervor of this saintly friar was very necessary in order to be able to teach them salutary doctrine" (*Crónica de la Orden de N.P.S. Augustin en Las Provincias de la Nueva España . . . por el P.M.F. loan de Grijalva . . .* , bk. I, chap. 1. Quoted by Robert Ricard, "Fr. Pedro Melgarejo," pp. 68–69). Bernal Díaz's dislike for the Franciscan may therefore have been due to his efforts to provide a measure of control over Cortés's unruly army. (Robert Ricard, *op. cit.*, and "Note sur Fr. Pedro de Melgarejo, Evangélisateur du Mexique.")

Julián de Alderete, appointed royal treasurer by the authorities in Santo Domingo, also arrived with the fleet, though, according to Cervantes de Salazar (bk. V, chap. 71), in a ship of his own, Bastidas having only two (see Orozco y Berra, vol. IV, p. 537). There is confusion as to how many men these ships actually brought. Cervantes de Salazar (*loc. cit.*) puts the figures at about two hundred men and eighty horses, but a captain of one of the ships said that there were four hundred men and more than sixty horses. In the parade held on April 28 Cortés counted a total of 818 foot soldiers and eighty-six horsemen. As he had had 550 foot soldiers and forty horsemen when he left Tlaxcala, the reinforcements must have numbered about 350 foot and forty-six horse, allowing a few extra to replace the dead. Bernal Díaz (chap. 148) gives a lower figure.

28. Tizapán (?), Mexicalcingo and Naucalpan, in the state of Mexico.

29. Tlalmanalco.

30. Yautepec (Morelos).

31. Jiutepec.

32. Cuauhnahuac ("Near the Trees" or "Near the Forest," according to Orozco y Berra, I: 494, and James Cooper Clark, *Codex Mendoza*, II: 1). The Spaniards corrupted this into Cuernavaca, the name by which the city is known today. Cortés built a house there after the conquest, and the city became the center of his marquisate (Wagner, p. 516, n. 44). It is now the capital of the state of Morelos.

33. According to Bernal Díaz (chap. 144), this feat consisted of clambering along the trunks of two trees growing toward each other from opposite sides of the ravine. Three soldiers fell into the water below and one broke his leg.

34. Xochimilco ("In the Place of the Xochimilca") was a tributary town of Tenochtitlan. The Spaniards arrived there on April 16.

35. Cristóbal de Olea, who was badly wounded as a result.

36. They left on the eighteenth. According to Bernal Díaz (chap. 145), the Mexica captured four Spaniards during these three days. They were sacrificed and their limbs sent to the provinces as a warning.

37. Huitzilopochco (now called Churubusco), Cuitlahuac (now Tlahuac) and Mizquic.

38. These were Francisco Martín Vendabal and Pedro Gallego.

39. Chinantla (Oaxaca).

40. Cervantes de Salazar (bk. V, chap. 101) says that the companion of Hernando de Barrientos was named Heredia. He also tells of Barrientos' ingenious use of gunpowder to frighten the unfortunate Indians into unquestioning obedience.

41. None of the Spaniards wished to become oarsmen. Bernal Díaz (chap. 149) says that Cortés forced into the brigantines all those who had been sailors, had gone fishing or were from any port or "parts where there are sailors." He also says that each ship had twelve crossbowmen and harquebusiers; Cortés is, however, more likely to be correct about the number. The captains and crews of the brigantines are discussed by Gardiner, *Naval Power*, pp. 133–154.

42. Cortés's dates are inaccurate. He says that the division of forces took place on the second day of the feast of the Holy Ghost, which fell that year on May 19. They could not, therefore, have left ten days previously.

Bernal Díaz gives the thirteenth (chap. 150), which is no better. Orozco y Berra (IV: 579) carefully examined both Cortés and Bernal Díaz, comparing them against Torquemada (bk. IV, chap. 189). He gives the twenty-second as the date of departure for Alvarado and Olid. Sandoval left on May 31.

Xicotencatl, the Tlaxcalteca chieftain, deserted at this time. The reasons for this are not clear. Cervantes de Salazar (bk. V, chap. 121), Bernal Díaz (chap. 150) and Herrera (dec. III, bk. 1, chap. 17) all give different versions, as they do of his end. Herrera, who spoke with both Marquez and Ojeda, who were sent to arrest Xicotencatl and were present at his execution, says that he was hung in public in Texcoco.

43. Fray Pedro Melgarejo and Luis Marín were sent to settle this dispute.

44. May 30.

45. Called Tepepolco. It was given to Cortés in 1529 and renamed El Peñon del Marqués. According to Bernal Díaz (chap. 150), the encounter took place four days after Corpus Christi, i.e., on June 3.

46. Xoloco. The first meeting between Cortés and Motecuçoma took place here.

47. Sahagún makes some interesting remarks on Mexica tactics. "But when the Mexicans could hold and determine where the gun [shots] and bolts would strike, no longer did they follow a direct course. Only from side to side would they veer; only sideways, at a slant, they traveled" (bk. XII, chap. 20, p. 84).

48. This probably took place somewhere between June 10 and 12. According to Sahagún (bk. XII, chap. 21, p. 85), the gate was the Eagle Gate (Cuauhquiyauac), where stood carved figures of an eagle, an ocelot and a wolf.

49. This gun, a lombard, was thrown into the water at Tetamaçolco, which, according to the Spanish text of Sahagún, was in a wood "called Tepetzinco where the baths are" (bk. XII, chap. 31, p. 86).

50. Ixtlilxóchitl tells a well-known story which Wagner (p. 348) believes to be a confusion with an earlier incident that took place during Cortés's first residence in the city. "They [Cortés and Ixtlilxochitl] climbed the tower and threw down many idols, especially in the principal chapel where Huitzilopochitl was. Cortés and Ixtlilxuchitl arrived at the same time and both attacked the idol. Cortés seized the gold mask encrusted with precious stones that the idol was wearing, while Ixtlilxuchitl cut off the head of one they had, a few years previously, worshipped as their God" (I: 360).

51. This is obviously false. Bernal Díaz (chap. 151) makes some interesting remarks about the fighting. The Mexica were using captured Spanish lances, or lances made from broken sword blades tied to long poles. "With those lances and the great showers of arrows and javelins which they shot at us from the lake, they wounded or killed the horses before they could do the Mexicans any harm; and, furthermore, the horsemen, who owned those horses did not wish to risk them, for a horse at that time cost eight hundred pesos, and some more than a thousand and this they did not have."

52. According to Ixtlilxóchitl (I: 361), Fernando Tecocoltzin was already dead by this time, and Ixtlilxochitl, also christened Fernando, was lord of Texcoco. The Mexican historian claims to have based his account on a relation of Alonso Axayaca, various native paintings, a manuscript written in Nahuatl and signed by the lords of Texcoco, and information received from eyewitnesses. He maintains that Fernando Ixtlilxochitl left Texcoco with the Spaniards and that "after God, [the country] was won with his help and favor." The Texcocan reinforcements must have arrived about June 10.

53. The Otomis.

54. It seems unlikely that the Xochimilca were with Cortés at this point. They could surely only have joined him after they had betrayed Cuauhtemoc (Wagner, p. 351. See n. 56 below).

55. June 1 (?). Orozco y Berra, IV: 579.

56. These people had betrayed Cuauhtemoc, presumably in order to curry favor with Cortés. Offering assistance to the Mexica, they had joined the defending armies and been given gifts of devices and shields, "To each one they gave a shallow gourd vessel of chocolate [cacao]. Thereupon he [Cuauhtemoc] said to them: 'Onward! let there be battle, O chieftains! For our foes already are come!' . . . But these people of Xochimilco then also raised a war cry and fell upon the boats [canoes]. In no wise did they help us, but only, then, robbed the people. They despoiled the beloved women and the small children, and the beloved old women. Then some they there slew; there these breathed their last" (Sahagún, bk. XII, chap. 33, p. 91). The Mexica, however, pursued them and killed or captured nearly all, although some survived to reach the Spanish camp. In 1563 the caciques and natives of the city put in a claim for privileges in payment for the aid they gave to Cortés. They maintained that they had given him two thousand canoes replete with provisions and twelve thousand warriors. It was also alleged that they had assisted Alvarado (their encomendero) in Honduras, Guatemala and Pánuco, and had gone with Nuño de Guzmán to Jalisco (*CDIR*, 13: 293–294).

57. Bernal Díaz (chap. 151) says this happened on a Sunday. Orozco y Berra (IV: 599) fixes the date as June 23.

58. This must have been June 24, the day of St. John the Baptist. Although Cortés makes no mention of it, Bernal Díaz (chap. 151) claims that Cuauhtemoc launched an offensive against all three camps, in commemoration of Cortés's first entry into the city.

59. Alonso de Molina gives four readings: Tianquiztli, Tianquizittoyan, Tlanamacoyan and Tiamicoyan (*Vocabulario de la Lengua Mexicana*, pp. 84, 113).

60. Julián de Alderete. According to Bernal Díaz (chap. 152), the attack was made on a Sunday. It must, therefore, have been June 30.

61. Cristóbal de Olea, whom Bernal Díaz (chap. 152) says killed four Mexica captains before being overpowered. Ixtlilxóchitl claims that his namesake was the one responsible for rescuing Cortés, and bickers about Spanish attempts to deprive him of the glory (I: 368). There is an old legend that an Indian did help save Cortés, though he is generally held to be a Tlaxcalteca.

62. Copal (Nahuatl *copalli*). A yellow resin widely used as incense throughout Mesoamerica.

63. Cortés's figures for the number of the dead are understated. Sahagún (bk. XII, chap. 35, p. 100) says that fifty-three men, four horses and a large number of Indian allies (including some from Xochimilco) were captured and later sacrificed. Bernal Díaz (chap. 152) says that sixty-six Spaniards were taken to be sacrificed. Orozco y Berra (IV: 609), after consulting numerous sources, gives "more than sixty Spaniards, seven or eight horses, two cannons, many weapons and a great multitude of the allies." The Spanish standard was taken by an Indian from Tlatelolo, called Tlapanecatl or Tlapanecatl hecatzin at a place "where now is [the church] named San Martín," a barrio in Parcialidad de Santa Maria la Redonda Cuepopan or Tlaquechiuhcan, according to Alfonso Caso (quoted by Dibble and Anderson in Sahagún, bk. XII, chap. 35, p. 99, n. 2).

Sometime around this date the Mexica succeeded in grounding one of the brigantines by driving stakes into the lake bottom. Juan Portillo, captain of one of the brigantines, was killed, and Pedro Barba was mortally wounded (Bernal Díaz, chap. 151).

After Cortés's defeat most of his allies deserted. According to Bernal Díaz (chap. 153), only Ixtlilxochitl and some forty of his friends and relations remained with Cortés. A cacique from Huexotzinco with about fifty followers stayed with Sandoval, and, with Alvarado, two sons of Don Lorenzo de Vargas (Xicotencatl the elder) and Chichimecatecle with some eighty men. Bernal Díaz adds this up and makes the total some two hundred men. Orozco y Berra (IV: 610) thinks that Bernal Díaz is exaggerating—which he undoubtedly is—and points out that Díaz himself (chap. 155) says that Andrés de Tapia left "with many allies." The Mexica had announced that their gods had promised them that the Spaniards would be annihilated within eight days. When the eight days had passed the allies began to return.

64. Cuernavaca. The messengers arrived on Tuesday, July 2 (Orozco y Berra, IV: 611).

65. Huitzuco (?).

66. Orozco y Berra (IV: 615) conjectures that Andrés de Tapia returned on July 11; the Otomis must therefore have arrived on July 13.

67. Huitzuco.

68. Ponce de León made a first expedition to Florida in 1512 in pursuit of the legendary Fountain of Youth, but failed to make a landing. (The chronology is obscure. The royal warrant for the expedition was granted in February, 1512, but it is possible that he did not in fact set out until the following year. On this point see Oskar Peschel, *Geschichte des Zeitalters der Entdeckungen*, p. 411 n.) He returned again in 1521, having secured a further warrant to colonize the "island of Florida" as well as that of "Beniny" (Bimine, probably Andros in the Bahamas). He equipped two ships and provided two hundred men and fifty horses. He was defeated by the Indians probably somewhere near Tampa Bay and was so badly wounded in the battle that he was forced to return to Cuba, where he died that same year (Vincente Murga Sanz, *Juan Ponce de León*, pp. 236–242). For an analysis of the mythology surrounding the Fountain of Youth, see Leonard Olschki, "Ponce de León's Fountain of Youth, History of a Geographical Myth."

69. Cervantes de Salazar says that it was Ixtlilxochitl who first suggested this idea to Cortés (Wagner, p. 349).

70. Cuauhtemoc. The last *Uei Tlatoani* of Mexico: *Cuauhtli* ("eagle") and *Temo* ("he swoops"), thus "Swooping Eagle" (*Codex Mendoza*, I: 35 n.). He was probably the son of Auitzotzin, lord of Tlatelolco.

71. July 25 (?).

72. August 1 (?).

73. Antonio de Sotelo, a native of Seville, was responsible for this machine. He claimed to have acquired a great knowledge of siege engines while on campaign in Italy with the Great Captain. According to Sahagún (bk. XII, chap. 38, p. 109), the catapult was aimed at Tlatelolco. The Mexica appear

to have been well aware that the machine was a failure and called it "the wooden sling." Sahagún (*loc. cit.*) says that the first stone fell behind the marketplace at Xomolco.

74. Thursday, August 8 (Orozco y Berra, IV: 632 n.).

75. Saturday, August 10 (*ibid.*).

76. The Ciuacoatl, called the "ruler's vicar" by Sahagún (bk. XIII, chap. 39, p. 115). Cortés appears to be confusing him with Tepanecatl, or captain of the armies.

   This was the last assault upon the city. Sahagún (bk. XII, chap. 40, p. 118) says: "And when the shield was laid down, when we gave way, it was the year count Three House and the day count was One Serpent." According to Orozco y Berra (IV: 636 n.), *Ce Coatl* ("One Serpent") is the month *Tlaxochimaco*. Ixtlilxóchitl (I: 376), using the Texcocan count, puts the date as the day *Macuili Toxtli* ("Five Rabbit"), the sixth of the eighth month, called *Micaylhuitzintli;* by the Christian calendar it was August 13, the day of San Hipólito. A church of San Hipólito was erected on the Tacuba causeway, and the anniversary of the fall of Tenochtitlan was observed as a national holiday throughout the colonial period.

77. It is impossible to compute the number of the Mexica or allied dead. Ixtlilxóchitl (I: 379) says that 240,000 of the Mexica perished, among whom were nearly all the nobility, a claim which was repeated in 1551 by the natives of Coyoacan (Wagner, p. 355). He also says that more than 30,200 Texcocans died out of the 200,000 fighting for the Spaniards. Gómara (p. 392) says that some 100,000 were killed, but that many more died of hunger or smallpox (*pestilencia:* On this subject see Alfred W. Crosby, "Conquistador y Pestilencia: The First New World Pandemic and the Fall of the Great Indian Empires"), in which he is followed by both Herrera and Torquemada. Bernal Díaz (chap. 156) gives no figures but claims to have read of the destruction of Jerusalem and doubts that fewer people were slain in Mexico. Oviedo (bk. XXXIII, chap. 30) claims to have talked to a number of the participants, who all made similar comparisons with Jerusalem. Perhaps this somewhat fanciful idea was popular among the army. Torquemada also adds that thirty thousand warriors surrendered (Oviedo and Ixtlilxóchitl put the figure even higher, at seventy thousand and sixty thousand respectively). These figures are probably exaggerated. Sherburne F. Cook and Lesley Bird Simpson (*The Population of Central Mexico in the Sixteenth Century*, pp. 22–27) estimate a preconquest population figure of one million for the entire province, but this is based largely on Spanish accounts and the population of Tenochtitlan itself must have been, in any case, very much less; furthermore, no count is made of the women and children who survived.

78. Sahagún (bk. XII, chap. 39, p. 116) says that the people in the canoe with Cuauhtemoc were only "the seasoned warriors Teputzitoloc and Yaztachimal, Cuauhtemoc's page. And the one who poled [the boat] was named Cenyaotl." Durán (chap. LXXVII), however, says that there was only a single oarsman with the *Uei Tlatoani* in the canoe. He also says that Cuauhtemoc had previously dressed all the women up as warriors and sent them out onto the roofs to decoy the Spaniards. Alexander von Humboldt (*Essai Politique sur la Royaume de la Nouvelle Espagne*, I: 192–193) says that the place of his capture is believed to have been close to the main square in Tlatelolco. Immediately after the capture, a dispute arose between Sandoval, as commander of the fleet, and Holguín, as to who should have Cuauhtemoc. Cortés put a stop to this argument and promised to let the emperor decide, but in the end it was Cortés himself who claimed the honor. He was granted the device of the heads of seven captive kings linked by a chain, among which was that of Cuauhtemoc.

79. The spoils, however, were few, although Bernal Díaz (chap. 157) says that there was a riotous celebration the evening after the fall of the city, each man boasting about the things he would do with his illusionary wealth. But looting failed to reveal any great quantities of gold, the booty being mostly human. The Spaniards took the good-looking women and all the strong young men they could find. Sahagún (bk. XII, chap. 40, p. 118) says that the men and women hid the gold on their persons. "[The gold] was everywhere in the bosoms or in the skirts of the wretched women. And as for the men it was everywhere in their breech clouts and in their mouths." He says that some of the women dressed in rags and covered themselves with mud to avoid capture, and that the Spaniards were not interested in precious stones, "the green stone [jade], quetzal feathers and turquoise," which to the Mexica were of greater worth than gold. In the following chapter (pp. 121–122) Sahagún describes the meeting between Cortés and Cuauhtemoc. Cuauhtemoc claimed that Cortés had all the gold there was. Cortés refused to believe this, and through Marina demanded two hundred ingots. Cuauhtemoc evidently could not provide this sum, and a search of the city was begun; this, however, revealed only a few objects of no great value. Bernal Díaz (*loc. cit.*) says they found some eighty or ninety *pesos*'s worth of jewelry and a wheel of gold. Cortés was accused of having first burned and then drowned an Indian during this search. Apparently he had been told that a gold statue of Huitzilopochtli and Cuauhtemoc's treasure were buried beneath the *Uei Tlatoani*'s home. When Cortés realized that he had been deceived, he had the Indian burned and then tossed into the lake, where he died. Cuauhtemoc, who was present, tried to hang himself in order to escape such a fate (*Sumario*, II: 303–304. The witness was Francisco de Zamora), and Cortés now had Cuauhtemoc and Tetlepanquetzaltzin, lord of Tacuba, tortured by burn-

ing their feet with oil. As a result of this, Cuauhtemoc was crippled (*li-siado*) and Tetlepanquetzaltzin died (*CDIR*, 27: 23). Cortés claimed that it was done on the insistence of Alderete, the royal treasurer (this at least was the excuse given by Garcia de Llerena, Cortés's agent at his residencia [*CDIR*, 27: 239–240]). Torquemada (bk. IV, chap. 103) and Cervantes de Salazar (bk. VI, chap. 2) also lay the blame on the royal officials. Bernal Díaz (*loc. cit.*) adds that Alderete and Narváez's men suspected Cortés of having taken more than his fifth, over which there was already some discontent. Ixtlilxóchitl (I:380–381) claims that his namesake remonstrated with Cortés over such cruelty (though he pretends that it was a servant of Cuauhtemoc who was tortured), whereupon Cortés put an end to it. He also claims that Ixtlilxochitl had to ransom his brother Cohuanacochtzin with what seems to have been almost the entire financial resources of Texcoco.

It is impossible to compute the exact amount of gold that was found. Bernal Díaz (*loc. cit.*) says that some 185,000 *pesos* had been collected before Cuauhtemoc was tortured, but this is probably an error. Bernal Díaz, a common foot soldier, had every reason to magnify what he considered to be the abuses of Cortés and the royal officials. He must, however, have been very conscious of his own lot, and he says that when the spoils were finally divided the horsemen received eighty *pesos* and the foot soldiers only fifty. As a sword cost fifty *pesos*, and a crossbow sixty, they were unwilling to accept such a paltry sum and suggested that it should be given to the sick, the crippled, the deaf and dumb, and those who had been burned by gunpowder. Once again there were complaints about Cortés's fifth (Wagner, p. 362), and he was even accused of receiving gifts of gold from which no fifth was paid to the royal treasurer (*Sumario*, II:218–221).

Cortés's own estimate of 130,000 *pesos* seems, however, to be a fair one. Wagner (pp. 361–362), working on this figure, concludes that Bernal Díaz's estimates of the amounts received by the soldiers are about right.

A further fifteen thousand *pesos* seem to have been extracted for the king "with the consent of the people," according to Cortés (*CDIR*, 27: 253). In all, Cortés claimed to have sent 37,000 *pesos* with this letter. But this was all seized by a French corsair before it could reach Spain (see the Fourth Letter, n. 64).

80. A force of three hundred men was left behind in Tenochtitlan under the command of Rodríguez de Villafuerte.

A charge for land usurpation was brought against the second Marqués del Valle in 1550 by the natives of Coyoacan. From this it seems that Cortés took possession of the main temple and some lands, the ownership of which was hotly disputed. He also appears to have appropriated the residence of the lord of the city for himself (*DIHC*, pp. 355 ff.; Wagner, pp. 364, 520 n. 19). The Spaniards frequently billeted themselves in the priests' quarters, presumably because they were the largest buildings available, and because the *teucalli* itself was militarily a strategic position.

81. According to Oviedo, the value of these things was some fifty thousand *pesos* (quoted by Wagner, p. 519 n. 11).

82. Michoacán. An independent Tarascan state. (See the Fourth Letter, n. 5.)
   The name of the province is Mechuacan and is Nahuatl in origin. Seler interprets it as "a Place of Fish" (*michi* or *michu*, "a fish" and the suffix *can*, "in the place of." Eduard Seler, *Gesammelte Abhandlungen zur Amerikanischen Sprach-und Alterthumskunde*, III:33–157). It was altered to Michoacán by royal decree on September 28, 1534.

83. One Spaniard who made this journey was Francisco de Montano, who told Cervantes de Salazar (bk. VI, chaps. 13 *et seq.*) the story of the expedition. The province was first discovered by a soldier called Porrillas, who had been sent to look for chickens with which to supply the army. When he returned to Mexico he took two of the Tarascans with him. Cortés then sent Montano "and his companions" with twenty Indians and a dog. The lord of Michoacán (the *Cazonci*) kept the dog but returned the Spaniards in company with a number of Indians and some gifts for Cortés. After receiving this embassy, he sent Montano back again with another Spaniard to explore the littoral of the Southern Sea.
   A different and undoubtedly more accurate story is given in a native manuscript entitled *Relación delas Cerimonias y rrictos* (sic) *y población y Gobernación delos Yndios dela Provincia de Mechuacan*, made in 1541 for the viceroy Antonio de Mendoza. First a Spaniard (Porrillas?) on a white horse appeared on February 23, 1522, followed by three mounted Spaniards, presumably Montano's company. They were well received, but a large number of heavily armed warriors were sent on a hunting party in an attempt to frighten them. The *Cazonci* kept their dog and some pigs (the easiest way to transport provisions over a long distance was on the hoof), which he took to be large rats, and then sent them back accompanied by two Indian women. Later Montano (?) with three other Spaniards returned but left again after two days, taking with them a large number of Tarascans. On July 17 Cristóbal de Olid came with a considerable force of Mexicans and so terrified the poor *Cazonci* that he tried to drown himself. When the Spaniards finally arrived they treated the Indians to the customary display of fire power and overturned their idols. No resistance was offered, however, and Olid remained 120 days (six "months") in the province, during which time he ransacked the *Cazonci*'s house in his search for gold. He then left with an Indian whom the *Relación* calls Don Pedro (it also says that he "is now a governor"), and who was to carry two hundred

loads (*cargas*) of gold and silver shields to Cortés at Coyoacan (chaps. XXIII *et seq.*, pp. 245 ff.). This last expedition was obviously a major undertaking and is therefore probably the one mentioned by Cortés. According to Beaumont, the first Spaniard to reach Michoacán was a soldier called Villadiego, who was lost there. This makes five exploratory expeditions in all (Pedro de Beaumont, *Crónica de Michoacán*, II:4).

84. Huatusco (Veracruz).

85. Orizaba.

86. Francisco de Orozco.

87. Sandoval seems to have been in Vera Cruz at this time, and Andrés de Monjaras was ordered to found the town and elect the alcaldes and regidores. Medellín, however, was probably founded after the arrival of Cristóbal de Tapia (see n. 94).

88. There were many complaints made against Cortés, alleging that the distribution of land had been unfair: the best plots were given to his relations and servants, while others were sent out into marshes and the edge of the city or given nothing at all (*Sumario*, I:235. See also n. 98). According to Ixtlilxóchitl (I:386), Motecuçoma's son Tlacahuepantzin, christened Don Pedro, was given the district of Atzacualco.

89. Alonso García Bravo and another unnamed Spaniard drew up plans for the new city. Bravo seems to have been the army's chief architect, planning the fortress of Vera Cruz and the city of Oaxaca as well as a palisade at Pánuco (see José R. Benítez, *Alonso García Bravo, Planeador de la Ciudad de México y su primer director de obras públicas*). There was much opposition to building the new city on the site of the old. It was marshy and unhealthy, communications were difficult and the land was poor. The soldiery wanted it built in Coyoacan, Texcoco or Tacuba, "where there was dry land and healthy places close to mountains, with plenty of water and lands and where the houses could be built without so much difficulty" (*Sumario, loc. cit.* Testimony of Rodrigo de Castañeda). Cortés himself was against it at first, and in 1521 declared that the city was to be depopulated and any Indian attempting to settle there would be hanged. His changed attitude was almost certainly due to the strategic advantages of having his capital on an island, as much as to the prestige of the old Mexica capital (George Kubler, *Mexican Architecture in the Sixteenth Century*, pp. 69–71).

According to Ixtlilxóchitl (I:386), more than 400,000 men were employed on the rebuilding. They constructed 100,000 houses of a better quality than the old ones and in all some forty thousand more than those that had been there before. These figures are probably exaggerated, but an adobe house does not take long to build, and the entire labor force of the valley seems to have been mobilized for the work. Motolinía lists the rebuilding of Mexico as the seventh of the "ten plagues."

"During the work of construction some laborers were killed by rafters, others fell from a height, and others lost their life under the buildings they were dismantling in one place in order to erect them elsewhere, especially when they dismantled the principal temples of the devil" (*History of the Indians of New Spain*, p. 91). Alva Ixtlilxóchitl says that Ixtlilxochitl was in charge of the work, and that all the laborers were Texcocans. He probably was in charge of the Alcolhua force, but the Ciuacoatl seems to have been entrusted with directing the operations (*loc. cit.* See the Fourth Letter, n. 51). It is nowhere stated exactly when the rebuilding began but March, 1523, seems a likely date (Wagner, p. 396). The city certainly took much longer to build than either Ixtlilxóchitl or Cortés suggest, but in 1555 Robert Tomson reported that there were 300,000 Indians and fifteen hundred Spanish families living in the city, a population figure of some 307,500 persons. This may well be an exaggerated guess, but the lowest sixteenth-century estimate, given in the 1570s by Francisco Hernández, physician to Philip II, is 100,000 Indians (*The voyage of Robert Tomson Marchant into Nova Hispania in the year 1555* . . . in vol. IX of Hakluyt's *Principal Navigations* . . . , p. 355. Francisco Hernández, *De Antiquitatibus Novae Hispaniae*, quoted by George Kubler, *op. cit.*, p. 72 n.).

90. *Cazonci.* The story may be found in Cervantes de Salazar, bk. VI, chaps. 25–28.

91. The number is missing in manuscript.

92. He arrived in early December, probably on the third or fourth.

93. Several members of the council of Vera Cruz were, it seems, prepared to accept Tapia. According to Juan Tirado, who was to become one of Cortés's most bitter opponents, Melgarejo tried to persuade Cortés to reach an agreement with Tapia. Sandoval was informed of what was happening by Simón de Cuenca, Cortés's factor at Vera Cruz. He immediately departed for the town, swearing to come down on the defectors "with fifty of the toughest men." Monjaras was left behind to found the town of Medellín, of which he appointed himself alcalde (*Sumario*, II:13–15; Orozco y Berra, IV:668).

94. Monjaras's testimony at Cortés's residencia throws some light on the machinations used by Cortés to dispose of Tapia. The town of Medellín, and probably even that of Mexico, was founded to supply representatives to protest against Tapia. Monjaras was ordered "to proceed with all haste to Guaulipan [Hueyotlipan] which is in the province of Tascaltecle, for it

had been agreed that all the representatives of the towns in the lands would meet there with Xpoval [Cristóbal] de Tapia who, it was said, had come as a governor. When this witness reached the province of Tascaltecle a servant of D. Fernando Cortés came to him with certain letters commanding him to go as swiftly as possible to Cenpual [Cempoal] for he had sent his own representatives there together with all the others for he did not think it wise to allow Xpoval de Tapia to come inland, for it would then be hard to send him away" (*Sumario*, II:54–55). These representatives, in addition to the ones named by Cortés, were Pedro de Alvarado from Mexico, Cristóbal Corral from Segura de la Frontera, and Bernardino Vásquez de Tapia from Vera Cruz. The meeting took place on December 24. Tapia's warrants were treated with due respect and sat on for four days. On December 28 Tapia was told that obedience was not in the best interests of the king, as His Majesty had been misinformed by Velázquez as to what had happened in Mexico. Two days later Tapia replied to this refusal, refuting the arguments of the municipal representatives point by point. Cortés's men remained adamant, however, and on the following day the sessions were brought to an end. Tapia departed for Vera Cruz, where, on January 6, he demanded a notarial copy of the proceeding: this was provided by Alonso de Vergara (Orozco y Berra, IV:672–673; *CDIR*, 26:36–58).

Tapia asked to remain in Mexico as a private citizen until he received further instructions from the king. Francisco Álvarez Chico then served him an order to depart at once in His Majesty's interests. Tapia delayed in Vera Cruz, however, on the pretext of selling his property (some Negro slaves, three horses and a ship were bought from him), until Sandoval threatened to send him home in a canoe if he would not go in his ship (*Sumario*, II: 56).

95. Tuxtepec, in Oaxaca.

96. Villafaña had been one of Narváez's men and, according to Diego Holguín, administrator of the goods of the dead (Wagner, pp. 336–337). Bernal Díaz (chap. 146) says that the conspirators had intended to go to Cortés while he was eating with his captains and give him a sealed letter, "like one that came from Castile, and say that it was from his father Martín Cortés. As he was reading it they would kill him, and not only him but all the other captains who were close and might come to his defense." After Cortés's death, Francisco Verdugo, a brother-in-law of Cortés, was to have taken command. Verdugo, however, claimed to know nothing about the plot. The date of this incident is uncertain. Bernal Díaz (chap. 167) agrees with Cortés that it took place while the army was at Texcoco, and Orozco y Berra (IV:559) fixes this date as April 25. Bernal Díaz (*loc. cit.*) also says that a ship belonging to Juan de Burgos arrived at this time,

and this may be the same ship that Cortés mentions as having arrived with much-needed supplies while he was in Texcoco. (See p. 181 and n. 12). Cervantes de Salazar (bk. V, chap. 50) says that it happened before the attack on Ixtapalapa, sometime in January, as does Gómara (p. 376). This would agree with Bernal Díaz's earlier statement (chap. 136) that Juan de Burgos arrived while Cortés was in Tlaxcala. It is possible, of course, that Díaz is borrowing from Gómara in the first instance and Cortés in the second.

As a result of this plot, Cortés is said to have kept constant watch on his companions and to have been accompanied by a regular bodyguard under Antonio de Quiñones (Wagner, p. 337).

97. For the succession of the last Texcocan kings see n. 11. "Don Carlos" followed Don Fernando Ahuaxpitzactzin, while Ixtlilxochitl, evidently too ambitious to be entrusted with the kingship, was granted Otumba, Atispan and the ruined city of Mexico, before Cortés decided to rebuild it. "Don Carlos" did not live long and was succeeded by Ixtlilxochitl.

98. This plea for the establishment in Mexico of the encomienda system (see the First Letter, n. 40) was ill-received in Spain. Previously, Cortés, or Cortés's representatives, had argued against the encomienda, and he now changed his mind just as the Crown had decided to abolish it; though it must be added that Cortés seems always to have been aware of the evils of the system, and he was probably acting under extreme pressure from his army, for whom the conquest of Tenochtitlan had brought little in the way of material wealth. In response to Cortés's request Charles sent, on June 26, 1523, instructions forbidding grants of encomienda and revoking those already made. The document (in *DIU*, 9:167–181) is illuminating of the Crown's attitudes toward its subjects in the New World for it suggests that Charles was as concerned with fulfilling his role as a Catholic prince as with preventing the conquistadors from establishing independent fiefs in America. Cortés's reaction was to write another letter explaining why the royal decree could not possibly be complied with. Although the Crown acquiesced in this, Cortés's insubordination was partly responsible for the inquiry which was later conducted into his affairs (Sanchez Barba, pp. 442–454. The duel between Cortés and the Crown is discussed by L. B. Simpson in *The Encomienda in New Spain*, pp. 56–64). Cortés's own encomienda was enormous, comprising Texcoco, Chalco, Otumba and Coyoacan. Texcoco was technically a province that included also Huexotla, Chiauhtla, Tezayuca and Coatlichan. Chalco was likewise a province and Otumba and Coyoacan were both large *cabeceras* (local capitals). Many of these later reverted to the Crown, and the area of Cortés's control was reduced to that of his marquisate, the Cuernavaca estates, which in 1519 covered two whole provinces, with cabeceras at Cuernavaca itself and at

Oaxtepec, and part of a third, Chalco-Tlalmanalco. Within the Mexican Valley, however, he retained a hold on only two cities, Coyoacan and Tacubaya, and their dependencies. These lay within the boundaries of the marquisate and were thus hereditary holdings (Charles Gibson, *The Aztecs Under Spanish Rule*, pp. 59–61. A comprehensive survey of the marquisate is given by Bernardo García Martínez, *El Marquesado del Valle*).

99. According to Wagner (p. 402), the original of this letter now lost was carried in the treasure ships under Ávila and Quiñones (see the Fourth Letter, n. 64). Juan de Rivera carried a duplicate. He sailed in the *Santa Maria de la Rabada*, under the command of Juan Bautista, and was accompanied by Alonso de Benavides. He reached Seville about November 8 and showed a number of the pieces of Mexican craftsmanship he was carrying to Peter Martyr, who gives a detailed description of them (*De Orbe Novo*, fol. LXXXV v. ff. trans. II:196 ff.).

Bernal Díaz (chap. 159) claims that the town council of Tenochtitlan wrote a letter to the emperor together with Melgarejo, Alderete, Cortés himself and most of the army. This letter has not survived. Díaz, however, gives a description of it which is worth quoting here, for it throws some light on Cortés's intentions at this time.

"And we all spoke of the many good and loyal services which Cortés and all the conquistadores had performed . . . and we besought His Majesty to send us bishops and clerics from every order that were of good life and sound doctrine, so that they might aid us to plant more firmly Our Holy Catholic Faith in these parts. And we besought Him as one, that He grant the government of this New Spain to Cortés, for he was so good and loyal a servant; and to grant favors to all of us, the conquistadores, and for our children. And [we besought Him] that all the official posts such as treasurer, *contador*, *factor* and notary public and the command of fortresses, should not be granted to others but remain with us. We also besought him not to send us lawyers because by coming to this land they would put it in turmoil with their books and there would be lawsuits and contentions."

They also asked that Fonseca should be prevented from meddling in Cortés's affairs and for permission to arrest Velázquez and send him back to Spain. On this last point see p. xxxiv above.

The register of the *Santa Maria de la Rabada* is printed in *CDIR*, 12:253–260. The inventory of the cargo of the ship is given in translation by Marshall H. Saville, *The Goldsmith's Art in Ancient Mexico*, pp. 86–96.

Notes to the Fourth Letter

1. See the Third Letter, n. 99.

2. Gonzalo de Sandoval (see p. 268).

3. This expedition took place early in 1520. Ordaz found "an extraordinarily large city, the richest in gold in the whole country." An account of this expedition is given in the tract *Newe Zeitung von dem lande das die Spanier funden ym 1521 lare genant Jucatan* probably printed in Augsburg in 1522 (H. R. Wagner, trans., in *HAHR*, vol. 9 [1929], pp. 198–202). Coatzacoalco, though a Nahuatl-speaking area, was not part of the Mexica empire, but seems to have been on more amicable terms with it than Ordaz's report might suggest (see Bernal Díaz, chaps. 102–103).

4. *Cazonci* (see the Third Letter, n. 83). This was his title, not his name, which according to the *Relación de Michoacán* (*op. cit.*, p. 246) was Tzintzicha. Beaumont (*op. cit.*, II:20) has Sinsicha.

5. According to *Relación de Michoacán*, the name of the capital of the province was Tzintzuntzan. I suggest that Huicicila, which Gómara (p. 394) calls Chincicila, is, in fact, a corruption of Cuyuacan-Ihuatzio (Çuyuacan is the Nahautl name), the former capital of the province. Tzintzuntzan lies on the banks of Lake Pátzcuaro.

6. At the mouth of the Río Balsas on the frontier of the modern state of Jalisco.

7. The modern state of Colima.

8. Núñez Sedeño and Gutierre de Badajoz were arrested: Sedeño was sentenced to death but was later reprieved. Afterwards he sued Cortés for three thousand *pesos* (Wagner, p. 388). For a brief account of this affair, see the testimony of Juan de Burgos, *Sumario*, I:157–158.

9. Tututepec (Puebla) and Metztitlán (Hidalgo).

10. This is a reference to the revolt of the *Comuneros* of 1520–1521. The *Comunidades* were the city councils of Castile and enjoyed considerable independence from Crown control. In June, 1519, Charles V was elected to succeed his grandfather Maximilian as Holy Roman Emperor. To finance the emperor-elect's journey to the Netherlands, Chièvres, Charles's Grand Chamberlain, demanded of the Cortes a *servicio* of 600,000 ducats, although the previous one, granted to Charles on his succession to the Spanish throne, had been intended to cover a period of three years. Toledo was the first town to revolt against these demands, setting up a commune headed by Pedro Laso de la Vega and Juan de Padilla, and it was soon followed by a number of others. The movement eventually collapsed as a

result of disagreements between the communes, and the rebels were finally defeated at the battle of Villalar on April 23, 1521 (J. H. Elliott, *Imperial Spain*, pp. 141–150).

11. The Casa de la Contratación de las Indias was established in Seville by royal decree in 1503 much along the lines of the Casa da India at Lisbon. Its purpose was to regulate the American trade, to check cargoes and collect duties. In this respect it functioned much like a modern customs-house. From 1503 Seville held a monopoly of Spanish trade; nearly all the fleets sailed from there and all, without exception, returned there. The Casa grew in importance and became responsible for fitting out fleets sailing on account of the Crown, inspecting private vessels for seaworthiness and setting limitation on their size. It also licensed navigation, and as early as 1508 a *piloto mayor,* or chief pilot, had been appointed for this duty. Amérigo Vespucci was the first to hold the office, and he was followed by Juan de Solís and Sebastian Cabot. (See Clarence H. Haring, *Trade and Navigation between Spain and the Indies,* pp. 21–45. See also Huguette et Pierre Chaunu, *Séville et l'Atlantique,* vols. II–VI of which record all the sailings to and from Seville between 1504 and 1650, and, on the office of the piloto mayor, José Pulido Rubio, *El Piloto Mayor de la Casa de la Contratación de Sevilla.*)

12. It seems likely that Cortés's expedition to Pánuco was primarily intended to forestall any effort by Garay to settle in that region. (Garay had been given permission to settle the area in 1521. The contract is printed in *CVD,* III:147 ff.) Francisco Verdugo testified that Rodrigo Rangel had written to Cortés from Vera Cruz saying that he had seen six of Garay's ships heading for the Pánuco. When he heard the news Cortés is reported to have said, "Let us go to Pánuco and drive Francisco de Garay out of the country" (*Sumario,* I:366). According to Bernal Díaz (chap. 158), when Cortés demanded that the royal officials compensate him for the cost of the expedition, they refused on the grounds that Cortés's purpose had been to drive away Garay.

13. According to Alonso Lucas, who knew Garay well, the *adelantado* had received letters from Cortés promising him assistance if his force should not prove strong enough to conquer the Pánuco area. Colón and Veláz-quez seemed to have gone to Cuba to help Garay recruit his army. They also raised objections to his going and warned him against Cortés's dupli-city (*Sumario,* I:275–276).

14. Coxcatlán (Puebla).

15. Chila is in the state of Puebla. The lakes mentioned are those of Tampico and Tamiahua.

16. This refers to the expedition of 1520 under the command of Pineda.

17. It is not certain when Santisteban del Puerto was founded, but it must have been sometime before March 1, 1523, for at that date Cortés issued a grant of encomienda from the town (Wagner, p. 411).

18. These figs were presumably *tunas*, the fruit of the nopal (Nahuatl, *nopalli*), or Mexican cactus called an *Higuera de India*.

19. Doctor Cristóbal Ojeda testified at Cortés's residencia that Cortés had taken sixty thousand castellanos from Diego de Soto, who had replaced Alderete as treasurer (*Sumario*, I:28, 127). Cortés himself claimed that part of this money was provided for the Pánuco expedition. Ojeda said that he was in Vera Cruz with Alderete when news reached him that Cortés had taken the money from Soto. This means that he must have been preparing for the expedition as early as the summer of 1522, although he could not have left before November 1, the day his wife Catalina Suárez died (Wagner, p. 410. On the death of Catalina Suárez see Alfonso Toro, *Un Crimen de Hernán Cortés*).

20. Colima (Michoacán).

21. The legend of the Amazons was a popular one at the time, and reports of such tribes occur well into the eighteenth century. They were "discovered" in a number of places as far apart as Finland and India, although, until the discovery of America, Asia Minor was the favorite place. Columbus claimed to have sighted them, and Orellana was so convincing in his description of them that their name, and not his, was given to the river he was the first to navigate. Cortés probably derived his knowledge of the legend from the romance *Sergas de Esplandían*, or *Deeds of Esplandían*. This novel, a sequel to the famous *Amadis of Gaul*, contains a description of the Amazons in which their locale is, for the first time, definitely identified with America or, "the islands of California." Velázquez's instructions to Cortés contain a command to search for the Amazons, "who are nearby according to the Indians [*i.e.*, the interpreters] whom you are taking with you" (Irving A. Leonard, "Conquerors and Amazons in Mexico," p. 24. See also the same author's *Books of the Brave*, and G. C. Rothery, *The Amazons in Antiquity and Modern Times*).

22. Tuxpan (Jalisco).

23. Xoconochco.

24. Utatlan. The Quiche name for the city was Gumarkaaj. It stood near the present-day town of Santa Cruz de Quiche.

25. The modern state of Chiapas.

26. Alvarado's two letters to Cortés describing the conquest of Guatemala may be found, in English, in Patricia de Fuentes, *The Conquistadors*, pp. 182–196.

27. See the Fifth Letter, n. 10.

28. Tierra-Firme, the northern coast of South America, was renamed Castilla de Oro ("Golden Castile") in 1513. Castilla de Oro was originally applied to the Isthmus of Panama and the coast as far as Cape Gracias a Dios. Diego de Nicuesa and Alonso de Hojeda were the first to establish a settlement there. As a consequence of this, Hojeda was granted the coast from Cape Vela to the Gulf of Urabá, with the name of Nueva Andalucia, and Nicuesa was given Castilla de Oro. Both of these men were ultimately unsuccessful. Hojeda was driven off by the local inhabitants and died penniless in Hispaniola. Nicuesa, believing that his colonists had established themselves in Darién, attempted to exercise his authority there. He was driven off in a leaking brigantine and never seen again (see Edward Gaylord Bourne, *Spain in America*, pp. 106–114. Documents are in *CVD*, III:337 ff.).

29. According to Alonso Lucas, Garay had eleven ships with 150 horses, four hundred foot soldiers and "much artillery and articles for trading." Navarrete, however, maintains that the fleet consisted of nine naos, two brigantines, 850 Spaniards, some Jamaican Indians, 144 horses, much artillery and arms of various kinds (see *CVD*, III:67–68).

30. According to Serrano de Cardona, one of the witnesses at Cortés's residencia, Rodrigo Rangel was sent first with some fifteen or twenty horse (*Sumario*, I:183).

31. This decree (*cédula*), dated April 24, 1523, may be found in *CDIR*, 26:72–74. It was read at a meeting of the town council of Mexico, September 13 (Wagner, p. 527, n. 33).

32. Diego Docampo met Garay in a town called Xicayahan (Xicapayan). Garay arrived sick in a hammock and in the opinion of one witness, "as though a prisoner" (*Sumario*, II:127, testimony of Domingo Niño).

33. Gonzalo de Ovalle.

34. Lucas calls the place Guazaltepec (*Sumario*, I:278). Lorenzana has a footnote which runs, "In the Huasteca they call the high smooth rocks of the mountains *lajas*." The Huasteca or Cuexteca are a branch of the Maya family (see Seler, *op. cit.*, trans., pp. 98 ff.).

35. Francisco de Orduña was an *Escribano de Su Majestad* and notary public. He had, in fact, come to demand that Garay obey the decree. This demand was made on October 4 (1523) and witnessed by Francisco de las Casas, Andrés de Tapia and Diego de Soto. Garay replied to it the following day in the town of Chiachacta. Orduña also gave orders, on Cortés's behalf, to Alvarado and Vallejo not to interfere in Garay's affairs, and he

issued a number of other orders concerning the roundup of Garay's men. They are printed in *CDIR*, 26:80 ff.

36. The secretary was Orduña. There is no mention of an alguacil mayor in Orduña's account, but an alguacil, Martín Sanz, is said to have brought in two or three of Garay's men and seems to have been in charge of the operations. Orduña's orders for the return of the deserters were issued on September 23 (*CDIR*, 26:80).

37. Presumably the letter written from Otumba on Sunday, November 8, advising Cortés that he intends to arrive on the Friday. It is printed in *CDIR*, 26:131–132.

38. Bernal Díaz (chap. 162) says that this daughter's name was "Doña Catalina Cortés or Pizarro." A Doña Catalina Pizarro is mentioned in Cortés's will: she was the daughter of Leonor Pizarro, who later married Juan de Salzedo. Leonor Pizarro seems to have been a Cuban woman, in which case she would have been too young for Cortés to have seriously considered marrying her (*Last Will and Testament of Hernando Cortés*, pp. 10, 35).

39. According to Alonso Lucas, Garay was taken ill after dining with Cortés on Christmas Eve. He spent the night vomiting, and on the following morning Cortés came to see him with a *licenciado* called Pedro López; then a barber was called to bleed him. Despite this attention, however, Garay died the following afternoon (*Sumario*, I:283–284). Naturally enough, Cortés was charged with having murdered him, a charge which he denied, saying that Garay had died of a well-known disease (Wagner, p. 413). From Lucas's evidence, it sounds as if he died of food poisoning, but the circumstances of Garay's death and that of Ponce de León (see the Fifth Letter, n. 111) are remarkably similar, and it is at least possible that Cortés killed them both.

40. Tanjuco.

41. Tantoyuca (?) (Veracruz).

42. Tancahuitz, the present-day Ciudad Santos.

43. See the First Letter, n. 40.

44. García de Pilar, who accompanied Sandoval, claimed that the "350 or 400 lords and principal persons" captured by Sandoval protested that they had killed the Spaniards, "because the Indians of Mexico had told them that Captain Malinchi, that is captain Ernando Cortés had ordered them to do it." When Pilar reported this to Sandoval, he told him not to listen and ordered the chieftains to be burned (*Sumario*, II:206–207). Since Pilar's evidence is corroborated by that of another witness (the *bachiller* Alonso

Perez, *Sumario*, II:89), it seems that Cortés was determined to be rid of Garay at all costs and had planned an Indian uprising in case all else failed (see Wagner, pp. 414–415).

45. San Juan de Ulúa.

46. The idea of a strait connecting the Atlantic and Pacific oceans may possibly have originated with the Schöner globe of 1515. This globe shows such a strait at about latitude 45° south which, in fact, proved to be the mouth of the River Plate. Schöner seems to have derived his knowledge from a Portuguese newsletter describing the voyage of two ships along the South American mainland and their claim to have discovered a strait. This newsletter, entitled *Copia der Newen Zeytung ausz Presillg Landt*, exists in a German translation of an Italian version. There has been some dispute about the date, but it now seems certain that it is an account of an expedition that returned to Lisbon in 1514. The original Portuguese version of the *Copia*, now lost, may well have appeared that same year. Schöner certainly appears to have known it, for in a pamphlet entitled *Luculentissima quaedā terra totius descriptio*, which he issued to accompany his globe, he gives a description of the strait taken directly from the *Copia*. Cortés's belief in a strait, however, was possibly based more on wishful thinking than actual cartographic information. Ever since America was discovered to lie between Europe and the lucrative trade of the East, efforts had been made to open a direct route. The search for a strait was to persist until further explorations north and south had demonstrated that no such thing existed. (Lawrence C. Wroth, *The Early Cartography of the Pacific*, pp. 143–145. For a description of the *Copia* see Henry Harrisse, *Bibliotheca Americana Vetustissima*, no. 99, pp. 172–174. Schöner's pamphlet is also described [no. 80, pp. 140], and the globe is reproduced in Joachim Lelewel, *Geógraphie du Moyen Age*, atlas, pages unnumbered.)

47. Utatlan.

48. Tehuantepec (Oaxaca).

49. Chinantla, Oaxaca and Coatzalcoalcos.

50. The Mixteca and Zapoteca occupied areas of what is now the state of Oaxaca, and part of the neighboring states of Guerrero and Puebla. The Mixteca were a people of high cultural achievement who, in the eleventh century, brought the whole of the Mixteca Alta under their rule. By his death in 1063, the Mixteca conqueror 8 deer "Tiger Claw" had extended his dominion to the Pacific-coast province of Tututepec. When Otomi and Nahua groups began to press down into the Mixteca lands, the Mixteca themselves migrated into the valley of Oaxaca.

The Zapoteca occupied the valley of Oaxaca before the Mixteca invasion but seem to have survived despite temporary exile in the isthmus of

Tehuantepec. As late as 1578 a missionary, Fray Juan de Córdoba, was able to write a detailed account of the Zapoteca language—which belongs to a group known as Macro-Mixteca or Otomangue—and include an encyclopedia of Zapoteca culture. (John Paddock, ed., *Ancient Oaxaca*, pp. 83–242. On the Mixteca see also Robert Ravicz and A. Kimball Romney in *Handbook of Middle American Indians*, 7:367–399; and on the Zapoteca, Laura Nader, *ibid.*, pp. 329–358.)

The bishop of Antequera (Oaxaca), writing about 1570, comments on the asperity of the land, and speaking of the town of Sancto Ilefonso says, "The Zapotecas . . . breed no cattle nor have anything else off which they live save the tributes that the Indians pay them, and these are some cotton wraps [*mantas*] and a little maize." Further on he remarks that the good land is only to be found near Tehuantepec, Tecomaxtlahuaca and Juxtlahuaca in the Mixteca (*Relación de los Obispados de Tlaxcala, Michoacán, Oaxaca y otros lugares en el siglo XVI*, pp. 61–64).

51. Ciuacoatl, the "Serpent Woman." His Nahuatl name was Tlacotzin, and he was baptized and christened Juan Velázquez. He was the first Mexica ruler under the Spaniards; and according to the *Aubin Codex* (pp. 61–62) he was confirmed in his position by Cortés in March, 1523. He died sometime before Cortés's return from Honduras in 1525 and was succeeded by Andrés de Tapia Motelchiultzin (Charles Gibson, *The Aztecs Under Spanish Rule*, p. 168. For the rebuilding of the city see the Third Letter, n. 89).

52. The lakes contained a variety of white fish, called *iztacmichin* in Nahuatl, none of which were very large. As already noted (the Second Letter, note 20), fishing was done with hand nets, spears or rods and lines. The Spanish gradually encroached on Indian fishing rights and soon drove the Indians into those areas of the lake which were contaminated by high salt content or filled with tule. The importance of the lakes as food-producing areas declined rapidly after the conquest. The scarcity of both fish and birds was noticed by Torquemada (bk. IV, chap. 14) as early as the beginning of the seventeenth century (Gibson, *op. cit.*, pp. 339 ff.).

53. Despite Cortés's statement, the Indians preferred maize and resisted Spanish attempts to introduce wheat cultivation; in some areas, however, they were obliged to pay a tribute in wheat, and there are many instances of Indians producing wheat for sale to the Spaniards. This reluctance to accept the establishment of Spanish farms provided an excuse for the appropriation of Indian lands. (An excellent study of the agriculture of the Mexican Valley is given by Gibson, *op. cit.*, pp. 300–334.)

54. None of the plans of Mexico City show any such building, and the "plan" is not, so far as I know, extant.

55. The Spanish area within the city was, in fact, surrounded by four barrios: Santa María Cuepopan (Tlaquechiuhcan) in the northwest, San Sebastáin Atzacualco (Atzacualpa) in the northeast, San Pablo Zoquipan (Teopan, Xochimilco) in the southeast, and San Juan Moyotlan in the southwest. Together they formed the district of San Juan Tenochtitlan. In addition to these Indian communities, there existed the Indian cabecera, or provincial capital, Santiago-Tlatelolco, which was separated from old Tenochtitlan by a canal called Tezontlalli (see Alfonso Caso, "Los Barrios Antiguos de Tenochtitlan y Tlatelolco"). Tlatelolco today is a dismal suburb.

56. The great market of Tlatelolco declined during the sixteenth century, the bulk of the trade passing to Tenochtitlan. A new Indian market at San Hipólito came into being in the 1540s. Cervantes de Salazar described it as a "square of such enormous size that it is wide enough for building a city." It was flanked by a Franciscan monastery—containing the Colegio de Santiago de Tlatelolco—the residence of the Indian governor and an Indian prison. Cervantes de Salazar estimated that the number of Indians using this market amounted to twenty thousand or more (Cervantes de Salazar, *Life in the Imperial and Loyal City of Mexico in New Spain*, p. 62).

57. Tasco. Cortés's statement about tin coins is open to question. In his description of the market of Tenochtitlan he includes tin in the list of metals sold, yet there is no evidence that tin was known to the Amerindians before the conquest. In an account of the province of Tasco compiled in 1581, no mention is made of tin, though silver and lead mines are said to exist (Francisco del Paso y Troncoso, *Papeles de Nueva España*, 6:263 ff.).

58. See the Third Letter, n. 68.

59. These ships may have been the ones that brought the royal officials.
    A number of witnesses at the residencia claimed that Cortés had had these guns made to resist any attempt by the Crown to remove him from office. They were more likely to have been made to put down any possible rising among his own men. Antonio de Carbajal claimed that whenever Cortés had any trouble he brought out his artillery (*Sumario*, I:417–418). In an inventory made by Cortés in 1528 and delivered to Alonso de Estrada, five small bronze guns are listed together with five smaller ones (all with carriages) and one very small one and one of cast iron (Wagner, p. 389).
    Sixteenth-century cannon varied enormously in length and caliber, though little in design. The types used in America in the early period were of necessity small. A culverin might fire a ball weighing twenty pounds which, on a horizontal trajectory, gave a maximum range of some four

hundred meters. The falconet was a swivel gun designed for mounting on a ship's gunnel. It had a removable breechblock which resulted in a great loss of power, making it both ineffective and dangerous to the gunner; the lombard was a similar weapon. The *pasavolante* (or *Cerbatana*), a small version of the culverin, fired a ball weighing between 1,560 and 3,220 grams and had a range of 435 meters on a horizontal trajectory. In all cases, with the exception of the culverin, the charge was the same as the shot. All these figures are estimations. Some culverins, for instance, were known to fire a ball as heavy as fifty pounds. The *media culebrina*, or medium-sized culverin, fired a ball weighing between 5,520 and 8,280 grams with a range of 870 meters on a horizontal trajectory. The *verso* resembled the pasavolante (Alberto Mario Salas, *Las Armas de la Conquista*, p. 234).

60. Francisco de Montaño, Juan de Larios and someone called Peñalosa climbed down into the crater of Popocatepetl. Cervantes de Salazar gives the best account of the event in bk. VI, chaps. 8–11. Humboldt maintained that the sulphur must have been taken from a lateral fissure rather than from the crater itself (Alexander von Humboldt, *Essai Politique sur la Royaume de la Nouvelle Espagne*, I:164).

61. The river mentioned by Cortés is the Río Canoas, and the town stood on the site now known as La Antigua.

62. The Spice Islands (*especería*), the Moluccas (Malucos), as they were more commonly known, was a name given to all those islands, about five in number, in the Indian Archipelago where spices grew or were thought to grow. The richest of these were Ternate and Tidore. The Moluccas lie north and south of the equator in about longitude 127° east; Acapulco— later to become the base of the silk trade with the Philippines—lies in longitude 100° west. The distance between these two places is approximately 133° or nearly nine thousand statute miles. Cortés appears to have accepted the idea, common in the early sixteenth century, that Asia lay close to the Pacific seaboard of the American mainland. Although the first map to show a broad Pacific, the hypothetically construed Waldseemüller-Stobnicza hemisphere, dates from as early as 1507, five years before Balboa's discovery, Cortés was probably unaware of the cartographical developments of the first two decades of the century. Maps for general circulation were not experimental, and left the extent of the Pacific at least vague. The Vesconte Maggiolo portolano atlas of 1511 omits 170° of longitude between America and Asia; and Waldseemüller himself was capable of labeling North America "Terra de Cuba-Asie Partis" as late as 1516.

Cortés does seem to have been well informed about events in Europe. How he heard about Magellan's voyage is uncertain. Most of his information, which seems to have been detailed, was almost certainly forwarded to him regularly by his agents in Spain. The first published account of the Magellan voyage, a little book entitled *De Moluccis Insulis*, was published in Cologne in 1523. It is unlikely that Cortés ever saw it, and Pigafetta's famous account appears to have first been published in 1525 and then only in French (see H. R. Wagner, *Spanish Voyages to the Northwest Coast of America*, pp. 94–98; Wroth, *op. cit.*, pp. 126 ff.).

63. These were Alonso de Estrada (treasurer), Gonzalo de Salazar (factor), Pedro Almindez Cherino (veedor) and Rodrigo de Albornoz (contador). It is not known exactly when they arrived. Cortés has already mentioned ships arriving at Vera Cruz with arms, and these are perhaps the same ships which brought the royal officials. It is likely that they did not all arrive at the same time. In 1547 Salazar claimed to have reached Mexico in 1523, although Cortés says (p. 331) that he arrived "two days ago," which would mean October 13, 1524. There is some evidence, however, that Cortés's letter was, in fact, completed some time before it was actually sent; it is possible, therefore, that Salazar came on the same ship, or in the same fleet, as Albornoz. Albornoz, who was appointed by royal decree on October 25, 1522, was a native of Paradinas, and had formerly been a royal secretary (Francisco A. de Icaza, *Conquistadores y Pobladores de Nueva España*, II:16). According to Peter Martyr, he was given a cipher in which he sent his reports, for: "From that time we were not without suspicion of [Cortés's] intentions [*animus*]. These [letters] were written against Cortés's mad designs, consuming avarice and partially revealed tyranny" (*De Orbe Novo*, fol. CXVr. *trans.* II:406). Albornoz was accompanied by a friend of Martyr's, Lope de Samaniego, whom Martyr calls Lupus or Lupicus Samanecus.

Estrada was evidently a man of some standing before his appointment as treasurer. He had served in Flanders and had been admiral of Malaga and later *corregidor* (magistrate) of Cáceres before coming to Mexico (Icaza, *op. cit.*, I:219).

Cherino was an agent of Francisco de los Cobos and had been assigned the task of collecting taxes from the mines. He was appointed on October 15, 1522 (Wagner, p. 434, p. 530 n. 14). In addition to these four royal officials, the licenciado Alonzo Zuazo came as assessor (see H. I. Priestley, *José de Gálvez, Visitor-General of New Spain*, pp. 78–79).

64. Antonio de Quiñones was in charge of the treasure. Cortés seems to have fleeced his men. Francisco de Orduña testified at the residencia that Cortés had published an order that "everyone who had gold in small quantities was to bring it to be melted down; and they did so and from the 35,000 *pesos de oro* which were melted down no fifth was taken" (*Sumario*, I:441). Peter Martyr (*De Orbe Novo*, fol. LXXXIII v. *trans.*, II:196)

gives the total value of the treasure as 150,000 ducats. Bernal Díaz (chap. 159) says that the ships carried 58,000 *castellanos*. According to Vázquez de Tapia, Quiñones, Ávila and Julián de Alderete, the royal treasurer who accompanied them, were each given three thousand *pesos*. Ribera and Pedro Melgarejo received fifteen hundred each and were entrusted with a further two thousand for Diego de Ordaz, who was then in Spain (*Sumario*, I:53). Juan de Burgos put the total sum at eight thousand or nine thousand *castellanos* and added that there was widespread discontent among the men, who had themselves received little or nothing.

Alderete died shortly after leaving Mexico, and it was widely rumored that he had been poisoned. Quiñones was killed in a fight in the Azores where two of the caravels of the treasure fleet were captured by the French. The third escaped to harbor in Santa Maria. In May, 1523, Captain Domingo Alonso Amilivia arrived to escort the remainder of the treasure home. He was attacked off Cape St. Vincent by six privateers led by Jean Florin of La Rochelle, who succeeded in taking two of the ships and all the treasure. According to Gómara (p. 394), he also captured a ship from the West Indies with sixty-two thousand ducats of gold, six hundred marcs of pearls and two thousand quarters of sugar (Cesáreo Fernández Duro, *Armada Española*, I:206). Ávila was captured and taken to France where he lay in prison until he was exchanged in 1525. As well as the gold, a number of gifts were sent to Spain. A list of these is given in Saville, *op. cit.*, pp. 56–86.

65. It was christened the Phoenix and bore the inscription:

> "Aquesta nació sin par,
> Yo en serviros sin segundo;
> Vos sin igual en el mundo."

According to Bernal Díaz (chap. 170), Charles gave it to Francisco de los Cobos, who smelted it.

66. See p. xxxiv above.

67. The famous "Twelve Apostles" had, in fact, arrived at San Juan de Ulúa May, 1524, and reached Mexico in June of that year. They belonged to the Order of the Friars Minor of the Observance; they were Martín de Valencia, Francisco de Soto, Martín de Jesús (or de la Coruña), Juan Suárez (Juárez), Antonio de Ciudad-Rodrigo, Toribio de Benavente (Motolinía), García de Cisneros, Luis de Fuensalida, Juan de Ribas, Francisco Jiménez, Andrés de Córdoba and Juan de Palos. The last two remained lay brothers; Martín de Valencia was their superior, and Francisco Jiménez was ordained shortly after arrival. (For the life of Martín de Valencia see "Vida de Fray Martín de Valencia, escrita por su compañero Fr. Francisco Jiménez.")

Their arrival was the final outcome of protracted negotiations. On April 25, 1521, Leo X had issued the bull *Alias felicis* authorizing the Franciscans Juan Glapión and Juan de los Angeles to go to Mexico. In 1522 Adrian VI issued another bull, *Exponi nobis feciste*, granting the Franciscan and Mendicant orders apostolic authority to do everything for the conversion of the Indians with the exception of acts that required episcopal consecration. Glapión died before the arrangements were complete, but in 1523 Francisco de los Angeles was appointed general of the Franciscan order and it was he who was finally responsible for organizing the mission of the Twelve (Robert Ricard, *The Spiritual Conquest of Mexico*, L. B. Simpson, trans. Berkeley and Los Angeles, 1966, pp. 21–22. The document [the *obedencia y comisión*] authorizing the Franciscan mission and signed by Francisco de los Angeles occupies fols. 326r–329r of the Vienna Codex. See also Gerónimo de Mendieta, *Historia Eclesiástica Indiana*, pp. 186 ff.).

68. The first Franciscans to reach Mexico came on August 30, 1523. They were the Flemings Johann van den Auwera and Johann Dekkers, known to the Spaniards as Juan de Ayora and Juan de Tecto, and a lay brother, Pedro de Gante. Ayora and Tecto died on the march to Honduras (see the Fifth Letter, n. 100). Tecto had been the emperor's confessor. Gante, who was said to have been related to Charles, remained in Mexico until his death in 1572 and was instrumental in founding the Indian schools (Ricard, *op. cit.*, pp. 20, 209. On Gante see García Icazbalceta, *Biblioteca Mexicana del Siglo XVI*, p. 35).

The Dominicans did not arrive until July 2, 1539. They were also twelve, under Fray Tomás Ortiz. He seems to have fallen foul of Cortés, for in a letter to the emperor dated January 12, 1527, Cortés claims that Ortiz tried to persuade him not to receive Ponce de León (see the Fifth Letter, n. 111) and later declared that Cortés had murdered the judge (P. Mariano Cuevas, *Historia de la Iglesia de México*, I:214–217).

69. These ordinances have been printed in *CDIR*, 26:135–148; in *Escritos Sueltos de Hernán Cortés*, pp. 26–39, and elsewhere. They make an interesting document which shows just how aware Cortés was of the damage done in the Antilles by the uncontrolled exploitation of the land and its inhabitants. The laws governing the treatment of the Indians are essentially the same as the laws already in force; although to some extent they anticipate the New Laws of 1542–1543. But other articles seek to impose a policy of fruitful colonization, which is a new departure. In an attempt to prevent absentee landlordship, Cortés forbade any encomendero to leave his land for a period of eight years following the promulgation of the ordinances; and article 17 obliges encomenderos to marry, or, if married, to bring their wives from Spain, within a period of eighteen

months, "so that the desire which the settlers of these parts have to remain should be made more manifest." Other articles provide for the defense of the land and exploitation of the soil—a matter of great concern for Cortés, as is testified by his constant plea for seeds to be sent from Spain.

He also issued some other ordinances, in the same year, to innkeepers on the road from Vera Cruz to Mexico, fixing prices. These may be found in *Escritos Sueltos de Hernán Cortés*, pp. 39–41.

70. This letter was carried to Spain in the fleet of two ships under the command of Diego de Soto. It is not certain when he arrived, but in a letter to the archbishop of Cosenza, Peter Martyr mentions that a ship has reached Coruña from Mexico with Samaniego aboard and "a tiger reared in a cage by a bitch and a culverin which report says is made of gold," presumably the Phoenix. His letter is dated March 29, and written from Madrid. If Martyr was in Coruña when the ship arrived, it must have come in early March (*Opus Epistolarum*, fol. CXCVIIIr. See also *De Orbe Novo*, fol. CXIIII r. *trans.*, II:399–400).

Notes to the Fifth Letter

1. This letter is the one often referred to as the Fifth. It has never been found. See p. lxiii.

2. The name of the gulf was variously spelled Honduras, Hibueras and Higueras. It was first discovered by Columbus in 1502 and called Punta de Caxinas because, according to Herrera, "there were many trees whose fruit is like an apple and good to eat." This may also explain "Higueras," which means "fig trees." What a *caxina* is I do not know, but it may have been an avocado or a *tuna* (see H. L. Bancroft, *History of Central America*, I:211, n. 6).

3. Cristóbal de Olid and Francisco de las Casas.

4. The Fourth Letter, however, is dated October 15 from Tenochtitlan. There are also two other letters sent from Tenochtitlan on the thirteenth and fifteenth respectively; in the latter, Cortés says that he has desisted from his plans to go to Honduras. Cortés's dates are frequently wrong, but the author of the *Memoria de lo acaecido en esta ciudad*, probably Estrada, confirms the date as October 12. Cortés probably camped somewhere near the city, but within the jurisdiction of the municipal council, before finally deciding to proceed to Honduras. It would be surprising if Cortés did not have doubts about the expedition, and he might well have decided to abandon it before going to Espíritu Santo (see *CDHM*, I:XLI, 512).

5. See the Fourth Letter, n. 63.

6. Bernal Díaz (chap. 174) says that in addition to Cuauhtemoc, Cohuana-coch, lord of Texcoco, and Tetlepanquetzal, lord of Tacuba, there were some caciques from Michoacán. He also says that Marina accompanied the expedition, as Aguilar was dead by this time. Alva Ixtlilxóchitl says that Ixtlilxochitl came along as well as Cohuanacoch, who was taken "for greater security." He names the regents as Alonso Izquinquani (Texcoco), Zontecon (Mexico), and Cohuatecatl (Tacuba) (I:403).

7. Francisco de Solís.

8. Coatzacoalcos.

9. According to Alva Ixtlilxóchitl (I:407), Ixtlilochitl and Cuauhtemoc were sent. Although Cortés is unlikely to have trusted either of them, they may have gone under heavy guard, for their presence would certainly have impressed the other Indians.

10. This is presumably a copyist's error for Ascension. It was along this coast that Olid had been sent to search for a strait leading to the Pacific. Cortés, however, is probably confusing Ascension Bay with Chetumal Bay, some ninety miles farther down the coast, for, previously, in the Fourth Letter (p. 301), he said that Ascension Bay was sixty leagues from the Cape of Honduras, which would place it somewhere in the region of Chetumal Bay. Gómara (p. 185) states that Chetumal and Ascension are one and the same place, and Oviedo (bk. XXI, chap. 8) calls Ascension Bay "the nearest [bay] to the Gulf of Higueras" (quoted by Scholes and Roys, p. 433. The Oviedo account was written sometimes prior to 1550 and is presumed to be based on the lost map of Alonso Chaves made in 1536). From this it would appear that Chetumal Bay was commonly confused with Ascension Bay in the early sixteenth century, and, in some instances, even up until the eighteenth. Cf. maps by Bellin, Hinton et al., in Carto-grafía de la América Central. Quoted by Scholes and Roys, loc. cit.

11. Pedro Arias de Ávila, or Pedrarias Dávila, as he is more commonly known, was the first governor of Castilla de Oro. A ferocious old man, he earned the name furor domini on account of his temper and El Gran Justador because of his skill in tournaments. He was descended from a noble family and was himself the brother of the count of Puñonrostro. He had distinguished himself in the Granada campaign and the African wars before going to Darién in 1514. (Fernández de Oviedo went with him as his veedor.) Nuñez de Balboa, who was then governor of Darién, was executed on a trumped-up charge by Pedrarias, who, after successive struggles with Gil González de Ávila, Hernández de Córdoba and Cortés's deputy Hernando de Saavedra, finally succeeded in gaining effective control of Nicaragua. He was later replaced in Darién by Pedro de los Rios but made governor of Nicaragua. He died suddenly while preparing to

return to Spain on March 6, 1531. Pedrarias has been widely and consistently condemned as embodying all the traditional vices of the Spaniards in America. A different view of his career and achievements is taken by Pablo Alvarez Rubiano in *Pedrarias Dávila*.

12. According to Gómara (p. 409), this map showed the route from Xicalango to Nito and beyond to Nicaragua. Herrera (dec. III, bk. VI, chap. 12) says much the same, but Bernal Díaz (chap. 175) says that it reached only as far as Gueyacala (Itzamkanac in Acalan). Cortés also says that he was given another map in Itzamkanac (p. 365), and it would seem from this that Díaz is right (Scholes and Roys, pp. 430–431).

13. It is uncertain what Cortés's final destination was to have been before his arrival in Acalan. The earliest reference to Nito as the place where he might find the Spaniards, which he mentions here, is made on p. 368. It seems likely, therefore, that, as he did not know the identity of the Spaniards, he assumed that they had belonged to one of the three previous expeditions and must, therefore, be living somewhere in the region of the "Bay of the Ascension."

14. These "secret orders" (*provisión*) have been published by Robert S. Chamberlain in *HAHR*, vol. 18 (1938), pp. 523–525. (They were not, however, issued in Espíritu Santo but in Culpico.) Salazar and Cherinos suppressed Cortés's original orders and deposed Estrada and Albornoz with the "secret orders." Once they had obtained control, they began to ravage the country, looting Cortés's home and hanging his cousin, Rodrigo de Paz, who had been in charge of his estate. On January 28, 1526, Martín de Orantes, Cortés's groom, reached Mexico with orders from Cortés displacing Cherinos and Salazar and appointing Francisco de las Casas as his lieutenant governor. After a brief struggle, the Cortés party regained power and imprisoned Salazar in a wooden cage. Cherinos took refuge in a monastery in Tlaxcala. I know of no detailed study of this period, but a full and fairly accurate description of the events is given by Bancroft, *History of Mexico*, II:193–237, who uses most of the published sources.

15. Bernal Díaz gives the size of the Spanish force as 250 soldiers, 130 of whom were horsemen and the rest harquebusiers and crossbowmen, "without counting many other soldiers newly arrived from Castile" (chap. 175). Albornoz claimed that Cortés departed with 120 horses, twenty harquebusiers and other crossbowmen and foot soldiers (Gayangos, p. 398). Cortés's figures are undoubtedly wrong, but this is probably the fault of the copyist.

16. Probably the modern Copilco. My authority for place names and for the route taken by Cortés until he left Acalan is Scholes and Roys, pp. 88 ff.

17. Tonala (also known as San Antón). According to Bernal Díaz (chap. 16), the first orange trees were planted there.

18. Ahualulco. It lay near the present-day Santa Ana and can undoubtedly be identified with an archaeological site of the same name at the eastern end of Lake Machona.

19. The Copilco River. A report of 1579 states that it was six leagues west of the mouth of Dos Bocas (now Río Seco). It must, therefore, have flowed into the western end of the Laguna Tupilco. The river has now shrunk to insignificant size, and it is difficult to locate, although it is probably the Tortuguero River, a tributary of the Tupilco (Scholes and Roys, p. 96, n. 24).

20. Bernal Díaz (chaps. 166, 169) talks of having traveled on two previous occasions by way of Tonala, Ahualulco, Copilco-Zacualco, Ulapa, Teotitan-Copilco and Nacajuca. Bernal Díaz (chap. 175) also supplies further information about this stage of the journey. He says that they passed through some small towns before reaching the Dos Bocas. Scholes and Roys (p. 97) identify these as Huimanguillo (originally Hueymango or Huimango), Iquinuapa and Copilco-zacualco. The name of the last appears to be Nahuatl in origin, and could be translated "Copilco, the place of the pyramid." Ixtlilxóchitl (I:408) says that the Indians were made to do all the construction work.

21. This must be the Grijalva itself and not a tributary.

22. Chilapa.

23. Nacajuca.

24. The crossing was made just below the present site of Villa Hermosa.

25. This road was cut along the banks of the Tacotalpa.

26. This was the town of Ciuatan. In 1579 it was said to be, in fact, three towns, Astapa, Jahuacapa, and Jalapa, also known as the three Ciuatans. They are now all three on the right bank of the Tacotalpa (Scholes and Roys, p. 98).

27. Chilapa. The modern town has been moved to the lower reaches of the Grijalva. Scholes and Roys (p. 98) estimate that its original position must have been on the left bank of the Macuspana, fifteen kilometers east of the town of Macuspana. Ixtlilxóchitl (I:408) describes Chilapa as subject to Texcoco, by which he probably means that they had special trade agreements; certainly the conquests of the Triple Alliance did not extend as far as Tabasco.

28. A spur of the Chiapas range.

29. Acumba (?).

30. Tepetitan. The modern town lies on the opposite (west) side of the river. There is some dispute over the original location of the town. Tepetitan may mean "in, near or below the mountains," and Tamacastepeque could be translated "mountain of the Tlamacazaque [a class of priests]." The mountains to which Cortés refers on page 348 are probably a low ridge called Los Cerillos, to the northeast of the Tulija River. If Tepetitan lay at the foot of these hills, it would have been somewhere near its present site (Scholes and Roys, pp. 99–100. Cf. S. G. Morley, "The Inscriptions of Peten," I:10; and Bernal Díaz [Maudslay, trans.], *The True History of the Conquest of New Spain*, 5:336).

31. Iztapa. It was probably situated on the left bank of the Usumacinta, near the modern town of Emiliano Zapata. (For a detailed discussion of the location, see Scholes and Roys, pp. 437 ff.)

32. These marshes are probably the Sabanas de Maluco, to the east of Tepetitan.

33. The Usumacinta.

34. The yuca (or yucca) is Adam's-needle. *Aji* is a small green pepper.

35. This village was probably located near the present site of Pobiluc, on the left bank of the Usumacinta.

36. The Candelaria.

37. There were two Flemings called Johann van den Avwera and Johann Dekkers. See the Fourth Letter, n. 68.

38. Ciuatecpan. Bernal Díaz (chap. 176) calls it Ziguatepecad. It probably lay in the region of Canizan. (For a full discussion of the location of the town, see Scholes and Roys, appendix B, pp. 442–448.) The name Ciuatecpan has been established by Seler and translated as "Palace of the Woman" (*Abhandlungen zur Amerikanischen Sprach-und Alterthumskunde*, III:583–584). In the Chontal text used by Scholes and Roys, the name is given as Tanodzic [p. 390]).

39. Usumacinta. It was probably situated near the present-day Balancan, at the junction of the Pedro Mártir and Usumacinta rivers.

40. This village was probably located a short distance downstream from Tenosique, which was almost certainly one of the three towns mentioned later by Cortés (Scholes and Roys, appendix B, pp. 442–448).

41. See n. 42. These are Nahuatl names. Cortés is probably recording a version of the original Chontal Maya provided by Marina, who accompanied the expedition.

42. Scholes and Roys (see appendix B, pp. 406–469) locate this province as lying next to the shores of the Laguna de Términos in the drainage of the

Río Candelaria. Acalan, which is derived from the Nahuatl *acalli* (canoe), was probably the name by which the Mexica merchants knew the province. As noted above, Cortés probably had all his information from Marina who, although she spoke Chontal Maya, would probably have used the more familiar Nahuatl versions of place names. According to the Chontal Maya text used by Scholes and Roys, this area was called Tamactun (p. 389).

43. According to Bernal Díaz (chap. 176), he and Gonzalo Mejía led one of these expeditions.

44. A section of the San Pedro Mártir. According to Scholes and Roys (appendix B pp. 459, 469), the crossing was made near Nuevo León (see Scholes and Roys, *loc. cit.* and map).

45. According to Ixtlilxóchitl, this bridge took six days to build and caused the death of large numbers of the Indians (I:411).

46. Bernal Díaz (chap. 176) gives more details. He says that the army seized all the food, leaving Cortés with none. Bernal Díaz, however, had hidden some away in the forest, and agreed to share it with Cortés and Sandoval. Díaz was then sent again to impress upon the Indians that they must keep the peace. This he did and, in addition, returned with over a hundred Indian bearers carrying supplies. Cortés, Sandoval and Luís Marín went out to meet them and organize the distribution of the food.

47. Paxbolonacha, the seventh ruler of Acalan and supposed founder of the capital, Itzamkanac (see genealogical table in Scholes and Roys, p. 85).

48. Çacchute in the Chontal text used by Scholes and Roys (p. 388). Seler translates Tizatepetlan, the form given by Gómara and Ixtlilxóchitl (I:412), as "village of the white earth" (quoted by Scholes and Roys in appendix B, p. 459). Tizatepetl is probably the correct Nahuatl form. Scholes and Roys (*loc. cit.*) suggest "white cedar" as a translation for Çacchute.

49. Ixtlilxóchitl gives Teotilac and elsewhere Teotlycacac (I:412, 417), which are both Nahuatl forms. Seler translates the name as "the upright standing god." The Chontal text has Tuxakha, "where the waters mingle." Scholes and Roys locate it on the Río San Pedro (see Scholes and Roys, pp. 107–108 and appendix B, 459–460).

50. Scholes and Roys (appendix B, p. 460) locate Itzamkanac on the south bank of the Candelaria, near the junction of the Río San Pedro and the Arroyo Caribe. Ixtlilxóchitl spells it Iztancamac (I:418 ff. *passim*).

51. Cohuanacoch of Texcoco, and Tetlepanquetzal of Tacuba.

52. There are several versions of Cuauhtemoc's death. Bernal Díaz (chap. 177) repeats the substance of Cortés's story, but says that the informers were two great "caciques" called "Tapia and Juan Velásquez." Torquemada (bk. IV, chap. 104), drawing from a Texcocan source, "which I hold to be true, for in other things that it has said I have found much truth and exactitude," says that there was no plot but only bitter complaints on the part of Cohuanacoch. These complaints were repeated by a "villainous commoner" to Cortés, who assumed that a conspiracy was being planned. Ixtlilxóchitl (I:413–416) says that the chieftains were celebrating the *carnestolendas*, pre-Lenten festivals (on these see Scholes and Roys, p. 112) and spent a long time in discussing their former glory. Cortés grew suspicious and sent an Indian, called Coxtemexi (Mexicalçingo), to find out what the Mexicans were talking about. Later Coxtemexi denied ever having told Cortés of a plot. Ixtlilxóchitl is not always reliable, but it does seem possible, at least, that Cortés took the Mexica leaders to Honduras, with the express purpose of murdering them where their deaths could not cause an Indian uprising. Nevertheless, the executions had to have a semblance of legality, and this was provided by the plot. According to the Chontal text used by Scholes and Roys (pp. 391–392) Cuauhtemoc attempted to enlist the help of Paxbolonacha. But the Acalan ruler remained loyal to Cortés and warned him of the plot. This version is suspect, especially as no other source mentions it: equally suspect is a claim made in a *Relación de Servicios* in 1605 that Marina was responsible for uncovering the plot.

The chieftains executed were Cuauhtemoc himself, Tetlepanquetzal, lord of Tacuba, and lastly Cohuanacoch of Texcoco, who, according to Alva Ixtlilxóchitl, was cut down hurriedly when Ixtlilxochitl began to call out his army. Within a few days, however, he had died from his wounds (Ixtlilxóchitl, I:416–417). It seems almost certain that they were hanged, though a Mexican manuscript, the *Mapa de Tepechpan*, shows the headless body of Cuauhtemoc hanging by its feet (Morley, *op. cit.*, I:15) and the Chontal text (p. 392) says, "They cut off his head and it was spiked on a ceiba in front of the house of idolatry" (see Josefina Muriel, "Divergencias en la biografía de Cuauhtemoc," pp. 107–114). The place of the executions are likewise disputed. Gómara (p. 413) says that it happened at Itzamkanac during the three days (the *Carnestolendas*) before Ash Wednesday. Ixtlilxóchitl (I:416) gives the place as Teotilac and the date as the eve of Ash Wednesday, which means February 28. Cortés intimates that the executions took place in Itzamkanac, and he may have told Gómara that they had. Certainly Itzamkanac would have been a more likely place than Teotilac, since the executions would also have served as a show of strength.

53. See the First Letter, n. 2.

54. For a detailed description of the province, see Scholes and Roys, chaps. 3 and 4.

55. In all probability, he left on Sunday, March 5.

56. Mazatlan is Nahuatl and was the name given to the Maya province of Cehache, here corrupted into Quiatelo. It probably lay in the Mocu-Cilvituk region, equidistant between the fork of the Champoton and Candelaria rivers (Scholes and Roys, pp. 128, 469).

57. Bernal Díaz (chap. 178) says that it was on an island in a shallow lake. He also says that the army had passed two villages burned by foreign invaders who, he says, were the Lacandon. On this point see Scholes and Roys, p. 462 n.

58. Tayasal, now called Flores.

59. Scholes and Roys (p. 463) place Yasuncabil in the region of Chuntuqui.

60. Puerto de Alabastro. It was probably near a small lake now called Laguna del Yeso (gypsum). The "alabaster" was almost certainly fine limestone (see Maudslay, *op. cit.*, p. 338).

61. Lake Peten. The people occupying the region were the Itza.

62. See the Second Letter, n. 26.

63. See the Second Letter, n. 21.

64. This is probably a mistranslation. Although it would have been feasible to reach Nito by sea, this would have meant making a long detour. Cortés was probably told that it would be easier to go by *water*. Cortés, however, appears to have ignored this advice and to have traveled in a southeasterly direction, following an established trade route (Scholes and Roys, p. 60).

65. According to Villagutierre, this horse was later venerated as a god of thunder and lightning. The Itza, assuming the horse to be human, had fed it on "chicken and other meats and had given it garlands of flowers, as they were wont to give to their nobles when they were ill." The horse died as a result of this treatment, and the Itza, fearing a reprisal by Cortés, erected a stone statue to it and worshipped it under the name Tziminchac. "For they had seen the Spaniards firing their muskets while out hunting deer on horseback, and had thought that the horses were the cause of the noise they had heard, which they took to be thunder; and the flash from the muzzle and the smoke of the powder they took to be lightning" (Juan de Villagutierre, *Historia de la Conquista de la Provincia de el Itza*, bk. II, chap. IV, pp. 100–102).

66. Maudslay (*op. cit.*, p. 338) identifies it as Lake Macanché.

67. Ixtlilxóchitl (I:423) calls it Axuncapuyn.

68. Ixtlilxóchitl (I:423) calls it Taxaytetl, undoubtedly the Nahuatl form.

69. Bernal Díaz (chap. 178) calls him Palacios Rubios, but later on (p. 387) Cortés calls him Juan de Avalos.

70. Probably the Río Sepusilha (Maudslay, *op. cit.*, p. 339).

71. The month is missing in the MS, but Easter fell on April 15. Cortés, therefore, must have actually arrived on the fourteenth.

72. Tahuican in Ixtlilxóchitl (I:424).

73. Ixtlilxóchitl has Azuculin (I:424).

74. Nito stood near the mouth of the Río Dulce and owed its importance to the cacao-producing areas in the vicinity. Like Naco (see n. 84), it seems to have been predominantly a Nahua trading post. A town called San Gil de Buenavista was founded by Gil González de Ávila on an island in the Golfete or Bahía de Amatique (*Relaciones de Yucatan*, I:403–406, in *DIU*, vol. ii. The wording is obscure). The area seems, however, to have been inhospitable, and the colonists soon moved into Nito (R. S. Chamberlain, *The Conquest and Colonization of Honduras*, p. 11).

75. Ixtlilxóchitl has Tunia (I:424); Bernal Díaz has Tania (chap. 178).

76. See n. 69.

77. The Río Sarstoon.

78. Gonzalo de Sandoval was in command. On his role in the Honduras expedition see C. Harvey Gardiner, *The Constant Captain*, pp. 144–170.

79. Gil González de Ávila left Santo Domingo in 1524 intending originally to reach the Caribbean coast of Nicaragua. After founding the town of San Gil de Buenavista, he moved inland toward Nicaragua only to encounter, in a district called Toreba, a force sent by Pedrarias's captain, Hernández de Córdoba. Ávila won the battle that ensued but returned to the coast where he learned of Olid's approach from the north. Ávila settled in the valley of Naco and came to an understanding with Olid. But Olid was only biding his time and finally sent a captain, Briones, who succeeded in capturing about half of Ávila's men. At this point Las Casas arrived and Briones had to be recalled. Finally Olid succeeded in capturing Las Casas, after which he moved to the valley of Naco and, in a surprise raid, rounded up the rest of Ávila's men and Ávila himself. When, after Olid's death, Las Casas returned to Mexico, he took Ávila along with him. Obviously, Cortés was ensuring that there would be no further threat to his

authority in Honduras (Robert S. Chamberlain, *The Conquest and Colonization of Honduras*, pp. 11–14).

80. The Río Lanlá.

81. This may be a copyist's error. Other readings give two leagues which, according to Maudslay, is more correct.

82. Probably the mouth of the Río Motagua.

83. According to Bernal Díaz (chap. 180), this ship had come from Cuba and belonged to Antón de Carmona, a buskin maker.

84. Naco, the principal trading center of the Ulúa basin, was situated near the Río Chamelcon. Archaeological evidence suggests that it was a Nahua trading station (Scholes and Roys, pp. 320–321).

85. Cortés seems to have sailed inland from Nito up the Río Dulce. The smaller of the two gulfs would be the one now known as El Golfete, and the larger Lake Izabal. Cortés then proceeded up the Río Polochic to Chacujal.

86. The Sierra de las Minas.

87. Bernal Díaz (chap. 180) calls this place Çinacantençintle. Maudslay (*op. cit.*, p. 341) says that when he visited the area his guide told him that Cha-ki-jal meant "ripe maize." This is probably the etymology of the word. It is not known where the town was situated.

88. See the Second Letter, n. 63.

89. The peoples of this area spoke Chorti. It seems likely, however, that Cortés had penetrated a Kekchi- or Pokonchi-speaking area; the former lay to the north of the Polochic River and the latter to the south, though these placings can only be tentative (see N. A. McQuown, "The Classification of Mayan Languages").

90. The Polochic.

91. For the career of Alvarado and the conquest of Guatemala, see J. E. Kelly, *Pedro de Alvarado, Conquistador*, pp. 121–153.

92. The date is missing in the Vienna Codex.

93. September 8.

94. Quimistlan is the present-day Quimistan, and Zula is probably San Pedro Sula. I can find no trace of Cholome.

95. Pedro Moreno had, in fact, been sent by the Audiencia of Santo Domingo as their *fiscal*, or Crown attorney, to find out where Olid, Ávila and Las Casas were. He was also granted royal authority to "settle the differences between the fleets that have gone to discover and settle the Gulf of

Higueras and other places." (The instructions from the Audiencia are only dated 1525. The royal authority [*poder real*] is dated February 25, 1525. The documents are printed in *CDIR*, 13:462–478.)

96. According to Bernal Díaz (chap. 165), when Olid landed in Honduras, he founded the town of Triunfo de la Cruz in Cortés's name and appointed the men Cortés had nominated as alcaldes and regidores, so that if the land proved not to be rich he could always return to Mexico and plea that his pact with Velázquez had been a ruse to gain more men.

97. Trujillo was founded on May 18, 1525. The charter (*testimonio de la posesión y fundación*) is printed in *CDIR*, 14:44–47.

98. So called because Gil González de Ávila had been hit by a storm there and was forced to throw some of the horses overboard to lighten the ships.

99. The region around Trujillo was predominantly of Macro-Mayan speech. The areas Cortés mentions, however, may have belonged to enclaves of Pipil, a now-extinct language of the Uto-Aztecan group (see McQuown, "Linguistic map of middle America").

100. On the death of Juan de Tecto and Juan de Ayora see D. Vincente de P. Andrade, "Disquisición Histórica sobre la Muerte de los Frailes Juan de Tecto y Juan de Ayora." The article is in a rather strange English translation.

101. In a letter to the emperor, dated December 15, 1525, Rodrigo de Albornoz claimed that, after receiving many conflicting reports of Cortés's death, Diego de Ordaz was sent to look for him. He was told by the natives of a place he calls Cucamelco, upstream from Xicalango, that Cortés was in fact dead and had been sacrificed (*CDIR*, 13:45 ff.). Moreno carried the news to Spain but seems to have doubted the truth of it (see *De Orbe Novo*, fol. CXVI v. trans., II:417).

102. Francisco Hernández de Córdoba had been sent by Pedrarias to explore the Pacific coast of Nicaragua in an effort to prevent Ávila from settling in the area. He founded three towns: Bruselas, in the Gulf of Nicoya; Granada, on the western shores of Lake Nicaragua; and León, to the north. Persuaded by Pedro Moreno to transfer his allegiance from Pedrarias to the Audiencia in Santo Domingo, he planned to make himself governor of Nicaragua. He soon ran into trouble, however, and, fearing reprisal by Pedrarias, turned to Cortés for assistance. But as soon as Cortés left for Mexico, Pedrarias moved up from Panama and captured and executed his erstwhile lieutenant. A struggle ensued between Pedrarias and Hernando de Saavedra, which was only settled by the arrival in October, 1526, of a royal governor, López de Salcedo (R. S. Chamberlain, *The Conquest and Colonization of Honduras*, p. 11).

103. Cortés's letter of instruction to Saavedra is printed in Sanchez Barba, pp. 455–458.

104. See n. 102.

105. Olancho (?), now a department of east-central Honduras.

106. Fray Diego de Altamirano was one of the first Franciscans to arrive in Mexico, together with Fray Pedro Melgarejo. Bernal Díaz (chap. 189) says that he was "a soldier and a man of war and knew about business." He did not achieve much in Mexico, although Cortés appears to have placed great trust in him. He returned in 1526, and on August 20, 1527, he was living in a monastery in Salamanca. The date of his death is unknown (P. A. López, "Los Primeros Franciscanos en Méjico").

107. Now called Utila. The other two islands in this group are Roatan and Guanaja. They are now called the Bay Islands.

108. The letter they carried has been printed by Lúcas Alamán in vol. IV, pp. 201–205 of the *Obras*.

109. Ponce de León was the juez de residencia. According to Peter Martyr (*De Orbe Novo*, fol. CXVI v. *trans.*, II:417–418), he had been sent to replace Cortés if Cortés were, in fact, found to be dead. If he were not, Ponce de León was instructed to "smother him in a thousand flatteries" and, apparently, to confer the Knighthood of Santiago on him. On Martyr's evidence, Ponce de León appears to have been sent as much to find out something about Cortés's motives and loyalty as to hold his residencia. He left Seville on February 2, 1526, and reached Mexico on July 2. His instructions, dated November 4, 1525, are printed in *DIU*, 9:214–226.

110. The notice of Cortés's residencia was read before the municipal council of Mexico on July 4. The document is printed in *CDIR*, 26:195–198. The proclamation (*acta de pregón*) is printed in *ibid.*, pp. 223–226. It was witnessed by Francisco de Orduña.

111. As soon as Ponce de León was dead, rumors began to circulate that Cortés had murdered him. Fray Tomás Ortiz seems to have been the first to spread this rumor. He is mentioned both by Bernal Díaz (chap. 192) and Cortés himself who, in a letter of January 12, 1526, speaks of "the aforementioned Fr. Tomás Ortiz . . . said and published some ugly things to my detriment, especially that I had killed Luis Ponce" (Sanchez Barba, pp. 472–474).

Dr. Cristóbal de Ojeda, who examined Ponce, said that he had died of a fever, *emitritea sincope humorosa*. Later, however, he claimed that the judge had been poisoned by Cortés at a banquet given on his behalf in Itztapalpa. As soon as rumors began to fly, the Dominican, Domingo de

Betanzos, threatened Ojeda with excommunication if he did not reveal the truth about Ponce's death. Ojeda then declared "that the truth was that Luis Ponce had been poisoned, or so it seemed to him, but as he had not seen it he did not know by whom or how" (*Sumario*, II:325–327). Other witnesses at the residencia also testified that a number of incriminating circumstances surrounded Ponce de León's death. The testimonies are those of Lucas (*ibid.*, I:289–290), Francisco de Orduña (*ibid.*, II:316–317), who claimed that someone called Aguilar had told him "that they were killing him in the medicines they were giving him," and Lope de Samaniego (*ibid.*, II:318–320). Ponce's death was a cause for concern for some time, for as late as 1545 Andrés de Tapia was questioned about his knowledge of the affair. Tapia declared that he had not seen the judge actually eat anything at the banquet in Itztapalapa, which is interesting in the light of the evidence given by Bartolomé de Zárate, who accompanied Ponce from Spain and was his cook; he said that the judge had decided in Hispaniola not to touch any food unless it were prepared by Zárate himself or Zárate's brother. (See Luis González Obregón, *Los Precursores de la Independencia Mexicana*, pp. 116–121). Ponce died on July 20, having handed over his office to Marcos de Aguilar four days previously (*CDIR*, 26:226–228).

There are striking resemblances between the death of Ponce de León and that of Garay (see the Fourth Letter, n. 39). Cortés, however, stood little to gain by Garay's death except the assurance that the adelantado would never again be able to threaten his authority. For Cortés, Ponce's death led to a partial recovery of his power, but he must have known that ultimately he would have to face a residencia. Cortés may once have thought of renouncing his allegiance to the Crown, but by 1526 he was both too tired and too insecure to have considered such a course; furthermore, he had just witnessed the disastrous careers of Olid and Hernández de Córdoba. I do not believe that there was sufficient motive for Cortés to have assassinated Ponce. Tropical fevers were many, varied and totally unfamiliar to Spanish doctors; both Ponce de León and Garay could have died from any one of them.

112. Cortés was required to resume office on July 20, the day of Ponce de León's death. As the members of the municipal council who presented this "requirement" to Cortés were mostly his loyal supporters, it is possible that Cortés engineered the whole affair. (The document is printed in *CDIR*, 26:256–267. Luis González Obregón has discussed these machinations at length, *op. cit.*, pp. 127–140. See also a letter of Estrada dated September 20, in which he claims that Marcos de Aguilar was "very sick and old." *CDIR* 2:85.)

113. See the Fourth Letter, n. 64.

114. Cortés's wish to create a new church in Mexico is derived from a medieval Messianic ideal that was widely shared among the Franciscans at the time; and it is no doubt from the Franciscans that Cortés took his idea. In the Fourth Letter (p. 333) he voices disgust with the clergy in Spain, a sentiment which won him the warm approval of Mendieta; but from the intensity of the conviction expressed in the Fifth Letter, it would appear that Cortés had only then become aware of his missionary obligations. During the intervening period, Juan de Tecto and Juan de Ayora had been constantly in his company. Cortés's Franciscan world vision is probably largely due to their personal influence, for his sense of his role in creating a new church becomes apparent at the very moment that Tecto and Ayora are beginning to be mentioned in his writings (see Fidel de Lejarza, "Franciscanismo de Cortés y Cortesianismo de los Franciscanos." For Mendieta's view of Cortés see J. L. Phelan, *The Millennial Kingdom of the Franciscans in the New World*).

115. Charles V sent Fray Garcia de Loaysa to contest his claims to the Moluccas (see the Fourth Letter, n. 62). A Casa de la Contratación de la Especería was established at Coruña, from where Loaysa's fleet of seven ships left on July 24, 1525 (*CVD*, V:3–5. Oviedo, bk. 20, chap. 4, lists only five. See, however, the *Relación* of Andrés de Urdaneta *CVD*, V:401). By the time it had reached the Strait of Magellan in February, 1526, the number of the ships had been reduced to four, and soon after entering the Pacific the fleet was scattered. The *Santa Maria del Parral* reached the Moluccas but was wrecked there. Loaysa, in the flagship, the *Santa Maria de la Victoria*, finally reached Zamafo on the island of Gilolo, on November 4, 1526 (*CVD*, V:57). One of the ships was lost and the other, the *Santiago*, reached Mexico after being separated from the flagship by a storm on June 1. Juan de Areizaga went to Tenochtitlan and gave Cortés a detailed account of the voyage, which he later repeated to Oviedo (Oviedo, bk. XX, chaps. 5–13; see also *CVD*, V:223–225).

On June 20, 1526, Cortés was directed to send the ships he was building at Sihuantejo on the Zacatula River. They left, together with the *Santiago*, on October 31, 1527, under the command of Alvaro Saavedra Ceron. The fleet, consisting of two caravels and a brigantine, was scattered in a storm off the Marshall Islands on December 15. Only the *Florida*, Saavedra's flagship, survived to reach Tidore on March 30, 1528. Two attempts were made to return to Mexico for help; during the second one Saavedra died, and the remainder of his crew settled at Zamafo on the island of Gilolo. Here they resisted the Portuguese (originally established at Ternate and Tidore) for several years but finally surrendered and were shipped back to Spain (see I. S. Wright, "Early Spanish Voyages from America to the Far East, 1527–1565," and the accounts of Francisco Granado, the fleet's secretary, and Vicente de Nápoles in *CVD*, V:465–486).

116. In February, 1525, Fray Pedro de Melgarejo and Rivera, who were acting as Cortés's agents in Spain, had agreed to pay the emperor 200,000 *pesos* over a period of eighteen months. In return Cortés was made a Don and given a coat of arms. Presumably it was at this time that he asked for the concession to settle the Pacific coast, which he did not receive until 1529 (Wagner, p. 427. *De Orbe Novo*, fol. CXV v. *trans.*, II:410).

117. The first and best known of the two treaties signed at Tordesillas on June 7, 1494, to define Spanish and Portuguese spheres of influence in the Atlantic, established a line of demarcation at a meridian 370 leagues west of the Cape Verde Islands. Although at the time this line applied only to the Atlantic, it was later extended round the world and, since no one could decide from where the 370 leagues were to be measured, sparked off the dispute between Spain and Portugal over the possession of the Moluccas. To contest his claim to the islands, Charles sent the Loaysa expedition, which was followed the next year (1526) by two more expeditions under the command of Diego García and Sebastian Cabot. In April, 1529, however, the Spanish Crown sold its rights in the Moluccas to the Portuguese for 350,000 ducats (Charles Edward Nowell, "The Treaty of Tordesillas and the Diplomatic Background of American History." The first treaty is printed in English in Frances Gardiner Davenport, ed., *European Treaties Bearing on the History of the United States and Its Dependencies to 1648*, pp. 79 ff.).

118. The Chichimeca were the peoples on the northern borders of the Mexica empire. They were nomadic hunters who proved far harder to subdue than the seed planters of the valley lands. Soon they were riding stolen Spanish horses and using Spanish weapons; like the Plains Indians of the north, they traveled in small bands against which the slow-moving Spanish forces could achieve little. The Chichimeca remained wholly independent until well into the seventeenth century, and sporadic uprisings occurred as late as the early nineteenth century (see Philip W. Powell, *Soldiers, Indians and Silver*).

119. The captain was Francisco Cortés. The instructions are printed in Sanchez Barba, pp. 367–371.

120. Near the foot of the page (fol. 287 r.) is a note by the copyist, Diego de San Martín, that reads, "This copy is in agreement with the original." The Vienna Codex is undated. See, however, p. lxiv.

Glossary

Adelantado. An *adelantado* was an army commander with administrative rights over the lands he conquered. Introduced during the reigns of Fernando III and Alfonso X, the office of adelantado (*adelantamiento*) was continued in the Indies with little alteration. The *Adelantado de Indias* was usually the commander of a sea-borne expedition, and as such resembled the *Adelantado de Mar*, an office created by Alfonso X for Juan García Villamayor when the latter proposed to mount a crusade.

Alcalde (Arabic, *al-ḳāḍi* [the] judge). The *alcalde* exercised judicial powers and served on the *concejo*, or civic council, and there were normally one or two attached to each town. The most powerful was called the *alcalde mayor*, and those under him were given specific duties. The alcaldes appointed by Cortés appear to have exercised little or no power during the conquest, except when Cortés found it convenient. Originally, appointments of alcaldes were made only by the king, but by Cortés's time certain classes of alcalde might be elected by the concejo.

Alguacil (Arabic, *al-wazīr* [the] vizier). The *alguaciles* were employed by the municipal council of a town to ensure that its orders were obeyed and, in a more general capacity, to preserve the peace. They ranked as auxiliaries to the *corregidor* and accompanied him in public. The nearest English equivalent is a constable: the *alguacil mayor* approximated a chief constable.

Audiencia. The Audiencia was a court of justice with a defined territorial area of jurisdiction. The Audiencia first appeared as a reformation of the ecclesiastical and royal courts, and was a tribunal appointed to the chancellery. In the Indies the Audiencias had far greater authority than in Spain and shared in the government of the colony to which they had been appointed. The first of such *Audiencias Indianas* was established in Santo Domingo in 1511, and it was with this body that Cortés had to deal.

527

Bachiller. A holder of the lowest of the Spanish university degrees. Like all Spanish degrees, the *bachillerato* carried valuable privileges, not least that of the right to be tried in an ecclesiastical court for most offenses. On May 7, 1870, the bachillerato was downgraded to a school-leaving exam.

Brigantine (*bergantín* from Catalan *bergant*, "mercenary soldier"). A term loosely applied to any vessel equipped with both sails and oars and designed for use in shallow waters or in conditions where great maneuverability was required. There is no record of the appearance of Cortés's brigantines; native drawings made after the conquest depict them as square-rigged and three-masted. This they certainly were not, and such drawings were probably inspired by Spanish caravels (*q.v.*). An eighteenth-century illustration shows them, more accurately, as single-masted, lateen-rigged longboats (see plate 13).

Caravel (*carabela*, med. Latin, *carabus*, a boat made of wands covered with leather). First used by the Portuguese on their African voyages, the caravel was probably derived from Arab models and closely resembled the modern sambuk of Aden and the Red Sea ports. Caravels were either lateen-rigged or square (*carabela redonda*) and carried two or three masts. They seem to have been carvel-built and were relatively small, not exceeding sixty or seventy tons and some seventy or eighty feet overall. Like the terms *nao* (*q.v.*) and brigantine (*q.v.*), caravel refers to no particular rig. The ships of the fifteenth and sixteenth centuries were classified according to the design and purpose of their hulls and to their size.

Contador. In Spain the *contador mayor* was the chief of the *Contaduría de Hacienda*, the center of the kingdom's financial administration. The contador of the Indies, however, in the absence of a Contaduría de Hacienda, was little more than an accountant, one of whose tasks was to look after the royal fifth.

Factor. A royal official appointed in the Indies to collect the rents and tributes owing to the Crown.

Hidalgo. From *hijo de algo*, probably meaning the son of someone of noble birth. The *Siete Partidas* describes *hidalgos* as "men of good lineage . . . [who] must be chosen from among those of direct lineage from both father and grandfather to the fourth generation." Only the paternal line was important, for elsewhere the *Partidas* rule that "if the mother is a commoner [*villana*] and the father an hidalgo, the son is an hidalgo" (part. II, tit. XXI, ley 2, 3). Although in the Middle Ages the term was often applied to all members of the nobility, the more general application was to the lesser nobility and *infanzones;* that is to say, those who had proved themselves noble by the purity of their blood and their prowess in arms but who lacked financial resources.

League. The Spanish league (*legua*) was calculated as one twenty-fifth of a degree of latitude measured on the earth's surface, about 2.6 miles. But there were no means of measuring this accurately, and the actual distance was variable and depended on the terrain. A day's journey on horseback, called a *jornada*, was usually considered to be seven leagues.

Licenciado. The holder of the second of the Spanish academic degrees. Its original derivation was from *licentia docendi*, and this gave the bearer the right to teach and to compete for the highest degree, the doctorate. A *licenciado* is now roughly equivalent to the English B.A.

Nao (Greek, *naus*, ship). The term *nao* was used to describe ships of some hundred tons or more. The Escorial MS of the *Siete Partidas* (part. II, tit. 24, ley 7) describes the nao, along with the carrack, as a ship with one or two masts, though by the sixteenth century most of them must have been three-masted and square-rigged.

Oidor. The judge or magistrate of an Audiencia (*q.v.*) or chancellery (*chancillería*). In the Indies the *oidores* had jurisdiction over both civil and criminal affairs and also made up the *Real Acuerdo*, an advisory council to the governor, viceroy or governor general. The oidores also had to perform various other functions; they were appointed by the *Consejo de Indias* and received a quarterly salary of five thousand *ducados*.

Regidor. A member of a municipal council (*regimiento* or *cabildo*) whose functions resembled those of the English alderman. *Regidores* were generally elected annually, although in some cases nominations for life were made by the Crown in recognition of outstanding service.

Residencia. An inquiry into the activities of Crown officials. It was usually held at the end of a term of office, and the holder was not allowed to leave his post without having submitted to it first. It might, however, be called at any time if charges of sufficient gravity were made against the holder; and this happened in Cortés's case. The presiding officer was either a judge, the *juez de residencia*, or the successor to the same office granted special judicial powers. A number of questions were put to selected witnesses. If the defendant were found guilty of mismanagement or injustices, he was required to make compensation or even suffer more extreme penalties, usually confiscation of lands and property.

Veedor. An inspector or overseer. In Spain there were *veedores* with a number of separate responsibilities, but their more general function was to uphold ordinances and inspect public services and fortifications. In the Indies they became also guardians of royal interests.

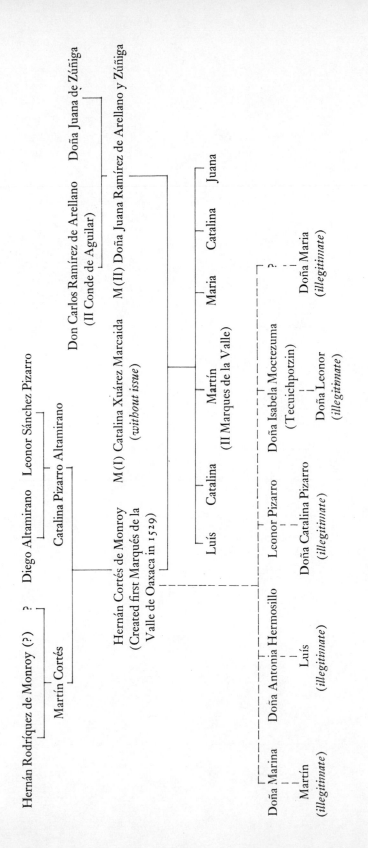

HERNÁN CORTÉS' FAMILY TREE

Key to Citations

(Because of the large number of available editions, references to the early histories are usually by book and chapter only. Further entries for some of the authors listed below may be found in the Bibliography.)

Bernal Díaz. Bernal Díaz del Castillo, *Historia Verdadera de la Conquista de la Nueva España*. Introducción y notas por Joaquín Ramirez Cabañas. 6a. ed. 2 vols. Mexico, 1960.

CDHE. Colección de documentos inéditos para la historia de España. M. F. Navarrete *et al.*, eds. 112 vols. Madrid, 1842–95 (discontinued).

CDHM. Colección de documentos para la historia de México. Joaquín García Icazbalceta, ed. 2 vols. Mexico, 1858–66.

CDIR. Colección de documentos inéditos relativos al descubrimiento, conquista y colonización de las posesiones españolas en América y Oceanía, [sic.], sacados, en su mayor parte, del real archivo de Indias. Joaquín F. Pacheco, Francisco de Cardenas and Luís Torres de Mendoza, eds. 42 vols. Madrid, 1864–84.

Cedulario. Cedulario Cortesiano, complación de Beatríz Arteaga Garaz y Guadalupe Pérez San Vincente. Publicaciones de la Sociedad de Estudios Cortesianos No. I, Mexico, 1949.

Cervantes de Salazar. Dr. D. Cervantes de Salazar, *Crónica de la Nueva España*. The Hispanic Society of America, Madrid, 1914.

Cuevas. *Cartas y otros documentos de Hernán Cortés novisimamente descubiertos en el Archivo General de Indias de la ciudad de Sevilla e ilustrados por el P. Mariano Cuevas S.J.* Seville, 1915.

CVD. Colección de los viajes y descubrimientos que hicieron por mar los Españoles desde fines del siglo XV. Con varios documentos inéditos con-

cernientes a la Historia de la Marina Castellana y de los Establicimientos Españoles en Indias. By M. F. Navarrete. 5 vols. Madrid, 1825–37.

DIHC. Documentos inéditos relativos a Hernán Cortés y su familia. Publicaciones del Archivo General de la Nación No. XXVII. Mexico, 1935.

DIU. Colección de documentos inéditos relativos al descubrimiento, conquista y organización de las antiguas posesiones de ultramar. Segunda Serie. 21 vols. Madrid, 1885–1928.

Durán. Fray Diego Durán, *Historia de las Indias de Nueva-España y Islas de Tierra-Firme.* 2 vols. and Atlas. Mexico, 1867.

Gayangos. Pascual de Gayangos, *Cartas y Relaciones de Hernán Cortés al Emperador Carlos V.,* colegidas é ilustradas por Don Pascual de Gayangos. Paris, 1866.

Gómara. Francisco López de Gómara, *Conquista de Méjico. Segunda Parte dela Crónica General de la Indias.* Enrique de Vedia, ed. Biblioteca de Autores Españoles, vol. 22. Madrid, 1946.

HAHR. Hispanic American Historical Review, vol. I. Durham, North Carolina: Duke University Press, 1918—

Herrera. Antonio de Herrera Tordesillas, *Historia General de los Hechos de los Castellanos en las Islas y Tierra Firme del Mar Océano,* 4 vols. Madrid, 1601.

Ixtlilxóchitl. Fernando de Alva Ixtlilxóchitl, *Obras Históricas de Don Fernando de Alva Ixtlilxóchitl,* publicadas y anotadas por Alfredo Chavero. 2 vols. Mexico, 1891.

Las Casas. Bartolomé de las Casas, *Historia de las Indias,* edición de Agustín Millares Carlo y estudio preliminar de Lewis Hanke. 3 vols. Mexico, 1951.

Orozco y Berra. Manuel Orozco y Berra, *Historia Antigua y de la Conquista de México.* 4 vols. Mexico, 1880. (The pagination of vol. IV is unreliable in many places.)

Oviedo. Gonzalo Fernández de Oviedo y Valdes, *Historia General y Natural de las Indias, Islas y Tierra-Firme del Mar Océano.* 4 vols. Madrid, 1851–1918. There is an onomastic index to this work by Isabel de la Peña Camara, "Indice onomástico de la 'Historia general y natural de las Indias' de Fernández de Oviedo," in *Revista Histórica. Organo de la Academia Nacional de Historia* (Lima) 29 (1966): 378–435.

Peter Martyr. *De Orbe Novo.* Peter Martyr (Anglerius), *De Orbe Novo, Petri Martyris ab Angleria Mediolanensis Protonotarii Cesaris senatoris decades . . .* Compluti . . . MDXXX.

Trans. Peter Martyr. *De Orbe Novo, The Eight Decades of Peter Martyr D'Anghera.* F. A. MacNutt, ed. and trans. 2 vols. New York, 1912. (This version is somewhat shorter than the original, and I have made my own translations for quotations.)

Peter Martyr. *Opus Epistolarum. Opus Epistolarum Petri Martyris Anglerii Mediolanensis Protonotarii Apostolici atque a consiliis rerum Indicarum . . .* Compluti, MDXXX.

Polavieja. *Hernán Cortés. Copias de documentos existentes en el Archivo de Indias y en su palacio de Castilleja de la Cuesta sobre la conquista de Méjico.* C. García de Polavieja y del Castillo, ed. Seville, 1889.

Sahagún. Fray Bernardino de Sahagún, *Florentine Codex, General History of the Things of New Spain.* Trans. from the Nahuatl by Arthur J. O. Anderson and Charles E. Dibble. Monographs of the School of American Research, Santa Fe, New Mexico, 12 vols. 1950–55.

Sanchez Barba. *Hernán Cortés, Cartas y Documentos,* Mexico, 1963. (The text of the *Cartas de Relación* is by Manuel Alcalá.)

Scholes and Roys. France V. Scholes and Ralph L. Roys, *The Maya Chontal Indians of Acalan-Tixchel, A Contribution to the History and Ethnography of the Yucatan Peninsula,* Publication no. 560. Carnegie Institution of Washington, Washington, D.C., 1948.

Sumario. Archivo Mexicano. Documentos para la Historia de México. *Sumario de la Residencia tomada a D. Fernando Cortés, gobernador y* Capitan General de la N.E. y a otros gobernadores y oficiales de la misma. Paleografado del original por el lic. Ignacio López Rayon. 2 vols. Mexico, 1852.

Torquemada. Fray Juan de Torquemada, *Ia—IIIa Parte de los veynte y un libros rituales y Monarchia Indiana con el origen y guerras de los Indias Occidentales de sus poblaçones descubrimiento, conquista conversion y otras cosas marvillosas de la mesma tierra.* 3 pts. Seville, 1615.

Wagner. H. R. Wagner, *The Rise of Fernando Cortés,* Documents and Narratives concerning the Discovery and Conquest of Latin America, New Series, no. 3, Berkeley, 1944.

ʬ Bibliography

This bibliography lists only those works referred to in the text. Rafael Heliodoro Valle has compiled a bibliography of Cortés's writings in *Bibliografía de Hernán Cortés*, Sociedad de Estudios Cortesianos, 7 Mexico, 1953. This, unfortunately, was left incomplete on the author's death, but it provides valuable references to Cortés material scattered through the published manuscript collections.

Alamán, Lúcas. *Disertaciones sobre la Historia de la República Megicana desde la epoca de la conquista que los Españoles hicieron a fines del siglo XV y principios del XVI de las islas y continente americano hasta la independencia*. 3 vols. Mexico, 1844–49.

——. *Obras de D. Lúcas Alamán*. 5 vols. Mexico, 1899–1911.

——, *et al.*, eds. *Diccionario Universal de Historia y de Geografía*. 10 vols. Mexico, 1853–56.

Alcalá, Manuel. *César y Cortés*. Publicaciones de la Sociedad de Estudios Cortesianos No. 4. Mexico, 1950.

Alvarado, Pedro de. *Proceso de Residencia contra Pedro de Alvarado, (y Nuño de Guzmán)*. Ilustrado con estampas Mexicanos, y notas y noticias biograficas . . . por Don José Fernando Ramirez. Lo publica paleografiado de ms. original . . . I. L. Rayon. Mexico, 1847.

Alvarado Tezozomoc, Fernando de. *Crónica Mexicayotl*. Trans. from the Nahuatl by Adrian León. Publicaciones del Instituto de Historia, ser 1. Mexico, 1949.

Anales de Tlatelolco. See Barlow, Robert H.

Andrade, D. Vincente de P. "Disquisición histórica sobre la muerte de los frailes Juan de Tecto y Juan de Aora." In *Congreso Internacional de Americanistas*. Actas de la Undécima Reunión, pp. 226–233. Mexico, 1895.

Archives Paléographiques de l'Orient et de l'Amérique, publiées avec des notices historiques et philologiques par L. de Rosny. Livres 1–4. Paris, 1896–71.

Aubin Codex. Charles E. Dibble, ed. Mexico, 1963.

Ballesteros Gaibrois, Manuel. *La obra de Isabel la Católica.* Segovia, 1953.

Bancroft, Hubert Lowe. *History of Central America.* 3 vols. (Works, vols. 6–8.) San Francisco, 1882–87.

———. *History of Mexico.* 6 vols. (Works, vols. 9–14.) Mexico, 1883–88.

Bandelier, A. F. "Art of war and mode of warfare of the ancient Mexicans." In *Reports of the Peabody Museum of American Archaeology and Ethnology,* (1877) 95–161.

Baudot, G., *Utopia et Histoire au Mexique. Les premieres chroniquers de la civilisation mexicaine (1520–1560).* Paris, 1976.

Barlow, Robert H. "Some remarks on the term 'Aztec Empire.'" In *The Americas,* I (1945) 344–349.

———. *The Extent of the Empire of the Culhua Mexica.* Berkeley and Los Angeles, 1949.

———, ed. *Analès de Tlatelolco. Unos anales históricos de la nación mexicana y códice de Tlateloco.* Mexico, 1948.

Bataillon, Marcel. "Hernán Cortés, autor prohibido." In *Libro Jubilar de Alfonso Reyes,* pp. 77–82. Mexico, 1956.

Beaumont, Pablo de. *Crónica de Michoacán.* 3 vols. Mexico, 1932.

Benítez, José R. *Alonso García Bravo, planeador de la Ciudad de México y su primer director de obras publicas.* Mexico, 1933.

Bernal, Ignacio, and Davalos, Hurtado, eds. *Huastecos, Totonacos y sus Vecinos.* Mexico, 1953.

Bourne, Edward Gaylord. *Spain in America 1450–1580.* Reprint. New York, 1962.

Bright, William. "Accent in Classical Aztec." In *International Journal of American Linguistics* 26 (1960)) 66–68.

Caro de Torres, Francisco. *Historia de los Ordenes Militares.* Madrid, 1629.

Carrión, Antonio. *Historia de la Ciudad de la Puebla de los Angeles.* 2 vols. Puebla, 1896.

Cartografía de la América Central. Guatemala, 1929.

Caso, Alfonso. "Los barrios antiguos de Tenochtitlan y Tlatelolco." In *Memorias de la Academia Mexicana de la Historia* 15 (1956) 7–62.

———. *The Aztecs, People of the Sun.* Lowell Dunham, trans. Oklahoma, 1958.

Castro Scone, José. "El P. Bartolomé de Olmedo, capellán del ejército de Cortés." In *Missionalia Hispanica* 6 (1949) 5–78.

Cervantes de Salazar, Francisco. *Obras que Francisco Cervantes de Salazar a hecho, glosado y traducido . . . La Segunda es un diálogo dela dignidad del hombre . . . comenzado por el maestro Oliva, y acabado por F. Cervantes de Salazar.* Alcala de Henares, 1546.

———. *Life in the Imperial and Loyal City of Mexico in New Spain and the Royal and Pontifical University of Mexico as Described in the Dialogues for the Study of the Latin Language.* Lee Barrett Shepard, trans. Carlos Eduardo Castañeda, ed. Facs. ed. Austin, Texas, 1953.

Chamberlain, Robert S. "Two unpublished documents of Hernán Cortés and New Spain, 1519 and 1524." In *HAHR* 18 (1938) 514–525.

———. "The concept of the 'Señor Natural' as revealed by Castilian law and administrative documents." In *HAHR* 19 (1939) 130–137.

———. "La controversia entre Cortés y Velázquez sobre la gobernación de la Nueva España, 1519–1522." In *Anales de la Sociedad de Geografía e Historia de Guatemala*, vol. XIX, 1943.

———. *The Conquest and Colonization of Honduras, 1502–1550.* Carnegie Institution of Washington. Publication No. 598, Washington, D.C., 1953.

Chaunu, Huguette et Pierre. *Séville et l'Atlantique, 1504–1650.* 8 vols. Paris, 1955–56.

Clavigero, Francisco Saverio. *Historia Antigua de México.* 4 vols. Mexico, 1945.

Códice Borgia. See Seler, Eduard.

Códice Chimalpopoca, Anales de Cuauhtitlan y Leyenda de los Soles. Traducción directa del Nahuatl por al licenciado don Primo Feliciano Velázquez. Mexico, 1945.

Codex Mendoza. James Cooper Clark, ed. 3 vols. London, 1938.

Códice Xolotl. Charles E. Dibble, ed. Mexico, 1951.

Columbus, Christopher. *Raccolta di documenti e studi pubblicati dalla R. commissione Colombiana*. Pt. I, vols. 1, 2. *Scritti di Cristoforo Colombo, pubblicati ed illustrati da Cesare de Lollis*. Rome, 1892–94.

Conway, G. R. G., ed. *La Noche Triste*. Documentos: Segura de la Frontera en Nueva España, año MDXX, que se publican integramente por primera vez con un prólogo y notas por G. R. G. Conway. Mexico, 1943.

Cook, Sherburne F., and Simpson, Lesley Bird. *The Population of Central Mexico in the Sixteenth Century*. Berkeley and Los Angeles, 1948.

Cortés, Hernán. *Codex Vindobonensis. S.N. 1600 of the Österreichische Nationbibliothek Vienna*. Introduction and bibliography by Charles Gibson [a facsimile]. Graz, 1960. Codices selecti phototypice impressi, vol. 2.

———. [*Cartas de relación*] Biblioteca nacional (Madrid), ms. 3202.

———. *Correspondance de Fernand Cortés avec l'Empereur Charles-Quint sur la conquête de Mexique*. Traduite par M. le Vicomte de Flavigny. Paris, 1778.

———. *Escritos Sueltos de Hernán Cortés*. Biblioteca Histórica de la Iberia, vol. 12. Mexico, 1871.

———. The Fifth Letter of Cortés. Translated from the original Spanish by Don Pascual de Gayangos. London: The Hakluyt Society, 1968.

———. *The Last Will and Testament of Hernando Cortés*. A facsimile and paleographic version together with an English translation. Edited with an introduction and notes by G. R. G. Conway. Mexico, 1939.

———. *The Letters of Cortés to Charles V*. Translated and edited, with a biographical introduction and notes compiled from original sources by Francis Augustus MacNutt. 2 vols. New York and London, 1908.

———. *Historia de la Nueva-España escrita por su esclarecido conquistador Hernán Cotés aumentada con otros documentos, y notas, por el ilustrissimo señor Don Francisco Antonio Lorenzana, Arzobispo de México*. Mexico, 1770.

Crosby, Alfred W. "Conquistador y Pestilencia: The first New World pandemic and the fall of the great Indian empires." In *HAHR* 47 (1967) 321–337.

Cuevas, P. Mariano. *Historia de la Iglesia de México*. 5 vols. Tlalpam, 1921–28.

Davenport, Frances Gardiner, ed. *European Treaties Bearing on the History of the United States and Its Dependencies to 1648*. 4 vols. Carnegie Institution of Washington, Publication No. 254, Papers of the Department of Historical Research. Washington, D.C., 1917–37.

Delgado, Jaime. "Hernán Cortés en la poesia española de los siglos XVIII y XIX." In *Revista de Indias* 8 (1948) 394–469.

Denhardt, Robert Moorman. "The equine strategy of Cortés." In *HAHR* 18 (1938) 550–555.

Díaz del Castillo, Bernal. *The True History of the Conquest of New Spain.* A. P. Maudslay, trans. 5 vols. The Hakluyt Society, 2nd. ser., nos. 23–25, 30, 40. London, 1908–16.

Elliott, John H. *Imperial Spain.* London, 1963.

———. "The mental world of Hernán Cortés." In *Transactions of the Royal Historical Society.* Fifth Series. 17 (1967) 41–58.

———. "The Spanish Conquest and Settlement of America." In *The Cambridge History of Latin America.* Edited by Leslie Bethell, Vol. I. Cambridge 1984, pp. 149–206.

Feliú Cruz, Guillermo. See Medina, José Toribio.

Fernández de Pulgar, Pedro. *Historia Verdadera de la Conquista de la Nueva España y evidente justificatión de el dominio que los Reyes Cathólicos tienen de el Reyno de México y su recto gobierno.* Colección de Don Juan Bautista Muñoz, LXVIII, Legajo 2.

Fernández Duro, Casáreo. *Armada Española desde la Unión de los Reinos de Castilla y de León.* 9 vols. Madrid, 1895–1903.

Flavigny, Vicomte de. See Cortés, Hernán.

Frankl, Victor. "Die Begriffe des mexicanischen Kaisertums und der Weltmonarchie in den 'Cartas de Relación' des Hernán Cortés." In *Saeculum* 13 (1962) 1–34.

———. "Hernán Cortés la tradición de las Siete Patridas." In *Revista de Historia de América* 53–54 (1962) 9–74.

———. "Imperio particular e imperio universal en las cartas de relación de Hernán Cortés." In *Cuadernos Hispanoamericanos,* 1963.

Fuentes, Patricia de. *The Conquistadors.* New York, 1963.

Gaither, R. B. "Government and jurisprudence of the Mexicans before the Spanish conquest." In *The Virginian Law Review* 6 (1920) 422–440.

Garciá Icazbalceta, Joaquín. *Biblioteca Mexicana del Siglo XVI: Primera Parte*. Catálogo razonado de libros impresos en México de 1539 a 1600, con Biografías de autores y otras ilustraciones etc. Mexico, 1886.

Garciá Martínez, Bernardo. *El Marquesado del Valle. Tres siglos de régimen señorial en Nueva España*. Centro de Estudios Históricos. Nueva Serie. 3. Mexico, 1969.

Gardiner, C. Harvey. *Naval Power in the Conquest of Mexico*. Austin, Texas, 1959.

———. *The Constant Captain, Gonzalo de Sandoval*. Carbondale, Illinois, 1961.

Gayangos, Pascual de. See Cortés, Hernán.

Gibson, Charles. *Tlaxcala in the Sixteenth Century*. New Haven, 1952.

———. *The Aztecs under Spanish Rule*. Stanford and Oxford, 1964.

———. *Spain in America*. New York, 1967.

———. *The Spanish Tradition in America*. South Carolina, 1968.

Giménez Fernández, Manuel. "Hernán Cortés y su Revolución Comunera en la Nueva España." In *Anuario de Estudios Americanos* 5 (1948) 1–144.

———. *Bartolomé de las Casas*. 2 vols. Seville, 1953–60.

Gómara. See López de Gómara, Francisco.

Gómez de Orozco, Federico, "Cual era el linaje paterno de Cortés." In *Estudios Cortesianos*, pp. 297–306. Madrid, 1948.

González de Barcía, Andrés, ed. *Epitome de la Bibliotheca de Leon Pinelo*. 3 vols. Madrid, 1737–38.

———. *Historiadores Primitivos de las Indias Occidentales*. 3 vols. Madrid, 1749.

González Obregón, Luis. *Los Precursores de la Independencia Mexicana en el Siglo XVI*. Mexico, 1906.

Goodwyn, Frank. "Pánfilo de Narváez, a character study of the first Spanish leader to land an expedition in Texas." In *HAHR* 29 (1949) 150–156.

Grijalva, Juan de. *Crónica de la Orden de N.P.S. Augustin en las Provincias de la Nueva España . . . por el P.M.F. Ioan de Grijalva*. Mexico, 1624.

Guzmán, Eulalia. *Relaciones de Hernán Cortés a Carlos V sobre la Invasión de Anáhuac*. Vol. 1. Mexico, 1958.

Hakluyt, Richard. *The Principal Navigations, voyages, traffiques and discoveries of the English nation made by sea or over-land to the remote ... quarters of the earth at any time within the compasse of these 1600 yeares.* 12 vols. Glasgow, 1903.

Hanke, Lewis U. "A aplicaçao do requerimiento na America Espanhola." In *Revista de Brasil*, 1938, pp. 231–248.

———. "The requerimiento and its interpreters." In *Revista de Historia de América* I (1938) 25–34.

———. Viceroy Francisco de Toledo and the just titles of Spain in the Inca empire." In *The Americas* II (1946) 3–19.

———. *The Spanish Struggle for Justice in the Conquest of America.* Philadelphia, 1949.

Haring, Clarence H. *Trade and Navigation between Spain and the Indies in the Time of the Hapsburgs.* Harvard, 1918.

———. *The Spanish Empire in America.* Oxford, 1947.

Harrisse, Henry. *Bibliotheca Americana Vetustissima, a description of works relating to America published between the years 1492 and 1551.* New York, 1886. Three volumes of additions have appeared, one in Paris in 1872 and two, by Carlos Sanz, in Madrid in 1960 with the title *Ultimas Adiciones.*

Hernández, Francisco. *De Antiquitatibus Novae Hispaniae authore Francisco Hernando medico et historico Philippi II et Indiarum omnium medico primario.* Facs. ed. Mexico, 1926.

Historia Silense, Francisco Santos Coco, ed. Madrid, 1921.

Humboldt, Alexander von. *Essai Politique sur la Royaume de la Nouvelle Espagne.* 2 vols. Paris, 1811.

Icaza, Francisco A. de. *Conquistadores y Pobladores de Nueva España.* 2 vols. Madrid, 1923.

Jiménez, Fr. Francisco. "Vida de Fray Martín de Valencia, scrita por su compañero Fr. Francisco Jiménez." In *Archivo Ibero-Americano* 26 (1929) 48–83.

Katz, Friedrich. "The evolution of Aztec society." In *Past and Present* 13 (1958) 14–25.

———. *Die Sozialökonomischen Verhältnisse bei den Azteken im 15. und 16. Jahrhundert.* Berlin, 1959.

Kelly, J. E. *Pedro de Alvarado, Conquistador.* Princeton, 1932.

Kirkpatrick, F. A. "Repartimiento-Encomienda." In *HAHR* 19 (1939) 372–379.

Konetzke, Richard. "Hernán Cortés como poblador de la Nueva España." In *Estudios Cortesianos*, pp. 341–381. Madrid, 1948.

———. *Mexican Architecture in the Sixteenth Century.* 2 vols. Yale, 1948.

Kubler, George. "The name 'Tenochtitlan.'" In *Tlalocan* I (1944) 376–377.

———. "The Behaviour of Atahualpa." In *HAHR* 25 (1945) 413–427.

Lamb, Ursula. *Frey Nicolás de Ovando Gobernador de las Indias* (1501–1509). Madrid, 1956.

Landa, Diego de. *Landa's Relación de las Cosas de Yucatan.* A translation edited with notes by Alfred M. Tozzer. Papers of the Peabody Museum of American Archaeology and Ethnology, Harvard University, vol. XVIII.

———. *Relación de las Cosas de Yucatan.* Jean Genet, ed. and trans. 2 vols. (discontinued). Paris, 1928–29.

Las Casas, Bartolome de. *Brevissima Relación de la Destrucción de las Indias.* Seville, 1552.

———. *Los Tesoros de Perú* (*De Thesauris in Peru*). Angel Losada García, ed. and trans. Madrid, 1958.

Lejarza, Fidel de. "Franciscanismo de Cortés y Cortesianismo de los Franciscanos." In *Missionalia Hispanica* 5 (1948) 43–136.

Lelewel, Joachim. *Géographie du Moyen Âge . . . Accompagnée d'atlas et de cartes dans chaque volume.* 5 vols. Brussels, 1852–57 [Atlas 1850].

Leonard, Irving A. *Romances of Chivalry in the Spanish Indies.* Berkeley, 1933.

———. "Conquerors and Amazons in Mexico." In *HAHR* 24 (1944) 561–579.

———. *Books of the Brave.* Cambridge, Mass., 1949.

Linné, Sigvald. "Hunting and fishing in the Valley of Mexico in the middle of the 16th century." In *Ethnos* (Stockholm) 2 (1937) 56–64.

———. *El Valle y la Ciudad de Mexico en 1550.* Stockholm, 1948.

Lockhart, James. *Spanish Peru.* Madison, 1969.

López, P. Atanasio. "Los primeros Franciscanos en Méjico." In *Archivo Ibero-Americano* 13 (1920) 21–23.

López de Gómara, Francisco. *La Conquista de México*. Saragossa, 1552.

——. *Cortés, The Life of the Conqueror by His Secretary, Francisco López de Gómara*. L. B. Simpson, trans. Berkeley and Los Angeles, 1966.

——. See Cortés, Hernán.

Lynch, John. *Spain under the Hapsburgs*. 2 vols. Oxford, 1965–69.

MacNutt, F. A. *Fernando Cortés and the Conquest of Mexico, 1485–1547*. New York and London, 1909.

Madariaga, Salvador de. *Hernán Cortés, Conqueror of Mexico*. London, 1942.

Maravall, Antonio. "La Utopia político-religiosa de los Franciscanos en la Nueva España." In *Estudios Americanos* I (1949) 199–227.

Mateu y Llopes, Felipe. *La Moneda Española*. Barcelona, 1946.

Maudslay, A. P. See Díaz del Castillo, Bernal.

McQuown, N. A. "The Classification of Mayan languages." In *The International Journal of American Linguistics* 22 (1956) 191–195.

——. "Linguistic Map of Middle America." In *Handbook of Middle American Indians*. R. Wauchope, ed. Austin, Texas, 1967. Vol. 5.

Medina, José Toribio. *Ensayo Bio-bibliográfico sobre Hernán Cortés*. Introducción de Guillermo Feliú Cruz. Santiago de Chile, 1952.

Mendieta, Fray Gerónimo de. *Historia Eclesiástica Indiana*. Mexico, 1870.

Menéndez Pidal, Ramón. "¿Codicia Insaciable? ¿Ilustres Hazañas?" In *La Lengua de Cristóbal Colón*, pp. 85–100. Madrid, 1942.

——. *La España del Cid*. 2 vols. Madrid, 1956 (*Obras Completas*, vols. VI–VII).

Molina, Alonso de. *Vocabulario de la Lengua Mexicana*. Facs. ed. Leipzig, 1880.

Morley, S. G. *The Inscriptions of Peten*. 5 vols. Carnegie Institution of Washington. Publication No. 437, Washington, D.C., 1937–38.

Motolinía (Fray Toribio de Benavente). *Motolinía's History of the Indians of New Spain*. F. B. Steck, trans. Academy of American Franciscan History, Documentary Series No. 1. Washington, 1951.

————. *Memoriales de Fray Toribio de Motolinía* in Documentos Históricos de Méjico, vol. I. Mexico, 1903.

Muñoz Camargo, Diego. *Historia de Tlaxcala . . . publicada y anotada por Alfredo Chavero*. Mexico, 1892.

Murga Sanz, Vincente. *Juan Ponce de León, Fundalor y primer gobernador del Pueblo Puertorriqueño, descubridor de la Florida y del Estrecho de las Bahamas*. San Juan, Puerto Rico, 1959.

Muriel, Josefina. "Divergencias en la biografía de Cuauhtémoc." In *Estudios de Historia Novohispana*, I:53–114. Mexico, 1966.

Nader. Laura. "The Zapotec of Oaxaca." In *Handbook of Middle American Indians* 7:329–358. Austin, Texas, 1969.

Navarra, Pedro de (Pierre d'Albret). *Diálogos de la preparación de la muerte* (part of the *Diálogos de la eternidad del anima*). Tolosa [1565?].

Newe Zeitung von dem Lande das die Spanier funden haben ym 1521 lare genant Jucatan. H. R. Wagner, trans. In *HAHR* 9 (1929) 198–202.

Newman, Stanley. "Classical Nahuatl." In *Handbook of Middle American Indians*. R. Wauchope, ed. Vol. 5, pp. 179–199. Austin, Texas, 1967.

Nowell, Charles Edward. "The Treaty of Tordesillas and the diplomatic background of American History." In *Greater America: Essays in Honour of Hubert Eugene Bolton*, pp. 1–18. Berkeley and Los Angeles, 1945.

Olschki, Leonard. "Ponce de León's Fountain of Youth, history of a geographical myth." In *HAHR* 21 (1941) 362–385.

Padden, R. C. *The Hummingbird and the Hawk*. Ohio, 1967.

Paddock, John. *Ancient Oaxaca*. Stanford, 1966.

Pagden, Anthony. *The Fall of Natural Man. The American Indian and the Origins of Comparative Ethnology*. Cambridge, 1982.

Paso y Troncoso, Francisco del. *Papeles de Nueva España*. Segunda Serie, 7 vols. Madrid, 1905–08.

Peschel, Oskar. *Geschichte des Zeitalters der Entdeckungen*. Stuttgart und Augsburg, 1877.

Phelan, John L. *The Millennial Kingdom of the Franciscans in the New World: A study in the writings of Gerónimo de Mendieta, 1525–1604*. Berkeley and Los Angeles, 1956.

Polanyi, Karl, *et al.*, ed. *Trade and Market in the Early Empires*. Glencoe, Illinois, 1957.

Porras Muñoz, Guillermo. "Martín Lopéz: Carpintero de Ribera." In *Estudios Cortesianos*, pp. 307–329. Madrid, 1948.

Powell, Philip W. *Soldiers, Indians and Silver, The Northward Advance of New Spain, 1550–1600.* Berkeley and Los Angeles, 1952.

Priestley, H. I. *José de Gálvez, Visitor-General of New Spain.* Berkeley, 1916.

Pulido Rubio. José. *El Piloto Mayor de la Casa de la Contratación de Sevilla.* Seville, 1950.

Ramírez Codex (bound with Tezozomoc's *Crónica mexicana*). José M. Vigil, ed. Mexico, 1878.

Ravicz, Robert, and Romney, A. "The Mixtec." In *Handbook of Middle American Indians* 7: pp. 367–399. Austin, Texas, 1969.

Relación delas cerimonias y rrictos [sic] *y población y gobernación delos yndios dela provincia de Mechuacan.* Biblioteca de El Escorial MS. ç. IV. 5. Published by José Tudela, Madrid, 1956.

Relación de los Obispados de Tlaxcala, Michoacán, Oaxaca y otros lugares en el siglo XVI. Mexico, 1904.

Ricard, Robert. "Note sur Fr. Pedro de Melagarejo, evangélisateur du Mexique." In *Bulletin Hispanique* 25 (1923) 253–256.

————. "Fr. Pedro de Melgarejo." In *Bulletin Hispaniqu*e 26 (1924, 1925) 68–69.

Riley, G. Micheal. *Fernando Cortés and the Marquesado in Morelos, 1522–1547. A Case Study in the Socioeconomic Development of Sixteenth-Century Mexico.* Albuquerque, 1973.

Robertson, William. *The History of America.* 4 vols. Dublin, 1777.

Rothery, G. C. *The Amazons in Antiquity and Modern Times.* London, 1910.

Roys, Ralph L. *The Indian Background to Colonial Yucatan.* Carnegie Institution of Washington, Publication No. 548. Washington, D.C., 1943.

Rubiano, Pedro Alvarez. *Pedrarias Dávila, contribución al estudio de la figura del "Gran Justador," gobernador de Castilla de Oro y Nicaragua.* Madrid, 1944.

Salas, Alberto Mario. *Las Armas de la Conquista.* Buenos Aires, 1950.

Saville, Marshall H. *The Goldsmith's Art in Ancient Mexico.* Indian Notes and Monographs. New York, 1920.

Seler, Eduard. *Gesammelte Abhandlungen zur Amerikanischen Sprach-und Alterthumskunde.* 5 vols. Berlin, 1902–03.

——. *Gesammelte Abhandlungen zur Amerikanischen Sprach-und Alterthumskunde, vols. I–V* . . . Unpublished English translations of German papers in the above work made under the supervision of Charles P. Bowditch . . . with slight emendations to vols. 4 and 5 by J. Eric S. Thompson and Francis B. Richardson, eds. Washington: Carnegie Institution of Washington, 1939.

——. *Códice Borgia.* A facsimile [with "Comentarios al Códice Borgia by Eduard Seler," Mariana Frek, trans.]. 3 pts. Mexico, Buenos Aires, 1963.

Siete Partidas. Las Siete Partidas de rey Don Alfonso el Sabio, cotejados con varios códices antiguos por la Real Academia de la Historia. 3 vols. Madrid, 1807.

Sigüenza, José de. *Historia de la Orden de San Geronimo. Nueva Biblioteca de Autores Españoles,* vols. 8, 12. Madrid, 1907–09.

Silva, José Valero. *El Legalismo de Hernán Cortés como Instrumento de su Conquista.* Mexico, 1965.

Simpson, Lesley Byrd. See López de Gómara, Francisco.

——. *Exploitation of Land in Central Mexico in the Sixteenth Century.* Berkeley and Los Angeles, 1952.

Strauss, Eberhard. *Das "bellum justum" des Hernán Cortés in Mexico,* Cologne and Vienna. 1976.

——. *The Encomienda in New Spain.* Berkeley and Los Angeles, 1966.

Suárez de Peralta, Juan. *Tratado del Descubrimiento de las Indias (noticias históricas de Nueva España).* Mexico, 1949.

Toro, Alfonso. *Un Crimen de Hernán Cortés. La muerte de Doña Catalina Xuárez Marcaida, estudio histórico y medico legal.* Mexico, 1922.

Toussaint, Manuel. *Justino Fernández y F. Gómez de Orozco, Planos de la Ciudad de México. Siglos XVI y XVII.* Mexico, 1938.

Vaillant, George C. "A bearded mystery." In *Natural History* 31 (1931) 243–252.

——. "Human sacrifice in ancient Mexico." In *Natural History* 33 (1933) 17–30.

——. *The Aztecs of Mexico.* Harmondsworth, 1965.

Vázquez de Tapia, Bernardino. *Relación del Conquistador, Bernardino Vázquez de Tapia*. Manuel Romero de Terreros, ed. Mexico, 1939.

Vetancurt, Fr. Augustin de. *Teatro Mexicano. Descripción breve de los sucesos exemplares, históricos, políticos, militares y religiosos del nuevo mundo occidental de las Indias*. Mexico, 1698.

Villagutierre Soto Mayor, Juan de. *Historia de la Conquista de la Provincia de el Itza reducción y progresos de la de el Lacandon, y otras naciónes de Indios barbaros, de la mediación de el reyno de Guatemala, a las provincias de Yucatan, en la America septentrional*. Primera Parte. Madrid, 1701.

Von Hagen, V. W. *The Aztec and Maya Papermakers*. New York, 1943.

Wagner, H. R. "The Discovery of Yucatan by Francisco Hernández de Córdoba." In *The Geographical Review*, 6, no. 5, 1918.

————. *The Spanish Southwest 1542–1794* (with annotated bibliography). Berkeley, 1924.

————. *Spanish Voyages to the Northwest Coast of America*. California Historical Society, Special Publication No. 4. San Francisco, 1929.

————. "The lost first letter of Cortés." In *HAHR* 21 (1941) 669–672.

————. *The Discovery of Yucatan by Francisco Hernández de Córdoba*. A translation of the original texts with an introduction and notes by H. R. Wagner. Documents and Narratives concerning the Discovery and Conquest of Latin America. New Ser., no. 1. Berkeley, 1942.

————. "Peter Martyr and his works." In *Proceedings of the American Antiquarian Society* 56 (1946) 239–288.

Winsor, Justin. *Narrative and Critical History of America by a corps of eminent historical scholars and specialists under the editorship of Justin Winsor LL.D.*, 8 vols. London, 1886.

Wolf, E. R. *Sons of the Shaking Earth*. Chicago, 1962.

Wright, I. S. "Early Spanish voyages from America to the Far East 1527–1565." In *Greater America: Essays in Honour of Hubert Eugene Bolton*, pp. 57–78. Berkeley and Los Angeles, 1945.

Wroth, Lawrence C. *The Early Cartography of the Pacific*. Papers of the Bibliographical Society of America, 38, no. 2, 1944.

Zavala, Silvio. *La "Utopía" de Tomás Moro en la Nueva España y otros estudios*. Mexico, 1937.

————. *Ensayos sobre la Colonización Española en América*. Buenos Aires, 1944.

Index

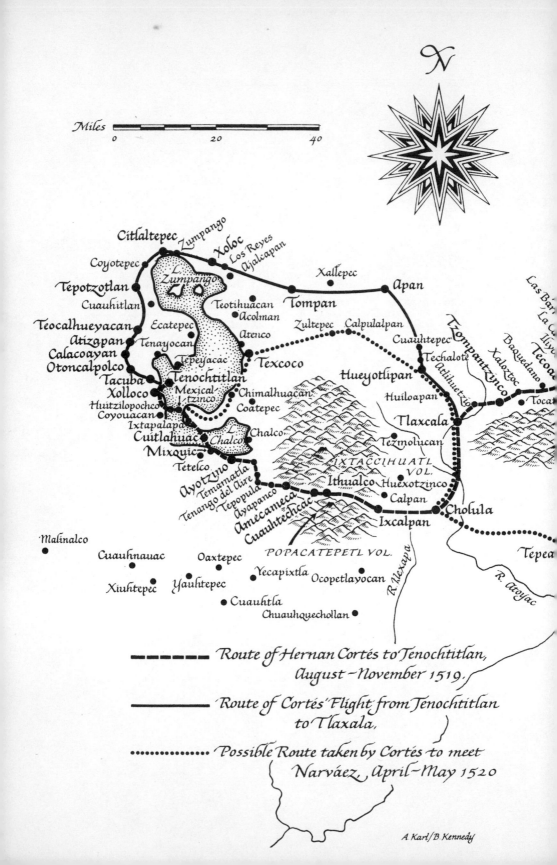

N

Miles

0   20   40

Citlaltepec
Zumpango
Coyotepec
Xoloc
Los Reyes
Ajalicapan
Xallepec
Apan
Tepotzotlan
L. Zumpango
Cuauhitlan
Teotihuacan
Tompan
Acolman
Zultepec
Calpulalpan
Las Bar
La C
Teocalhueyacan
Ecatepec
Atenco
Cuauhtepec
Techalote
Xaloxtoc
Tecoa
Atizapan
Tenayocan
Tompantzinco
Baquedano
Calacoayan
Texcoco
Hueyotlipan
Actihuetzio
Otoncalpolco
Tepejacac
Huiloapan
Toca
Tacuba
Tenochtitlan
Xolloco
Mexical-
Chimalhuacan
Tlaxcala
Huitzilopochco
Itzinco
Coatepec
Tezmolucan
Coyouacan
Ixtapalapo
L.
Chalco
IXTACCIHUATL
VOL.
Cuitlahuac
Chalco
Ithualco
Huexotzinco
Mixquic
Calpan
Cholula
Tetelco
Ayotzinco
Temamatla
Tenango del Aire
Tepopula
Amecameca
Ixcalpan
Ayapanco
Cuauhtechcac
Malinalco
POPACATEPETL VOL.
Tepea
R. Alexapa
Cuauhnauac
Oaxtepec
R. Atoyac
Yecapixtla
Ocopetlayocan
Xiuhtepec
Yauhtepec
Cuauhtla
Chuauhquechollan

— — — — — Route of Hernan Cortés to Tenochtitlan,
August–November 1519.

——————— Route of Cortés' Flight from Tenochtitlan
to Tlaxala.

·············· Possible Route taken by Cortés to meet
Narváez, April–May 1520

A. Karl / B. Kennedy

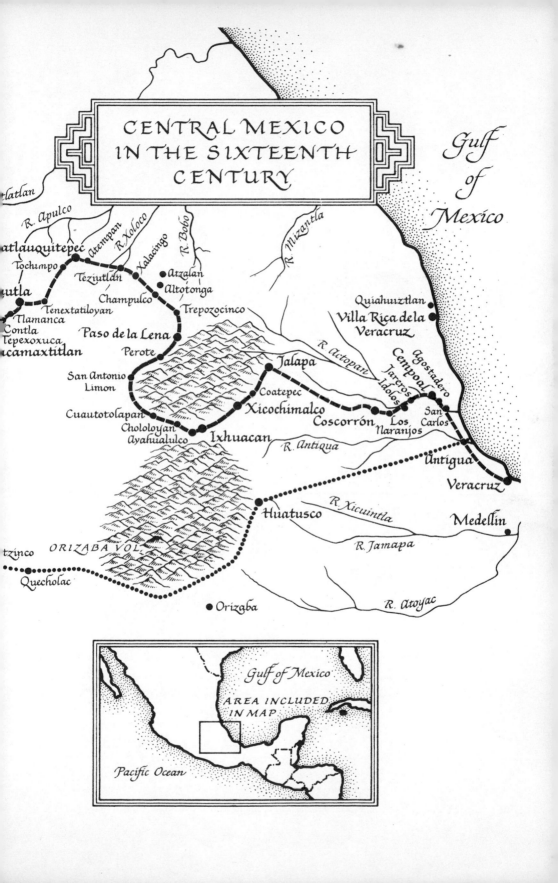

CENTRAL MEXICO IN THE SIXTEENTH CENTURY

Gulf of Mexico

...latlan

R. Apulco

...atlauquitepec

Tochimpo

...utla

Teziutlan

Tenextatiloyan

Tlamanca

Contla

Tepexoxuca

...camaxtitlan

Champulco

Paso de la Lena

Perote

San Antonio Limon

Cuautotolapan

Chololoyan

Ayahualulco

Ixhuacan

Atempan

R. Xoloco

Xalacingo

R. Bobo

Atzalan

Altotonga

Trepozocinco

R. Mizantla

Quiahuiztlan

Villa Rica de la Veracruz

R. Actopan

Cempoal

Jarros Idolos

Agostadero

Jalapa

Coatepec

Xicochimalco

Coscorrón

Los Naranjos

San Carlos

R. Antiqua

Antigua

Veracruz

Huatusco

R. Xicuintla

Medellin

...tzinco

ORIZABA VOL.

Quecholac

R. Jamapa

R. Atoyac

Orizaba

AREA INCLUDED IN MAP

Gulf of Mexico

Pacific Ocean